The Way It Was in the South

'The Way It Was in the South,

The Black Experience in Georgia

by **Donald L. Grant**, 1919–1988
ııı

Edited with a foreword by Jonathan Grant

The University of Georgia Press

Athens and London

Published by the University of Georgia Press
Athens, Georgia 30602
© 1993 by Mildred Bricker Grant
All rights reserved

The paper in this book meets the guidelines for
permanence and durability of the Committee on
Production Guidelines for Book Longevity of the
Council on Library Resources.

Printed in Canada
05   04   03   02   01   P   5   4   3   2   1

Library of Congress Cataloging-in-Publication Data
Grant, Donald L. (Donald Lee), 1919–1988.
The way it was in the South :
the Black experience in Georgia / by Donald L. Grant ;
edited with a foreword by Jonathan Grant.
p.   cm.
Originally published: Secaucus, N.J. : Carol Pub. Group, ©1993.
Includes bibliographical references and index.
ISBN: 0-8203-2329-2 (pbk.: alk. paper)
1. African Americans—Georgia—History.
2. Georgia—Race relations.
3. Georgia—History. I. Grant, Jonathan. II. Title.
E185.93.G4 G75 2001
975.8'00496073—dc21   2001021350

British Library Cataloging-in-Publication Data available

To Mildred Bricker Grant
who made this book possible

Contents

Editor's Foreword	ix
1. The Formation of Georgia	3
2. A System of Bondage	27
3. The Civil War and Reconstruction	77
4. Post-Reconstruction Horrors	137
5. The New South and Further Degradations	172
6. Black Institutions and Advancement	238
7. The Search for a Decent Living and a Better Life	274
8. The "New Negro"	297
9. The Depression, New Deal, and World War II	341
10. Postwar Progress	364
11. The Civil Rights Movement	386
12. Modern Politics	434
13. The Struggle for Economic Advancement	460
14. Social Problems	489
15. Modern Education and Culture	523
16. Civil Rights and Race Relations	549
Notes	567
Select Bibliography	591
Index	605

Editor's Foreword

Since the days of Spain's first explorations of Guale in the 1500s, blacks have contributed heavily to Georgia's development and dominated its political thinking. Georgia contained more blacks than any other state for a long time, and the argument can easily be made that they influenced its history more than that of any other state. Unfortunately, Georgia often held an unsurpassed reputation for violent racism. Despite proscriptions and their brutal enforcement, Georgia blacks consistently refused to accept the white definition of their "place." Georgia produced the nation's most honored civil rights leader, and Atlanta became a citadel of black education. Georgia's contrasts of racial oppression and counteracting black achievement may be unmatched.

The writers of history were often slow to recognize such truths. As a result, whites and blacks have been presented with a horribly inaccurate portrayal of African-Americans, fed by racist stereotypes and romantic illusions of "good old days" that never were. These accounts supported mistaken theories and led to bad policies with fatal consequences. Many of Georgia's problems stem from economic inequality that has given the upper classes illusions of grandeur and has brutalized its lower classes. No culture is healthy if many of its people are on the outside looking in, as has been the case for most blacks during most of Georgia's history. Some of Georgia's most prominent historians have been hostile toward blacks or neglectful of their contributions to the state. The need to correct many of the falsehoods that have been accepted as long-established fact led my father to write *The Way It Was in the South: The Black Experience in Georgia.*

There is also a history behind this book. My father began work on it in the early 1970s, when, as a middle-aged man, he had received his doctorate and had begun teaching at Fort Valley State College, a small, predominantly black school in Middle Georgia. A man of boundless energy, he worked on the manuscript in his spare time for nearly fifteen years. He retired in 1985 and kept working on the book until 1987, when he went with my mother to spend a year teaching American history and the English language at Zhejiang Normal University in the People's Republic of China. He died a few months after his return to the United States without knowing the fate of his two-thousand-page manuscript. Our last conversation concerned his final push to update and complete the work.

Little did I know then that the job would fall to me. Mildred Bricker Grant (who also had devoted countless hours to the project as a researcher and proofreader) did not want her husband's great work to die with him. So she turned to me, her youngest son and a writer by trade, and asked me to consider taking over and completing the project. (During my college days, I had done some research for Dad at the University of Georgia.) I agreed to look at the manuscript, and when I saw it, I caught his zeal for the project. I spent two years editing this monumental work. *The Way It Was in the South* covers more than 450 years, from the early 1500s to the 1990s. It is unique in this regard, and it is the most exhaustive state history of blacks that has yet been produced. This book is intended for a general audience. I have updated the manuscript to make the text as current as possible.

Both of us owe a great debt to those who have toiled in the field before us. Over the years, several of my father's friends and colleagues were helpful. While it is impossible to mention all of those worthy souls, Dr. Arvarh Strickland of the University of Missouri was a constant inspiration to him, and professors Fred van Hartesveldt and Donnie Bellamy of Fort Valley State College also provided encouragement and assistance. Dr. Bellamy graciously consented to assist me by critiquing portions of the manuscript. The greatest gratitude goes to my mother, Mildred Bricker Grant. Without her devotion to the cause, there would simply be no book. Lastly, I want to thank my wife, Judy, for her patience, support, and assistance.

Jonathan Grant
Stone Mountain, Georgia
July 1993

The Way It Was
in the South

1

The Formation of Georgia

Beginnings of Evil: An English Experiment Gone Awry

The history of blacks in Georgia began long before their enslavement by British colonists. Blacks were intimately involved in the Spanish exploration and conquest of the New World from the beginning. One, Pedro Nuñez, was a pilot for Columbus. Cortez, Balboa, and Pizarro also had significant contingents of blacks. It is likely that most, if not all, of the several Spanish expeditions to what is now the South Atlantic Coast of the United States had blacks in their ranks.

The first of these expeditions, that of Juan Ponce de Leon, governor of Puerto Rico, discovered Florida for the Spanish in 1512. Thereafter the Spanish restlessly probed northward from their bases in the Caribbean. On April 14, 1528, Pánfilo de Narváez landed near Tampa Bay and from there marched north and west for ten weeks, arriving back on the coast near Tallahassee on June 25. One of the scouts for this five hundred-man Spanish expedition was a black named Esteban de Dorantes, affectionately called Estevanico, or "Little Steven," and he may have been the first black to set foot on what is now the soil of Georgia. After Narváez, the De Soto expedition established a base at St. Augustine, Florida, and visited Georgia in 1540. De Soto left a cannon with the Indians near what is now Macon after demonstrating its power by toppling a tree with a well-placed shot. In the 1550s, the Spanish ventured into Georgia on hearing rumors from the Indians of gold deposits in what is now Lumpkin County, near Dahlonega. These developments eventually led to the creation of the

3

first Spanish settlement in Georgia, when a base was established on St. Catherines Island by an expedition from St. Augustine.

The Spanish hold on Georgia and the Carolinas was tenuous at best. The area was on the outer fringes of Spain's empire. Repeated efforts to find wealth there proved disappointing, and since Spanish efforts elsewhere in the New World were paying off handsomely, these northern outposts drew little interest and attention. When Georgia was included in the grant of Charles II of England to the eight Lords Proprietors in 1663, the Spanish took little note of the event. By 1686, the Spanish abandoned their Georgia missions and presidios because of trouble with the English, Indians, and pirates.

The youngest of the original thirteen British colonies began with an official ban on slavery. This prohibition was not instituted out of any respect for the rights of Africans, however. The compelling reasons for the ban were military and economic, not moral. The experiment was never successful, and within twenty years of the fledgling colony's founding, slavery was officially sanctioned with a shrug of the shoulders by Georgia's Trustees.

Before James Edward Oglethorpe founded Georgia in 1733, the British were interested in extending their control of North America south from Virginia and the Carolinas. In 1716, they established a fort on the Savannah River, and from 1721 through 1727 they maintained Fort George on the Altamaha River near what is now Darien as a defense against the French. By 1730, British influence was sufficient to bring an acknowledgment from the Cherokees of British supremacy in this area.

The British wanted to settle Georgia for several reasons. They needed a buffer between the English Carolinas and the Spanish in Florida, partly to resist possible future Spanish claims and to help secure the frontier against Indians but more importantly because Florida was already a haven for runaway slaves who fled the Carolinas and passed through Georgia on their way to safety in St. Augustine. The Spanish encouraged runaways as a tactic in their struggle against the British. In 1699, a Spanish decree promised protection "to all Negro deserters from the English who fled to St. Augustine and became Catholics." One English sea captain was discomfited when he chanced upon two of these runaway slaves while in St. Augustine. They made faces and laughed at him, secure in the knowledge that the Spanish would do nothing to help an Englishman.

The British moved tentatively to establish the buffer colony of Georgia in 1716 when the Carolina Proprietors granted land between the Savannah and Altamaha rivers to Sir Robert Montgomery; however, his proposed Margravate of Azila—a grand scheme for a feudal colony— failed to materialize. In 1729, title to the area was surrendered back to the king by the Proprietors. Three years later, Oglethorpe and a score of his associates secured a charter for the region between the two rivers, with the charter extending all the way from the Atlantic Ocean to the Pacific.

The philanthropic nature of Oglethorpe's colony as a haven for the poor and oppressed—and as a chance for prisoners to make a fresh start—has been greatly exaggerated. Although sermons delivered to annual meetings of the Georgia Trustees opposed the concept of man merely as an economic being, business motives were uppermost in the minds of Trustees and colonists. They saw Georgia as a money-making agricultural venture. Crops would be produced and sold by the corporation the Trustees directed. The imprisoned debtors who came to Georgia to start life anew did not number over a dozen, but the Trustees used this appealing concept to raise funds.

The theory that Oglethorpe founded Georgia as a philanthropic and eleemosynary colony had been encouraged by the fact that Oglethorpe tried to exclude both slaves and liquor at the beginning. There were, however, economic and strategic motives for this. Since Georgia would be a buffer protecting the Carolinas from the Spanish to the south and the French and Indians to the west, a compactly developed settlement of sober, hardworking white Protestant Englishmen was considered the best way to meet this strategic need. Therefore, no individual grants of over five hundred acres were to be made, and only Protestants were allowed religious freedom in the new colony.

Georgia was the only British colony that made an attempt to prohibit slavery. If settlers were to be sturdy yeomen, they should not have slaves—that would induce idleness among the settlers and make work seem degrading. Also, if the English were to defend the area effectively, they should have only small farms in a tight pattern. Small farms would not justify the expense of slave labor. Another reason the Trustees tried to exclude slavery was the logical belief that black slaves would cooperate with the Indians and Spanish in attacks on the English colonies and would not only escape to Spanish Florida themselves but would also help and encourage the slaves in South Carolina to do so. The Trustees also said slavery was "against Gospel as well as the fundamental law of England," but they would change their minds about this.

In addition, the Trustees originally anticipated that silk and wine production would be the mainstay of the Georgian economy. They saw these occupations as requiring more skill than strength, and therefore not compatible with slave labor. As with succeeding generations of whites, they ignored or were ignorant of the high levels of craftsmanship that had existed in Africa for centuries.

The Trustees' original charter said unequivocally that any kind of slavery, black or otherwise, was forbidden and that all in the new colony who shall

> inhabit or reside within our said province, shall be and hereby are declared to be free.... that all and every person which shall happen to be born within the said province, and every (one) of their children and posterity, shall have and enjoy all the liberties, franchises, and immunities of free denizens and natural born subjects...as if abiding and born within this our Kingdom of Great Britain....

Which did not mean the Trustees intended for blacks to have the status of free Englishmen. They made this clear by stating in their original prohibition against slavery that it was forbidden "to hire, lodge, board, or employ within the limits of the province any black or negro."

Oglethorpe had no moral or personal scruples against slavery, however. He owned slaves in the Carolinas and was a deputy governor of the Royal African Company, founded in 1672 to win for England a larger share of the slave trade between West Africa and the New World. By the time it was dissolved in 1752, the company had transported 100,000 Africans to New World slavery. The Trustees' support of slavery outside of Georgia was further indicated by their promise to return to their owners any runaway slaves found in Georgia.

The Trustees recruited settlers with extravagant promises of prosperity if they went to Georgia: All one had to do was "scratch the earth . . . (and) cover the seed in order to be rewarded with unbelievably large yields." The first settlers sent from England by Oglethorpe's company arrived at Yamacraw Bluff, now part of Savannah, on February 12, 1733. They were small businessmen, tradesmen, and unemployed laborers. There were no released convicts in the group. Oglethorpe returned to England the following year to enlist more support for the fledgling colony and for the ban on slavery. Back in England, he told the London Trustees: "I have brought all our people to desire the prohibition of negroes and rum." An act of Parliament had been passed June 24, 1735, entitled "An Act for rendering the colony of Georgia more defensible by prohibiting the importation and use of black slaves or (free) negroes into the same." Violations of this act would draw a fine of fifty pounds; the law also provided for the confiscation and sale outside the colony of any slaves who might be there. This showed that Oglethorpe had renewed his determination that Georgia would not follow the Carolina model of a tiny planter elite supported by slave labor. He also reaffirmed the Trustees' ban on hard liquor and continued to try to limit land grants to create a society of white yeoman farmers.

Oglethorpe, the Trustees, and Parliament might make pronouncements, issue regulations, and enact legislation, but that did not mean

Georgia's white settlers would abide by them. As often happened, when the mother country's rules interfered with the profits of the colonists, the rules were flouted. Actually, settlers in Carolina moved across the Savannah River with their slaves even before Savannah was founded. Within days of Oglethorpe's landing, Col. William Bull brought four black sawyers from Carolina to do the heaviest work building Savannah's first houses. More slaves were used to work on roads. Oglethorpe sent them back to Carolina when their work was done and hoped that the new rules would keep all other blacks from the colony.

However, the law's enforcement was lax, and the punishment was only a fine. Settlers circumvented the letter of the law from the very beginning by leasing slaves from Carolina for periods of up to a hundred years. The price of the lease equaled the sale price of the slave, and when they spoke of "leasing," all parties understood it was a euphemism for slavery. The courts closed their eyes to the practice, and in rare cases where it was challenged, the slave was sent back to Carolina as a "runaway," and the "lessee" was reimbursed by the Carolina "owner." This clever arrangement ensured that no one dealing in slaves would be financially hurt if the laws and regulations were enforced.

When Oglethorpe returned from England in 1736 with more settlers, he found both slaves and rum being smuggled in from South Carolina and a movement among many of the settlers to make this contraband fully legal. In the 1730s, slaves were widely used in the Augusta region, and there is no record of any legal prosecution. By 1740, there were many complaints by whites around Augusta that the widespread use of slaves made it difficult for whites to find employment. One informant of the Trustees estimated there were a hundred slaves in Augusta in 1740, and Thomas Causton, one of the settlers, wrote the Trustees in 1741 that around Augusta the ban was largely ignored. The Trustees took no action on this information.

Oglethorpe and the Trustees not only had these individual acts of defiance to deal with, but they also faced a rapidly growing organized resistance. In 1735, seventeen residents of Savannah petitioned the Trustees for the "use of negroes" on the spurious grounds that "their constitutions are much stronger than white people's." The freeholders found that white indentured servants were unwilling to work for no pay and were leaving before their terms of indenture had expired. South Carolina's failure to return runaway white indentured servants increased the pressure for the introduction of black slaves into Georgia. Georgia officials had been active in seeking to return South Carolina's fugitive slaves who escaped to Georgia and resented the lack of reciprocity.

In 1738, 117 freeholders, led by Patrick Tailfer, a lowland Scot, petitioned for the introduction of black slaves and complained they had been tricked by the Trustees into believing they would earn six times as much in Georgia as in London. The Trustees rejected the request six months later on the grounds that other Georgia settlements had petitioned for the maintenance of the ban against slavery because they believed that slavery would create an aristocracy and drive out the poor whites needed to defend the colony against the Spanish and Indians.

The Trustees might deny petitions, but they could not stop the influx of slaves or prevail upon local officials to support the ban. One example of the refusal of local authorities to support the exclusion of blacks from Georgia occurred in 1737 when Captain Davis, a Savannah merchant, fired his ship's captain because the man had mistreated Davis's black mistress/administrative assistant. The discharged captain took the case to court, but the court did not question the black woman's right to live in Savannah.

By 1740, pro-slavery pressures were mounting. The majority of Trustees reaffirmed the ban even though the lack of slaves was cited by the settlers on the Ogeechee River as the reason they abandoned their lands. Part of the Trustees' stand was based on the fear of slave insurrections. South Carolina had recently experienced several slave revolts, including the 1739 Stono Revolt in which eighty slaves burned several buildings and killed twenty-five whites before they were defeated in a pitched battle by the better-armed white militia. The following year, fifty slaves were hanged in Charleston for insurrection, and the entire colony was on the verge of hysteria. Oglethorpe and the Trustees felt that conditions in Georgia would be even more conducive to slave revolts if many slaves were brought into the colony.

The petitioning freeholders were not impressed with the authorities' reasoning and in August 1740 repeated that they still wanted slaves, claiming they thought only slave labor would guarantee a prosperous economy. They said a white servant cost three times what he could produce and that Savannah was languishing in contrast to Augusta, founded in 1736 and prospering with the help of eighty slaves imported from Carolina.

By 1740, settlers were leaving Georgia in large numbers for Charleston. There they published an eighty-page book of complaints and accusations against Georgia Trustees. The main complaint concerned "denying the use of negroes and persisting in such denial after, by repeated applications, we have humbly demonstrated the impossibility of making improvements to any advantage with white servants."

Thomas Stephens, leader of the attack on the antislavery ban, came from England in 1737 to join his father and to assist in supervising his father's Georgia holdings. By 1739, he had concluded that a slave would bring in £75 more profit than a hired white worker. The next year, he said that a landowner using white labor would always be much poorer than one who used black slaves. Stephens returned to England to promote the introduction of slavery against the desires of Oglethorpe and the Trustees. He returned to Georgia in 1741 and, with the support of the colonists opposed to Oglethorpe's ban on slavery, published a tract in London the following year that forced Parliament to debate the subject. By then, some of the Trustees were moving to support the introduction of slavery. Other Trustees and Oglethorpe continued to oppose slavery on the grounds that it would endanger the colony, cause deaths, and necessitate unproductive guard duty for whites, who would be better engaged in producing commodities for the corporation.

The Trustees' position was reinforced by petitions supporting their ban on slavery from the Scotch Highlanders and the Germans from Salzburg, Austria, who had settled in Georgia. One small group of Salzburgers came to Georgia in 1734 by way of South Carolina where they saw slavery in action and did not like it. (However, twelve slaves from Carolina helped them build their town of Ebenezer northwest of Savannah.) They engaged in silk production and logging and did not need slaves to prosper. When the Scotch Highlanders arrived in Savannah in February 1736, Oglethorpe settled them at Darien. This group numbered about 150 by 1739, when they and the Salzburgers petitioned for the maintenance of the ban on slavery.

In 1739, Oglethorpe had other matters to tend. The War of Jenkins' Ear broke out that year—so named because the Spanish cut off the ear of the unfortunate English Captain Robert Jenkins, who then carried it about with him to fortify his crusade against the Spanish. This war merged into the War of the Austrian Succession and most of the fighting took place in Europe. Georgia was only a backwater in this global conflict, but Oglethorpe, a loyal Englishman, was interested in doing anything to weaken Spain, the Catholic enemy. He raised a small army, which included five hundred troops from South Carolina (it had not yet overcome the shock of the Stono rebellion), and invaded Florida. He marched toward St. Augustine, where, among the Spanish troops, there were two hundred blacks, many of them runaways from Georgia. One of his goals was to wipe out Fort Mosa, built by the Spanish two miles north of St. Augustine to protect a colony of slaves who had run away from the Carolinas. This action, though unsuccessful, was consistent with one of the reasons for founding Georgia—insulating Carolina slaves from Spanish enticements.

The fighting in Georgia that most influenced the lifting of the ban against slavery was the Battle of Bloody Marsh, where Georgians beat off Spanish counterattacks on St. Simons Island in 1742. This repulse of the Spanish effectively ended the Spanish threat to Georgia and thus partly negated one of the reasons for banning slavery—that slaves in Georgia would be potential allies of the Spanish.

The pressures resisting the establishment of slavery were too weak to prevail. De facto slavery had existed from the colony's inception, and well before the ban was lifted, slaves were sold openly in Savannah while magistrates refused to enforce the ban. The Salzburgers and the Highland Scots argued that Africans had natural rights, but these settlers were minorities far from the seat of power. The ban on slavery was lifted as of January 1, 1751, due to several factors: Immigration had slowed, many settlers had left for the Carolinas, Oglethorpe paid little attention to Georgia after 1742, and clerical support for the legalization of slavery had increased.

The proponents of black slavery dusted off the old environmentalist doctrine that the Enlightenment had picked up from classical Greece and passed on to the New World. This held that climate determined a people's nature, abilities, attitudes toward freedom, and even intelligence. The French political philosopher, Baron de Montesquieu, circulated the environmentalist notion that people would work in hot climates only if forced to do so; therefore, slavery was rational in such places. The Rev. Alexander Hewat of Savannah used the environmentalist theory to argue for the introduction of slavery.

More religious support for slavery came from George Whitefield, who brought religious revival to Georgia in 1738. Whitefield was the first "American" public figure to be well known in all the colonies. A disciple of John Wesley's, Whitefield was a remarkably effective preacher who had greatly stimulated the Great Awakening, a revival movement that started in New England and swept through the colonies in the early eighteenth century.

When he came to Savannah in 1738 to found an orphanage, Trustees gave him five hundred acres for his project, which he named Bethesda. It was partly funded from the profits earned from slave labor on the eighteen hundred acres Whitefield owned in South Carolina. By 1742, he had joined those clamoring for more slavery in Georgia. Whitefield argued that God made Georgia for black labor because He made the climate so hot. "If they should see good to grant the limited use of Negroes," Whitefield said, "Georgia would be as flourishing a colony as South Carolina."

Whitefield did more than anyone else in Georgia to ease the troubled minds of those who wondered if Christianity was incompatible with slavery. Christians often said they believed they had a duty to convert non-Christians. If slaves were converted, could they remain slaves, or did Christian brotherhood require their freedom? Many believed so, and this inhibited conversion of the slaves. Whitefield helped convince Georgians that blacks could be good Christians and yet remain slaves. The brotherhood of man, he argued, did not apply on earth, but only in heaven. Although Whitefield criticized the brutal treatment of slaves, his recommendation to the Georgia Trustees to legitimize slavery carried great weight and influence.

In 1750, the Trustees petitioned the British government to rescind the 1735 ban and recommended that there be one white for every four slaves, religious instruction for the slaves, and as little Sunday work as possible. To ensure that skilled white workers would not have to compete with blacks, they urged that black labor be used in agriculture only, except that coopers and sawyers might have black apprentices. The end of the ban was recognition that slavery already existed in Georgia and that the profit-minded colonists would prevail despite Oglethorpe's desires.

After the ban was lifted in 1751 and Georgia became a royal colony, the revision of land policies opened the door to large plantations, and the number of black slaves increased dramatically. In 1750, the six hundred blacks in Georgia comprised 16 percent of the total non-Indian population. By 1760, there were thirty-five hundred blacks constituting 35 percent of this population. The 1763 victory of the British over the French in the Seven Years' War further stimulated Georgia's development. By 1773 there were fifteen thousand blacks in Georgia constituting 45 percent of the colony's population.

Throughout the New World, whenever opposition to slavery or pleas for better treatment of Native Americans and Africans conflicted with the quest for greater profits, the humanitarian impulse was overwhelmed. While the English tried for a few short years to avoid black slavery in Georgia, their failure to do so guaranteed a growing dependence on slave labor. This dependence quickly grew so strong that maintaining slavery became more important to Georgia's officials than victory over the British in the American Revolution.

The American Revolution in Georgia

Revolutionary fervor seized Georgia somewhat later than it did other colonies. In 1769, a mass meeting of Savannah merchants resolved to protest implementation of the Townshend Acts and curtail imports of British goods, emulating the boycotts initiated by other colonies. Georgians vowed to admit no American slaves after January 1, 1770, or import African slaves after June 1 that year. In May 1770, when South Carolina was boycotting Britain to protest the Townshend Acts, it refused to accept shipments of slaves from British merchants. The slaves were then brought to Georgia and sold just under Georgia's self-imposed deadline.

A few years later and still lagging a bit, Georgia sent no delegates to the

First Continental Congress in the fall of 1774. However, the following January, Georgians approved the resolutions of that Congress. Georgia was represented at the Second Continental Congress, which organized the war effort against the British and adopted the Declaration of Independence.

Thomas Jefferson's original draft of the declaration contained a section condemning the slave trade and castigating King George III for his resolve "to keep open a market where MEN should be bought and sold" and then inciting the same slaves to rebel and murder their masters. Jefferson's position was too radical for South Carolina and Georgia delegates. They refused to sign any declaration that criticized slavery or the slave trade lest it encourage slave rebellions and strengthen the movement for abolition. The offending paragraph was removed from the final draft. Georgians wanted to preserve slavery for the same reason they established it: It was profitable. "We cannot do without slave labor," explained one Georgian. "Our whole economy would be ruined."

The American Revolution proved that slaves were willing to fight and die for freedom and did not much care for whom they fought. Personal freedom was their goal, not political independence from Britain. If the Americans offered freedom in exchange for military service, fine; if the British offered it when the Rebels did not, as was the case in Georgia, then some slaves joined them.

The British and their German mercenaries, the Hessians, were well aware of American black soldiers. One Hessian officer wrote in his journal, "No regiment may be seen in which there are not Negroes in abundance and among them are able-bodied, strong and brave fellows." This was not the only Hessian experience with black soldiers. The Hessian State Archives at Marburg, Germany, contain records of 6 black Georgians among the 115 blacks who served King George III during the Revolution as drummers, musketeers, military police, fifers, and wagon hands. The Hessian commanders were apparently pleased by their performance, and they continued to welcome blacks into their forces throughout the Revolution.

Blacks also helped the revolutionary cause, but the Patriot leaders' attitude toward black soldiers was ambivalent. Shortly after the Battle of Bunker Hill, George Washington took command of the revolutionary forces. On July 9, he signed an order prohibiting blacks, either free or slave, from enlisting in the Continental army. In September 1775, Georgia's delegates to the Continental Congress supported an abortive move to discharge all blacks already in the army. In response to the November 7 proclamation by the British governor of Virginia, Lord Dunmore, to free slaves who fought for the British, Washington recommended the reenlistment of blacks who had already seen service. By war's end, slaves and free blacks were sought after and welcomed into military units in all the colonies except Georgia and South Carolina. Georgia's leaders consistently placed the preservation of slavery above victory over the British and refused to enlist blacks into the Patriot cause as soldiers.

The war also offered many opportunities to run away from slavery. Estimates on the number of runaways vary from a low of 50 percent of the fifteen thousand slaves that were in Georgia at the outbreak of hostilities to a high of 83 percent. Historian John Hope Franklin estimated that Georgia lost three-quarters of her slaves. Of the thousands who escaped (at least temporarily) during the American Revolution, many fled to the frontiers in western Georgia and south to Florida, where they often found refuge among the Indians.

There was widespread fear in Georgia that the British might declare an end to slavery. Georgia's delegation to the Second Continental Congress believed that if a British force of one thousand were to land in Georgia and unfurl the banner of freedom for slaves, they would be joined by at least twenty thousand blacks within two weeks. American Tory leader Joseph Galloway thought the British could enlist three times as many blacks as whites in an army to suppress the Americans. Maj. Gen. Robert Howe was also concerned about this when he wrote John Hancock early in 1777 that he would need seven or eight thousand troops to prevent the British from coming from Florida to Georgia and inducing slaves to revolt. Howe's request was impossible to fulfill, for Washington had only thirty-six hundred soldiers in the Continental army then.

British field officers in the South informed London that abolishing slavery would end the rebellion. The idea of abolition was seriously debated in England, but there were too many Tory planters in the South who felt that a victory that deprived them of their slaves would strongly resemble a defeat. Another reason the British never raised the standard of general abolition was that their stake in the British West Indian plantation-slave economy was too great. The 750,000 black slaves who labored there to enrich the British outnumbered the total in the thirteen colonies. The British feared that to arm and free all slaves in the Rebel colonies could lead to a chain reaction in the other colonies that might bring independent black governments into power in the Caribbean. This happened in French Haiti fifteen years later.

Early in 1776, British officers on the Georgia coast promised freedom to defecting slaves of Rebels who would fight against their former masters and encouraged them to board ships at Tybee Island. Soon many did. Several fearful Georgia planters took their slaves to other places to prevent defections to the British. George Haverick, for example, removed sixty of his slaves to Virginia for safekeeping. Knowledge of the British offer became widespread among slaves. Whites had long been amazed at the speed and efficiency of the slaves' underground "grapevine." A Georgia delegate to the Second Continental Congress commented that "the Negroes have a wonderful art of communicating intelligence among themselves; it will run several hundred miles in a week."

Nowhere were the results of Georgians' refusal to enlist blacks more obvious than in the events in and around Savannah. The city was protected by Continental troops and the Georgia militia from the outbreak of the war until its capture by the British on December 29, 1778. Blacks played a large role in this reversal of American fortunes.

General Howe, commander of Georgia's defense of Savannah, was expecting a frontal attack, which would give his sharpshooters an opportunity to slaughter the British. However, the British, who had landed unopposed a short distance from the city, had an offer from a slave, Quamino Dolly, to guide them up a secret path and take the Americans by surprise. The British kept their main force in front, where they were expected by Howe, but out of range of the guns of Savannah. The completely distracted Howe was surprised by a flank attack of the British Highlanders guided by Dolly. When the Highlanders fell on Howe's flank, the main British force began a frontal assault that completely routed Georgia's thousand-man force. Dolly was only one of several blacks who assisted the British as spies, guides, and couriers in this action. Had the Georgians held their position for only a few more days, reinforcements from Charleston might have prevented Savannah's fall.

From their victory at Savannah, the British pushed north up the Savannah River and captured Fort Cornwallis and Augusta on January 29, 1779. One-third of the British forces occupying Fort Cornwallis were runaway slaves who played a vital role in defending against Georgian counterattacks at Briar Creek in March. Georgia lost over 350 men in this battle, while the British lost only 20 soldiers. In 1781, when Georgians recaptured Augusta, Thomas Brown, a British officer, escaped to Savannah with a contingent of two hundred black troops that became the nucleus of the famous King of England's Soldiers.

After the British captured Savannah, they continued to use blacks to hold their prize. Sir James Wright, the reinstalled Tory governor, had the legislature approve the impressment of four hundred blacks to construct fortifications and the arming of blacks in a crisis. Historian Benjamin Quarles estimated that from one thousand to four thousand blacks, mostly slaves who fled from Rebel masters, assisted in fortifying Savannah. That fall, when Georgians besieged Savannah in a vain effort to retake it, several hundred blacks, armed by the British, played an active role in skirmishes. When Savannah was finally surrendered to the Americans, black troops made up 10 percent of the total British force.

The British continued to follow the policy of freeing Rebels' slaves when they sought refuge with the British. However, the slaves of loyalists remained chattel, and if their masters wanted to take them to the British West Indies, they remained in bondage there. Patriot Georgians also used slave power to help with the Revolution, mainly as labor for the military. As early as November 4, 1775, the Georgia Council of Safety ordered a hundred slaves impressed to help Gen. Charles Lee prepare Savannah's defenses against the anticipated British attack. Two years later, in a more general impressment act, masters were ordered to submit lists of male slaves aged sixteen to sixty-one. One-tenth of them could then be impressed, with the master receiving three shillings per slave for the twenty-one-day term of service. Although fines might be levied against masters who failed to furnish the lists, the act was difficult to enforce, and compliance was poor. In June 1776, the Council of Safety authorized the hiring of slaves to build entrenchments around Sunbury and had Col. Andrew Williamson hire Negroes from their masters to repair the road between the Ogeechee and Altamaha rivers. He was empowered to impress slaves for ten-day periods but had to use them in their home districts. This action was unpopular among slave owners, whose private interests outweighed patriotic sentiments.

Overall, more blacks served the Patriot cause than the British, but this was not the case in Georgia. The main reason blacks in Georgia served the king rather than the cause of the Revolution was that the British freed Rebel-owned slaves who defected to their ranks and were willing to fight. While the Continental Congress declared all white indentured servants free and the states made provisions to pay their masters for the time remaining in the indentures, not only would American forces in Georgia return captured slaves to their American masters, but they consistently refused to free the slaves of Tories, although the New England states did so. Tory-owned slaves were usually spoils of war in Georgia. Sometimes they were even returned to their Tory masters by Rebels—for a fee.

The slaves Patriot Georgians captured from the enemy were used in various ways. Some worked in lead and salt mines, and some were forced to build military fortifications, as, for example, the twenty axmen taken from the British and forced to construct batteries at Tybee Island. In June 1778, the General Assembly authorized the use of two hundred confiscated Tory-owned slaves for labor service in a Continental army expedition against East Florida; hundreds of others labored for the Georgia militia.

The Georgia Executive Council in 1780 ordered the slaves captured at Savannah to be sold and the proceeds divided among the soldiers taking part in the action. On one occasion, Georgia donated a slave to every soldier taking part in one campaign. Georgia also used captured slaves as money to buy provisions and pay soldiers. In 1782, Gov. John Martin received ten slaves in lieu of his salary, and one month earlier, the entire Executive Council took its pay in slaves. Altogether, more Tory slaves were seized by the Rebels in Georgia than in any other state. The Tory plantations in the coastal region, including those of Governor Wright, who owned 523 slaves on eleven plantations, were especially vulnerable to Rebel raiders. The final stages of the Revolution in the South were largely financed by the sale of slaves confiscated from the Tories.

The best clear chance for Georgia to use black soldiers to shorten the war and ensure victory came in March 1779, when Congress agreed to pay masters up to $1,000 for each slave under thirty-six years of age who passed muster. The blacks would remain slaves while fighting in the Continental army, and upon discharge they would receive their freedom and a fifty-dollar bonus. That year, Congress sent John Laurens, one of Washington's staff officers and son of the Continental Congress's president, Henry Laurens, to Georgia and South Carolina to raise three thousand slave soldiers for the Revolution. This and later attempts in 1782 ended in failure. Both colonies held that arming slaves was too high a price to pay for victory. Rather than weaken slavery in Georgia, the planter class preferred to weaken the struggle for independence.

Georgia not only refused to let her slave power be used to win the war; ever fearful, she passed a law in 1778 requiring that one-third of the state's troops remain in their home counties to provide manpower to guard against insurrections and for slave patrols to prevent runaways. After the war was over, Georgia did come around to using free blacks in the military as a labor force, as pioneers, and as musicians in the state militia. But they were not used extensively and were not armed. Decades before the Revolution, blacks, both slave and free, had been used occasionally in Georgia's colonial militia, but Georgia never had more than a few free Negroes in the militia, and it had never armed slaves. Provisions made in 1755 for accepting slaves in the Georgia militia included granting freedom for acts of valor. An unimplemented 1772 legislative act provided for arming slaves in an emergency and for awarding freedom for outstanding examples of heroism by slave soldiers.

Not all Georgians opposed the use of blacks in the revolutionary cause. The general policy of the time permitted one to send a substitute in his place when called to service. Many Northern slaves went as their master's substitute and exchanged their uniforms for freedom when the conflict was over or when their terms of service expired. This happened occasionally in Georgia. The most famous surrogate was Austin Dabney, born a slave and brought into Georgia from South Carolina by his owner, who freed him to enlist as his substitute. Georgia permitted this occasionally for free blacks but not for slaves. Dabney served the state militia well and was in several engagements, including the crucial Battle of Kettle Creek in North Georgia on February 14, 1779. One of the bloodier battles fought in Georgia, Kettle Creek was a great victory for the Americans, who surprised and defeated a force of seven hundred Tories, ending a long string of Rebel defeats that started with the fall of Savannah.

Dabney was badly wounded in the fighting. He suffered a broken thigh and was mustered out a free but crippled man. He was befriended by a white man, Giles Harris, whose family nursed Dabney back to health. In the early 1800s, Dabney moved to Madison County and became a racehorse fan. When Georgia gave land to revolutionary war veterans in the 1819 land lottery, Dabney was excluded because he was black. However, a special act of the legislature in 1821 awarded him 112 acres in Walton County. He also received the same federal pension that white veterans received.

The names and deeds of blacks were often left out of Colonial and revolutionary war records—which also are incomplete for whites. However, records show that two other black Georgians won their freedom by fighting for the Americans: David Monday, a slave whose owner was paid 100 guineas by the state in order to emancipate him, and Joseph Scipio, a private in the Fourth Regiment. Others will be forever anonymous.

One interesting example of the use of blacks on the American side occurred when an effort was made to recapture Savannah from the British in 1779. France had entered the war on behalf of the colonies in 1778, and on September 23 the following year, the French fleet, commanded by Adm. Charles Henry d'Estaing, joined fourteen hundred American troops under Gen. Benjamin Lincoln to besiege the three thousand-man British garrison in Savannah where Tory general Augustine Prevost had five hundred blacks in his force. The French brought four thousand soldiers with them, including the black 545-man volunteer Chasseurs Brigade from Haiti. Although this combined operation did not succeed in recapturing Savannah, it was the prime example during the Revolution of blacks fighting on both sides in the same battle.

Blacks worked on strengthening fortifications and collected naval stores throughout the British occupation. When the British were forced to evacuate Savannah in July 1782, at the end of the war, they took the blacks, who were in two fundamentally different categories: the slaves of Tories and those who ran away from Rebel masters to join the British. Most of the Tory slaves were taken by their masters to the British West Indies or to Florida, which Britain wrested from Spain as part of the fruits of her victory in the Seven Years' War, concluded by the Treaty of Paris in 1763. British planters who fled to Florida believed the area would remain

British. This hope was shattered the following year when England returned Florida to Spain as part of the overall settlement of 1783 that ended the American Revolution.

In 1783 there were seven thousand black slaves and one thousand free Negroes in Florida. Many of the slaves were taken by their owners back to Georgia when Florida was returned to the Spanish. There they were either kept by ex-Tories who made their peace with the new nation and settled down as planters or were sold to planters who had been Rebels during the war. In some cases where identification could be made, slaves who had defected to the British were reclaimed by their masters.

What happened to the slaves of the Rebels who fled to the British in response to the British promises of freedom? Although the Rebels tried to stop this flow of runaways by telling slaves that the British would only sell them into slavery in the West Indies, this did not happen to most of them. The Georgia legislature sent emissaries to buy escaped slaves back from the British prior to evacuation, but the British refused to sell them. Individual Georgians also tried to buy back slaves who had taken refuge with the British, who insisted the blacks who voluntarily joined them were free.

The British evacuated 1,568 blacks from Savannah to Jamaica in six ships. Later, about two thousand were taken to St. Augustine. Altogether, some four thousand blacks were evacuated from Savannah. Just after the evacuation, the price of slaves in Georgia more than doubled, but the shortage was so great, they were hard to obtain at any price. Rice production suffered for years due to the labor shortage.

Although a few free blacks stayed in Florida or the British West Indies, the British eventually took most of them to Canada, where they were given land and an opportunity to start new lives as free men. However, life there was a disappointment. While better than slavery in Georgia, it had drawbacks. The climate was severe, the land they were allotted was not the best, and there was prejudice and discrimination against them by the white British Canadians. Some were sent back to Africa and established communities in Sierra Leone.

One of the major diplomatic problems of the new nation was that of prevailing upon Britain to return the blacks who had deserted the Rebels and sought refuge with the British during the Revolution. The controversy raged for decades. The Continental Congress considered the question before the British actually started their evacuation. Georgia's delegates led the fight in 1782, and they were joined by all the states except New Hampshire, New Jersey, and Maryland to pressure the British to return the refugees. In 1783, George Washington was instructed to get the runaways back, and Congress resolved that the British were not to remove the blacks. James Madison's notes on the congressional debate on May 8, 1783, indicate that delegates were interested in a proposition according to which the United States would not release any British prisoners until the runaways were returned. All U. S. diplomats were instructed to make the return of these blacks a high priority in negotiations. As early as May 26, 1783, U. S. ministers in Europe protested the failure of Britain to return these blacks, whom the United States considered still slaves. Britain was denounced as a "slave stealer" time and time again.

Another way blacks tried to obtain freedom and independence was to escape to the wilderness and establish communities there. Formation of these enclaves, or maroons (from the Spanish, "Cimarron," meaning wild and unruly) had been a long-established method of resisting slavery. Slaves would desert their masters and go off and eke out a subsistence from the game and food plants of the area, sometimes supplementing this with booty taken by raids on settlements. Maroons existed in Georgia even before the American Revolution. In 1771, Georgia's acting governor, James Habersham, who had earlier been the most active importer of slaves to Georgia, sent militiamen and Indian warriors to wipe out several slave maroons between Savannah and Ebenezer. He said they were marauders, preying on the countryside, and he feared the number of maroons would multiply if not promptly destroyed. The militia had to be called out the following year for the same purpose.

Of the free Negroes with the British at the time of the evacuation, there was one group that chose not to leave Georgia, a group of three hundred runaway slaves who had answered the British call to fight for their freedom. Some had joined the British at Savannah; others, at Augusta. When that city fell, they succeeded in making their way back to safety in Savannah, calling themselves the King of England's Soldiers. They elected to try to make an independent life for themselves by building armed camps on the river between Savannah and Augusta instead of leaving with the British. This band was described as the "best disciplined band of marauders that ever infested (Georgia's) borders." Finally, on May 6, 1786, militia from Georgia and South Carolina, guided by Catawba Indians, surprised the fortified maroon and destroyed it. Many of the blacks fought to the death; others were captured, and some escaped.

The great irony of the American Revolution is that it was not revolutionary enough. In 1775, Thomas Paine's newspaper article, "African Slavery in America," called for ending the slave trade, abolishing slavery, and providing land for blacks so that they might have true independence and the economic opportunity necessary for the pursuit of happiness. However, there were few, if any, gains from the Revolution for most blacks in the United States. Black initiatives, the need for soldiers, plus the rhetoric of freedom and liberty did encourage the weakening of slavery in the North, and most of the five thousand blacks who fought on the American side, if they were not already free when they enlisted, received freedom as their reward for patriotic duty. Also, the view of the slave trade as an unmitigated evil grew during the Revolution.

In Georgia, the worst was yet to come. The war for liberty was followed by an increase in slavery and a reduction in the liberties of blacks. A few blacks were freed as a result of the Revolution and were permitted to remain in the state, but the institution of slavery was not weakened, nor was the status of blacks improved. On the contrary, an ever-tightening and constricting net was thrown over the blacks of Georgia during the next eighty years. By the outbreak of the Civil War, blacks had fewer freedoms than they had before and during the Revolution.

During the war, as slavery was undermined in the North, it was made more binding in the South, and the seeds of later sectional conflict were sown. The Revolution's failure to develop a commitment to freedom for blacks has led many historians to conclude that the Civil War was a consequence of the American Revolution. Perhaps Jefferson regretted not taking a stronger stand in his final draft of the Declaration of Independence, for later, when referring to the slavery issue's divisiveness, he said, "I tremble for my country because I know that God is just."

Reds, Blacks, and Whites

The Cherokees' history was intricately interwoven with both blacks and whites in Georgia. When the European settlers first came, the Cherokees were a seminomadic people who lived by hunting, gathering, and farming. They did not then own any "slaves" in the European sense of the word. Indeed, slavery would offer no economic benefits to their subsistence economy.

Indians were not united against Europeans, and Indians often fought tribe against tribe and even helped one or both sides in Europeans' conflicts. Whites were similarly divided. In 1670, the British started buying Indians captured by other Indians to sell into slavery in the Carolinas, giving Indians an economic incentive to wage war. In the earlier Colonial wars with the French, the British also bought black slaves the Cherokees stole from the French, and the French bought those the Cherokees stole from the British. This led to the Treaty of Dover in 1730, when the Cherokees agreed to return captured and fugitive slaves to the British for a fee. Creeks were also paid. A 1763 agreement provided £5 in trade goods for each returned slave. This increased in 1774 as the British sought to increase antipathy between blacks and Indians.

However, not all Europeans were dedicated to despoiling the Indians. Christian Priber, a German-born legal scholar who came to Georgia in 1735, advised the Cherokees to make no more land concessions to the British but to establish a communal republic that, among other things, would be a haven for all runaway slaves. The British viewed this unique individual as a threat to both their land and slaves and sent an expedition to capture him in 1739. It failed because the Cherokees protected him. The Creeks, never overly friendly with the Cherokees, succeeded in capturing Priber and turned him over to the British in 1743. James Oglethorpe had him imprisoned, and he died the following year.

Early in Georgia's history, whites frequently complained that Cherokees offered refuge to fugitive slaves. Before 1800, refugees often learned Indian ways, intermarried with them, and became members of Cherokee society. The revolutionary war had a great impact on the Cherokees and altered their relationships with blacks. It accelerated the stream of fugitive slaves into Cherokee territory and brought many more blacks into closer contact with other Indian groups. The war also greatly accelerated the rate of white contact with Indian cultures and increased the hostility between the two peoples.

When the revolutionary war broke out, the Cherokees, encouraged by the British, attacked Rebel frontier villages in both Georgia and South Carolina. In August 1776, a Rebel counteroffensive using almost five thousand troops laid waste Cherokee country and drove the Indians south and west. When this large American force was augmented by two thousand more, the Cherokees signed treaties with the Rebels and sat out the rest of the war. The Cherokee War of 1777 involved many Georgians and was one of the most disastrous for Indians in the total history of Indian-white relations. One reason Rebel Georgians attacked the Cherokees all out was to confiscate slaves some Tory planters had taken into Indian territory for protection. Moreover, the Indians provided a haven for many slaves who escaped from their Rebel masters, and this became a major problem.

The first treaty with the Indians made by the United States (the Treaty of Hopewell, signed with the Cherokees in 1785) pledged them to return all fugitive slaves. Georgians were especially interested in this treaty, and William Few, Georgia's first congressman, was one of its most outspoken proponents. Similar treaties were soon made with other Indian nations.

Georgians who were dissatisfied with the slow pace of federal policies from 1789 to 1794 formed state militias and private armies to raid the Indians. They were "land hungry" and welcomed a good fight. To provoke these encounters, Georgians stole horses and blamed the Indians or hid their own and claimed that Indians had stolen them. When Georgia settlers seized Indians' land, they also took their slaves.

The use of black slaves had developed slowly among the Cherokees in the latter part of the eighteenth century. As colonists and frontiersmen gradually encroached on the Cherokees' traditional hunting ground and their lands were further reduced during the Revolution, Indians were forced to abandon their communal hunting economy and became increasingly dependent on agriculture. Some Cherokees, enslaved by Europeans, learned plantation agriculture. When opportunities to have their own plantation agriculture developed, some Cherokees adopted black slavery. As with most hunting groups, agricultural tasks were considered women's work. As the Cherokees turned more to agriculture, their women welcomed the acquisition of slaves to ease the burden in the fields. By 1790, black slavery was well established among the Cherokees. Some full-scale Southern-type Cherokee plantations existed in northern Georgia by 1800. Slavery thus became a part of the Cherokee culture until the end of the Civil War.

As among whites, only a small elite among the Cherokees ever owned slaves. Plantation owner James Vann was probably the best-known Cherokee owner of black slaves. Another Cherokee, Major Ridge, owned thirty black slaves in the 1820s. John Martin, treasurer and chief justice of the Cherokee Supreme Court, reportedly owned a hundred black slaves. In 1811 there were 12,395 members of the Cherokee Nation, with only a small handful owning a total of 583 slaves. By 1825, the Cherokee elite in Georgia, Alabama, North Carolina, and Tennessee owned 1,217 black slaves. The development of this elite was encouraged by the treaties that gave fee-simple titles of up to 640 acres of land to individual Indian leaders as bribes. This action encouraged the development of the concept of private property and greatly altered traditional Cherokee society, which had been based on communal ownership of land.

As black slavery developed among the Cherokees, so did their legal and extralegal methods of controlling slaves. Vann had one of his slaves burned alive at the stake for theft. In 1819 and 1820 the Cherokee Nation emulated white attitudes and adopted Black Codes that forbade slaves from engaging in trade or from marrying either white or Cherokee women. They also provided for organized slave patrols and excluded free blacks from Cherokee country.

Cherokees and blacks were up against the same dilemma. Whites said neither blacks nor Indians were sufficiently developed to run their own lives. But in neither case did adapting to white culture lead to acceptance or independence. The goal of whites was not to acculturate Indians and blacks but to use the differences in culture as an excuse to appropriate for white use the most valuable thing that the Indians and blacks had: land and labor, respectively. The more Cherokees adopted white culture, the greater were the white attacks on them. Vann, the successful Cherokee planter, was seen as a greater threat to white domination of the new land than the nomadic hunting and gathering Indians of earlier times.

The Cherokees were the victims of misfortune when gold was discovered on their land by whites in 1828. Among the first miners was a slave of Major Logan who panned gold in White County. Shortly thereafter, another black found gold in nearby Dahlonega. Within a year, the nation's first gold rush brought five thousand rough-and-ready miners into the area. They attacked and were attacked by the Cherokees, who resisted the invasion. Georgia responded by extending its sovereignty over the Cherokee lands and unilaterally declared that the laws of the state of Georgia applied in the Indian nation and that Georgia's police powers extended through it.

In 1830, the Georgia legislature created the Georgia Guard to police the area and forbade units of the Cherokee government from meeting *except to cede territory.* Later that year, Congress passed President Jackson's hotly debated Indian removal bill, and Georgia ordered the rest of the Indian lands surveyed for the land lottery of 1832—the last of a series of six land lotteries that began in 1802 and turned the Indian lands over to private white ownership. While the Georgia Guard was an instrument aimed primarily at the Indians, it also had an antiblack bias and enforced the law forbidding traders to employ blacks in their dealings with the Indians. On one occasion it forced a white missionary teacher to expel two black students who were among her Indian pupils. In an 1831 incident, the Guard arrested eleven missionaries to the Cherokees who were tried and convicted of violating Georgia's laws. The matter went to the U. S. Supreme Court in 1832 (*Worchester v. Georgia*), which ruled against Georgia. Georgia defied the ruling.

Another result of the policies that extinguished land ownership by Indians in Georgia and drove most of them from the state was the expansion of the plantation system and the increase in the demand for black slaves. To most white Georgians, this required the removal of the Indians. The instrument justifying the final removal of the Cherokees was the 1835 Treaty of Echota, which ceded to the United States all Cherokee lands and provided for their removal beyond the Mississippi River by 1838. Though most Cherokees would not agree to leave Georgia, a small minority of five hundred of the wealthier Cherokees led by Chief Martin Ridge signed the treaty and left the state in 1836. The leaders of this minority were later killed as traitors by other Cherokees.

The failure of the Indians to unite effectively with each other and with blacks had made it impossible to resist white aggression. The actual removal of the remaining majority of Cherokees, appropriately known as the Trail of Tears, was a bloody and brutal military operation. Sixteen hundred blacks were included with the fourteen thousand Cherokees who were herded by the army; of this number four thousand died of fatigue, starvation, exposure, and disease.

Although the territory south of Georgia was finally organized as the separate state of Florida and admitted into the Union in 1845, it was intimately involved with the black experience in Georgia from the beginning. In Florida, blacks and Indians were able to resist enslavement and eviction longer than those in Georgia because of divisions of Florida's white ruling class into American, British, and Spanish factions. Moreover, a much better working relationship between blacks and Indians contributed to the Florida Indians' ability to resist aggression by the United States longer, though the end result was similar. It took the full weight of U.S. military forces in a protracted struggle to solve the "problem."

In the 1740s, English and Georgian military units began making incursions across the border into Florida to attack the Spanish. Lower Creeks, from their villages on the Chattahoochee and Flint rivers in Georgia, cooperated with the British in laying waste the northern Florida Indian communities that had been Christianized by the Spanish. From about 1750, some Creek Indians moved into Florida from Georgia and established a society which lived mainly by hunting, fishing, and gathering wild plants for food. Although they practiced some agriculture, they did not develop it or own land privately to the extent that the Cherokees in Georgia eventually did. Consequently, they lacked the Cherokees' economic motivation for enslaving blacks. These Creek Indians became known as the Seminoles and defended themselves in three wars initiated by the United States primarily because the Seminoles had welcomed fugitive slaves from Georgia.

England acquired title to Florida from Spain in 1763. When the American Revolution broke out, Florida was a haven for Georgia's Tory planters and their slaves as well as slave fugitives. The flight of black slaves to relative freedom in Florida, which began before the revolution, continued after it was over. This problem was recognized as a national issue, not just a local concern of Georgia. The state's planters used the War of 1812 as an excuse to attack the Seminoles because they did not help return fugitive slaves. The runaways who escaped to Florida lived in their own agricultural villages and paid the Seminoles rent in the form of small tributes of grain and cattle. During the war, the United States also mounted attacks on Florida's fugitive slave encampments. When the War of 1812 broke out, the British resumed their practice of encouraging slaves to escape to British territory. The British also renewed the promise of freedom to slaves who defected in exchange for military service. Georgians, in turn, used slaves to construct fortifications.

Some 17,500 Creeks, living in a confederation of villages in western Georgia and eastern Alabama in 1812, cooperated with the British in attacks on the United States. With the help of Cherokee allies, Gen. Andrew Jackson crushed the Creeks at the Battle of Horseshoe Bend in 1814, and the Creeks were forced to cede two-thirds of all their remaining land to the United States. This cession included the last Creek claims in Georgia. Jackson was then appointed commander of the Southern District, ostensibly to defend Georgia from Seminole Indian raids from their Florida bases. It was generally known in Washington that Jackson wanted to obtain Florida for the United States, and it was not surprising when he exceeded his authority and invaded Florida, for he believed this was the only way to safeguard Georgia planters from the loss of large numbers of slaves.

The main actions of the War of 1812 that involved Georgia after the Creek War were border raids. Parties of Georgians, with their Indian allies, would raid Florida and engage groups of British with *their* black and Indian allies. According to historian John D. Milligan, blacks in Florida maroons "were openly eager for battle; they often planned and struck the first blow and then defied the Americans and the Indians to counterattack."

As was the case during the American Revolution, blacks fought on both sides during the War of 1812. And for several years, in a replay of the diplomatic conflict that followed the revolutionary war, the United States unsuccessfully pressed the British for the return of defecting slaves. In March 1815, President James Madison sent documentary evidence to the Senate naming seven Georgia slaveholders who had lost a total of 535 slaves in one British raid on plantations around Savannah during the War of 1812. The British did relinquish custody of some slaves, and U. S. officers used troops to prevent other fugitive slaves from embarking with the British from their Georgia bases. Still, 1,483 blacks left Cumberland Island on seventeen British ships early in 1815. Georgians claimed that 833 of them were stolen slaves.

The British took refuge slaves from New Orleans and the Chesapeake, but most of them were taken from British bases at St. Marys and St. Simons and Cumberland islands. Many slaves risked their lives to get out to the British ships, and several Georgia planters were ruined by the defections. Negotiations in the Anglo-American dispute continued to drag out as they had after the Revolution. Old claims, some going back to the revolutionary period, were settled eventually. One such involved twenty-eight slaves who deserted the Du Bignon plantation on Jekyll

Island and sought refuge with the British on Cumberland Island. The owner filed suit against the British for $69,418 when the revolutionary war was over and in 1828 received $10,920 from them in full settlement of his claim. Disputes with the British over the return of runaway slaves were never settled completely. Time's passage gradually stilled the planters' protests.

Georgian slaves continued to seek asylum in Florida; this situation was intolerable to Georgia and the U. S. government. Both were committed to supporting, strengthening, and extending the institution of slavery. As usual, force was employed to solve the problem of runaways to Florida. Three wars (1816–18, 1835–43, and 1855–58) were initiated and fought by the United States against the Indians and blacks. These protracted conflicts, called the Seminole Wars, came about for two main reasons: The United States wanted the land of the Seminoles and to end the use of Florida as a refuge for runaway slaves. As a result, the institution of slavery was protected and enhanced.

The complex interaction of blacks, reds, and whites in Georgia resulted in continual bondage for blacks, exile for the Indians, and supremacy for whites. Blacks and Indians would have been natural allies to make common cause against the Europeans, but relationships and attitudes were warped by slavery, twisted by racism, and exacerbated by the white practice of pitting blacks and Indians against each other. Georgia's founders did fear a black-red alliance, which did happen sometimes, but too often the Indians enslaved blacks despite their common status as victims. After the Civil War, African-American soldiers were used to help kill Native Americans.

2

A System of Bondage

The Slave Trade

Georgia's history is inseparable from the development of slavery, and Georgia's leaders were among the staunchest defenders of the slave trade that fed it. They consistently fought federal attempts to undermine the trade prior to the 1808 ban on it, and Georgia continued as a major center for slave trafficking until the Civil War.

Though slave ships from Africa did not go directly to Georgia before 1766 due to the small size of the Georgia market, merchants in Savannah had little trouble obtaining slaves directly from Africa via Charleston. While Georgia volunteered to go along with the First Continental Congress's 1775 ban on the slave trade as part of the general boycott of British goods, it refused to make this temporary ban a part of its 1777 Constitution. In 1779, the Continental Congress lifted its four-year old ban on the slave trade, but by 1788, every state except Georgia had outlawed or suspended the trade. In recognition of the shortage of slaves due to runaways during the Revolution, Georgia's 1789 Constitution specifically allowed the foreign slave trade to continue.

The most fundamental issues at the 1787 Constitutional Convention concerned slavery and the slave trade. Georgia's planters interpreted proposals to ban the slave trade as attacks on slavery itself. Abraham Baldwin, Georgia's delegate to the Constitutional Convention, stated that Georgia would never yield her right to import slaves and agreed with C. C. Pinckney of South Carolina that neither state could do without fresh supplies of slaves. During negotiations, Northern interests agreed that Congress should be prohibited from considering a ban on the slave trade for twenty years.

Georgians also fought mightily against any federal regulation of slavery. The new United States government under the Constitution was barely born when Georgia's representatives began to threaten disunion over the slave issue. In May 1789, during the first session of the First Continental Congress, Rep. James Jackson of Georgia repeated the idea that agriculture was impractical in Georgia without slave labor. In a 1790 debate over a Quaker petition against the slave trade, Jackson said that interference with the slave trade would lead to emancipation and jeopardize all property. Jackson concluded, "Anyone who attacks slavery might be in danger in Georgia." This remained a strongly held and consistent attitude among Georgia's plantocracy. In 1794, in the face of several abolitionist petitions to Congress, Jackson continued to voice Georgia's opposition to any ban of the slave trade by arguing that the Bible and Jesus favored slavery and that if Congress persisted, it would endanger the Union; furthermore, Georgia never would have joined the Union if Georgians had known that by so doing they would endanger slavery.

In 1793, Georgia banned the importation of slaves from the Bahamas, West Indies, and especially Haiti. There was a special horror of slaves from this French colony as French Revolutionary ideas about liberty, equality, and fraternity had begun to circulate there. Confirming planters' worst fears, the most significant slave revolt in the New World broke out in Haiti, led by Toussaint L'Ouverture. In 1795, responding to rumors that the importation ban was being violated, fearful citizens of Savannah turned out for a mass meeting to demand its enforcement.

When Georgia adopted her third constitution in 1798, it prohibited the importation of slaves from foreign shores. The law enforcing this provision assessed a $1,000 penalty for each slave brought in. However, the slave trade continued. According to congressional debate, 20,000 slaves were imported into Georgia and the Carolinas in 1803, mostly by New England merchants hiding behind a foreign flag. While Georgia imported many, it also exported a few slaves. In 1805, three different ships carrying slaves went from Savannah to Cuba.

Federal legislation, signed into law March 2, 1807, banned the slave trade effective January 1, 1808, and provided for the forfeiture of the vessel and cargo, an $800 fine for anyone knowingly buying a smuggled slave, and a $20,000 fine for equipping a slave ship. The law gave the states permission to dispose of the slaves as they saw fit; they could be returned to Africa, but they seldom were. Henceforth, most smuggled slaves were resold into slavery by the states in which they were captured. Georgia congressman Peter Early voted for this bill, but he successfully amended it to protect the domestic slave trade by permitting the ocean transport of slaves from one part of the United States to another.

The United States failed to take vigorous action to enforce its own ban on the Atlantic slave trade. It also sabotaged England's efforts to do so.

There is no doubt that hundreds of thousands of slaves were smuggled into the United States between the enactment of the 1808 prohibition and the Civil War. In one day in 1819, hundreds of slaves were unloaded in Savannah, including 109 from the schooner *Politana*.

Following the federal ban on the slave trade, the main avenue by which slaves were being smuggled into the United States then was from Spanish Florida into Georgia. Andrew Jackson charged in 1819 that David Mitchell resigned as governor of Georgia to become an Indian agent, then used his post and federal funds to encourage the Creek Indians in Georgia to smuggle in black slaves. Jackson further stated that William H. Crawford (who, with George M. Troup, led the planter faction against the small farmers in Georgia), was the moving force and silent partner in the illegal activities. John Clark, leader of the small farmer faction, was elected governor in 1819. Clark accused Mitchell of smuggling in slaves and subsequently sent his indictment to President Monroe, who found that the charges were substantiated and dismissed Mitchell from his post.

Georgia remained a center for smuggled slaves until the Civil War. Ex-slaves interviewed in the 1930s remembered the landing of Africans in the 1850s. Wallace Quarterman, who was born near Darien in 1844, recalled slaves from Africa being landed near his home before the Civil War. In the late 1850s, a Georgia agricultural society offered a twenty-five dollar prize for the most physically perfect African imported that year. The last slave ship to smuggle slaves into Georgia was the *Wanderer*, one of many vessels operating out of New York involved in the illegal trade. The *Wanderer* arrived at Jekyll Island on November 28, 1858, with a cargo of 409 "salt backs," as the smuggled slaves were called. Seventy-eight more perished during the passage from Africa. This venture was the work of Charles A. L. Lamar, a prominent Georgian who had engaged in the slave trade for some time. He was able to distribute the Africans before the government could act.

As the smuggling continued, so did efforts to legalize the slave trade. Reopening the trade was a hot topic of conversation in Georgia all through the 1850s. The *Macon Georgia Citizen* editorialized in 1859 that the African slave trade should be reopened because there was "no chance" for a poor man to obtain slaves at the current high prices. A move to modify the state constitution to permit reopening the trade failed by only one vote in the legislature. The actual end of the slave trade came with the Civil War and the Union blockade of the South.

Slave Economy and Society

Slavery insulated the South from the three great shaping forces of the nineteenth century: urbanization, industrialization, and emigration. Lacking these modernizing influences, the South was retarded before the

Civil War and continued as a backwater for a century afterward. Nowhere is this more clearly seen than in Georgia.

Slavery delayed Georgia's development by establishing negative attitudes toward work. It deprived the slave of the incentive to improve traditional work methods, and the master was apathetic toward labor-saving methods or technological innovations. Plantation records show a dependence on muscle power. Of a $42,660 total investment in a plantation in Stewart County, Georgia, in the early 1800s, only $300 was invested in tools and machinery. The Tooke plantation in Georgia had a total investment in implements and machinery, other than the cotton gin, of just $85. This lack of machinery was typical. Slavery also stultified the South, inhibiting the growth of the domestic market, since slaves and their poor white counterparts had little purchasing power. The weakness of the domestic market in Georgia restricted the growth of a progressive nonplanter middle class that would have supported industrialization, played a greater role in the abolition of slavery, and opposed secession.

Slaves have always been the best source of information on slave life. Many wrote their life stories after escaping to the North. Others told their stories to abolitionists who printed them in their extensive press, and many ex-slaves recounted their trials and tribulations after the Civil War. Emerging from this surprisingly large body of literature is the fact that the treatment of slaves varied greatly depending on time, place, and master.

The ninety-six narratives of Georgia ex-slaves, collected by the Federal Writers Project during the New Deal, indicate that the slave's life was one of unremitting toil, that educational opportunities were rare, but that harsh punishments and whippings were the exception. All recalled pleasant moments. Twenty-one said they had good masters, though often they said the overseer was harsh. Eight said their masters were bad. The remainder called their masters fair. Some who said their masters were good also told of being whipped. Others left their "good" masters at the first opportunity to be free.

There are many accounts of good and bad treatment. One thing is certain, however: Inhumanity was inherent in the system. Too many Georgia bondsmen testified to the brutality of slavery for there to be any question concerning it. Mr. Johnson, a slave who was emancipated by his master in the North, told the Massachusetts Anti-Slavery Society in 1837 that, although his owner "was more a father than a master," other masters in Georgia were exceedingly brutal: "I have seen a Christian professor, after the communion, have four slaves tied together and whipped raw, and then washed down with brine." Johnson stated he knew of another Georgia slave, Tom Buckine, who was given 150 lashes for going to a meeting.

John Sella Martin also testified on the cruelty of the "peculiar institution" in Georgia. To pay a debt of his owner, he was torn from his mother when he was nine years old and sold separately to a new master who lived sixty miles away. His mother tried three times to go and see him, but each time she was caught and severely whipped. When he was older, he went to see her, and she was almost beaten to death for "harboring" a runaway—her son. The same master, a Mr. Terry, did beat another slave to death with four hundred lashes because the slave had resisted a clubbing. Martin escaped to Chicago in 1856 and became a noted abolitionist and cleric who worked with Frederick Douglass. After the Civil War, he served in Louisiana as a superintendent of a school district, where he fought segregation.

A similar story was supplied by the Rev. W. B. Allen, born a slave in Georgia in 1850, who became a Methodist preacher in Columbus. He knew of slaves beaten to death for traveling without a pass, passing as white, assisting fugitives, or any of fifteen other reasons. Many Georgia slaves recounted the brutality and omnipresence of the slave patrols, which they called "paddy rollers," among other names. The patrols routinely whipped slaves traveling without proper passes.

Just as slaves disagreed on the brutality of slavery, they also disagreed on where slavery was the worst. Being sold "down the river" meant to be sent toward the frontier where new lands were opening up and life was cruder. There cotton was more profitable, slaves were worked harder, and discipline was more severe. Georgia itself was "down the river" until the 1850s, and Frederick Douglass once said that to be sold to Georgia was the worst fate possible.

Abolitionist pressures could apparently bring out the worst in masters, too. "In 1851, Garnet Andrews warned the Southern Central Agriculture Society of Georgia not to allow unscrupulous masters to use the abolitionist agitation to excuse undue severity toward their slaves," slavery historian Eugene Genovese wrote in *Roll, Jordan, Roll*. When Georgia's 1798 Constitution stated, "Any person who shall maliciously dismember or deprive a slave of life shall suffer such punishment as would be inflicted in case the like offence had been committed on a free white person," the state recognized that such excessive cruelty conflicted with the interests of the master class. In an 1827 case, a Georgia grand jury did indict a slave owner for manslaughter for beating a slave to death, but the owner was .acquitted. By the 1850s, Georgia law prohibited certain treatment of slaves, such as "cutting, or wounding, or...cruelly and unnecessarily biting or tearing with dogs."

However, there was no recourse for slaves who had been mistreated. A slave could not testify in court against a master—or any white, for that matter—and few white Georgians would contradict any master who said a given punishment was necessary. Punishment could be for any reason, real or fancied. Short of actually killing a white person, the most infuriating slave behavior was resistance to orders or running away. This frequently resulted in cruel reactions by owners.

Slave accounts indicate that overseers were often a bigger problem than masters, since the former were directly accountable for the operations' profit or loss. Masters might temper the acts of a brutal overseer, but if the overseer showed a satisfactory profit, his methods would not be questioned closely. One way the slaves could have some control over their lives was to sabotage their work and make a cruel overseer appear incompetent. Overseers had to have some support from the slaves to keep their jobs.

Many slaves were supervised by black drivers who were responsible for their work and conduct. Usually, they were large, strong slaves in the prime of life. One study indicated that only 20 percent of all Southern plantations had white overseers. Seldom would a small operation of under fifteen slaves have a white overseer, and only about one-fourth of the larger plantations with fifty or more slaves had them. Where there was no overseer, the master would delegate one or more slave drivers to organize the work. Occasionally, a driver might have a mean streak and flaunt his authority over the other slaves, but slaves usually preferred supervision by a black driver.

By the time Georgia's ban against slavery was lifted in 1750, the number of slaves had grown to about a thousand. This doubled in the next five years, and after that the increase was even more dramatic, as table 2.1 indicates.

Table 2.1 Population of Georgia

Year	Blacks	Whites	Total	% BLACK
1790	29,662	52,886	85,248	35
1800	60,425	102,216	162,641	37
1810	107,019	145,414	252,443	42
1820	151,419	189,570	340,989	44
1830	220,017	296,806	516,823	43
1840	283,697	407,695	691,392	41
1850	384,613	521,572	906,185	42
1860	465,608	591,550	1,057,158	44

Source: Table 13, "Geographic Distribution and Increase," James M. McPherson, *Negro Population in the United States* (New York: Arno Press and the *New York Times*, 1968), pp. 43–45.

The average number of slaves owned by Georgia's slave-owning families rose from eleven in 1755 to twenty-three in 1777, greater than the average for all such families in the United States at that time. In 1860, about 40 percent of all white families in Georgia owned slaves. Fifty-seven percent of the slaves were in units of twenty or more; 24 percent, in units of fifty or more. The larger concentrations were in the eastern part of the state, in the rice swamps and on the Sea Islands, although other centers of slavery, such as Macon, later developed. Macon's founding father, John Davis, owned twenty-one slaves in 1826. By 1860, Maconites owned 6,890 slaves, and half of the white Savannah households had slaves.

Most slaves were occupied in agriculture. As the nation grew, the geographic center of the U. S. slave population moved from Virginia in 1790 to northwest Georgia by 1860. This reflected the southwestern movement of the cotton frontier, a shift that was required because the slave-based cotton monoculture was constantly exhausting the soil and impelling masters to look to distant places for new plantation lands.

Rice and indigo were the main cash crops of Colonial Georgia. Some tobacco was grown in the hill country by small farmers. Coastal Georgia was also home to a modest sugar industry in the 1800s. On the rice plantations near the coast, the slaves saw less of their masters, who might live on the plantation for half a year but only visited occasionally during the malaria season, from May until the first frost. The slaves were isolated and developed a close society with a high degree of autonomy under black drivers.

In the 1840-60 period, there were up to thirty thousand acres in Georgia devoted to rice culture. Only South Carolina produced more than Georgia's 52 million pounds in 1859. Much of this work required great skill, and Frederick Law Olmsted reported that on one Georgia rice plantation, a slave engineer received higher pay (in the form of presents) than the white overseer—an interesting example of using pecuniary incentives with slaves. The average rice plantation was four hundred acres, had about sixty field hands, and required an investment of $100,000. The slaves were usually given individual tasks each day, and when they had completed them, they were free to till their gardens and care for animals or quit work for the day. Custom set the size of the task, and most slaves refused to let it be increased. The best workers could finish their daily tasks in eight or nine hours. Children were expected to do one-half a task from the age of ten, and younger children would shoot birds or catch rats.

On some plantations the regimen was more severe. An English traveler in 1842 reported that on a rice plantation near Savannah the slaves worked in gangs from daylight to dark, six days a week, and were furnished only one peck (two gallons) of corn a week for rations. They had to get the rest of their food on their own somehow, and none of them held hope for a better future.

Cotton was Georgia's main cash crop after 1812. Sea Island cotton was introduced into Georgia in the late 1780s and proved profitable in a small area along the coast where it could be grown. The hardier, shorter-fibered upland cotton that could grow throughout the state was known at this time but was unprofitable because the sticky fibers adhered to the seeds so tenaciously that it was a good day's work for a slave to separate one pound of cotton fiber. This process of separation, called "ginning," was necessary before the fiber could be spun into thread. Sea Island cotton was profitable because it could be easily ginned, since the fibers did not stick to the seeds. The expansion of the upland cotton culture awaited the invention of the mechanical cotton gin.

The standard account of the invention of the cotton gin credits it to Eli Whitney, a young Yale graduate student who was visiting a plantation near Savannah in 1793. Other sources have credited unknown slave mechanics for this important invention. Since slaves were the mechanics and craftsmen of the plantations, it is likely that some ideas Whitney incorporated into the gin came originally from discussing the problem with slaves.

The first of Whitney's gins enabled one slave to separate fifty pounds of cotton fiber from its seeds in one day. Subsequent models were far more efficient. This machine laid the basis for the cotton kingdom, and production increased spectacularly from a few bales before the Revolution to 150,000 bales in 1826 when Georgia became the world's leading cotton producer. By 1860, Georgia's production had soared to over 700,000 bales a year, but Alabama, Mississippi, and Louisiana produced more.

Slave narratives reveal that a host of jobs kept the agricultural slaves busy when they were not doing crop work in the fields. Harvests were hauled and stored, animals were tended, fields were prepared for the next crop, land was logged and cleared, rails were split to build and repair fences, wagons and carriages were built and maintained, buildings were constructed and repaired, and ditches were dug and cleaned out. On many larger plantations, slaves wove cloth, sewed garments, and made and repaired shoes. Often these jobs were done after the regular day's work. Blacksmiths, ironworkers, and coopers were seen frequently at work. As if this were not enough, there were also the routine tasks of cooking, mending, and cleaning after the regular day's work, and if the slave had a wise master, there was a kitchen garden to tend.

Not all slaves did agricultural work. In Georgia, in 1860, 88 percent of the male slaves were field hands, 6 percent were artisans, 4 percent performed unskilled labor, and 2 percent served the big house. Some slaves worked in the cities, especially Savannah, while others did industrial and construction work throughout the state.

While white workers did not object to slaves doing agricultural work, they did not want to compete with skilled slaves in urban areas. In 1758, when up to 10 percent of Georgia slaves were skilled workers, a law was designed ostensibly to keep skilled slaves out of the towns. However, the General Assembly allowed enough exceptions to actually encourage competition between white and black workers, which helped keep urban wages down. Pitting the two groups against each other would be a major theme in Georgia's history. In the 1800s, white mechanics and artisans constantly protested against having to compete with free Negro or slave labor and obtained unwieldy laws, such as an 1845 legislative act forbidding blacks from working in cotton mills. In 1845 and again in 1848, the Georgia legislature provided a $200 fine for Negro mechanics contracting jobs. This was warmly supported by a resolution of Macon mechanics against black competition on the grounds it would lessen the dignity of white labor. Despite the laws, in 1858, 200 white artisans protested to the Atlanta City Council that black artisans were underbidding them.

There was widespread use of slaves in transportation and public works. Slaves built over a thousand miles of railroad in Georgia and helped build the Brunswick and Altamaha Canal while working for private contractors, although the canal never operated. In 1836, work started on the Central of Georgia Railroad, and slaves gradually replaced white workers during the depression. The Alabama, Florida, and Georgia Railroad contractors advertised for five hundred slaves for construction, and the Macon and Forsyth Railroad wanted three hundred. In the 1830s several other railroads owned slaves, and the state appropriated $50,000 to purchase 207 slaves for road construction and maintenance. This experiment ended the following year because runaways, sickness, and deaths made it too costly.

Slaves not only built railroads but helped operate them as engineers and firemen. The Macon Steamboat Company used slaves to transport cotton to Savannah and Darien, and in 1831 a company was organized to insure the slave boat workers. Several municipalities used slaves for public work. All males, free and slave, were supposed to donate a few days a year to road-maintenance work, but few actually did. Macon owned ten slaves for routine street maintenance and hired others as needed, as, for example, when Mulberry Street was repaired in 1831.

Slaves were also promoted for industrial use and manufacturing. In 1830, half the millworkers were slaves. Slave labor was used in the Augusta cotton factory, one of the largest and most modern of its time. In 1838, blacks and whites worked side by side in the Athens cotton mill.

The *Macon Telegraph* praised slave labor in textile mills as "more docile, more constant and cheaper than freemen." The 1851 cotton planters' convention promoted an increase in the state's cotton mills and recommended slaves as operators. The Increase Cotton Plant owned six slaves.

Slaves worked in the lumber industry, especially around Savannah. Logs were rafted downriver by three- to five-man interracial crews from as far away as Augusta. Of the two hundred people employed in the Savannah lumber mills in 1849, most were black. Free Negroes also did logging and sawmilling on the plantations. Elbert Heard, a slave born in Georgia, worked on one of the first steam sawmills in the state for the Macon and Forsyth Railroad in 1836. He became a prosperous home builder in Americus after the Civil War.

Slaves preferred working in the cities to working on the plantations because they could keep more of the income produced by their labor. In rural areas this "pay" was mainly in the form of food, clothing, and shelter. In the cities, there were more opportunities for a slave to hire out, receive money, and manage his own life a little, because many of the constraints associated with the close supervision on the plantation fell away. Free blacks were concentrated in the cities, and whites often could not tell by looking who was slave and who was free.

Sometimes the owner would let the slave pick his job, with the stipulation that he return a certain amount of money regularly to the owner. If the slave earned more, he often could keep the extra money. The number of slaves who could sell their own time was increased by wills that provided that funds for the support of widows and for the education of the master's children would come from the money brought in by hiring out the slaves. In Atlanta, slaves with permission to hire themselves out would, along with free blacks who were looking for work, congregate on what is still known as "Hungry Corner," which used to be a park on what is now Central Avenue.

Savannah boomed after the Central of Georgia Railroad was completed in 1843. By 1850, Savannah replaced Charleston as the third-largest cotton-exporting port in the nation. In these boom conditions, slaves could hire themselves out, and free blacks could find employment more readily. Hiring out began before 1760, and the different municipalities adopted a host of regulations governing slaves who were hired out. They had to wear distinctive identification badges that cost the owner $2.50–$10.00. In an effort to control blacks, a curfew was instituted from 10:00 P.M. to midnight, and there were regulations prohibiting more than seven blacks meeting together at any one time except for church or funerals. These regulations reflected the fear of rebellion and refute the myth of a peaceful antebellum atmosphere. Court records also show whites striking and beating blacks and blacks fighting back.

Some of this excitement was no doubt stimulated by the liquor that was readily available. Demon Rum had his enemies, and when he raised his head in antebellum Georgia, it was smartly slapped around by forty temperance societies, three of which were black. In Bryan County, two hundred slaves promised to stay on the wagon, and the local Baptist church refused membership to all, including slaves, who would not take the pledge. Liquor remained a popular beverage, and the state temperance society proposed to run two thousand grog shopkeepers out of the state in 1855.

Slaves often appropriated white-owned property. Liquor shops were often fences for the receipt of property "liberated" by the slaves in and around Savannah. To the white, this was stealing. To the slave, it was reclaiming a small portion of what was due for unpaid labor. In any event, this transfer of goods was a fact of life in Georgia. By one estimate, this stolen property included forty to sixty bales of cotton a week. One planter kept a store where he bought anything the slaves wanted to sell and paid them with simple necessities to keep them from taking the goods into town and trading them for liquor at the grog shops. Masters often despaired over what they perceived to be the dishonesty of slaves. Much of what the slaves appropriated was to try to make an inadequate diet better or to get things they could have easily purchased had they been paid for their labor.

Slaves in Athens had little supervision and had the run of the town after work each day. Some had skilled jobs, and they dominated the mechanical and building trades. Some were hired out by their masters, while others hired themselves out and returned most of their earnings to their master. If they lived away from the master's property, the master had to pay the city a fee. Sometimes, to escape this fee, the master would let the slaves live just outside the town, where they had even less supervision. Macon tried to ensure the close supervision of the slaves by requiring that they live on the same lot as their owner whenever possible. Masters who were too lax in supervising their slaves were sometimes called to task. The owner of Sinai and Silas Reynolds, the great-great-great-grandparents of Lena Horne, was cited by a Coweta County grand jury in 1839 for permitting them to live off by themselves.

These urban environments created possibilities for slaves to buy their freedom with their savings. Some fortunate ones who did so also bought their wives and children, who might remain on the record as slaves of their husbands or fathers rather than run the risk of being reenslaved if they were freed. This possibility of forced reenslavement was omnipresent. Another reason a black might "own" his family as slaves was that as the Civil War approached, it grew increasingly difficult to obtain legal manumissions in Georgia. Often a special act of the legislature was required for each manumission.

One of the most astounding cases of self-purchase involved Dimmock Charlton, a slave in Savannah. He was born in Africa, captured in an intertribal war, and sold into slavery when he was only twelve years old. The slave ship taking him to the United States was captured by the British and he became a cabin boy on the HMS *Peacock*, later captured by the USS *Hornet* in the War of 1812. Taken to Savannah, he was sold into slavery but was permitted to hire himself out. After he had saved $800 by working many years as a stevedore, he bought his freedom, or so he thought. His master took the money but defrauded him of his freedom by selling him to another owner, who also bought Charlton's wife and children. The new master agreed to let Charlton buy himself and his family for $1,500. This took more long years to save. The second master also proved deceitful. He took the money and then sold each member of the family separately. Charlton's third owner kept his word and really did free him when the agreed-upon price had been saved. By this time Charlton had lost track of his family and, old and worn out after forty-five years of labor in a futile cause, he made his way to England in 1857, where he later became a public charge.

In all of Georgia's cities there was a deep suspicion that blacks had too much freedom. An endless list of city ordinances tried to limit liberties by curfews, registrations, special taxes, identification badges, and regulations limiting the right of assembly in groups. Usually such regulations claimed to be aimed at curbing boisterous behavior, but they were more likely inspired by fears of revolts and insurrections. A different apprehension was expressed by whites in Columbus, where so much of the skilled work was done by slaves that whites were unable to get their children started in skilled trades.

The peculiar institution was a profitable one for the slaveholders. F. N. Boney, professor of history at the University of Georgia, stated that the large cotton plantations in Georgia, cultivated by gangs of slaves, were more profitable than most other economic enterprises. The rice plantations on the Atlantic Coast were the most profitable slave enterprises in the early history of the new nation.

The average price of prime field hands in Georgia ranged from $300 in 1792 to $1,800 in 1860. The total cost of maintaining a male slave in the prime of his life during the two decades before the Civil War was less than thirty dollars a year, or less than one cent per hour for many slaves. Such a slave would produce about five bales of cotton that the planter could sell for around $200. A female slave produced less cotton, but she produced children who could be worked or sold.

In the 1850s, the labor of the average slave created over twice as much wealth as the master paid to buy, maintain, and provide for the reproduction of the typical slave, according to historians Roger Ransom and Richard Sutch. The profitability of slavery was a direct result of the low living standards of the slaves. James D. W. De Bow, pro-slavery editor and statistician, said that a slave's food cost his owner two cents a day. Frederick Law Olmsted, who traveled extensively in the antebellum South, said that the slaves' food was not as good "in quality or quantity as that which we furnish rogues in our penitentiaries." Slaves built their cabins from local material, usually available without cost to the owner. Often they had dirt floors, and "windows" were holes in the wall that could only be closed by wooden shutters. Fresh air poured in abundantly through the cracks, even in winter, and many slaves reported that they could see the stars at night through the holes in the roofs.

Slaves were not only profitable on the plantations, but their use in Georgia's industry increased steadily for the simple reason that they cost less than free labor. In 1845, the DeKalb Mill reported that a slave worker cost seventy-five dollars a year, two-thirds of what a white Georgian worker would receive—and only a third of a skilled Northern mill hand's wages.

A well-functioning domestic slave trade was vital to the profitability of slavery. The entire slave system depended on the shipment of surplus slaves to newer cotton areas where slaves were in demand and higher priced. As a result, families were more likely to be torn apart in those states producing surplus slaves. Georgia began to produce surplus slaves before 1830 and by the 1850s was exporting considerable numbers to the West. Texas was the final destination for the greatest number.

The largest single sale of slaves recorded in U. S. history came when James Bond, Georgia's largest planter, sold 566 slaves in 1860 for $580,000. Pierce Butler, another large Georgia planter, sold four hundred slaves in 1859 to pay his debts. Savannah had an active slave market, and the process of auctioning off human beings, once seen, was never forgotten. One of the bitterest memories of Susie King Taylor, a slave born in Georgia who became prominent during the Civil War for her work for the Union, was the recollection of handcuffed slaves being sold on the block at the corner of Brayton Street and Court Lane in Savannah and in Bryant Street near the Pulaski House. Macon was also one of the principal slave markets in the South.

Georgia planters were always glad to sell surplus and "troublemaking" slaves to other states, but Georgians frequently worried that the state would become a dumping ground for the South's black criminals. In 1851, the editor of the *Milledgeville Southern Recorder* fretted about "the introduction into our state, of the Negro felons and desperadoes of all the other states." Several times, Georgia's lawmakers tried to prohibit the importation of slaves from outside the state, but the convenience and economic necessity of the domestic slave trade always outweighed its drawbacks.

Of all the criticism directed against slavery, outcries against the breakup of slave families made planters squirm most. Some Georgia masters may have tried to avoid this heartbreaking practice, and some sale advertisements did specify that slaves be sold as families, but Georgia placed few restrictions on the breakup of families when slaves were sold to satisfy creditors and none at all when the master voluntarily sold his slaves, as when surplus slaves were sent "down the river" to the frontier.

It is likely that these minor restrictions offered no protection to slave families. Since the laws did not provide for the marriage of slaves, slave children had no legal fathers, and descent was reckoned through the mother. When a slave family was sold "together," this usually only meant that the mother and her children went as a unit. It was easier to sell the members of a slave couple separately. Many masters and masters' sons fathered children by slave women. However, if the white father owned the mother, the child was his by virtue of this ownership, not biology. A slave child's black father was legally ignored.

Generally masters encouraged monogamy among their slaves, and there is much evidence of strong family ties developing; however, since Colonial slave mothers averaged less than two children, the master's encouragement of family life left much to be desired. Another factor limiting the natural increase of slaves was the sex ratio during the Colonial period, when there were 146 males for every 100 females. When white men appropriated some of the black women, this made the ratio even more unbalanced.

There were some instances of white fathers acknowledging and providing for their black children. Moses Nunes acknowledged in his will that he was the father of four children by his slave mistress and left them land and personal property when he died in Savannah in 1797. David Dickson, a prominent and progressive Hancock County planter, took Julia, a black slave, as his wife and lived openly with her and their daughter Amanda. He was socially ostracized for his unconventional lifestyle. When he died in 1885, he left his estate to his daughter, thereby making her the wealthiest black in Georgia at the time.

Michael Morris Healy, a prominent planter near Macon, and his beautiful slave wife, Mary Eliza, had ten children. He sent them all north to escape insult and persecution and to acquire an education. Several of them became prominent and successful. The eldest, James Augustine Healy, became the first black Roman Catholic bishop in the United States. Two sisters became nuns, one a convent superior, and two brothers also became clerics. Another brother, Michael A. Healy, became a captain in the U. S. Coast Guard. Dickson and Healy were exceptions, and tolerance for miscegenation often depended on discretion. When Ben Perley Poore, who later became a nationally known correspondent, was the editor of the *Southern Whig* in Athens, he reportedly was fined $400 and driven from town in 1845 for hosting an orgiastic dinner dance for white men and mulatto women.

A common saying throughout the South was that the white mistress of a plantation knew the father of every child on the neighboring plantations but had no idea who fathered those on her own. This referred to the fact that she could not admit that her father, husband, or sons might be the fathers of the black children under her nose. Dolly Madison, wife of President James Madison, said that the Southern wife was "the chief slave of the master's harem." Mary Boykin Chesnut, in her Civil War *Diary from Dixie*, said that a Southern slaveholder could remain respectable while putting the children of his black harem into the same house where he lived with his wife. Fanny Kemble, wife of Georgia planter Pierce M. Butler, described this situation well in her *Journal of a Residence on a Georgia Plantation in 1838-1839*. Sometimes the black slaves resented the children with white fathers, and one former slave stated to a Federal Writers Project interviewer that slave children with straight hair would have it cut very short by their mothers to avoid calling attention to their white parentage.

Legend also has it that miscegenation in the slave South was only between white men and black women and that it resulted from the men's lechery and the women's powerlessness. In fact, some black women welcomed white lovers, and some white women welcomed black lovers. Genovese stated, "Despite the legend, white women of all classes had black lovers and sometimes husbands in all parts of the South, especially in the towns and cities." Most of these unions were clandestine. Modern scholars agree that miscegenation was common and worked both ways. Historian John Hope Franklin said, "The practice of white women mixing with Negro men was fairly widespread during the Colonial Period and had not entirely ceased by 1865." Georgia-born John Blassingame, black studies chairman at Yale University, said that the white women were infuriated about their husbands' slave concubines and "on innumerable occasions" took slave lovers themselves. In any event it was not against the law in Georgia, which did not adopt an antimiscegenation statute until 1865.

* * *

The slaves' poor living standards affected their health, well-being, and life expectancy. Considering their substandard diet, poor housing, and lack of sanitation, it is surprising that the rate of natural increase among slaves was so high. Many slaves relate in their narratives that, as children, they ate "like pigs" from a common trough that often had dirt mixed with the food. Standard fare for adult slaves consisted of about two pounds of corn meal or corn weekly and up to a half pound of low-grade pork a day. This was sometimes supplemented by vegetables from the slave's garden and by fishing or hunting. Such a diet was deficient in protein and "must be judged immensely damaging," as Genovese stated. The slaves' opportunities to improve their diet were limited. There was not much free time to hunt, fish, or garden. Owners were reluctant to allow very much land for gardens for slaves, for this would reduce the amount available for the cash crops.

As the treatment of slaves varied greatly from one owner to another, some plantations experienced less trouble due to sickness than others, but on even the best it was a problem. In the Georgia rice country, few plantations produced as many slaves as died; therefore, periodic purchases had to be made to maintain the work force. One South Carolina planter, on the verge of buying two hundred acres of rice land on the Savannah River, backed out of the deal because of what he said was the "great mortality" among the slaves there. In other sections of the state, smallpox and yellow fever were considered the worst diseases.

The average planter allowed three dollars a year for medical expenses for each slave. This was generally inadequate, so slaves were forced to rely on their own knowledge of folk remedies and medicinal plants. Quite a few preferred this to the dubious ministrations of the overseer or the master's family. Two Georgia pharmacists found references to the use of ninety medicinal plants in the narratives of Georgia slaves, ranging from alder root for boils to yellowroot for ulcerated mouths.

In addition to their contribution to folk medicine, slaves contributed, albeit unwillingly, to the advance of medical science by serving as guinea pigs for doctors trying out experimental treatments and new surgical techniques. John Brown, in his narrative of slave life in Georgia, told of medical "experiments" performed that more resembled torture than science. Once Brown's skin was blistered to see how deep his blackness went. Since whites did not like the idea of their loved ones being dissected by medical students, the Atlanta Medical College routinely had its students practice on the bodies of blacks. In 1852, the Medical College of Georgia at Augusta purchased Grandison Harris, who was assigned the task of obtaining cadavers by gift, purchase, or grave robbing. He did good work and continued for almost forty years after slavery ended.

In the South, the general level of physicians' training was low, and the doctor was often no more skilled than the master or overseer. Many planters complained of slaves coming down with respiratory diseases in the winter. They did not understand then that the sickle cell trait, common among blacks, while protecting against malaria, predisposed them to pneumococcal infections.

Because of the unending toil and poor diet and living conditions slaves grew old before their time, and despite protestations from the master class that the aged and infirm were always kept on the plantations as respected retirees, some were cast out when they were no longer productive workers. Thomas M. Williams tried to meet this need by providing in his will for the establishment of a Negro hospital in Savannah in 1817. Another proposal recommending that the state of Georgia pay for the support of old and infirm slaves, with the cost to be passed on to the owners, was made in 1816. These proposals led to the establishment of the Georgia Infirmary in Savannah in 1832. This first state-supported hospital founded in the United States for blacks was chartered by the General Assembly, which provided twenty dollars a year for the maintenance of each patient. It fell far short of meeting the need. Macon had two infirmaries for blacks by 1856. Some attention was paid to the handicapped, though less than 1 percent of Georgia's slaves were classified as deaf, dumb, insane, or idiotic, in contrast to 5-10 percent of the state's whites.

From early on, slavery became the most important fact of life in Georgia. It determined the political actions of the state's leaders, and its problems dominated the thinking of all, both slave and free. Though slavery was an ancient institution, Southern slavery acquired an extremely racist defense that was carried to extremes. This inhibited Georgia's development before the Civil War and laid the foundations for the brutal society that followed.

Slavery was not monolithic or uniform. There were great variations in how Georgia's slaves were treated, but the slave who was treated best was still a slave, while those on the other extreme endured hell on earth. The benefits of slavery to the few masked a culture that was degrading to all other Georgians, white and black. As the ex-slave Mr. Johnson concluded, slavery was the "cruelest ting in de world." Still, slaves developed strong, stable, complicated personalities and adapted to a broad range of conditions.

In addition to the knowledge of herbal medicine, there were other African "survivals" throughout the slave culture. In Georgia, they were strongest in the rice country around Savannah on the Ogeechee River where the slaves were left more to themselves, thanks to the whites' fear of contracting malaria. One evidence of African survivals is in language, especially the Gullah and Geechee dialects. Many African words became incorporated into dialects, and some are now a part of standard English: okra, gumbo, and tabby (a building material made with oyster shells), for example. African survivals are more significant than many previously thought; as late as 1940 it was still possible to find blacks whose parents or grandparents had remembered life in Africa and passed these recollections on as part of the oral tradition.

Resistance and Rebellion

The most telling judgment of the peculiar institution was the unremitting resistance of slaves to their bondage. Despite the romantic vision of the antebellum South many people have, slaves were not happy and contented, and they showed their disaffection constantly. Fear of slave revolts was a paramount concern of Southern whites, and runaways were a fact of life; the massive numbers of slave runaways during the Revolution and northern Florida's armed camps of fugitive slaves from Georgia offer compelling evidence of this. Georgia resembled a police state in its efforts to guarantee slave docility and obedience. Nevertheless, slave resistance and rebellion varied from trickery to lighten their work load to revolutionary acts, including organizing to kill the white overseer or master, escaping to freedom in the North, or establishing and maintaining a maroon.

Whites liked to recall how slaves in Savannah protected their masters property from looting when many whites fled the city during the epidemic of 1820. Incidents of slaves' loyalty to whites are numerous, but they tell a half-truth that is contradicted by a larger truth: Countless thousands of incidents showed whites that blacks resented servitude.

Plantation records indicate that slaves constantly matched wits with masters and overseers to ease their burdens. They frequently used a "divide and conquer" strategy to make trouble between the overseer and the master and often had the pleasure of seeing a hated overseer pack his bags and leave. By resisting unusually harsh treatment, the slaves were often able to modify it.

Malingering and sabotage—such as breaking tools and abusing livestock—were common among slaves. In 1855 Dr. Samuel W. Cartwright, a respected Southern medical man, diagnosed this as a disease, *dysaethesia aethiopica*, which caused the slave to work "in a headlong, careless manner, treading down with his feet or cutting with his hoe the plants." Feigning illness or pregnancy was also typical. The most publicized form of slave resistance was running away, and the good Dr.

Cartwright also invented a syndrome to explain that behavior: drapetomania, or in simpler terms, "the disease causing Negroes to run away."

The slaves' actions in resisting slavery encouraged the development of the Northern abolition movement. When thousands of the most vigorous, militant slaves left the South, their exodus may have acted as a safety valve, letting off the steam of slave discontent and saving the whole system from explosion. Efforts to downplay slave resistance fail to properly credit this "venting." In any case, runaways shook the confidence of masters in their ability to maintain and strengthen the system. We will never know the exact number of fugitive slaves because secrecy, not record keeping, was the key to their success.

Most masters were reluctant to admit that their slaves ran away and minimized the number, believing that public discussion of the problem would only encourage more slaves to make a break for freedom. The 1850 census states that Georgia had only eighty-nine fugitive slaves, an incredibly low number. In the next ten years the runaway problem became more acute as the abolition movement matured, but the 1860 census indicated that runaways from Georgia had declined to an absurdly low twenty-three—a total whose accuracy is easily discounted.

Usually the only record left on most runaways was a brief notation in the plantation books that one disappeared. We have few records of what happened to those who were successful. The Talbot County owner of Mabin, a runaway, posted a twenty-dollar reward, but his will noted that Mabin was still unrecovered seven years later. Some escaped slaves, such as John Brown of Georgia, dictated their life stories to abolitionists after they achieved freedom. James Madison, a slave of John T. Snypes, recounted his adventures to Henry Bibb, a black abolitionist. Madison, born in 1827 in Georgia, set off for Canada one day. His owner and a slave catcher caught and manacled him to the back of their buggy and went into a tavern to celebrate. While they were getting drunk, Madison picked the lock of his manacles with a nail and completed his trip to Canada.

Georgia was powerless to obtain the return of determined slaves who had the support of Northern abolitionists. Two famous runaway slaves played a part in Georgia's decision to secede from the Union by showing the state it could not prevent such escapes. Ellen Craft was her original master's daughter and light enough to pass as white. This annoyed her mistress, for it led Ellen to be mistaken for her daughter. When Ellen was eleven, she was given to the mistress's daughter, Mrs. Robert Collins of Macon, as a wedding present. William Craft belonged to a neighbor. The Crafts fell in love and were married in a slave ceremony in 1846. Though relatively well treated, they were disturbed by their recent separation from relatives due to sales. William had been trained as a mechanic and carpenter, and his master let him keep a small portion of his earnings. Using his skills, he worked nights and Sundays to accumulate money for an escape. They both applied for a Christmas pass in 1848, claiming they would visit Ellen's sick aunt. This gave them a head start before they were missed, since their owners would be preoccupied during the holiday.

The Crafts developed a daring plan. Ellen would dress as a young gentleman and pretend to be sick. William, who was much darker, would then pose as her slave coachman, and she would say she was going to a medical specialist in Philadelphia. The plan included three nights on the road. To avoid arousing suspicions, Ellen stayed in the best hotels; her "coachman slave" slept in the stables. Ellen could not write, so the problem of being exposed when asked to sign her name in hotel registers was avoided by putting her right arm in a sling. To complete the masquerade, her face was covered with poultices to add credibility to the story that she was going to see a skin specialist. The plan worked. In Charleston they stayed at the same hotel in which former vice president John C. Calhoun and the governor of South Carolina stayed when they were in the city.

Once across the Mason-Dixon line they were met by William Wells Brown, an escaped slave who had become an active abolitionist writer and lecturer. To Ellen's dismay, they were first sent to the home of a white abolitionist near Philadelphia for safekeeping. Ellen was suspicious, but she soon realized that fugitives had some true friends among Northern whites. Using Boston as home base, they went on the abolitionist lecture circuit with Brown beginning in January 1849, only a few days after their arrival in the North. They became such drawing cards that sometimes admission was charged, "an almost unprecedented practice in abolitionist circles," according to Benjamin Quarles.

On learning the Crafts were in Boston, Dr. Collins hired a Macon jailer and a laborer to recapture them. The two men arrived in Boston and obtained warrants for the arrest of the Crafts, but their efforts were thwarted by abolitionists. Shortly after this, on November 7, 1850, Theodore Parker, a white Unitarian minister, "officially" married the Crafts in a solemn ceremony in which he placed a Bible in one of William's hands and a weapon in the other. The Bible symbolized William's duty to save his and his wife's souls. The weapon symbolized his right to defend himself from being returned to slavery. Parker said he had no right to fail to defend his wife from being returned to Georgia even if he had to take a thousand men with him to the grave. Fearful for their safety on American soil, the Crafts went to England and continued their work as prominent abolitionists.

Another fugitive from Georgia, Thomas Simms, was not as fortunate as the Crafts. In the first court test of the hated 1850 Fugitive Slave Law, he was seized and jailed in Boston pending a hearing on his slave status. Simms begged for a knife so that he could kill himself if the court ruled he must be returned to Georgia. Three hundred policemen were required to prevent his release by abolitionists when he was escorted to a ship to take him back into bondage. With tears in his eyes but walking erect, he heard friends shout, "Simms, preach liberty to the slaves." Simms had little immediate opportunity to do this. As soon as his ship reached Savannah, he was dragged through the streets in chains and publicly whipped. However, he escaped to Boston again during the Civil War.

More slaves sought refuge near the plantation than tried to flee from Georgia to the North. Many slaves would take to the swamps or woods to escape work or whippings. They could find caves or dig dens and live off the land or raid a plantation, where they would be supplied by other slaves, who kept their secret. Celestia Avery, born a slave to Peter Heard in Troup County, recalled that when her uncle William was whipped by a patrol, he ran away to the woods, dug a cave, returned for his wife, and raised two children undetected. He came out after the Civil War. Roland Hayes, famous as a concert singer from the early 1920s to the late 1950s, had a maternal grandfather who, as a slave in Georgia, hid out in the woods one time for eighteen months, living on food smuggled to him by fellow slaves. Sometimes when a slave's success hiding out became known, others would join him, creating a maroon.

While Georgia planters disliked admitting it, if they were to get the slaves back, it was necessary to advertise the fact that they had run away. There were many advertisements in the antebellum press that told more about slavery than was intended. Notices often told of fugitives who only wanted to rejoin their families, broken up by sale:

> *Macon Messenger*, November 23, 1837. $25 Reward. Ran away a Negro man, named Cain. He was brought from Florida, and has a wife near Mariana, and will probably attempt to make his way there.

> *Savannah Republican*, September 3, 1838. $20 reward for my Negro man Jim. Jim is about 50 or 55 years of age. It is probable he will aim for Savannah, as he said he had children in that vicinity.

One advertisement advised readers that Lawrence, age fourteen, was trying to make his way back to Atlanta, where "his mother was supposed to be," after he was sold to Florida. Another planter advertised for Will, aged fifty, who was suspected of trying to return to Savannah, "where he has a wife and children." Advertisements for runaways often included a reward for information about the white person who helped slaves escape. Usually this reflected the master's incorrect opinion that the slaves were incapable of escaping on their own.

Resistance to being sold to a distant place often meant escaping and returning home. This way slaves could hamper family breakups by sale. A Georgia owner who took his slave to Alabama grew tired of the prospect of going back to Georgia repeatedly to reclaim him. The owner finally sold him to a neighbor near the place the slave was determined to live.

Some desperate slaves resorted to self-mutilation and even suicide. Cases are on record in which a slave cut off a finger, or even a hand, to escape excessively arduous labor. Some slave mothers killed their children rather than see them grow up to be slaves. A group of Ibos, fresh from Africa, were taken to St. Simons Island for plantation work. At the first chance, led by their chief, they walked into Dunbar Creek and drowned themselves. This point is now called Ibo (Ebo) Landing, and local legends still say it is haunted.

There was outwardly directed violence also. Some slaves resisted by turning on their masters or overseers and killing them. Revenge for a whipping was one motive; historian Ralph Flanders noted, "There are many cases recorded of slaves having murdered their master or overseer for this reason." One Dougherty County overseer was enticed into a swamp and killed for threatening to whip a slave. In 1797, a planter in Screven County was killed by a group of new slaves from Africa. Also that year, two Georgia slaves were burned alive for killing whites, and in 1806, one slave was burned and another hanged for killing an overseer. Many planters confessed in their journals that they feared their slaves might try to kill them. This feeling intensified during the Civil War, as illustrated by a letter from Margaret E. Harden of Athens to her son in 1863 advising him to sell an "outrageously impertinent" slave named Sally. "I would not own her if she was worth her weight in gold," the mother wrote. "I should be afraid that she might kill me."

Slaves found another way to express their true feelings—by burning their masters' buildings and fields. Georgia had many unexplained fires during the antebellum period. In 1804, there were arrests and imprisonment of slaves for arson in Georgia and a strengthened patrol system. A slave named Coot, or Coco, was executed as the leader of a conspiracy to burn Augusta in the spring of 1819.

The ultimate form of resistance and the act most likely to terrorize whites was the slave revolt. The few slaves who engaged in these violent acts profoundly influenced the institution of slavery. Georgia's history was influenced by such insurrections beginning in 1526, when a Spanish settlement on the Pee Dee River in South Carolina failed because slaves revolted and joined the Indians. This revolt helped to discourage the Spanish occupation of the South Atlantic Coast, and their withdrawal facilitated later British control of Georgia. Slaves fighting their way down from Carolina on their way to freedom in Spanish Florida killed several Georgians in 1738. The most serious slave revolt in the Colonial era, at Stono, South Carolina, came in 1739. It occurred when the Georgia Trustees were under intense pressure to relax the ban on slavery in Georgia. The revolt gave them an opportunity to avoid legally sanctioning slavery longer on the grounds that they wished to avoid the tumult that slavery would bring.

A slave named Captain James, of Greene County, Georgia, corresponded to a slave in North Carolina regarding a general insurrection that could have been a model for Nat Turner twenty-one years later. Beginning at midnight on April 22, 1810, the slaves planned to kill the nearest whites, seize arms, and watch their forces grow from slave volunteers as the rebellion spread to encompass the entire area of slavery. In 1827, there were reports of a plot organized by a Frenchman who led three hundred slaves into revolt near Macon. Interestingly, many of the accounts of slave plots include a white leader. While this shows it was generally known that some whites were in sympathy with the slaves, it also means many whites could not accept the fact that blacks were capable of planning revolts. If there was no white leader (and usually there was none), one had to be invented.

David Walker was a significant figure in the early Northern abolition movement who had a profound effect on Georgia. His writing sparked hysteria among the state's top officials, which in turn led to the passage of severely repressive laws. A free Negro who settled in Boston about 1817 and became a secondhand clothes dealer, Walker was active in the abolition movement and contributed to *Freedom's Journal*, the first black newspaper published in the United States. On September 28, 1829, he published a small book, *David Walker's Appeal*, which blamed the wretchedness of blacks on slavery, ignorance, religion, *and* the colonization movement aimed at sending free blacks back to Africa. The *Appeal* said that slaves were "the *most wretched, degraded, and abject* set of beings that *ever lived* since the world began." Walker counseled resistance by slaves even if it meant taking the life of an oppressor. This was not the kind of literature planters wanted circulating in Georgia.

Walker's business brought him into contact with many sailors, both black and white, and by the late fall of 1829, they carried copies of the pamphlet to Savannah, where the *Appeal* immediately inspired fears of slave revolts. In December, Savannah authorities seized a shipment of sixty copies of the *Appeal* brought in by a white ship steward and delivered to a Negro minister named Cunningham, who was arrested. The mayor then urged a quarantine of all seamen and a ban on the interstate slave trade. A group of Georgians offered $1,000 for Walker dead and $10,000 for him alive, a sum matched by the legislature. (Walker died mysteriously in 1830.) Blacks were not the only ones persecuted for owning copies of *David Walker's Appeal*. E. H. Burritt, a white Milledgeville printer and editor of the *Southern Recorder*, was arrested for possessing copies of the *Appeal*. He fled to Connecticut for fear of his life.

The distribution of the *Appeal* in Georgia was the catalyst for the passage of laws against slave literacy and slaves working around printing plants and for the death penalty for circulating literature "tending to incite rebellion." Walker's *Appeal* also led to further legislative enactments that caused conflict between the United States and Great Britain, whose merchant marine employed many free blacks. Georgia's leaders had always been leery of black seamen.* The new laws called for a ship to be quarantined for forty days if it had free Negro employees or passengers. The ship could be released from quarantine if all blacks on board were lodged in jail and bond was posted for their expenses and transportation out of the state, for legislators feared they might stir up rebellion if they remained. The 1829 law also forbade contact between Georgia's free Negroes and seamen.

The damage done by these acts is inestimable. In the 1840s, the British Foreign Office protested to the United States that such measures violated the 1815 commercial convention between the two countries. The Georgia legislature, appreciative of the fine champagne sent by the British consul in Savannah, responded in 1854 by modifying her laws so that free Negro seamen could come ashore if they had a special passport. By then the fear engendered by *David Walker's Appeal* had subsided.

The Nat Turner insurrection in Southhampton County, Virginia, in 1831 had repercussions throughout Georgia. Maconites were especially frightened by news from Virginia. Many rural families came into town for protection, white sentinels were posted at the city outskirts, and a temporary cavalry was organized. Even the *Messenger*, Macon's newspaper, was reduced to skimpy issues, as most of its staff was out on patrol duty. When six blacks got into a fight among themselves, Gen. Elias E. Beall, from his headquarters at Fort Forsyth, signed an order declaring that Bibb, Baldwin, and Jones Counties were in a state of insurrection. Around the same time, six slaves suspected of organizing a revolt were

---

*An 1818 law allowed for the sale of a free Negro seaman into slavery if he was in Georgia twenty days after his ship left port, and in 1826, the Georgia legislature, suspicious of black seamen, required that they stay aboard their docked vessels at night.

arrested near Dublin, and four were executed. In reaction to Turner's rebellion, the Macon City Council put a price of $12,000 on the head of prominent Northern abolitionist Arthur Tappan, and the Georgia legislature offered $4,000 for the arrest of William Lloyd Garrison, the nation's most prominent abolitionist editor.

Although the fears engendered by Nat Turner died down after a few months, Georgians remained apprehensive. They seemed to be hysterical over the prospect of slave revolts during the 1830s, with 1835 being a particularly nasty year. Newspapers were filled with warnings to be vigilant against revolts, and an antiabolitionist meeting was held in Lumpkin County. That year, a white was lynched in Jefferson County for "seditious activity," and another was driven from Twiggs County for the same reason. The ever-apprehensive Macon City Council then offered a $1,000 reward for the arrest and conviction of anyone distributing abolitionist literature. A white named Grady was sentenced to four years in prison for plotting to help three slaves escape to Boston.

In 1841, several slaves and a white schoolteacher named Hawes were arrested in Augusta and charged with planning to burn down the town and seize the arsenal. One execution resulted. In July 1849, a group of three hundred slaves planned to seize a steamboat near St. Marys, on the Georgia coast, and use it to escape to the British West Indies, where slavery had been abolished four years earlier. This plot failed because the ship was late arriving at St. Marys, and the plan was exposed. All these events contributed to the overall climate of fear. The accusation of abolitionist sentiments brought attack. L. F. W. Andrews, editor of the *Georgia Citizen*, was so accused and driven from Macon in 1850.

Georgia's editors frequently warned of insurgency plots throughout the 1850s. There was a general slave insurrection panic throughout the South in 1856 in connection with the just-born Republican party's first effort to elect a president. Its candidate, John C. Frémont, was suspected of being antislavery. To make Georgia more secure, the *Athens Southern Watchman* asked the legislature to clamp down on free Negroes.

The Civil War brought an increase in slave unrest, mainly manifested in a huge increase in the number of runaways. In August 1860, a group of slaves planned to burn Dalton, seize a train that would take them the seventy miles to Marietta, and complete their escapes from there. Thirty-six slaves were imprisoned in this ill-fated break for freedom. Many Georgians were openly talking secession by this time. They felt that as long as they were a part of the United States, they would live in fear of slave revolts and escapes. No part of the state seemed immune. Other plots were uncovered that year in Cobb, Floyd, and Crawford counties. A few months later, a black charged with inciting a riot was hanged in

Kingston and another in Sumter County in 1862 for planning the escape of several slaves. The following year, when the war was half over, eighteen slaves were imprisoned in Hancock County for planning a revolt. One white and three slaves were hanged in Brooks County in August 1864 after what turned out to be the last slave revolt in Georgia. The last two in the Confederacy came in Mississippi and Alabama later that year.

The record of slave revolts in Georgia will never be complete. Although plots and rumors of plots abounded, most incidents were not mentioned in the newspapers. Editors firmly believed that published accounts about these events might fall into the hands of slaves and encourage greater resistance. Most of this information appears in the private letters and journals of whites, who, despite their rhetoric about the docility, natural inferiority, and lack of initiative in the slaves, never overcame their fear that somehow, sometime, the slaves would rebel and perhaps destroy the entire master class. In an effort to maintain a white united front against the slaves, the planters also worked to convince poor whites that they also would be included on the slaves' slaughter lists.

Slave Control Systems

The proper treatment of slaves was much discussed in the South. Planters wrote articles, sent lengthy instructions to their overseers, and mused about the problem of slave discipline frequently in their journals. The idea that all blacks were children was encouraged by law and custom. The *Southern Agriculturalist* advised owners against threatening slaves: Either punish them or don't, but don't give them time to brood over impending punishment. This advice was often ignored, and many runaways were motivated or galvanized into long-contemplated action by the threat of some severe or unfair punishment. The paper also advised to show no passion before slaves; always keep one's word to slaves; show no favoritism; do not let their good behavior lull one into relaxing discipline; and never, never trust a slave.

To keep the peculiar institution functioning, an elaborate legal and extralegal control system evolved, for such an all-encompassing system of domination was necessary for slavery to survive. There were three categories of mutually reinforcing methods. First were the legal controls, functioning through the courts, police, and sheriffs to enforce constitutional and legislative regulations. Second was the masters' discipline on the plantation. Finally, there was the mob.

In the eyes of the law, the slaves were more than chattel; they could be held responsible for their actions, tried, and even executed. However, the law did not permit a black to testify against a white. Slave codes applied equally to Africans, those who were part white, and blacks who were part Indian. While statutes governing slavery were important, they did not necessarily determine how slaves were treated. The law represented the collective judgment of the ruling class, but it did not necessarily govern what each individual master did. The white community as a whole attempted to make individual masters conform with the consensus and tried to influence an overly harsh master toward moderation in his punishment—and conversely, to persuade an overly lenient one to be more harsh. Masters had great leeway to do more or less than the law stated. In most cases, the master obeyed the law if it suited him. The laws were most likely to be enforced during crises.

At first, the masters' security was considered greater if the slaves on any one plantation came from different areas of Africa and spoke different languages. Another security idea was branding slaves with the owner's initials, a practice of treating human beings as cattle that started among traders in Africa. In the late 1740s, as it became clear that black slavery would become legal in Georgia, the belief by whites in the need for special laws grew. In 1748, an assembly met in Savannah to draw up a slave code; the regulations became effective on January 1, 1751, when the ban on slavery was rescinded.

To counter whites' fears of slave revolts, the regulations were designed to ban large concentrations of slaves by setting a population quota of no more than four blacks for each white man. The code also forbade miscegenation. The first code gave slaves the right to religious instruction and the right to trial according to the laws of England. However, it provided for a fifteen-pound fine to be levied against anyone who taught a slave to write and stated that any slave refusing to be searched, or who struck a white, could be lawfully killed. Whites were given standing warrants to search any black home for weapons. The code also provided penalties for masters who unnecessarily killed or mutilated a slave, denied slaves the right of a jury trial, and provided that owners of slaves who were executed according to court orders would be reimbursed for the value of the slave.

This first Georgia slave code, which was not as detailed as the codes of the older slave colonies, was quickly determined to be too lenient. Thus began a long process of making the slave codes increasingly strict, a tightening of shackles that continued until 1865. After Georgia became a royal colony, a more complete and severe slave code was adopted. This 1755 code was patterned after the one South Carolina adopted in the wake of the Stono Revolt. Under the new Georgia code, though slaves might be tried, they were no longer protected by the laws of England governing the rights of the accused. Slaves could be killed for destroying commodities, and the penalty for killing a slave was reduced. Rewards were authorized for killing runaways and bringing the scalp and ears back as proof, though the reward was higher if the slave was returned alive.

The 1755 code also initiated the pass system, which provided that no slave might leave the plantation without the written permission of his master or overseer. It also authorized the use of the militia to destroy maroons. In 1757, the pass system was reinforced by the establishment of a system of rural patrols to challenge and, if necessary, apprehend slaves who were abroad without the required pass. The patrols were authorized to administer up to twenty lashes to any suspect slave.

Because overly abusive treatment would encourage more militant slave resistance, the 1755 code *limited* the slave's workweek to six 16-hour days and slaves were to receive "sufficient" food and clothing. However, the law limiting the work week to ninety-six hours was repealed in 1765, when slave codes grew harsher and added crimes for which slaves might be executed. The new laws continued to reflect white fears of slaves by providing the death penalty for any slave who knew about a case of poisoning and did not report it or taught another slave the use of poisons.

As the number of blacks in Georgia grew, so did fears among whites. Every instance of real or suspected slave revolt led to harshly detailed slave codes aimed at controlling blacks and preventing insurrections. In 1767 theft by a black became a capital crime. In 1770, whites felt it necessary to enact an even more complete and complex slave code. To alleviate fears that blacks might "plot and confederate together," it forbade groups of seven or more to go on the highway unless accompanied by a white.

Black-on-white rape was among the planter's main concerns. In 1770, Georgia added rape to the growing list of crimes for which a slave could be executed. In 1806, the Georgia General Assembly made the death penalty mandatory for any black who raped or attempted to rape a white woman in Georgia. Although there was no basis for castration as a punishment in English law and the 1755 Colonial regulations and later Georgia codes specifically prohibited it, a Jasper County court sentenced a Negro to castration and deportation in 1827 for attempted rape. The *Macon Telegraph* considered this punishment too lenient. Contrary to the general custom after the Civil War, it often took careful legal work and hard evidence to convict a slave of the rape of a white woman in the antebellum period. Black-on-black rape was not thought sufficiently serious to end up in court; the master would handle such cases on the plantation.

Although slaves were ordinarily "tried" on the plantation, with the master being the judge, jury, and administrator of punishment, Georgia slaves occasionally received their day in court for alleged violations of the laws. Eighteenth-century laws permitting slave punishment without trial changed after the Revolution as the safeguards for whites were extended, in part, to slaves. However, the penalties given slaves were usually more severe than those assessed against whites for the same crimes.

Slaves tried for lesser offenses appeared before a justice of the peace, but for capital cases, a jury was required in a county court, or sometimes a panel of three judges handled the case. There are few records of slave trials because the slaves were usually punished by their masters, or, when tried, the records were kept separately. There were no appeals, not even of death penalties. One study of slave justice in four Georgia counties showed that twenty-one accused slaves had jury trials, and of six charged with theft, two were found not guilty, two were flogged, and two were executed. One of the latter unfortunates, Jack, a slave of Barnes Holloway of Lincoln County, was executed in 1814 for a ten-dollar theft. Three-quarters of those charged with murder were executed.

While blacks could not give testimony against whites, they were permitted to testify in cases involving other blacks. In 1837, a slave named Peter knifed to death a slave named Ben because Ben had been disparaging him. Peter was tried, and partly on the basis of the testimony of another slave, was hanged. In a trial two years later where two whites and seven slaves testified, a slave named Edmond was convicted of the theft of seven dollars and was sentenced to pay the costs of the prosecution and receive sixty lashes. Whippings were the most frequent form of punishment of slaves convicted in the courts. In *Georgia v. Adeline* (1849), a slave who had previously run away was convicted of theft and arson and sentenced to endure fifty lashes on each of three consecutive days and to have her owner's initials branded on her cheeks.

The daily efforts of masters and overseers to control all aspects of the slave's life were even more important than the laws and the courts. The master was almost completely free to mete out whatever punishment he saw fit, ranging from deprivation of pass privileges to assignment of extra work, or as a last resort, selling a slave to a place that was even worse. However, force was the main tool used to ensure submission. The black slave driver was also a factor in the control system. These were men selected for their strength and leadership qualities. While they often had to do the master's and overseer's dirty work in disciplining the slaves, they were also in a position to mitigate the severity of discipline.

In one case in which a master killed his slave coachman, he only needed to say he did not intend to, since the Georgia Supreme Court ruled that even if an owner should "exceed the bonds of reason... in his chastisement, the slave must submit...." While many owners acted with restraint, their license to brutalize slaves with impunity led to degradation of everyone's life. Prominent whites could ensure that any slave who offended them would suffer, and the master's children quickly learned to copy these behavior patterns. When political figure Nelson Tift knocked down a white woman in the street, he made sure the female slave who came to the woman's defense received fifty lashes.

Planters always wanted their slaves home in bed at night so they would be ready for the next day's work, stay out of trouble, and not have opportunities to plot. Since Colonial times, the main control mechanism guaranteeing this was the slave patrol, whose members would ride the roads at night and apprehend any slave they found. A 1758 law required that all white males between the ages of sixteen and sixty ride one night in fourteen or pay a proxy to do this. Georgia law provided that the patrols could give up to twenty lashes to any black, either slave or free, caught at night without proper papers. The patrols, a common feature of ante-bellum slave states, were often composed of poorer whites and frequently assumed the aspects of lynching bees—whipping and even killing inoffensive slaves. Yet an 1851 court decision held that patrol members were not liable for any slaves they might kill. The pass and patrol system remained a vital part of the overall slave control system until the end of the Civil War. Planters were so convinced of its value that they tried to force it on freedmen after slavery ended.

The mob was just a step down from the slave patrols. While planter punishment and the court system were deemed sufficient to deal with individual acts of slaves, when the peculiar institution was threatened by slave insurrection or the abolitionist movement, mobs often took matters into their own hands. Blacks were lynched in Georgia before and during the Civil War. A mob in Columbus lynched a black in 1851 who had been pardoned by the governor; in 1860 an Oglethorpe County Negro was burned alive at the stake after being accused of murdering a white man; and a slave in Athens was burned alive in 1862 for assaulting the wife of a white overseer.

Georgia tried desperately to close itself off from outside influences that might criticize or undermine slavery. This attitude increased as the militant abolitionist movement grew in the North. Efforts to destroy abolitionist opposition to slavery became more frequent as the Civil War approached. Finally, even to question the peculiar institution became a crime. One writer stated in 1846: "The suppressive system of the South has turned every Southern community into a mob which enacts lynch-law and speedy vengeance against all who do not support slavery."

As pro-slavery opinion became more unified, the pro-slavery mobs in the South came to be known as "vigilance committees," or "Committees of Safety" which were granted quasi-legal status. This status was later transferred to the lynch mobs of the post-Reconstruction period. These vigilante committees tended to be "democratic" in that they elected their officers and claimed to represent the whole people and therefore were above the law. These groups became more powerful and intolerant with time's passage, and as 1860 approached, they challenged the court system at will. It was not difficult to raise a mob in the South; popular dread of racial amalgamation, Negro equality, and most of all, the specter of slave revolt would energize white Southerners to go outside the law.

It is no wonder that in this climate of hysteria a Georgia subscriber to the *Liberator*, the leading abolitionist organ, was tarred, feathered, horsewhipped, and half-drowned. John Hopper, a New York merchant, was almost lynched in Savannah in 1836 because he was suspected of being an abolitionist. The police rescued him from the mob, and the mayor allowed him to leave town. As the Civil War approached, actions against white abolitionists increased in Georgia. Lewis W. Paine was jailed for six years for aiding fugitive slaves. After Joseph L. Blodgett received eighty lashes in Florida in 1856 for teaching a black to read and for helping fugitive slaves, he escaped to Savannah, where he was jailed by local authorities and then was shipped on to New York City to save him from a lynch mob. Joseph Ribero, a Savannah carpenter, was whipped and run out of the state in 1860 for informing slaves of Lincoln's election.

Regardless of the methods used, ensuring black subservience was the dominant theme in white thought from the appearance of the first slave until after the Civil War, when controlling the behavior of freedmen became the major preoccupation. Even prior to emancipation, the presence of free Negroes added to the problem of slave control. While never present in large numbers, these blacks were always viewed with deep suspicion by most whites. The roles of religion and education (or rather the lack thereof) were also crucial to the maintenance of slavery. All of the control systems illustrated what historian Herbert Aptheker has called "the deep-seated schizophrenia of the South, where the right hand held the Bible and the left the bullwhip."

Religion

In the South, the master class used religion as a tool for slave control. The use of Christianity as a defense of the peculiar institution can be seen from the beginnings of the Georgia colony. One argument against Christianizing slaves held that they would have to be taught English and could then plot resistance and rebellion. This objection to conversion was abandoned early in Georgia's history on the strength of the teachings of the Great Awakening and the experience of the older slave colonies, especially Virginia and South Carolina, which showed that Christianity could be used to uphold the system of bondage.

John and Charles Wesley, the founders of Methodism, accompanied Oglethorpe on his second trip to Georgia, arriving in Savannah in February 1736. The Wesleys were agents for the Society for the Propagation of the Gospel in Foreign Parts, whose goal was to bring Christianity to the English colonies. Charles Wesley served as Oglethorpe's secretary for a few months before returning to England. John Wesley remained in Georgia and worked to convert both whites and blacks until he returned to England in 1737. Although both Wesleys remained clergymen in the Church of England, the missions John established in Georgia developed independently of the Anglican Church and by 1784 the missions were chartered as a separate church. Although John Wesley became an outspoken opponent of slavery, Methodism, as it developed in Georgia and the South, was largely used to buttress the institution.

Methodism got off to a slow start among blacks in Georgia. There were only 148 black Methodists in 1797. White ministers had catechisms printed and taught the slaves to read them. The catechisms were used to brainwash the slaves into accepting slavery; the Episcopal catechism taught that God had given the slave to his master and mistress and that He wanted the slave to obey them and work hard because "God is always at work."

The Presbyterians attracted even fewer blacks than the Methodists. The Presbyterian synod of Georgia and South Carolina devoted few resources to the education and religious instruction of blacks. Before they got their separate Presbyterian church, blacks in early Macon attended the white church and sat in the gallery, as they did in the Methodist and Episcopal churches. Joseph Williams, a black who had been active in promoting the Presbyterian church from the 1840s, was attached to a white Presbyterian church on a segregated basis. His message: Bide your time for a better day is coming. After the Civil War he was an outspoken advocate of black equality.

The Baptist faith proved to be the most appealing to slaves and free blacks in Georgia. The Baptist denomination spread into Georgia rapidly, taking root in the ground prepared by the Great Awakening, especially in the Georgia backcountry, which was more egalitarian than the planter-dominated coast. The Great Awakening and subsequent early Baptist teaching encouraged individualism and equality, as did the Protestant Reformation originally. Since this subversive message appealed to slaves, the planters had some preachers whipped and jailed, and a few were killed for their beliefs.

David George and George Liele were the two most prominent early Baptist slave preachers in Georgia. They began preaching at Silver Bluff Church on the Galphin plantation in Aiken County, South Carolina, near Augusta. After the British captured Savannah in 1778, David George and his congregation of forty slaves fled to the coastal city. Liele, from Burke

County, also was moved to Savannah, where in 1779 he organized the first black church in Georgia, now the First African Baptist Church, in the Yamacraw section of Savannah. He preached liberation and support for the British. In July 1782, Liele left with the British for Jamaica, where he continued his role as an influential minister. David George went with the British to Nova Scotia and later led a group of ex-slaves who had been freed by the British to their colony of Sierra Leone in Africa.

Liele's last act before embarking for Jamaica was to baptize Andrew Bryan, a slave who continued what Liele had started in Savannah. Bryan and his congregation were persecuted because of the liberation message in his sermons and because so many blacks gathered at one place at night alarmed whites. Bryan was jailed twice and was whipped at least once along with fifty of his followers. The persecutions ended when the church was approved by Abraham Marshall, a much-admired white Baptist minister in Georgia, and Bryan was ordained by white ministers in 1788.

Bryan had an indulgent master who supported him in his work and helped him buy the freedom of his wife, Hanna. Once, when he was arrested, the magistrate ruled that blacks were entitled to religious freedom only during daylight hours, so his master gave him the use of a building about three miles out of Savannah called Brampton's Barn, where he could hold services between sunrise and sunset. By 1791, the church had two hundred regular members. In 1792, Bryan moved his congregation back to the city, where his flock quickly doubled in size. The members paid him a salary and, after his master's death, helped him raise his self-purchase price of fifty pounds. Bryan owned a sixty-five-acre farm near Savannah and brought abused slaves there to work out their freedom. At one time he had eight such unfortunates under his wing.

Bryan's work continued to bear fruit, and another Negro Baptist church was started in Savannah in 1803 by Henry Francis, a slave of Col. Leroy Hammond, when he took over a branch of Bryan's congregation. Since the two churches could not accommodate all of the blacks willing to embrace the Baptist faith in Savannah, a third church was started there in 1805. In 1793, Jesse Peter, an associate of George and Liele in Savannah, moved to Augusta, where he organized the Springfield Baptist Church.

When blacks went to church (often their masters' church after the whites held their service), the same white minister would stay and preach a different sermon to the slaves. These ministers were strong advocates of the view that the Bible sanctified slavery, and they were fond of quoting Biblical passages that called for obedience by servants to masters.

Sometimes the slaves might attend the same church service as whites, as they did in Wilkes County in 1805. At such times, they would sit by themselves in a balcony, if there was one, in a back corner or behind a partition, but the separate service was more common. Most whites did not want their slaves to see them in the throes of an emotional religious experience.

Actually, many slaves went to no church at all. The Methodists only claimed about 5 percent of the slaves of Georgia in 1860, and they were the second-largest denomination. Some planters forbade their slaves to attend church, claiming an inherent danger in the practice. Many slaves in Georgia were unable to attend church because they had to work even on Sundays, except in the slackest periods.

Slaves were taught that suffering should be endured for the sake of the heavenly reward and that to rebel would jeopardize their ticket to paradise. It was this "pie in the sky when you die" fundamentalist approach to Christianity that the planters encouraged. Slaves and free Negroes who preached this type of religion were given a free hand by masters, who appreciated the value of letting slaves work off their bitterness and frustration in religious services. Hiding their true feelings out of necessity, some only preached this way when the master or his agent was around and at other times preached a more social gospel, saying that the Lord did not intend his people to suffer bondage forever and suggesting that it might be good to leave the land of Egypt soon.

Some black ministers had whites in their congregations. Jacob Walker of Augusta, a black minister who preached mostly to slaves, frequently had whites in his congregation because they enjoyed his services. Whites often had another reason to listen to a black minister preach: to monitor the message to be sure that submission, not liberation, was being preached.

With every slave rebellion or rumor of insurrection, the planter class moved to limit the freedom of the black minister along with the freedom of all blacks. In 1833, in response to Nat Turner's revolt, Georgia adopted a law that forbade Negro preachers from preaching to more than seven blacks at one time. In addition, the minister had to have recommendations from three white ministers, a license, and special permission to use the place of worship. But the laws against Negro preachers often could not be enforced, even though planters suspected liberation was being preached in their absence. Perhaps a significant number of black ministers were literate, and slave narratives speak of literate preachers who taught others how to read. Robert Toombs, one of Georgia's most powerful planters and politicians, taught his coachman to read and write and allowed him to preach almost anywhere he wished.

Some defiant black preachers were whipped or even lynched. In the 1830s, George, a slave preacher in Georgia, was ordered by his master to stop sermonizing or he would receive 500 lashes. George ignored the order and, on learning that his master had found out about his disobedience, fled to South Carolina, where he took refuge in a barn when the owner tried to apprehend him. George fought when captured, was subdued, and after a brief stay in jail, he was publicly burned alive. A large number of slaves were brought from as far away as twenty miles to witness the execution. James Smith was another Georgia slave who incurred whippings in order to preach. He received 100 lashes for ignoring an order not to preach and then ran away. He was caught and whipped again. Finally, after two more unsuccessful escape attempts, he made it to safety in Ohio, and later, Canada.

James G. Birney, 1840 presidential candidate of the Liberty Party, quite properly termed the churches "the bulwark of American Slavery." The Quakers were the main exception. A group of Quakers settled in McDuffie County in 1767 but were unpopular because they supported England in the Revolution and opposed slavery. Unable to compete with Georgia's labor system, they left around 1800, and Georgia lost an antislavery force. Birney's charge was true of all the organized churches in the South and many in the North. As the nation later divided over the issue of slavery, the major religious institutions likewise split and became sectional organizations.

Convinced that there was more to Christianity than submission, blacks sought to establish their own churches where ideas of freedom and equality could be developed away from white control. This tendency toward religious independence troubled masters. They tried to stamp it out or subjugate it, but the spark of freedom found in the teachings of Christianity grew into a flame that guided many slaves through the worst times of their lives. The black church grew up in the shadow of the white church and finally achieved independence after the Civil War, when it became the most significant institution blacks could call their own. The later independence of the black church could not have been so complete if blacks had not tried to control their own religion during slavery.

Education

Keeping slaves in ignorance was another means of control. The master class was always, in theory at least, opposed to educating slaves. Although the education of slaves was legally forbidden, there were enough exceptions so that by 1860 at least 1 percent (and perhaps as many as 5 percent) of the slaves could read and write. Perhaps two-thirds of free blacks were literate then.

In 1750, Dr. Thomas Bray and the Society for the Propagation of the

Gospel in Foreign Parts raised £40 to hire Joseph Ottolenghe as a schoolmaster for black children in Savannah. He taught for nine years, and his students "graduated" as soon as they could repeat the catechism in English. The rector of Christ's Church in Savannah also taught blacks, and when he died he left his estate, including his slaves, to support the work of Negro education.

An occasional planter or his wife taught the slaves, and some slaves learned from the master's children. However, most planters were convinced that literate slaves would not only be more discontented but better able to act on their dissatisfaction. The ·attitude that education spoiled workers carried over to penalize poor whites also. As a result, Georgia spent little on education for *anyone*. There would be no organized system of common schools supported by public taxation until the 1870s.

Georgia had many laws against slave literacy. The Colonial statute of 1770, providing for a twenty-pound fine for teaching a slave to read or write, was reinforced after the Revolution. The fear of slave insurrections brought further educational proscriptions throughout the antebellum period. Following the appearance of *David Walker's Appeal* in 1829, a law was adopted forbidding any teaching of blacks. If a black taught, he was to be fined $500 and whipped. White teachers of blacks were to be fined and jailed. The Nat Turner revolt two years later brought another wave of repression. Georgia later added a $100 fine for employing a Negro in a printing plant, where literacy was easily acquired. There were, in addition, a number of city ordinances, such as Savannah's 1833 provision of a $100 fine and thirty-nine lashes for any black teaching another black to read and write.

Sometimes a slave caught in the act of reading or writing would have a finger or thumb cut off. These laws, like others regulating free Negroes and slaves, were often evaded or disregarded except in times of crisis. Some free Negroes of Savannah circumvented these strictures by sending their children to Charleston. The secession crisis increased fear among whites of slaves and led to increased agitation for further crackdowns on slave literacy. The *Macon Telegraph* condemned the selling of books to slaves in 1860 and called for an investigation of the practice.

Most blacks who became literate acquired their learning from other blacks. Festus Flipper, the father of African Methodist Episcopal Bishop J. S. Flipper and West Point graduate Henry Flipper, was a slave in Atlanta who was taught to read and write by another slave with the full knowledge of his master. Julian Froumontaine, a black Haitian, opened a school for blacks in Savannah in 1818 and operated it openly until December 22, 1829, when the new laws, brought on by the reaction to Walker's *Appeal*, went into effect. Then he took his school underground and taught clandestinely until 1844. Another black, Mrs. Deveaux, taught

secretly in Savannah from the 1830s to the end of the Civil War. Susie
King Taylor, who became a teacher after the Civil War, recalled going to a
Mrs. Woodhouse's illicit school. Mrs. Woodhouse was a free Negro and
had her students bring their books to her home wrapped up in clothing so
that they would be presumed to be carrying laundry and not attract
attention. If a stranger came while the school was in session, the children
would quickly hide their books under their pile of clothes and pretended
to do mending. In Augusta, black Methodist preacher Ned Purdee ran a
clandestine school for seven years. William J. White, who became the
leading advocate of black education in Georgia after the Civil War, was
taught by his slave mother with the knowledge of his white master-father.
The first black school in Macon was supported by some planters who
wanted some of their slaves to market tobacco better. It was taught by
Lewis Williams, a slave of L. N. Whittle's, and at least five other blacks
shared in the teaching duties.

Slaves developed many ingenious ways to learn to read. John Sella
Martin was brought to Georgia with his mother and sister when he was
six years old. Three years later, the family was broken up and sold
separately to pay their owner's debts. Young John became a errand boy for
gamblers in a hotel. He became an expert marble shooter and took a
white boy on as partner on the condition that he teach John to read.
Martin then made extra money by reading to slaves who were anxious to
hear the news, especially about abolition.

Attitudes toward the education of slaves began to soften a little in the
1850s. A few of the more progressive whites adopted the position that an
ignorant labor force might be all right for an agricultural peasantry, but
business, industry, commerce, and scientific agriculture needed intelligent and educated workers. As efforts were made to introduce scientific
methods to agriculture, the leaders of this modernization movement
began to support more education for blacks. In 1850, a series of articles
appeared in the Savannah newspaper regarding the desirability of
educating slaves.

The subject was introduced in an agricultural conference in Macon
later in 1850, and two years later a bill passed the lower house of the state
legislature to repeal the severe laws of 1829 and 1831 forbidding the
teaching of slaves to read and write. The bill failed by a small margin in
the state senate. These efforts were supported by some churches. The
Presbyterians urged masters to enlighten their slaves, and in 1856, their
publication, *Presbyterian Witness*, favored teaching slaves to read in
1856. With the coming of the Civil War, this would be considered
subversive.

The great majority of whites firmly believed that to keep blacks as work
animals, they must be treated as such. Educating slaves endangered the

system of slavery. So Georgia, always low in any ranking of states according to interest in education, remained opposed to the education of blacks both before and after the Civil War. It was not until after World War II that black pressure and Northern influences began to change this.

In the Shadow of Slavery: Free Negroes

Free Negroes were never independent in the sense whites were. Their degree of freedom varied. Some lived almost without restriction, but others led lives little better than those of slaves. On a continuum from slavery to freedom, the average free Negro occupied a position closer to slavery. Law historian Lawrence Friedman stated:

> In Georgia, free Negroes could not own, use, or carry firearms, dispense medicine, set type, or make contracts for repairing buildings. They could not deal in agricultural commodities without permission. They could not acquire land or slaves in Savannah or Augusta; in some Georgia cities, they could not operate restaurants and inns. . . . and might suffer punishment more severe than whites who committed the same crime.

Taking into account the ever-increasing barriers placed in their way, free Negroes did remarkably well and thus helped show that blacks could live and work outside the bonds of slavery.

The presence of free Negroes was always discouraged in Colonial Georgia, in part because their presence made it more difficult to identify the runaways from the Carolinas that Georgia was committed to return. The first record of a free Negro is in a 1745 court case in which an enslaved black established that he was a free citizen of the Netherlands' Caribbean island possession of Curaçao.

The number of free Negroes slowly grew to 398 by 1790, when they constituted 1.3 percent of Georgia's black population. When the revolutionary fervor and rhetoric about freedom and liberty subsided, the climate encouraging manumission changed, and chances grew slimmer that an individual slave could look forward to freedom in his or her lifetime. There was a decline of free Negroes as a result of the War of 1812, when blacks, both free and slave, fled Georgia. Although the number of free blacks increased to thirty-five hundred by 1860, the free population of Georgia had declined to 0.75 percent of all blacks, barely more than half the 1790 percentage. This was a much lower ratio than that of the other slave states, where the average was 6 percent.

Free Negroes were disliked because they constantly disproved the slaveholders' claims that blacks were incapable of surviving on their own. A class of free blacks who survived and occasionally prospered proved to slaves that the masters' ideology was wrong. The masters assumed, usually correctly, that free Negroes would help the slaves to become free by serving as role models, by teaching slaves to read and write, by bringing in dangerous ideas about liberty, by helping slaves escape, or even by arming them or otherwise promoting insurrections. State Supreme Court Chief Justice Joseph E. Lumpkin stated part of the planters' case against free blacks in 1857 when he said they "facilitate the escape of our fugitive slaves. In the case of civil war, they would become an element of strength to the enemy." Frederick Douglass said that abolitionists were the spark, the free Negroes the fuse, and the slaves were the powder keg that would someday explode.

The free Negro population grew during the Colonial and revolutionary periods for several reasons. There were no restrictions on manumission before 1750, and no laws limiting freeing slaves before 1801. Runaways from South Carolina plantations could sometimes lose themselves in the cities and become free for all practical purposes. Those slaves freed by provisions in a master's will were a major source of the free Negro population of eighteenth-century Georgia. Meritorious service could lead to freedom, as in a 1792 case of a slave who was freed by her master in recompense for nursing his wife throughout her terminal illness.

Some slaves earned enough, mainly by hiring themselves out, to buy their own freedom, and even that of their family. The first record in Georgia of self-purchase occurred when Peter Fleming bought his freedom for five shillings in 1772. Early Georgia law permitted slaves in the militia, though they were not to be armed except in the event of a crisis, and then, if their contribution had been unusual, they might be freed. However, there is no evidence in Colonial records of any black militiamen obtaining freedom. In 1765, when Georgia was threatened by both the Spanish and the Indians, free blacks were encouraged to come to Georgia and were promised all the rights of "persons born of British parents"—except voting or holding office. There is no record of anyone taking advantage of the offer. A few years later, Austin Dabney and a few other blacks were freed in Georgia for military service during the American Revolution. After 1800, the most significant way the number of free blacks grew was by natural increase.

The Georgia colony quickly became concerned about the free Negroes even though their numbers were few. In 1755, much of the first slave code was applied also to the free blacks who worked side by side with slaves in Savannah doing blacksmithing, coopering, carpentry, and mechanical and other work on the same dawn-to-dark schedule as the slaves. They had to wear badges and buy licenses to pursue their occupations. All had to pay a poll tax and have a white guardian. This tax was six times the amount of tax a master had to pay on a slave. It was raised to one dollar in

1783, four dollars in 1807, and five dollars in 1852—twenty times the poll tax that a white man had to pay for himself! Consequently, a free black needed to earn more than a white to meet this added expense. Many got jobs only because they were skilled, and they had to produce more than a slave or a white to keep their jobs. In addition to special taxes, free blacks had to carry papers proving their status. As one scholar noted, "Generally the free Negroes worked harder for the little freedom they had than the white people for all the freedom they took for granted. To be a free Negro was a much harder job than being a free white citizen."

In 1761, free blacks were specifically barred from voting. Earlier, some may have voted provided they owned fifty acres of land. However, in most cases it is reasonable to assume that custom discouraged this practice. As the number of free Negroes increased, so did restrictions. During the American Revolution, the free Negro's status did not improve in Georgia as it did in New England. Georgia's first Constitution, adopted in 1777, continued the ban against voting by free blacks, although all other states except South Carolina permitted them to vote. In 1789, the Georgia Assembly confirmed the ban when it declared free blacks could not vote or serve on juries.

The number of slaves who were freed increased during the revolutionary period as more masters manumitted children they had fathered with slave mistresses and other special favorites. They also heartlessly turned out some older, less productive slaves to shift for themselves. Some free blacks were able to accumulate property, and by 1789 there were four in Georgia whose average holdings were worth $2,500. The climate of increasing freedom began to change in the 1790s. The *Savannah Advertiser*, reflecting this in 1796, said that manumission was "not a prudent subject of discussion in Georgia."

The slave revolt in Haiti hurt the status of all Georgia blacks, especially free Negroes. By 1792, the Haitian mulattoes, who had fought with the whites against the slaves, were forced to flee, and some came to Savannah, one of the main Atlantic ports, but Georgians feared they brought the virus of revolution and closed the port to them. The state began requiring free blacks to give proof of their honesty and industry within six months of their arrival. Those who failed to do so could be deported from the state.

In 1799, one-third of Georgia's free Negro population was concentrated in Savannah, which passed a free Negro registration law. From then on, blacks were more harassed by the necessity of carrying "free papers" than they had been during the Colonial period. The registration caused problems for whites also: Papers could be forged, or a free Negro could claim to lose them and get a duplicate set, which could be passed on to a slave to aid an escape.

Beginning in 1801, amid growing concern over the increase of free blacks, a special act of the legislature was required to free a slave. The master could no longer on his own free a slave. Some masters did so anyway, and this created a small class of blacks who were neither slave nor legally free; they were free as far as their masters were concerned but still slaves according to official records. The law was repealed in 1815, then reinstated in 1818 with even more severe penalties, including a $500 fine for each violation. The new law specifically forbade the practice of self-purchase, though it did not end the opportunities for the unusually enterprising and lucky slave to buy his freedom, since this law, like so many, was not always enforced.

The 1818 law had the effect of requiring freed slaves to leave Georgia; slaves could be sent from the state and then freed, but they could not be freed first and then sent from the state. Even the former practice was forbidden by an 1859 enactment. As in so many other cases, enforcement of the laws was not uniform. The legislature occasionally acted to free slaves. In 1823, a slave named Sam was freed when the legislature appropriated $1,600 to buy him from his master as a reward for having saved the state Capitol at Milledgeville from burning. Ransom, a slave who saved a railroad bridge from fire in 1839, was purchased by the legislature, which could not bring itself to actually free him, but did allow him to retire and required the railroad to pay him a pension. An 1855 act of the legislature freed a slave in tardy recognition for his service in the War of 1812. However, the legislature was always reluctant to free slaves, and most manumission bills never came to a vote after 1830.

Slaves who were freed without the approval of the legislature were known as "nominal slaves." Some lived for years by hiring out their labor or by their own farming abilities and were hard to distinguish from the slaves who hired out their own time. Recognizing that a significant number of these blacks existed, Georgia moved in 1850 to tax them $150 apiece. (Only two actually paid the tax.)

Around 1806, following Virginia's lead, Georgia's crackdown on slaves affected free Negroes also. Free blacks were made increasingly subject to the slave codes, especially in towns and cities, where they were denied jury trials and stood before justices of the peace as slaves did. An 1808 law required that free blacks between the ages of eight and twenty-one be bound out as apprentices if they had no guardian. The lower age limit was dropped to five years in 1854.

The entry of free Negroes into Georgia was made more difficult in 1810, when the registration law of 1793 was strengthened with the requirement that a twenty-dollar registration fee be paid within ten days for the dubious privilege of entering Georgia. Yet some free Negroes did come. The 1850 census indicated that 339 (almost 12 percent of the 2,931 free Negroes then in Georgia) were born outside the state. Some, of course, may have been freed after arriving. In 1818, the law was tightened by requiring that all unregistered free blacks entering the state illegally be sold into slavery or turned over to the American Colonization Society (ACS) for removal to Africa and that any free Negro convicted of enticing a slave to run away or who sheltered a fugitive slave would be sold into slavery. The same law required that free blacks donate twenty days of labor to public work each year. In Savannah, black women met this requirement by working in a hospital. Free blacks were forbidden to own slaves, nor could they own real estate under penalty of a $1,000 fine. This last provision was repealed in 1824 but reinstated in 1859. This law was often evaded by free blacks who could transact business in their guardian's name.

Earlier, slaves were permitted to have firearms during the weekdays when they had the permission of their owner, but in 1833, in the wake of the terror inspired by Nat Turner, the legislature forbade slaves or free blacks to have firearms at any time. The penalty was thirty-nine lashes. Also in 1833, the registration fee was raised to $100 on all free Negroes coming into the state. If they could not pay it, they were subject to sale as slaves. Also, any free Negro who left the state for as long as two or three months was not permitted to return. Later, for a short time, free blacks were again denied entry into the state altogether. Since few, if any, blacks wanted to come to Georgia, this legislation did not affect blacks so much as it reflected the state's growing paranoia about outside influences, which contributed to Georgia's developing closed society. As the Civil War approached, efforts to enslave free blacks would increase. Georgians also used their influence in the national government to limit the activities of free blacks. Georgia representatives in Congress supported the Fugitive Slave Act of 1793, knowing that it could be used to force some free blacks back into slavery.

Blacks had shown an ability to do good work and helped build Georgia from the time they constructed the first houses in Savannah in 1733, but there was always jealousy on the part of many white workers, who constantly pressured for action to limit black opportunities for the better jobs. White laborers, especially in the cities, complained of having to compete with free Negro and slave labor. They frequently agitated for restrictions on blacks to remove this competition. White workers had some success in their efforts during the Colonial period and even more after Georgia became a state. In 1796, the legislature forbade the licensing of free blacks as river captains and pilots, thus forcing blacks out of a good-paying, high-status line of work they had come to dominate. White protests in Atlanta, Rome, Augusta, and Columbus increased toward the Civil War and often led to discriminatory licensing fees for skilled black workers. In 1845, the legislature forbade black mechanics from making contracts, thereby severely hampering their ability to do business. In the 1850s, white workers united against black mechanics in Savannah and helped pass high licensing fees for black mechanics there. Free Negro stonemasons and other artisans had to have their work approved by white artisans, which effectively reduced black employment in skilled labor.

By 1840, white Georgians were worrying about who was black. Miscegenation had produced all shades of folk, including those light enough to pass for white. Ticklish problems were sometimes raised by efforts to define who was black. In Georgia a higher percentage of the freed slaves had a white parent than in the upper South; therefore, free Negroes in Georgia tended to be lighter in color than those in the upper South. Some states, perhaps fearful of treading on the toes of the powerful who may have had an African among their ancestors, never defined "black." The question was not resolved in Georgia during the Colonial period but in 1788 and again in 1840 the Georgia legislature ruled that anyone who had a black ancestor in the past three generations would be defined as black. This law stayed on the books until 1927, when it was broadened to define as black anyone with *any* African ancestry. The 1840 law even provided for channels by which suspicious neighbors could take persons to court and make them prove their ethnic purity. No other state had such a "skeleton-rattling" provision.

Free blacks had no guarantee they would not be reenslaved. Because free Negroes could not testify against whites, they were subject to being kidnapped and sold into slavery. Some kidnapping rings had hundreds of victims, and these kidnappings increased as the price of slaves went up. Free Negroes who ran afoul of the many regulations circumscribing their lives were sometimes heavily fined and sold into slavery if they could not pay the fines. This also could happen if they did not pay the discriminatory taxes that were levied on them. Before the Civil War ended, there were five attempts to enslave all of Georgia's free Negroes.

Most free Negroes lived in the cities. Savannah had the largest free black population in Georgia, and Atlanta, Columbus, Augusta, and Macon also had significant numbers. Most of Savannah's blacks lived in the Oglethorpe Ward; unlike nearly every other ward, it had no public square. Land and rents were cheap there between the railroad and the river, where it was dirty and unhealthy. By 1850 the area contained hundreds of workshops and warehouses. The elite of the free Negro population lived in the Yamacraw section. Both free blacks and slaves followed a variety of occupations in the cities. The 1840 Savannah census shows both groups represented as mechanics, butchers, barbers, engineers, pilots, and preachers.

Many cities and towns in Georgia had a host of special rules and regulations limiting the conduct and daily life of free Negroes. In Savannah they were not supposed to rent property; they were to live on the premises of their guardians. They could not sell wares on the streets except on certain holidays. There were fines and whippings if they were caught gambling. Playing a musical instrument after sunset required special permission. They were not supposed to own dogs, follow parades, smoke in the streets, or ride horseback on Sunday. Free Negroes had to wear an identifying badge and pay special taxes. Despite all these regulations, the city was considered a better place than the plantation. Historian Richard H. Haunton painted a picture of antebellum Savannah as a bustling, crime-ridden, boisterous, brawling, growing city in which a runaway slave could escape detection.

In Savannah, as elsewhere, a higher percentage of blacks were in the labor force than whites. A larger percentage of black women worked than did white, and black children usually went to work at an earlier age than did white children. Despite the obstacles, a few free blacks were able to accumulate some wealth. In 1860, though most were penniless, the elite blacks of Savannah owned $92,280 in property, and whites were surprised at the opulent funeral pageantry in 1855 when a deacon of Savannah's Third African Baptist Church was buried. There were four uniformed black fire companies, a porter's association, three benevolent associations, thirty-five "well-filled" carriages, and many mourners on horseback among the multitude that turned out for the funeral procession.

Free Negroes were viewed with alarm throughout Georgia, and they were subject to a never-ending stream of regulations. In Athens, the *Southern Watchman* asked the legislature to do something about the nuisance of the free Negroes, as they were "incompatible with public safety." In Sparta, free blacks could not keep a place of entertainment or sell merchandise. This was also true in Clinton and Macon. Augusta had the usual restrictions: A typical ordinance stated in 1843 that free blacks could not ride or drive for pleasure, carry canes, smoke, or sell merchandise. The penalty for violations was a fine or whipping.

In 1840, Atlanta was called Terminus; it was a railroad community with fifty slaves and two free Negroes. In a typical action there, white workers petitioned the city council to limit the work of the hired slaves. Whites expressed resentment when blacks drank liquor, rode horseback, or traveled in horse-drawn gigs, engaged in trade, smoked cigars, or even carried a cane. By 1850, Atlanta had a $200 head tax on free Negroes to discourage their presence.

Although the obstacles set up to prevent an individual free black from prospering were great, a sizeable number were moderately successful. A few free Negroes owned land in Colonial times. In the 1850s, though the population of free blacks went up only 20 percent, their landholdings increased 60 percent. McPherson Bowman and William Lucas were two prominent black landowners. Of the 184 free Negroes in Chatham County in 1826, 67 owned property, and 25 owned from one to twenty-five slaves. In the entire state in 1830, sixty-one free blacks owned 207 slaves in thirteen counties. In the 1850s, though the population of free blacks went up only 20 percent, their landholdings increased 60 percent. Whereas whites owned slaves to exploit their labor, the most important reason blacks owned them was to keep their families together. When a free black man married a slave, his wife remained the slave of her master, as did their children, unless he could buy them. Since the legislature would not permit free blacks to free the slaves they purchased, those purchased remained "nominal slaves," though in fact they were members of a family.

Three brothers, Ralph, Robert, and Roderick Badger, were born slaves; they all had the same white father but different mothers. The three learned dentistry from their father. Roderick, the best known of the brothers, practiced in Atlanta. In 1859, a group petitioned the city council to stop him from competing with whites. As a result, the city passed an ordinance requiring a $200 fee for a free Negro to come to Atlanta. If the fee was not paid, the black was to receive thirty-nine lashes every day he was in town. The regulation was not enforced, and Roderick continued to practice dentistry. Another petition was circulated against him in 1861. During the early part of the Civil War, he served as an aide to a Confederate colonel. Roderick and Robert escaped to the North with their families and went to Chicago when Sherman came in 1864. Roderick returned to Atlanta and continued to practice dentistry until his death in 1890.

James Boisclair was a free Negro gold mine owner-operator and merchant in Dahlonega in the 1830s. He was expelled from a white Baptist church for selling liquor on Sunday but was readmitted the following year on evidence of a sincere repentance. He later became one of the "49ers" who took part in the California gold rush.

Wilkes Flagg, born a slave in Virginia in 1802, was brought to Georgia, where he learned to read and write and became a blacksmith. He was able to buy his own freedom and that of his wife and family. Although a Democrat, he was an abolitionist and acquired property worth $25,000 by 1860. He was trusted by the whites of Milledgeville, where he was a minister during the Civil War and withstood torture rather than disclose to soldiers in Sherman's army where he had buried the money entrusted to him by his former master. He was a welcome visitor in the home of his ex-owner as long as he observed the rules of racial etiquette: "On such occasions Flagg would always stand, hat in hand, never in the least presuming," according to one account.

In most Georgia cities, a black who rode in a gig, a type of horse-drawn carriage, was considered to be "putting on airs" and would usually be roughly treated by whites until he got back in "his place" again. Andrew Marshall was a successful drayman in Savannah who was worth $5,000 by 1850 and was sufficiently respected so that he could drive his own gig without inciting undue protest from whites. Other free Negroes, such as Jeffery Moore (Augusta) and James Oliver (Savannah), also flouted the racial mores by driving gigs. In 1853, Atlanta made it illegal for a black to own a gig.

In 1809, before restrictions on manumission had grown too rigid, Anthony Odingsells was freed by his father, who was also his owner. He worked hard and acquired skills in the fishing business and amassed an estate by 1860 in Chatham County that included two hundred acres and fifteen slaves, one of whom he sold in 1833 for $335.

Macon's most prominent free black was Solomon Humphries, known as "Free Sol." He became a wealthy merchant and cotton broker who had a $10,000 line of credit with New York wholesalers and was known there and in Savannah and Charleston as a "merchant of reliability and honor." He purchased his own freedom, but it took a four-year campaign in the legislature before he could free his wife, Patsy, and his father, Cyrus. He received white guests in his home for dinner but was careful not to sit down in their presence and join his guests at the meal. Instead, he served them as a waiter. He was worth $20,000 at one time, but his hired white clerks, whom he trusted unduly, speculated with his money and lost most of it for him by the time he died. The city council declared a day of mourning, and Macon shut down for his 1855 funeral, to which many whites, including fellow merchants, came. He is now buried in Macon's Fort Hill Cemetery. Another prominent free black Maconite was Edward Woodliff, a barber-entrepreneur who came to Macon in 1832 and prospered. He purchased his slave wife, Mahala, for $800 in 1843 and accumulated property through the agency of a white guardian as required by law. After the Civil War he was active in Reconstruction politics.

Outside events sharpened the crisis for free Negroes just before the Civil War. The 1857 Dred Scott Decision, which stripped free blacks of any citizenship rights, led to intensified persecution in Georgia. If Dred Scott proved to white Georgians that blacks had no rights they must respect, John Brown's raid on Harpers Ferry in 1859 scared them into even more repression. That year, the state established a fine of $1,000 for bringing a free Negro into Georgia. As the secession crisis mounted, Georgia passed draconian laws against free blacks and slaves and enforced old ones. Laws against whites arming or selling poison to blacks were tightened. In 1859, the 1851 vagrancy laws permitting the sale of free blacks into slavery were strengthened and more rigidly enforced. In 1859, the legislature decreed that slaves could not be freed by will, even if they were sent out of state first. The Georgia legislature even established procedures that permitted free Negroes to petition to become slaves. Needless to say, few blacks volunteered for this fate, although two cases are documented.

After the Civil War started, attacks on and complaints against the free black population increased. In June 1861, the *Savannah Daily Morning News* charged that all free blacks were "drones." Perhaps in response to this, sixty free blacks wrote Gov. Joseph E. Brown volunteering their services "in any capacity," and a hundred free black women volunteered to make clothes for the Confederate army. A number of free blacks did work on the fortifications at Fort Pulaski and were honorably discharged in July 1861, when the work was completed. Joe Clark, a free Negro barber in Columbus who had earlier served in the 1836 Seminole War, offered to raise a company of soldiers for the state. Wilkes Flagg of Milledgeville contributed twenty-six dollars to a local white military company. Historian Clarence L. Mohr regarded these efforts as attempts by free blacks to avoid enslavement more than as evidence of any sincere good wishes for the Confederate cause.

Many free Negroes—demonstrating remarkable resilience despite constant attacks, proscriptions, and disabilities—went on to lay the basis for black churches, fraternal orders, schools, and other institutions. Some free blacks had acquired a respectable amount of property, so that their children had an advantage over the offspring of those freed at the end of the Civil War. A study by Horace Mann Bond in the 1960s showed that descendants of free Negroes dominated the intellectual and professional classes among blacks in the United States.

While Georgia's free blacks demonstrated that slavery was not a necessary condition for blacks, neither was absolute bondage necessary to ensure a racial caste system. Free Negroes were exploited and kept subordinate before the Civil War. This reduced resistance to the Thirteenth Amendment by helping whites visualize the possibility of continuing to exploit blacks after emancipation. The laws permitting temporary slavery set a precedent for the widespread institution of peonage after the Civil War, when many blacks were for all intents and purposes enslaved for failure to pay their debts, however unjust they might be. There was very little difference in status between slavery for a free Negro who was trapped into debt by credit buying and dishonest accounting before the Civil War and the sharecroppers who fell into debt after the war because they were unable to pay court fees and fines or meet store bills.

Back to Africa: The American Colonization Society

After the 1808 law banning the slave trade, Congress wanted to establish an area in Africa where slaves liberated from apprehended slave ships could be taken, as the British did in Sierra Leone. The American Colonization Society (ACS) was organized in 1817 to take free blacks back to Africa. Its founders included prominent white Georgians. The ACS became the main promoter of the back-to-Africa movement, and it wanted Congress to authorize it to direct this activity as an agency of the U. S. government, but congressional opposition was too strong. President James Monroe did authorize agents supervising the suppression of the slave trade to be agents of the ACS.

The ACS selected an area in Africa on the coast just southeast of Sierra Leone. The land was purchased in 1822 from King Mannah Funaral whose grandson, Dr. Cornelius McKane, was later a prominent black physician in Savannah. The name Liberia (Latin for "place of freedom") was selected. The area was covered by a dense tropical forest. The ACS immediately established a capital city, Monrovia, named in honor of President James Monroe. That same year, Jehudi Ashmum, an ACS agent, sailed to Liberia on the *Strong*, with thirty-five freed slaves from Georgia in this first group going to Monrovia and freedom. The new colony experienced great difficulties and many deaths. The colonists were attacked twice by indigenous Africans but, because they had cannons, they won the battles. The young colony went through trying times, but in 1847, Liberia declared itself an independent republic and tried to model its government on that of the United States.

The Georgia legislature barely tolerated the ACS. Although it initially agreed to turn manumitted slaves over to the society if the ACS would pay their costs back to Africa, it did not support the society financially and later restricted the ACS's right to hold slaves pending their shipment to Liberia. In 1827 the Georgia legislature protested to Congress against federal funding of the ACS. The 1828 legislature resolved that the ACS was an evil and viewed with "jealousy and distrust all associations having for their object the abolition of slavery."

The efforts of the ACS to get funding from the state of Georgia never materialized because too many slave owners mistakenly equated the society with abolition. However, those planters who understood that the ACS's major aim was to remove free Negroes (and thus strengthen slavery) approved of it. The society played on this fear of free blacks. The Putnam

County ACS pointed out that removing free Negroes would remove "the most fruitful source of discontent."

Some planters emancipated their slaves so that they could be taken to Liberia. In 1830, Joe Early, brother of the governor, freed thirty of his slaves to make the trip. Another group had left Georgia three years earlier under the auspices of the ACS. This group included some of the forty-eight slaves that Richard Tubman of Augusta freed in his will, which also provided $10,000 for their removal from Georgia and their support afterward. Alexander, taking the surname of his master, later married Elizabeth Rebecca Barnes, a slave freed in Atlanta on the condition that she go to Africa. Their grandson, William V. S. Tubman, served as president of Liberia from 1943 to his death in 1971. He was honored by Atlanta's black community when he visited there in November 1954. Georgia furnished an earlier president for Liberia in the person of J. J. Cheeseman in 1895. Further evidence of the ties between Georgia and Liberia may be found in the fact that the second oldest town was named Savannah. The third oldest was founded in 1826 about five miles north of Monrovia and was named New Georgia.

The ACS had several agents in Georgia at various times and established branches in Jackson County, Augusta, Eatonton, Waynesboro, Mille-dgeville, and Savannah. By 1837, there were eighteen local branches in Georgia and South Carolina. These were apparently built on sand, however. The *African Repository*, official organ of the ACS, reported in 1846 that there had been in Georgia "no agent for many years past."

Although many who went to Liberia found disappointment and hard-ship, others were successful in carving out new careers. Adam Anderson, the son of a black preacher in Savannah who had once been a slave in Chatham County, went to Liberia in 1833 as a missionary to the Vai tribe and helped to found a Baptist church in Monrovia where he became a minister and an editor. Freed slaves named Harris and Savage went to Liberia from Georgia in 1840 and became successful farmers there. Joseph Clay left Georgia in 1848 and became a Liberian Baptist minister. Of a group of 181 who sailed from Savannah in May 1849, 103 were literate and 24 were self-purchased at an average price of $624. The Rehoboth Baptist Association of Augusta sent African-born Caesar Frazer back to Liberia and followed with $186 in supplies to show their continuing support of that country. One of the last Georgians to make the trip before the Civil War was Silas Pope, born a slave in Georgia in 1813. He was able to buy his own freedom and that of his wife and daughter for a total of $1,739 and left for Liberia in May 1860 on the *Mary Caroline Stevens*.

Less than one-quarter of 1 percent of Georgia's black population left Georgia for Africa. Although by 1835 only 200–300 left, the pace quickened somewhat in the next two decades, so that by 1856, 1,030 black Georgians had departed for Africa. The decade 1846–55 saw an increase in interest in colonization. In the peak year of 1853, 796 blacks left Georgia for Liberia. White Georgians contributed $12,670 to the ACS between 1846 and 1855, and some Georgia ACS branches were revitalized. In 1856, the Georgia legislature passed a bill "to aid the colonization of free persons of color," but this small swell of support for the ACS died as tensions over slavery mounted in the late 1850s. Later in 1856, Savannah voted to tax the ACS $200 for every black bound for Africa under the society's auspices. In 1860, the *African Repository* reported that a total of five Georgians had donated an average of eighty-five cents apiece for the work of the ACS. The following year, as the Civil War began, this measly contribution dropped to zero.

3

The Civil War and Reconstruction

Prelude to Conflict

By the time Georgia legalized slavery in 1750, the decision regarding black servitude seemed settled for all time. It required another 115 years of increasing tension and a great war to reverse this decision. There were many steps on the road to armed conflict. However, the fundamental reason for the Civil War was the South's intransigence on slavery. The South's unwillingness to alter its "peculiar institution" and enter the modern world made a major convulsion unavoidable. Southern fears of the power of the federal government to interfere with slavery increased to the climax of 1860-61, when, one by one, states entered into open rebellion against the Union.

When Abraham Lincoln opposed the expansion of slavery into western territories, he was, as far as the Southern oligarchy was concerned, pronouncing the death knell of slavery. With Georgia in the front ranks, the South marched off to war to preserve and extend slavery under a cloak of "states' rights" rhetoric. Although the slave interests did not start hostilities against the Union until 1861, they had been prepared to leave it over the issue of slavery time and time again ever since the nation was founded. In 1830, the *Milledgeville Federal Union* said, "The moment any improper interference is attempted with our slaves, we say, let the Union be dissolved," and the *Macon Georgia Messenger* said prophetically that only a bloody civil war could end slavery. Prompted by an antiabolitionist convention in Athens, the Georgia legislature in 1835 resolved that the preservation of the Union depended on the North crushing the abolition movement by denying abolitionists free speech and extending slavery into the territories.

The Compromise of 1850 was an effort to reconcile pro-slavery and antislavery interests that disputed over the disposition of Mexican War spoils. A five-point package was worked out in Congress that would admit California as a free state but not close the door to slavery in other western territories taken from Mexico. The compromise agreed to abolish the slave trade, but not slavery, in the District of Columbia. The provision that did the most to heighten tensions over slavery was the agreement to enact a new and far more severe fugitive slave law, one planters hoped would put an effective end to the underground railroad.

Georgia played a leading role in the Southern debate on the acceptability of the Compromise of 1850 when its leading citizens met in the capital at Milledgeville on December 13–14, 1850, and resolved, though reluctantly, to accept the compromise. In what became known as the Georgia Platform, the delegates warned the nation that the life of the Union was secondary to their right to keep slaves and that Georgia would secede if slavery was abolished in the District of Columbia without the consent of the slave owners, if the domestic slave trade was limited in any way, or if Congress refused to admit new slave states or abolished slavery in the territories. They viewed the new Fugitive Slave Act as the crux of the matter and resolved: "That it is the deliberate opinion of this convention, that upon the faithful execution of the Fugitive Slave Bill by the proper authorities, depends the preservation of our much loved Union." The poor enforcement of the Fugitive Slave Law of 1850 was a source of bitterness in Georgia. The Craft case (see pp. 45–46) especially reinforced Georgia planters' doubts concerning its practicality.

In the territories, tensions continued to rise over the issue. Georgians watched events in "Bleeding Kansas" with interest, but they were horrified when they learned of militant abolitionist John Brown's raid at Pottawatomie Creek on May 25, 1856. In 1857, the legal position of all blacks in the United States was greatly weakened by the Dred Scott Decision, which opened the way for the expansion of slavery into the western territories. The Supreme Court ruled that slaves had no rights and that the federal government had no authority to regulate slavery or to interfere in state regulation of slaves.

The single event that most shocked the slave society was Brown's raid on Harpers Ferry, Virginia, on October 16, 1859. News that Brown had seized the federal arsenal and intended to arm slaves in a chain of counties extending through Georgia and other states to bring an end to slavery spread like wildfire throughout the South and caused panic in Georgia. In one typical reaction, Rome organized a hundred vigilantes to march to the aid of Virginia. Northern travelers, always under suspicion for kindling the fires of abolitionism among blacks, became even more suspect and were often forced to leave. Mob violence broke out in Savannah against a white accused of reading accounts of the raid to local blacks, and a mob seized a Yankee ship docked there. The *Savannah Republican* and the *Columbus Sun* both reported in November that a "squad of Brown's emissaries" in Meriwether County were waiting to give battle. The burning of numerous cotton gins that same month was called "Kansas work in Georgia," though such fires were common during the ginning season. Gov. Joseph E. Brown, who earlier had difficulties getting money appropriated for the state's militia, had no problem getting $75,000 from the legislature after the news came from Harpers Ferry.

The single-minded abolitionist's daring raid engendered a climate of hysteria that led to a flood of rumors regarding slave insurrections throughout the South. In the spring of 1860, mysterious fires broke out in Macon and six other Georgia towns. All were blamed on a slave conspiracy, with white abolitionists supposedly directing the operations. "Confessions" of insurrection were whipped out of blacks all over Georgia in late 1860. Rumors of slave revolts were especially rife in Northeast Georgia, though no part of the state was immune.

Fueling the already intense emotional climate was a new popular song. "Dixie" was first performed in 1859 and expressed Southern intransigence so well that it became for all practical purposes the Confederate anthem. H. S. Stanton of Georgia is credited with turning it into a war song. Among the many original verses of "Dixie" was:

> Hear the Northern thunders mutter!
> Northern flags in South winds flutter!
> Send them back your fierce defiance!
> Stamp upon the accursed alliance!

Lincoln's election in November 1860 increased the fears of slave revolt and led to a strengthening of the patrol system and tightened security over slaves. Mob violence against blacks and an occasional white considered sympathetic to abolition became a wave of terror. Frequent lynchings served to keep most slaves cowed, although the number of runaways increased. Trusted slave drivers had their hunting guns confiscated. Passes, especially for railroad travel, were severely restricted, and separate church services for blacks were curtailed. Some cities, like Macon, greatly enlarged their police forces in response to insurrection scares.

Georgia's leaders had greeted Lincoln's election with dismay. Lincoln, in his first inaugural address, promised to support a constitutional amendment that would guarantee slavery where it already existed. However, Lincoln would not agree to any extension of slavery. Southern planters were in basic agreement that slavery must expand or die. They believed that new lands had to be opened to slavery for three reasons: to replace lands worn out (by poor agricultural practices); to provide out-of-state markets for the continual increase in the slave population in order to prevent a class of idle blacks from appearing; and to enter new slave states into the Union at least as often as new free states so that slaveholding interests would not grow politically impotent in Congress. They foresaw a day, not too distant, when the ever-expanding and dynamic North would outvote them in Congress on every issue. This, the Southern oligarchy feared, would mean the demise of slavery.

To Georgia leaders such as Howell Cobb and Robert Toombs, the election of Lincoln was the last straw. However, secession by the Southern states was neither unanimous nor simultaneous. The Georgia legislature debated the secession issue on November 13 and 14, 1860. Toombs led the firebrands, urging headlong action. He anticipated that lacking new markets to receive the surplus of 500,000 slaves he thought Georgia would produce through natural increase by 1900, the state would be impoverished. "We must expand or perish," he declared, and demanded "resistance to Lincoln and his abolition horde." Alexander Stephens headed those with a more moderate "wait-and-see" attitude and was labeled a "submissionist" and "crypto-abolitionist." The legislature decided to refer the matter to a convention. Delegates to this convention were elected on January 2, 1861, when secessionists' "propaganda skillfully exploited the voters' racism, employing everything from vague rumors of slave insurrections to (Governor) Brown's warning to non-slaveholders that submission to Lincoln would mean abolition, ethnic equality, and intermarriage," according to historian F. N. Boney.

Delegates to the convention would decide if the state was to secede or not. Although Governor Brown stated that the popular vote for electing delegates was 50,243 for immediate secession and 37,123 for a more moderate course, later research indicated the margin "was paper thin, if it existed at all," and the vote was no more than 44,152 for immediate secession to 41,632 against. Some evidence suggests a slight majority of voters favored cooperationist, not secessionist, candidates. Historian Michael P. Johnson concluded:

> Georgians were so equally divided by the question of secession that the voters' judgment can be justly termed a paralyzing indecision...when the delegates listened to the voice of the people and made the final decision to secede, their ears were more closely attuned to the shouts for secession than to the almost equally numerous whispers of doubt.

Interestingly, Brown did not announce the vote totals until April, three months after the convention had done its business; official records of the vote do not exist.

Governor Brown, a thin, teetotaling Baptist lawyer from the hill country with a Yale law degree, called for the convention to meet at Milledgeville on January 16, citing as reasons the failure of the North to enforce the Fugitive Slave Law and the election of Lincoln, though he earlier had said Lincoln's election by itself was insufficient reason for Georgia to secede. The move for secession was strongest in the plantation country, and convention delegates disproportionately represented slavery interests. Of the 301 delegates, 259 (86 percent) were slave owners; seven owned more than a hundred slaves, sixty-seven owned more than fifty, and almost half owned more than twenty slaves. In all, the delegates owned 7,660 slaves. Had the delegates been typical of Georgia's white population, most would have owned no slaves at all. Proceedings were closed to outsiders, and the first convention vote on secession was only 166 in favor to 130 opposed. Terrific pressure was then put on the 130, and 41 were persuaded to switch their votes three days later.

Not only did planters want to maintain slavery, they also wanted to continue controlling yeomen and poor whites. Many who voted for secession did not foresee a war; Brown had said that secession before Lincoln's inauguration would reduce the chance of war. Brown told non-slave-owning poor whites that without secession the Union would buy and free the slaves and planters would use the money to buy their land and reduce them from landowners to tenants. Thirty percent of the delegates still voted to stay in the Union despite secessionist leaders' propaganda, manipulation, and deception. On January 19, 1861, Georgia became the fifth state to pass an ordinance of secession, which was never offered to the people of Georgia for approval. The *Augusta Chronicle and Sentinel,* then the largest newspaper in the state, deplored the action. Georgia joined with other states to form the Confederate States of America on February 9, 1861, at Montgomery, Alabama. Georgia's convention reconvened in March to adopt the Confederate Constitution (which also did not get popular approval) and to write the 1861 state constitution, which was approved by less than 52 percent of the voters in a very light turnout.

Secession resolved the tension and quelled the slave insurrection panic. The planter class again felt secure, in charge of its own destiny, and in the heady days of the secessionist enthusiasm, saw only a rosy future. As the Civil War proceeded, the rigor of the plantation system softened. Slaves remained a "troublesome property," and lynching and burnings still occurred, but the paranoia diminished.

In Savannah in March 1861, Alexander Stephens, chosen to be vice president of the Confederacy, expressed the fundamental beliefs white

Southerners had been busily teaching each other for generations. He said of slavery: "Its cornerstone rests upon the great truth that the Negro is not equal to the white man; that slavery—subordination to the superior race—is his natural and normal condition." It was this racist bedrock, born of self-deception and assiduously cultivated since Georgia was founded, that obscured the relatively simple fact that slavery was an economic institution created to exploit the black worker. It was this racism that took Georgia out of the Union in 1861, that killed so many of its sons on the battlefields of the Civil War, impoverished its economy, and brought needless suffering to countless people, both black and white.

The Civil War

The Civil War is surrounded by many myths. One of them is the belief that an idealistic and courageous South, unified in the conviction that its cause was just, with its sons stumbling over each other in their eagerness to get up to the battle lines, fought wholeheartedly for the preservation of a gracious way of life until Northern materialism, with its preponderance of men and supplies, wrote the final chapter at Appomattox. This myth ignores the facts that the South was divided about slavery, secession, the war, and how to fight it—and that the "gracious way of life" was enjoyed by only a tiny minority that had to impose conscription a year before the North did. As for morale, the Confederate army had more desertions than the Union army. In 1864, Jefferson Davis admitted, "Two-thirds of our men are absent... most of them absent without leave." Another myth states that it was an unnecessary war brought on by bad statesmanship— fought to preserve a dying institution that soon would have disappeared, anyway, because it was economically unsound. Considering how little economic relations between black and white changed after the South was defeated on the battlefield, it is difficult to imagine that any great changes would have occurred had there been no military defeat. Outside force was required to change the South's race relations in the 1860s, just as it was a century later.

The participation of blacks in the Civil War was enormously important. It changed the war from one aiming merely to preserve the Union and prevent the extension of slavery into one to abolish slavery. Slaves and free Negroes worked and fought on both sides; however, their contribution to the Union cause was far greater, made willingly and often joyously, while black support for the Confederacy was forced.

Despite efforts by masters to keep slaves ignorant and uninvolved in the conflict, the grapevine telegraph that ran from the slave quarters on one plantation to the next ensured that slaves were often as knowledge-able of major events as their masters. Literate slaves, such as Minnie

Davis, stole newspapers in Savannah and read them in the quarters. Of 180 Georgia ex-slaves interviewed in the 1930s, 178 (99 percent) knew about the Civil War long before it came to their plantations.

The myth of black docility during the Civil War was no more true than it was before the war. During the war many slaves shook the dust of the plantation off their feet at the earliest opportunity. In one effort to stop runaways, the legislature in 1862 tried to get all white males from age eighteen to sixty-five to do patrol duty. As an added precaution, some masters locked up their slaves at night. To slow defections to the Union, slaves were often fed false atrocity stories about Yankees drowning, shooting, or burning slaves alive. However, other slaves contradicted these tales. In addition, there were many plots and rumors of plots by slaves that kept white Georgians on edge throughout the war. For a true measure of slaves' feelings, consider this: Whenever the Union military forces approached, the nearby plantations would suffer mass desertions of the slaves. W. E. B. Du Bois referred to this as the General Strike of the slaves against the Confederacy.

Though they were often forced to help the Confederacy, blacks were nearly unanimous in hoping for a Yankee victory. This unwilling help took three forms: as the main labor force in agriculture and to a lesser extent in industry, as impressed labor on military projects, and last and least, as soldiers for the Confederacy. Perhaps 80 percent of the slaves stayed on the plantations of Georgia, going about their customary tasks through the first three years of the war. While the South at first viewed the slaves as an asset in the war effort, as the fighting proceeded, slaves turned on their masters by the tens of thousands and helped decisively to bring the Union victory. Ultimately, the help the Confederacy received from forced labor was far less than that received by the Union army from the hundreds of thousands of black volunteers who worked as civilian laborers and soldiers. Of this number, an estimated fifty thousand were from Georgia.

Black women did their part to help the Union war effort. Susie King Taylor recalled that Negro women by the hundreds assisted Union soldiers by hiding them and helping them to escape. There was a stockade in Savannah where captured Union soldiers were imprisoned. There the prisoners had no shelter from sun and rain and very little food. Mrs. Taylor wrote:

> Many were punished for taking food to the prison stockade for prisoners. The colored women would take food there at night and pass it to them through the holes in the fence. The soldiers were starving, and these women did all they could toward relieving those men, although they knew the penalty, should they be caught giving them aid.

*   *   *

Three wartime developments would weaken slavery in Georgia: the impressment of slaves for military labor; "refugeeing," whereby masters moved their slaves away from battle areas; and the breakdown of the pass and patrol system.

Highly skilled slaves already had been working in Georgia's industries, such as the Columbus Naval Iron Works, and after the war started, many more were used for military work. Masters were exceedingly reluctant in most cases to hire out their slaves for military work; however, as the war became more serious, so did official actions to impress slaves. On August 1, 1863, Brig. Gen. H. W. Mercer of Savannah, on the authority of the secretary of war, signed an order impressing 20 percent of Georgia's slaves if the masters would not volunteer them. Masters were to be paid $25 a month for each slave's labor and $2,500 if the slave was killed, injured, or captured. As the war drew to a close, efforts to impress slaves increased. Thousands, some drawn from as far away as Macon, were used in the summer of 1863 to fortify Atlanta and Columbus after the fall of Vicksburg. Twenty percent of the nearby slaves were impressed to work on the fortification of Macon, and bondsmen were also used to fortify Athens and Augusta. Nine hundred worked on the construction of the infamous prison camp at Andersonville. In December 1864, Georgia was assigned a quota of twenty-five hundred more slaves to be impressed. Free Negroes were also dragooned into serving the Confederacy. Historian Clarence Mohr estimates that "altogether at least 10,000 slaves and free Negroes probably labored at various times on Georgia's military defenses." Many fell victim to disease, especially measles and smallpox. Impressment helped weaken slavery because it provided more chances for escape. It also increased the slaves' sense of grievance by tearing them from familiar surroundings.

Another factor weakening slavery during the war was "refugeeing," as planters fled with their slaves from areas menaced by Union forces. It started with the removal of some slaves from Georgia's Sea Islands early in 1861. The process accelerated toward the end of the year as planters learned of events surrounding the Union navy's capture of Port Royal, South Carolina on November 7, 1861. Planters there were caught by surprise and made frantic last-minute efforts to move the slaves, who resisted and remained behind, to be freed by invading forces. With the perils of delay so dramatically underlined, Georgia island planters completed the refugeeing process by December 1861. The subsequent surrender to Union forces on April 11, 1862, of "impregnable" Fort Pulaski impelled planters to flee the Savannah area, taking their slaves with them. The capture of these prizes encouraged slaves to desert the plantations and come to the islands for refuge.

In March 1862, the Union navy had started a colony for runaway slaves on St. Simons, which, along with Skidaway Island, had been deserted by the Rebels. Within nine months some six hundred slaves had sought refuge there. Then they were all sent to Port Royal, where an army regiment was formed that contained some runaway slaves from Georgia. Amelia Island, Florida, also served as a haven for runaway slaves from Georgia after its capture by the Union early in 1862.

Union successes along the Georgia coast were a psychological boost to blacks who saw their doubts confirmed about the masters' tall tales of Confederate invincibility and Union weakness. There would have been a far greater defection of slaves to the Union lines had it not been for the active presence of six Confederate cavalry companies between them and the Georgia coast. The Confederate army there was converted into a gigantic slave patrol to prevent blacks from escaping to the Union-held islands. These troops limited but did not completely stop runaways. Perhaps a thousand slaves escaped to the Union-held coast between December 1861 and October 1864. Many were killed, wounded, or captured trying to make the break to freedom. The dangers inherent in trying to escape are illustrated by the case of Paul, a slave of a wealthy planter and former Savannah mayor, Edward C. Anderson. When Paul started to run away to the Union forces, he killed a white who tried to stop his escape. He fled to the home of a slave couple, who took him in even though they knew the risks involved. Paul was found and died of the wounds he received, and the good Samaritan hosts were almost lynched. They each got thirty-nine lashes.

By early 1863, well over half of the thirty-four thousand slaves in the coastal areas were moved inland. Toward the end of that year, as the tide of war turned against the South, slaveholders in northern Georgia began fleeing to the south and west. Valdosta and other cities soon had a surplus of slaves whom the masters could no longer provide with food and shelter.

Refugeeing weakened slavery in several ways. As the slaves traveled, their sense of isolation diminished, and their horizons broadened, contributing to their growing perception of the master's weakness. Moreover, many slave families were broken up in the process, which increased the slaves' sense of grievance and oppression. Sometimes, when the slaves did not want to move, the owners would make refugeeing more attractive by paying cash for the property slaves accumulated in household items, furniture, and livestock.

Many slaves were now in towns and cities, where it was easier to conceive of freedom. The abandonment of plantations meant new jobs for many slaves. Atlanta, with its rapidly expanding industrial base, had the greatest wartime growth of all Georgia cities. Between 1860 and 1862, its population doubled to seventeen thousand, largely because it was a major destination for refugee planters and their slaves. Urbanized blacks found work in many occupations, serving as hospital attendants, mechanics, carpenters, smiths, wheelwrights, molders, laborers, and domestics. The number permitted to hire themselves out increased, and the detailed supervision of the plantation gave way to the looser constraints of the city. This also occurred in many other Georgia cities, such as Macon, and the black populations in the smaller rural towns also increased.

Slaves, ever alert to improve their lot, could find themselves jobs better than their masters could. This led to an even greater degree of freedom. Since masters of refugeed slaves had no home for them in the cities, they could find their own lodging. This led to the beginning of segregation in Georgia's cities as slaves began to congregate in peripheral enclaves. Blacks chose these areas so they could be by themselves, escape white surveillance, live in relative physical and psychological security—and because there was no other place to live. Some masters, after taking their slaves to town, abandoned them for all practical purposes, and they experienced what was tantamount to freedom.

Meanwhile, the pass and patrol system broke down, and complaints against urban blacks' "insolence and impudence" increased as the war neared its end and the "structure of urban bondage slowly crumbled under the stress of the war environment," according to Mohr. Following the Northern invasion of Georgia, rural slave patrols faded away and supervision on plantations and in towns relaxed. Those sent to Atlanta to help fortify it were left without white supervision, and Atlanta became a center for wandering slaves.

Accounts of black Confederate soldiers were exaggerated both in the North and South. Southerners boldly pointed to their existence to show that blacks did not oppose slavery. On the other hand, Northern abolitionists used the stories to prod the federal government into accepting the many blacks anxious to fight against slavery. Black troops were used by the Confederacy first because the free Negroes of the North who volunteered when Lincoln issued his first call for troops were rejected at the outbreak of hostilities on the grounds that the war did not concern them, whereas pressure was applied to the South's free Negroes to enlist in the Confederate army. Some did, mainly to defuse the sentiment to enslave all free Negroes. However, most accounts of black Rebel soldiers died away soon after the war started and were not heard again until the Confederacy grew desperate toward the war's end.

Slaves were never used as Confederate soldiers. However, some Georgia slaves went to the war with their masters to work as servants: to cook, mend, take care of the horses, and work around the camp. George Brooks was one such. Born in 1833, he went with his master as a body servant and served him for six months before he defected to the Union.

Many of the men of the Troup Artillery took their slaves with them to the war, but the slaves all ran away. A few were more faithful to their masters. Dave served R. H. Nesbit, son of Georgia's Supreme Court chief justice, and once helped save his master's commanding officer's life and helped capture Union soldiers.

Georgia considered using black troops in the war's last, desperate days, but the contradiction of a slave/soldier could not be resolved, and nothing came of the proposal. Maj. Gen. Howell Cobb of Georgia explained:

> I think that the proposition to make soldiers out of our slaves is the most pernicious idea that had been suggested since the war began... you cannot make soldiers of slaves or slaves of soldiers... the day you make soldiers of them is the beginning of the end of the revolution. If slaves will make good soldiers our whole theory of slavery is wrong.

Governor Brown agreed: "If the Negro is fit to be a soldier, he is not fit to be a slave."

On March 20, twenty days before the final surrender to General Ulysses Grant, the Confederate Congress relented and enacted the necessary legislation authorizing the enlistment and freedom of 300,000 slaves. The Georgia legislature opposed this decision. In any case, the Confederate action came too late. The cause was already lost. Some black companies were formed but they saw no action.

In the North, blacks rushed to enlist when Lincoln called for seventy-five thousand volunteers on April 15, 1861, two days after the surrender of Fort Sumter. They were everywhere rejected on the grounds that the war was "white man's business." It was not until January 1863 (the month the Emancipation Proclamation went into effect) that the first ex-slaves were formally mustered into lasting military units. Among the first of these was Gen. Rufus Saxton's First South Carolina Volunteers, with Thomas W. Higginson as commander, which included some slaves who had escaped from Georgia. Several runaway slaves from Georgia served in the most famous black regiments, the Massachusetts Fifty-Fourth and Fifty-Fifth.

Of the one hundred eighty-six thousand black soldiers in the Union army, ninety-three thousand came from the Confederate states, with a significant number from Georgia. Another forty thousand came from the border states that did not secede, and fifty-three thousand were from the free states. In addition, almost twenty thousand blacks served in the Union navy. The Sable Arm served in 449 engagements, of which 39 were major battles. Sixteen black soldiers and five black sailors won Congressional Medals of Honor. Thirty-eight thousand black soldiers lost their lives—40 percent more deaths in proportion to their numbers than white

Union troops suffered. Contrary to customs of war, the Rebels executed some of their prisoners out of fear and hatred of black soldiers and their officers.

Black units saw little action in Georgia, as the Union army was usually farther north or west until 1864. Although Sherman had thousands of blacks helping him march through Georgia, they were not organized as military units. Georgia's black Union soldiers were scattered throughout the Union army. Some Georgia slaves who had run away and joined the Union forces at St. Simons and were evacuated to Port Royal in 1862 served in the First South Carolina Volunteers under Colonel Higginson. Though sometimes brutally mistreated, they became good soldiers. An account in the February 11, 1863, *New York Times* of a raid by these volunteers into Georgia and Florida concluded that the Negro was a good soldier and that arming the slaves was the key to victory. The Second South Carolina Volunteer Regiment, which contained many black Georgian soldiers, participated in the destruction of Darien in a raid on June 11, 1863. Through much of Georgia's history, Darien had rivaled Savannah as Georgia's chief city. Two other engagements in Georgia in which black units saw action were at Dallas on May 31 and Dalton on August 19, 1864.

The Civil War, or "The War Between the States" to white Southerners and "the Late Unpleasantness" to their descendants, came with frightful losses in lives and wealth. Georgia remained relatively unscathed until the final campaigns, when, in the words of Julia Ward Howe's "Battle Hymn of the Republic," it, too, felt "the fateful lightning of His terrible swift sword."

The single event giving the slaves of Georgia the greatest opportunity to react to the Civil War was Sherman's march to the sea. Gen. William Tecumseh Sherman was no stranger to Georgia. He had been stationed there in 1844. Twenty years later, after marching down from Chattanooga, he laid siege to Atlanta on July 20, 1864. Despite the fortification work done by thousands of impressed slaves, he captured the city of twenty thousand on September 2. This helped ensure Lincoln's reelection in November. Sherman left Atlanta with fifty-five thousand hardened troops on November 15. His destination was Savannah, and his purpose was to destroy the economy of Georgia. Despite local shortages, Georgia was a surplus food producer for the Confederacy, and the Union leaders rightly concluded that the blows that Sherman could deliver would be decisive in ending the war. Sherman's soldiers burned some plantations and confiscated food stocks; they left many lonely chimneys—"Sherman's sentinels"—standing above the smoking ruins of the manor houses. And they tore up railroad tracks, built bonfires with the ties, heated the middles of the rails red-hot, and then wrapped them around trees, making "Sherman's neckties." The army reached the outskirts of Savannah on December 14 and entered the city a week later. If they could, planters in Sherman's path took their slaves with them, at least their able-bodied ones; as Sherman approached Savannah, some slave owners tried to flee with their slaves and were shocked when the slaves refused to go with them.

The reaction of the slaves to Sherman was somewhat mixed. Most greeted the Yankees with joy. They were glad when the Union troops were winning. However, even though they enjoyed seeing their masters discomfited, they sometimes resented the destruction. Although Sherman did not enlist any, for fear of alienating North Georgia Unionists, some nineteen thousand slaves flocked to the wake of his army. This mass defection was facilitated by the fact that Georgia recently had canceled all military deferments to overseers and planters. Many planters expressed surprise and shock at this "ingratitude." Some furious whites hanged several blacks to prevent them from joining the Union forces.

The large mass of refugee blacks who fell in behind Sherman posed both problems and opportunities for the general. Southern observers were amazed at the Union army's speed as it rolled through Georgia, especially when the weather was sometimes rainy and the dirt roads were turned into a succession of mudholes. Blacks, anxious to speed the march, would be stationed by the mudholes and would bodily lift army wagons over the worst places. Sherman had deliberately not taken many supplies so he could travel more quickly. Slaves were a great help to the troops, who had to live off the country and get their food wherever they could. Who knew better than the slaves where the smokehouses were or where the food and other valuables were hidden? Most of the slaves were glad to point out these hiding places to the Union foraging parties.

In addition to finding and preparing food for the Yankee soldiers, slaves supplied invaluable intelligence, built and destroyed railroads and bridges, took care of horses and equipment, and helped in numerous other ways as servants, scouts, teamsters, foragers, and pioneers. Some of the Union privates acquired volunteer servants who carried their packs for them. General Grant, Sherman's commanding officer, encouraged the use of black labor. The Union paid some blacks for their labor, and a few got bounties for military service.

However, the reaction of the slaves to Sherman's army was not total approval. To a certain extent the Union army reflected the mixed feelings of the North towards blacks and slavery. While Sherman opposed secession, he had never objected to slavery, and some high Union officials thought he had an almost criminal dislike of blacks. Sherman was troubled by the host of refugees that fell in behind his columns; he feared them as a military liability and did not object when his officers tried to get them to go away. When temporary bridges were thrown across rivers and streams for the Union army, they would sometimes be destroyed by their builders after the army had crossed but before the refugees were able to attain safety on the other side. Thus, hundreds of blacks were left to perish at the hands of Confederate patrols. This happened at Ebenezer Creek, between the Savannah and Ogeechee rivers, on December 8, 1864. Moreover, there were charges that Northern troops raped black women. Sherman downplayed such charges. One account of Sherman's troops concluded: "They did make free with Negro women and set special value on shapely mulattoes."

Liberty County, thirty miles south of Savannah, was settled by Puritan Congregationalists and had a milder form of slavery than most of Georgia. Family breakups and cruelty were at a minimum, and many of the slaves were allowed to accumulate property. Sherman's forces sequestered the property of both blacks and whites, and because blacks in Liberty County had more to lose, they were hurt more than blacks elsewhere in the path of the Yankee juggernaut. Of forty-four claims from the county that were later filed against the federal government, twenty-seven, with an average value of over $1,000, were pressed by blacks. A congressional commission was established in 1871 to reimburse those who lost assets helping the Union.

Despite such incidents, blacks generally welcomed the Union army as a deliverer. When the troops entered Milledgeville, the whites had fled, but blacks lined the streets in welcome. Sherman's soldiers often told the slaves to help themselves from the smokehouses and manors. Soldiers often shot the dogs kept by the masters to track down runaway slaves and would wreak greater destruction on those plantations where the slaves told of cruel treatment. And Negro troops would sack and sometimes burn the mansions of the crueler masters. Such vindictiveness, while understandable, was the exception, not the rule. Many observers were surprised at the lack of bitterness on the part of most blacks in Georgia, both during and after the war.

On Christmas Day, shortly after Sherman entered Savannah, he met with a group of black leaders who had been called together by Secretary of War Edwin Stanton to discuss some of the charges and rumors of brutality against blacks that had been directed at the Union forces. At one time in the discussion, Sherman was asked to leave the room so that the black leaders would be encouraged to speak frankly. Their spokesman, the Rev. Garrison Frazier, an ex-slave who had purchased freedom for himself and his wife in 1859 for $1,000, told the federal officials that the blacks' greatest needs were to own land and to be free from white oppression.

The "March Through Georgia" was long remembered. White Southerners tended to remember it as an unnecessary blow by a vindictive enemy. Blacks were more likely to remember it in the context of deliverance and retribution. Fifty years later, many blacks still dated events from "the time Tecumsey was here." Some of Savannah's blacks were happier to see the Union army than the host of black refugees, which meant more competition for jobs. The war brought more suffering to blacks in Georgia than to whites. Most commodities came to be in short supply, and blacks first felt the pinch of privation. Those who survived learned to make it on their own, and this increased their sense of independence.

General Lee surrendered to Grant at Appomattox, Virginia, on April 9, 1865. If there had been any doubt in the minds of Georgians about the outcome of the war, it was dispelled when Jefferson Davis was captured a month later near Irwinville, Georgia, while attempting to escape to Florida. He was brought to Macon as a prisoner and lodged with his wife in a comfortable room in the Lanier Hotel. Then, by way of Atlanta, Augusta, and Savannah, he was sent to two years' imprisonment at Fortress Monroe. While traveling by rail from Macon to Atlanta, he was joined by fellow prisoner Alexander Stephens.

The Civil War was long, brutal, and bloody. However, the length and severity of the conflict were factors that ensured the large-scale entry of blacks into the struggle as partners of the North and required emancipation as a war aim. With the restoration of peace, all looked to the future with mixed feelings of hope, despair, and trepidation. Black Georgians expected a far brighter future, and whites were apprehensive about the changes they foresaw. Both groups would learn that their anticipations were ill founded. Georgia remained so dedicated to white supremacy that the North's feeble efforts to effect change had little influence on fundamental patterns of race relations.

The Failure of Presidential Reconstruction

After Appomattox, there was confusion, uncertainty, and sometimes despair. There was also hope, confidence, and a desire to rebuild. Blacks wanted to reunite their families, enjoy freedom by working for themselves, and live without the constraints and abuse that previously had dogged their lives. Whites wanted to restore their world and their prewar relationships with blacks. These conflicting goals meant Reconstruction in Georgia would be almost as violent as the war had been. Georgians could rebuild from war's destruction, but they could not forget the legacy of slavery. White supremacy was still the dominant ideology and would be the main impediment to progress.

When possible, planters told blacks they were still slaves and treated them accordingly. Henry McNeal Turner, then one of the few black Freedmen's Bureau agents in Georgia, was infuriated by blacks who said that they were not free because "Mas ain't tol me so yit." The Rev. James Lynch, who became a black political leader in Mississippi, traveled in Georgia four months after the war was over and found blacks who did not know they were free—or feared discussing the subject.

But things certainly had changed. Military defeat had increased white animosity toward blacks, and whites deeply resented the attitudes of freed people, many of whom no longer stepped off sidewalks or performed the acts of deference that had been required of slaves. It was an emotional shock and a severe blow to their egos when whites saw that their slaves did not love them, after all. Planters could not understand how "loyal" slaves could just leave, sometimes without even thanking the master for many years of employment. Stunned mistresses were suddenly left to do their own housework—and even carry water!

Besides denials that slavery had ended in 1865, there was also much violence against blacks who thought it had. Black lives were cheap during the summer of 1865. For twelve dollars any Negro could be killed in the swamps, according to one Georgia farmer. A planter told a Freedmen's Bureau official in June, "If we cannot whip the Negro, they and I cannot live in the same country."

Just after the war, armed bands of mounted ex-Confederate soldiers, called the Black Horse Cavalry, Jayhawkers, or Regulators, sprang up in the South to deal with "unruly" blacks. The terrorist groups were very active in rural Georgia. Members beat, mutilated, and murdered freedmen, sometimes drove them from plantations to avoid paying wages, and often practiced simple brigandage. These bands were later absorbed into the Ku Klux Klan.

Northern newspaper journalists traveling through Georgia after the Civil War reported many acts of antiblack violence. Some of the murders and lynchings had strong economic motives, for they were intended to discourage blacks from migrating to Mississippi and Arkansas for better-paying jobs. Despite intimidation, former slaves left the plantations. While some blacks hated their former masters, others felt they could do better elsewhere. Some wanted to test their freedom. Others wanted to seek out members of their families from whom they had become separated by sale or the confusion of war. Such reunions often required much travel. Thousands of couples who had been living as man and wife rushed to get married. One white woman complained: "I never heard of so much marrying among the negroes in my life. I am getting tired of their weddings, for all of them think we must give them a big supper...."

One problem blacks had in reuniting their families was finding their children. Antebellum law permitted whites to bind the children of free

Negroes to apprenticeships until they were twenty-one years old, and this practice continued after emancipation as a means to obtain cheap labor. The Freedmen's Bureau encouraged the practice to help solve the problem of orphans, of whom there were many. It found a hundred orphans in one Atlanta shantytown in 1866. A problem arose when a family found one of its children and the white to whom he or she was apprenticed did not want to give up the child, especially if he or she was old enough to work. Some apprentices had whip scars, and whites also would lie about an apprentice's age to keep him or her past the age of twenty-one.

Many blacks immediately began to make their own decisions even if they did not switch employers. Blacks on the David Barrow plantation moved and rebuilt and expanded the old slave cabins to get more "elbow room" and to be farther away from the big house. They also brought more variety into their diet with hams, tinned fish, candy, and cheese.

Since most Georgians gained their livelihood from the land, it was on the issue of land tenure that the real struggle for black freedom would be won or lost. Owning their own land would give Georgia's blacks control over their lives and a chance for economic progress. Without land, they would have lives of dependency, subservience, and poverty. When black leaders met with Sherman in Savannah, their leader, Garrison Frazier, said, "The way we can best take care of ourselves is to have land, and turn in and till it by our own labor. . . . We want to be placed on land until we are able to buy it and make it our own." This goal of economic self-sufficiency was embodied in the phrase "Forty Acres and a Mule." Blacks were encouraged to believe that each black family would be endowed with land and tools. After all, a Colonial precedent had provided indentured servants with these assets at the end of their three-to-five-year indentures. It seemed even more logical to reward *generations* of unpaid labor this way when slavery ended. The Confederates, to rally their fading forces, had claimed the Union's war aim was to confiscate and redistribute Southern land. Further fueling the idea of free land, Congress established the Bureau of Refugees, Freedmen, and Abandoned Lands in March 1865 to confiscate abandoned lands and distribute them to freed people. Pennsylvania congressman Thaddeus Stevens, the blacks' best friend in Congress, introduced a bill in 1867 to grant forty acres and fifty dollars to every former slave who was head of a household. The bill did not pass.

In January 1865, Sherman responded to the Savannah meeting by issuing Field Order Number Fifteen, which set aside the Sea Islands from Charleston to the St. Johns River and an area thirty miles inland for distribution in forty-acre plots to black families. Any three Negro families could get a license for a settlement. White ownership was to be excluded from the area. A February 1865 meeting of ex-slaves at Savannah's Second African Baptist Church cheered the order. When the Freedmen's Bureau was slow to implement Sherman's order, blacks took matters into their own hands. Under the leadership of Abalod Shigg, blacks seized two major plantations along the Savannah River on the assumption they would be a part of the general distribution. The Rev. Ulysses L. Houston led his congregants to Skidaway Island to take advantage of Sherman's order.

Rumors were rife throughout the South that the federal government would make a general land distribution to blacks on Christmas Day, 1865. One Georgia black was so certain he would receive land that he offered to sell part of it back to his former master. Another pervasive rumor predicted a general uprising of disappointed freedmen to take the land if it was not distributed. On the basis of the insurrection rumor, volunteer whites patrolled around Macon, in Lumpkin County, and in several other areas of the state. Christmas came and went, and nothing extraordinary happened.

Black hopes for land turned out to be futile. President Andrew Johnson had been busy in Washington undermining these aspirations by granting amnesty to thousands of former Confederate leaders. His amnesty of May 29, 1865, restored land covered by Sherman's order to its former owners and gave blacks until the end of the year to relinquish it and leave. The Freedmen's Bureau and the army enforced Johnson's policies by letting the former white owners return and initiating a policy of evicting any blacks who would not sign a labor contract with a white planter. The bureau collected rent from the dispossessed blacks and turned the money over to the white owners. Groups such as those led by Shigg were driven off by federal troops.

Quite understandably, intransigent Georgia whites were encouraged by the new president. Lincoln picked Andrew Johnson to be his vice president in 1864, and he was sworn in after Lincoln's death on April 14, 1865. Unlike Lincoln, Johnson held little respect for black rights. He opposed the black vote because he thought it would be used against the poor whites he claimed to champion. Johnson had at first talked tough to the planter class, accusing them of being war criminals who should be punished and impoverished. He had Governor Brown arrested and brought to Washington, but he soon shifted his views. His pardons left few white Georgians without full citizenship rights and the voting franchise. These few were not silenced or restricted except for a ban on holding political office. In March 1866, the Georgia legislature passed a resolution citing Johnson as "a wise and patriotic statesman."

Whites did not want life for blacks to change much. On October 25, 1865, a Constitutional Convention met at the Milledgeville Capitol and drew up a new constitution that nearly duplicated the 1861 Constitution except for provisions voiding the secession ordinance, abolishing slavery, and reluctantly repudiating the state debt. These changes were made only because they were required by the federal government. Georgia's leaders sounded the old theme that the national government had no right or business interfering with race relations.

When the new legislature, chosen in a whites-only election, convened in December 1865, race relations were the main order of business. Gov. Charles Jenkins said that readmission into the Union required accepting the Thirteenth Amendment abolishing slavery. He recommended doing this so "we may once again present to mankind the spectacle—the pleasant, happy spectacle, of brethren dwelling together in unity." The amendment was approved the next day with a proviso, recommended by the governor, that only the state could give blacks the right to vote and sit on juries. Even so, fourteen of forty senators voted against ratification on the grounds that the constitutional amendment was too liberal. The legislature then reluctantly abandoned the Constitutional Convention's hope for compensated emancipation and went on to bar blacks from voting or testifying in court except for or against each other. Blacks were, however, accorded the right to own property, marry, and legitimize their children. The legislature also passed the state's first antimiscegenation law, which provided a $1,000 fine and six months' imprisonment for anyone convicted of performing a wedding ceremony uniting white and black. "Black" was defined as anyone who was one-eighth or more African—a black great-grandparent made a person legally black in Georgia then. The law was sometimes enforced by mob action. A white man was tarred and feathered for trying to marry a black woman, and Tempy Ann Holton, a white woman married to a black, was stripped naked and whipped by a white gang in Ware County in 1866.

The 1865 legislature next turned to vitiating the Thirteenth Amendment it had just ratified by passing "Black Codes" to regulate black labor. They included laws permitting whipping as punishment for misdemeanors and, by means of laws on labor contracts, set up enforcement machinery to drive blacks back to agricultural work at starvation wages. The labor-contract legislation included a stipulation that the hours of labor would be from sunrise to sunset except on Sundays. *Servants* (the term slave was frowned on, although the term *Master* was still used) were to rise at dawn, do their chores, and be in the fields at sunrise. They were required to obey all lawful orders of the master or else be discharged and forfeit wages already earned.

This provision permitted an employer to fire black workers on any pretext to avoid paying them. Freedmen's Bureau records are filled with complaints of black workers who were turned off the plantation at the end of the growing season in 1865 and 1866 by landowners who did not want to pay them for their work. Often naked terror was used in this robbery. Henry McNeal Turner stated that the terms in written contracts were misrepresented to illiterate freed people. Although the Freedmen's Bureau recommended $144 a year plus food and shelter, actual contracts would often provide rations and $50 to $75 a year in pay with a deduction for every day not worked: $5 if it was for political activity and at least $1 if the reason was illness. Under such a contract, if no days except Sundays were taken off, a black worker would earn two cents an hour. Some of the ex-slaves recalled earning as little as $35 to $40 a year plus rations right after the war. Even this was too much for some planters, who only wanted to pay $25 a year. In effect, many masters were getting their labor more cheaply than they did during slavery.

By putting blacks at the mercy of whites, the codes restricted the mobility of blacks and weakened their ability to bargain for higher wages, thus hindering their entry into a free labor market. The Black Codes' worst provision authorized the arrest and conviction on vagrancy charges of any jobless black. This tended to force an unemployed black to accept the first job offered, no matter how low the pay. Otherwise, he could be fined and sentenced to serve time. Then a planter could pay the fine, and the black worker would be bound to work for him until the debt was paid. The overcharges for food and shelter, high interest rates, and fraudulent bookkeeping that often entered into such deals meant that the unfortunate black might find that he still owed as much at the end of the year as he did at the start. He had to stay on in virtual slavery. This was the foundation of the peonage system that developed and continued in Georgia for nearly a century.

While the vast majority of blacks stayed in the country, many saw no future in agriculture and left the plantations for the cities. Whites usually disliked the influx, large or small. Despite the military's attempts to force black newcomers out of Macon and back to the plantations, between April and December 1865, the city's black population more than doubled, to more than six thousand.

City life held many problems for blacks. Initially, many were reduced to scavenge garbage dumps and steal food, clothing, and fuel. Inadequate medical attention, malnutrition, and urban squalor contributed to high mortality rates. Blacks were often charged higher rent than whites for similar accommodations. Many, unable to pay any rent, built shantytowns called "Sherman Towns" on the outskirts of the cities. These became breeding grounds for crime and disease, especially cholera and smallpox. In December 1865, five hundred blacks died in Macon, some on the streets. A black carpenter with four helpers could not make coffins fast enough for the dead. Macon officials had its shantytown burned and sent sixty whites to round up the residents and ship them back to their former masters. Other cities took similar drastic actions. In January 1866, Governor Jenkins proposed to fund relief for black paupers with a special tax on working blacks, since he believed there was no white responsibility for this misery or its relief.

Many blacks died due to malnutrition and disease following the war. The Freedmen's Bureau, which helped provide relief to blacks in 1865, reported an astronomical 22 percent death rate for Georgia blacks in 1865, though more modern researchers have declared such estimates may be twelve times too high. Some whites predicted the extinction of blacks. Judge C. H. Sutton of Clarkesville wrote in July 1865 that he believed Negroes would die out as a race in fifty years.

The freed people "were in rags and wretchedness, but the unquenchable longing of the soul for liberty has been satisfied," Northern journalist Sidney Andrews reported. Despite their humble condition and low status, Georgia's blacks did not meekly accept the deplorable conditions they faced or the white politicians' proscriptions against them. In Georgia, blacks held political meetings in Augusta, Columbus, Macon, Savannah, and many smaller places in 1865, and they organized protest into constructive activity. On January 10, 1866, a hundred black delegates from eighteen counties convened in Augusta at the Springfield Baptist Church. The Rev. James Porter, a freeborn Negro who had been with the group that met with General Sherman in Savannah, was chairman of the freedmen's convention. The delegates, generally conciliatory toward whites, did not make radical demands, but they did go on record favoring equal pay and called for voting rights, jury duty, equality in public accommodations, and universal education. The convention formed the Georgia Equal Rights Association, headed by white Republican J. E. Bryant, which established branches in several cities to advocate black rights and to notify the North of the reign of terror against blacks.

Congress did respond to the outrages that were occurring across the South. In July, Congress overrode President Johnson's February 1866 veto of the extension of the Freedmen's Bureau and authorized it to extend military protection to freed people, a duty the bureau was unable to fulfill. From its inception, the bureau incurred the opposition and wrath of Georgia's leaders. To get rid of it, Georgia would have to behave more moderately. Governor Jenkins told the legislature on March 12, 1866:

> It is essential to our restoration that (blacks') capacity to contract, to sue and be sued, to hold property, to testify in the courts... should be made full and complete, that in this respect they should be

placed on the footing of the citizen. If we are to get rid of military rule—and the Freedmen's Bureau—if we are to have the laws administered by our own courts... these things must be done.

The bureau's first and most immediate job had been to provide for war refugees, many of whom were white. When the bureau moved into Savannah with Sherman, at first it gave relief only to whites, including some of the six thousand poor white refugee families that had been in Sherman's path. Blacks were told to return to the plantation and go to work, even though many of the plantations were abandoned. Even so, the bureau stood between blacks and even worse exploitation. By late 1865 the bureau had two hundred agents scattered throughout Georgia; it issued three pounds of bacon, a peck of cornmeal, and a pint of molasses per adult per week, equivalent to poor slave rations. The fact that *any* federal relief was available to blacks incensed planters. They wanted hunger to drive freed people into signing the one-sided labor contracts which at first offered only one-tenth of the bureau's recommended minimum wage.

After Congress overrode the president's veto (the first of his many efforts to undo the more liberal congressional policies), the bureau continued its work of relief, regulation of black labor, administration of justice for blacks, and the management of abandoned and confiscated land and property until July 1, 1869. It continued what turned out to be its main contribution, the support of black education, for three more years.

President Johnson, after failing to kill the bureau, emasculated it by replacing agents who were sympathetic to blacks. If the Freedmen's Bureau had been strongly supported by the federal government, it might have made reforms that could have prevented much of the suffering of the century following the Civil War. Instead of sounding a clear call for social reform, it spoke with an uncertain voice due to the attitudes of those in high places. In 1865, Johnson sent General Grant on a fact-finding tour of the South. Grant did not talk to blacks or visit places such as the Sea Islands, where independent freed people were successfully and profitably cultivating lands abandoned by planters during the war. Instead, Grant listened only to the views of the planters who were getting the land back. Through intimidation, Grant also prevented bureau head Gen. O. O. Howard from confiscating more land for freedmen.

The Freedmen's Bureau turned out to be a mixed blessing for black Georgians. Its benefits came due to some able local administrators and because of its support in Congress. It prevented immediate starvation for many, and its influence raised the average amount planters would pay black workers. To the chagrin of some whites, suspicious freed people often took the bureau's word over the planters' on the legality of the contracts they were offered. Gen. Rufus Saxton, who had worked with blacks in South Carolina, was put in charge of the bureau in Georgia by Lincoln, but President Johnson replaced him with Gen. Davis Tillson in July 1866. Far less sympathetic to the plight of blacks, Tillson opposed black land acquisition and picked agents who shared his prejudices. He also used the policy of withholding rations to drive blacks to work and refused to let them quit one job to take a better one. More than in any other state, the bureau in Georgia favored the appointment of local whites as agents in a vain attempt to build goodwill for Northern policies. When Tillson left the bureau to become a Georgia planter in January 1867, there were few blacks in the Georgia bureau, and almost 90 percent of the agents were native whites. Most of them flouted bureau regulations and accommodated their friends with cheap labor. His replacement said Tillson's native white agents "had shamefully abused their trust, inflicted cruel and unusual punishment on the blacks, and were unfit from their education and belief in slavery to promote the interest of free labor."

According to Cuthbert agent Charles Raushenberg, about one-half of the labor contracts were being honored in November 1867. He believed this represented an improvement and reported that blacks wanted to be partners in agricultural production, but that white employers were "tyrannical" and would not employ blacks who did not vote the way whites wanted. While many whites complained about the quality of freed black labor, others noticed that blacks did poor work if they were treated as slaves; when well-treated, they were diligent and honest.

A year later Raushenberg reported that many blacks were complaining of being defrauded of their earnings and assaulted for their politics. The bureau could sometimes attach the crops, but it did little about the assaults. Gen. George Meade, hero of Gettysburg but no abolitionist, had become head of the bureau in Georgia in 1868 and turned all cases over to the planter-dominated civil courts. Any black who complained was subject to violent reprisal; therefore, they often feared to seek justice.

In too many cases, hard work by blacks did not contribute to their material well-being any more than it had during slavery. One study made in 1865 and 1866 indicated that an average year's crop produced by the labor of one person was worth $385. Few blacks received as much as the bureau recommended: $144 a year, plus food and shelter (together worth maybe another $80 a year). The planter who paid the bureau's minimum had a gross profit of $161 per worker, or twice that if he treated his help poorly. Even Tillson noted that planters were only willing to pay a freedman half what they paid to hire a slave: "The trouble is, these (planters) wish to make everything there is to be made, and leave the freedmen nothing." The bureau reported some wages as low as two dollars a month for black men. The standard wage for a white foreman then was $800 a year and for a black foreman, $200. Techniques of defrauding freed people were developed to a high art that benefited the landlord and merchant class for the next century: dishonest crop weighing, excessive fines for absences, and overcharges for food, clothing, and supplies. Some planters overcharged fivefold for food despite promises to the bureau to sell it nearer cost.

White Georgians strenuously objected to black soldiers in the army of occupation. On February 15, 1866, the Georgia Senate passed a resolution addressed to General Grant and Secretary of War Stanton:

> ...(O)ur towns, cities, and villages are now being garrisoned by United States' colored troops, thus placing our former slaves, with arms in their hands, to arrest, fine, or imprison, and lord it over their former owners and as a necessary result of their recent emancipation and self-aggrandizement, to maltreat our citizens and insult their wives and daughters; and whereas such conduct will inevitably tend to irritate and inflame the public mind, and produce scenes of disorder, violence, and bloodshed; and whereas, if garrisons are deemed necessary, no such results would ensue by placing white troops, under competent officers....

General Grant was sympathetic to this plea, and he generally opposed the use of black troops in the South because it would make the blacks "uppity." Also he thought the black soldiers would be attacked by whites and consequently would need to be stationed in large units in order to defend themselves. Indeed, black troops and white police clashed in Savannah in 1865 and 1866. In January 1866, the 137th Regiment of the U.S. Colored Troops (USCT), based in Macon, was disbanded. This left only the 280-man 103d Infantry USCT. One altercation with whites led to one of the troopers bayoneting Robert Bass, son of a Confederate colonel. This led to a thirty-minute shootout in which four black troopers died. The army did not back up its black soldiers; in April, this unit was transferred from Macon. Contrary to widespread belief, there never were many Union soldiers in Georgia after the war. By October 1865, they numbered 3,108, and the great majority of them were white. In 1871, there were only 396 federal troops in Georgia outside permanent military installations. In 1868, when a hundred black Union veterans in Savannah tried to form a militia company, white Republicans joined with Democrats in the legislature to defeat enabling legislation. A black militia was out of the question. (However, black militia companies would be formed in Georgia's major cities within a few years.)

With black power nipped in the bud, whites could go about their business. In 1866, when it became apparent that President Johnson's policies of appeasement of the Southern ruling class would prevail, whites continued to use terror against the most minimal black gains and aspirations. That year, the head of the Freedmen's Bureau in Georgia complained of "the most fiendish and diabolical outrages" against former slaves.

The reign of terror that the Georgia Equal Rights Association complained of in 1866 was later formalized by the Ku Klux Klan, the most effective organized movement representing militant white supremacy. The Ku Klux Klan, essentially organized by leaders of the Confederacy, opposed black economic, political, and social advances, and it especially fought the Republican party because, for a while, the party appeared to be the means through which advances would come. The Klan was opposed to black voting, and black Republican leaders were especially targeted. The first Klan existed officially from 1867 to 1870, but it had its roots in nightriding antebellum slave patrols that often inflicted summary punishment on hapless slaves.

In March 1868, Klan Grand Wizard Nathan Bedford Forrest went to Atlanta, ostensibly on business. Klan organizational notices soon went up in Atlanta, Columbus, Macon, and Milledgeville, and newspapers in the state began to report Klan activities beginning on March 14. The timing is significant, for Georgians were preparing to vote in a highly charged atmosphere on a new Constitution, legislature, and governor. The Klan grew rapidly, and before the year was out, Forrest estimated that the total membership in the South was 550,000. Many were Confederate veterans, including Georgia's grand dragon, Gen. John B. Gordon, the unsuccessful Democratic gubernatorial candidate in 1868.

Reconstruction-era Klansmen in Georgia used dark robes that blended into the night. Dark horses were preferred for the same reason. Klan riders often used speaking trumpets, believing they made their voices more sepulchral and fitted with the image they tried to project that they were the ghosts of the Confederate dead returned from hell. The mythology of the Klan emphasized the gullibility and superstitions of blacks, and many Klansmen thought that blacks believed their ghost stories. However, it wasn't simpleminded trickery that enabled the Klan to accomplish its purpose—it was the whip, the gun, and the lyncher's noose.

While many blacks were intimidated by the Klansmen, some blacks did resist terrorism. Militant slaves or free Negroes were often militant during Reconstruction. There were dozens of leaders, such as Aaron A. Bradley, Tunis G. Campbell, Sr., and Henry McNeal Turner, who advised armed resistance. William H. Harrison of Hancock County threatened to set fire to the property of Klansmen who threatened him. The Rev. James M. Simms of Savannah—a former slave who had escaped during the Civil War and brother of famous fugitive slave Thomas Simms—used his newspaper *Freemen's Standard* to return threat for threat. The Republican Loyal League of Savannah issued handbills warning all "BADMEN" that violence against blacks would be met with counterviolence. In March 1869, there were rumors that blacks in Lexington resolved to burn the town in revenge for the death of Warren Haynes, whose "crime" was the refusal to work for whites, but nothing came of this. Sometimes black militancy brought results, but with a few notable exceptions, the issuance of counterthreats marked the limit of black resistance.

At first numbed by the shock of defeat, the planter aristocracy had been resigned to accepting a few changes. But as time passed and President Johnson showed his sympathies through a lenient amnesty policy, the return of confiscated land, and his commitment to white supremacy, former Rebels became bolder in their resistance to change. On November 9, 1866, by a lopsided vote of 36-0 in the Senate and 131-2 in the House, the Georgia legislature rejected the Fourteenth Amendment. This amendment made freedmen citizens, guaranteed them due process of law, penalized any state that denied them the franchise, denied federal office to those who broke their oaths to uphold the U. S. Constitution by rebelling, and forbade the payment of Confederate war debts or compensation to masters for the loss of their slaves.

Throughout the South, the rejection of the Fourteenth Amendment, along with the adoption of Black Codes and organized antiblack violence, gave credence to the belief in the North that though the Union had won the war, it was losing the peace. Northern Republicans also feared that if the freedmen did not vote, Democrats would soon control the federal government.

Southern terror and repression, Northern humanitarianism and black racial solidarity, partisan politics, and businessmen's greed combined when Congress assembled in December 1866 to energize that body to wrest control of the Reconstruction process from the president. Congress passed the Reconstruction Act of March 2, 1867 and then easily overrode Johnson's veto. The act divided the South into five military districts, nullified the states' constitutions, and called for new constitutional conventions whose delegates would be elected on the basis of universal manhood suffrage. When no such conventions were called by the states, Congress authorized the U. S. Army to call conventions and enroll voters. Georgia, along with Alabama and Florida, was in the Third Military District commanded by Gen. John Pope.

The second meeting of the Georgia Equal Rights Association was held in Macon on March 26, 1867. Its main purpose was to urge blacks to register and vote in the upcoming referendum on the Constitution. For their third meeting, the delegates returned to Augusta and passed resolutions pledging support for Congress, universal education, and the right of blacks to vote. Georgia blacks also became active in the state's Republican party, which developed from a merger of the Georgia Equal Rights Association and the Union Leagues, which spread to Georgia from the North, where they had originated to mobilize support for the Union war effort. In Georgia the leagues were strongest among the poor whites in the hill country. The party was an uneasy coalition of diverse groups, some of which never supported black landownership, voting, or office holding. Yet blacks bent over backward to conciliate white allies; although they dominated the Republican party convention in 1867, black delegates chose a mainly white executive committee of those allied with Rufus Bullock.

General Pope supervised the registration of all voters, black and white, for the election of delegates to a Constitutional Convention and worked to overcome the Democrats' efforts to keep blacks from voting. Georgia was divided into forty-four districts for the registration of voters and for the subsequent election of delegates to the Constitutional Convention. Each district was administered by a team of registrars consisting of two whites and one black. The voter lists contained the names of 102,411 eligible whites and 98,507 blacks. There were some 10,500 whites who were temporarily disfranchised by their failure to take the "Ironclad Oath" or "Test Oath." The oath was applied to all public officials and military personnel who had served against the Union and required the former Rebel to swear he had not broken an earlier oath to uphold the U.S. Constitution. The oath actually had little importance in Georgia. Many of these 10,500 whites ignored the prohibition against voting.

The process moved swiftly, and by late October 1867 voters were trooping to the polls. Prominent Democratic leaders, such as Benjamin H. Hill, urged whites to boycott the election of delegates to the Constitutional Convention and then vote against any Constitution the convention might produce. Governor Jenkins went to Washington to appeal to the Supreme Court for an injunction against Pope's administration of the congressional mandate, but the court dismissed his plea.

Some twenty-four thousand blacks stayed away from the polls due to intimidation. Blacks would have been in a minority in the 1867 vote if all eligible whites had voted, but most eligible white voters took Hill's advice and boycotted the election, thinking that if less than 50 percent of the eligible voters turned out, the election would be voided. Statewide, more than half of those eligible did vote, including 36,000 whites, and the convention was approved by an overwhelming margin of 102,283 to 4,127. When all the ballots were counted, 169 delegates were elected; 33 (nineteen percent) were black. Had blacks been elected in proportion to their share of the general population, there would have been twice as many. In 1868, blacks constituted 44 percent of the population of Georgia but made up 49 percent of the registered voters. Nowhere in the South, and especially not in Georgia, did blacks dominate the Reconstruction process or institutions.

The convention site was moved from Milledgeville to Atlanta because the innkeepers of the old capital would not accommodate black delegates. Governor Jenkins was removed from office because he refused to use state funds to pay for the Constitutional Convention. Jenkins went to Washington again to try for another Supreme Court injunction, taking the state executive seal and the treasury of $400,000. He was again unsuccessful. The seal and the money disappeared until he returned them in 1872, when Georgia was firmly back in Democratic control. Four days before the Constitutional Convention convened, opponents of political equality for blacks founded the Conservative party. They charged the state had fallen under the control of Negroes and carpetbaggers and called for a reassertion of white supremacy—even though 74 percent of the convention's delegates were native white Georgians.

On December 9, 1867, the black delegates joined 136 white delegates and began deliberations, which lasted until March 15, 1868. The white majority was composed of 9 Northerners and 127 native Georgians, most of whom were poor farmers from North Georgia who favored self-help economics, debt relief, and homestead exemptions and opposed seeing blacks advance or hold office.

The result of the meeting—highlighted by the expulsion of controversial black delegate Aaron A. Bradley—was the most democratic constitution Georgia ever had up to then. Its provisions included universal suffrage for all adult males, prohibition of slavery, support for the principle of free public education for all children, abolition of imprisonment for debt and whippings as a form of punishment, provisions for a poll tax, and moving the state capital from Milledgeville to Atlanta. The 1868 Constitution also provided for the right of women to own property, which could not be taken for a husband's debts; it democratized the lower house by reapportionment, and provided for homestead exemptions for all except tax and mechanics' liens. It ignored the issue of the Ironclad Oath and did not disfranchise any whites.

The Constitution contained a subterfuge to limit black political power masterminded by Joseph Brown, a postwar convert to the Republican party. The convention had debated whether or not the Constitution should state that all voters were eligible to hold office but decided that such a provision was unnecessary. Blacks were told they could assume that if they were eligible to vote they were eligible to hold office. Whites understood otherwise. When Brown campaigned in North Georgia for the ratification of the Constitution, he told poor whites that they had been born with the right to hold office, but blacks needed to have that right spelled out, and the Constitution did not do this. Democrats understood that later, when the federal presence was removed, though blacks might still vote, they could not hold office.

The Constitution was submitted to an April 1868 popular vote. Republicans supported it with the slogan: "Let the slaveholding aristocracy no longer rule you." It was adopted by a majority of eighteen thousand over the bitter opposition of conservative whites. Not surprisingly, blacks enthusiastically supported the new Constitution, sometimes to excess. The *Macon Telegraph* reported that Jefferson Long, later to be elected Georgia's only black Reconstruction congressman, told a rally of one thousand blacks supporting the referendum on the Constitution that any black who failed to register to vote should receive thirty-nine lashes and if he failed to vote Republican, he should receive two hundred. George Wallace, soon to be elected one of three black state senators, told this audience that any black who did not vote Republican should be hanged and denied a Christian burial. A banner at this rally repeated the dire threats and was illustrated by a picture of a black dangling from a noose as the penalty for failure to vote Republican.

While the Klan was not yet sufficiently well organized in Georgia to interfere significantly with the April 1868 constitutional referendum or state elections, it tried. Efforts were made to intimidate black politicians by sending them notices that they would be killed if they stayed in politics. Thomas Allen of Jasper County was warned not to stand for election. He ignored the warning and won. The threats were deadly serious. In April, a plot to blow up a Republican meeting in Valdosta was thwarted. In Columbus, the Klan was deeply implicated in the March 31 murder of white Republican leader George W. Ashburn.

Blacks voted for the Constitution, state legislators, U. S. congressmen, and a new governor. The new legislature contained Georgia's first black officeholders, who were elected by the black-white Republican coalition that ratified the Constitution and elected white Republican Rufus B. Bullock governor. Three black state senators were elected along with twenty-nine black state representatives.

The new legislature, the most democratic one in Georgia up to that time and for a century after, convened on July 4, 1868. One of the first acts was to ratify the Fourteenth Amendment, which was believed at the time to protect the civil rights of blacks. This action permitted Georgia's readmission into the Union. Many of the members of this legislature were ineligible, since they had not taken the Ironclad Oath, but the legislature investigated itself and found that it was a fine group of fellows. The election and seating of ineligible white legislators further undermined the later fraudulent complaint that whites were disfranchised wholesale

Table 3.1

Georgia's Black Representatives and the Counties They Represented—1868

Thomas M. Allen	Jasper	William H. Harrison	Hancock
Eli Barnes	Hancock	Ulysses L. Houston	Bryan
Thomas Beard	Richmond	Philip Joiner	Dougherty
Edwin Belcher	Wilkes	George Linder	Lowndes
Tunis G. Campbell, Jr.	McIntosh	Robert Lumpkin	Macon
Malcolm Claiborne	Burke	Romulus Moore	Columbia
George Clower	Monroe	Peter O'Neal	Baldwin
Abram Colby	Greene	James Porter	Chatham
John T. Costin	Talbot	Alfred A. Richardson	Clarke
Madison Davis	Clarke	James M. Simms	Chatham
Monday Floyd	Warren	Abram Smith	Muscogee
F. H. Fyall	Macon	Alexander Stone	Jefferson
Samuel Gardner	Warren	Henry McNeal Turner	Bibb
William A. Golden	Liberty	John Warren	Burke
		Samuel Williams	Harris

and rendered politically powerless during Reconstruction. From the beginning of Reconstruction and under the new Constitution, Georgia was controlled by conservative whites.

Fleeting Hope: Blacks in Reconstruction Politics

Radical Reconstruction was one of the nation's great reform movements. Had its reforms survived, the nation might have arrived a century earlier to where it is now in race relations. Unfortunately, it was destroyed by a reign of terror that its perpetrators and apologists labeled "Redemption." The more modern, democratic society that was trying to emerge from the ashes of the Civil War was almost drowned in blood.

The duly elected black convention delegates and legislators became among the most vilified figures in Georgia history. They were derided in their time as "unlettered" and "ignorant" and later accused of all manner of high and low crimes and personal shortcomings by conservatives in their attempts to justify Reconstruction's overthrow. Thus a flood of innuendo and plain lies formed the basis for traditional historical views of the era. Contrary to such views, the black lawmakers' level of education and their commitment to public service were on a par with white lawmakers. Indeed, considering the threats and the physical abuse many of them received, their commitment and courage were probably much greater. In each group were some illiterate men, some mediocre, and some who were outstandingly able. The literacy rate of Georgia's black legislators was about 75 percent.

While the entire period from 1867 to 1877 was often called Radical Reconstruction, precious little that would be considered radical today characterized the era. The term was used generally to describe the Republican party faction that favored political and economic rights for blacks. While the majority of Georgia's Republicans were black, most white Republicans in Georgia never favored these progressive measures. Attempts by blacks to form political alliances with whites generally proved futile, and the white Republican leadership's failure to support militant blacks was one reason why the party lost control of Georgia so quickly. By 1870, Georgia's Republicans had been routed at the polls.

Recent histories have regarded Georgia's black Reconstruction leaders as more conservative than their counterparts in other states. Historian Edmund Drago argued that the large proportion of ministers among Georgia's black legislators was one reason for "a certain conservatism." However, Georgia's blacks were never in a strong position to pursue radical demands. They never came close to forming a majority in the state legislature. No blacks held major offices in Georgia, nor did they hold many local offices. Still, militant blacks played key roles in Georgia during this period.

When President Johnson ordered the dispossession of blacks from their farm plots along the coast, planters going on their own to retake their plantations were met by armed resistance and driven back. According to one member of a white party, their group was "surrounded by fierce black faces and leveled guns, captured and not permitted to regain their boat. Their lives were spared only because a government official was with them." Gen. Davis Tillson of the Freedmen's Bureau sent troops to enforce the white claims. To make the evictions more palatable, the bureau often used its few black officers for this disagreeable job.

While blacks were rebuffed in their efforts to acquire land, these struggles gave some militant black politicians their start. Aaron A. Bradley and Tunis G. Campbell, Sr., were prominent leaders of the black struggle for landownership. Although they were ultimately unsuccessful in their attempts to hold on to confiscated lands, they were elected state senators in 1868.

Aaron A. Bradley was born a slave in South Carolina in 1815. When he was hired out as a shoemaker in Augusta at age nineteen, he escaped to the North. There he acquired an education and became a lawyer. Like many blacks, he returned to the South after the war to cast his lot with his people. Bradley arrived in Savannah in late 1865, just as the government was revoking land claims by blacks. Leading the resistance to this regressive measure, he advised seizure of abandoned plantations by force if necessary and called for President Johnson's impeachment. Bradley often was armed and led blacks against gangs of whites—even white police forces. He was soon arrested and tried by military authorities. In his defense, he argued that the Second Confiscation Act of July 17, 1862, had in effect freed the slaves and that their unpaid labor from that date to December 18, 1865 (the effective date of the Thirteenth Amendment) would more than pay for the lands they occupied. The government was unimpressed by his reasoning, and he was sentenced to serve one year at Fort Pulaski for using "insurrectionary language." However, he was soon paroled. Undeterred, Bradley continued to organize blacks for action to secure land titles. He also led black suffrage drives. Bradley quickly established himself as the number-one troublemaker in the minds of white Georgians.

The confrontational Bradley was indeed a troublemaker. According to historian John Blassingame, he was "probably arrested more times than any other politician in the nineteenth century." Bradley supported the eight-hour day for labor and the inclusion of blacks in the ranks of organized labor, woman's suffrage, an interracial militia, and an end to the convict-lease system and the chain gang. He favored constitutional provisions against Jim Crow seating in public transportation. When threatened, he made equally ferocious counterthreats and warned that if blacks did not achieve equality, there would be a new civil war. Bradley became a leader because he articulated blacks' feelings and acted out their suppressed desires. He was an apostle of black power who said whites were not completely trustworthy. His behavior attracted the lightning of white backlash. This hatred was expressed in physical attacks on his person and property and constant vilification in the white press from December 1865 until he was finally rendered ineffective in 1872, after Reconstruction's collapse in Georgia.

With a base of support from urban and rural black laborers, he was elected to the Constitutional Convention from his base as president of the Lincoln Council of the Chatham County Union League. At the convention, Bradley tried to neutralize planters by allying with the poor up-country whites and supporting their desires for stay laws and homestead exemptions in exchange for their support for his programs. During the course of events, Bradley was accused of being an unfit delegate, based on charges he had seduced a woman in New York in 1851 and been imprisoned for the offense. A committee investigated the charge, and its majority report concluded that even if the charge was true, seduction was not a crime in Georgia and that perhaps half the members of the convention had been guilty of the greater offense of treason. However, in defending himself, Bradley insulted white delegates. He stated he had evidence that the Gordon County delegate and the convention's president were also guilty of seduction and that one member had impregnated his wife's sister. Bradley introduced a resolution "to enquire into and report on all delegates who have been guilty of seduction, of either black or white women," and he named five delegates who could testify on the matter. In turn, Bradley was accused of outrageous behavior and on February 12, 1868, was expelled from the convention by a vote of 130-0. When Bradley was attacked in January, delegate Henry McNeal Turner spoke on his behalf, but after Bradley's breach of racial etiquette, he failed to garner a single black vote.

Although the other black delegates deserted him, he was elected in April 1868 to the state Senate by voters in Chatham County, then 60 percent black. Later that year, after he was expelled from the Senate on the old seduction charges, he tried unsuccessfully for the Republican nomination to Congress, then ran as an independent. While on his way to Savannah accompanied by a band of his supporters on Election Day, November 4, 1868, Bradley was met by a group of armed whites; one of them, Samuel Law, was killed in the confrontation. Bradley was accused of murder and had to go underground and escape to the North. The murder indictment was quashed in 1870, and Bradley was able to return to Savannah and resume his controversial career.

In 1870, he again campaigned for Congress as an independent. He attacked the traditional Republican party's paternalism. He assailed Governor Bullock for not giving blacks a fair share of public offices and accused him of murder by leasing convicts to the Western and Atlantic Railway. Bradley charged that children as young as ten were leased convicts guilty of such petty offenses as taking potatoes when they were hungry. Running a desperate campaign, Bradley threatened to support the Democrats, who quickly turned from vilifying him to cheering him when he began to attack the machine Republicans. This sparked a confrontation with another militant black leader, Tunis G. Campbell, Sr., whose supporters ran Bradley out of Campbell's stronghold in Darien during the campaign. This division of Republican ranks enabled a Democrat to win. Such splits—coupled with concentrated attacks by conservatives—doomed the party in Georgia.

Although he had been reseated along with other black legislators in 1870, Bradley was not reelected to the legislature in 1872. He campaigned vigorously for President Grant's reelection, and when the Klan attacked him, he printed and posted handbills in Savannah attacking the Klan. He further antagonized the hooded order by advising blacks to carry hatchets and to use them if their voting rights were hampered.

Unfortunately, hatchets were a poor defense against the Klan, whose well-organized armies of ex-Confederate soldiers had come to dominate Georgia. (By then, white supremacist terror had seized complete control of the election process.) The following year, perhaps in disgust with events in Georgia, Bradley promoted the emigration of blacks from around Savannah to Florida, where opportunities appeared brighter. In 1879, Bradley supported a black exodus to Kansas. He died on October 19, 1882, in St. Louis, with only twenty-five cents to his name.

Tunis G. Campbell, Sr., the militant black leader of Darien who opposed Bradley when he bolted from the Republican party, was born free in New Jersey on April 1, 1812, the son of a skilled blacksmith. Campbell, the seventh of ten children, was very bright and caught the attention of a white patron who sent him to a private Episcopal school in Babylon on Long Island, New York, when he was only five years old. Young Campbell remained in the school as the only black student until he was eighteen. While his teachers had hoped to train him as a missionary to Africa, he chose the cause of abolition and temperance and became a member of the A.M.E. Zion church.

The early 1830s, when Campbell became an abolitionist lecturer, was a period of increasing antiabolitionist violence. He sardonically reported that "except being mobbed many times while lecturing or preaching, and nearly killed once, there was nothing of note that occurred." As a part of his work, Campbell helped several fugitive slaves complete their escapes. Campbell also found time to organize churches and schools in New Jersey and New York.

By 1861, Campbell was a partner in a bakery that supplied bread to the Union army. He was one of many blacks rejected when they responded to Lincoln's call for volunteers. When William H. Seward, Lincoln's secretary of state, advised him that he was "premature" in his efforts to join the army, Campbell bided his time, and when he sensed that attitudes toward blacks had changed, he wrote to Lincoln in 1863 outlining a plan in which freed people could become self-sufficient and productive members of the new society he envisioned. After Campbell tried again, Lincoln saw merit in Campbell's ideas and ordered him to report to Gen. Rufus Saxton at the Hilton Head, South Carolina, experiment in Reconstruction. Campbell stayed there until after February 18, 1865, when Charleston fell to Sherman's forces.

The war's end was imminent, and the Union would be replacing Rebel governments throughout the Confederacy. As a move in this direction, Campbell was appointed military governor of five of Georgia's Sea Islands: Burnside, Ossabaw, Sapelo, Colonel's Island, and St. Catherines, where he had his headquarters. His assignment was to protect freed slaves in the area covered by Sherman's order distributing land and to assist them in the transition from slavery to freedom. Campbell established schools, brought in two teachers at his own expense, and by 1867 had 270 students enrolled. Knowing he would face considerable opposition from planters, he also organized a 275-man black militia. Campbell used his militia in another case to resist a Yankee who had purchased St. Catherines Island from its former Rebel owner. This resistance was futile, however, for the tide had turned against blacks who hoped to hold the land. The Freedmen's Bureau arrested twelve black leaders who had taken their followers to Sapelo Island to claim the "Forty-Acre" allotments, and General Tillson subsequently removed Campbell from his post. The schools were broken up, and blacks were driven off unless they signed one-sided labor contracts that "were purposely made to cheat the Freedmen out of their labor," Campbell charged.

Campbell kept his dream alive, however. With a $1,000 down payment on the $17,500 price, Campbell purchased the 1,250-acre Belleville plantation in McIntosh County as a home for the dispossessed blacks. Because of continued white harassment, many of the blacks did not want to go there until Campbell announced that he, too, would make it his residence. This operation lasted until 1870.

Under provisions of the March 1867 Reconstruction Act, Campbell was appointed one of three registrars of Georgia's Second Senatorial District, which encompassed Liberty, McIntosh, and Tattnall counties. On April 22, 1867, he addressed the largest meeting ever seen in those parts at the Newport Church in Darien. Mrs. Charles Colcock Jones, wife of one of Georgia's best-known planters, was afraid that Campbell's enthusiastic support of the Republicans and bitter castigation of the Democrats would so polarize attitudes that "a war of races" would result. Elected as a delegate to the Constitutional Convention, he introduced the provision forbidding imprisonment for debt, opposed all discrimination against blacks, and supported proscriptions against leading Rebels until freed people were secure in their liberty. As a member of the education committee, he strongly supported the proposals for universal free public education that were adopted.

The convention finished its business on March 11, 1868, and in the subsequent seven weeks, Campbell effectively organized the black vote. In the April election, Campbell was elected to the Georgia Senate along with Bradley and George Wallace, whose district included Baldwin, Washington, and Hancock counties. Tunis G. Campbell, Jr., was elected to the lower house to represent McIntosh County. The elder Campbell was Georgia's most effective black Reconstruction lawmaker, next to Henry McNeal Turner.

Not only was Turner the most important nineteenth-century black leader in Georgia, but for decades after Reconstruction he was one of the most prominent blacks in the nation. Turner was born in South Carolina on May 1, 1834. He was never a slave; his mother, an African princess who had been sold into slavery, was freed by the British. As Turner explained, "They did not believe in enslaving royalty." His black father had a German mother. As a child he worked in the cotton fields around Abbeville, South Carolina, and when his father died, he was apprenticed to a blacksmith. He learned to read and write while employed by a law firm to run errands and clean up the offices. He astounded people with his keen mind and memory.

Turner was licensed to preach by the Methodist Episcopal church in 1853 and preached in Georgia and other Southern states. In 1858, he joined the A.M.E. church and learned Latin, Greek, and Hebrew at Trinity College in Baltimore. From there he went to Washington in 1862 to accept the pastorate of the Israel Church. That August, Turner predicted that the Union could not win the war without black soldiers. This was a dangerous and unpopular doctrine at the time, and the trustees of the church were told that the church would be burned down if he continued in this vein. Turner was not deterred and later raised a regiment of black soldiers. Lincoln commissioned him as its chaplain, with the rank of major. Before the war was over, Turner saw action in thirteen battles and thirty skirmishes. President Johnson renewed his appointment in the regular army and assigned Turner to work with the Freedmen's Bureau in Macon, where he enjoyed seeing deferential whites seek rations.

Turner was no stranger to Macon. In 1855 he had preached there so powerfully that many whites came to hear him, but enough of them were sufficiently disturbed by his message that he was forced to leave. In 1866, he picked up in Macon where he had left off. He chided freed people on their inability to shed the habits of slavery and develop racial pride. "We want power, it only comes through organization, and organization comes through unity," he admonished. He characterized the developing share-cropping system as a means to cheat blacks and attacked President Johnson for failing to protect freed people, saying in the *Loyal Georgian* in March 1866, "I charge Mr. Johnson with the murder of thousands of our people; for though he does not kill them personally, yet he abets, or gives aid to those murders, so that it actually amounts to a direct encouragement." At one of his lectures during this period, whites threatened to shoot him through the window. Turner defied them and went on speaking. When he urged black men in Greensboro to keep white men away from their women, whites in the audience drew their guns. Since the blacks were also armed, nothing came of this incident.

He soon resigned his army commission to devote himself to building the A.M.E. church and politicizing Georgia's blacks. Turner was very influential. He made his home in Macon but traveled over fifteen thousand miles, making over a thousand speeches in 1867 and 1868 to advise blacks of their rights and to help them understand current issues. In recognition of his leadership role, Turner was elected to the Constitutional Convention, where he took a favorable stand toward whites and hoped that "soon the prejudice will melt away, and with God for our father, we will all be brothers." He favored the pardon of Jefferson Davis. He opposed the confiscation of white-owned land, "social equality," and miscegenation. He voted to remove all voting restrictions on Rebels and favored an educational requirement for the franchise that would apply equally to blacks and whites. He thought this last proscription should not be adopted until five years after the public school system had become fully operational and effective, however. He supported a one-dollar-a-year poll tax in the belief that it would be used fairly to fund education for all. Looking back from 1871, he said he made a great blunder, for he had not anticipated that the poll tax would be used to disfranchise blacks.

Turner was elected by a narrow margin in 1868 to the Georgia House of Representatives, where he would, in time, introduce bills supporting the eight-hour workday and eliminating Jim Crow seating on common carriers. He continued to push for Davis's pardon, the creation of a state police force, convict-lease reform, support for orphan's homes, women's suffrage, the use of the Milledgeville Capitol as a college, regulation of fees for magistrates and constables, and legislation designed to prevent tax foreclosures and bank failures. Like many black lawmakers, Turner was ahead of his time. Though none of these proposals passed then, Georgia adopted most of his ideas eventually, though it took until the 1980s to finish regulating the pay of court officials. Turner tried to do the impossible: to win conservative confidence, yet still be a fearless, outspoken defender of black rights. He became "the most articulate—and most disliked" Negro member of the General Assembly. In the end he was almost universally disliked by white Georgians. He was not endeared to Democrats when the National Executive Committee of the Republican party printed 4 million copies of his pamphlet explaining Reconstruction laws and the differences between the two parties.

The General Assembly convened on July 4, 1868, and almost as soon as Georgia was readmitted into the Union on July 21, the legislature turned on its black members. The first resolution to oust the three black senators was introduced on July 25. Though it was voted down strictly along party lines by a vote of 21-14, its supporters argued that the Constitution, by failing to specifically state that blacks were eligible to hold office, barred them from office. Then seduction charges were brought against Bradley again. Campbell reported that the evidence against Bradley "was not sufficient to convict a fly." White reporters covering the proceeding then suggested that Campbell should be framed on a chicken-stealing charge. Eventually he was railroaded to prison on more serious, though equally baseless, charges.

On August 16, Bradley was forced to resign, and on September 3, twenty-five black representatives were ousted by a vote of 83-23. The blacks were not allowed to vote on the issue. The Senate soon moved to expel the two remaining black senators. Campbell stood alone in the Senate for eight days arguing against this. "At different times when I was speaking I could see Democratic members with their hands on the butts of their pistols, with their teeth shut hard together, and using threatening gestures at me," he said. "On the ninth day I gave way, seeing no hope for us in the Georgia legislature." Campbell and Wallace were ousted on September 16 and protested "in behalf of ourselves, our constituents, and also in behalf of nearly five hundred thousand loyal citizens of this State... against the illegal, unconstitutional, unjust and oppressive action of this body." In all, forty-six Republican legislators voted with the Democrats or abstained. By permitting the expulsions, Republicans gave up their majority in the House. Although many of them had been threatened with death if they voted against the expulsion, many probably disliked the concept of black lawmakers as much as the Democrats did. In another blow, the legislature specifically barred blacks from jury duty.

Meanwhile, as University of Georgia historian Charles E. Wynes stated, "Some of the white members, as former Confederates, sat unchallenged and in plain defiance of both the Reconstruction Acts and the Fourteenth Amendment." Four very light-skinned blacks who could pass for white escaped expulsion: Madison Davis of Clarke County, Edwin Belcher of Wilkes County, F. H. Fyall of Macon County and Thomas Beard of Richmond County. At the time, Davis denied he was a Negro, but both blacks and whites in Clarke County considered him black, and blacks there reelected him in 1870. Belcher, a former Union army captain and Freedmen's Bureau agent, though generally considered black, was less than the legal one-eighth Negro.

When Henry McNeal Turner was expelled along with his black colleagues, he realized there were irreconcilable differences between the wishes of the white majority and black desires for fundamental civil rights. In a ringing speech to the legislature that marked his increasing militancy, he said that while some blacks tried to keep their seats by obsequious behavior, "I shall neither fawn nor cringe before any party, nor stoop to beg them for my rights.... I am here to demand my rights and hurl thunderbolts at the men who would dare to cross the threshold of my manhood." If being black was an offense, he said, it was "an offense committed by the God of Heaven Himself." He accused the "Anglo-Saxon race" of deception, cowardice, and treachery. He reminded lawmakers that the legislature in which they sat was the creation of blacks. After all, only 12 percent of the eligible whites but 80 percent of the eligible blacks had voted to adopt the new Constitution. Turner argued that he and his black colleagues were being thrown out of the house they built. He continued:

> We have pioneered civilization here; we have built up your country; we have worked in your fields, and garnered your harvests, for two hundred and fifty years! And what do we ask of you in return? Do we ask you for compensation for the sweat our fathers bore for you— for the tears you have caused, and the hearts you have broken, and the lives you have curtailed, and the blood you have spilled? Do we ask retaliation? We ask it not. We are willing to let the dead past bury its dead; but we ask you now for our *rights*.

Turner concluded by stating that with money, land, and education on their side, it was "extraordinary" that whites would "make war upon the poor defenseless black man." As an indication of the white legislators' attitude, Turner's stirring speech was not included in the House journal.

Black legislators did not take their expulsion meekly. The Campbells went to Washington and conferred with Charles Sumner and other senators who shared his idea for a Fifteenth Amendment to prohibit voting discrimination. One of the main purposes of the trip to the Capitol was to forestall the seating of the Georgia congressional delegation when Congress convened in December and to encourage a deeper probe of conditions in Georgia that would lead to reform. When the Campbells returned to Georgia, the father was appointed to the state Republican committee. He went back to Washington to lobby Congress for measures to improve conditions in Georgia. Rebel sympathizers warned him that if he made this trip he would be killed on his return.

Recognizing the need for black Republican allies for his administration, Governor Bullock pleaded with Congress to send troops to reinstate the expelled black legislators. Meanwhile, Turner called a convention to meet in Macon in October to protest the expulsion and to initiate counterattacks by mobilizing public opinion, and approximately 130 delegates representing eighty-two counties came, while others remained at home in fear of their lives. Many delegates, too poor to come by train, walked 50-60 miles to reach Macon; one walked 105 miles. They met "to inaugurate war against the foul and base action of the so-called legislature and to oppose the principles of all men who oppose equal rights." With rhetoric such as this, the *Atlanta Constitution* said the convention was "venomous" and "incendiary," and the *Macon Telegraph* called the speeches "false and inflammatory."

A Committee on Murders and Outrages was appointed and a Civil and

Political Rights Association of Georgia was formed. The convention sent a synopsis of recent violence against blacks in Georgia in a memorial to Congress. A more militant Turner was elected president of the convention. Along with James M. Simms and other black leaders, Turner was delegated to carry the memorial to Washington. Mostly Turner's handiwork, this memorial was entered into the *Congressional Globe*. It denied that black legislators were incompetent and noted that all power was then in the hands of the old slave-owning class that regarded blacks as "having no rights a white man is bound to respect." Georgia's leaders hoped to restore the conditions of slavery and deny blacks education by burning schools and slandering, ostracizing, and abusing their teachers and political friends, it said. This memorial was supported by Governor Bullock and thirty-four white Republican legislators who petitioned Congress on behalf of the ousted blacks. A similar memorial to Congress, written by the Rev. Robert Cromley and State Rep. Philip Joiner, came from a black convention that met in Albany in December. Around Albany, blacks reported there had been forty-six murders or attempts to murder blacks by whites in a three-month period in 1868.

Soon after this, a case moved up in the courts from Savannah that resulted in a Georgia Supreme Court decision that held that the black legislators' expulsion was illegal. In a January 1869 contest for the position of clerk of superior court in Chatham County, Richard W. White, a black, defeated William J. Clements, a white. However, a jury decided that because White was one-eighth Negro, he was ineligible to hold office. White appealed, and on June 15, 1869, he was upheld by the state's highest court on the grounds that Negroes were citizens and citizens could hold office. The legislature ignored this decision, and there were rumors that Federal military rule might be reimposed. As if willing this outcome, Georgia's Democrats vowed that only force could reseat the black legislators.

The expulsion of blacks from the General Assembly paved the way for a reign of terror that enabled the Democrats to win the November 1868 elections and marked the beginning of the end of Georgia's Reconstruction. Democrats pulled out all stops to carry the fall elections to choose legislators, congressmen, and the president. They wooed blacks with promises and barbecues and warned them that they would be jobless if they voted Republican. While the loyalty of blacks to the Republican party was natural, it enraged Democrats, who were accustomed to blacks doing as they were told. Throughout the fall, the violence escalated, and outrages became more widespread against blacks who vied for political power and their white friends in the Republican party.

Such events influenced life outside the political arena. As the ruling class saw its position strengthened by the expulsion of the black legislators and the increasing effectiveness of the Ku Klux Klan on the political front, planters grew bolder and even less fair in their business dealings with black workers. In August 1868, the Freedmen's Bureau agent in Columbus reported a hundred complaints in Butler by blacks who were unable to collect their wages or crop shares. Many were fired for asking for pay or for attending Republican meetings. The agent concluded that they were often swindled. The Cuthbert agent said in October that he spent most of his time trying to collect wages for blacks driven from plantations and noted the "increased boldness of the planter in his fraudulent and violent proceedings." The Americus agent concluded: "There seems to be a determination to control, or let starve, the colored people. . . . Any one assisting to ameliorate the conditions of the Freedmen being considered guilty of treason to the 'lost cause.'" Many blacks were driven off the land just before the 1868 harvest so the landlord could take the entire crop. Freedmen's Bureau records of Georgia would probably contain many more such accounts except that most agents were native whites who were unsympathetic to the bureau's aims.

The worst single incident of violence came at Camilla on September 19, 1868, when a group of more than three hundred blacks, including a few who were armed, were marching into town behind a band to attend a political rally in support of Ulysses Grant in the upcoming November election. Mitchell County Sheriff Munford Poore was determined that no Republican meeting would be held in Camilla and organized a heavily armed force that went out to intercept the blacks. The first shot was fired by James Jones, a drunken white. The blacks returned fire, wounding six. In the ensuing battle, between seven and nine blacks were killed, and thirty were wounded. The *Nation* called it "a shocking massacre" and said that following the skirmish, blacks were hunted down with dogs and unknown numbers were shot.

All over Georgia, an atmosphere of intimidation hovered over blacks who planned to vote. Murder was commonplace, and in several counties the violence went on nightly for two weeks before the election. Perry Jeffers, a prospering black sharecropper with five sons in Warren County, refused to join the Democrats and said he would vote for Grant. Shortly before the election, six Klan ghouls fired on his cabin; the shots were returned, killing one Klansman and wounding three others. The raiders then retreated and came back with reinforcements four nights later. Jeffers had taken to the woods with his four able-bodied sons, thinking that the fifth one, who was bedridden, and Mrs. Jeffers would be safe in the cabin because they were helpless. The Klan shot the son eleven times, burned all their possessions, and hanged his wife, who remarkably survived. The five remaining male Jefferses fled, but the Klan caught up with them on a train and killed four; one son escaped. In another incident, expelled legislator Thomas Allen of Jasper County was home on the night of October 15, 1868, when a group of men came asking for matches so they could make a fire to bring down an opossum they had treed. Allen's brother-in-law, Emanuel Tripp, opened the door and was instantly gunned down by mistake.

During the elections on November 3, large bands of armed whites gathered at the polls to intimidate all black and white Republicans. If threats and the show of force were not sufficient to scare off would-be Republican voters, they would then be challenged to produce evidence that they had paid their poll taxes. In Fort Valley, 169 blacks were denied the right to vote because their poll taxes had not been paid despite a proclamation by the governor that the payment was not necessary. Where blacks were induced by bribery or threats to vote Democratic, the poll-tax-receipt requirement was ignored. Many blacks who voted Republican were dismissed from their jobs the day after the election. In some places blacks were told that the Democratic ballot was the Republican one, and in Savannah the Democrats put pictures of Republican candidate Grant on Democratic ballots. A riot erupted there when police and other whites attacked black voters as they lined up to vote, killing several blacks and wounding twenty others. Black leaders then advised their followers to return to their homes and give up the effort to vote. Perhaps only 10 percent of Savannah's blacks were able to cast ballots. In the November election, blacks won only seventeen local elected offices, nine being uninfluential coroners.

The fall elections "convinced conservative whites of the political usefulness of intimidation and fraud," according to historian John Michael Matthews. Terror and intimidation all over the state kept most eligible black voters from the polls. In a partial picture of the violence against black Republicans and their white allies, the Freedmen's Bureau reported thirty-one killings, forty-three shootings, five stabbings, fifty-five beatings and eight whippings from August through October. In Oglethorpe, Warren, and Columbia counties, where the regular Republican ticket had received 3,490 votes in April, it got only 305 in November. In twenty-two other counties where the Klan was active, the Republican vote in November was only 3 percent of what it had been in the spring; in eleven counties, *Grant failed to get a single vote.*

On December 19, 1868, Congress opened hearings on the condition of affairs in Georgia. Henry McNeal Turner, James M. Simms, and Gen. J. R. Lewis of the Freedmen's Bureau all testified on the hundreds of outrages that occurred in connection with the 1868 election. Freedmen's Bureau official Dr. S. P. Powell, a native white Georgian, testified that in the seven months before the expulsion of blacks from the legislature, the murder and attempted murder of freedmen occurred at the rate of seventeen per month; in the three months after the expulsion, they averaged forty-seven a month, almost three times as many. The congressional committee took depositions from eighty Republican party officials, Freedmen's Bureau agents, and blacks who all agreed that election-day violence had carried the day for the Democrats.

Despite having a Republican governor and president, the horrors of 1868 repeated themselves the next year. Governor Bullock told Gen. Alfred Terry, military commander of the Georgia district, that a widespread reign of terror existed in the summer of 1869. Bullock said he was powerless to organize a militia or replace local authorities. Only two sheriffs, Ruffin of Richmond County and John Norris of Warren County, dared oppose the Klan, and Ruffin had been assassinated in the November 1968 election. Norris was partially crippled in a December ambush, but stayed on as sheriff. Bullock could not ask the legislature to appeal to the federal authorities. It was not recognized in Washington because it expelled its black members; besides, it was under Democratic control and therefore was part of the problem. Bullock offered rewards for the apprehension and conviction of terrorists but got no takers.

Warren County was a hotbed of Klan activity in 1869. In March, Klansmen took Dr. George W. Darden out of the Warrenton jail and lynched him. Darden was being held on a charge of murdering Charles Wallace, the editor of the county Democratic paper, the *Clipper*, and an active local Klansman. Two months later, when white Republican state Senator Joseph Adkins returned from Washington, where he had gone to report on conditions in Georgia and to request the reestablishment of military control over the state, he was lynched by the Klan on May 19. General Terry sent troops to Warren County then, and the Klan's nightriding was temporarily curtailed, but efforts to try and convict the terrorists failed.

Violence and intimidation against politically active black Republicans continued. Turner testified that in a dozen instances he had to hide, sometimes in the woods, once in a hollow log, to escape assassination by bands of night prowlers and stated, "I have seen men who had their backs lacerated... who had bullets in them; I have seen others who had their arms shot off... I have heard of any quantity of horrible deeds." Legislators were especially targeted. Abram Colby, the black representative of Greene County, after refusing a $5,000 bribe to resign, barely escaped one lynching attempt in 1869 and was later whipped and left for dead by the Klan. He survived but was crippled. Eli Barnes of Hancock County, who had asked for military protection for a black school, was whipped by a band of thirty Klansmen. Following a threat from the Klan, Romulus Moore of Columbia County packed up his family and left his district.

Alfred Richardson of Clarke County was badly beaten by the Klan and left for dead. Others had false charges of rape and murder brought against them. Overall, twenty-one of the sixty-nine blacks elected to the Constitutional Convention or the legislature between 1868 and 1872 were threatened, intimidated, attacked, or killed for their political activity.

In 1869, Turner was named temporary chairman of the National Colored Convention, which met in Washington. Frederick Douglass became the permanent chairman. President Grant appointed Turner postmaster of Macon that same year; however, he was only able to hold this position for a few weeks due to opposition from Georgia Democrats. An unsubstantiated case involving counterfeit money was brought against Turner and was dismissed for lack of evidence. However, the frame-up served to make Turner even more controversial in the press and contributed to the withdrawal of the postmastership. Turner proclaimed that the white newspapers that constantly vilified him and other black leaders "have no more regard for the truth than the devil does for Holy Water."

Political pressure by Georgia's black Republicans and their white allies helped bring about a change in late 1869. The Klan-directed violence in the presidential election of 1868 and political pressure from Northern Republicans had forced President Grant to take action. In his December 1869 message to Congress, Grant said that the expulsion of black legislators and failure to ratify the Fifteenth Amendment required federal action to reconvene the original 1868 Georgia legislature.

Congress quickly complied with Grant's request, and what happened next was unique in the annals of Reconstruction. Congress assumed Georgia whites accepted none of the implications of their military defeat and were trying to turn the clock back to the days of slavery. Deciding that a reign of terror, not constitutional government, existed in Georgia, Congress placed the state under congressionally directed military rule for a second time on December 22, 1869. This happened in no other state; then again, no other state had shown Georgia's extreme intransigence about granting the most basic civil rights to blacks. General Terry reinstated the ousted blacks to their legislative seats and expelled the whites who had replaced them. Congress also began new hearings on the state of affairs in Georgia.

When the Georgia General Assembly met on January 10, 1870, there were several unreconstructed Rebel legislators who had not met the requirements of the federal loyalty oath. Senator Campbell, despite threats to kill him if he did, protested their presence. His action forced federal authorities to check the eligibility of the unpardoned Rebels. Six ineligible senators were purged. According to historian Russell Duncan,

Campbell "was essentially responsible for all the deposings" and "made the 1870 session more radical." Campbell said, "It now became the common talk that the old Negro Senator of the Second (District) was destroying Georgia, and that the Negroes would be unruly unless he was put out of the way."

The more properly constituted legislature then ratified the Fifteenth Amendment, and Georgia was restored to the Union for a second time on July 15, 1870. When Georgia's black state legislators were reseated, they were more active than they had been previously. When Turner returned to the House, he no longer went out of his way to appease the white power structure. Instead, in an effort to broaden the franchise and undermine the oligarchy, he introduced a bill for women's suffrage—fifty years ahead of his time. He also opposed the milking of the state treasury by the railroad companies. In a generous gesture aimed at letting bygones be bygones, one of the reinstated blacks introduced a measure to continue to pay the whites who had to relinquish their seats. While this sop for politicians passed, much of the progressive legislation blacks introduced died in committee.

Ironically, after Reconstruction, Turner and other blacks were accused of running the state heavily into debt in a "carnival of extravagance" by those same supporters of the railroad interests who were most responsible for the debts incurred during Reconstruction. Critics of Reconstruction often blamed blacks for corruption during this period. However, most of the wrongdoing was associated with railroad bonds that blacks had nothing to do with. This myth of black corruption colored the thinking of generations of white Georgians and emerged again in the 1960s to bolster opposition to the Voting Rights Act.

The Klan's 1868 tactics were put into effect on a bigger scale in 1870 to effectively dismantle the Republican party, complete the murder of Reconstruction in Georgia, and dash the political hopes and aspirations of blacks. Georgia's state elections, set for December 22-24, 1870, ushered in the most extreme period of Klan violence in Georgia history. Historian Drago noted:

> It is true that divisions within the Republican party hastened its demise as a majority party, but external pressures exerted against it by the conservatives reduced it to almost complete impotence. To crush their opponents, the conservatives employed demagoguery, social ostracism, intimidation, fraud, violence, and the Ku Klux Klan.

Klansmen rode extensively in the week before the election, intimidating those they could and injuring or killing those they could not.

Violence occurred throughout the state, although most of the 1870 Klan activity came in three major areas: Northwest, East-Central, and Southwest Georgia. The greatest Klan activity was probably centered around Wilkes County. These tactics, known as the "Georgia Plan," were later copied in other states, especially Mississippi, where Gen. John B. Gordon went in 1875 to help the Klan terrorize Republicans and return that state to Democratic control.

The poll tax was used again to ensure a Democratic victory in 1870, and in some areas Republican poll watchers and election managers were jailed. After military rule was reimposed, the reconstituted legislature passed the Akerman Bill, which was signed into law on October 3, 1870. This provided that voters did not need to pay poll taxes to cast ballots in the December elections. Democrats in towns like Sparta refused to acknowledge the new state law and swore out arrest warrants for black voters who would not pay their poll taxes and election managers who encouraged "illegal" voting.

All over Georgia white supremacists armed themselves and gathered at the polls on election day to prevent Republicans from voting. In some counties blacks had Republican ballots taken away from them and were forced to vote Democratic. Sometimes they were paid. Many blacks concluded that if they were going to have to vote against their principles, they might as well take whatever money was offered.

Despite widespread fraud by Democrats, Henry McNeal Turner was reelected by twenty-eight votes—and then was threatened with death if he did not immediately leave town. That night, 150 armed blacks protected his home and told city fathers that if one black was killed they would torch the town. It was peaceful in Macon that night. Later, Turner and other black leaders were convicted on charges of inciting to riot, but the convictions were overturned on appeal. Turner was denied his seat in the legislature, however.

In 1870, Georgia Democrats won 86 percent of the Senate and 81 percent of the House. Despite the overwhelming election of white Democrats, five blacks were elected to the Senate, two more than in 1868, and eighteen to House, as compared to twenty-nine in 1868. One, Abram Turner of Putnam County, was soon murdered, and the Klan initiated a race riot at the special election that was called to replace him, ensuring a Democratic victory. Even before the Democrat-controlled legislature assembled a year later, in November 1871, eleven of the remaining black members came under fire. Their elections were disputed by Democrats, and the Klan sent them notes saying they would die if they did not resign. Governor Bullock did resign and fled the state to avoid prosecution on charges of corruption. In "An Address to the People of Georgia," he said, "My successful effort in restoring the Negro members to the Legislature against the opposition of General Toombs and his Ku Klux is the cause of the slanders." (Bullock was later tried and acquitted of the charges.)

The 1870 election, while generally a disaster for the divided Republicans, did see some gains at the local level for blacks. At that time, Atlanta and Macon elected city officials by wards instead of at large, or citywide. This meant that majority black wards could elect black officials to local offices. In Macon, three blacks were elected in 1870: City Councilman Edward Woodliff, Bibb County Treasurer Peter Perkins, and Coroner Lewis Smith. In 1870, Atlanta had two black wards, which elected William Finch, a tailor, and George Graham, a carpenter, to the city council. Finch promoted universal education and prevented Mitchell Street from being extended through the campus of Atlanta University long enough for the school to get a court injunction to prevent the campus from being divided and its buildings destroyed. The return to at-large voting plus Democratic fraud and violence impelled Finch to drop out of politics.

When Georgia was restored to the Union for the second time in July 1870, its delegation was admitted to Congress. The group included Jefferson Long, Georgia's only black congressman until the election of Andrew Young a century later. Long was born a slave near Knoxville, Georgia, in 1836. His master brought him to Macon and taught him to be a tailor, and later he opened his own shop. He was self-educated and after the war became active in politics. In September 1868, he was elected to the Macon Republican Convention and was nominated to represent the Fourth Congressional District. He did not win the election, but none of the state's congressmen were seated that year. Long was renominated in 1870, and despite the violence and fraud by Democrats and the Klan, he won by nine hundred votes over W. J. Lawton, the Democratic candidate. The victory came at great cost. On election day, seven of Long's followers were killed, and Long had to take refuge in a belfry to avoid the same fate. Friends then spirited him away to a hiding place in an uncompleted section of a sewer until the immediate danger passed.

Long served only the short second session of the Forty-first Congress, from January 16, 1871, to adjournment on March 3. On February 1 he gave his one and only speech, the first ever delivered in the House of Representatives by a black congressman. It was a part of the debate on lifting the Ironclad Oath. Long opposed lifting this restriction from "the very men who were leaders of the Ku Klux Klan." He charged: "Why, Mr. Speaker, in my state since emancipation there have been over five hundred loyal men shot down by the disloyal men there, and not one of those who took part in committing these outrages has ever been brought to justice." Long was arguing for a lost cause because the Supreme Court had already ruled that such oaths were unconstitutional. He was not reelected because the violence he spoke against had put Georgia firmly under the control of the Klan-led Democrats by the next election, but he remained active in the Republican party until his death in Macon in 1900.

After Turner was denied the seat in the legislature to which he had been reelected in 1870, he called a Colored Convention to meet in 1871 in Columbia, South Carolina, to protest the growing terror against blacks. There he stated there had been more than fifteen hundred murders of blacks by whites in Georgia since the Civil War. Turner later served a short time as customs inspector in Savannah and then left for Philadelphia in 1876 to manage the A.M.E. Publications Department. While in Savannah, he also served as pastor of St. Phillips A.M.E. Church and supported the efforts of James M. Simms to get the legislature to approve the establishment of a bank for blacks. Turner became increasingly militant. He led armed blacks in marches for voting rights and promised to kill the whites who threatened him. Turner grew to national prominence as a bishop of the A.M.E. church, chancellor of Morris Brown College in Atlanta, and a promoter of a return to Africa for disillusioned American blacks. He died in Canada in 1915. He was buried in Atlanta, and in belated tribute, his portrait hangs in Georgia's Capitol.

The 1870 election signaled the end of Reconstruction in Georgia for all practical purposes. The short-lived experiment was in shambles, destroyed by massive violence against blacks and those whites who stood with them. Similar events occurred in all of the ex-Confederate states. However, Georgia has the unenviable distinction of being the state where it happened first and most completely. That Georgia was the least reconstructed state helps explain why it led the lynching parade between 1883 and 1932, surpassing even Mississippi's wretched record. Authorities generally agree that the Klan was more violent in Georgia than in any other state during the 1867-71 period. Allen Trelease stated, "Terror probably accomplished more in Georgia than in any other state to subvert the Republican party and Reconstruction."

Countless blacks were murdered in Georgia in the first decade after the Civil War, but the murderers faced no consequences. Violence kept blacks from the courts, the courts themselves were steeped in racism, the judges were white supremacists, the juries were often filled with Klansmen, and the witnesses were intimidated. In the extremely unlikely event they were brought to trial, it was virtually impossible to convict whites of crimes against blacks.

Georgia had only one black congressman in Washington for a few weeks and no blacks in high executive or judicial positions. Blacks rarely held local offices, either, and black state legislators were so powerless, they could be expelled. There never was a chance of black domination anywhere in the South, Georgia least of all.

Despite this gloomy picture, blacks achieved gains during Reconstruction in Georgia in education, economics, and politics and also in the social, religious, and psychological areas. Although most of these gains were slight, the promise of more had been made, and the groundwork was being laid for further advances. The Fourteenth and Fifteenth amendments, although largely ignored, stayed on the books, to be enforced at a later day. The public education of all Georgians was promised in the 1868 Constitution. Blacks were able to keep a slightly larger share of the wealth they produced than they had as slaves, even though most of them remained dependent on white sufferance for their daily bread. Reconstruction created the opportunity for blacks to establish their own social and religious institutions.

On the other hand, the Ku Klux Klan had laid down a blueprint for terrorism that would continue randomly and effectively for generations. The Klan's activities accelerated urbanization by driving blacks from rural areas, where they could be productively employed, to the cities, where they were often unemployed and sometimes destitute. As a result of violence in Chattooga County, some two hundred blacks fled to nearby Rome. East of Atlanta, hundreds were whipped in a massive intimidation effort just before the 1870 election, and many fled to Atlanta, losing their meager possessions and their share in the crops.

Nathan Bedford Forrest, the Klan's founder and leader, officially disbanded the organization in Georgia in March 1869. However, most Klansmen continued their terrorism and assumed the claim that the Klan was breaking up was simply a ploy to defuse Northern calls for intervention. Gen. Dudley M. DuBose, grand titan in charge of the Fifth Congressional District, said he dissolved the Klan in his area early in 1871 with a statement that its job was done. Georgia's Democratic press generally agreed. The *Rome Courier* editorialized, "The time had passed for the Ku Klux." Henry Grady's *Commercial* declared, "The good cause has triumphed; the enemies of Georgia are beat to the dust." However, Grady—who was implicated in some Klan activities—advised against completely disbanding the Klan, since it might be needed in the future.

Although the Klan vitiated black input into Georgia politics, it did not end it. Blacks continued to influence the state's political life to the extent they were able. Few black leaders ever gave up totally on this path to reform. Tunis Campbell, Sr., returned to his home and to his old position as justice of the peace in Darien, where his past rulings upholding freed people's rights had made many white enemies. These rulings were resurrected by Judge Henry Tompkins, a vindictive white Democrat, to whittle away at Campbell's effectiveness. If one charge against Campbell did not stick, Tompkins tried another, until he finally sent the black leader to prison. Campbell then fell victim to the convict-lease system and was leased out to J. T. Smith to work on his Washington County plantation near Oconee. Black efforts to free him, in the form of a resolution sent to Gov. James M. Smith by the Southern Georgia Conference of the A.M.E. church asking for his pardon and a petition signed by seventeen of the most prominent blacks in the state, proved futile. A similar resolution by the state Senate on January 25, 1875, to pardon Campbell by reason of his age and feeble health was also ignored. He was still too much of a threat to Georgia's white rulers. Campbell never lost the loyalties of the blacks in his district. His endorsement ensured black Republican Hercules Wilson's election to the legislature in 1882. Campbell spent his last years in Boston doing missionary work for the A.M.E. church. He died on December 4, 1891, and was buried in Boston's Woodlawn Cemetery.

Counterattack of the "Redeemers"

Conservative Democrats, whom the Republicans called Bourbons, consolidated their position after Governor Bullock fled the state. Democratic control was both complete and vengeful. James Milton Smith was inaugurated as governor on January 12, 1872, and spoke of the "long and cheerless night of misrule." So began the myth that the Redeemers and leaders of the New South would propagate so assiduously.

Triumphant Democrats, united mainly by white supremacist ideology, continued to carry elections by fraud, intimidation, and terror, but their methods would not be quite as bloody as in 1870. Fraud replaced violence as a principal characteristic of Georgia politics. Fear of federal interference all but vanished with the success of a five-day filibuster in Congress against disciplining Georgia for the conduct of the 1870 election.

Blacks continued to win elections, though in ever-decreasing numbers. On the political front, they fought for laws opposing lynching and segregation and for an end to the convict-lease system. They also worked for improved landlord-tenant relationships, better treatment of prisoners, the right of blacks to serve on juries, and other improvements. White Republicans, interested in political power, not change, usually failed to support measures that would primarily benefit blacks. Consequently, Georgia saw little legislation aimed at improving race relations.

Whites who had joined with blacks at the beginning of Reconstruction began to return to the Democratic fold in 1870 in part due to social ostracism by other whites if they did not do so. In one of countless examples, Savannah physician James J. Waring was expelled from the Georgia Medical Society because he was a Republican. This killed his practice. Confederate vindictiveness lingered on. When Lt. Gen. James Longstreet, often called Robert E. Lee's "most distinguished lieutenant," died in 1903, the Savannah chapter of the United Daughters of the Confederacy refused to send a wreath because he had turned Republican—even though he never favored racial equality and tried to make the Republican party "lily white."

Looking back on the period from 1870 to 1915, one might wonder why so many blacks trailed along in the wake of the Republican party so faithfully, since white Republicans' duplicity and coldhearted indifference became so apparent. It was not so obvious to the average black voter back then. There was always a chance that the next set of promises might be kept or that blacks might gain influence within the party. Besides, the Democratic party was much worse. Nevertheless, some blacks did support the Democrats in Georgia. Democrats were in power and might actually do something worthwhile. Conversely, black support might limit the damage Democrats would do. Some blacks supported Democrats because it was the only way they would be allowed to vote. There were also bribes for voting Democratic—and the fear of reprisals if they did not.

Northern support of Southern blacks withered away during the 1870s. Congress did not heed Jefferson Long's one speech in the House of Representatives against restoring full civil rights to Confederate leaders and instead passed an amnesty act in May 1872 that reduced the number of Confederates excluded from office to about three hundred. Among those granted amnesty in Georgia were Alexander Stephens, former vice president of the Confederacy.

The three Enforcement Acts of 1870 and 1871 were aimed at safeguarding black political rights under the Fourteenth and Fifteenth amendments. However, these laws were poorly enforced, especially in Georgia. When the Supreme Court ruled that the acts applied to federal elections only, Georgia reacted by scheduling state and local elections about one month before the national elections so that Democrats could discourage blacks from voting, yet avoid federal scrutiny.

Only four blacks were elected to the General Assembly in the October 4, 1872, election, which was marred by the usual fraud and violence. On election day several blacks were killed in a riot at polls in Macon. One white and three blacks died in Atlanta. Election violence also broke out in

Savannah. In Athens, the polls closed while a hundred blacks were still lined up to vote. The Democrats won Houston County by throwing out eight hundred Republican votes and Liberty County by refusing to count votes from the two largest black precincts. The black assembly candidate protested, and as the fraud was too much even for the state legislature, he was later awarded the contested seat. However, Tunis G. Campbell, Sr., was defrauded of his rightful Senate seat, representing Liberty, McIntosh, and Tattnall counties, and *his* protest failed. The new legislature began what was to be a long series of measures whittling away the black vote. It raised the residency requirement from six months to a year in the state and from one month to six months in the county—a restriction aimed at the black voter, who was less likely to own land and stay in one place.

Election violence continued in the 1874 state contests. Several blacks were killed when they were driven away from the polls in Macon. Three unarmed blacks were killed for voting Republican in Screven County, and several more were beaten, yet blacks who voted Democratic were unmolested. Violence in Columbus, Quitman, and Hogansville was serious enough to convince the U. S. marshal in Savannah to recommend U. S. troops for the federal elections in November—a request that was not heeded. Simple fraud continued, and blacks were helpless to prevent or even protest it. Morgan County had 1,300 black and 600 white voters, yet Democrats won by a margin of 230. In a case of "enforced apathy," blacks refused to vote in Troup and Wilkinson counties, centers of Klan activity. They were able to vote on the coast and won House seats in Glynn and Liberty counties and elsewhere helped to elect four white Republicans to the state's lower house and one to the Senate. Campbell had concentrated his efforts in his home county of McIntosh and won his contest for a post in the House of Representatives, but the General Assembly later threw out the results and seated his white Democratic opponent instead.

In 1874, Sen. Charles Sumner (R-Mass.) introduced a bill to prevent racial discrimination in public accommodations, such as inns, theaters, and public transportation. It also forbade the exclusion of blacks from jury duty. When the bill was being considered by Congress, Georgia whites "reacted hysterically," according to historian Horace Wingo. The white press said the issue was a choice between white supremacy or Negro domination. The 1874 legislature, over black protests, passed a resolution stating that Georgia's blacks did not support the Sumner Act. In tribute to Sumner, who died in 1874, Congress enacted his bill the next year. Its passage was the national Republican party's last gesture to support black rights until the Eisenhower years.

At first the Sumner Act appeared to threaten the developing pattern of segregation in Georgia. Whites furiously denounced it and exaggerated its purported bad effects. The *Atlanta Constitution* said that Georgians should resist enforcement of the act but should not provoke the return of federal troops. The Sumner Act stimulated a discussion of black genocide. This extreme manifestation of white supremacist ideology received support in the highest circles. Ex-governor Joseph E. Brown warned blacks in 1874 that the act's enforcement and efforts for "social equality" on their part would lead to the "extermination of the Negro race." This position helped ensure his final acceptance as a loyal Democrat. Meanwhile, the *Atlanta Daily News* warned that any struggle between the races would result in a victory by whites "even if they had to destroy the Negro." Democratic concern over the issue evaporated when it became apparent that the act—like other legislation aimed at benefiting blacks—would not be enforced.

Although the Republican party of Georgia did not support the Sumner Act, Democrats accused it of advocating "social equality"—a code term for miscegenation. This charge further weakened Republicans. In 1874, the accusation helped unseat Republican congressman Richard H. Whiteley of Bainbridge, who did support the Sumner Act. The bill's passage influenced the 1876 election in Georgia and hurt the gubernatorial bid of Jonathan Norcross, who was badly beaten by Democrat Alfred H. Colquitt. Colquitt received up to twenty thousand black votes, and even more blacks failed to vote due to fear, indifference, or resignation.

As the nation celebrated its centennial in 1876, Custer was making his last stand at Little Big Horn, and so were Republicans in the South. That year, the U. S. Supreme Court gutted the Enforcement Act of 1870. The Republican party in Georgia, still 90 percent black, sent several blacks including John H. Deveaux of Savannah, Henry McNeal Turner, George Wallace, Jefferson Long, and Madison Davis to the party's national convention in Cincinnati. Delegates were pledged to battle for the "holy principles of justice and liberty." Rutherford B. Hayes was the Republican presidential nominee.

The *Savannah Tribune*, founded by Deveaux in 1875, had predicted that if Republicans could avoid splitting into factions, they could poll 100,000 votes in Georgia in the 1876 presidential election, which would be enough to win. However, black turnout was low. Only six hundred of six thousand potential black voters in Chatham County were registered. In addition to other hindrances, registration fell during the busy planting season and often required a walk of five to fifteen miles. Republicans in Macon were harassed by police. Throughout Georgia such factors suppressed the Republican vote.

Democrats stole Georgia's October 1876 state election. In some counties, blacks were forced to vote Democratic or not at all. The entire Republican vote was thrown out in predominantly black Camden County, and as a result blacks lost a representative and a senator. A similar loss resulted from Democratic activities in Athens. Remarkably, blacks were elected that year to the state legislature from Dougherty, Lee, Glynn, and Liberty counties. Georgia militia units were mobilized against militant black voters. In Americus, the all-white Sumter Light Guards turned out when armed blacks were reported at the polls on November 7. In Augusta, black Republicans were fired from their jobs for voting for Hayes.

Hayes won the famous disputed election of 1876. Both the Republicans and Democrats claimed the electoral vote of three Southern states following widespread irregularities, and Hayes needed all of the disputed votes to gain the White House. To obtain the acquiescence of the Democrats, Republicans agreed to several concessions, including the withdrawal of the few remaining federal troops on police duty in the South. The terms of the "Compromise of 1877" meant that Georgia's blacks no longer could hope for federal intervention or assistance. They were to be delivered into the hands of their tormentors.

The election further weakened blacks politically in Georgia. The division of the Republican party into lily-white and black-and-tan factions widened. White Republicans increasingly believed racism caused Democratic election dishonesty and violence. Blaming the victim for the crime, white Republicans came to the ignoble conclusion that if Georgia blacks were eased out of the party, the white faction could survive in peace and perhaps even win some elections. The lily-whites echoed Democrats' arguments that the North should trust the South to treat blacks fairly.

For some time Georgia's 1868 Constitution had been under attack. Democrats were dissatisfied with the comparatively liberal document, which had been influenced by blacks. In 1874, Robert Toombs called it "the handiwork of Negroes, thieves, and Yankees." In 1876, he offered to help write a new constitution to ensure that "the Negro shall never be heard from." Democrats wanted to secure control of Georgia by eliminating the black vote, yet they had to avoid obvious violations of the Fourteenth and Fifteenth amendments that would invite national attention. After the 1876 election, Democrats had so solidified their position that they could call for a new Constitutional Convention.

While Republicans nominated some blacks as convention delegates, none were elected, so the convention was an all-white affair. The new Constitution, ratified in 1877, included a poll tax and a residency requirement to make it more difficult for blacks to vote. Power was vested in the rural counties by weakening the executive and judicial branches while strengthening the legislature and adopting the county unit system. These changes guaranteed that backward rural sections would dominate the state for decades to come. The new Constitution provided for low public salaries and low taxes, which meant that social services would be paltry and that the government's weakness would prevent it from assisting in developing the state's economy.

The new Constitution fostered an elite Bourbon-controlled state run by "a Democratic machine that was both ruthless and corrupt... whose record was so offensive that by the end of the 1880s the white masses—some even willing to accept Negro support—rose in political rebellion against it," according to historian Kenneth Stamp. Opposition to oligarchic control, known as the Independent Movement, began to form in the early 1870s. The Independents were led by William H. Felton of Bartow County and his wife, Rebecca Latimer Felton. In their region of Northwest Georgia, there were relatively few blacks, and the poor farmers did not worry about white disunity leading to black gains. The Independents tried to get blacks to join them at the polls to trim the power of the corrupt Bourbon regime. In 1874 elections, Felton won his congressional race in the "Bloody Seventh" District, horrifying area planters. With black support, fourteen Independents won seats in the General Assembly.

In 1876, blacks and whites met together in Pierce County to nominate Independents for the legislature. In 1878, Felton won a third term, and the Independents elected Emory Speer to Congress. To the relief of the Bourbons, this represented the high-water mark of the Independent Movement, though Bourbon control of Georgia was slightly weakened by an investigation of the government in 1879, which included exposure of convict-lease scandals.

During the same period, smoldering black resentment against the white leadership of the Republican party resulted in a revolt by the blacks, who elected a new state committee of twenty-four blacks and eight whites. Black leader William A. Pledger led the revolt and replaced John E. Bryant as party chairman. Pledger, one of the most important black political leaders in Georgia during the nineteenth century, was born to a slave mother and a white father near Jonesboro in 1852. He acquired an education, attended Atlanta University, and taught school in Athens in the early 1870s. When the Democrats closed his school in 1872, he stumped the state for the Republicans. By 1880, he was editor of the *Athens Blade*. He was a delegate to every Republican national convention from 1876 to 1900 and remained on the state Republican committee until his death in 1904.

In 1880, Republicans did not nominate a candidate for governor. White Republicans hoped to join Independents to defeat incumbent Alfred H.

Colquitt, but the new state committee prevented the Republican endorsement of Thomas M. Norwood, the Independent candidate. Blacks preferred Colquitt, a paternalistic lay preacher, to Norwood, who had a strong racist reputation. The black vote was still important; Democrats and Independents both vied for it. Colquitt assumed a moderate role before the election. He went to black Sunday School meetings and spoke at black churches, proclaiming equality before God and promising equal justice to blacks. Blacks voted three to one for Colquitt in the fall election; though this may have been self-defeating for them, it did not affect the outcome, for Colquitt would have won without the black vote, which had been considerably reduced from its 1868 peak. In 1880, blacks from five counties were elected to the General Assembly, the most since 1870: Anthony Wilson of Camden, Ishmael Lonnon of Dougherty, Frank Johnson of Lee, John McIntosh of Liberty, and Thomas Goodrich of McIntosh.

Republican James A. Garfield was elected president in 1880 and was assassinated not long after his inauguration. His vice president, Chester A. Arthur, was less sympathetic to black aspirations and started the national Republican "Southern Strategy" of building an all-white Republican party in the South. Whites regained control of the Georgia Republican party in 1882 when Pledger was ousted from his position as state chairman and replaced by a white, Alfred E. Buck. However, the new chairman opposed the lily-whites, led by Jonathan Norcross and General Longstreet, because he needed black support. While blacks continued to be a factor in Georgia politics, they could not control the Republican party even though they represented 90 percent of its constituency. President Arthur did not deal with the "black-and-tan" faction led by Buck and Pledger, but with the lily-white faction. By then, the Republican party was of little importance in Georgia except as a job-dispensing patronage machine; therefore, competition centered on appointments to federal jobs, not election to office. The president tried to neutralize and placate Pledger by appointing him surveyor of customs in Atlanta.

While Felton had been defrauded of a fourth term in 1880, the 1881 success of the Readjuster Movement of the Virginia Independents energized the Feltons to try harder in Georgia. In 1882, in an open bid for black support, Rebecca Felton denounced the Democrats for their "crusade against the colored race," and she exposed convict-lease barbarities. (However, later in her career, she would advocate lynching blacks.) Independents also charged Democrats with impeding industrialization of the state. The Independents indirectly encouraged black political participation by calling for a free ballot and an honest count. In 1881, under the name of the Georgia Syndicate, the Independents hoped to organize a coalition of Republicans, disaffected Democrats, and blacks for the 1882 election. The staunchest black Republicans, such as Madison Davis, condemned this move. Black Democrat Thomas Harden of Savannah called the Independents "soreheads," and Bourbon U. S. Sen. Benjamin H. Hill warned that if Independents got the black vote, they would lead the state back to Republican control. Appeals to white racism plus the Democrats' control of the black vote assured the election of their gubernatorial candidate, former Confederate vice president Alexander H. Stephens, in 1882.

Although the Georgia State Convention of Colored Men endorsed the Independents, fifty-two thousand blacks voted for Democrats, who spent money on the black vote and hired some black speakers. Only thirteen thousand blacks voted Republican. The 1882 election was the death knell for the Independent Movement, which expired largely due to its failure to achieve Republican-Independent fusion. Due to this disunity and the usual voting frauds, Pledger lost his bid for the position of secretary of state, and Felton and Speer lost their races. Soon after that, Speer was appointed a federal district attorney. In 1883, several whites were found guilty of whipping blacks who voted for Speer in Banks County; Speer was the prosecutor in that case. He went on to have a remarkable career as a federal judge.

Several national issues of great concern to Georgia's blacks were decided in the Supreme Court, usually in an unfavorable way. In addition to the Georgia courts' undermining the rights of blacks, the U. S. Supreme Court delivered a major blow in 1883 when it invalidated the Sumner Civil Rights Act of 1875. This decision signaled that the judicial branch of the federal government had joined the executive and legislative branches in turning its back on blacks. Bishop Henry McNeal Turner commented bitterly: "The Supreme Court is an organized mob against the Negro and every subordinate court in the land has caught its spirit."

By 1883, Georgia Democrats were finding ready acceptance to their myth that race relations were good and that white leaders treated blacks fairly. The *Constitution* said, "There are simply and absolutely no political outrages committed in Georgia." The newspaper later claimed that the decline in the black vote was due to lack of Republican organization, not intimidation. In a national-magazine article in 1887, Colquitt denied that the black vote was suppressed or that Georgia's elections were anything but honest.

The 1884 elections showed that Georgia blacks had some political clout. William Jefferson White, a black educator and the editor of the *Georgia Baptist*, ran a write-in campaign for governor and won in

Camden and McIntosh counties. Three blacks—Anthony Wilson, J. B. Frazier, and Hercules Wilson—were elected to the legislature.

Over the decades, Georgia Democrats charged that blacks were the main corrupting political influence in the state. They believed that black voting required that Democrats use violence and other illegal means to steal elections, and they severely condemned blacks for taking the bribes they offered. The 1886 "bitter and corrupt" governor's race between two Democrats, Augustus O. Bacon and Gen. John B. Gordon, in which "the Negro was completely uninvolved," demonstrated that it was primarily the white leaders' lust for power that was the corrupting influence, according to historian Wingo.

Most blacks continued to vote for Democrats in Georgia state elections through the 1880s. However, black disaffection with the major parties continued to grow. By 1886, Bishop Turner favored a new party to promote reform and prohibition. So far as blacks were concerned, he saw no difference between the Democratic and Republican parties: "One holds and the other throttles, one robs and the other looks on with a smile, one steals and the other conceals. . . ."

The size of the black vote continued to decline as a new state law disfranchised all who owed any taxes levied since 1877, the year the new Constitution was adopted. By 1888, the number of black legislators was cut to two: Anthony Wilson of Camden County and S. A. McIvor of Liberty County. William A. Pledger was defeated in his effort to represent Clarke County in the legislature. Only half the eligible black voters there were willing to risk the reprisals that could follow voting. Democratic leaders attacked Pledger for his role in the Afro-American League, a national black organization then being proposed to defend blacks against white attacks. Though not officially born until 1890, the league was being talked up in the black press starting in 1887, and Pledger played a prominent role in its organization. The conservative Democratic newspaper of Sparta warned: "The people of Georgia are very patient and long suffering, but there is a limit to their forbearance." The *Augusta Evening News* was more explicit: "Some of these days Pledger's smartness will lead him to take a step that will bring him to the end of his career very suddenly." This was an invitation to lynching: "Very suddenly" referred to the jerk of a rope.

Georgia Baptist publisher White devoted much effort to organizing blacks at the state level. He organized the Union Brotherhood to promote Negro rights and presided over its 1888 convention in Macon. That same year, he chaired the Georgia Consultation Convention, a Macon meeting of Georgia's black leaders, including Pledger, Augusta attorney Judson W. Lyons, and E. K. Love, then pastor of the First African Baptist Church of Savannah. Love was born in 1856 and was one of the best-known Baptist preachers and religious writers of his time. The Rev. Charles T. Walker was another politically active preacher. Of unmixed African ancestry, this fiery evangelist was a perennial member of the Republican State Committee and a delegate to several national conventions. Lyons was born in Burke County in 1858. He received a law degree from Howard University and was admitted to the Georgia bar in 1884. He was a delegate to the Republican National Convention four times and a member of the Republican National Committee for eight years. For a short period he served as the Augusta postmaster, until white prejudice forced him out.

The Macon meeting condemned lynching and passed resolutions against jury exclusion and railroad Jim Crow. Condemning the convict-lease system, one resolution stated, "The present chain gang and penitentiary system of Georgia is simply barbarous, and yet no past legislature has removed this foul blot." Delegates also protested dishonest elections, withdrawal of state funds from Atlanta University, the exclusion of blacks from the legislature, their small role in the state militia, and the "totally inadequate state funding of public education."

Georgia's blacks were encouraged by the election of Republican Benjamin Harrison as president in 1888. In appreciation of what appeared to be a greater regard for them by the president, black parents in Atlanta named seventeen newborn black babies after him. In return, President Harrison sent letters of thanks to the parents. He also appointed more blacks to federal offices than Grover Cleveland, his Democratic predecessor. Black Georgians who received appointments included C. C. Wimbush as Georgia surveyor; John H. Deveaux as collector of customs at Brunswick; and David A. Dudley as the postmaster in Americus.

White Georgians resented the presence of blacks in such high-profile jobs. In a typical white reaction of this time, the Americus mayor opposed the appointment by trumpeting that Dudley was "incompetent, ignorant, and vicious." When Madison Davis was appointed postmaster in Athens, the white citizens draped the post office with black cloth as a sign of mourning. When Atlanta's white Republican postmaster, Gen. John R. Lewis, hired a black assistant, both he and the clerk were burned in effigy by outraged Democrats, who considered the appointment an outrage to white womanhood. Black journalist and civil rights leader T. Thomas Fortune accused the *Atlanta Constitution* of trying to start a race war over the appointment.

Pledger, undeterred by the white threats or countervailing black advice, was prominent at the January 1890 organizational meeting of the Afro-American League in Chicago. Lynching was viewed as the primary obstacle to black progress and antilynching activities were at the top of the league's agenda. Voting rights and ending discrimination in public accommodations and transportation were also important. During the meeting, Pledger said that blacks were killed in Georgia for being "impolite, indolent, or impertinent," and whites were never punished for these murders. The black who protests respectfully, Pledger said, is called "'insolent' or 'an incendiary,' and forthwith he is marked for destruction." He said Georgia's Democratic leaders only tolerated blacks who "appear in a cringing, menial attitude" and who have "no views and no aspirations above the hoe and plow, and walking behind a mule in the furrow from one year's end to the other."

4

Post-Reconstruction Horrors

Tenant Farming: The New Slavery

The Southern ruling class's desire for a docile, cheap labor force continued after emancipation, and for many decades after the Civil War, most blacks in Georgia continued to eke out their livelihood in agriculture, living in poverty or on its fringes. Lacking realistic alternatives, most blacks picked up the hoe, harnessed the mule, and went about the simple agricultural tasks that had occupied them during slavery. They went to work on white-owned land under financial arrangements that robbed most of them of the hope that hard work and planning for the future would improve their circumstances.

As W. E. B. Du Bois said in 1912, the black farmer was "consciously and carefully trained to irresponsibility." This led to living for the present, which served as "confirmation" of the stereotypical black as lazy and improvident. Such behavior only reflected the blacks' forced status— a condition sufficiently familiar to their antebellum status to deserve the title "the New Slavery." The control over labor by Southern capital interests meant the new relationship that developed between blacks and the elite was much like the old—the new "slaves" were merely rented, not owned.

While Reconstruction brought some advances and laid the groundwork for others later, its failure to provide the freed people with an economic base meant they would be at the mercy of those who held economic power. Conditions could have been different, for there were more equitable proposals advanced when the Civil War ended. The most logical was "forty acres," with or without a mule. This could have been accomplished through traditional conservative capitalist means or by a more radical program of land confiscation and redistribution, such as Sherman attempted in Coastal Georgia. The more conservative method was possible because there was cheap unclaimed land in the state, and many other tracts were selling for prices considered "ruinously low" by planters. As late as 1870, Georgia land was selling for less than half of 1860 prices. Values did not fully recover until the 1880s. With land selling for $2 to $8 an acre after the war and a mule costing around $50, a forty-acre farm with poultry, a mule, hogs, and equipment could be obtained for $200 to $300. However, few blacks had this amount of capital, and there was no source of credit that would have permitted a black to pledge the land as security for the loan required to buy it—even though whites had bought and sold land this way from Colonial times.

The federal government's failure to provide land outright or to make low-cost loans available to freed people was a profound mistake. Although lower-ranking Freedmen's Bureau officials thought former slave owners should be forced to offer life leases on as much land as each black family could cultivate, the attitude of Brig. Gen. Davis Tillson prevailed. He believed the Negro was better off as a wage hand than as a landowner and ordered all freedmen to make contracts by January, 10, 1866, or he would make contracts for them.

Some blacks, reluctant to abandon the dream of ownership, took matters into their own hands. Shortly after the war, blacks near Augusta seized land but were not allowed to keep it. In 1867, rumors of an impending land distribution swept the state, triggered by Thaddeus Stevens's legislation, which would have provided every freedman who was head of a household with forty acres and fifty dollars. Though it was defeated, discussion of it revived the dream of "Forty Acres and a Mule." Unscrupulous promoters sold phony land titles for one dollar around Savannah. Impatient Albany freedmen practiced military drills to prepare for seizing land. Union Leagues encouraged such militancy, and in 1868 armed blacks took control of some Chatham County rice lands. When a sheriff arrested the leaders, blacks forced their release. This brought a 120-man posse from Savannah that killed an innocent black teenager. Twenty-five blacks were indicted for the insurrection.

In another incident, Cudjo Fye, who was born a slave in 1823, became president of the Louisville Union League and organized fellow blacks in Jefferson County for self-protection, fair settlement from landlords, the vote, and ultimately, land redistribution. In 1870, when one follower was put into the Louisville jail, Fye led a group that battered down the door and freed him. Thousands of whites poured in to aid federal soldiers in quelling this uprising, and twenty-one blacks were sentenced by an all-white jury to from one to twenty years. Fye was among those who received the maximum sentence.

Most of the few blacks who did have a little capital often found the door to landownership slammed shut in their faces by hostile whites, who did not want to lose their cheap labor and resented independent blacks. Whites who might have sold land to blacks faced social ostracism, economic reprisals, and even violence from other whites if they tried to make the sale. Blacks who did acquire land were prime targets of the Ku Klux Klan.

Federal policy from the time of the Articles of Confederation had been to make public land available to the yeoman farmer on increasingly easy terms. By the time of emancipation, statutes were already on the books which theoretically provided land for all. Because of ignorance or intimidation, very few blacks took advantage of the Homestead Act passed in 1862 and extended to the former Confederate states between 1864 and 1872, which allowed the acquisition of 160 acres by anyone who paid a filing fee and lived and worked on the acreage for five years.

Therefore, most Georgia blacks went back to their prewar positions as agricultural laborers for the lords of the land. When the war ended, many planters, lacking cash, offered the freedmen deferred pay in the form of a share of the crop when it was harvested. However, blacks quickly realized their earnings were in jeopardy, and many preferred receiving their pay in cash frequently and regularly. Northerners who took up agriculture in the South instituted the "standing wage": Laborers received about $100 a year and certain fringe benefits. Another arrangement was called the "four-day plan": The freedman labored four days each week on the landlord's land and received as pay the use of land he could work for himself the other three days. This system was attractive to the man with a large family that could work "his" land while he worked for the owner. This system did not last as long as the standing wage. In the most common system during the first two years of freedom, blacks worked in gangs for a share of the crop. In one such arrangement, ten men and seven women affixed their "Xs" to a contract in Putnam County; the former master agreed to furnish food, clothing, and humane treatment, plus one-sixth of the 1865 crop. In exchange, the freed people agreed not to leave the plantation without permission and to stay on the job through Christmas. Some laborers got one-eighth or one-twelfth shares, and others got virtually nothing, especially in Brooks, Clinch, and Ware counties in South Georgia, where planters denied that blacks were even free.

By 1867, due to Freedmen's Bureau activity and the greater freedom of congressional Reconstruction, most blacks were able to increase their share of the crop to at least one-quarter. It soon doubled to one-half of the crop as individual family sharecropping replaced the gang labor that freedmen rejected—it was too reminiscent of slavery. Freedmen withheld labor, broke contracts, and forced changes. There was much violence attending this increase in income, for landlords, not wanting to pay more, resisted the efforts of blacks to move to the land of fairer-minded whites. Gradually the many plans were reduced to three general arrangements: cash wages, sharecropping, and cash rent. Those who sharecropped or paid an annual cash rent for land were called tenants. The others were laborers. In 1879, the average sharecropper received 56 percent of the wealth he produced.

Blacks demanded and got a larger portion of the crop in the late 1860s because they reduced the total amount of labor they were willing to do. The average freedman spent about two-thirds as much time in the fields as he had as a slave. This reduced his workday to near the national norm. Whenever possible, black women and children gave up field work altogether, often at the insistence of the husband and father. This produced a labor shortage that planters complained about. In an 1869 publication, one Georgian thought more than half the black labor had disappeared: "not dead, nor gone...but they have very much *quit the fields.*" In 1870, agricultural expert David Dickson thought that the decline was close to 40 percent. The actual decline in the number of "hands employed" in Georgia's cotton regions was 25 percent from 1866 to 1869, from 116,489 to 87,396.

The wage system also failed because planters would not or could not pay the agreed-upon amounts. Landlords of larger plantations were interested in letting their land out on the sharecrop system, for then they did not have to supervise the work as closely as when they hired wage hands. Blacks also preferred less supervision, and this facilitated the trend to sharecropping. A frequent black complaint, however, was that even under sharecropping, the landlord constantly tried to supervise the tenant's daily life.

Though most black farmers were sharecroppers, they would have preferred to rent their land for a fixed annual amount, payable at the end of the year, so they would be less likely to be cheated in the annual settlement. But this also meant that they would have to supply their own tools, mules, equipment, seed, and fertilizer and support themselves from one year's harvest to the next. Those who were able to do this were better off than any other group in agriculture except those who owned their land outright.

By 1890, nine out of ten black farmers in Georgia were sharecroppers. However, after 1890, many landlords moved to town, and since they could no longer conveniently supervise, they changed many of their sharecroppers to cash renters. This was in a period of declining cotton prices; as a result, the Black Belt grew blacker and poorer. Whereas sharecroppers increased only 149 percent in the 1880-1910 period, renters increased 343 percent. In 1900, 60 percent of all cash renters were black, and 42 percent of all black farmers in Georgia rented their land. After 1910, as land grew more scarce and expensive and Jim Crow tightened its hold, it was more difficult to move up from sharecropping to renting.

Why were so few blacks able to own their own land? One answer is low wages. Different studies have shown that wages in Georgia were significantly lower on average than those in other states. In 1880, an average family consisting of father, mother, and three working-age children, all working for pennies per hour, could seldom expect to earn more than twenty dollars a month. There was little change in the next forty years. According to a 1917 study of 217 black farmers in Sumter County, the average family income was forty-two dollars a month. This would buy no more than twenty dollars would in 1880. Most blacks locked into this culture of poverty had no chance of climbing the agriculture ladder.

Wages declined in the 1880-95 period, especially during the 1893 depression, the worst the nation had endured up to then. By 1899, though up from the 1893-94 lows, wages were still in the neighborhood of eight to ten dollars a month for a man. This changed little until 1917, when war-induced migration led to a labor shortage and the boll weevil weakened the earlier dependency on cotton and led to crop diversification. In the four years before the boll weevil infestation, Georgia's average cotton yield was 230 pounds per acre. Afterward, it dropped to 117 pounds per acre.

The low wages also forced women and children out into the fields. Women received one-third or one-half a man's wages; working children, even less. By 1890 there were 50,300 black female agricultural workers in Georgia. In 1900, 47 percent of black women sixteen years of age or older were gainfully employed, mostly as domestics to eke out the family's subsistence earnings—in contrast to 13 percent for white women in Georgia. By 1910, it had risen to 58 percent for black women. It was not unusual for the landlord to interfere with school attendance by pressuring black parents to make their children work in the fields, especially during the rush periods of cotton chopping in the spring and picking in the fall. Landlord pressure would usually take the form of threats to cut off credit or to evict. Sometimes threats of bodily assault were carried out in Klan-style attacks.

The permanent depression for black agriculturalists was also shared by a smaller percentage of whites unfortunate enough to have sunk down to, or never risen above, the necessity of doing agricultural work for others. The oligarchy decreed that blacks would occupy the position of mudsill supporting its mansion and ensured that poor whites would occupy a level not much higher. One of the tragedies of Georgia's history was the failure of poor whites to realize their low position was determined by that of the blacks. A recent study of the economic consequences of emancipation concluded that racism encouraged the development of institutions which kept the entire South in poverty: "It removed the incentive to self-advancement, not only for blacks, but for whites as well." Another historian noted: "In time, sharecropping would take on the onus of a curse... it was, or became, a system that beggared all the South."

One institution that developed to keep both white and black tenants in permanent depression was the crop lien system. Lien laws functioned to keep tenants forever poor and dependent. As with the other instruments of oppression, the system's effects fell more disastrously on blacks than whites. A lien was a legal claim of the landlord or merchant on the tenant's share of the next crop, which served as collateral for what the tenant borrowed to live on and produce that crop. Because the anticipated crop was usually the only asset the tenant had, he had to pledge it to obtain credit. Having done this, he could only get credit from the party holding the lien. This put each tenant at the mercy of the landlord or merchant who held his lien, thus depriving the tenant of any chance to shop around for better deals. He became the powerless victim of unconscionable interest rates, and his bargaining power at settlement time was destroyed. In 1913, Georgia blacks paid over twice the interest rates whites paid.

Georgia's first lien laws were passed by the unreconstructed 1866 legislature so that planters could finance the 1867 season after two poor harvests. Money was obtained from as far away as New York City as liens were sold to wholesale houses and banks. Liens on the tenant's share gave the lienholder full authority and discretion to dispose of the tenant's crop share. The fiction that the tenant was in any way independent was abandoned in 1872 when Georgia courts ruled that sharecroppers were wage hands paid in kind. By 1873 the merchants had gained sufficient power and influence to get the law amended to permit them to deal directly with the tenant when the merchant, not the landlord, furnished the sharecropper with life's necessities. The provision was deleted in 1874, perhaps due to the strength of the Independent Movement, but it was restored the following year.

As black political power diminished, the legislature passed laws even more opposed to the tenant's interests. The Georgia legislature refused to pass a bill that would have protected tenants when landlords foreclosed liens before they were due. In 1889, a law was approved to let the landlord keep title to the tenant's share of any crop until settlement time instead of paying the tenant at the time of harvest. If the landlord believed his tenant wanted to leave, the settlement could be delayed until the following spring planting. Then it was too late to move, and the tenant probably had used up his share in the crop by credit purchases to sustain his family through the winter. Broke and helpless, he then had no choice but to remain and repeat the same depressing cycle for another year. To further increase the tenant's dependency, in good years the landlord or merchant would pay the tenant less so that he would not have enough money to consider leaving. In bad years, more than the market price might be paid to keep the tenant's hopes up.

Black bargaining power was weakened by a white united front. Gradually, merchants and planters became one interlocking establishment of capital. Planters became merchants, and merchants became planters involved as ginners, millers, cotton buyers, and investors in railroads, lumber, and other enterprises. This trend meant "all possibility of dispute between landlord and merchant from which the tenant might benefit was extinguished," according to historians Roger L. Ransom and Richard Sutch.

As a larger proportion of tenants became black, Democratic politicians agreed that tenant grievances would neither be remedied by law nor become political issues. Moreover, local constables, sheriffs, and the state court system worked together to enforce lien laws as interpreted by the landlords. To further reduce the ability of a tenant to improve his position by moving, in 1901 the legislature formalized a long-standing practice by making it illegal for a landlord to employ a tenant who had a written contract with another landlord or merchant. In 1903, this law was extended to cover oral agreements. The contract terms were what the lienholder said they were.

Du Bois stated in 1912 that at least three-fourths of the black worker's crop shares and wages earned since emancipation were illegally withheld. Some blacks tried to revolt against the stacked deck. In 1869, Cane Cook's landlord beat him senseless when Cook tried to argue about his share of the crop. In the spring of 1876, two blacks were reported murdered near Savannah for protesting their annual settlement terms. When two blacks near Augusta took their protests to court, the evidence was so blatant that the court awarded them a share of the 1876 corn crop they had produced. They were murdered when they went to claim it. In the main, protest was futile.

The plantation store was an integral part of the system of exploitation. The company store increased the cost of living by driving up the prices of goods the tenant bought while driving down the prices of the things he had to sell. Bills were padded by high markups and credit charges. Because the tenant had to live on credit and because the harvest settlement was seldom more than his outstanding bill at the store, he was fated to start each year with virtually nothing. Studies show that black tenants produced more per acre than white tenants but worked fewer acres and had less in the end. In one Georgia county Du Bois studied in 1898, 26 of 271 families cleared at least twenty-five dollars each for their past year's labor, but 118 ended the year losing that much or more and fell deeper into debt. Even Henry Grady, who usually spoke about how well blacks were treated, said that the store credit price was 30-70 percent higher than the cash price. The *Savannah Tribune* claimed in 1876 that the interest charge was 100 percent. Detailed modern studies place the interest rates at 60 percent in Georgia for the 1880s.

Even if the tenant was technically free to take his business elsewhere, he was inhibited from shopping around to get lower prices for fear of angering the landlord or merchant, who was his main backer, and also by the distance to the next store. Rural stores were over six miles apart and constituted monopolies. One could seldom afford the time and energy required for the round trip when a mule and wagon would mosey down the road at two miles an hour. Such a trip would take all day, and the whole county would know it had been made. The development of transportation and communication technology helped to weaken the high-interest merchant lien system. Rural free delivery of mail started in 1896, postal savings in 1910, and by 1913 one could order out of the Montgomery Ward "wish book" and have items delivered by parcel post. In the 1920s, as more blacks bought automobiles and roads were improved, the territorial monopoly of separate stores tended to disintegrate. Ironically, in the prosperous years of 1917 to 1920, merchant-landlords sometimes encouraged tenants to purchase Model Ts, hoping that the expense would keep them in debt. It did. But it also weakened the lienholders' power.

In search of a better life, frequent moving from one landlord to another was common among black tenants, but most failed to improve their condition. Landlords and merchants often expounded on blacks' ingratitude and irresponsibility. The *Atlanta Constitution* said that the "irresponsible" cropper who moved without notice was the bane of the South and called on blacks to be more dependable. The *Southern Cultivator* recommended that the way to deal with such "irresponsibility" was to starve blacks into submission, because "all leniency and kindness are thrown away upon" them. Sometimes blacks were lynched for jumping a contract.

Merchant control of Georgia's agriculture led to another evil, the overemphasis on cotton production. Merchants wanted the maximum amount of cotton and pressured tenants to devote all their land, time, and energy to the cash crop. Cotton monoculture exhausted the soil, led to erosion, and contributed to the poverty of the individual farmer and the state. The emphasis on cotton increased after the Civil War. In the late 1860s, only 31 percent of the state's cropland was in cotton; by 1880, 41 percent was, and the percentage continued to rise. Tenants would have been far better off if they had raised most of their own food instead of planting cotton "to the doorstep." By raising more food and buying less from the company store they would more likely have some cash left over at settlement time.

One of the best views of a black community after it had fallen victim to postwar exploitation is found in Du Bois's study of Dougherty County. The rural area surrounding Albany, the county seat, was 83 percent black. There it was common to have up to eight people living in a one-room cabin. Du Bois said that living conditions were worse than in the worst slums in New York City he had seen. Eighty-eight percent of Dougherty's blacks were farmers; the rest worked in turpentine camps or for the railroad. Tenants bought five dollars worth of food on credit that could be bought for three dollars cash or grown for one dollar, but the landlords' insistence on cotton to the doorstep discouraged kitchen gardens. "If cotton rose in price, the rent rose even higher. If cotton fell, the rent remained or followed reluctantly," Du Bois noted. If a tenant worked hard and raised a large crop, his rent was raised the next year. If the crop failed, his corn and mule were sold to cover his debts. The worker received a house and garden site and thirty to sixty dollars a year. Of the total black population of nine thousand, only six percent had risen to peasant proprietorship. The other 94 percent struggled and failed.

The poverty imposed on most blacks produced many individuals with no or limited literacy, narrow horizons, ignorance of great issues, poor nutrition and health, short lives, and with no ability to ensure that their children's status would be measurably better. The tenant was not inclined to make permanent improvements (such as erecting fences or clearing brush) on land that he knew would never be his. Another powerful incentive not to do well economically was the fear of arousing the jealousy of whites. Many blacks have written of this fear of appearing prosperous and inviting the lynch mob. A white journalist described the tenant system as one that "a cynic might have imagined to have been deliberately devised in order to inculcate in the tenants the very traits of shiftlessness and irresponsibility which were attributed to the Negroes."

Sharecropping, which should have been a stepping-stone to landowner-ship, instead became a scheme to maintain the status quo. The agricultural ladder did not work for blacks. Not many whites got to the top rung of landownership either, because ownership was concentrated in the hands of a few. The myth that the large antebellum plantations were broken up following the Civil War was given credence by the 1880, 1890, and 1900 censuses, which counted each sharecropper's or tenant's holdings as a separate farm. Just as most whites in antebellum Georgia owned no slaves, most had no tenants after the Civil War. In 1900, of the small percentage that did, 32 percent had one, 36 percent had two to four, 17 percent had five to nine, 10 percent had ten to nineteen, and 6 percent had over twenty tenants. The average was under four.

Blacks in Georgia were never able to acquire title to land in anything commensurate with their proportion of the population. Reflecting the consequences of Georgia's especially nasty Reconstruction experience, through 1910, a smaller percentage of blacks owned land in Georgia than in any other ex-Confederate state. By 1874, freedmen owned 338,769 acres, worth $6 million, or a little less than 1 percent of Georgia. Most holdings were concentrated on the coast. Other holdings were scattered around in all counties in the Black Belt except Warren County, an especially vicious center of Klan activity. There were black landowners in all other counties except Fannin and Union counties in the hill country of North Georgia. Most of the holdings were south of the Columbus-Augusta fall line. By 1880, blacks owned 586,664 acres, 1.6 percent of Georgia's total acreage, and in the peak year of 1920, 130,131 blacks owned a total of 1,838,129 acres; blacks then constituted over 40 percent of the state's population, and their holdings amounted to only about 5 percent of Georgia's land. However, even this was viewed by whites as a looming problem. Then the boll weevil and the depression of the early 1920s reduced the number of black landowners to 84,187 by 1925.

There were many reasons why blacks did not own more of the land they worked. In the beginning, few had capital to buy, and many factors worked to ensure that they did not accumulate the necessary money later. White supremacy, low cotton prices, and high interest rates kept the agricultural ladder from working. White farmers often refused to sell land to blacks because it was more profitable to have it sharecropped; then they could rob the tenant of the fruits of his labor. In addition, the marketing process worked against the tenant. Usually in debt at harvest time, the black tenant would have to turn over his portion of the crop to the landlord-merchant for whatever the price was then. Had he been able to hold it until the price advanced seasonally, he would have been better off. Cotton prices swung seasonally, just as corn prices did. Tenants could not hold their crops off the market to take advantage of regular upswings. Most poor white farmers could not do so, either, and one of the main attractions of the Farmers Alliances and the Populist Movement of the

1880s and 1890s was the Sub-treasury Plan that would enable them to delay marketing their crops (see p. 173).

Moreover, blacks were often asked to pay several times what land was worth. Actual prices were low; in 1870 land sales averaged $2.87 an acre in Georgia. Many blacks were paying that much in rent and crop shares every year, but it was difficult to find whites who would sell land to blacks or banks that would loan them the purchase price.

Despite all the difficulties—bad weather, defective seed, poor live-stock, lack of experience, outdated equipment and methods, poor land, and ignorance and superstition—there were some blacks who by dint of extra-hard work, good management, and fortunate circumstances, or a combination of these and other factors, were able to prosper as farmers because they did own their own land. The wonder is not that so few became landowners but that so many did. Blacks obtained land in several ways. Some were given it by former masters; others had honest landlords and were able to accumulate enough money to buy it; still others pooled their resources for initial purchases. According to one study, in 75 percent of the cases in Georgia where blacks acquired land, a white, often a former owner, encouraged the purchase. Of those who bought, 60 percent purchased from former owners and 15 percent from a merchant the black had dealt with. Tenancy usually preceded ownership for the more fortunate blacks. Unfortunately, while many blacks had the requi-site "Puritan virtues," they lacked lucky circumstances and the help of sympathetic whites.

Some counties offered more opportunities than others. With its more liberal Congregational background and high percentage of blacks, Lib-erty County sent black representatives to the state legislature long after Reconstruction was overthrown. In April 1876, the *Savannah Tribune* carried a resolution from Liberty County inviting black victims of violence in other parts of Georgia to come there, "where there is plenty of good cheap land for rent or sale." By 1908, Liberty County blacks owned fifty-six thousand acres.

Where blacks could not acquire land by individual effort and luck, they could sometimes do so by pooling their resources in a land club. A pioneer development in this area was the Old Midway Church farm cooperative in Liberty County, which received help from the American Missionary Association of the Congregational church. One group of freedmen from Wilkes County bought about two thousand acres in Thomas County. The Freedmen's Bureau also encouraged cooperatives. A land club near Sandersville in Washington County helped six blacks buy small farms in the 1907-12 period. In Athens, schoolteacher Judia C. Jackson organized a mutual benefit society in 1900 to help blacks pool their resources to buy land and divide it up. By 1908 they had acquired four hundred acres.

Not only was it difficult for blacks to acquire land, but hanging on to it presented many problems also. Beginning around 1890, white resistance to black landownership increased. This was considered by many African-Americans to be a conspiracy to keep blacks as sharecroppers. Whitecapping (driving off so-called "undesirables"), lynching, peonage, and the convict-lease system all were methods used to force blacks to relinquish their land.

When the Civil War ended, there were more blacks in Georgia than in any other state. Georgia could have taken the lead in showing the nation that blacks, given an opportunity to achieve economic independence unencumbered by discrimination, could make the New South a prosperous and wholesome place. Instead, black advances during Reconstruction were reversed with unparalleled ferocity, and an edifice of discrimination, proscriptions, and exploitation was erected on the foundation of white supremacy. As a consequence, progress was slowed, the economy was retarded, and amicable race relations were delayed for over a century. As the United States was still basically an agricultural nation in the second half of the nineteenth century, it would be expected that if blacks were to achieve independence anywhere, it would be as landowning farmers. Some did; most did not. The problems of tenancy lingered on, gradually being attenuated by the economic developments of a more modern society in the twentieth century. Meanwhile, no method was too brutal to maintain the status quo.

Peonage

"A Georgia peon camp is hell itself!" reported one black caught up in the peonage system. Peonage—the holding of persons to forced labor to pay off debts—was common in Georgia from the end of the Civil War to recent times. The debts were often fictitious and fraudulent, which only exacerbated the injustice of peonage. Sharecropping, peonage, the convict-lease system, and lynching were strands in a web of oppression. While tenancy and sharecropping kept blacks on an economic plane approximating slavery, peonage and the convict-lease system were especially reminiscent of the peculiar institution's more brutal aspects. The vast majority of peons were black, though alien workers and poor whites were also exploited.

While debt slavery existed before the Civil War, it became common in Georgia with the passage of the Black Codes by the state legislature in 1865 and 1866. Code provisions required blacks to sign contracts to work for a year for a particular employer. The contracts were often vague about the rate of pay and frequently offered only one-third (or less) of the Freedmen's Bureau recommendation of twelve dollars a month plus rations. Failure to sign such a contract could lead to a vagrancy conviction for the freedman.

In an 1867 article in *Harper's* magazine, the Freedmen's Bureau chief, Gen. O. O. Howard, called national attention to Georgia's vagrancy laws, which he said gave blacks little time to look for better jobs and "will occasion practical slavery." He described the practice of arresting a black on any pretext and trying him before a white justice of the peace: After that came "the sale of his services at public outcry for payment of the fine and costs, without limit as to time. Whipping, and working in chain gangs, present some of the obnoxious features of the irregular law." Howard noted these were a continuation of antebellum laws allowing the sale of free Negroes into slavery for minor crimes or debt. Congress passed an antipeonage law in 1867 that provided for ten years' imprisonment and a $10,000 fine for violators. This law and the 1868 Georgia constitutional provision forbidding imprisonment for debt were generally ignored, however.

It was a short step from evading the Fifteenth Amendment, which was supposed to protect blacks' political rights, to violating the Thirteenth Amendment, designed to prevent involuntary servitude. As the political power of Georgia's blacks declined toward the end of the nineteenth century, the degree and intensity of their victimization increased. Robert Toombs said in 1886 that blacks in the South were still essentially slaves and that their ultimate condition would be that of peonage very similar to that which existed for the peasants of Mexico. Toombs's prediction held true for decades.

There were several ways a black could slip into peonage. He could be arrested on a trumped-up charge and fined. Not having the money to pay, he would be turned over to a white employer who would pay his fine, and he would then have to work until the debt had been paid. However, workers had no control over pay or the price or the number of items charged against them, and they were swindled by being forced to pay exorbitant prices for goods they might not have received, so it often took years to pay off a ten-dollar fine. The entire system was obviously corrupt. Landlords and merchants profited greatly from the unpaid labor of peons, and the practice depended on the cooperation and collusion of law enforcement officials, courts, and planters, all of whom stood united to return any laborer who tried to escape from bondage.

Another way blacks sank into peonage was through the "furnish system." The worker who had no money at the start of the growing season would be furnished supplies and food by the landlord until settlement time—usually between completion of the harvest and the next year. If the worker tried to leave before the bill for his "furnish" was settled, he could be arrested and fined and forced into peonage under the "false pretense" law, which was designed to circumvent the constitutional provision against imprisonment for debt. This law stated that anyone who did not pay debts owed to his furnisher was guilty of obtaining money under false pretenses with intent to defraud. This law was not declared unconstitutional until the 1940s. Even so, it remained a guiding principle for peon masters for many years after that.

Peonage doomed the individual peon and his children to perpetual poverty, ignorance, and poor health. While peonage was widespread, no definitive count of its victims can be made. Peons labored far from public view in turpentine camps, sawmills, and on plantations. There was no way for the vast majority of peons, who lacked financial and legal resources, to escape the trap they had fallen into, because local law enforcement officials conspired against them.

In April 1905, the *Atlanta Independent*, one of the state's leading black newspapers, charged that hundreds of blacks were in peonage in Georgia under the false-pretense contract law. In 1905, an Atlanta grand jury investigated fifteen complaints. In South Georgia, one Miller County operator had twenty-three on his private chain gang. He purchased peons for two years' labor from the local sheriff.

Contributing to the ranks of peons were children who were apprenticed under provisions of an 1866 act designed to provide orphans with guardians. Edwin Belcher, a black Freedmen's Bureau agent and politician, said that whites would "drive off the father and then go to the ordinary and make affidavit that the father is out of the county and the mother unable to support the child." Children could be apprenticed until they were twenty-one years old and forced to work for their appointed guardian, who generally was interested only in cheap labor. The practice was widespread. Belcher said that one-third of the black children in Monroe County were bound out in this manner in 1867. In Dougherty County, the orphan apprentice law was used to virtually reenslave black children.

The first test of the constitutionality of the 1867 federal peonage statute began on February 11, 1901, when Samuel M. Clyatt, with two other Georgians and a cooperative Florida deputy sheriff, kidnapped two blacks, Will Gordon and Mose Ridley, who had fled from Clyatt's employment in a Tifton, Georgia, sawmill for what they hoped would be safety in Florida. Clyatt claimed they owed him money and took them at gunpoint back to Tifton. They were never seen again. (Many peons who fled were recaptured and severely beaten or murdered as a lesson to others.) Clyatt was tried and convicted in early 1902 before Judge Emory Speer under the 1867 federal statute. Because the case threatened to undermine their forced-labor system, the Georgia Sawmill Association and the naval-stores industry raised $90,000 to defend Clyatt and hired U. S. Sen. Augustus O. Bacon and Rep. William G. Brantley to represent him. Clyatt's conviction was appealed to the Supreme Court, which, in March 1905, reversed the lower court and remanded the case for a new trial on the grounds that it had not been proved that Gordon and Ridley had actually been returned to peonage. There was no new trial because the witnesses had "disappeared." Clyatt went unpunished. But the Supreme Court did rule peonage illegal, theoretically invalidating Georgia's contract labor law. As a matter of practice, peonage continued.

Speer, the former Independent politician, was an unusual man to grace the Southern bench at this time. Until his death in 1918, he did more to oppose peonage in Georgia than any other court official. Speer was strongly convinced that peonage undermined the yeoman farmer and the small businessman. Judge Speer's power was limited, since white juries were reluctant to convict whites for crimes against blacks. In a case tried in Macon, he "practically ordered a verdict of guilty" and was angered when the jury took just five minutes to acquit. In his charge to a federal grand jury in 1904, Speer called for the end of both peonage and the leasing of convicts and urged the formation of interracial law-and-order leagues. Speer even violated the tenets of racial etiquette by publicly rebuking a Georgia state official for using the term "nigger."

The Clyatt case encouraged more prosecutions. On November 23, 1902, a Savannah grand jury indicted seven men on twenty-six counts of peonage. Three McRee brothers, of Valdosta, were brought before Speer's court. State legislator Edward McRee owned thirty-seven thousand acres in South Georgia and operated a large forced labor camp whose inmates included both peons and leased convicts. His family controlled local law officers who helped him obtain and keep unpaid labor. McRee pleaded guilty and was fined $1,000. Meanwhile, McRee signed a lease for one hundred more convicts. Despite a law stating that no one convicted of a felony could sit in the legislature, the conviction did not affect McRee's position.

While McRee's case did little to discourage peonage in Georgia, it led to increased investigations and more press coverage. In April 1904, the U. S. Secret Service found that a white Madison County farmer had held eight black children in slavery for six years because their father owed him two hundred dollars. At four dollars a year per child, it cost the planter less than the child labor of slaves. The white was also accused of murdering the father, so the case became a murder trial.

The practice of employers paying court fines and costs of accused blacks and then forcing them to pay them back with labor led to many more abuses. Du Bois stated that the whole court system degenerated into a scheme to rob blacks of any cash they might have. In other instances, blacks were arrested on trivial or trumped-up charges to swell the ranks of peons and leased convicts. In one 1905 case, when Putnam County cotton growers were short of labor, seven blacks were charged with assault. Six of them were sent to farmers who paid their fines and the seventh to a county chain gang because the county was behind on its road maintenance.

Despite an occasional prosecution, peonage continued with the full support of most local courts and officials, who were active partners in the conspiracy. A typical 1912 case involved a fourteen-year-old girl who received a seven-dollar advance when she signed a contract to pick cotton. She was arrested when she quit the job after earning this amount because her employer said she still owed him money. She was convicted, fined seventy-five dollars, and sentenced to a year in jail under the false-pretense law.

The sheriff of Macon County jailed a hundred blacks in 1911 because they would not go to work for certain employers. When Sam Sadler of Hartwell refused to continue to work to repay his "debt," he was taken to jail and beaten by his employer as the sheriff held a gun on him. Lath Horne was beaten to death by whites in the Houston County cemetery in 1910 because he was trying to help his sister escape from peonage. Mob action to enforce peonage was not uncommon. King Moore, a black in Vienna, was charged with assault, jailed, and threatened with lynching because he tried to quit his job when his white employer raped his wife.

Few Georgia peons were able to tell their story to the world. One who told his story to Hamilton Holt in 1905 illustrated the fine line that existed between the status of peon and leased convict and how easy it was to slip from the former into the latter. The victim was born during the Civil War, and when he was eight his mother died, and an uncle took care of him. Two years later the uncle apprenticed him to the former owner of his mother. The child did not know at the time that his uncle had contracted for him to work until he was twenty-one. The former slave owner was paying three dollars a week for men, two dollars a week for women, and less for children. His uncle drew his pay for the eleven-year period and gave him ten to fifteen cents a week as spending money.

In the early 1880s, not knowing he was bound for three more years, he hired out to a neighboring plantation for forty cents a day and one meal. His original employer summoned the sheriff to reclaim him the first day. He was given thirty lashes and returned to his former condition. When he was twenty-one, he signed a contract for $3.50 a week and a place to sleep. This contract was renewed yearly for five years; then he made his "X" on a ten-year contract similar to that which the employer required of his other workers. Shortly after that, the employer's son, then a state senator, brought in forty leased convicts for which he paid the state two hundred dollars each per year. This made all the free workers want to quit, but they found out that they would be held to their ten-year contracts or be made convicts also. Six months later, more black convicts were brought in, including eight women. The senator then bought another thousand acres, built two sawmills, and started a company store where the free laborers were forced to trade because they were paid in script that was not accepted anywhere else.

When their ten years were up, they refused to sign new contracts but were told that they owed the company store and if they would all come up and sign papers acknowledging their debts, they would be free to leave. He was told that he owed $165, accumulated over a four-year period, and he dared not question the white bookkeeper. "We had been told that we might go if we signed the acknowledgments. We would have signed anything just to get away," he explained. That night, they were all locked up as convicts. Their pay was stopped, and their wives became the mistresses of the white guards. His nine-year-old son was given away and never seen again. In the convict barracks the food was poor, and quarters were nasty and dirty. After three years he was told his debt had been paid off and was released—by the white man who was living with his wife. Compared to many, he fared well, for he survived.

Unequal Justice: The Convict-Lease System

Being a peon was not the worst thing that could happen to a black in Georgia. After the Civil War and until it was abolished in 1908, the convict-lease system became, next to lynching, the most brutal manifestation of black oppression in the South. The forced labor of its mostly black victims mainly benefited a small ruling elite. Leased convicts were prisoners who were given, rented, or leased by a governmental unit to individuals and companies that forced them to work, usually under atrocious conditions. Lessees wanted to maximize profits and were not held accountable for the prisoners' condition. As a result, the brutalization of prisoners was unparalleled. Driven to work by the lash—often when sick, underfed, and provided with miserable quarters—many died while serving their sentences. Southern historian Fletcher M. Green called it "a system that left a trail of dishonor and death that could find a parallel only in the persecutions of the Middle Ages or in the prison camps of Nazi Germany."

Most of Georgia's antebellum penitentiary inmates were white. Slaves were usually disciplined on the plantations or, when incarcerated, were placed in a local jail. Legislators thought the state penitentiary should be self-supporting, and some politicians hoped that it might even make a profit. Georgia began to use white convict labor in the mid-1840s to build railcars for the state-owned Western and Atlantic Railway. The 1866 Georgia legislature provided for farming out prisoners on five-year leases to the highest bidder. In 1868 the provisional military governor, Brig. Gen. Thomas H. Ruger, leased one hundred black convicts to the Georgia and Alabama Railroad for one year for $2,500. Later that year he leased another hundred to the Selma, Rome, and Dalton Railroad for $1,000. Gov. Rufus Bullock continued the practice. In 1868 he agreed to lease 100 to 500 a year to the Grant, Alexander Company for ten dollars apiece to work on the Macon and Brunswick Railroad. The following year, Bullock leased all of the state's convicts to this same firm at no cost to it except for the salary of an inspector. Democrats confirmed the lease when they regained control of the General Assembly.

At first viewed as a temporary solution to the problem of prison overcrowding, the convict-lease system grew as it became profitable to state leaders, the courthouse rings, and New South entrepreneurs. Only after Reconstruction was overthrown did the system became the heartless, profit-making machine of the Bourbon elite. Eventually, the lease system weakened Bourbons' control of the black vote and contributed to their loss of power. In *Origins of the New South*, C. Vann Woodward stated that more than anything else, their support of the convict-leasing system lost the Bourbons their reputation as paternalistic protectors of blacks.

Tenancy and sharecropping produced certain poverty for most Georgia blacks. "Proper" behavior for these peasants meant working long and hard and keeping silent when cheated or tricked out of what little they were legally entitled to. To enforce this "proper" behavior, the alternative had to be grim indeed. The convict-lease system was a part of that alternative, as was lynching. The General Assembly's infamous Black Codes forced freed people to work on whatever terms were offered and to increase the number of convicts. The legislature authorized leasing convicts to dispose of the increase. The laws provided severe penalties for vagrancy and petty offenses such as cursing, fighting, or just being an annoyance to whites. Frequently, to escape imprisonment as vagrants, blacks took any work that was offered. Trying to get out of a bad contract could yield a two-year sentence as a leased convict for the tenant under Georgia's false-pretenses law.

Generally speaking, Georgia's Black Codes accomplished their purpose. The freed person was offered the choice of a slavelike status or conviction under the codes. As a result, most blacks stayed on or returned to the plantations, but enough were caught up in the system's mill to greatly increase the number of convicts. Since the vast majority of convicts were black, the convict-lease system's growth was encouraged. It is unlikely that it would have grown to its full size and horror had the victims been white. In a frank explanation that the convict-lease system's function was to force blacks to accept work, Clark Howell's *Atlanta Constitution* offered a cure for a shortage of cotton pickers: "Drive the vagrants toward the cotton fields or send them to the gang."

The convict-lease system started as a temporary solution to the routine problem of taking care of prisoners as inexpensively as possible. It gradually became an important source of income to the favored few and a source of revenue to the state. Corporations, influential planters, and politicians all united to increase the number of leased convicts, and laws against blacks were more stringently enforced. This slave labor helped build the fortunes of several politically powerful Georgians, notably the "Bourbon Triumvirate" of Gen. John B. Gordon and governors Joseph E. Brown and Alfred H. Colquitt.

There is no doubt that the state's justice system discriminated against blacks. As demand for convict labor increased, the inherent corrupting influence of the system worked back into local politics and courts. The rich and powerful Bourbon leaders who benefited from convict leases greatly influenced the lower echelons of the Democratic political machine and used their weight to coerce and encourage petty officials constantly to swell the numbers of convicts. Judicial promotion was often influenced by the number of blacks sentenced to serve private interests. Rebecca Felton stated in *My Memoirs of Georgia Politics* that judges with political ambitions would curry favor with the corporations, planters, and prominent politicians, such as the Triumvirate, by meting out long sentences to blacks. Democratic bosses would then show their appreciation by supporting the judges for seats in Congress. Because they sent many blacks to prison in the 1880s, Judge John W. Maddox of Rome and Charles L. Bartlett of Macon received such support.

Instead of receiving a salary, many law enforcement and court officials were paid by fees for each arrest, trial, and conviction. The fee system gave them an incentive to run the greatest possible number of prisoners through the courts. The more powerless blacks were less able than whites to resist this inclination of officials to line their pockets.

Living conditions in convict camps were hell. The prisoners' arduous work went on seven days a week. Some convicts lived in tents year-round, and some slept in cages with tin roofs that broiled the prisoners in summer and froze them in winter. In 1891, black sociologist William Scarborough stated, "There is no system of penal punishment...so degrading, so inhuman, so barbarous, so revolting in all aspects." Prisoners were constantly chained, brutally and frequently whipped, and lived in an unsanitary, filthy, disease-ridden environment made worse by heat, rain, cold, vermin, rotten food, bedbugs, and other detriments to health. Sentences for minor crimes often became sentences of death by torture. In one private *misdemeanor* camp, 25 percent of the prisoners died before their sentences were up; in another, 17 percent died. Only three of the twenty-four camps had *any* medical facilities in the 1870s. The *Augusta Chronicle* said in 1887 that prisoners would be better off hanged "than to suffer the tortures and lingering death" in the camps.

George Washington Cable, Confederate army veteran and later an astute critic of the white South's racial attitudes, noted that in Georgia in 1880, about one-half of the almost twelve hundred convicts had sentences of ten years or more and that the average black sentence was double what a white would receive for the same crime. "Ten years, as the rolls show, is the utmost length of time a convict can be expected to remain alive" in a Georgia convict-lease camp, he reported.

The Dade County coal-mining convict camp owned by Joseph E. Brown, former governor, state Supreme Court justice, and U. S. senator from 1880 to 1890, was considered one of the best managed, yet conditions remained so bad that on July 12, 1886, the desperate convicts mutinied, and over a hundred of them refused to work. Their meager rations were cut off completely for three days, and they were starved into submission. An investigating committee of the legislature found filthy bunks, wet blankets, a brutal whipping boss, and dangerous working conditions. Interest in investigations rose when it was reported in 1888 that whites were also being brutalized in the camps. An investigation in 1892 of the Dade mining camp showed that many convicts were sick because they were forced by threat of floggings to work while standing in water, were frequently injured by falling slate, slept on wet blankets, and breathed air poisoned by underground gasses.

Women and children were not immune to the ghastly system's horrors. Women were whipped if they did not extend sexual favors to guards and overseers. Rapes of girls and women in camps were routine. By 1894, twelve black women had borne children of white fathers in one camp. In 1884 there were 137 boys aged eleven to seventeen who were leased. One, Ryder Hillard, received a life sentence when he was nine years old and worked in the coal mines for nearly twenty years, seldom seeing daylight. The *New York Freeman* reported that in 1886 there were boys and girls as young as six years old working on convict-lease gangs, and the *Atlanta Defiance* reported: "The feet of a colored boy rotted off a few days ago. This was caused by his being worked in the county chain gang all winter without shoes."

These terrible conditions were exposed by several black legislators, who began opposition to the convict-lease system during Reconstruction. Peter O'Neal of Baldwin County introduced a bill to require payment to convicts for their labor. Henry McNeal Turner also sought reforms. Other blacks, including Edwin Belcher and Aaron A. Bradley, condemned the system outright at that time. Sen. George Wallace, Turner, and Rep. James M. Simms served on a joint committee investigating the treatment of prisoners. Though they were unable to abolish the system, their recommendations influenced Governor Bullock to pardon some convicts. Contractors and the legislature continued to support the system. Few Georgia voices were raised against the system after the overthrow of Reconstruction until black Rep. James Blue introduced a bill for some minor reforms in 1876. This bill was enacted. In 1879, a bill by black Rep. Thomas M. Butler to improve inspections of the convict-lease camps failed by eight votes. Butler introduced another reform bill that year that would have abolished the lease system in favor of a central penitentiary, but the legislature refused to consider the change. In 1881, black Rep. Ishmael Lonnon's attempt at reform also fell short.

The camps continued to grow as a political issue. In 1882, the controversy heated up even more as Tom Watson jockeyed for the support of blacks and poor whites in his successful bid for a seat in the legislature. Despite increased attacks—and its own previous reports detailing poor conditions—the General Assembly claimed that Georgia's prison system in 1884 was "the most humane and least expensive of any in the United States, if not the world."

By then, the Northern press had picked up on criticism of Georgia's convict-lease system and helped focus the nation's attention on this "murderous machine managed by thugs." In a national magazine article in 1886, Rebecca Felton charged that convicts were sometimes beaten to death, that women were stripped naked and whipped, and that the entire system was "selling the poor to the highest bidder." As the principal exploiters of convict labor, she named Brown and Gordon, who, along with Colquitt, had been the primary beneficiaries of the infamous twenty-year leases that brought the state a lump sum of $25,000 a year for all convicts beginning in 1876.

Black pressure against the convict-lease system mounted in the late 1880s. A mass meeting in Augusta on August 8, 1887, heard local attorney Judson Lyons and two other blacks, A. W. Wimberly and P. H. Craig, denounce the convict system. Later that month, Governor Gordon pardoned some convicts, ordered the prosecution of one whipping boss, and filed damage suits against two minor lessees. *Georgia Baptist* editor William Jefferson White said Gordon was merely responding to Northern political pressures, and that nothing had really changed.

However, more and more groups and individuals joined the fight against the convict-lease system. All labor unions opposed the system because convict labor depressed the wages of free labor. Except for Southern Democrats, all political parties eventually took a stand against the system. Finally, criticism of the convict-lease system began to take its toll. In 1897, Gov. William Y. Atkinson urged the abolition of the system. During his term, he imposed $25,000 fines on lessees for abuse of convicts. That year, the General Assembly approved the establishment of a prison farm two miles west of Milledgeville. In 1911 the main building was constructed.

Court cases, adverse publicity, and political pressure combined to weaken the convict-lease system. Northern blacks continued to support efforts for reform in Georgia, and in Atlanta, Du Bois lobbied for a reformatory for the young as an alternative to sending them to a convict-lease camp or chain gang. In 1899, Clarke County stopped leasing prisoners because they competed with free labor and began to use them for its own road work. This was part of a trend. Although the number of leased convicts increased from 405 in 1870 (86 percent black) to 4,528 in 1902 (92 percent black), by the turn of the century, misdemeanor convicts on county chain gangs often outnumbered leased felony convicts. In 1902, 51 percent of all sixty-five prisoner gangs worked for counties; the rest were leased to private contractors.

After Harry Jamison, a black, was sentenced to the chain gang without a trial in a Macon recorder's court for allegedly violating a city ordinance, Judge Emory Speer ruled in 1904 that such courts lacked the power to do this. Speer's decision released Jamison, and the Georgia Supreme Court made a similar ruling in 1906. A 1908 law forbade leasing misdemeanor convicts, and throughout Georgia, persons convicted of misdemeanors were then sent to city and county work camps, where, in chain gangs, they led lives often little better than those in a lease camp.

Populist and Progressive pressures, earnestly supported by blacks, finally brought an end to the convict-lease system. When the legislature failed to abolish it in 1907, Governor Hoke Smith called a special session for 1908 that did. Smith was aided by ministers, labor unions, newspapers, the Prison Reform Association, blacks, the Farmers Alliance, Greenbackers, the Southern Sociological Congress, other progressive groups, and public opinion aroused by a series of mass meetings that detailed the system's atrocities.

The convict-lease system's demise did not improve prisoners' lives much. The public-road chain-gang crews that replaced convict leasing, while not quite as barbarous, were still terribly inhumane. The only real change put prisoners under the control of guards on the state payroll. Blacks were still rounded up and convicted not for crimes but to fill the labor needs of private and public employers.

The black prisoner in chains became a more obvious part of the Georgia scene after 1908 as more convicts were put on public works in plain view rather than hidden away in private work camps. When the American

Road Congress met in Atlanta in 1914, delegates were called out of the auditorium to view a parade of seven hundred chain-gang Fulton County convicts marching by to dramatically underscore the state's explanation of its ability to get so much road work done at so little cost to taxpayers.

Lynching in the New South

After the Ku Klux Klan won its battle to maintain white supremacy, the lynch mob of the New South assumed a major role in maintaining blacks as a caste of peasants and serfs. Between 1889 and 1918, Georgia had more lynchings than any other state, and 94 percent of the victims were black. By no coincidence, Georgia had the South's lowest cotton-field wages during this time. The post-Reconstruction reign of terror was nearly totally demoralizing. With good reason, blacks saw lynching as the worst form of their oppression. Henry McNeal Turner summed it up cogently: "Until we are free from menace by lynchings ... we are destined to be a dwarfed people." Lynching was significant not only for what it did to the victims and their immediate families, but for the damage it did to the entire culture, for it poisoned the shallow well of good feeling between blacks and whites.

While blacks were occasionally killed during slavery by being burned alive, this practice did not become common until after the Civil War. At least three blacks were lynched in 1866: two in Polk County and Pompey O. Barrow, accused of killing a white woman, in Jonesboro. He was burned at the stake, and his body was fed to dogs. Just how many blacks were murdered and lynched in Georgia from 1865 to 1875 will remain a mystery. Most mob murders then were well known locally but were not widely publicized; no records were kept.

After 1875, the record became clearer as press coverage improved. In 1876 a gang of six whites set out to capture Amos Bines when he was suspected of shooting a white woman in Effingham County. The mob killed Monday Roberts while looking for Bines. When Bines was captured, he was murdered in the jail, and a third black was killed in the neighborhood a week later for not answering when called. In 1880, a white who had been tried and fined for having whipped a member of a black family led a Georgia mob that murdered the entire family in retaliation. Jerry Hamilton was lynched in 1883 near Savannah. Leaders of that mob were indicted and brought before the U. S. Circuit Court in Savannah, but the indictment was dismissed and the case returned to the state courts, where nothing happened. This case was a particular blow to blacks who had hoped for federal protection under the 1875 Sumner Civil Rights Act.

Lynchings increased after 1882, and as the collective position of blacks grew weaker, white mobs grew more ruthlessly aggressive. The *Atlanta Constitution* reported four lynchings of blacks in Georgia in the six weeks preceding August 26, 1884. In 1888, Allen Sturgis was accused of rape and lynched in McDuffie County, and Henry Pope was lynched on the same allegation in Chattooga County even though five whites testified he was not in the county at the time. Such incidents led a black writer to conclude that Southern whites were "usually suspicious of everything except a hysterical woman."

In 1919, the National Association for the Advancement of Colored People (NAACP) found that of 3,224 recorded lynchings in the past thirty years, 405 occurred in Georgia, more than any other state. Of these, 379—or 94 percent—were black, including five women. Walter White, Georgia-born chief NAACP lynching investigator, unearthed 549 lynchings in Georgia in the 1882-1927 period, and 93 percent of the victims were black. However, black sociologist Allison Davis thought less than half were reported, and many who lived through the worst times of lynching agree. Sometimes the lynch mob would try to disguise its work to make it appear that the victim had died from other causes. One way was to place the body on a railroad track and let it be mangled by a train.

The New South myth that black men constantly raped white women and therefore justified lynching for purposes of punishment and prevention was supported by a massive press campaign. Although many Southern whites went to their graves thinking (or at least saying) that the only reason for lynching was rape, the NAACP found that rape was not even alleged in 71 percent of the cases. Sometimes white men blackened their faces to commit rape and then framed black men. Other reasons reported for lynchings in Georgia included murder and attempted murder, arson and incendiarism, rioting, theft and burglary, turning state's evidence and informing, insulting whites or disputing their word, resisting arrest, living with a white woman, being lazy, enticing a servant away, illicit distilling, using inflammatory language, resisting arrest, window peeping, and throwing stones. Sometimes merely "race prejudice" and "unpopularity" were reported in white newspapers as the reasons for brutally taking black lives.

One motive for some lynchings was to force blacks to give up jobs or land that whites coveted. William A. Pledger testified before a 1902 congressional committee, "Men have been lynched simply that their crops might revert to the landlord." Some blacks were lynched for trying to claim the pay that was due them, protesting low wages, or not observing the etiquette of deference that white supremacy demanded.

The rape myth held that blacks never raped white women during slavery and that even during the Civil War, when many of the white men were away and opportunity was greatest, the slaves, in the words of Booker T. Washington, had with "fidelity and love" protected the planters' families. Spokesmen for the New South claimed that Reconstruction made blacks forget their place and engage in a "frenzy of rapine." Actually, during slavery the white rape of black women was far more common than black rape of white women.

Occasionally, whites would touch closer to the real reasons for lynching. Governors Allen Candler and William Northen suggested in the 1890s that lynching was related to black voting. Black sociologist Oliver Cromwell Cox noted, "Disfranchisement makes lynching possible and lynching speedily squelches any movement among Southern Negroes for enfranchisement." The NAACP's White said, "Lynching has always been a means for protection not of white women, but of profits."

Another frequent justification for lynching involved the "law's delay"— the argument that trials were long and costly and often a guilty rapist was acquitted or given a light sentence. In reality, the trials of accused blacks were swift and usually resulted in convictions. Furthermore, rape had carried the death penalty in Georgia since the early 1800s. Seldom was the defendant presumed innocent until proven guilty; rarely was a black on the jury. Courts tended to follow the adage: "Give him a fair trial and then hang him."

Murder, not rape, was the most common offense that resulted in a lynching. Often the murder victim was a white law officer killed when trying to arrest a black who knew torture and lynching could follow his arrest—or he could receive a convict-lease sentence that was tantamount to a slow, agonizing death. Ironically, the frequency with which arrested blacks were denied due process of law and turned over to lynch mobs tended to make blacks resist arrest and even kill lawmen.

Georgia's peak year of lynching was in 1899, when twenty-seven persons, all blacks, were lynched. Though only 14 percent of the nation's blacks lived in the state then, 31 percent of the blacks lynched that year died in Georgia. The state was the scene of a number of sensational cases that attracted national publicity.

In March 1899, the case of the Palmetto Five erupted. In late January, there was a serious fire in the Palmetto business district in what is now south Fulton County; losses were uninsured. Four days later, a second fire burned out twelve property holders, and fears of black insurrection created a climate of hysteria. In March, eight blacks were jailed on the uncorroborated evidence of a white who said he crawled under a black home and heard blacks discuss the fires. On March 16, a masked mob of fifteen broke into the jail after brushing aside six guards who offered no resistance. The mob killed five black prisoners and wounded two. Gov. Allen Candler ordered out the militia and offered a $500 reward, the legal maximum, but no information was forthcoming, and no arrests were made. National black protests to President McKinley were futile. The federal government continued until the 1960s to maintain a hands-off attitude and to hold that lynching was a state matter.

On April 23, Sam Hose was the victim of one of the most publicized lynchings in U. S. history. His death was surrounded by wildly false charges of rape, and the publicity nourished the myth that lynching was a just punishment. Governor Candler described the crime as "too horrible for publication.... the most diabolical in the annals of crime." Georgia congressman James M. Griggs described Hose's crime on the floor of the House of Representatives in lurid terms. While the Cranford family was peacefully seated for supper,

> a monster in human form, an employee on the farm, crept into that happy little home and with an ax knocked out the brains of that father, snatched the child from its mother, threw it across the room out of his way, and then by force accomplished his foul purpose. More than that, Mr. Chairman, he was afflicted with the most loathsome disease known to human kind.

After a two-week search, Hose was found in his mother's cabin near Marshallville and was placed in the Newnan jail, about thirty-five miles southwest of Atlanta. When the mob came to get Hose, the sheriff surrendered the keys to the jail. The mob took Hose out of town and tied him to a tree. The impending lynching was publicized in the newspapers, and when the story spread that a special train had left Atlanta at 1:00 P.M., the mob assumed it was bringing the militia and advanced the time to start torturing Hose for fear that they might have to kill him quickly if they delayed until the militia appeared. There *was* a train on its way from Atlanta. It carried not militia but sightseers who had struggled to obtain tickets for the special excursion to Newnan to see "the show." The *Atlanta Journal* covered the lynching as though it were a festival.

The mob went about its work. First, Hose was stripped of his clothes, and then the torture began. His ears were cut off, then his fingers, and finally his genitals. He was then doused with oil and set afire. Desperate in his agony, Hose almost slipped his bonds, so the fire was quenched, he was retied to the tree, and after more oil was poured on him and lit, he finally died. Then the sightseers showed up: "But for the fact that the program was changed... fully five thousand people would have seen the burning near the Cranford home and of these nearly half were from Atlanta," complained one reporter. Parts of the body were taken as souvenirs, and pieces of bone sold for twenty-five cents. His heart and liver were also cut up and the pieces passed out to the mob or sold as souvenirs. The disappointed Atlantans did get to the scene before the ashes were cool and managed to pick up or buy some of the grisly tokens. The mob left, but the blood lust was not yet satisfied.

Unfortunately, thinking that a response to the mob's demands for a confession would shorten his agony, Hose blurted out that Elijah Strickland, a black minister, had given him twenty dollars to kill Cranford. Later that day Strickland was taken from his cabin on the plantation of ex-state senator W. W. Thomas near Newnan. Thomas hurried after the mob and in a dramatic confrontation pleaded to let Strickland stand trial. Thomas said that it was unlikely that Strickland could have given Hose twenty dollars, since Strickland never had that much at any time. The mob paid no attention and went ahead with their plans, which included torture. Strickland's fingers were cut off before he was hanged. Twice he was drawn up in the air by the rope and twice let down as a means of trying to extract a confession. Strickland maintained his innocence and was drawn up a third time and left to strangle slowly.

W. E. B. Du Bois, then teaching at Atlanta University, was on his way to see Joel Chandler Harris of the *Atlanta Constitution* concerning the case when he learned that Hose had been lynched. On his way to see Harris, Du Bois passed by a grocery store that already had a knuckle bone of Hose displayed in a jar. Deeply upset, Du Bois returned to the campus without meeting Harris. This lynching helped draw Du Bois away from his academic detachment and toward greater involvement in the civil rights struggle. Up to then Du Bois was committed to the idea that blacks were mistreated by a minority of whites and if the majority realized what was actually going on, conditions for blacks would improve. The Hose case convinced him that lynching and other brutality toward blacks in Georgia would not be stopped simply by exposing their details, because the oppression was part of a white conspiracy to retain, as fully as possible, the subordination of blacks. The *Constitution* had offered a $500 reward for Hose's capture. After the Hose lynching, the newspaper proudly proclaimed, "The *Constitution* never issued a check with greater pleasure."

Reverdy C. Ransom, a militant black activist, financed an investigation of the Hose lynching from his base as an A.M.E. minister in Chicago. He hired a white detective who went to Georgia and obtained a statement from Mrs. Cranford. She said Hose had come to the Cranford house for pay due him and had quarreled with her husband, who ran into the house to get his revolver. Just as Cranford was about to shoot him, Hose picked up an ax and threw it at Cranford, killing him instantly. Hose then fled. Mrs. Cranford attested that Hose had not entered the house or assaulted her. Ida B. Wells, then the leader of the antilynching movement, also investigated the incident and confirmed Ransom's version. The results of these investigations did not appear in the white press. If they had, they probably would have caused the lynchings of suspected black informants.

Black editors often suffered when they challenged that part of the rape myth that held that no white woman would have sexual relations voluntarily with a black man. Francis Grimké, distinguished black Presbyterian minister and one of the leading intellectuals of his day, wrote of a Southern white woman, "one of the bluest of the blue blood," he spoke with in 1898. She said she knew of several cases where a white woman with a black lover cried "rape" when the affair was discovered and sacrificed her paramour on the altar of her reputation. John Hope documented the case of John Will Clark, a Cartersville, Georgia, black. He was taken out of the bed he shared with his common-law white wife and lynched. This relationship was not unique; Ida B. Wells detailed fourteen cases of white women with black lovers in 1892.

When black editors wrote on this subject, some were lynched themselves, or they were driven out of town, and their presses were destroyed. This is what led to the 1892 destruction of Ida B. Wells's newspaper in Memphis. In 1886, the editors of the *Atlanta Defiance* were jailed and fined for criticism of white violence. In 1900, William J. White, editor of the *Georgia Baptist*, was forced to repudiate and apologize for an article critical of lynching.

Another major myth held that only poor whites supported lynching. The Associated Press dispatches covering lynchings were written by Southern white reporters, and they often ended thusly: "The best people deplore this sad affair." Yet lynching, the ultimate bulwark of the caste society, was defended by all who benefited from that society. Perhaps the "best people" were not in all the mobs, though they certainly were in many. Even if they were not, as jurors they uniformly refused to convict known mob leaders, and they "explained" to the nation that lynching could not be prevented because it was the righteous reaction to an unspeakable crime. They fought tooth and nail against any effective antilynching legislation. Du Bois stated, "Whenever an aristocracy allows the mob to rule the fault is not with the mob." Most white Georgians justified lynching even when they knew the real reasons behind the mob murders.

In Georgia, as lynching increased in the 1890s to an average of more than fifteen per year, an increasing effort by propagandists of the New South was required to minimize its implications. The dual but contradictory ideas that blacks were content, yet were inhuman, vengeance-wreaking brutes that only white Southerners knew how to handle was successfully promoted into general national acceptance by 1889. In the

1890s, few white Georgians condemned the barbarity of lynching publicly.

At the same time lynchings became more frequent, they became more savage as more and more blacks were burned alive after being tortured before the fire was lit. The threat of lynching for trivial reasons was also part of the overall campaign of terror and intimidation. Between 1891 and 1904 there were several stories in the *Atlanta Constitution* regarding lynching threats against blacks who were involved in bicycle and automobile accidents. No doubt countless similar incidents went unrecorded.

Some joked about lynching. "Mr. Dooley" (Peter Finley Dunn), a well-known humorist, wrote: "The black has many fine qualities. He is joyous, light-hearted, an' aisily lynched." One of these "easy" lynchings occurred in 1901 in Rome, Georgia. George Reed, charged with rape, was ordered released by the judge for lack of evidence and the inability of the rape victim to identify him. The mob learned of the impending release, took him from jail, and lynched him.

"The Statesboro tragedies" were among the nation's most highly publicized lynchings. In 1904, Paul Reed and Will Cato were tried and convicted of the murder of the white Hodge family in Statesboro. The two were sentenced to hang on September 9, and though "protected" by a 125-man militia unit, they were seized by a mob that knew that the militia's guns were not loaded. Reed and Cato were brutally tortured before being burned alive. There followed a reign of terror, with nightriding and whippings, throughout the county for several weeks. Three blacks were shot for "making remarks" about the lynching, Albert Roger and his son were lynched the next day, and blacks were whipped for no other offense than their color. One of the nightriders' victims was Sebastian McBride of Portal, who was killed trying to prevent the whipping of his wife, who had given birth just three days before. The mindless rage against all blacks was carried on in ignorance of the fact that blacks had apprehended Reed and Cato in the first place. There were at least ten other Georgia lynchings in 1904, including the lynching of John Ware, who was charged with murder and lynched in Franklin County on September 18. The next year, eight blacks accused of murder were lynched on June 29 at Watkinsville.

Between 1908 and 1914, an average of twelve blacks were lynched in Georgia each year. Occasionally, the lynchings were accompanied by the mob destruction of black property. This happened in 1911 at Ellaville in Schley County when a black killed the town marshal. The mob lynched three blacks, then burned the buildings of three black lodges, two churches, and a school. Two women were among the thirteen Georgia blacks lynched in 1912, a year when more than a quarter of all U.S.

lynchings occurred in the state. In another interesting 1912 case, Henry Etheridge was lynched near Jackson in Butts County for trying to recruit blacks to go to Africa. This was in an area of low pay for blacks, even for Georgia, and the white farmers objected to the possibility of losing their cheap black labor.

In 1913 seven blacks were lynched in Georgia, according to a 1919 NAACP study. In Americus, William Redding was accused of firing a shot that missed the police chief when the lawman was attempting to arrest him. Redding was taken from the jail and strung up. As often happened, the body was riddled with bullets. Some accounts say that thousands of shots were fired into the corpse. In this incident, four other blacks who were in the crowd were wounded by stray bullets. Blacks were often on the fringes of lynch mobs to gauge the possibility of the lynching turning into a pogrom against the entire black community. If it did, someone had to carry the warning so that plans to fight or flee could be made. There was also a slim hope that, by identifying mob members, they might be brought to justice. It took special courage combined with righteous anger to take up these lookout positions. Two months after Redding was lynched, Virgil Swanson was lynched in Meriwether County for the murder of a planter. A few days later, another black, Walter Brewster, confessed that he had killed the planter in a rent dispute, but the blood lust of the white community was apparently slaked, and he was not lynched.

There were at least three lynchings in Georgia in 1914: that of Nathan Brown for murder; Charley Jones was lynched in Grovetown on May 6 while under suspicion of shoplifting a pair of shoes; and a Hawkinsville black was lynched for the murder of a white man. Later, the murdered man's nephew confessed to the crime.

However brutal, lynching never completely intimidated blacks. Opposition to it often took the form of organized political pressure to influence the federal and state governments. Henry McNeal Turner, Jefferson Long, and James M. Simms were among the black leaders in 1876 who called for the prosecution of lynchers. Many Georgia blacks wrote or visited presidents to urge resistance to mobs. In addition to his involvement with the Afro-American League and its antilynching efforts, William Pledger once led armed blacks to the Athens jail and successfully defied a mob bent on lynching two prisoners.

As in South Carolina, the Klanmen in Georgia came to realize that blacks could retaliate against them in the coastal counties with black majorities and traditions of black political power; consequently, there were fewer lynchings on the coast than elsewhere in Georgia. In 1899, Governor Candler had to send the militia to quell a "riot" in McIntosh

County in which one white and several blacks were killed. Some blacks were flogged there later for "incendiary speeches." The trouble occurred in Darien, where Henry Delegale was arrested on a rape charge and the sheriff said he was going to remove him to Savannah for safekeeping. Local blacks did not believe he would do this and armed themselves to guard the jail. One white and several blacks were killed in a confrontation with the mob that came to lynch Delegale. Governor Candler sent the militia and praised the black leaders for their cooperation. Then fifty-nine of the black "rioters" were arrested; some were released and others were tried and convicted. Delegale's son, John, was convicted of killing a white deputy and was sentenced to life as a leased convict. Delegale was tried and acquitted on the original rape charge, made when a white woman gave birth to a mulatto child. Accusing Delegale of rape was the best way she could avoid social ostracism.

The *Indianapolis Freeman* cited the 1890 case of Nelson Jones, who twice fought off a Georgia mob and survived his wounds. "If we had more men of the Nelson Jones stamp, we would be better off," the editor concluded. To resist a mob or not was always a dilemma. While the question was academic for the victim, made prisoner by overwhelming force, the desirability of resistance by the black community as a whole was debated frequently. Many black leaders counseled greater militancy, and there were many calls for retaliation.

Right after the brutal lynching of Reed and Cato at Statesboro in 1904, rumors abounded in Georgia about the organizations of "Before-Day Clubs," black organizations pledged to execute lynchers before the next day following a lynching. Such clubs did not exist, however. The stories probably represented a combination of black fantasy and white paranoia.

Atlanta's role as a center for black-led protest against lynching was reinforced in 1904 by the establishment of a significant journal of culture and politics, the *Voice of the Negro*. Its editor, J. Max Barber, was one of the militants who joined Du Bois in the Niagara Movement when it was founded in 1905. The Statesboro rampages radicalized Barber; the *Voice* devoted considerable space to lynching and the problem was discussed, referred to, or mentioned in at least 25 percent of all the pages in its first year. Barber was driven from Atlanta because he protested the false rape stories that helped set off the 1906 Atlanta riot.

Although they seldom did so, local officials could request troops to guard prisoners and trials. In 1900, 150 soldiers were used to escort Sam Robinson, convicted of rape, to the gallows to prevent his being lynched en route. Some impending lynchings in Georgia were avoided by the timely actions of courageous white sheriffs who were willing to risk losing their next election. Sheriff Miller of Ware County prevented a lynching in 1891 by moving two black prisoners to a safe location. In

1897, when a mob tried to lynch a white and a black in Jonesboro, the sheriff summoned guards and saved the prisoners by removing them to Atlanta. Later that year, the jailer at Augusta successfully resisted the attempt of a mob to take one of his prisoners. In 1901 Sheriff J. L. Merrill of Carroll County killed one person and wounded several when preventing a mob from lynching Ike Williams. These incidents are notable mainly as exceptions, for in Georgia's 152 pre-World War I counties, seldom would a sheriff or jailer resist a mob.

Paradoxically, it was always popular among white politicians to denounce crimes against blacks, and there was some antilynching activity by Georgia officials beginning with the extension of the franchise to blacks in 1867. Republicans, Independents, Populists, and Democrats all inveighed against lynching but did little but talk. When Governor Northen pushed an antilynching bill through the legislature in 1893, Georgia was one of only two states to have such a law on the books. It authorized sheriffs to deputize persons to protect prisoners and made failure to do so a misdemeanor. This law accomplished little or nothing, however.

All governors were protective of their state's image, and Georgia's image was tarnished more by lynching than any other state's. The British Anti-Lynching Committee sent a petition to Gov. William Y. Atkinson in 1896 condemning Georgia. Atkinson asked the legislature to consider the matter and informed lawmakers that he believed some mob victims were innocent of the crimes of which they had been charged. "To adopt lynch-law," he said, "is to put the life of every man in the power of any woman who for any reason might desire his death." Various governors from time to time dispatched the militia to stop lynchings, as Governor Candler did in eight different counties in 1899. Sometimes they also offered rewards for the conviction of lynchers, but no rewards were collected. A 1911 Georgia statute required judges to order a change in venue for trials where there was a threat of mob violence. Gov. John M. Slaton invoked the statute in 1913 to prevent a triple lynching in Louisville by having a trial moved to Fulton County.

The Southern white press was of little help, for it was reluctant to recognize that most lynchings were for crimes other than rape. Despite its frequent failures, the *Atlanta Constitution* was probably the most fair. Yet in 1890, a story concerning a white shot by a black burglar carried the headline *"Lynching Probable,"* with nothing in the article to suggest it would be wrong. The *Constitution* opened its pages to a debate on the subject in 1903 when Methodist Bishop Warren A. Candler wrote that 75 percent of all lynchings were not linked to rape in an article entitled *"Must Put Down the Mob or Be Put Down by It."* This article drew many responses from whites and blacks. Black religious leaders, professionals and educators, including Du Bois and other faculty of Atlanta University, hailed Candler as a "noble champion." By the end of the year the discussion had run its course, with no real change.

Removing "Undesirables" Through Whitecapping

Property and landownership were a major cause of friction between the races. In addition to the extralegal executions of individual blacks by mobs bent on maintaining white supremacy, blacks had to contend also with whitecapping—the use of terror, intimidation, and violence to kill or drive away from the community persons deemed undesirable. Whitecapping was one more reason blacks did not own their own land in Georgia. While lynching was intended to keep blacks "in their place," whitecapping was used more to drive blacks out of the area than to ensure the docility of those who remained. It was used primarily to remove blacks as competitors of poorer whites.

Blacks who did not accept second-class citizenship and aspired to improve their status were frequently victims of the whitecappers, armed terrorists who rode in the Ku Klux Klan tradition. These gangs of marauders were often small white farmers who did not want blacks to become landowners and thereby pull themselves out of the cheap black labor pool from which whites hired during the rush seasons. A black tenant or sharecropper might be available for occasional employment, but the black who had sacrificed to own his own land would more likely stay at home and improve his own place. Moreover, when blacks bought land, such purchases would tend to drive up the price of the remaining land and make it more difficult for whites to become landowners. Planters often preferred the more exploitable black tenants to white ones, and this was another source of friction as landless whites, dependent on seasonal employment, resented the preference for black labor.

The very first issue of John H. Deveaux's *Savannah Tribune* noted that white brutality was driving blacks out of Brooks County in 1875. In 1876, white mobs virtually stopped land acquisition by blacks in Georgia. In 1883, thirty masked whites killed Bill Jackson in Walton County because he was "infecting" other blacks with ideas of independence. Such occurrences became widespread in Georgia.

There was an upsurge of whitecapping in 1889, when hundreds of blacks in Fulton County were terrorized by gangs. The governor offered a reward, and a Fulton County grand jury did indict six whites, including a reporter, a policeman, two merchants, and a ticket agent. Whitecappers were active around Macon at this time, and a boy preacher was taken into the woods and whipped. Later that same year, near Mountain Hill in Harris County, Regulators terrorized the "best and most intelligent" blacks by chalking the outlines of coffins on their doors and then shooting into their houses. This time, the governor offered a $1,000 reward for information in the case, to no avail. There were several reports of whitecappers attacking black tenants and landowners near Fort Valley in 1893. Blacks fought back and killed one. Whitecappers were active in Pike, Fayette, and Floyd counties around the turn of the century.

In the spring of 1889 a white mob stoned the homes of blacks in Lyerly in Chattooga County in an effort to rid the community of all blacks. W. J. Johnson, a black in Walker County, wrote Gov. John B. Gordon that year about the whippings of three blacks, the burning of a black home, and the threat to shoot another unless he left the county within twenty-four hours. The governor futilely offered a $250 reward. That same year, when whitecappers tried to force blacks to leave Griffin, they flogged Dan Franklin almost to death and gave him twenty-four hours to leave town. Meanwhile, mobs in Decatur, Early, and Miller counties in Southwest Georgia, after forcing blacks to surrender their arms, whipped men, women, and children.

In 1901, something remarkable happened. When whitecappers murdered Sterling Thompson, a Fairburn black, an Atlanta jury sentenced two of them to life imprisonment. In 1904, when whitecappers terrorized Lincoln and Franklin counties, so many blacks left the area that despite offers of high wages, the area was short of agricultural labor. This response to brutality was to become a powerful brake on such activities during World War I, when whole counties were sometimes stripped of black labor due to migration to the North in the wake of atrocities. In 1907, whitecapping in Banks and Habersham counties forced Frank Grant, Henry Scism, and Marshall Davenport to leave. Whites appealed to Governor Terrell, who offered rewards—which went uncollected, as usual. Turner County in South Georgia was a center of such activity in 1911.

In 1912, a Dawsonville mob burned a black church and drove off some tenants. That year, nearby Forsyth County witnessed what was probably the worst outbreak of whitecapping in the century. When Edward Roberts was lynched for rape and two others hanged for complicity after trials in Cumming, the county seat, it triggered whitecapping attacks on blacks throughout the county. Nightriders told them all to leave. Storekeepers would not sell to them, and by October 11 all were gone. In this successful effort to drive all 1,150 blacks from Forsyth County, some $90,000 worth of property belonging to whites who employed blacks was put to the torch. The blacks, having to leave suddenly, were forced to sell their property at no more than 25 percent of its value.

There was concern over similar events coming to pass in Oconee and Oglethorpe counties near Athens, and whitecapping continued the following year in counties north of Atlanta. In January 1913, all the white farmers near Marietta received mailed notices to dismiss their black tenants. A store selling to blacks was burned, and the Kennesaw Marble Company was told to discharge all black employees. Signs were posted reading "Hurry up niggers and leve this town if you don't leve you will wish you hadder got out." Shortly thereafter, the homes of three black families were dynamited. A month later, the killing of several blacks in Jackson County was linked to whitecapping. A white Georgian complained that if the whitecapping was not stopped, "Our wives will have to do their own cooking and washing."

5

The New South and Further Degradations

Failed Attempts at Reform: The Alliance and Populist Movements

Although the struggle for political supremacy in Georgia was decided by 1870, blacks did not meekly surrender. They continued to fight rear-guard skirmishes that had some influence on how the state developed. Blacks continued to elect a few representatives to the state legislature and to positions in local government, most notably on the coast.

No sooner was the Independent threat to Bourbon control eliminated than a new agrarian challenge cropped up. For a while, at least, this movement seemed to encourage black political participation in exchange for beneficial programs. A deep undercurrent of agricultural unrest swelled after 1870 and reached tidal-wave proportions in the 1890s as both black and white farmers suffered from increasing costs for the goods they purchased and declining prices for the goods they sold. Farmers rightly believed they were the victims of profit-hungry financial and business interests, and they tried to organize to redress their grievances. Southern farmers especially resented the protective tariff. They sold their goods on the open world market but had to buy the goods they needed at inflated prices due to tariffs that sheltered domestic industry from world competition.

Farmers developed several organizations to cope with their problems. The Patrons of Husbandry, better known as the Grange, was organized in the North after the Civil War and moved into Georgia in 1872, where it encouraged railroad rate regulation and cooperative buying and cotton marketing. The National Grange did not exclude blacks but left their admission to local branches. As a result, a segregated but parallel organization of black farmers, the Council of Laborers, was organized, with two white advisers for each local. By 1875, there were twenty-five thousand Grangers in Georgia, including some blacks who saw the Grange as an alternative to the business-minded Republican party. By then, farmers were ready for a more radically militant organization. Farmers organized several groups in Texas that emerged as the Farmers' Alliance in 1884. The first Alliance organized in Georgia was in Troup County in 1887, and a statewide Alliance of white farmers was organized in Fort Valley in February 1888.

By February 1889, a Colored Farmers' Alliance with eight chapters was formed in Screven County by local black minister J. W. Carter. Although it was segregated, the fact that some white Alliances were able to cut the farm supply markups from 50 percent down to 25 percent helped make the Alliance Movement attractive to blacks. A statewide organization of the black Alliances was organized at Macon by R. M. Humphrey, a white Baptist minister, in July 1889. By then there were 240 local chapters in thirty-nine counties. Edward S. Richardson, a prominent Marshallville black, was elected state president. By December 1890, there were eighty-four thousand members of the Georgia Colored Farmers' Alliance, many of whom were women. Black Alliance members were welcome at white Alliance camp meetings.

The two groups worked together denouncing monopolies and successfully attacked the jute bag trust with a boycott and a switch to cotton bagging that forced the trust to cut prices drastically in 1889. They supported the "Sub-treasury Plan," which would have helped all farmers who were free of the crop-lien system. Under this plan, instead of selling crops at harvest time, when prices were lowest, the farmer would put his crop into government-supervised storage and receive a loan equivalent to 80 percent of the crop's value. The immediate worth of such a program was readily apparent: Cotton was seven cents a pound in autumn 1889 but over eleven cents six months later. (Such a program was actually put into practice during the New Deal in the 1930s.)

The Georgia Colored Farmers' Alliance sent several delegates to the national Alliance's meeting in December 1889 in St. Louis. They were received as comrades and heard much talk of brotherhood. At the next national meeting in Ocala, Florida, in December 1890, the Southern white Alliance and the black Alliance met separately. Members of the black Alliance and some representatives of the Knights of Labor addressed the white group.

In an early manifestation of the Alliance spirit, Sandersville blacks in Washington County put up $1,000 for a cooperative grocery, and the Rev.

E. K. Love of Savannah urged the development of cooperatives at a Macon convention of black Baptists. Black Alliance units in Georgia bought and sold through a central exchange and warehouse established at Mobile, Alabama. It was financed by a two-dollar-per-capita contribution of the members.

Some of the twelve cooperative general stores that the Alliance had in Georgia in 1889 were established by blacks. In September 1889, three hundred members of the Colored Farmers' Alliance at Eatonton opened a general store; it did so well it was robbed of $400 four months later. Georgia's black Alliance continued to grow; in 1891, it had an estimated ninety thousand members in all counties except Banks. Humphrey reported a membership of 1.2 million nationally, of which 300,000 were women.

The cooperative store movement was a declaration of independence and a threat to white supremacy. Consequently, it was a source of potential racial trouble. The fundamental conflict of interests between black and white farmers surfaced at the December 1889 meeting of the white Alliance in Screven County. The white Alliance maintained that blacks must continue as sharecroppers. Some blacks threatened to leave before submitting to such exploitation.

Farmers began to measure legislators by their promise to uphold Alliance principles, known as the "Alliance Yardstick." In July 1890, Georgia's white Alliance defeated six incumbent congressmen in the primary election. In the October general election, more than three-fourths of the successful state legislative candidates had Alliance backing, as did Democratic Gov. William J. Northen. Two blacks, Lectured Crawford of McIntosh County and J. M. Holzendorf of Camden County, were also elected. Crawford, an old adversary of Tunis Campbell's, was one of five legislators who voted against Alliance principles. His vote, not calculated to strengthen the much-needed black-white unity on economic issues, was probably a grievous error, as was the Georgia black Alliance's decision to sit out the political campaign that year.

Just as they differed on the issue of black economic rights, white and black Alliance members disagreed on black political rights. The "Farmers' Legislature" of 1891–92 implemented part of the Alliance program, but it disappointed many of its rural constituents when it elected Bourbon John B. Gordon, who opposed many Alliance programs, to the U. S. Senate. It also passed a long list of antiblack measures, including Jim Crow car laws requiring segregation on railroads. Instead of ending the convict-lease system, it increased the number of leased convicts and restored whipping as a punishment. It authorized county and city governments to hire whipping bosses for convict gangs and relieved them of liability for any injuries they might inflict. It strengthened lien laws that bound tenants and sharecroppers to their landlords. Adding to the injury, the legislators (of whom over two-thirds were Confederate veterans) promoted segregation by overturning the Reconstruction public accommodations law. Georgia's black Alliance, then meeting in Atlanta, sent a delegation to the legislature to protest, to no avail.

The sharpest difference of interests between black and white Alliances surfaced in the 1891 cotton-picking strike. White farmers who depended on hired black labor to get their cotton picked did not want anything to delay the harvest or increase its cost. When national Colored Farmers' Alliance leaders called for a general cotton-picking strike throughout the South to start on September 20, 1891, white Alliance members were furious. Richardson, president of the Georgia black Alliance, disapproved of the strike, as did J. W. Carter, the Alliance's state lecturer. When their nonmilitant advice was followed, the strike failed to materialize in Georgia. The black Alliance, having little practical help to offer members, lost rank-and-file support and began a rapid decline. It collapsed almost completely by 1893. Only seventy-five members came to Dublin for the 1894 meeting.

While the Alliance Movement was strong, it was unable to improve the status of Georgia's poor because it failed to unite blacks and whites to produce economic changes that would benefit both groups. Due to its members' racism, the white Alliance ended up with little to offer blacks. Many blacks could not overcome the belief that the poor white, the Alliance's backbone, was their worst enemy. For many, the exchange of good and faithful service for the protection of a "boss man" was often considered vital for survival. Blacks knew Bourbons opposed the Alliance, and the way to please the "boss man" was to refute the Alliance.

Although white racism and black suspicions were too strong to overcome Alliance divisions, for a while it seemed that a new national political party might achieve the necessary unity. The People's party, commonly known as the Populist party, sprang from the Alliance when many of its members bolted from the business-dominated Democratic party. Populists in Georgia followed Thomas Edward Watson, one of the most controversial figures in Georgia's history.

As an attorney representing the Alliance in its successful fight against the jute-bag trust, Watson emerged as a popular hero with great sympathy for poor farmers, both black and white. In a December 1889 speech at Stellaville, he said blacks were freed in 1865; subsequently, however, both black and white farmers were enslaved. In 1890 he won a seat in Congress from the Tenth District.

In 1891, Watson joined the Populist Movement and took a daring political step. He decided that if the Populists were to get anywhere at the polls they would have to break the color bar and woo black voters as well as whites. He denounced the convict-lease system and declared that Populists would "make lynch-law odious to the people." Watson's strategy was to replace race hatred, political repression, lynching, and terrorism with tolerance, cooperation, justice, and political rights for blacks. Quite naturally, blacks were attracted to the Populists.

As early as 1880, when he ran for a state legislative seat, Watson had called for a revolt against entrenched financial interests even if it meant splitting "the white man's party." While running for Congress in the 1892 campaign, Watson encouraged interracial meetings and had whites hold up their hands to pledge to defend black rights. He told blacks and whites:

> You are kept apart that you may be separately fleeced of your earnings. You are made to hate each other because upon that hatred is rested the keystone of the arch of financial despotism that enslaves you both. You are deceived and blinded that you may not see how this race antagonism perpetuates a monetary system which beggars both.

At Populist political picnics, blacks and whites ate together. When the new party nominated William L. Peek to run for governor, a black man, John Mack, was on the committee to notify him. To their credit, Populists demanded a secret ballot, which theoretically would help protect black voters from intimidation. Populists in this campaign took a strong position against lynching and the convict-lease system. The black delegate who introduced a resolution favoring honest elections was supported by a huge majority. These radical moves engendered intense opposition from the ruling Democrats.

When H. S. Doyle, a young black preacher whom Watson had hired to make speeches on his behalf, was threatened with lynching, he came to Watson's McDuffie County home for protection one evening. Watson's followers heard there was trouble afoot, and the next morning there was a crowd of hundreds of armed white farmers (some estimates reach as high as two thousand) at his doorstep to see that no one would be harmed. Blacks then regarded Watson nearly as a savior, according to Doyle. Despite these progressive moves, all was not harmonious between blacks and Populists. When Doyle, who had made sixty-three speeches for Watson in the 1892 campaign, came to Watson for protection, he was not invited into Watson's home but had to sleep in a shed in the rear. It turned out that the farmers who had rushed to Watson's home to prevent a threatened lynching did so because they believed *Watson* was endangered. A week before this incident, Doyle was almost killed by a white in Sparta, but no one came to his rescue then.

Watson only spoke against the political color line, never the social barrier, and voted against funds for black education before 1892. Many Populist leaders had, as Alliance men, voted for segregation and voting restrictions in the 1891–92 legislature. When black Liberty County legislator William H. Styles tried to repeal the railroad Jim Crow law in 1892, his bill was referred to a committee with five Populists on it. They all voted against his proposal, as did the Democrats. Populists organized segregated clubs for blacks in Bibb, Wilkes, and Houston counties. At some Populist meetings, whites sat on one side of a central aisle, and blacks sat on the other. Moreover, Populists, like Democrats, sometimes practiced violence and intimidation against blacks.

Some blacks supported Democrats in 1892 out of a sincere conviction that they would do more for blacks in the long run than another party would. William Pledger favored Populist candidates for the legislature while supporting William J. Northen, the Democratic governor who was running for reelection. Northen, first elected in 1890, called for anti-lynching legislation and the removal of sheriffs who permitted lynching in their counties. Pledger, Henry McNeal Turner, and Joseph S. Flipper supported Northen for his position against anti-black violence and his support for Negro education. They overlooked the fact that Northen had signed all of the discriminatory legislation that the 1891–92 legislature had passed. R. H. Carter and J. E. Tate were two blacks who led in organizing supporters for the governor's "Northen Club."

Although Henry Grady had declared in 1889 that "the Negro as a political force has dropped out of serious consideration," three years later Democrats were positively hysterical on the subject of "Negro domination." They distributed a circular to white farmers inferring that a Populist victory would mean higher wages and shorter hours for black workers and strikes against white employers; it asked them to use the "power which your situation gives you over tenants and sharecroppers" to defeat Populists. Charging that Populists threatened Georgia with "anarchy and communism," Democrats resorted to bribery, fraud, intimidation, assault, lynching, and murder to keep blacks from voting their true interests. Democrats sponsored revelries for blacks on plantations the night before Georgia's October 1892 general election. Blacks were plied with food, whiskey, and "beer by the barrel," according to historian William F. Holmes. On Election Day they were marched to the polls and required to vote Democratic, some doing so repeatedly. Of the fifty thousand blacks who voted, 80 percent were for Northen and only 20 percent for Peek. Sixty-four percent of potential black voters did not or were not allowed to cast ballots. The *Savannah Tribune* said that

Democrats spent $50,000 bribing black leaders. The newspaper called blacks who worked for Democrats at the polls "traitors" and said they contributed to the defeat of blacks running for the legislature, including Lectured Crawford in McIntosh County. Only two blacks, Anthony Wilson of Camden County (who had worked with Watson) and Republican Styles were elected to the legislature. Only sixteen Populists won General Assembly seats. When the returns were in, two and a half times as many blacks voted for the Democrats as for the Populists.

Where bribery and fraud did not work, violence did. A few Populists attacked blacks for supporting Democrats, but Democrats may have killed as many as fifteen blacks in connection with the state elections. There was fighting between white Democrats and black Populists in Elbert County, and five blacks were killed or wounded at the polls in Ruckersville. In Augusta, Isaac Horton, a black Populist, was shot dead by a white Democrat, and a local deputy sheriff was shot while trying to arrest a black Populist official.

Watson, running for reelection to Congress in the November federal elections, was defeated by the massive fraud. While Populists were not above such tactics, Democrats were more successful in their efforts. Conservatives justified their methods on the grounds that these were necessary to maintain white supremacy, just as they had when the same methods were used to overthrow Reconstruction two decades earlier.

Although the Populist effort in 1892 was largely a failure, the movement did not die. The conditions that gave birth to agrarian discontent became more intense as the agricultural slump merged into the second most severe general depression the nation has ever experienced. Cotton, which had been one dollar a pound at the end of the Civil War, fell to five cents in 1893, when the cost of production was seven cents a pound. Blacks and poor whites slid backward economically, and their desperation in searching for alternatives increased.

The state Populist convention of 1893 supported free silver, the Australian (secret) ballot, and free public school books, and it opposed lynching and the convict-lease system. Drawing crowds that numbered into the thousands, Watson and Doyle continued to campaign together and spoke before 150,000 Georgians in thirty-five counties that summer. Watson said those who feared that the Populists would lead to black domination of Georgia were "detestable cowards."

The Populists encouraged blacks to join them even more than they had in 1892. There were twenty-four black delegates at the May 1894 state convention of the Populist party, which nominated James K. Hines for governor and pledged to repeal the Jim Crow car law, to reform the convict-lease system, and to adopt the secret ballot. Ephraim White, a black minister of McDuffie County, was elected to the state executive committee, and Watson seconded his nomination.

As Populists geared up for the 1894 election, they attracted more whites. This caused both Populists and regular Democrats to view the black vote as more important. The *People's Party Paper* in Atlanta said in August 1894 that Democrats were preparing to buy the black vote, without which, according to Atlanta black politician Henry A. Rucker, they could not win. *Georgia Baptist* editor William J. White believed the Populists had made it possible for blacks to vote to a degree never before possible, and he also believed Democrats were preparing to buy the black vote. Black editors warned their readers not to participate in such schemes.

The 1894 election was, impossible though it may seem, even more crooked than the one of 1892. It was perhaps the single most corrupt election in Georgia history. Fraud and intimidation again provided the decisive margin for some of the Democratic victories. The Democrats got six thousand votes in one county which had only fifteen hundred registered voters. A Democrat later said, "We had to do it! Those damned Populists would have ruined the country!"

While there was much rank and file support for Watson, in one Augusta ward his opponent got 989 black votes and Watson only 9. There were three election murders in Augusta, including the killing of a white Populist who challenged a black voter. In all of Augusta, James Black, Watson's opponent, received 13,780 votes when there were only 11,240 registered in both parties. The Democrats hired blacks to vote repeatedly. They paid ten cents a vote, and some blacks earned six dollars that day. While the Populists actually polled the majority of the votes in Augusta in the October election for governor and received many black votes there, Richmond County had four times as many ballots counted in the November federal elections. The fraud was so blatant that even the Democrats admitted that the election was stolen, and Black resigned to run against Watson in a special election the following year. But Augusta's Democratic registrars and precinct officials again used fraud to beat Watson. These two defeats helped to bring Watson's latent racism to the forefront. As for the movement, historian Barton Shaw stated, "The notion that the black man had somehow betrayed Populism would constantly haunt the Georgia People's party." Blacks had their own misgivings: "(They) found it impossible to trust white Georgians, especially those of the laboring class," another scholar noted.

In the Black Belt, more blacks voted Populist in 1894 than at any other time. Statewide, the Democratic majority was reduced from eighty thousand to twenty thousand. This was too close for the Democrats' comfort. So, in December 1894, the legislature "reformed" the state's election machinery by decreeing that a three-man registration committee in each county would decide who was qualified to vote. These committees, dominated by Democrats, purged Populist voters from the rolls. Black Populists were purged, but not black Democrats; they could continue to vote for their oppressors.

In 1896, the Populists still encouraged blacks to vote for them but offered less in return. The year before, Watson had begun to attack blacks and accept the myth that the Democrats would have permitted honest elections had it not been for their fear that blacks might gain some influence. By this specious reasoning he thought blacks had cost him his bid for reelection as congressman in 1892 and his attempt to regain his seat in 1894. The 1896 Populist platform was more antiblack than the Democratic program. The Populists accused Governor Atkinson of being pro-rape because he had pardoned a black who had been convicted twice of raping a white woman—a man everyone believed to be innocent.

Black ardor for the Populists cooled. Black editors A. A. Gordon, of the *Atlanta Reporter*, and John H. Deveaux deserted the Populists. A disgusted and cynical Henry McNeal Turner advised blacks to vote the way that would weaken the country the most. The Populists continued to denounce lynch law, the Klan, and the prison system, but many blacks did not think Populists were sincere, and they could not see how supporting the Populists had brought them any gains. The black vote was smaller in 1896 than earlier, and the Populists made less effort to corral it. As the Populists approached fusion with the Democrats and endorsed their presidential candidate, William Jennings Bryan, black voters drifted away from the People's party and back into the Republican fold in greater numbers. The old lily-white, black-and-tan division continued in the Republican party. White Republican leader Alfred E. Buck wanted to join with the Populists and alienated many blacks with his persistence. Many fusion-minded white Republicans entered the Democratic party when it absorbed the Populists.

In 1896, the Populists, who did not run any black candidates, polled 42 percent of the Georgia vote. Four black Republicans were elected to the state legislature. This election marked the last large black turnout in Georgia until the 1908 referendum on constitutional disfranchisement. By some accounts, whites' fear of Negro rule caused the decline of Populism. The return of prosperity in the late 1890s also helped to kill the movement, which sputtered to a halt in Georgia at the turn of the century.

In the early 1900s, Watson's racism, submerged in the campaigns of 1892 and 1894 for reasons of political expediency, surfaced. His black comrades in the struggle of the early 1890s became "niggers" a decade later. Perhaps the "change" in Watson's attitude should not be surprising.

As a member of the planter class, Watson grew up imbued with a hatred of Republican Reconstruction and its black component. As the Populist presidential candidate in 1904, Watson supported black disfranchisement. He opposed the literacy test as a disfranchising tool because he feared it would only spur blacks to seek education. Instead, he felt that voiding the Fifteenth Amendment would be the best way to deprive blacks of the vote. He became the greatest enemy of blacks in Georgia. "Lynch law is a good sign," Watson later explained. "It shows a sense of justice yet lives among the people." He also turned increasingly anti-Catholic and anti-Semitic. He rejoined the Democratic party in 1910 and became a political kingmaker in his later years, winning a U. S. Senate seat in 1920. It was only fitting that the Klan should send an eight-foot-tall cross of roses to his 1922 funeral. As an indication of the strength of racism in Georgia then, it should be noted that only after Watson attacked blacks did he become a power. As their political ally, he sat on the sidelines.

Rebecca Felton echoed Watson's Negrophobia. The determined wife of the Independent Movement's founder made the same intellectual journey. She moved from promoting convict-lease reforms and supporting black voting rights to recommending lynching blacks "a thousand times a week if necessary." Killing these "ravening beasts" would protect white womanhood, she believed.

Understanding that black power was never a realistic goal, blacks continually looked for allies, beginning with the Republican party, the party associated with their initial liberation. It proved to be a weak reed. Small hopes were later offered by the Independent Movement and larger hopes by the Populists, but they, like the Republicans, were unwilling to accept blacks as equal partners and viewed them instead as inferiors who were only useful as the foundations for white political careers.

C. Vann Woodward stated that the failure of the Populists to achieve interracial unity constituted "a tragic chapter in Southern history." The Independent Movement led directly to the Populist Movement and in both cases, the gains of the poor whites were limited by their inability to cast off their racism. After their respective failures, many in each group began attacking the blacks they earlier sought as allies.

After 1890, Georgia's race relations deteriorated, and the few whites who spoke out against the sorry state of affairs were dealt with harshly. Despite the halting attempts at reform, Georgia would remain a state dominated by a clique that had only contempt for the common people, no matter what color. Georgia remained backward in education and culture, with a political system devoted to the preservation of this backwardness. The wealth the freed people produced was siphoned off by a white elite, and blacks continued to wander in the wilderness as an impoverished peasantry for many more decades.

A Policy of Deception: The New South's Mythology

The New South was many things: a historical period beginning at the end of Reconstruction and lasting as long as one hundred years; an ideology, even a religion; a dream for the future; or an imagined present. For blacks, however, it was a nightmare. Bourbon leaders first thought they were "redeeming" a war-prostrated region from the "ruin" of Reconstruction. Then they believed they had charted the path to a happy and prosperous future. Finally, mistaking rhetoric for reality, they imagined they had actually achieved progress. Above all, the New South was a time of a great brainwashing designed to convince the North that good and constantly improving race relations prevailed in the South. Its message, a complex of myths, was designed to salve the conscience of the North, which gradually abandoned Southern blacks, and stimulate Northern investment in the South's embryonic industry.

For all practical purposes, Reconstruction ended in Georgia with the election of 1870, and the already deplorable race relations deteriorated gradually from then to well after 1901. The downward trend accelerated in the 1890s as the voice of the New South became more pervasive. The final breakdown was evidenced by constitutional disfranchisement in 1908 and the almost total apartheid of the early twentieth century. The weakening of black political power was accompanied by and closely related to the deterioration of the economic and social status of blacks. Georgia did not stop its descent until World War I.

The Democrats governing post-Reconstruction Georgia advocated oligarchic rule that strengthened peonage and the leasing of convicts and institutionalized lynching while denying blacks adequate education, equitable wages, and a chance to live in dignity. The Bourbons did little more for poor whites, who were also chained to dead-end jobs in agriculture and industry. The would-be entrepreneurs of the New South, who wanted to create the climate necessary to encourage investment needed to establish the South as a land of peace, order, and justice—and to destroy dissenters. As things worsened, fewer and fewer whites dared to speak out in protest. Those who did were categorized as "disreputable" and treated with increasing harshness that recalled the treatment accorded white abolitionists earlier.

To create a proper investment climate, an enormous body of myths was propagated for dissemination in the North. Georgians took the lead in this endeavor. First of all, the bloody death of Reconstruction was labeled

"Redemption" and the return to home rule. The victory of white supremacy was characterized as a triumph of civilization over barbarism and anarchy; of honesty and efficiency over graft and corruption; and of racial purity over "mongrelism." Reconstruction was depicted as a time of rotten government propped up by bayonets. Black suffrage was presented as a great mistake forced on the South by a few vindictive, hate-filled Northern radicals whose influence had since been replaced by the sweet reasonableness of the Compromise of 1877.

The New South, like the Old South, opposed all efforts of blacks to advance. New South spokesmen looked back with maudlin sentimentality to a romanticized, magnolia-scented vision of the good old days and were quick to defend the culture that slavery produced. Some even claimed that blacks longed for the return of those older, happier times. The spokesmen claimed that all racial problems stemmed from Reconstruction, which caused blacks and whites to hate each other; during slavery, slaves and masters held only the deepest mutual respect and devotion for and to each other. Unfortunately, Reconstruction gave blacks ideas that were beyond their ken or status. It made them "uppity," and when their foolish ambitions were thwarted, they promptly began to murder and rape, according to the New South's version of history: In short, Reconstruction transformed the docile, obedient, and naturally humble slave into a monster. In *The Tragic Era*, Claude Bowers' widely read white supremacist view of Reconstruction, rape was Reconstruction's foul daughter.

The New South advanced a dual and contradictory theory on the personality of the Negro: a happy, contented, and useful worker in the new society—yet at the same time, he was a ravening beast preoccupied with lusting after white women. Spokesmen for the New South said that blacks were naturally humble, realized their inferiority, did not want to vote, and were most comfortable when whites were in charge. They said that blacks and whites agreed that the Negro's best friend was the Southern white and that race relations in the South were better than in the North. On the other hand, they pictured the Negro as lazy, improvident, stupid, and criminal in order to justify harsh repression and the lynch mob; blacks were accused of all manner of depravity, and those who did not take part in criminal actions were believed to shelter those who did.

The New South presented itself as peaceful and law-abiding since Reconstruction: Antiblack outrages were rare after the Compromise of 1877, and blacks voted freely. When contradictory evidence filtered out of the South, the violence was excused as the necessary reaction to the lustful criminal nature of the Negro. In this period of increasing social Darwinism, the New South claimed that the natural inferiority of blacks was proved by their failure to have risen to a higher status. After all, had not the federal government done everything possible for them during Reconstruction? If that failed to help blacks, what could? The answer: kindly supervision of blacks by Southern whites. Reconstruction *proved* that Northern intervention in Southern race relations only made matters worse. If the intervention was renewed, Civil War and Reconstruction animosities would be revived. The white South said that blacks were well treated and advancing while it insisted they were incapable of achievement. This contradiction went unnoticed.

Before the Civil War, the economic, political, and social development of Georgia was controlled by the planter elite, which had formed connections with manufacturing and merchant interests in the North beginning in the Colonial period. Antebellum planters had become increasingly dependent on Northern money, shipping, and manufacturing as they concentrated on agriculture and invested most of their capital in slaves and land. These ties were not fully severed even during the Civil War. After the war, the South became an economic frontier, as did the West. The New South's sponsors wanted Northern capital invested in their region. These investors, or "carpetbaggers," were welcomed with open arms, provided the investors accepted white supremacy and would be reluctant to disturb the economy by calling for enforcement of the Constitution.

Leading Georgian fabricators of the New South's mythology were heavily involved in economic development as agents for Northern investors. Chief among them was the triumvirate of Gen. John B. Gordon, Alfred H. Colquitt, and Joseph E. Brown. They and their associates, the Bourbons of Georgia, built railroads, promoted foreign immigration, and encouraged business and industry while demanding and getting reductions in taxes and social services.

The Bourbons "worshipped business success and asked few questions about the methods used. . . . (They were) more interested in the accumulation of wealth, however, than in respecting human rights," stated one scholar. The Bourbon Democrats also were more interested in industrial development than agriculture, the mainstay of most Georgians. During the 1870s and 1880s, only two Georgia congressmen were planters. The oligarchy used government to further business interests wherever possible. Since profits were based on the exploitation of labor, both black and white, this meant that state government was used against the best interests of over 90 percent of all Georgians. Georgia's oligarchs sold out their own state and people to become personally rich and powerful by catering to the needs and wishes of the even more powerful financial interests in the North. By guaranteeing low wages, the Bourbons persuaded units of the textile industry to move to Georgia.

The most prominent Northern financier operating in Georgia then was Hannibal I. Kimball, "the most extraordinary man in the Reconstruction history of Georgia," according to W. E. B. Du Bois. Kimball was a prime example of the Northern capitalist whose bribes bought the willing cooperation of leading Georgians for his schemes to control development. Along with Brown, Alexander Stephens, and others, Kimball was heavily involved in Georgia railroad frauds. In one deal, the North and South Railroad, built from Columbus to Rome during Reconstruction with state backing and convict labor, was sold to a Boston financier in 1878 for a "paltry" sum.

To make the New South attractive to Northern investors, it was necessary to show that the labor force was docile and contented and that investments were safe. The most articulate propagandist for this message until his death in 1889 was Henry Grady, who as managing editor of the *Atlanta Constitution* built it into the state's most influential newspaper, with a national circulation of 120,000. Grady, son of a prosperous slave owner who died in the Civil War, propagated the mythology of the New South and gave special attention to the role of Georgia's blacks. His type was described by Mark Twain as having "the dollar their God, and how to get it their religion."

Grady made a career out of convincing the North that the New South was the best friend blacks ever had, and he tried to create the belief that blacks were happy and contented and were treated with equal justice. Grady contended that neither whites nor blacks wanted "intermingling"; and though whites paid 95 percent of the school system's costs, they insisted on the "perfect equality" of the two school systems; public transportation was separate but equal; blacks were on over half of the federal juries; and if there were no blacks on a jury, the Negro would get a lighter sentence than a white for the same crime. Grady also said that mutual confidence and goodwill between blacks and whites had replaced the doubt and distrust of the past: "Each has his place and fills it, and is satisfied." He explained, "As a matter of course, this implies the clear and unmistakable domination of the white race in the South... the assertion of the right of character, intelligence, and property to rule."

The 1884 Republican revival of "Bloody Shirt" political rhetoric concerned Northern investors who worried about the possible revival of sectionalism that could affect their extraction of profits from the South. John H. Inman, who had supervised the investment of $100 million in the South, mainly in railroads, steel, and coal, obtained for Grady an important speaking engagement in New York City in December 1886.

There Grady addressed the nation's most important manipulators of money and public opinion: men like J. P. Morgan, H. M. Flagler, and even Gen. William T. Sherman. Grady was so well received by these mainstays of the Republican party that some Democrats considered him as a possible vice presidential candidate.

In his New South speech, Grady said that the Southern cavalier and the Northern Puritan had been merged into something greater than both— the American. The South was glad slavery was gone; its recovery from war's ravages was swift, and the New South was progressive. The South, Grady continued, if left alone, would solve the race problem. "No section shows a more prosperous laboring population than the negroes," he explained, and emphasized that "the relations of the southern people with the negro are close and cordial." On the hundredth anniversary of Grady's speech, one scholar stated that Grady "was either lying or stupid" when he declared the South held no racial prejudices. Black editor T. Thomas Fortune bluntly said at the time, "Grady stands up and lies about these matters."

Grady's swan song was a speech, "The Race Problem in the South," given in Boston in 1889 to an audience that included President Cleveland and the leaders of the business world and the Republican party. One of Grady's goals was to undermine possible support for the Lodge Bill, which would have placed federal officials at the polls in the South, as the 1965 Voting Rights Act actually did. The Lodge Bill conceivably could have done much to ensure a free vote and an honest count in Georgia's elections that, in turn, could have endangered the Bourbons. The speech was received with acclaim and was interrupted by applause twenty-nine times. Grady was not surprised. Before coming to Boston he had tried out the speech on an Atlanta neighbor, Mrs. W. L. Peel. When the neighbor sobbed at one emotional passage, Grady "screamed with laughter," pleased that he had plucked the heartstrings.

Grady reiterated his spiel with emphasis on how well blacks were treated: "What people, penniless, illiterate, has done so well? For every Afro-American agitator, stirring the strife in which alone he prospers, I can show you a thousand negroes, happy in their cabin homes, tilling their own land...." He proclaimed that only white Southerners under-stood blacks, and to show the harm that could result from Northern tampering with the race relations that undergirded the Southern econ-omy, Grady noted that the annual value of the products produced by blacks was $1 billion and that blacks were able to accumulate one-fiftieth that amount in twenty-five years. Even though he claimed these figures showed that blacks were *not* oppressed, the tacit message was that most of the wealth created by black labor went to others, some of whom were in his audience. This was not news to any of the two hundred blacks who met in Atlanta in December and contradicted Grady and denounced Georgia's wage system, lynching, and disfranchisement.

While Grady was the most talented and effective spokesman for the New South's intricate racial mythology, there was a small army of reporters, magazine writers, book authors, and even poets and humorists who joined in trying to prove to the rest of the nation that blacks were well treated, happy, and contented in Georgia and the rest of the South. Blacks were convinced that there was a conspiracy of silence against their good deeds, advances, and progress that was coupled with a campaign of falsehoods and innuendo calculated to harass and defame them. A.M.E. Bishop J. W. Hood believed that these efforts were designed to prepare the minds of the American people for the disfranchisement of black voters.

Blacks believed one of the worst elements in this conspiracy was the newspaper press and wire services. The most important was the Associated Press (AP), formed in 1848. The AP covered the United States and hired Southern journalists to cover the South. These reporters often promoted race segregation, the subordination of black folk, and "have excused at times mob law and even lynching," according to Du Bois.

Black journalists were outspoken in rebuttal. One editor noted the convict-lease system was a "cesspool of degradation and crime...under the very nostrils of the prophet Grady." *Savannah Tribune* editor John H. Deveaux attacked the AP in 1899 for its exaggerated stories blaming the Negro for all violence and cited an AP report that blamed a train wreck near Atlanta on a black when the cause was unknown. William A. Pledger charged that the AP was manipulated by Southern Democrats: "There is such suppression of truth, that were all the facts known, the Christian people of the North would be worse shocked than by the inhumanities of Andersonville and Libby prisons."

After Grady's death in 1889, a legion of Georgia editors carried on the New South's campaign to persuade the nation to accept white supremacy. John Temple Graves edited several Georgia newspapers and won a wide reputation as a public speaker. With the help of General Gordon, Hoke Smith bought the *Atlanta Journal* in 1887 for about $10,000 to compete with Grady's *Constitution* and hired John Temple Graves as editor. Graves became editor of the *Rome Daily Tribune* in 1888 and later became a popular lecturer. Graves said Grady died "literally loving a nation into peace." While Graves agreed with Grady on basic race relations in Georgia, Graves was more virulent against blacks. In 1906, Graves became editor of the *Atlanta Georgian*, where he promoted fear and distrust of Georgia's blacks and saw the fruits of this policy ripen to help produce the Atlanta riot that year. Wesley J. Gaines, founder of Morris Brown College in Atlanta and a bishop in the A.M.E. church, said that among the greatest enemies of blacks in 1906, Graves was in his estimation "the most dangerous of the group because he is the most educated."

Graves, a spellbinding orator, lectured extensively on the chautauqua circuit. The chautauqua movement for adult education grew out of a program organized in 1873 at a Baptist summer camp at Chautauqua, New York. Local groups sprang up in hundreds of towns and cities and provided ready-made audiences for authors, explorers, performing artists, magicians, and political personalities. Graves traveled the circuit giving a set lecture called "The Mob Spirit in the South." He contended that the lynch mob acted only against rapists and if it were not for the mob, rape would increase a hundredfold. Graves argued that blacks only feared the mob; they apparently enjoyed trials because then they were the center of attention. Graves once said that four blacks (any four) should be hanged for each rape. He called for the legalization of lynching and for sending blacks to other countries and replacing them with cheap European immigrant labor. Until then, he wanted total segregation and constitutional disfranchisement of blacks. At the same time, he dwelt rapturously on how happy and contented everyone was in Georgia.

General Gordon also had a stock lecture, "The Last Days of the Confederacy," which he gave far and wide. He asserted that the Southern white man was the Negroes' best friend. The Bourbon leader praised the convict-lease system for building industry, since most prisoners worked in mines, railroads, and coke or brick plants. He did not mention the horrible treatment of convicts or say they were an important source of his personal fortune.

Others sold Northern leaders on the benefits of leaving Southern race relations to white Southerners by pointing out that the nation's economy benefited from the cheap black labor that produced cotton for export; if not for this, the United States would have an unfavorable balance of trade. Cheap cotton helped fuel the Industrial Revolution then going on in the North and was one reason the robber barons could accumulate their millions.

As it turned out, the nation was quite willing to accept the New South's message. The campaign to discredit and degrade blacks had its first national victories in Northern magazines. Influential molders of opinion such as *Harper's*, the *Century*, the *Nation*, and *Outlook* began to change from their position that blacks were oppressed in the South to one in line with the thinking of Grady and Graves. *Outlook* carried an article in 1907 blaming Georgia's poor race relations on federal interference and the Fourteenth and Fifteenth amendments. Without this interference, the author argued, Georgia would restore the Negro "to a condition of morals and industry as good, and an enjoyment of personal virtue as complete, as were his in 1866." Some whites degenerated to viciously anti-Negro positions. By 1890, few white Northerners attacked the Southern position publicly.

After the New South converted national magazines to its cause, it won the battle of the books. Publishers stumbled over themselves to print white Southern views. A major opening shot was Hilary Herbert's 1890 work *Why the Solid South? Or Reconstruction and Its Results*. Herbert feared that the Republicans' push for the Lodge Bill meant a revival of Reconstruction. His book was a collection of essays on the ideology of the New South, with special emphasis on the "horrors of Reconstruction." Significantly, he dedicated the work to "the businessmen of the North." To persuade Northerners to leave Southern race relations alone, the book tried to show how much Northern business was profiting from the South. The work was a huge success, influencing political leaders, the general public, and historians.

One of the essays in *Why the Solid South* was written by Georgia congressman H. G. Turner. His "Reconstruction in Georgia" was a rather dull chronology of events that he interpreted as all bad until "Redemption." Things were fine during slavery, but in 1866 "aliens and strangers disseminated among the Negroes hate and rancor towards the white citizens." Things went from bad to worse until the election of 1870—"a contest for supremacy between those who had always been masters and those who had been their slaves." He stated that what was actually a Klan-induced bloodbath was "totally without disorder or violence." Turner concluded, "Reconstruction accomplished not one useful result and left behind it, not one pleasant recollection."

Herbert was regarded as an expert on race relations and was chosen to be the permanent chairman of the 1900 Conference of the Southern Society for the Promotion of the Study of Race Conditions and Problems in the South, which had several Georgians among its founders, including Atlanta corporate attorney Alexander Campbell King and Clark Howell, publisher and editor of the *Constitution*. No blacks were invited to this conference. One speaker explained, "The cause of the Negro can be advocated much more effectively by the white man who is his friend, than by the Negro himself." In his closing remarks, Herbert noted how much brighter the atmosphere was than at an earlier conference he attended in 1868 to consider new Reconstruction laws. During the conference, King stated: "It is to the credit of the white man that he treats the Negro with perfect justice except when the Negro by an ignorant ballot or by criminal act threatens the integrity of white civilization."

Along with Graves, Bishop Gaines placed Thomas Dixon, Jr., among the worst enemies of blacks. Dixon wrote *The Leopard's Spots* (1902) and

The Clansman (1905). Both were runaway bestsellers. In a few months *The Clansman* sold over a million copies. It glorified the Ku Klux Klan and gave the New South's view of Reconstruction in vivid prose: Blacks were depicted as ignorant barbarians, lusting after fair young white maidens, corrupting the political process, and swaggering domineeringly over the good white citizens who were trying to rescue the vestiges of their superior civilization. Fortunately, according to Dixon, the Klan was born and performed its heroic mission of restoring order and decency. Dixon said in *The Clansman*, "A brave Reb is worth more to this nation than every negro that ever set his flat foot on this continent."

The *Voice of the Negro* stated that *The Clansman* showed that Dixon "should be incarcerated in a madhouse. Surely the man's mind is unhinged." Dixon, not one to buck a trend that was bringing him fame and fortune, rewrote the novel into a play; it was performed by two companies that played for five years and set touring records. White Atlanta doctor Len G. Broughton called the play "un-Christian and un-American." After seeing the play at Bainbridge, audience members broke into the jail and lynched a black prisoner. Dixon went on the chautauqua circuit where 5 million people heard him advance his racist doctrines. In 1915, *The Clansman* was redone as a film, *The Birth of a Nation*, which helped stimulate the rebirth of the Klan that year.

While Dixon and others were poisoning race relations, Du Bois, then a young scholar teaching economics and history at Atlanta University, wrote *The Souls of Black Folk*, a moving collection of essays that would have done much to counter such writers as Dixon—had it been widely read. Though *Souls* eventually went through more than twenty American editions and has become a classic of American literature, it was little noticed at the time outside a small circle of black intellectuals and their white friends.

Blacks grew discouraged by the increasing racism they saw. Feeling helpless in the face of widespread attacks on their political rights, black clergymen called for a day of fasting and prayer on May 3, 1903. On that day, the prominent black intellectual clergyman Francis Grimké delivered an address, "God and the Race Problem." In it he contrasted the reception given to the writings of Du Bois and Dixon. *The Leopard's Spots*, "a vile publication that seeks to hold the Negro up to ridicule and contempt...was put into all the libraries; it was to be found on the shelves of all booksellers; it was taken up and reviewed by all the papers and magazines," Grimké said. "It is almost impossible to conceive" of widespread publicity for Du Bois's book, he pointed out, because black writers were ignored. To underline the downhill trend, Grimké noted that *Uncle Tom's Cabin* had just been banned by the New York City Board of Education. This pleased white Georgians. For two generations they had been taught that Harriet Beecher Stowe's famous book was a wicked libel.

Benjamin Mays, Georgia's most distinguished black educator in the period after World War II, reviewed racist literature and concluded, "Perhaps no writings in anybody's lifetime did as much to engender prejudice against the Negro as the writing and works of the minister, Dixon, did in mine." Dixon's works signaled a torrent of racist literature, with each work seemingly vying to be more scurrilous than the others. Taken together, their popularity throughout the nation was a telling comment on how deeply the period's racism went. Ideas that would not have been generally accepted a generation earlier were touted as gospel truth in the early twentieth century.

Newspapers, magazines, and popular books piled calumny after calumny on the heads of helpless blacks who could not respond in the general media. Two works appearing twenty years apart illustrate how deeply the nation had accepted the New South's worldview and sunk into the morass of racism. The first, *Our Brother in Black*, published in 1881 by Methodist Bishop Atticus G. Haygood two years before he became president of Emory University, presented blacks in sympathetic terms. In 1901, Charles Carroll wrote *The Negro a Beast*. These two titles indicated what had happened by the turn of the century. Not even the *Encyclopaedia Britannica* disputed Carroll's premise.

Haygood was often described as the best friend of blacks in the South. Though opposing secession, he supported the Confederacy and believed that giving the vote to blacks in 1868 "was a terrible mistake." He said in a national magazine article in 1893 that lynching was wrong but was due to black men raping white women. He said that Northern teachers had made blacks insubordinate and blamed black teachers and ministers for not speaking out more against rape. He adopted the New South view that lynching would only end when rape did. If Haygood was one of Georgia's best white voices speaking in behalf of blacks, one can imagine what the worst were saying.

Contributing mightily to the nation's change of heart were the "quill drivers" of Georgia. During this time, Georgia produced two humorists and folklore philosophers who acquired national reputations and contributed to acceptance of the New South's claim of rosy race relations. Charles Henry Smith was in the Confederate army and later became mayor of Rome. He created the homespun cracker-barrel philosopher Bill Arp and had his material published in the *Constitution* in the 1870s and 1880s. Smith put all the white supremacists' prejudices into Arp's mouth in a way thought humorous by many at the time, and consequently his writings spread throughout the country. His popularity gave him "license to damage the entire Negro race as he chooses," stated anti-lynching activist Ida B. Wells.

Far better known was another white Georgian, Joel Chandler Harris, whose "Uncle Remus" stories, songs, and sayings have become ingrained in American culture. Whites regarded Harris as the nation's greatest expert on the Negro. He wrote, "It was to the glory of the American character and name, that never before in the history of the world was human slavery marked by such mildness, such humanity, as that which characterized it in the United States." As Smith created Bill Arp to articulate his philosophy, Harris created Uncle Remus, the kindly "darkie" grandfather who told stories to children about Br'er Rabbit, Br'er Fox, and other animals children like to hear about. In one story, Uncle Remus explains that black children need not go to school, as they cannot profit from the classroom: "As to education, I kin take a bar'l stave and fling mo' sense into a nigger in one minute dan all de schoolhouses." Uncle Remus stories were widely read, and the protagonist came to be considered an actual person. If the Negro sage did not value formal education for black children—well, what right did whites have to contradict him?

Minstrel shows carried negative Negro stereotypes down to the lowest level of popular culture. These acts probably originated on the plantation, where slaves entertained themselves and their masters. By 1769, Northern whites in blackface parodied drunken blacks to amuse other whites. Both blacks and whites in blackface developed this form of popular entertainment. The Brooks Negro Minstrels were organized in Macon in October 1861. To obtain permission to use the Macon concert hall, they had to donate the proceeds from the first performance to Confederate soldiers' relief. Admission was fifty cents for whites and half that for "servants."

After the Civil War, white actors in blackface would do cakewalks, "coon songs," and "darkie" dialect jokes. They did not portray blacks; they played their stereotypes of blacks. The audiences, most of whom had little honest contact with blacks, often did not know the difference and assumed the caricatures accurately depicted blacks as brutish, lazy, stupid, and dishonest, but with a streak of cleverly dissembled cunning.

Historians reflect their times, and many during the late nineteenth and early twentieth centuries used New South sources uncritically. One of the most influential scholars was Archibald Dunning, who taught history at Columbia University from 1886 to 1922 and influenced generations of graduate students, who went on to elaborate on his ideas, which were founded on racist assumptions. His most influential student was Ulrich B. Phillips, who was raised in the plantation country of the Georgia cotton belt and graduated from the University of Georgia before going to Columbia to pursue his studies. Phillips noted that the central theme of Southern history was the maintenance of white supremacy.

The capstone of racist historiography was *The South During Reconstruction*, published in 1947 by longtime (1919–58) University of Georgia history professor E. Merton Coulter. He wrote, "(T)he most spectacular and exotic development in government in the history of white civilization was to be seen in the part the Negroes played in ruling the South— longest to be remembered, shuddered at, and execrated." In Coulter's view, blacks had their opportunity to participate in politics during Reconstruction and had blown their chance by messing things up; therefore, wisdom dictated they should not have another chance. Historian Vernon L. Wharton noted, "This interpretation became the standard of general histories, college and high school textbooks, and popular fiction." Many Georgians who led the fight against civil rights and desegregation after World War II were strongly influenced by Coulter.

It was difficult to buck the trend, and scholarly refutations were mostly confined to works by blacks. George Washington Williams, who enlisted in the Union army at the age of fourteen, went on to become the greatest black historian of the nineteenth century. He included in his two-volume monumental work published in 1883 much evidence that contradicted what New South spokesmen were saying. The next year, T. Thomas Fortune published *Black and White: Land, Labor and Politics in the South*, which built on Williams's foundation. Black scholar and attorney David Augustus Straker was born in Barbados in 1842 and came to the United States in 1868 to help educate freed people. In 1888, he published *The New South Investigated*, which contended that conditions in Dixie were oppressive for blacks.

Presentation of dissent from the New South's mainstream thought was encouraged by the American Negro Academy, founded in 1897 by the Rev. Alexander Crummell, the leading black intellectual before the age of Du Bois. Crummell had studied at England's Cambridge University. The first of the academy's five stated objectives was "defense of the Negro against vicious assault." The second was "the publication of scholarly works." One of these, a study of black disfranchisement, was published in 1899. Du Bois wrote about the positive side of Reconstruction in the *American Historical Review* in 1910, thus continuing his scholarly attack on the ideas and programs of the New South that he began with the *Atlanta University Studies* in 1896. Booker T. Washington's *Story of the Negro* appeared in 1909, but Washington was very cautious about biting the white hand that fed him, and many of his criticisms of the New South were so veiled and bland that they went unnoticed.

Macon-born classics scholar and university president William S. Scarborough had his ideas sometimes accepted by national magazines. He wrote of the Negro in *Forum* in 1889: The New South "proscribes and persecutes him in countless ways. Fraud, intimidation, violence, and constant depreciation of him as a man... make freedom a mockery and life simply a terrorized existence." If a black took up arms in self-defense, it was called "insurrection," Scarborough said, and if he voted, it was called "Negro Supremacy."

Unfortunately, the total audience for this black counterattack on the New South's mythology was minuscule. A little additional help came from the few white voices crying in the wilderness. The most prominent Southern white to take issue with the New South's developing ideology was George Washington Cable. Among his essays were one exposing the convict-lease system in Georgia and a sympathetic look at the Negro and the Congregational church in Georgia. A prolific writer, Cable turned his back on a promising literary career and spent the 1880s developing a case for unrestricted civil rights for blacks, but by 1890 he concluded that the cause was lost. Cable argued that because slavery was wrong, the Southern rebellion was wrong and the postwar caste system symbolized an ongoing rebellion. He contended that the South was firing into its own ranks when it suppressed the Negro because "it is the first premise of American principles that whatever elevates the lower stratum of the people lifts all the rest, and whatever holds it down holds all down." He visited and spoke at Atlanta University, and the American Missionary Society helped distribute his writings. T. Thomas Fortune prophesied: "It will take the South a century to reach Mr. Cable's position." Cable himself said, "We may reach the moon one day, not social equality." Although he was a bona fide white Southerner, twice wounded fighting for the Confederacy, he was eventually driven from his native land.

Georgia and other Southern states became a closed, conformist society that would no more tolerate dissent from the official ideology of the New South than the Old South would allow criticism of slavery in its waning days. More than one brave soul who spoke honestly was persecuted. Andrew Sledd, a professor of Latin at Emory University and son-in-law of Bishop Warren A. Candler, lost his position because he mildly denounced prejudice in a 1902 *Atlantic Monthly* article. In "The Negro: Another View," he said blacks were brutalized and that the motive for lynching was to make all blacks servile. Rebecca Felton led the attack on Sledd until he was fired. The *Atlanta Constitution* denounced his "northern foolosophy," and the *Atlanta News* labeled him a traitor. J. D. Hammond, the white president of Paine Institute, the black college in Augusta, was forced out of his job in 1915 after four years because he and his wife challenged some of the New South's racist assumptions. This fear of and rage against those who challenged the myths of the New South was characteristic of all the ex-Confederate states, not just Georgia, and other noteworthy white professors were dismissed throughout the region.

The New South was a great success if measured by how completely its attitudes toward blacks were accepted in the North. When Mary Church Terrell, a key organizer of the National Association of Colored Women, lectured to Northern audiences in 1896, she found that they knew little or nothing about Negro disfranchisement, the convict-lease system, or lynching. Fannie Barrier Williams, another activist black clubwoman, said in 1904, "Our special reason for fear today is that the colored people have not as many friends to do their fighting as they had fifty years ago." Hoke Smith supplemented his income on the chautauqua circuit after he was governor of Georgia and spoke in 1912 of the growing prejudice against blacks in the North without mentioning his part in the New South's campaign to stimulate the growth of prejudice—which included a full-page ad in the *New York Times* he bought to "prove" the Negro was a burden to Georgia.

The South, which produced 10.3 percent of the nation's manufactured products in 1860, produced 10.4 percent in 1904, during a period when the nation's industrial output increased 900 percent. C. Vann Woodward noted, "For the South...to have held its own in this march of giant strides, was no inconsiderable achievement." Despite the New South's attempts to industrialize, the region remained primarily agricultural. However, the drive to industrialize was not the New South's real goal. Its highest priority was the subordination of the Negro. Georgian apostles of the New South worshiped not modernization but low taxes and the trinity of the Lost Cause, the "horrors" of Reconstruction, and white supremacy. Despite its triumphs, Georgia's leaders did not feel totally secure. There was one more thing to do: legally disfranchise black voters.

Disfranchisement in the "Progressive" Era

"First we would vote: with the right to vote goes everything: Freedom, manhood, the honor of your wives, the chastity of your daughters, the right to work, the chance to rise and let no man listen to those who deny this," proclaimed a speaker at the Niagara Movement's Harpers Ferry meeting in 1906. The founders of this black protest organization were painfully aware of the importance of the voting franchise. Voting determined what streets were to be paved and lit, the fairness of courts, and even who would be beaten by law officers. To the extent blacks lost the power to influence elections, they also lost the ability to prevent the further relative decline of their schools, the security in their property, the right to work at an occupation of their choice, and even the right of self-defense: Disfranchisement made lynching possible, and lynching kept blacks from speaking up for the right to vote.

The disfranchisement of Georgia's blacks developed gradually and was never complete. From 1870 to 1900, black political participation in Georgia's affairs was lower than in other Southern states because blacks in Georgia faced greater obstacles to voting, yet a longer period of turbulence preceded constitutional disfranchisement in Georgia than in any other state. In retrospect, efforts by blacks to achieve political equality during this period would seem largely futile. Blacks had exerted enormous efforts, and hundreds had died for their convictions, but the results were slight.

The real problem white Georgians had with the black vote was the idea that blacks would use it to improve their status, gain political power, and attack white supremacy. John H. Deveaux wrote in 1897 that whites would let blacks vote for things that whites wanted but whites would not help blacks in return. Richard R. Wright, Sr., who replaced Louis M. Pleasant as "Mr. Black Republican" in Savannah in the early 1890s, dropped out of politics in 1900, saying that the time and trouble were not worth the results. By 1906, only thirty-seven blacks in Augusta bothered to register and pay their poll taxes; only twenty-seven in Clarke County bothered. Of the 6,000 potential black voters in Bibb County, only 250 took the trouble to register.

There were many ways to discourage blacks from voting. Obviously, violence and fraud were significant factors. Following a reasonably fair election in early 1868, when federal troops and the Freedmen's Bureau held off white attacks on blacks, a period of intense violence, spearheaded by the Ku Klux Klan, ensured that absolute control of Georgia would remain in the hands of white Democrats for a century. The massive terror from 1867 to 1877 gave way to other forms of intimidation. Coercion was reinforced by a steady increase in legal discrimination that culminated in 1908 with the adoption of a state constitutional amendment that effectively barred blacks from the polls.

The first legal disfranchising tool was the poll tax, which was not intended to raise revenue so much as it was designed to disfranchise blacks and other "undesirable" voters. Ironically, the poll tax was written into the 1868 Georgia Constitution with black support. Henry McNeal Turner voted for it thinking it was the best way to raise money to fund a public school system. He did not foresee that payment would not be enforced and that the lack of a poll-tax receipt would be used to keep blacks from voting. Gov. Rufus B. Bullock ordered the suspension of the requirement of a poll-tax receipt for the 1868 and 1870 elections, but Democratic poll watchers nevertheless enforced it illegally and effectively. The tax had a disastrous effect on the Republican party.

There were other tools to keep blacks from voting. Sometimes blacks were not allowed enough time to cast ballots. Whites went to the head of the line and stalled; when they had voted, it was time to close the polls. In 1873, the legislature changed residency requirements from six months in the state to one year and from one month to six in the county. This restricted voting by uprooted tenant farmers, most of whom were black. Georgia's failure to adopt the secret ballot also cut off black voting rights. By 1892, Georgia was one of only five states that failed to take this progressive step. As long as whites could watch blacks mark their ballots, intimidation was easy, for few blacks were sufficiently strong and financially independent enough to withstand reprisals.

After the 1877 Constitution went into effect, Georgia's Bourbon leaders dominated and limited the Negro vote by intimidation, fraud, the cumulative poll tax, and the county-unit system, which gave disproportionate power to the rural areas, where the majority of blacks lived. Rural blacks were less educated, less organized, and less prosperous than their city cousins; therefore, they were more easily intimidated and controlled. With a cumulative poll tax, blacks would have to pay for several years in order to vote in any subsequent election. The poll tax was effective because a few dollars was an impossible sum for most blacks to pay. The per capita income of the bottom 76 percent of all Georgians was an estimated fifty-five dollars in 1880, and most blacks were in the bottom third of this group, with an average income of only thirty-seven dollars. Many blacks saw no cash at all from one year to the next, for they received their meager pay in goods at the "company store." One observer called the cumulative poll tax "the most effective bar to Negro suffrage ever invented."

One of the poll tax's charms for Georgia's leaders lay in the fact that it did not appear to the North as a measure aimed specifically at violating the Fifteenth Amendment by disfranchising blacks. As long as Georgia's white supremacist leaders feared federal intervention, they claimed that barring blacks from the ballot box was the furthest thing from their minds. Macon's A. O. Bacon, later U. S. senator and three times unsuccessful candidate for governor, introduced a resolution in the 1876 state legislature stating that Georgia had no intention of abolishing Negro suffrage. Three years later, Alexander Stephens said that disfranchisement was impractical and undesirable.

Georgia's Bourbon and New South leaders fought on the national level to keep the federal government from protecting black voting rights. The Compromise of 1877 that put President Rutherford B. Hayes in office included the implicit recognition by the North that Southern race relations would be left to the South. However, Republican President Benjamin Harrison, in his 1889 message to Congress, proposed that the rights of blacks as litigants, jurors, witnesses, travelers, and voters be protected. To protect voting rights for blacks (and thereby protect the Republican party), Massachusetts Sen. Henry Cabot Lodge introduced in 1890 the Lodge, or "Force," Bill to provide federal supervision of national elections in the South where one hundred or more voters requested it. Blacks strongly favored the bill, although some considered it too weak.

Georgia politicians feared the North was reneging on the 1877 compromise. Although the Lodge Bill applied only to federal elections, they claimed it was a Northern effort to "Africanize" Georgia by placing the state under black control—as they insisted it had been during Reconstruction. Democrats were apprehensive that any precedent of federal intervention to protect black rights might later be extended into state politics or even into social and economic spheres. The Lodge Bill was one issue that divided the Farmers' Alliance from the Colored Farmers' Alliance and later split black and white Populists.

Democrats were united against the proposal and appealed to Northern business interests to protect their Southern investments by lobbying Congress against it. Democrats promised economic warfare if the bill passed. The business interests responded favorably to Southern appeals, since they were more interested in stability than democracy. The *Atlanta Constitution* reported: "The merchants of the North and the capitalists who have investments in the South are sending in petitions by the score protesting against the bill." Should the bill pass, the *Constitution* threatened that the South would organize a massive boycott of the North that would stimulate industrial development in the South. The paper's editors knew Northern industrial barons did not want the South to escape from its self-imposed colonial dependency on Northern manufactured goods.

The Lodge Bill passed the House of Representatives in July 1890 by a margin of six votes. Then Southerners filibustered in the Senate until Democratic senators came to an agreement with western senators to vote for the greater use of silver coinage in exchange for western votes against the Lodge Bill, which was defeated in January 1891 by a 35-34 vote. Fearing that the Lodge Bill would come up again if Republicans won the off-year election of 1892, Georgians continued to campaign nationally to discredit it. Hoke Smith wrote an article entitled "The Disastrous Effects of the Force Bill" and said it would hurt blacks whose "hope of development rests upon the kind feelings which now exist between the two races in the South, which is constantly increasing to the benefit of Negroes as outside interference decreases." Smith explained that few blacks voted in Georgia because they were disappointed with the Republican party. In addition, Smith said that the Lodge Bill would cut in half the value of Northern investments in the South.

Many people in the North, not knowing or caring about such matters, accepted Smith's statements as gospel truth. Meanwhile, in addition to seventeen lynchings of blacks in Georgia that year, fifteen others were killed while trying to vote as the Bourbons stole the election from the Populists. The principle behind the Lodge Bill died and was not resurrected until the Voting Rights Act of 1965 was passed.

The United States became an industrial nation between the Civil War and World War I. The development of the factory system in the North also brought terrible working conditions for the laboring poor, great economic injustice, and political machines that favored the rich. The depression of 1893 made many people aware that the country was run by a few arrogant business leaders who bought and paid for state and national legislators and executives. The Progressive Movement was a revolt against this inefficient oligarchic control. In the North, the movement manifested itself in exposés by investigative journalists (muckrakers) of corporate arrogance, big business politics, and the inefficiency that resulted from putting private profit over public welfare. The Progressive Movement led to a realization that there were many poor in this land of plenty and that the political system was unresponsive to the needs of the general populace.

In the South, the Progressive Movement was characterized by a new breed of politician who claimed to speak for poor whites against the Bourbons. This revolt in the South was centered in the rural areas, whereas in the North the Progressives were mainly urbanites. The revolt of the poor whites in Georgia began with the Independents. After the Independents failed in 1882, the Democrats became increasingly secure, and they believed that Negro suffrage increased the party machine's power; in the elections of 1884 and 1888 they did not object to blacks voting, especially if they voted Democratic.

As the Independent Movement died, the Alliance Movement was born and changed into the Populist Movement as poor whites sought to gain on the political front what they were unable to gain in an economic struggle by the use of boycotts and cooperatives. Populists made a greater effort to enlist blacks in their cause but were eventually defeated by their inability to see blacks as equal partners—and by corrupt Bourbon control of much of the black vote. As a result, white Southern Progressives decided that political progress could only come with the exclusion of blacks.

The adoption of the primary election to select the party's candidates for the general election was considered a democratizing step. Primaries did away with the old convention system that kept the power to nominate in the hands of a caucus of the few in the fabled "smoke-filled" back rooms. Ironically, along with the poll tax, primary elections became the most effective disfranchising tool by the turn of the century. Local primaries in which blacks could vote were first used by Democrats in 1874, but Georgia soon found a way to turn the new method against blacks by ruling that only whites could vote in primary elections. With the state's political power concentrated in the Democratic party, the Democratic primaries became the only meaningful elections. When blacks were excluded, they were effectively disfranchised for all practical purposes, even if they paid their poll taxes and met residency requirements. The effect of the white primary on black political power was devastating.

In 1880, blacks were driven away from primary-election polling places in Oglethorpe County. The white primary began in other counties after the 1882 election. In 1891, when the legislature said the Democratic party could make what rules it pleased for the nominating elections, the white primary spread. The move to exclude blacks from primaries was centered in the cities, where there were fewer but more independent and better organized blacks. Atlanta introduced the white primary in 1892 but removed it in 1895 so that Democrats could use the black vote against the Populists. It was reinstated in 1897, when that threat had passed. Augusta adopted the white primary before 1900; Macon, in 1901; Savannah, in 1904. Despite black protests, the white primary had become statewide by 1900.

Along with the other proscriptions, the white primary enforced the attitude among blacks that there was little or no use taking the risk of voting. As political apathy was enforced on blacks, whites also became less interested in voting, as table 5.1 indicates.

Table 5.1 Percentage of Georgians Voting in Presidential Elections

Year	Overall %	Black %
1876	54	53
1880	50	37
1884	40	36
1888	37	20
1892	53	42
1896	44	18
1900	24	8
1904	24	4
1908	22	10

Source: J. Morgan Kousser, *The Shaping of Southern Politics: Suffrage Restriction and the Establishment of One-Party Rule*, 1880–1910 (New Haven: Yale University Press, 1974), p. 212.

In 1876, 53 percent of the eligible black males voted. The white vote was only slightly higher. By 1880, after the poll tax had been made cumulative, the black vote declined sharply to 37 percent. The next large decline, in 1888, was partly due to the more general use of the white primary and the collapse of the Independent Movement. The Populist upsurge in 1892 increased the black vote to 42 percent, but with the defeat of the Populists, blacks were effectively removed from Georgia's political equation. Black voting declined to new lows by 1904. The fight over constitutional disfranchisement in 1908 stimulated an increase in political participation by blacks as they organized to defeat it.

Only 18 percent of Georgia's blacks voted in the 1896 election, and whites were elected even in counties with black majorities. This did not keep newly elected Gov. Allen D. Candler from saying in 1899 that the black vote was "a constant menace" that "tainted society." In the name of reform, he called for new election laws to eliminate the black vote. Acceding to the call, State Sen. Thomas Hardwick of Washington County, "the father of disfranchisement in Georgia," introduced a bill requiring a literacy test to qualify as a registered voter, with an escape provision in the form of a "grandfather" clause that would permit the 12 percent of the whites who were illiterate to vote.

A petition from John Hope, William A. Pledger, Du Bois, and other black leaders endorsed the general idea of limiting suffrage to those who met an educational qualification, if free schools were provided for all children. The petition further stated that if Georgia's leaders wanted to enact laws against bribery, vote selling, ignorance, and crime, they should do just that and not legislate against blacks. Black leaders protested the "grandfather clause," which would permit grossly ignorant whites to vote, and the "understanding" clause, which would let any petty official decide if a black understood the state constitution after reading it. This was "a direct invitation to injustice and fraud," the petition stated.

The charge of the petitioners was well founded. It was not so much the laws on the books but their administration by officials plus the vast body of unwritten laws that disfranchised blacks. Hardwick did not mince works and explained to the *Atlanta Journal* that even an educated black would not get by his literacy clause.

Booker T. Washington came to Georgia to help organize resistance to the Hardwick Bill. He did not object publicly to educational and property tests for voters as long as they were applied justly, although the experience of Mississippi, South Carolina, and Louisiana proved that such requirements were not applied fairly. Washington wrote T. Thomas Fortune in disgust at the lack of initiative he found in Georgia:

I am almost disgusted with the colored people of Georgia. I have been corresponding with leading people in the state but cannot stir up a single colored man to take the lead in trying to head off this movement. I cannot see that they are doing anything through the press. . . . It is a question how far I can go and how far I ought to go in fighting these measures in other states when the colored people themselves sit down and will do nothing to help themselves. They will not even answer my letters.

Washington apparently wrote to the wrong people, for he did not contact the militants.

Hardwick's bill was overwhelmingly defeated in 1899 by a 137–3 vote because the Bourbon Democrats felt they safely controlled the black vote and poor whites feared that it might be used to disfranchise them. Besides, the white primary, poll tax, and the lack of secrecy in voting had practically eliminated the black vote anyway, so why stir up racial trouble and invite the attention of the North? Candler still believed the Hardwick Bill was a good idea. In his second inaugural address in 1900, he said that Georgia would not prosper until capitalists were convinced that the Negro could never control the state. The Hardwick Bill was again defeated in 1901 by a 114–17 margin.

While Candler took credit for authoring the white primary law, he admitted that it did not end electoral corruption. Then again, how could it? Whites caused the corruption. Election dishonesty continued despite the great decline in the black vote. In the 1904 election, when few blacks voted, the Rev. A. M. Williams, pastor of a large white Methodist church in Savannah, charged that there were four thousand fraudulent ballots cast in his district during the white primary.

The white primary was effective, but only as long as there was no danger of white political factions bidding for black support. When that happened, other methods of disfranchising blacks were needed. Rebecca Felton had urged disfranchisement in 1902, and Tom Watson had written her, "The rich educated white man who debauches the poor white and the nigger—isn't he the really dangerous man?" Those opposed to Bourbon control, such as Watson and former Independent Felton, believed they had lost their elections because the "rich educated white" used blacks to vote against them and "miscounted" the election returns out of their fear of actual black influence developing. Black educator John Hope said as much in 1905: "Populism was defeated by the colored voters espousing the Democratic side." Constitutional disfranchisement was touted by whites as a progressive measure. If there were guarantees that blacks could no longer vote, then those such as Watson and Felton, who considered themselves the progressive forces, believed their side could win offices.

Watson was the Populist presidential candidate in 1904 and made constitutional disfranchisement a popular issue when he announced he would support any gubernatorial candidate who favored the measure. Hoke Smith was such a man. Born in 1855, Smith passed the bar examination when he was eighteen and rose to fame and fortune quickly. He bought the *Atlanta Journal* in 1887 and was worth $300,000 by the time he was thirty-five. He played a role in the 1892 nomination of President Cleveland to a second term and was rewarded with the position of secretary of the treasury. He resigned in 1896 over the silver issue and sold the *Journal* in 1900 to a friend, James Gray. Smith had opposed Watson and the Populists in the 1890s, but after 1900, as Watson became more and more bitterly antiblack, they were drawn together, representing a joining of rural and urban poorer whites.

Hardwick and John Temple Graves prevailed on Watson to support Hoke Smith in the 1906 governor's race, with the understanding that Smith would make constitutional disfranchisement his highest priority. Leading Populists also supported Smith's move in this direction. Smith began his fourteen-month campaign in June 1905 with a platform centered on black disfranchisement and economic reform. "I favor a constitutional amendment which will insure a continuation of white supremacy," he proclaimed, thereby sealing his bargain with Watson, who pledged his support three months later. Following a Smith speech in Valdosta, local blacks called a meeting and canceled their subscriptions to Smith's old newspaper, the *Journal.*

Smith represented the "progressive" wing of the Democratic party. Bourbon Clark Howell, editor of the *Atlanta Constitution*, was considered the other leading candidate in a crowded field. Howell's need to compete for the poor white vote led him to drop the traditional Bourbon paternalism for a more anti-Negro stance. The *Voice of the Negro* noted in August 1905 that Howell, who previously condemned lynching, had become silent on the subject.

Howell did not support a constitutional amendment, arguing that it was unnecessary. After all, the poll tax and white primary had eliminated the black threat to the Bourbon oligarchy. Howell admitted as much when he said, "The Negro vote in Georgia is already disfranchised." Besides, Bourbon Democrats might need black votes to beat back future challenges. Howell thought the "grandfather" escape clause was unconstitutional, as indeed the Supreme Court would rule in 1915. He tried to scare white voters by stating that Congress would reduce Georgia's representation in Congress by enforcing the Fourteenth Amendment if the state disfranchised blacks. He also claimed that a literacy clause would stimulate black education and hurt poor whites. "Make the ballot the prize of education and every Negro child in Georgia will trot straight from the cabin to the college," he said. When whites were divided, he claimed, "Educated Negroes graduating by the thousands each year from richly endowed institutions will hold the absolute balance of power."

Smith needed the votes of the poor whites, and he and Watson understood that the Bourbon machine could always change the rules—by dropping the white primary, for example. The only protection for Progressives, Smith and Watson agreed, was the complete elimination of blacks from the political process. Smith argued that the literacy qualifications under his plan would be so restrictively applied to blacks that "if they brought every teacher from New England for ten years, it would not give ten percent of the niggers in Georgia the privilege of voting." One way would be to require potential black voters to interpret Latin phrases in the Constitution, whereas whites would only have to read English.

Smith and Howell tried to "out-Nigger" each other; that is, they competed to see who could say the worst things about blacks. Genuine Progressive issues, such as railroad regulation were neglected, as the candidates concentrated on the Negro menace and how to attack it. In Smith's speeches, "The Negro voter was ignorant, illiterate, savage, vicious, inhuman, unendurable, venal, arrogant, brutish, venomous, (and) lust-ridden," by one account. Smith stood on the verge of calling for violence: "Shall it be ballots now or bullets later?" He had warned blacks that "the black quest for 'political equality' inevitably moved toward 'social equality' which in turn led either to deportation or extermination." Linking the black vote with dreams of race mixing guaranteed white support of disfranchisement. In the only election that mattered in Georgia in 1906, the August 22 Democratic primary, Smith won the gubernatorial nomination with more votes than his four rivals combined. Howell came in third behind Richard B. Russell, Sr.

Newspapers involved in the Democratic factional struggle fed prejudices and increased racial tensions to a fever pitch in the summer of 1906. Civic and religious leaders made the situation worse by advocating new restrictions on blacks. The long, grueling racist political campaign combined with long-standing racial tensions and antiblack propaganda to yield a frenzy of violence starting on September 22, 1906, in Atlanta. The Atlanta race riot was one of the worst attacks on blacks in the United States in the twentieth century. Historian Charles Crowe estimated that twenty-five blacks were killed and several hundred were injured in the rampage, which lasted several days and also claimed at least one white life.

During the campaign, the media had sensationalized the issue of "social equality" with lurid front-page stories of assaults by blacks on white women. Graves, then editor of the *Atlanta Georgian*, intensified the race-baiting campaign on Smith's behalf in July 1906. The *Atlanta Evening News* called for a reappearance of the Klan and congratulated lynchers. The *Atlanta Journal*, which had promoted violence against blacks for some time, also supported Smith. Graves's inflammatory editorials advocating lynching were later condemned by a Fulton County grand jury, which said they incited the lynch-mob spirit and "encouraged citizens to act outside the law in the punishment of crimes."

Many factors contributed to the buildup of racial tensions in Atlanta. Thomas Dixon's play, *The Clansman*, did much to inflame white sentiment against blacks. One reviewer predicted it would have the force of "a runaway car filled with dynamite." During Smith's campaign, it played to packed houses in Atlanta and to the applause of a crowd that included Gov. Joseph M. Terrell.

There were economic reasons behind the riot also. In Atlanta, blacks had been making advances that white supremacists wanted to take away. Atlanta had a relatively well developed black middle class growing up along "Sweet Auburn," which was reinforced by Atlanta University and a black press. The relative prosperity of the time led to a labor shortage in Atlanta, and blacks were able to earn up to $1.50 a day in 1906 as compared to one-third of that a few years earlier. This was a source of white resentment because higher income for black men meant that fewer black women had to go to white homes to do kitchen and domestic work and a greater proportion of black children could go to school. Crowe noted that racial disturbances during the Progressive era "were rooted in the common white desire to arrest Negro progress and to drive blacks into greater docility and subjugation." President Taft's secretary of war, J. M. Dickinson, later told an Atlanta audience that the lid on Negro aspirations would always lead to violence.

Blacks were sometimes militant in their opposition to repression, which Du Bois believed was also a factor that fueled the Atlanta riot. Blacks protested against disfranchisement and segregation at the new Carnegie Library and boycotted railroads, streetcars, and stores that practiced discrimination. One of several efforts blacks made to develop ways to fight the impending disfranchisement was the convocation of the Equal Rights League by William Jefferson White in Macon on February 17, 1906.

The climate of racial tensions continued after the election, as Atlanta newspapers, locked in a circulation war, spread rumors and fabricated accounts of numerous rapes of white women by blacks. Few, if any, actually took place. During the week immediately preceding the riot, "scattered and largely inconsequential incidents between Negro men and white women were transformed by press and public discussion into 'an intolerable epidemic of rape' which had to be ended 'immediately,'" according to one historian's account. In one case, a white woman claimed she had been assaulted and her throat slashed by a black. She later confessed that family troubles had led her to a suicide attempt. Some reports of attacks on white women were pure inventions. One "rape" came when a woman peeked out her window and screamed when she saw a black man walking on the sidewalk.

The flashpoint occurred when Atlanta newspapers each ran several extras on September 22 featuring sensational rape charges and articles attacking "Negro Dives." The *Evening News* alone published five extras. Heavily armed Atlanta whites, already brought to a fever pitch of antiblack emotions by the rhetoric of the election campaign, collected downtown near the saloon district and exploded into mob violence that Saturday night. White mobs, numbering in the thousands, descended on innocent blacks and murdered them in the streets. Some of the first victims included a lame bootblack and a barber. The rioters then dumped the bodies in front of the Henry Grady statue, thinking this "constituted a proper tribute to 'the statesman of the New South,' who had lectured so often on the need to keep the Negro in his place," according to Crowe.

Twelve trolleys were attacked, and several passengers were killed, though one got away by firing a gun point-blank into a crowd of attackers. Several blacks who were downtown or in white neighborhoods were killed, and many more were wounded on the first day of the riot. For the most part, police refused to protect victims or joined in the violence. Blacks fled the city, and finally, early on Sunday morning, "the ranks of the rioters were thinned after one o'clock by physical exhaustion, the lack of victims in the central city, and a partial satiation of the lust for blood."

On Sunday, whites feared reprisals, and the city was comparatively quiet. Historian Crowe contended that "every Atlanta Negro who could buy, borrow or steal a weapon did so in fear of his life." Monday evening, whites invaded the black middle-class community of Brownsville and were met by armed resistance. Walter White, who was then thirteen, told a dramatic story about how his father handed him a gun as they crouched inside an open window in their darkened house and told him to shoot the first white who stepped through their yard gate. He did not have to pull the trigger, for shots from a home nearer the mob caused it to retreat.

On Tuesday morning, police and militia, accompanied by other whites, disarmed middle-class blacks in their own neighborhoods whenever possible and then stood by or sometimes joined the mob as whites continued their attacks. But by then blacks were shooting back even more. Around Clark University and the Gammon Theological Seminary, "The respectable colored citizens had formed armed patrols. . . . they were threatened and fired on by a mob-like group of police and other armed whites," according to John Hope's biographer. One white and four blacks were killed in this battle. Gammon President J. W. E. Bowen was beaten and black homes were looted and burned.

If black militancy was a cause of the riot, it also helped end it. There were many instances of self-defense by blacks. Du Bois stated that the riot was stopped when the blacks began to fight back. A few days after the riot, Lewis H. Douglass, son of Frederick Douglass, wrote, "Our people must die to be saved and in dying must take as many along with them as it is possible to do with the aid of firearms and all other weapons."

The black press was also a riot victim. During Tuesday's riot Graves telegraphed a report to the *New York World* stating that the riot was a result of "a carnival of rape" and the deaths and property destruction, while regrettable, were justified. He said that only criminal Negroes who were guilty of raping white women had been killed. When J. Max Barber read of this, he sent the *World* a report of events leading up to the riot and told how the newspaper's stories of rape were lies. Barber said that Hoke Smith hired men to blacken their faces and knock down white women and these incidents were then reported as rape, as were the hysterical screams of some women, frightened by all the false rumors. James W. English—president of the Fourth National Bank, member of the city police commission, and Governor Terrell's chief of staff—called Barber to his office and told him he would either have to retract his account of the causes of the riot or go on the chain gang. Barber chose neither and moved with his magazine to Chicago, where The *Voice of the Negro*, a significant record of Negro life and thought, soon died. William Jefferson White, editor of the *Georgia Baptist*, was forced to leave Augusta temporarily because he denounced the rioters and those behind them.

Although he had to leave town, Barber's position was supported by Atlanta Mayor James G. Woodward, whose investigative committee found no confirmed cases of rape and concluded that the mob had killed innocent blacks. Even conservative Governor Terrell admitted that ten of the eleven murdered blacks he knew about had not been suspected of any crime. Woodward told the city council he blamed the riot on "inflammatory sensational newspaper extras" and that some of the stories were "utterly without foundation." Woodward had a reputation for drinking, supported lynching, and generally lacked respect. On September 22, the mob had taken his pleas to stop rioting as a joke.

After the riot hundreds of blacks refused to go to work in Atlanta. Hundreds more moved to other cities, including Macon, where blacks were buying guns. To reduce tensions, the Macon mayor canceled performances of *The Clansman* and closed the saloons. Atlanta's mayor also closed down saloons for ten days after the riot. The riot had an economic cost above the loss of property and productive lives. Many blacks lost wages, and some had to mortgage their homes to pay for medical and funeral bills or the fees of lawyers to defend them in court. A number of blacks were tried for killing whites but were acquitted, and fifteen young whites were sentenced to thirty days in the stockade for their role in the violence. Charles T. Hopkins, a member of the Atlanta Chamber of Commerce, said shortly after the riot that earlier, Atlanta's credit was good for millions in the North but "today we couldn't borrow fifty cents and our credit, so laboriously built up, was swept away by hoodlums and white criminals."

The Atlanta riot did stimulate some white leaders to move against the conditions of mutual hostility. Hopkins and ex-governor Northen organized the Christian League, an interracial group to combat the causes of mob violence, which became statewide. Hopkins and the Rev. Henry Hugh Proctor, pastor of the black First Congregational Church, organized a "Colored Cooperative Civic League" in Atlanta to ease racial tensions. This league, founded on Thanksgiving, had a membership of three thousand by Christmas. It raised money to help riot victims and obtained the release of sixty blacks who had been arrested. The two organizations joined to secure a trial for Joe Glenn, a black accused of rape. They thought him guilty but wanted to establish the precedent of due process of the law in such cases. Glenn had been misidentified by a white woman and was proved innocent. Nevertheless, he had to give up his farm and flee to avoid a possible lynching. The leagues also helped to secure the dismissals of some culpable Atlanta police officers.

Many mass meetings in the North protested the Atlanta riot. Several black citizens' groups as well as Booker T. Washington had asked President Theodore Roosevelt during the riot to send troops. But Roosevelt said he "had absolutely no authority under the circumstances to send troops to Atlanta." While Washington publicly praised Clark University President William H. Crogman and Bowen for organizing the self-defense of the Atlanta University campus, Washington told the Afro-American Council the following month in New York City that blacks needed to be patient and get rid of the criminals in their own ranks. The council ignored Washington's emphasis and vigorously condemned the riot, ballot restrictions, Jim Crow, and mob violence. A.M.E. Zion Bishop Alexander Walters, president of the council, said, "It is nonsense for us to say Peace! Peace! when there is no peace." The riot weakened Washington's influence, for it further undermined the faith blacks had in his theory that as they acquired more education and property they would gain greater white respect. After the initial downtown Saturday night bloodletting, educated, property-owning, middle-class blacks became the primary target of Atlanta's rioting mobs.

Washington also was blamed by militant black opponents for helping to create the climate that produced the riot. In August 1906, he was in Atlanta to attend a meeting of the National Negro Business League (NNBL), which he had founded in 1900, and was called to the office of Graves, who advised him to urge his people to stop the wave of rapine that the editor claimed was sweeping the country. Although no such "wave" existed, Washington dutifully addressed the NNBL on August 29: "Our leaders should see to it that the criminal Negro is got ride of. . . . The Negro is committing too much crime." The *Constitution* reported the speech under the headline *Law-Breaking Negroes Worst Menace To Race.*

In the year after the riot, Northen traveled the state in behalf of interracial good feelings and asked for justice for blacks. The *Journal* charged he was trying to undo Hoke Smith's campaign to disfranchise blacks. Northen's type of interracial cooperation, based on white guilt and paternalism, was ineffective. The Christian League survived for a few years in Atlanta but quickly died outside the capital. It was not until blacks attacked the economy of Georgia by leaving the state in great numbers during World War I that a more permanent, effective interracial organization could function.

The riot did yield some justice to one of Atlanta's white newspapers. In January 1907, the *Atlanta Evening News* went into receivership—"its failure being due largely to the strong public sentiment against its course before and during the riot," contemporary white journalist Ray Stannard Baker noted.

The move to disfranchise black voters was only strengthened by the Atlanta riot. The Hardwick disfranchisement bill to amend the Constitution was reborn in the 1907 Georgia legislature as the Felder-Williams Bill. The amendment had a property qualification that required the ownership of forty acres or property assessed at $500, a "grandfather" escape clause for whites, a "good character clause," and a literacy qualification. The bill's supporters knew disfranchisement could be enforced against blacks by fraudulent means, which they believed would keep 75 percent of the graduates of even Atlanta University from passing the literacy test. Blacks organized in protest, but their actions were futile. The disfranchising bill passed on August 17, 1907 without serious opposition in the General Assembly. The only votes against the bill were from fifteen legislators representing poor whites who feared the bill would disfranchise their class and the one black in the legislature, Atlanta University graduate William Rogers of McIntosh County.

Rogers introduced an amendment in the form of a grandfather clause that would exempt all who had been slaves and their descendants from the literacy requirement inasmuch as those whites who had served in the armed forces during the Civil War and their descendants were excused by their grandfather clause. This amendment received one vote—his. Rogers resigned when the bill went into effect. He was the last black legislator in Georgia until Leroy Johnson of Atlanta was elected to the state Senate in 1962.

The disfranchisement amendment was submitted to the people in a statewide referendum in 1908. The *Constitution* opposed it because the oligarchy for which it spoke felt secure in its ability to manipulate the black vote. Some white Republicans probably supported the disfranchisement of blacks on the mistaken theory that they would then have the party all to themselves and no longer would have to share its offices and patronage jobs with blacks. Blacks registered, paid their poll taxes, and organized to defeat the amendment. Over twice as many voted as had voted four years earlier, but they were too few. Whites responded in the traditional way by stuffing ballot boxes, threatening would-be black voters, burning thirteen black churches, and by lynching several blacks. In a light voter turnout, the amendment passed by a two-to-one margin on October 7, 1908 and went into effect the first of the following year.

Georgia, which had pioneered legal and illegal disfranchisement of blacks, became the seventh Southern state to incorporate the principle into its Constitution. Voters and politicians ignored the July 1868 congressional requirement for the state's readmission to the Union—that Georgia never amend its Constitution in a way to deprive the Negro of the vote.

Negro registration in the state declined from over 28 percent in 1904 to under 5 percent in 1910, with that mostly in urban areas. The rural black vote practically disappeared, and the urban vote drastically declined. The disfranchisement of blacks not only encouraged black political apathy, but most whites also quit bothering about elections, and only about 20 percent would show up even for the more exciting ones. This surrendered Georgia more and more to the demagogues who had only one issue—keeping the black down. Whoever rode this issue the hardest was usually elected. On the day after the constitutional referendum, the *Atlanta Journal* might crow, "Georgia takes her place among the enlightened and progressive states which have announced that the white man is to rule," but in reality disfranchisement brought control of Georgia to a small group of narrow-minded men with limited vision who retarded the state's development. On the national level the same men kept getting reelected to Congress, where they rose through the seniority system to chair many of the more important committees and opposed almost every truly progressive idea that came along.

Blacks did not go down without fighting. Despite all the machinations, some blacks still voted, and others continued to struggle to win this basic democratic right. The black press mounted a drumfire of criticism against Georgia's voting restrictions, calling them, among other things, taxation without representation. When one black managed to vote in the 1912 Atlanta white primary, the secretary of the Fulton County Executive Committee moved to throw the vote out as a matter of principle. Joseph Butt of Fannin County sued the registrars who kept him from voting in 1912. These acts, while showing spirit, accomplished little. Laurens County was typical for Georgia that year. There were over twenty-five hundred black males of voting age, but only fifty-four were registered, and none of them expected to vote.

Over the years, the literacy test served the disfranchisers' wishes well. The test required voters to be able to read and explain any paragraph in the federal or state constitutions. Blacks who might have known that the Thirteenth Amendment to the federal Constitution ended slavery would not necessarily be able to explain Section 10 of Article 1 concerning bills of attainder and ex post facto laws. The literacy clause was enormously abused through the years, and registrars' questions grew ridiculous. Those who could give a proper explanation could then be asked an irrelevant nonsense question. In Telfair County in the 1950s, one well-educated black minister was asked, "How many drops are in this glass of water?" He did not know, and his application for registration was denied.

Historian David H. Donald argued that constitutional disfranchisement was the final effort of the Civil War and Reconstruction generations to ensure that the coming generations would live in the same world they knew. Those leaders wanted to confine the next generation "in a prison with four walls: racial separation, disfranchisement of blacks, allegiance to the Democratic party, and reverence for the Lost Cause." The 1909 call of the NAACP for its founding convention acknowledged their success by saying that Georgia had just joined the Second Confederacy of ex-Confederate states.

"Southern Progressivism" was an ironic term when blacks were concerned. As disfranchisement proceeded, laws became more harsh and unfair, education for blacks was curtailed and discouraged, and mob violence continued. While whites had argued that blacks would be treated more fairly once they were removed from active participation in electoral politics, the truth was a different matter. "It has on the contrary," Du Bois said, "stripped them naked to their enemies."

Jim Crow: Keeping Blacks Down and Distant

Segregation—the physical separation of the races—was not a defining feature of the antebellum South. The lives of slaves and whites were closely intertwined. They worked together, prayed together, often slept together, and house slaves sometimes lived in the manor house. While blacks and whites had a certain degree of intimacy, the social distance between master and slave was so great that customs and laws to keep blacks physically apart from whites were not needed to impress his or her status upon the slave. It was not until Reconstruction and afterward, when blacks began the long march toward equality, that whites felt compelled to impose Jim Crow customs and laws on Southern society to keep blacks down and distant.

"One of the strangest things about the career of Jim Crow is that the system was born in the North and reached an advanced age before moving South in force," historian C. Vann Woodward pointed out. As slavery ended in the North, Jim Crow regulations began. By 1830 there remained only about thirty-five hundred slaves in all the Northern states. By 1860, the 250,000 free Negroes in the North lived mostly in separate sections of cities and towns. If they went to school, it was usually a separate school, and blacks were buried in a segregated cemetery.

The nation's dedication to white supremacy was not altered sufficiently by the Civil War to prevent similar developments in the South when the smoke of battle cleared away. Just as the North emancipated slaves, then segregated them, so did the South. However, the process was not sudden, and as in the North, it was never complete.

In post-Civil War Georgia, there was no period of integration that was later discarded in favor of segregation; blacks moved from exclusion to admission to society on a segregated basis. White supremacy was so completely assumed that the 1865 Constitution did not address the question of segregation except for including a prohibition on intermarriage. An 1866 law further discouraged intermarriage by forbidding any Negro minister from marrying any white or mixed couple and a Negro. As with all laws, it was occasionally ignored. An 1885 newspaper account reveals that progressive planter David Dickson paid a young University of Georgia graduate $25,000 to marry his mulatto daughter. After a Boston wedding, the couple returned to Georgia and lived in peace.

While Georgia's apartheid developed mainly by custom, not law, congressional Reconstruction temporarily slowed the growth of Jim Crow. The federal Civil Rights Act of 1866, the Reconstruction Acts of 1867, and the Fourteenth Amendment seemed to indicate that the nation opposed segregation and anticipated an open society. Furthermore, Georgia's 1868 Constitution said: "The social status of the citizen shall never be the subject of legislation." However, recognizing that segregation was to be the practice, black Savannah legislator James Porter introduced a bill that required equal facilities for all races on public carriers. While the bill passed the legislature, the law was ignored. Additional hope for Georgia's blacks came from Washington when the

Sumner Civil Rights Bill passed in 1875. As a practical matter, the Sumner Act was meaningless. It was not enforced, and the U. S. Supreme Court overturned it in 1883, making official what was already fact and sanctifying the caste system.

Prior to the 1890s, there were relatively few attempts by the legislature to write segregation laws; the most notable of these concerned education. The state's 1877 Constitution required school segregation and made provisions for establishing Jim Crow institutions for the blind, deaf, and dumb. In the 1880s private discrimination grew, and Jim Crow was institutionalized even though a system of laws was not yet in place. Bourbons believed such laws were unnecessary because they thought blacks could be manipulated; therefore gratuitous insults in the form of Jim Crow laws might be counterproductive.

By some accounts, race relations were more friendly prior to the 1890s, despite political terrorism and economic hardships. In addition to interracial political alliances, there was social mingling. Racial attitudes hardened with time. The first generation of blacks after slavery was less servile and did not accept the low status of its parents, and the flexibility in Georgia's black-white relationships from Appomattox to the 1890s disappeared as the intensity of racism increased. Whites came to realize that customary ways of keeping blacks down might be insufficient. Discrimination could no longer be enforced simply by economic means, and political terrorism and fraud might not be successful much longer. Fearful for the future, the generation led by Confederate veterans was determined to pass its world on unchanged to the next generation and seized on a legislative solution to preserve the society it cherished.

During the period of Populist influence in the early 1890s, Georgia's law books began to fill with Jim Crow regulations aimed at keeping whites from having contact with blacks. To blacks, "social equality" meant equal civil rights guaranteed by law, with the opportunity to use any public accommodation on an equal basis with whites. Whites deliberately misunderstood and tried to equate "social equality" with an imagined desire of blacks to marry whites.

Over time, whites became increasingly vigilant in enforcing the Jim Crow structure, and more laws defining details of segregation went on the books. "By 1908, the color line had become a color wall: high, thick and seemingly impenetrable," according to historian Horace Wingo. Like political disfranchisement, economic restrictions, terrorism, and unequal justice, segregation rendered blacks more powerless and less able to become equal members of society.

Jim Crow laws were more complex, stronger, and more completely enforced than antebellum slave codes. The most publicized white supremacy laws applied to the railroads. They affected articulate middle-class blacks, who frequently reacted with bitter protests and lawsuits. Before the Civil War, slaves rode on the railroads for one-half fare. In 1866 the Georgia House of Representatives passed a bill that required separate railroad cars for blacks, but the Senate failed to ratify it. Some conservative whites believed that blacks who could afford first-class tickets were entitled to first-class accommodations. The 1870 law requiring equal railroad accommodations provided for a fine of $10,000 for violations, although it was never enforced.

The 1875 Sumner law inhibited the legalization of railroad conductors' growing practice of assigning black passengers to a separate car. Former governor Joseph E. Brown, as head of the Western and Atlantic Railway, stiffened the enforcement of segregation after the Sumner law was voided in 1883. In 1885, black Camden County legislator Anthony Wilson introduced a public accommodations bill that would have banned discrimination on Georgia's common carriers, in hotels, and at circuses and theaters. It got only three votes—those of the black legislators.

Lacking refinements that would come later, railroad discrimination in the 1880s was hit or miss, and individual black victims found several ways of protesting. The Interstate Commerce Act of 1887 contained a nondiscrimination clause. The white press denounced it as giving carte blanche to blacks to ride on any railroad car they pleased. As the *Macon Telegraph* phrased it, "Any dirty buck negro may demand admission to any ladies' car running upon the railroads of Georgia." Interstate Commerce Commission (ICC) rules only slowed the development of segregated public transportation for a couple of years. Soon thereafter, the *Savannah Tribune* concluded that the ICC would not help and blacks would have to fight for their rights on their own. The federal government's failure to enforce its own laws soon convinced whites that they could kick out blacks from first-class cars. Georgia's 1891 separate car law legalized the growing practice of railroad segregation. An exception was made for black nurses and servants accompanying white employers. A 1901 law gave railroad conductors police powers to enforce segregation, and this was done vigorously.

Between 1870 and 1891, most railroads had a "white only" first-class car, but many also continued to offer prime accommodations to blacks. However, the practice of jamming blacks into filthy, dilapidated, segregated cars was growing. The *Savannah Tribune* noticed the trend in 1889. The 1891 law legalized and encouraged the spread of second-class treatment for blacks; soon there was only one railroad in Georgia that still provided first-class accommodations for blacks.

Pullman cars were the one significant exception to the 1891 law. In 1888, the Georgia Railroad Commission decided it did not have jurisdiction over Pullman cars, and George Pullman, the manufacturer and leaser of the cars, refused to order segregation on them. The Afro-American League won several suits involving the ejection of blacks from Pullman cars in 1891. These were temporary victories, for the Supreme Court's "separate but equal" ruling in *Plessy v. Ferguson* (1896) rendered futile all efforts to resist such treatment.

Over black protests, the Georgia legislature extended the segregation law to include Pullman cars in 1899. Du Bois, Atlanta Congregational minister Henry H. Proctor, and Gammon theology professor John W. E. Bowen met with Gov. Allen D. Candler to urge him to veto the bill, to no avail. Du Bois and Booker T. Washington tried to see Robert Todd Lincoln, son of Abraham Lincoln and president of the Pullman Company, when the ICC suggested to Du Bois in 1901 that he challenge the 1899 Georgia law in the courts. The suit was initiated but later dropped, and railroad segregation remained complete and inflexible in Georgia until after World War II.

The struggle with the railroads turned to an effort to acquire the "equal" accommodations the Plessy case seemed to promise. The two hundred members of the Georgia Equal Rights League, which met in 1906, protested Jim Crow conditions for black travelers. In 1913, the Georgia Federation of Colored Women's Clubs filed a petition with the Georgia Railroad Commission complaining that Negro cars were dirty, swept while occupied, and both sexes had to use the same lavatory; white smokers, news vendors, and law officers with convicts occupied more than half the seats. Jim Crow cars were so bad that Georgia sheriffs protested having to ride in them when traveling with black prisoners.

In 1891, Georgia was the first state to adopt a statute to segregate streetcars, which came to Georgia's larger cities by the 1870s. At first, they were single horse-drawn cars and were the most integrated Georgia facility for three reasons. Whites could more readily accept the idea that blacks were entitled to ride on streetcars than on trains. Such trips were necessary for shopping in the local white-owned stores and for working in white homes and businesses, whereas a train ride did not obviously benefit the white community—it was more likely to be considered an unnecessary excursion. Also, black protest against streetcar Jim Crow was better organized and more effective. These factors combined to produce a third reason: Traction company owners opposed segregation because it was bad for business.

Savannah's older, more stable, and better-organized black community resisted streetcar segregation until 1906. Horse-drawn cars were introduced in Savannah in 1869 with separate cars with black drivers for blacks. Blacks immediately challenged the segregation; radical black Republican James Habersham was arrested on May 1870 for riding in a white car. The case against him was dismissed, however. To forestall a suit by blacks in 1872 that would enforce the 1866 federal Civil Rights Act, the traction company abandoned the separate-car system, and blacks then rode on the formerly all-white cars. This soon led to racial clashes. In 1872 a riot broke out in July when blacks who got on the "white" cars were thrown off. Crowds of angry whites and blacks confronted each other with guns and clubs. Eleven whites and twenty blacks were injured, and some accounts reported the deaths of three blacks. A black lost the court case he brought against his attackers, and the separate Negro cars were reinstated. Then a black boycott of the traction company was instituted. It was so effective that it forced the end to segregated cars within two months. When Warsaw, a suburb of Savannah, segregated its cars in 1899, a two-month boycott forced a return to integrated cars. A similar effort to segregate the cars by city ordinance in 1902 was also defeated by another boycott by the unified and determined black community. Savannah streetcars remained integrated until 1906.

In 1906, Savannah whites were inflamed by Hoke Smith's viciously antiblack gubernatorial campaign. This led Savannah to reimpose segregation on its streetcars. The racial climate had so deteriorated that whites were determined to make segregation stick despite another boycott. As with most black boycotts, the ministers organized it, and the black press supported it. Sol C. Johnson's *Tribune* said "WALK," and helped organize the short-lived Negro Transport Company, which utilized the city's black hackmen, who charged twenty-five cents for whites and ten cents for blacks. Many blacks used it; others walked. The boycott was almost total and lasted over eighteen months, longer than the Montgomery bus boycott of the 1950s. As late as 1908, some blacks were still walking. But it was futile, for white attitudes had so hardened that the streetcar company and police saw no choice but to enforce segregation. One scholar concluded, "The failure of the Savannah boycott marked the demise of effective protests throughout the state."

In 1916, three white Savannah women were killed when the front end of a streetcar caught fire. Blacks were then told their section would be moved to the front and whites would ride in the safer rear section. As late as 1918 there were reports of racial clashes "almost daily" on Savannah streetcars. Everyone knew there was a color line, but no one knew exactly where it was or how much it could be bent.

There were similar events in other Georgia cities. Macon opted for segregated transportation, and a black boycott of segregated streetcars failed in Rome. In 1900, an altercation on an Augusta streetcar resulted in the shooting death of a white by a black. The black was lynched, and the city reacted by passing an ordinance requiring total segregation on streetcars.

Atlanta got streetcars in 1871. A boycott in 1892 by the city's blacks resulted in non-enforcement of the segregation requirement. However, in 1896, when F. A. Turner refused to sit in the back of a streetcar, he was sentenced to twenty-six days in the stockade, and the judge ruled that the back two rows of streetcar seats were the Jim Crow section. A 1900 boycott failed. Historically, the most successful transportation boycotts were supported by black alternatives to public transportation. Though some blacks were willing to walk, Atlanta was too spread out by then, and blacks' efforts to form their own transport company failed. Several Atlanta University faculty members continued to walk or ride their bicycles for years rather than sit in the back of a streetcar.

Segregation continued as new forms of public transportation developed. When taxis appeared, they were also segregated in most cities. When buses began to replace streetcars, they usually carried signs stating, "Whites Forward, Negroes Rear."

The 1875 Sumner Civil Rights Act encouraged blacks to be more insistent in receiving equal treatment in bars and restaurants. Atlanta's Union Station had a freedmen's saloon in 1872. Augusta's Planters Hotel seated blacks at separate tables. Some Atlanta establishments countered the Sumner Act by raising prices for blacks to ten dollars for a glass of beer and fifteen dollars for a shot of whiskey, with a "liberal" discount to whites, who paid five and ten cents for those drinks. The Sumner Act's 1883 demise weakened resistance to segregation in public accommodations. By 1885, every public place in Atlanta where patrons sat down was segregated except for two integrated saloons, according to the *Constitution*. Atlanta had sixty-six other saloons then: five for blacks and sixty-one for whites. By 1910 the Atlanta city code required a restaurant or bar to serve one race only and signs to be posted accordingly. Blacks could not eat at any downtown restaurant or use any downtown toilet facilities except those at the railroad station. Careful planning was required for what should have been simple shopping trips.

Jim Crow governed all facets of life. The practice of having segregated restrooms developed, with many places having three: one for "Ladies," one for "Gentlemen," and a unisex one for "Colored." This probably happened first in Atlanta, but in 1895 the Savannah Post Office had segregated restrooms. When Atlanta had a bad fire in 1917, its auditorium was set up by blacks and whites as a relief center. Following objections by whites, all blacks had to use the back door.

The ambition for self-improvement that drove many blacks was thwarted by segregated second-class schools and libraries. Atlanta received a Carnegie Library in 1902. Blacks contributed to the tax receipts that the city used to pay for the $5,000 site and to maintain the library, but they were excluded from the facility, although any black servant with a note from a white could obtain any book the white requested. Carnegie offered $10,000 in 1904 for a building for blacks if the city would supply the site and the $1,000 annual operating costs. Although blacks agreed to furnish the site, the city refused to help, and Atlanta's blacks did not get a library until 1921.

The availability of virtually all services was affected by Jim Crow. Hotels and boardinghouses adopted the color line. A few separate facilities exclusively developed to accommodate those blacks who traveled. The Union Hotel in Augusta advertised that it catered to "the traveling public of color." Black barbershops that had been fairly well self-segregated earlier were the targets of laws later. In 1926, Atlanta enacted an ordinance against black barbers working on the hair of white women or any white child under fourteen years of age. This was challenged in the courts, which ruled that the provision applying to children was unconstitutional.

Stores were not as segregated as much as black merchants would have liked; many blacks shopped in white-owned and white-clerked stores despite often being treated shabbily and waiting until all whites had been served. Blacks could not ride the elevators in stores; they had to use the stairs. Some blacks who could do so spoke French or Spanish and pretended to be from another country in an effort to avoid racial insults.

The idea of sharing recreational facilities became unthinkable to white Georgians. In 1865, Savannah closed its park rather than see it integrated. The next year, Savannah's city council found a solution by prohibiting blacks from going into the park unless accompanied by a white child. When bicycles became popular in the 1890s, Savannah hastened to forbid blacks the use of its bicycle paths. Atlanta did not have separate parks in the 1880s, but when blacks went to Ponce de Leon Springs, they were expected to use a separate dance pavilion and refreshment stands. Georgia passed the first segregated-park law in 1905. When blacks were barred from parks, seldom were separate facilities made available for their children. In 1911, Atlanta had no Negro parks. By 1915 there were two parks for blacks and eleven for whites. In 1926 blacks could use only three of the city's twenty-four parks. In 1940, Atlanta passed an ordinance putting all of Grant Park off limits to Atlanta's blacks except the zoo, and no blacks were allowed in the other white parks, or whites in the black parks. Several blacks were arrested for walking through parks on their way to work rather than detouring around them. Macon did not take down its symbol of park segregation, a bust of Sen. A. O. Bacon, until 1986. Bacon died in 1914 and willed fifty-five acres for Baconsfield Park to the city for the perpetual use of whites only.

Macon's blacks could attend events at the Grand Opera House only by climbing the fire escape to reach their balcony. The *Savannah Tribune* protested when a theater manager forced blacks to sit in the balcony at a performance of an all-black musical group. Circuses and fairs were segregated before and during Reconstruction. Thomasville blacks did boycott a street carnival in 1906 when they were barred from a special holiday presentation of the fete. Blacks not only protested these inequities but tried to provide recreational facilities with their own resources.

Residential segregation was never absolute in any of Georgia's cities. It developed first in the cities, where refugee slaves had to find their own housing during the Civil War. Slaves in Athens had lived among whites, but with freedom they gradually segregated. Ten small enclaves in the less desirable parts of town developed as exclusively black. In Savannah, integrated housing remaining from slavery continued into the 1870s at least. Atlanta, starting over after Sherman's visit, developed segregated housing earlier.

W. E. B. Du Bois reported in 1910 that fifty white Atlanta realtors had agreed not to sell or rent to blacks in certain areas. Atlanta and Augusta adopted residential segregation laws in 1913. In 1916, Atlanta Mayor James G. Woodward signed a segregation ordinance forbidding blacks from moving into any neighborhood that was mostly white or whites moving into black neighborhoods. While such local ordinances were routinely overturned by the Supreme Court, judicial rulings did little to slow residential segregation, and it continued to grow under coercive tactics and privately sponsored restrictive covenants, which were not outlawed until 1948. Whites behaved foolishly in their attempts to distance themselves from associating with anything black. During World War II, whites living on Uncle Remus Avenue in Atlanta thought their street was named after a black and had it changed to Lawton Place.

Most cities had a vice-ridden area called the "tenderloin" district. In 1888, white and black prostitutes lived in separate blocks. Whites often wanted to move tenderloin districts into black neighborhoods. They did this in Macon before 1913 and as an added indignity placed it next to a church. Black ministers in Savannah prevented the city from moving its red-light district into a black neighborhood in 1917.

White Georgians often behaved as if sex between a black male and a white female was the greatest crime on earth, as the myths used to justify mob murders attest. Yet both races crossed the color line for sex. An 1891 book on race relations noted, "Even men in high religious circles ran no risk of ostracism when it became known they were the fathers of children by colored concubines." While society was lenient toward white male dalliance with black women, a white woman's black lover was in constant danger of lynching.

Intermarriage, as with other segregation proscriptions, was not enforced uniformly, and despite the 1865 legislature's enactment of an anti-miscegenation law, the old Georgia custom of interracial cohabitation continued. (If interracial couples wished to get married, they usually went to Charleston.) Georgia's law was upheld in the courts in 1869 when the marriage of a white, Leopold Daniels, to a black, Charlotte Scott, was declared invalid by the Georgia Supreme Court. Yet such couples sometimes lived openly. Black children with white fathers often had problems when they tried to benefit from the provisions in their fathers' wills. After a long court battle, a black Savannah woman was finally awarded the $3,000 left to her in her white father's will. Georgia strengthened its antimiscegenation law in 1927 and changed the definition of "Negro" from one-eighth black to "descent from any Negro," with a provision that the State Health Department of Vital Statistics maintain a "color profile" on every citizen that the clerks had to consult before issuing marriage licenses.

Georgia justice was only selectively blind and certainly was not color-blind. In 1876, the *Savannah Tribune* reported that the Mayor's Court had separate Bibles for swearing white and black witnesses. This practice continued and was adopted by Atlanta and other cities. In 1891 the General Assembly officially segregated black and white convicts; they were not to be chained together. The state prison farm was officially segregated in 1897, and the federal penitentiary in Atlanta had a segregated dining hall by 1912.

During Reconstruction, ballot boxes were often segregated, and blacks served on Georgia juries, sometimes under the direction of a black judge. The opportunity for blacks to serve on local juries declined markedly when the Bourbons came to power, and the rare black juror was required to eat separately. In 1888, when blacks in Eastman demanded to be placed on the jury lists and were, a mob burned the lists. In Macon, a black who had been on twenty-five juries was dismissed from the panel for the twenty-sixth in 1889 on the grounds that he was not the peer of the white being tried. In 1894, separate taxpayer lists were being kept. By 1912, voting lists and polling places (where blacks still could vote) were segregated.

Professional and middle-class blacks were subject to the same demeaning treatment as the poorest, most unlettered and unwashed black. Black physicians endured Jim Crow restrictions, and black patients suffered from the practice of separate and unequal medicine. When a black doctor with white patients was appointed to a city medical position in Savannah in 1895, white doctors' fear of competition led to an ordinance two years later requiring that black doctors treat only black patients and white doctors treat only whites—a horribly unfair restriction, given the scarcity of black doctors. Juliette Derricotte, dean of women at Fisk University, was returning to her home in Athens by car when she was badly injured in a head-on collision near Dalton in 1931. A white doctor gave her emergency treatment, but the Dalton hospital would not admit her because she was black, so she had to be driven to a Chattanooga Hospital. She died the next day.

When Walter White headed the NAACP in 1931, his father, a light-skinned Atlantan, was struck on a city street by a car driven by a white doctor, who rushed him to Grady Hospital. Thinking he was Caucasian, "the best doctors in the hospital worked feverishly to save his life," White said. Then they learned that he was a black when a darker-skinned relative came to inquire about his condition, and he was hurried across the street in the rain to the Negro annex. Other than a twelve-bed private sanitarium, this annex was the only hospital facility available to Atlanta's ninety thousand blacks. The Grady annex had dirty, run-down buildings with huge cockroaches and aggressive rats. White wrote that when his father died, "he was ushered out of life in the meanest of circumstances an implacable color line had decreed for all Negroes, whatever their character or circumstances might be."

Whites may have occasionally attended black funerals and vice versa, but they did not share last resting places. Many city ordinances required segregated cemeteries. Atlanta had integrated cemeteries during Reconstruction, but an 1877 ordinance required that blacks buried in white cemeteries be dug up and reburied in segregated sites. Indeed, most Georgia cities required Jim Crow gravesites. Savannah passed such an ordinance in 1888, Augusta, in 1889, Rome, in 1894, Thomasville, in 1902, and Albany, in 1911.

While prejudice was never able to erase completely contacts between blacks and whites, segregation cast a pall over all aspects of society. Blacks were born segregated, went to segregated schools, enjoyed segregated entertainment, got sick and died in segregated facilities, and were buried in separate cemeteries. Then the obituaries were kept separate in the newspapers. Blacks had three responses: They could protest and try to integrate, withdraw into an all-black circle as much as possible, or when among whites, "wear the mask that grins and lies."

Throughout the Jim Crow era, leaders from Georgia and other Southern states attempted to make segregation a national policy. At the state level, new Jim Crow laws were added as late as the 1950s. By then "White" and "Colored" signs were everywhere, and the only contact most whites had with blacks was with servants and workers. As Jim Crow developed, most whites forgot that there had been an earlier period in Georgia lasting over a hundred years during which blacks and whites worked in intimate association. By the 1950s white Georgians assumed that segregation was an innate idea, a condition of birth. In Georgia, though most of the laws had been overturned by the federal courts and were no longer enforced after the civil rights struggles of the 1960s, they remained on the books through the 1970s.

Separate and Unequal Education

"Of all the civil rights that the world has struggled and fought for, for five thousand years, the right to learn is undoubtedly the most fundamental," declared W. E. B. Du Bois. Unfortunately, a good education—the first necessity for a free people—was denied to most blacks in Georgia for a century after the Civil War, and more blacks had obstacles placed in their path to education than had them removed. Georgia's white elite-dominated society had little or no use for educated blacks. Consequently, many blacks were robbed of the incentive for formal schooling: Education meant "overqualification" for available jobs, not advancement.

Despite difficulties, Georgia's blacks did make progress. Proscriptions against slave literacy increased the freed people's desire to learn. They recognized the value of education and chose their leaders after the Civil War by this one criterion over any other. A study of Savannah indicated that in the 1880s, 96 percent of black leaders had been slaves and that education, not hue or wealth, was the most important factor in their rise to leadership.

Simple terror was one of the greatest obstacles to education for blacks after it became legal. Although the original Ku Klux Klan's short-range goal was to return Georgia to undisputed Democratic control, when an opportunity presented itself, it also attacked blacks' long-range efforts for self-improvement, for the Klan was used as a means of social control as much as political dominance. Therefore, black schools were a favorite target in the years following the Civil War. In Walton County, the Klan burned the books of a Negro teacher and announced that it would tolerate no Negro schools and would whip any black who sent a child to school. Reports surfaced of teachers being shot, beaten, and threatened in Warrenton, Andersonville, Greensboro, and Macon, in Elbert and Walton counties, and numerous other places. For many blacks, going to school was an act of political defiance. Terrorism against black schooling gradually gave way to white efforts to control and direct it.

When the Civil War ended, Georgia needed a state-funded public school system, something it had never had before. In December 1866 a law was enacted, but not funded, for the free education of white children at state expense. This act also provided free college education for maimed or indigent Confederate veterans and guaranteed teaching jobs to those who graduated. Meanwhile, impatient blacks started their own schools, sometimes to the astonishment and irritation of Northern missionaries. Shortly after General Sherman arrived in Savannah, a group of blacks including James Lynch, later Mississippi secretary of state, conferred with him and got his blessing to start schools. They helped organize the Savannah Educational Association, which established schools for freed people and their children. They located ten black teachers and started two schools; one at Bryan's Slave Mart and another at the Oglethorpe Hospital opened within three weeks of Sherman's capture of the city. These schools had five hundred pupils and thirty-eight teachers between them in 1867. The teachers were paid fifteen dollars to thirty-five dollars a month from tuition charges and contributions of $1,000 from the black community. The American Tract Society, the American Missionary Association and other missionary groups, the Quakers, and the National Freedmen's Aid Society also helped. Some native whites established schools on their plantations to attract better workers.

Before the end of 1865, blacks had organized fifty schools in Georgia. During the next three years this network was extended into seventy counties, where over two hundred blacks (some of whom had been literate slaves who taught clandestinely before and during the Civil War) conducted 191 day schools and 45 night schools. Thirty-nine were in buildings blacks built for the purpose. Others were in existing structures or buildings furnished by the Freedmen's Bureau. Ninety-six of these schools were wholly or partly supported by blacks. Blacks preferred black teachers and would ask the Freedmen's Bureau or Freedmen's Aid Societies for a teacher only if they could not find one of their own.

Independent black schools depended mainly on monthly tuition charges—usually between fifty cents and a dollar—for their support. As schools became more numerous, rival groups competed with each other, and some, for example, Susie King Taylor's, were forced to close. Taylor, born a slave in 1848, was taught by two blacks and two whites in Savannah and joined the Union forces in 1862, teaching soldiers and caring for the wounded. After the war she opened up a school in Savannah for black children. This prospered, and she lived on the tuition fees (a dollar a month per pupil) until Beach Institute opened in 1867. It did not charge tuition, and she lost pupils to it and moved to Liberty County and opened another school. She later moved to Boston.

As the Freedmen's Bureau came into Georgia in the wake of Sherman's troops, it established schools in buildings it erected or repaired in some sixty towns. It also tried to enforce its apprenticeship regulations that were originally designed to place orphans with suitable guardians who would teach the children to read, write, and cipher. Whites resisted these efforts at education, just as they opposed the bureau's attempts to get fair labor contracts for freedmen. As federal troops withdrew, such resistance grew more fierce. In 1869, L. Lieberman, a white agent at Hawkinsville, wrote John Randolph Lewis at the Freedmen's Bureau in Atlanta and said he feared for his life because whites disliked the school so much—"yet it will thrive." Lewis received many such letters and concluded the following year that education for blacks was resisted by Klan-like elements in half of Georgia.

The Freedmen's Bureau was a big help before the state assumed a role in education. By 1867 it was paying $2,000 a month for schools and teacher salaries. Blacks themselves were furnishing $3,000 a month; Northern philanthropy, $5,000. By 1869 about 7 percent of the black school-age population attended Freedmen's Bureau schools in the Deep South. The schools themselves were simple to the point of crudeness, and students often walked miles in all weather to ramshackle classrooms. Northern missionary groups staffed eighty-two schools that year but the majority of Georgia's 131 counties had no schools for blacks in 1867.

The most important philanthropic group to help educate freed people was the American Missionary Association (AMA), organized in 1846 by the Congregational church in New England. Eighty percent of the 367 teachers—the "New England schoolmarms"—sponsored by Freedmen's Aid Societies who came to Georgia were AMA representatives. The Methodist Freedmen's Aid Society sent the second-largest group of teachers. In a missionary spirit of self-sacrifice, the teachers worked under difficult conditions for pay that was meager and often late. Dedicated and able, they viewed themselves as holy warriors; Du Bois called their efforts the "Ninth Crusade."

The teachers taught Puritan virtues, self-worth, and the importance of voting Republican. They faced a lack of books, chairs, slates, paper, and buildings. One AMA school was an awning stretched over poles. Sometimes teachers had to supply food, clothing, and medical care to students. Teachers also had to contend with superstitions and tardiness on the part of the students, whose crowded classrooms sometimes included whispering, pinching, and "mirthfulness and want of order." There were attendance problems, especially when election violence scared the children. The January contract signing meant much moving by black families from one plantation to another, which disrupted their children's education. Another impediment to regular attendance was the use of child labor in the fields, a practice blacks resisted, sometimes unsuccessfully.

Terror, poverty, and the shortage of schools, teachers, and classroom space limited attendance to 13 percent of the black school-age population in 1873. Classroom space was often the major obstacle. In 1873, there were 360 black schools in Georgia, mostly with one teacher, for 207,000 children—one school for every 575 children. Due to the lack of teachers and facilities, many would-be students did not go to school. Attendance rose to 37 percent in 1880 and to 56 percent in 1909, when two-thirds of those actually enrolled were in the classroom on any given day of the school term.

The Northern white teachers enjoyed the appreciation of blacks but often incurred the hatred of whites, who shunned them or screamed profanities at them, spat, and jeered. They were called "Sherman's camp followers" and "Nigger teachers." Some AMA teachers were threatened with having their houses burned or even with death by white Southerners, especially if the teachers tried to influence elections. Some were driven from rural to urban schools by such threats. Black children were pelted on the way to school, and their teachers were denied service at stores, post offices, and banks. The teachers were sustained by the conviction that their cause was righteous, for they believed it was vital to change Georgia, an especially important state due to its prominence in the Confederacy.

The AMA teachers also had problems with the military and the Republican party, which they often (with good reason) believed were not sufficiently committed to advances by blacks. This charge certainly applied to Gen. Davis Tillson when he headed the Freedman's Bureau in Georgia. Tillson countered by labeling the AMA teachers at Augusta "damned whores."

Native white Georgians resented the fact that Northern money was going to educate blacks when many whites also needed educational assistance. (AMA schools were open to whites, too, but they chose to stay away.) More basically, most white Georgians opposed education for blacks because they believed it would make the former slaves less subservient.

Although many in the AMA could be accused of cultural imperialism, their attitudes were far more advanced than those of most white Georgians. The New England teachers came mainly from abolitionist strongholds, and when they first arrived, they espoused the idea that blacks should and could achieve equality. They combined evangelical zeal with cultural self-righteousness and were convinced that for the time being, blacks should acknowledge New England's superiority in education, moral philosophy, and way of life. This led to conflicts, especially with those blacks who preferred black teachers. The AMA did not encourage black teachers, because the association thought they were less able. AMA personnel were disgusted that some blacks would pay a dollar a month to send their child to a black teacher when AMA schools were free. They also expected the blacks to join Congregational churches, but the freed people's Baptist and Methodist ties were too strong.

After the 1870 overthrow of Reconstruction in Georgia, the AMA began to compromise its radical position on black equality. In 1871, one

AMA official said that the North should stop trying to influence the South's racial mores. The AMA gradually became a cautious defender of its vested interests rather than the advocate of black advancement it started out to be.

Northern teachers taught 5,630 blacks in 1867. In 1873 the AMA had five normal schools, seven churches, three common schools, and one college. It founded schools in Atlanta, Andersonville, and Macon and it continued to support them through 1888. Three years later, it still maintained eight common schools in Georgia. Some of the AMA schools continued into the twentieth century under state support. The Dorchester Academy in Liberty County, supported by the black members of the old Midway Congregational Church, became a regular graded school. The AMA was instrumental in the founding of Howard University, Hampton, and Fisk, and in Georgia, Storrs Academy in Atlanta, Knox Academy in Athens, Albany Institute, and Atlanta University, among others.

Black leaders saw a strong link between education and political power. As the AMA quickly found out, freed people wanted to maintain authority over their education. When the AMA tried to replace black teachers in the Savannah schools that blacks started, it ran into resistance, and the AMA responded by denouncing militant black power advocates such as Aaron A. Bradley for "seditious harangues" against whites. However, the Savannah Education Association accepted some Northern white direction in order to obtain much-needed AMA funds.

The main institution that struggled to keep the education of black children under black control grew out of the Georgia Equal Rights Association. With the support of the more progressive white Republican leaders, such as John Bryant and Rufus Bullock, the Equal Rights Association developed into a statewide organization in 1866 to fight for civil rights for blacks. In the fall of 1866 it changed its name to the Georgia Education Association (GEA). By late 1867 there were 120 schools in 53 of the state's 131 counties affiliated with the 3,500-member GEA. The GEA did not confine itself to the "3 Rs" but added a fourth, "Rights," and was a base for the political careers of many blacks, including James Porter, William Jefferson White, and Tunis G. Campbell, Sr. The GEA held its first convention in Macon in October 1867. Following the previous legislature's approval of funding of schools for whites only, the convention resolved to support only those delegates to the federally mandated Constitutional Convention who pledged their support to schools for blacks also.

Two blacks sat on the seven-man Constitutional Convention's Committee on Education. The 1868 Constitution, reflecting Northern and black influences, required the next session of the legislature to provide for education to all children. State Rep. Philip Joiner of Dougherty County and Henry McNeal Turner wanted the old Milledgeville Capitol building and $100,000 for a Negro college. (Instead, it became a private white school that was still receiving state funds into the 1990s. By that time, the school had some black students, but its admission policies and status as a state-funded private school drew heavy criticism.) Black lawmakers were ousted soon after the 1868 session convened. Without their influence, the legislature did not act on the issue of universal education. When black legislators were restored to their seats in 1870, the legislature did act, and Governor Bullock signed the law establishing Georgia's first statewide public school system.

The 1870 measure provided that local schools would be controlled by county boards supervised by a state panel headed by the governor. The law provided for "separate but equal" facilities. The public school system would be funded by a property tax that was supposedly enough for a three-month term. County school boards were expected to furnish school buildings; the state would pay the teachers. Even this inadequate state support for black education was opposed by many whites.

John Randolph Lewis, former Freedmen's Bureau superintendent of education for Georgia, was the first state commissioner of education. Prejudice and lack of funds were his great handicaps. Many teachers went unpaid, since the 1870 legislature provided only 12 percent of the funds needed and diverted $200,000 to other purposes; lacking funds, Georgia schools did not operate in 1872. When the Democrats took control in 1872, the "separate but equal" provision was modified by the addition of "so far as practical," and Lewis was replaced by Gustavus John Orr, who held the post until his death in 1887. The schools reopened in 1873, and in 1874 there were 1,379 schools for whites and 356 for blacks. Recognizing the inadequacies in Georgia's educational system, an interracial mass meeting in Liberty County was called in 1876 to support an increase in the school term from three to six months.

"Separate but equal" became more separate and less equal. When Democrats rewrote the state constitution in 1877, many delegates wanted to abolish public education altogether or limit the state's commitment to elementary education only. An overwhelming majority did approve the provision that schools should be segregated or closed. "Separate but equal; as far as practical" became just "separate" under the new Constitution.

The belief that if blacks were to go to school those schools should be under white control helped keep white support for black schools from disappearing. White paternalism and the desire to control black minds led many whites to besiege the state superintendent of education for jobs teaching in black schools. Influencing the decision against ending state support of public education were such warnings as that of Emory President Atticus Haygood, who said that if Georgia did not provide public education for Negroes, "radical" Northerners would. However, the absence of any state compulsory school attendance law shows that many whites thought it was better if blacks did not go to school at all. A 1910 study that showed 75 percent of the state's illiterates were blacks also reassured whites that compulsory attendance was unneeded. Georgia finally adopted a compulsory attendance measure in 1916. It was the next-to-last state to do so.

Efforts by blacks to educate their people were often nothing short of heroic, for attacks on black schools and teachers continued throughout the late nineteenth century. William and Ellen Craft, Georgia's most famous runaway slaves, returned from England in 1870 and managed a plantation just across the Georgia line in South Carolina but were burned out by nightriders. They then tried again on the Woodville plantation in Bryan County near Savannah, where they established a school patterned after the Ockham School they had attended in England. They attempted to make Woodville a successful farming operation despite resistance from local white planters. The farm failed following Ellen's death in 1891, although the school lasted into the next century.

Repression could be especially harsh in rural Georgia. There were many plantations with twenty to a hundred black families where schools were not allowed. In 1871, when Wesley Shropshire's black tenants in Chattooga County built a school, the Klan rode through and whipped the black teacher and threatened to whip Shropshire. The school then moved into a Negro church, which was promptly burned to the ground. The blacks persevered and built another church and school. In 1876, when a black minister was whipped and a black schoolteacher had his teeth filed down to the gums, the *Savannah Tribune* asked in despair, "Is there no one in Georgia who will take the lead in denouncing such crimes?" In 1899 promoters of black education in Twiggs County were whipped along with their children; homes of black teachers were gunfire targets. Such incidents proliferated.

Keeping schools for blacks open in Georgia's cities also required courage and perseverance. Beach Institute had opened in Savannah in 1867 through a gift of $13,000 from Alfred Beach, inventor and editor of the *Scientific American*, and received continuing support from the AMA. Both Beach Institute and the Lewis School in Macon were burned by arsonists in the 1870s. Macon's white firemen stood by and watched Lewis School burn to the ground. Both schools were rebuilt and reopened, however. Lewis later became the Ballard Normal School, which continued as a private school until the 1950s. The Connecticut

Industrial School for Girls in Georgia, founded in 1885 for blacks through the gift of a $10,000 hotel in the heart of Quitman, was torched by whites six weeks after it opened; teachers and students had been harassed from its first day. It reopened in Thomasville two years later.

Throughout Georgia, black educators struggled on. Not all schools were attacked, and some were later incorporated into the public school system. One example is the Lamson Normal School at Marshallville, founded by Anna Wade in 1886. Wade was born a slave in 1862, entered a work-study program at Atlanta University when she was thirteen, and after a few years spent in Boston, where she attended the Boston's Girl's Latin Grammar School, she returned to graduate from Atlanta University in 1885. Then, with funds from Mrs. Kate G. Lamson and other Boston friends, she opened her school, which ran with AMA funding until her death in 1914. Her husband, Edward Richardson, then became the principal. The school was later renamed the Lamson-Richardson School and in 1957 became a part of the Macon County public school system. There were a number of such schools begun by dedicated black teachers such as Wade. The Rev. M. W. Reddick graduated from Morehouse College in 1897 and founded a school in Americus with two teachers. In 1915 it had fourteen teachers and seven buildings worth $40,000.

Although black schools in Georgia's cities were inadequate, they were better than the one-room ungraded rural schools where one teacher taught everyone. Atlanta's first elementary school for blacks was founded by two ex-slaves, James Tate and Grandison B. Daniels, on Jenkins Street. It and another were absorbed by Storrs Academy later that year. By 1872, Atlanta had two black elementary public schools. Whites had five elementary schools plus two high schools then. William Finch, Atlanta's first black city councilman, and twenty-five other blacks petitioned the city council for a black high school, or as an alternative, for the city to pay Atlanta University's three dollars a month tuition so students completing the primary grades could go on. The city refused, but it did take over Storrs Academy. A close race for mayor in 1888 permitted black voters to bargain and gain another school. By the 1890s there were four graded elementary schools for blacks in Atlanta. Blacks did not get a high school in the city until 1924.

Macon's first school for blacks was opened in 1865 by Ariadine Woodliff, the Philadelphia-educated daughter of prominent free Negro businessman and Reconstruction politician Edward Woodliff. In January 1866, Eliza Miller established a school at the Freedmen's Hospital that had thirty-seven students attending weekly classes. By October there were ten black and two white teachers for five hundred pupils. By the end of 1867, Bibb County had twelve black schools, with freed people raising most of the money for their support. Together these schools raised the black literacy rate to 28 percent by 1870, no mean feat for such a short time. The first library for blacks in Georgia opened that same year in the city. As in other places, Macon saw a struggle for control of these schools. E. E. Rogers, an AMA teacher in Macon, complained in 1869 that Henry McNeal Turner was encouraging distrust of all white teachers.

Black initiatives supplemented inadequate public schools. In 1899, under the prodding of the Rev. E. K. Love, then president of the Missionary Baptist Convention of Georgia, the Baptists organized Central City College in Macon, which offered elementary and secondary schooling and opened a college department in 1920. Its buildings burned in 1921. The Methodists established the South Macon Orphan Home and School in 1900 in what is now Ballard Heights. As in other places, the public schools for blacks in Macon began and ended with the elementary grades. Seventh grade was not initiated until 1917. The eighth, ninth, and tenth grades were added in 1918, but to go further, students had to attend the private Ballard Normal School or Central City College. In 1921, the Beda-Etta Business College, the first such institution in Georgia, was founded in Macon by Minnie L. Smith, a public school teacher. This school, named after the founder's sisters, taught typing, shorthand, bookkeeping, and banking to many of Macon's future black leaders.

William Finch established a freedmen's school in Athens during the summer of 1865 and moved to Atlanta in 1868. Public schools for both blacks and whites began in Athens in 1873. Blacks there had long been interested in education and liked to attend the University of Georgia commencement exercises until they were made to feel unwelcome (a black was shot during a program in the 1880s). By 1887, each group had a two-story, ten-room brick school building. In 1892, as the political power of blacks declined, their children were moved into frame buildings, while 177 white students took over the brick building that had accommodated 537 black children. By 1900 there was room for only half of the black children in Athens public schools. The private Jeruel School was started by Baptists to supplement Knox Academy, which had been opened by the AMA in 1867. Knox received some tax money when whites wanted black support to pass a bond issue in 1873. Later, disfranchisement robbed the black community of such influence.

Augusta got its first school for blacks in 1867 when William Jefferson White and Richard C. Coulter, an ex-slave, opened the Augusta Baptist Institute. When it moved to Atlanta in 1879 and eventually became Morehouse College, it left a void. As the black vote was still important there, the Richmond County School Board established Georgia's first public high school for blacks, named after Atlanta University president Edmund Asa Ware. In 1897, with the advent of the white primary and greatly reduced black political power, the school board decided to convert Ware High School into a primary school to accommodate the increasing number of younger black students. The Cumming, Harper, and Ladeveze families, all members of Augusta's black elite, then sued for equal treatment under the terms of *Plessy v. Ferguson*. They argued that no money could go to a white high school if there was not one for blacks. Augusta officials contended that blacks could attend one of the private black schools in the city. The Supreme Court decided it could not question local school board decisions, and Georgia's only public black high school disappeared. The Augusta court case, *Cumming v. Richmond County Board of Education*, was very important because it was the first time the Supreme Court ruled on school segregation. By sanctioning it, the court encouraged further educational discrimination nationwide and indicated that the word "equal" in the *Plessy* "separate but equal" decision could be ignored. In 1901 the Augusta public schools could only accommodate one-third of the black school population.

Augusta's leading private black school was the Haines Normal and Industrial Institution, founded by Lucy Craft Laney, who learned to read when she was four and was in Atlanta University's first normal graduating class in 1873. Du Bois noted in 1911 that after the Ware school was closed, the academic content of the lower grades in Negro schools was reduced. On the other hand, he lauded Haines: It "was no pretense of a school with dishwashing substituted for English, but a home and center of learning." After Laney's death in 1933, dwindling support forced the school to close in 1949. A public facility, the Lucy C. Laney High School, now stands on the site of Haines Institute, and Laney's portrait hangs in the state Capitol in honor of her contribution to black education.

The thrust for education was strongest in the cities where apostles of the New South promoted industrialization and economic development. Even they did not fully appreciate the value of an educated working class, however. Agrarian interests were less supportive; education was bad for farmhands if only because it made them dissatisfied. Agrarian views were strengthened by the county-unit system, which gave rural areas dominance in the legislature. The Industrial Revolution required intelligent labor, and the South's caste system required ignorance and subservience; these separate goals created "an impossible contradiction," Du Bois pointed out. In 1890, and for the next twenty-five years, the state's emphasis on Negro education declined as Jim Crow and disfranchisement increased. Moderate voices were ignored, and the last Northern teachers drifted away in the face of increasing racial animosity.

When the "Redeemers" came to power they reduced taxes and accused blacks of not paying their share of educational costs. The *Atlanta Constitution* charged that blacks received more from the school fund than whites and that white children had to go to work in the fields to replace black children who were in school. However, many counties spent less on black education than they received from the state for that purpose. In 1892 Georgia blacks paid $100,000 in poll taxes and $171,500 in property taxes. That year, the state made a net profit of $17,000 from the convict-lease system.* All of this $288,500 total went to the school fund, but the state only paid out $167,857 on black education. Not only were blacks paying all their education costs; they were subsidizing white education by over $120,000. By 1908, this black subsidy of white education was over $140,000. *In no other state was this subsidy so large.* Not only did the property owners who controlled Georgia's government bitterly resist any efforts to raise taxes to support a more adequate system; they also adamantly opposed federal funds for education, for they feared the money would be divided equitably among the races.

The New South's mythology about blacks included the belief that vast amounts of money had been spent on the Negro but had not brought any improvement. Charles E. Dowman, former president of Emory, cited what he saw as an increase in crime, rape, immorality and the "failure of education" to explain what "turned the feelings of many white men from sympathetic helpfulness to strained toleration." When a visitor to Bishop Henry McNeal Turner asked a white man in 1894 which streetcar went to Atlanta University, he got a lecture on the futility of "nigger colleges" instead of directions.

As whites came to understand less and less about blacks due to the growing Jim Crow, they assumed the worst. Governor Candler wrongly claimed in his 1899 message to the legislature that the rising crime rate was due to the increased education of blacks and that 90 percent of all black crime was committed by those who were educated. In one sense, whites were correct when they argued that education would "ruin" blacks. It did ruin them for the roles whites envisioned for them, and it threatened the status quo. A common remark in the black press from the late 1880s was that the new generation was too educated to accept the kind of treatment that was meted out to slaves: "That's why so many get killed." It is worth noting that the most outspoken proponents of lynching were also the most shrill opponents of schools for blacks.

Even while they tried to convince themselves that education bred crime and bad manners, Georgia whites appeared to talk themselves into believing that the state spent a great deal on the education of blacks. Rep. Charles Bartlett of Georgia told Congress in 1912 that white Georgians were taxing themselves "to a burdensome degree" for the education of Negroes. White Georgians maintained the delusion that they were

---

*Beginning in 1883, the net receipts of convict leases were added to the school fund, and most of this money came from leasing black convicts. The state's twenty-year lease (1876–96) grossed the state $25,000 per year, regardless of the number of convicts leased. Lease rates increased dramatically when the twenty-year lease expired.

selflessly generous by developing the myth that segregated schools were more expensive than integrated ones would have been.

Actually, the dual school system gave those in control the opportunity to support one system by robbing the other. While Bartlett was extolling the largesse of Georgia's white taxpayers, 45 percent of the money due blacks for education was misappropriated by the counties and diverted to white schools. The dual system let Georgia cut costs without impairing the education of whites quite so much as it did for blacks. It was not until the early 1950s—when Georgia was resisting outside pressure to desegregate schools by trying to make the separate systems more equal—that the dual system became more costly than one integrated system would have been. Before World War II, the dual system was significantly less costly. The 1877-78 school year in Columbus was probably typical. There, 48 percent of the 2,872 pupils were black, but they only received 20 percent of the total spent on heating schools, 17 percent of the amount spent for teacher's salaries, and 1 percent of the total spent on books and supplies. In 1909, Houston County spent $1.43 on each black pupil and $10.23 for each white student.

Throughout the state, funding inequities continued, and black education suffered a relative decline. In 1901 blacks comprised 47 percent of the population but received only 25 percent of the money spent on education in Georgia. By 1911, Du Bois could write that "common schools are worse off than they were twenty years ago." In 1913, Georgia spent less than 20 percent of the amount the U. S. Bureau of Education recommended for a moderately good public school system, with blacks getting the short share of this inadequate expenditure. One study shows that in 1915, Georgia spent six times as much in educating a white child as a black. (Proportional expenditures for school buildings and repairs, supplies, and equipment show even greater disparities.) Gov. Hugh M. Dorsey said in 1917 that only 3.5 percent of the state's expenditures on education went to blacks. The results were predictable. Martin Luther King, Sr., was barely able to read and write after he graduated from a rural school before World War I; to get a high school diploma, he had to attend the private Bryant Preparatory School and pay for his studies.

The higher the percentage of blacks in any Georgia county, the smaller their share of the school fund. Where blacks made up less than 10 percent of the population, 57 percent of what was spent on each white child was expended for the education of each black child. Where blacks comprised 10-25 percent of the population, they received 42 percent as much per student as whites. Where they were 25–50 percent, they received 22 percent, and where they were over 75 percent, only 8 percent of what was spent on the education of each white child was spent on each black child.

Although rural blacks were defrauded in the school-fund distribution more than those in the cities, all was not well in town, either. By 1908,

Atlanta was letting blacks have their share of the state fund, but the city found another way to cheat them. Cities had local tax assessments in addition to the state property tax. In 1908, Atlanta collected $330,000 for white schools by taxing all real property. Atlanta's blacks owned $1 million in property then, but the taxes they paid on it went to educate white children only.

One important way black education was shortchanged came with teacher pay. Not only were black teachers forced by lower pay into a meager existence, but the low pay made the position of teacher unattractive to the more able. On the other hand, opportunities for better-paying jobs were not that great for blacks, so many dedicated black teachers did teach, but the greater portion were ill prepared for the job. Many had little more than a third-grade education. Only one in five of all public school teachers had more than a grammar school education in 1890. Around 1900, while 80 percent of the white public school teachers had some teacher training, only 20 percent of the black teachers had any. In 1900, teacher pay ranged from sixty-five dollars a month for a white male to ten dollars a month for a black female. The cycle started: Poorly trained teachers taught students poorly, and the students grew up to be teachers who also were not able to train the next generation properly.

White school boards did not care if the teachers were competent. Principals and teachers, to keep their jobs, had to avoid making waves. Local school officials, fearful that well-educated black teachers would not teach their students to be subservient, often believed that if two black teachers applied for the same job, the least qualified one should be hired. To make matters worse, sometimes black teachers had to pay salary kickbacks to the county school commissioners to get and keep their jobs. Although they would have obtained superior teachers, many counties refused to hire the graduates of Atlanta University because they were afraid that the graduates, having socialized with whites, would not uphold racist mores.

The school boards and Confederate veterans committees banded together to ensure that course contents would only support traditional white supremacy. As William E. Dodd, one of the few Southern educators with a Ph.D. degree before 1900, said in 1904, "The very best books we have on history are ruled out of the South by these committees." One book in wide use to which black teachers particularly objected was a history of Georgia by popular columnist Charles H. Smith (Bill Arp), who thought education made blacks lazy and insolent.

Black teachers generally taught larger classes than their white counterparts, thus further increasing the discrepancy. In 1906, black teacher pay averaged three cents per pupil per day, while white teachers averaged ten cents. With growing uneasiness, black leaders realized how clearly teacher salaries, the quality of education, and the right to vote were related. In 1905, three years before constitutional disfranchisement, white teachers averaged $214 a year, and blacks averaged $124—58 percent of the white scale. Three years after disfranchisement, blacks received only 38 percent of the white scale; the average salary for blacks had *declined* $5 a year, whereas the average white teacher's salary had increased more than $100. In 1916, Georgia's appropriation for white teachers' pay was over five times as much as for black teachers.

School buildings for blacks were also substandard. In 1910, only half of the classrooms were in school buildings. The rest were in churches, lodges, or abandoned buildings. There were many complaints about leaking roofs, rotten floors, and cold, drafty classrooms. There were not nearly enough of even substandard quarters to accommodate all those wanting to attend school. This was especially true in the cities. In 1889, five hundred were turned away in Savannah. The problem continued; in 1916, seven hundred were turned away even though Savannah classrooms were overcrowded and double-shifted.

The problem was even greater in Atlanta. Despite protests from black leaders, classes were double-shifted. One group came in the morning and another in the afternoon to meet in the same overcrowded classroom with the same (and by then weary) teacher. As many as fifteen hundred black children could not be accommodated. In 1913, one thousand of these children went to makeshift private schools. In 1904, black parents "literally begged" the city council to allocate $650 to secure space in a building so five hundred children could have three months' schooling. The city refused, citing a lack of money. When fifty white students needed space, the city found $10,000 to accommodate them. The overcrowding continued, and Du Bois noted in 1917 that there was plenty of tax money to develop Druid Hills, an upper-class white neighborhood, but none to remedy Atlanta's inadequate black schools.

Northern philanthropy helped fill *some* gaps. Much of this funding was in a sense the conscience money of robber barons who had accumulated vast fortunes by fraud, deceit, violence, and corrupt politics. As investors in the South, they appreciated the value of a literate working class. They contributed mostly to the education of whites but also contributed to black schools, for they also realized the value of two mutually hostile groups of workers who could be pitted against each other.

The funds accomplished good by supplementing teacher salaries, erecting school buildings, purchasing equipment, encouraging attendance at teacher-training institutes, and financing long- and short-range research and development. Unfortunately, the managers of the various Northern funds accepted the New South's view of the Negro and the caste system and thus reinforced oppression. William H. Baldwin, prominent fund manager, said that blacks "will willingly fill the more menial positions and do the heavy work at less wages," leaving "the more expert labor" to whites.

In 1867, wealthy merchant George Peabody donated $1 million to a fund that by 1914 had invested $3.5 million in Southern education. The fund's administrators included Confederate general Henry Rootes Jackson of Georgia, and the trustees avoided AMA teachers, whom they thought too radical. In 1882, stimulated by the success of the Peabody Fund, the Slater Fund was established, and some of the money went to train black teachers for the one-room schoolhouses. By stimulating primary education, pressure was built for secondary education. The General Education Board was created by a gift of $1 million from John D. Rockefeller in 1902. All of these funds supported the education of whites more than blacks and opposed academic freedom, especially if it led to attacks on the Southern caste system.

In 1905, the Anna T. Jeanes Fund was founded to improve the education of rural blacks in the South. It was unique in its exclusive devotion to black education. Two years later, Jeanes added $1 million to the fund, which concentrated on raising the quality of black teachers, for only 30 percent of them had more than six years of elementary education as late as 1915. The most dedicated and able teachers were selected, and they received support to go out in the field and train their colleagues. The program started in Georgia in 1908. To be a Jeanes teacher was an honor and carried considerable prestige in the black community. The job also paid better than regular teaching positions. Jeanes teachers received $320 a year in 1910, which gradually increased to $1,000 in 1929. Many of them actually functioned as county supervisors of black schools. Because the Jeanes program improved black education, many whites opposed it. Mrs. Catherine J. Duncan, Peach County Jeanes supervisor, had to sell schoolbooks to blacks out of her car because no store would handle them as late as 1930. Most blacks in public schools had no books at all then. This worthy endeavor died out after 1954.

The Rosenwald Fund, established from the profits of Sears, Roebuck and Co., functioned as a catalyst for building construction. The fund would give 15 percent of the costs to build schools for blacks if others would contribute the remainder. Blacks themselves contributed about 17 percent of the costs of construction in a flood of small contributions. By the time Julius Rosenwald died in 1932, the fund helped construct 5,387 buildings, over 25 percent of all the black school capacity in the rural South. The last school built with help from this fund was the Eleanor Roosevelt School at Warm Springs.

Despite this help, the responsibility for providing a decent education to Georgia's children fell to state and local officials—a task they were unable and often unwilling to fulfill. In 1906, the General Assembly established a white agricultural high school in each of the state's eleven congressional districts. Since the legislature would not make similar provisions for blacks, $30,000 was raised by private subscription to support the plan of the Interdenominational Union of Colored Ministers of Atlanta to establish similar high schools for blacks. Unfortunately, the plan was not implemented. Five years later, in 1911, only Athens, Columbus, Milledgeville, and Vienna offered even the ninth grade for blacks, and Athens had Georgia's only four-year public black high school in 1914. There were 169 white high schools in Georgia in 1920. By 1928, when Georgia was 37 percent black, whites had 213 high schools and blacks had 47. Less than half the black schools were accredited.

Though it was better than what blacks received, the education Georgia provided whites was not good. Low standards for black education pulled down standards for whites. In 1920, Georgia was forty-seventh in school attendance, forty-fourth in length of school term, and first in the number of children aged ten to fifteen who were employed. All factors considered, it is not surprising that the illiteracy rate for all Georgians remained two to three times the national average.

6

Black Institutions and Advancement

Higher Education: Raising "The Talented Tenth"

Just as there was disagreement among black leaders on how to cope with segregation, there was also dispute over the proper goals of education. The debate was initiated by militants opposing Booker T. Washington's philosophy of industrial and vocational training. W. E. B. Du Bois used his base at Atlanta University to put forth a view of society counter to Washington's. "The Negro race, like all races, is going to be saved by its exceptional men," declared Du Bois in his classic essay "The Talented Tenth." In arguing that broadly educated black college graduates would be the ones to improve the status of the entire black community, Du Bois was trying to build general support for a liberal arts education as an alternative to the agricultural and industrial classes offered at Tuskegee Institute. For his part, Washington blamed the decline in the number of blacks holding skilled artisan jobs on the rise of liberal arts education.

In 1895, Washington made his famous "Atlanta Compromise" speech, considered by many to represent a surrender of civil and political rights by blacks in return for more economic opportunities. Du Bois became the spokesman of those who believed that economic progress was dependent on progress on all other fronts. The white who would not abide a cultured black bishop sitting next to him in a Pullman car would not hesitate to cheat his black sharecropper out of a year's earnings; to Du Bois, gaining respect as a human being and getting a fair day's pay for a fair day's work were inseparable. While at Atlanta University, he became the leader of the anti-Washington forces when he organized the Niagara movement in 1905. Leaders of this organization pointed out the catch-22 aspect of Washington's economic theory, the contradiction between black economic advancement and increased persecution. Du Bois was not the first to raise a banner of opposition to Washington, however. In 1896, ten years before he became president of Morehouse College, John Hope was one of the first to speak out against Washington's limited view of black aspirations.

When Du Bois publicly attacked Washington's positions, the General Education Fund cut off its support of Atlanta University and blamed Du Bois for "conveying to his students a feeling of unrest, which is not helpful to them." Du Bois struck back in his 1911 novel *The Quest of the Silver Fleece* in which a "Negro Education Board" is formed by white planters to ensure that Northern philanthropic funds were not used so as to make blacks "restless and discontented" with their position in society.

Time has proved Du Bois and Hope correct. Washington died a disappointed man because he could see little, if any, improvement in race relations in the two decades from the Atlanta address to his death. And unfortunately for many of his students, the industrial training Washington promoted was rapidly becoming obsolete. While Tuskegee and similar schools trained blacks for nineteenth-century manual jobs, the industrial training for twentieth-century jobs was going on at places such as the Massachusetts Institute of Technology.

Atlanta would become a preeminent center of higher education for blacks. Importantly, blacks and their educational allies did not wait for the state of Georgia to help them build or run colleges. As with primary education, blacks did much for themselves and were assisted by Northern philanthropy. The American Missionary Association (AMA) realized in 1866 that it could not send enough teachers to the South to fulfill the demand and promoted the development of colleges and normal (teacher-training) schools. The capstone of these schools was Atlanta University, which started its first class in 1869. Most of its first classes were at the elementary level, with a few at the high school level. It graduated its first normal school students in 1873 and initiated a college department in 1872, with its first graduates in 1876. Northern missionaries transplanted the classical New England curriculum to their Georgia schools. The reading of Caesar, Vergil, Cicero, and Homer was common.

With the help of black legislators during Reconstruction, Atlanta University began to receive $8,000 annually as its portion of the federal funds Georgia received under the 1862 Morrill Act. This largesse also encouraged blacks to stay away from the University of Georgia. This sum was 20 percent of Atlanta University's income, with 80 percent coming from tuition and gifts. Atlanta University was under attack from its inception. Black City Councilman William Finch led the successful fight in 1871 to keep Democrats from running Mitchell Street through the university campus and destroying a new classroom building and dormitories. State Commissioner of Education Gustavus Orr did not like its development of the liberal arts—considered a useless luxury by most of the best white supporters of Negro education and a positive evil by the rest—because such studies encouraged blacks to take their place in the middle class. Orr was also concerned that Atlanta University was teaching "social equality." White teachers freely socialized with black teachers and students, and some of them had children who attended the school. Gov. James Smith and Orr tried to divert Atlanta University's share of federal funds to establish a normal school in 1875, but the legislature did not act on their proposal.

In 1887, state officials were shocked to find out there were white students at Atlanta University, even though it should have come as no surprise. In response, the legislature considered the Glenn Bill to punish those who allowed integrated classrooms with a year on the chain gang and a $1,000 fine. This passed the House but not the Senate. Blacks and a few whites opposed the Glenn Bill. Although the Glenn Bill failed, the federal money was withdrawn by the state because the school would not abandon its commitment to integration. In 1890, the legislature diverted the Atlanta University funds to Savannah, where it was used to found the Georgia State Industrial College for Colored Youth (later Savannah State College).

Other colleges were started in Atlanta. Clark University was founded by the Freedmen's Bureau and the Freedmen's Aid Society of the Methodist Episcopal church in 1869 as a primary school and grew as Atlanta University had, later opening its college department with four freshmen. Gammon Theological Seminary began as a division of Clark in 1883 and became a separate institution under Walter Thirkield in 1886. With Wesley J. Gaines as a prime mover, Morris Brown College was founded by the A.M.E. church and chartered in 1885 with 107 students and nine faculty members. It was the first all-black college in Georgia and was able, at least temporarily, to get the funds that had gone annually to Atlanta University. Morris Brown graduated its first class in 1890 and started college courses in 1894. In 1913 it combined with the Turner Theological Seminary, which was also in Atlanta. Spelman was founded in 1881. Three years later, John D. Rockefeller paid its debts, and it was named after his wife's family. Its college department opened in 1890, and the high school department was abolished in 1930.

Morehouse College was founded and staffed by blacks as the Augusta Institute in 1867 "for teaching colored ministers rudimentary English," according to John Hope. It moved to Atlanta in 1879, where its name was changed to the Atlanta Baptist Seminary, then Atlanta Baptist College. It assumed its present name in 1913. Through the work of C.M.E. Bishop Lucius Henry Holsey, Paine Institute was founded in Augusta in 1883. Holsey, born in 1842, was the son of his owner and the owner's slave, Louise. Southern Methodist women started helping Paine in 1901, when Paine's president, the Rev. George Williams Walker, asked for funds to train black girls in domestic skills to help relieve "the servant problem." By 1912, Paine College had 337 students, but only nine were doing college-level work. Its white president then, John D. Hammond, did not support higher academic education for blacks because he did not believe them capable. He thought they should receive training that would make them acceptable to whites. School officials bragged that Paine's graduates were not rapists—which really meant they did not challenge white supremacy and get lynched. Yet even Hammond was too extreme for the Southern whites who controlled Paine, and he was driven from Augusta in 1915.

Smaller towns also saw the rise of colleges. Fort Valley State College began about 1890 as a school in Usher's Temple, C.M.E. It later moved to the Masonic Lodge Hall and was chartered in 1895 as Fort Valley High and Industrial School. As with many black schools, the word "Industrial" or "Agricultural" was incorporated into the name because doing so facilitated white financial support and supported the impression that the school's goal was training better black workers or farmers, not thinkers. Even so, funds were hard to come by. As late at 1907, not even the kitchen had running water. Henry Alexander Hunt became principal in 1903 and served ably until his death in 1938. Support by the Methodist Episcopal church did much to sustain the school in its early years, when it struggled to help the 200,000 blacks who lived within fifty miles. The charge for tuition, room, and board, which was twelve dollars a month in 1912, was too high for most. In 1939 it was merged with the State Teachers and Agricultural College of Forsyth and incorporated into the University System of Georgia under its present name, with Horace Mann Bond as its president. The Forsyth school was founded by William M. Hubbard in 1902, with four students and the support of the AMA. Fort Valley State College did not graduate its first four-year class until 1941.

Albany State College began as the Albany Bible and Manual Training Institute in 1904 due to the work of Joseph W. Holley, who served as its president until 1943. He worked well with the white power structure. According to one biographer, "Holley was perhaps more accommodating than his hero, Booker T. Washington." In 1932 the Albany School became a junior college and was incorporated into the state-supported university system as the Georgia Normal College. In 1943 it became a four-year college with its present name.

* * *

All the black colleges had problems stemming from the poverty and limited backgrounds of many of their students. Though tuition was low, it was out of reach for many, and most students who started were unable to graduate for lack of funds. In 1891, Atlanta University students paid about 34 percent of the school's total costs, the same relative amount Harvard students paid. Black colleges had to start out as elementary schools, since there was no pool of public school graduates to draw on. This detracted from their ability to focus their resources on developing a larger group of college-educated graduates. Clark, Paine, and Morehouse colleges were not able to drop elementary work until 1920. Public schools, by not providing a high school education for blacks, forced the colleges to do their work. Unfortunately, the excellent work done in the high school departments of the black colleges contributed to the continuance of educational inequities by reducing the pressure for more and better public facilities.

Black college students in Georgia had limited curricula, paternalistic administrations, and closed lives against which they occasionally protested. Chapel was often compulsory, dress codes were strict, and relations between the sexes rigorously circumscribed. In 1917, Morehouse students staged a four-day strike against the requirement that they go to the study hall every evening and demanded the right to study in their dormitory rooms.

In 1916, the U. S. Office of Education found only one school in Georgia open to blacks that was worthy of the name "college"—Atlanta University. From 1867 to 1899, it graduated ninety-four from its college department: of these, forty-three became teachers. Later, the percentage of teachers increased. In 1903, 75 percent of Atlanta's black public school teachers were Atlanta University graduates. Although the school ended its elementary department in 1894, even after World War I it continued to grant more high school than college degrees. However, by 1910 at least, its college-department entrance requirements were higher than those of the University of Georgia.

In 1920, 466 students graduated from approximately 110 black colleges nationwide. That year, Paine graduated only two, but Georgia had more than its share of college graduates thanks to the Atlanta institutions. Morehouse, for example, had seventeen who received bachelor's degrees that year. In 1920, the state spent over $1 million on higher education for whites and $15,000 on black colleges, with two-thirds of that going to the Georgia Agricultural and Industrial College at Savannah and the rest to Holley's Georgia Agricultural, Industrial, and Normal School at Albany.

With most white universities closed to blacks, graduate work developed slowly. Atlanta University offered a modest master's degree program beginning in 1924. However, without well-developed graduate programs, there was little opportunity for scholarly distinction for black professors, who were "overburdened instructors of underprivileged undergraduates, with crushing teaching loads, inadequate libraries, and departments without research budgets," noted historian Richard Bardolph. The colleges that were controlled by white Georgians gave the presidencies to deserving black politicians or men "who knew how to play the white politician's game," Bardolph pointed out. Still, these leaders frequently challenged white supremacy and maneuvered skillfully within the system to improve the status of blacks.

Before the 1960s, black academics had special problems. At first, they were not hired even in the white-controlled black colleges. It was not until 1895 that Atlanta University added blacks to the faculty. The first hired were Adrienne Herndon, wife of Atlanta businessman Alonzo Herndon, and Georgia-born Harvard graduate George Towns. John Wesley Gilbert, an archaeologist and classical scholar, was the first black on the Paine College faculty. With few exceptions no white institution would employ black academics. Du Bois, a brilliant scholar, never got an offer to teach in any but black colleges.

Despite the barriers, some Georgia blacks were scholars in the highest sense of the word. Leading the "Talented Tenth" was Du Bois himself. Born in Great Barrington, Massachusetts, in 1868, he graduated from Fisk and after study abroad he became the first American black to receive a doctoral degree from Harvard. Du Bois taught at Atlanta University from 1897 to 1910 and from 1934 to 1944. There he set standards for scholarship that have not been exceeded. When he was not teaching, he was educating the world through his vast writings. One bibliography includes 1,827 articles, 34 governmental publications and proceedings, 38 contributions to the books of others, and almost 75 books written or edited by Du Bois. The cumulative impact of this body of work is enormous. Du Bois was a longtime editor of the *Crisis*, the official organ of the NAACP, and in 1940 he founded *Phylon: The Atlanta University Review of Race and Culture*.

The Atlanta University faculty, student body, and alumni were in the forefront of the battle for human rights in Georgia. The faculty of the black colleges taught their students that they were important and had a duty to resist racism and improve the world even though there was often a price to pay for trying. Looking back three decades, John Hope thought that much of the progress that Atlanta's blacks made in the early part of the twentieth century was due to the strong black leaders associated with Atlanta University. He included Leigh Maxwell, William H. Crogman, William Pledger, Henry Lincoln Johnson, H. H. Porter, and Du Bois, to mention a few. E. Franklin Frazier, the leading black sociologist of his generation, taught at Atlanta University and Morehouse from 1922 to 1927. He was driven from Atlanta that year by whites who objected to his article, "The Pathology of Race Prejudice," which appeared in a national magazine.

Several Georgia blacks, representing the ultimate of the Talented Tenth, including Richard R. Wright, Sr., of Savannah, Hope, artist Henry O. Tanner, Crogman, Jesse Max Barber, and Du Bois, were members of the American Negro Academy (ANA), which was organized in 1897 by Alexander Crummell. The original impetus for the ANA came from Crogman and Wright. The ANA published twenty-two scholarly papers that are still of great value; John Hope's paper on disfranchisement in Georgia and T. G. Steward's paper on the black role in the siege of Savannah during the American Revolution are of special interest to Georgians. Du Bois was president of the ANA from 1898 to 1904. It faded away in 1929.

The annual Atlanta University Conferences, which began in 1896, were one reason the school had influence far beyond its size. Du Bois took over their direction in 1898, and by the time the last one finished its work in 1915, 2,172 pages of the best and most scientific data on the black condition had been published. These works are today found in libraries throughout the world and retain their value. The studies reflect Du Bois' interest in sociology and his overly optimistic belief that the disclosure of "the facts" would lead to their remedy for blacks.

In the age of segregation, white-imposed obstacles to advancement were not as great for lighter-skinned blacks. John Hope was light enough to pass as white but insisted on being identified as a Negro. He was born in Augusta in 1868, the same year as Du Bois, where he finished the eighth grade. In 1894 he was the class orator when he graduated from Brown University. He joined the faculty of Atlanta Baptist College (Morehouse) in 1898 and became its first black president in 1906. Under Hope, it developed a reputation as an outstanding school. His long association with Du Bois, who was next door at Atlanta University, was one of mutual admiration and respect. In 1929, Hope was the architect of the reorganization of the Atlanta colleges and the creation of Atlanta University as the first black institution offering only graduate work.

John Wesley Edward Bowen was born in 1855 in New Orleans, where his father was a carpenter. When Bowen received a Ph.D. from Boston University in 1887, he became the nation's second black to earn this degree. In 1892 he became the first Negro on the Gammon Theological Seminary faculty. His high position did not keep him from being clubbed by police during the 1906 Atlanta riot, however. He became Gammon's president for four years and taught there until his 1932 retirement. He died the following year. Always a vigorous opponent of segregation and unequal treatment, he influenced a wide audience through his sermons and writings. His first wife, Ariel, who died in 1904, was also an accomplished writer and lecturer.

William Henry Crogman (1841-1931), a Latin and Greek scholar, traveled the world as a sailor for eleven years and then completed the four-year college work at Atlanta University in three years, in time to be a member of its first graduating class. He began teaching at Clark University in 1876. Crogman was largely responsible for the Negro exhibit at the 1895 Cotton Exposition in Atlanta (the site of Washington's "Atlanta Compromise" speech). From 1903 to 1910 he was Clark's president and then a teacher until 1921. Rather than be segregated on the streetcars, he walked the several miles from his home to the campus.

Benjamin Griffith Brawley was born in 1882 in South Carolina, where his father taught at Benedict College and pastored a Baptist church. He graduated from Atlanta Baptist College (Morehouse) in 1901 and returned there the following year for a ten-year teaching stint. During this time he obtained a master's degree from Harvard. Except for a two-year period teaching at Howard University, he remained at Morehouse until 1920. Then, after eleven years of travel in Africa and teaching in other black colleges, he returned to Howard in 1931, where he remained until his death in 1939. Altogether he wrote forty scholarly articles and books (including a history of Morehouse) dedicated to the intellectual and social development of blacks and to educating whites to throw off the stereotypes of the New South.

James Weldon Johnson is best known as the author of "Lift Every Voice and Sing," which came to be known as "The Negro National Anthem," and for his work with the NAACP from 1916 to 1930. He left the NAACP, which he headed from 1920 to 1930, to teach literature at Fisk. He remained in this position until his accidental death in 1938. Born in Florida in 1871, he came to Atlanta in 1887 to complete his education and graduated from Atlanta University in 1894. He taught in rural Henry County in 1891 and 1892, where poor conditions led to his resolution to concern himself with the problems of blacks. This experience molded him into a resolute civil rights activist, one who was convinced that it was up to blacks to prove that they were not inferior.

The influence of the many talented blacks teaching in Atlanta can be gauged by the number of college presidents who studied there, notably under John Hope, who has been called the "maker of college presidents." Mordecai W. Johnson studied at Atlanta Baptist College, returned to teach there after it was named Morehouse, and became the first black president of Howard University in 1926. John W. Davis was born in Milledgeville in 1888, grew up in Savannah, and married a granddaughter of Jefferson Long. He studied at Morehouse and later became president of West Virginia State College; he did his job so well that blacks became a minority student group there. Zachary Taylor Hubert graduated from Atlanta Baptist College and went on to be the president of Jackson College in Mississippi and later of Langston University in

Oklahoma. His brother, Benjamin Franklin Hubert, was president of the Georgia State Industrial College in Savannah.

William S. Scarborough was born a slave in Macon in 1852. He finished Lewis school at Macon and went to Atlanta University and Oberlin. On graduation from Oberlin in 1875, he returned to Macon and taught at the Lewis School until it burned down. He went on to a career as a classics scholar and became president of Wilberforce University and a lifetime civil rights activist.

All black colleges in Georgia attracted members of the Talented Tenth. Frank S. Horne, an uncle of the famous singer Lena Horne, was a published poet and writer of the Harlem Renaissance when he came to Fort Valley. There he started an elementary school and taught for ten years, working with Henry Alexander Hunt. Hunt (1866-1938) and James H. Torbert (1868-1911) at Fort Valley are also good examples of the group. When Torbert came to Fort Valley High and Industrial School, it was a small, struggling institution with a four-month term. At great personal sacrifice, he devoted himself to fund-raising, the greatest problem of the early black schools, and was the first to interest Anna T. Jeanes in helping Southern black schools. When Torbert died, the school was one of the most important of its kind.

The valedictorian of Atlanta University's first graduating college class epitomized Du Bois's ideal of the Talented Tenth. Richard Robert Wright, Sr., (1855-1947) was born a slave in Dalton. In Atlanta, Wright attended Storrs Academy. When Gen. O. O. Howard, head of the Freedmen's Bureau, visited the school and asked what he should tell the children of the North, young Wright, then twelve, responded, "Tell them, General, we're rising." This became the basis for a famous poem, "Howard at Atlanta," by the abolitionist poet John Greenleaf Whittier. After graduation from Atlanta University, Wright became the first principal of Augusta's Ware High School. While there he also edited a newspaper, the *Sentinel*.

The second Morrill Act (1890) demanded that states divide federal educational funds equitably between the races or lose their share. Georgia's leaders were not about to send money to Atlanta University, so the legislature responded by passing a bill to establish a normal school as a branch of the University of Georgia. The state did nothing further until the federal government declared Georgia would get no money for the school until it was in operation. Savannah was picked as the site, and in 1891, Wright was appointed the first president of the State College of Industry for Colored Youth (now Savannah State College). He held this position for thirty years.

During this time Wright became a power in the Republican party and was able to attract the interest of highly placed people. President McKinley spoke at his school in 1898 and William Howard Taft visited the

campus two years later. Wright steered a course between the philosophies of Du Bois and Washington. He fought a constant battle to include
liberal arts courses in the curriculum and enjoyed some success despite
continuous opposition to his goals by white leaders. Also knowing that
blacks were expected to confine their efforts to agriculture, he sought to
improve race relations by displaying black talents at agricultural fairs. He
organized farmers' cooperatives and conducted the first Negro county fair
in Georgia. He testified before a congressional committee in 1912 that as
president of the Georgia Negro State Fair he had raised $100,000 from
blacks for the festival, which had been held annually in Macon since
1906. Booker T. Washington and Henry McNeal Turner were featured
speakers at the first fair, and George Washington Carver often attended.

Wright, like Booker T. Washington, also worked to improve the
farmers' incomes by showing them how they could improve their
practices. In 1900 he initiated farmers' conferences on the Savannah
campus patterned on the Tuskegee model. Wright would go out and visit
the farmers before each conference to encourage attendance. In 1905 he
said "more than 120 prosperous farmers, owning from 100 to 2,000 acres
of cultivated land, have promised to attend." Other colleges did similar
work. Clark had week-long summer schools for farmers; Fort Valley had a
demonstration wagon that went to the farmers with ideas and practical
advice to pay more attention to vegetables, fruit, dairy products, and
livestock and less to cotton.

The Rise of the Black Middle Class

Behind the wall of segregation, black colleges produced educated
professionals, and other forces worked to elevate the mass of largely poor
and illiterate blacks in Georgia. Blacks built their own churches, fraternal
and civil rights organizations, and press, and these institutions served as
cohesive forces in the community. Whites were generally unaware that a
class-structured black society—similar to that in the white world—was
growing up around them. When the age of Jim Crow began to crumble,
many whites were surprised to find that a respectable black middle class
had grown up under their noses. There were differences, of course: The
black middle class was poorer, smaller in comparison to the total black
population, and opportunities for upward mobility were far fewer.

Independent black businessmen like Solomon Humphries of Macon
existed in antebellum Georgia; many free Negroes were skilled workers,
and some acted as independent contractors. Favored slaves were carpenters, blacksmiths, coopers, metalworkers, seamstresses, cooks, and teamsters. Some were able to parlay these skills into small businesses after the
Civil War: in fact, blacks dominated the skilled-artisan work at first. Since
whites no longer had to compete with the unpaid labor of slaves, they

gradually moved into these occupations. This increased competition helped lead to the increasing Jim Crow that began in the 1880s. One goal was to force blacks from the more desirable jobs that were beginning to elevate some of them into the middle class's lower ranks.

The black middle class usually developed in an urban setting. As urbanization increased after the war, so did chances for black merchants, although the vast majority of blacks still worked for others. There were certain businesses blacks could enter with more prospects of success than others, such as providing personal services to blacks that whites either would not provide or only furnished on insulting terms and conditions.

Draying, undertaking, shoe repairing, tailoring, catering, real estate, and barbering provided some of the best opportunities. Most barbershops, livery stables, or food-catering services were quite modest, although in some cases, enterprising blacks invested tens of thousands of dollars in business ventures. Some AMA teachers encouraged their students to enter business. One helped Ruben Richards open a grocery store in Cuthbert in the late 1860s, when black businesses were exceptionally rare. A few firms survived, and the owners prospered, but only the fortunate few were not thwarted by white hostility and/or a lack of capital and experience. These factors, coupled with the black worker's inability to achieve decent wages and the tenant farmer's continual miseries, retarded the growth of a middle class. Savannah was home to Georgia's largest black community and developed the state's strongest black middle class following the Civil War. While there were more civil liberties for blacks in the North, some people believed that there were greater opportunities for the accumulation of property in the South. As evidence, Susie King Taylor pointed to Savannah's suburb of Brownsville, which she said was nearly all owned by blacks.

A study of Savannah's black community by Georgia-born scholar John Blassingame showed that in 1870, sixty-six blacks operated twenty-seven different kinds of businesses there. A decade later, 253 people were engaged in forty-one different businesses. Daniel Button owned the largest black business in town, a livery stable worth $15,000. Ninety-six blacks owned land in 1870; in ten years the number had risen to 648. While blacks doubled their land holdings, land values fell more than 50 percent during this decade, which contributed to the decline in per capita wealth from $17.79 in 1870 to $7.31 in 1880.

Athens, Columbus, Macon, and Augusta also had growing middle classes. In 1870, two hundred of eleven thousand black Maconites owned real property. Seven blacks were worth over $3,000; in comparison, sixty-one whites were worth over $30,000. The richest black, Charles Damon, was worth $10,000; however, the richest white was worth thirty-five times that.

Atlanta was rebuilt after the Civil War, and blacks entering the life of the city did not have to buck an established black elite to succeed. It overtook Savannah as the center of black economic progress. Atlanta's "new men" of the nineteenth century became the old guard of the twentieth: the Rucker, Cunningham, Cater, Yates, Milton, Harper, Trent, Hopkins, Faulkner, Penn, Pitt, Thomas, and other families. Atlanta's black community developed around Auburn Avenue, with its many black businesses. John Wesley Dobbs coined the expression "Sweet Auburn" to denote the street's vigor and promise. The Rev. Maynard Jackson, Sr., father of the future mayor, married one of Dobbs's daughters and used the phrase in his sermons. Later, it became a Tin Pan Alley song—anyone who succeeded on Sweet Auburn "could go to the stars." Like Harlem, Auburn Avenue was first a white enclave. In 1884, only nineteen of its forty-three residents were black. In 1890, only fifty-two of Atlanta's almost thirty thousand blacks lived in the Auburn community. By 1909 they outnumbered whites, who had accelerated their flight to the suburbs in what one wag called a demonstration of black power—one black could move a thousand whites. However, it was still integrated as late as 1930.

By 1911, Atlanta had some two thousand black-owned establishments representing over a hundred types of business, including one bank, three insurance companies, twelve drugstores, sixty tailor shops, eighty-three barber shops, eighty-five groceries, eighty hack lines, and 125 drayage places. *The Negro Business Directory and Commercial Guide of Atlanta* listed forty professional men.

While the cities seemed more promising, there were opportunities for economic advancement in rural Georgia for blacks if they were able to purchase and hold on to their land. By 1891, half of the blacks in Marion County owned their own homes, and some had large plantations. One of the most successful black families of the period in Georgia was the Hubert family. Three brothers, Zach, David, and Floyd, who had all been slaves, bought land soon after the Civil War. They paid for 165 acres in the first three years. This was one of the first black landholdings in Middle Georgia. Other members of the family bought land nearby, and by 1940 they collectively owned twenty-seven thousand acres—the largest holding of its kind in the South. Two of Zach's sons, Benjamin Franklin Hubert and Zachary Taylor Hubert, became college presidents.

Some black farmers became major landlords. Isaac Miller, born a slave in Georgia in 1856, inherited part of the land that his former master gave to his father during Reconstruction. By dint of hard work and sacrifice, Miller became a prosperous landlord of fifteen hundred acres near Fort Valley. Black landowner Deal Jackson was unusual in that he had both white and black tenants. Du Bois reported proudly that Jackson harvested and sold the first bale of the 1912 season on the South Georgia market— the sign of a superior grower. Du Bois met a prosperous black farmer,

Bartow F. Powell, in 1900 and followed his career with interest. Powell, born in 1865, acquired some land, and then won government dredging contracts. When he died in 1918 he reportedly owned ten thousand acres, employed up to five hundred people, and marketed up to a thousand bales of cotton a year.

After emancipation, black financial institutions became very important. Many of these organizations grew out of the small self-help societies associated with churches and fraternal groups. One fire company in Athens invested the pooled funds of its members for railroad construction in 1871. Blacks also had "penny banks" before the Civil War. Such banks were stimulated during the war by the savings of black soldiers. As the funds increased, management grew more professional and produced black banks and insurance companies. These institutions facilitated the growth of the middle class by accumulating capital for investment in the black community and by providing professional jobs.

Black banks would have grown more rapidly had it not been for the debacle of the Freedmen's Bank. The success of banks for black troops led Congress to charter the Freedmen's Savings and Trust Company in 1865 for the exclusive use of black depositors, whose investments would be safeguarded by the requirement that two-thirds of deposits were to be invested in government securities. The Freedmen's Bank absorbed many of the penny banks. Thousands of blacks, including many in Georgia, deposited their nickels and dimes; many of them were saving up for a down payment on a home. The bank prospered and grew in its early years. The Savannah branch was the largest, with Atlanta's not far behind. Edward Woodliff helped organize the Macon branch, which paid 5 percent interest in 1869; the minimum deposit was five cents. The Rev. T. G. Steward, founder of Steward Chapel A.M.E. Church, was president and cashier. Deposits totaled $330,000 in the state's four branches in 1874, when the bank had thirty-seven branches in seventeen states—thirty-two in the South—and deposits of more than $3 million.

The bank was mismanaged at the top by its white directors, who, in the depression of 1873, allowed unscrupulous robber barons to borrow huge sums on bad security. Jay Cooke borrowed $500,000 at low interest, posting worthless railroad bonds as security. After the bank was already ruined, Frederick Douglass was appointed president in March 1874. Although he invested $50,000 of his own money, he was helpless to prevent its final collapse three months later. With the bank's failure, the hard-saved nickels and dimes of sixty-one thousand black depositors went down the drain. The Macon branch had $54,342 deposited when the bank failed. Eventually, depositors received 62 percent of their money, but this did little to restore their confidence in the value of savings.

Over time, black banking associations moved into the void created by the Freedmen's Bank failure. By 1913 there were fifty-seven black banks in the nation doing an annual business of $20 million. The first black-owned and managed bank in Georgia, the Georgia Workingman's Loan and Building Association, was founded in Augusta in 1889. It only survived a few years. In 1890, twenty-one men, headed by Henry A. Rucker, a prominent black Atlanta businessman and politician, organized the Georgia Real Estate Loan and Trust Company, capitalized at $10,000, the first Negro land company in the state. In 1904, Rucker became the first black to build a professional office building in Atlanta. Alonzo Herndon joined with Richard Wright, Sr., to form the Atlanta Loan and Trust Company in 1891. Both of these ventures were intended to help blacks become homeowners. Herndon also was involved with the Atlanta State Savings Bank, which opened in 1909 and was chartered by the state in 1913. The Atlanta Savings Bank had $104,000 in deposits in 1916 but collapsed in 1922 following a series of large withdrawals that followed the August 1921 opening of the black-owned Citizens Trust Company. After the Crash of 1929, many borrowers were unable to repay loans. Citizens Trust was the only black bank in Georgia to survive the depression. It continues operations to this day.

In Waycross, the Laborers' Penny Savings and Loan Bank opened in 1917, and Heman Perry opened the Penny Savings Bank of Augusta before 1920. In Savannah, the Wage Earners Savings Bank was founded in 1900 by L. A. Williams and proved to be a strong institution. By 1917 it had over nine thousand depositors with accounts averaging twenty-five dollars. By 1919, Savannah also had Mechanics Savings Bank and Fidelity Savings Bank.

Black insurance companies in Georgia played a key role in developing an entrepreneurial class. White-owned companies did not want to insure blacks after the Civil War. Actuarial tables had not been developed for the black population, but white companies charged that blacks were bad risks due to poverty, disease, and short life spans. This exclusion fostered the development of all-black organizations that provided this service to members. Black fraternal lodges and church benevolent associations often offered health, death, and burial insurance. Some of them had their beginnings before the Civil War, when free Negroes paid their pennies, nickels, and dimes into funds that provided for their burial and helped provide for them in sickness and hard times. Early-twentieth-century black insurance companies often faced hostile regulators and competition from well-capitalized, politically well connected white firms.

Georgia's most successful black insurance company was founded by Alonzo F. Herndon, born a Walton County slave in 1858. He moved to Atlanta in 1879 and became a barber. He was frugal and industrious and soon owned several barbershops. In 1902 he opened a luxuriously appointed shop on Peachtree Street, said to be the largest in the world. Remodeled and enlarged in 1913, it had twenty-five chairs and eighteen baths with tubs and showers and catered to the white elite of Atlanta. Herndon's shop was one of the first targets during the Atlanta race riot of 1906. When the Atlanta City Council passed a Jim Crow ordinance in the 1920s prohibiting black barbers from cutting whites' hair, his influential clientele helped him get it repealed. Herndon invested in real estate, banking, a cemetery, a theater, and a drugstore. In 1905, he purchased the Atlanta Benevolent Protective Association from two Atlanta ministers for $140. Under his management, it grew into the Atlanta Life Insurance Company, which, by the time of his death in 1927, had $25 million in policies and over $1 million in assets. Herndon preached Washington's philosophy that economic advancement was the path to equality; he also was one of the original twenty-nine members of Du Bois's Niagara Movement.

Norris B. Herndon (1897–1977) took over Atlanta Life and built it into the nation's largest black-owned stockholder insurance company. He continued his father's policies of building the black community and providing jobs. Atlanta Life financed many black businesses and home-owners when white financial institutions were turning their backs on investments in the black community. Atlanta Life offices were used as headquarters for the civil rights movement in the 1960s in small towns where even the black churches were intimidated. When Norris Herndon died in 1977, he was reputed to be the richest black in America.

The rise and fall of Standard Life Insurance Company provides a contrast to Herndon's Atlanta Life. Heman E. Perry was born in Texas in 1873 and came to Atlanta at the turn of the century to enter the insurance business. He was on the verge of starting a reserve life insurance company when, in 1909, the state began to require $100,000 capitalization for such a business. With tireless effort he met this requirement, and Standard Life began operations in 1913. In 1915, the company paid a $2,000 death claim on which premiums of only $47.10 had been paid. To impress the public with the company's soundness, the payment was publicized as "the check that made history" and the "largest payment ever made by a colored life insurance company." By 1917 the company had written 6,172 policies in nine states.

Like the Herndons, Perry was interested in the advancement of civil rights, and he was a charter member of the NAACP. Perry, like Herndon, absorbed other insurance firms into his company to make sure claims were paid. In 1924, *Forbes* magazine described him as "the busiest, brainiest Negro in the South." When his empire was at its peak, he controlled assets reputedly worth $30 million, drew a salary of $75,000, and employed twenty-five hundred. However, he did not follow

Herndon's conservative path and overextended himself into other businesses, including construction, real estate, banking, laundries, pharmacies, and printing. His overexpansion meant he had to borrow from a white insurance company, which absorbed Standard Life.

Standard Life's 1925 failure "shook the black world in the same way as had the failure of the Freedmen's Bank in 1874," stated historian Alexa Benson Henderson. Although Perry died broken and discouraged in 1928, he did much to promote the black middle class. While he lived, he was a source of funds for many black businesses that outlived him. Several fragments of his empire remained in black hands and continued on a sound basis.

In addition to exclusion, white merchants' second-class treatment of black customers provided opportunities for African-American entrepreneurs. Black-owned clothing and shoe stores were necessary for those blacks who would not endure the humiliation of shopping where the clerks hid them behind curtains or waited on whites who came in the store after the black customer had entered. Likewise, there were opportunities for black businesses to provide services to blacks which whites did not want to provide, as well as to provide personal services to whites on terms that did not threaten the caste system.

Throughout Georgia, several black businessmen made their fortunes providing funeral services for the community. David T. Howard was born a slave in Crawford County in 1849. He worked in a railroad shop and as a Pullman porter after the war and learned to read and write. With his savings and $200 from his former master he established a successful undertaking business in Atlanta. With the help of his Atlanta University-educated son, Frank, he manufactured coffins and obtained a state embalming contract. By 1890 he was worth over $9,000, which put him in the top 1 percent of Georgia blacks in terms of wealth. He was an early civil rights leader and one of Atlanta's leading black philanthropists when he died in 1934. Alexander Toles was a prosperous Columbus black undertaker and property owner when he died in 1916. Edward Seabrook, born in 1869 in South Carolina, came to Savannah and became an undertaker there in 1895. J. C. McGraw and the Rev. J. W. Johnson bought the Waycross Casket Company for $10,000 in 1919.

Sometimes a small business was a springboard to bigger things, often in real estate. By 1890, Thomas Goosby had a $6,000 inventory in his Atlanta grocery store and with his son entered the real estate business. James Tate, another early Atlanta black grocer, was well established by 1867 and branched out into real estate. He was worth $90,000 by 1890. J. G. Lemon, president of the Consolidated Realty Company in Savannah, built a hotel, theater, and a department store on West Broad Street around World War I. In Macon, Clarence E. Jackson, Sr., built a successful drayage business early in the century and later successfully invested in real estate.

Providing retail goods and services could be profitable. In 1890 there were fifty black merchants in Atlanta, thirty in Savannah, twenty-seven in Macon, eighteen in Americus, six in Griffin, and scores of others scattered around the state. Ronald Edwards managed the black-owned Eureka Furniture Company in Savannah. R. T. Carter headed the Pioneer Mercantile Company of Atlanta, which opened its fourth clothing store in 1919. There were several black restaurant owners in Athens and other major cities. Moses Calhoun, a great-grandfather of Lena Horne, opened a restaurant on Decatur Street in Atlanta. While blacks often shopped at black-owned stores to avoid demeaning treatment, black restaurateurs often excluded black customers to attract a white clientele. Lexius Henson was Georgia's most prominent black restaurateur in the nineteenth century and served whites exclusively. Shortly after the Civil War, he built a large restaurant in Augusta complete with white linen tablecloths, a wine steward, and monogrammed silver. By 1890 he was worth almost $20,000, a fabulous amount back then.

Barbering was a good path to middle-class status. Like Alonzo Herndon, Edward Woodliff used the profits from his Macon barbershop to deal in real estate and banking. In 1872, he was the most successful of Macon's seven black barbers. Edward A. Johnson, who went on to a significant career outside Georgia as an attorney and writer, helped finance his education at Atlanta University in the 1880s by barbering. At one time, all Athens barbershops were run by blacks. They catered to their patrons' needs, advertising, "Ladies will be waited on in their homes." Barbers often had a certain amount of respect in the white community; for example, two Athens barbers, Eugene Brydye and Richmond Harris, stayed on local jury lists from 1882 through 1894, when nearly all other blacks were excluded.

As the age of Jim Crow approached, some black businessmen cut off their black customers thinking that doing so would enable them to keep the white ones. To signal whites that he was on their side, black barber Frank McArty of Albany draped his shop in mourning for Jefferson Davis's funeral in 1889. However, with the spread of Jim Crow, blacks began to lose white customers and were forced to acquire black customers or fail.

The 1890s saw the greatest development of white solidarity, a movement that accelerated with the 1893 depression. Many whites claimed blacks should not be doing skilled work—or at least should not be paid as much as whites. Extending the argument, white workers argued that for the sake of racial solidarity, whites should patronize white businesses. To the extent that this attitude prevailed, black artisans, businessmen and tradesmen who were dependent on white customers were forced out of business and down to the status of wage laborers or sharecroppers. Some black businessmen kept white customers longer; black barbers did not lose most of their white trade until 1920.

Black businesspeople also tried to achieve racial solidarity. C. M. Howell, a prosperous Atlanta tailor, started with fifteen dollars in 1886 and had seventeen employees by 1905. He delivered a paper on his progress at the 1905 convention of the National Negro Business League (NNBL), founded by Booker T. Washington in 1900 to encourage blacks in business to develop good practices and to exhort rank-and-file blacks to patronize black entrepreneurs. The NNBL's first Georgia branches were in Atlanta and Savannah. By 1912 there were fifteen local branches, and a statewide organization was formed in 1917. By 1920, Georgia had twenty-one local chapters.

Unfortunately, black professionals faced a double-barreled racism. Seldom would a white call on a black doctor or lawyer for services and many blacks did not trust them, believing they were less well-trained and competent than whites. A few blacks were able to obtain the education necessary to enter the health services. There were 27 black doctors in Georgia in 1891, 65 in 1905, 146 in 1915, and 193 in 1930. They were barred from white medical associations and from practicing in all but a few hospitals. They responded by founding the Georgia State Medical Association in 1893, which later became the Association of Colored Physicians, Dentists and Pharmacists. Black physicians in Savannah and Atlanta also formed local groups.

The Freedmen's Bureau operated several hospitals in Georgia. In Savannah, the Lincoln Freedmen's Hospital was headed by a black doctor. After its demise at the end of Reconstruction, hospital and nursing services for blacks were slow to develop. The unique husband-wife team of black physicians, Dr. Cornelius McKane and A. Woodby McKane, founded McKane Hospital in 1893. Charity Hospital in Savannah grew out of a nurses' training center founded in 1896. The two-year course was taught by black doctors. By 1908, there were twenty-five in the graduating class. Charity Hospital treated up to five hundred patients a year. Before 1920, it was the only public hospital in Georgia where black doctors were permitted to practice. It had an all-black staff and a high rate of success but was always plagued by a shortage of funds.

Many of the early hospitals were associated with the black colleges, and with time, training for nurses accelerated. Florence Johnson Hunt, wife of the principal at the Fort Valley school, obtained Northern funds for an infirmary that opened in 1934. It was used by both blacks and whites, for Peach County did not have a hospital until 1953. Fairhaven Hospital was made a part of Morris Brown in 1916, and a school for nursing opened at Spelman in 1919. Earlier, Grady Hospital began to train black nurses, and the first class graduated in 1917. By 1930, there were 595 black nurses in the state. White resistance to the training of black health officials had diminished drastically with the growing realization that contagious diseases were nondiscriminatory. Fearing the spread of contagion, the Atlanta Rotary Club asked the mayor to support a Negro hospital in 1915.

William H. Harris (1867–1934) was among the first generation of black physicians to practice in Georgia. He was born in Augusta, completed his college undergraduate work in Atlanta, and was valedictorian of the 1893 Meharry Medical College class. He set up practice in Athens, founded a hospital, and edited a newspaper. He selflessly used his reputation and financial resources during the Great Depression to prevent the closing of Morris Brown College, of which he was a trustee, and an Athens bank. He constantly exhorted blacks to become educated and vote. He helped organize the NAACP in Athens in 1917 and helped other blacks to go into business. He was an excellent example of a member of the Talented Tenth "raising the race."

In Macon, black medical professionals organized a dental clinic for schoolchildren. Savannah's black doctors organized an antituberculosis league in 1908 that made two thousand home visits a year. Many of Georgia's other early black doctors had distinguished careers highlighted by devotion to public service. Dr. E. H. Martin began practice in Atlanta in 1910 and the Army sent him to LaGrange during the 1918 flu epidemic as the only black on an otherwise all-white medical team. Dr. F. S. Belcher of Savannah was appointed city physician in 1920. Louis T. Wright (1891–1952), the best-known black physician from Georgia, was born in LaGrange, where his father, a Meharry graduate, was a doctor. He graduated from Clark College in 1911 and Harvard Medical School in 1915. He practiced in Atlanta until commissioned by the army as a doctor. His later career was outside Georgia, where his medical research and civil rights activism made him a national figure.

By 1905 there were seven black dentists in Georgia and sixty by 1930. Roderick D. Badger, a free Negro, was the first black to practice dentistry in Atlanta in 1854 and later became Clark University's first black trustee. Ezekiel Jones practiced in Augusta during Reconstruction, and Alonzo Wilkens did well enough as a dentist in Griffin to purchase a $32,000 downtown property by 1920.

Blacks were almost totally excluded from Georgia's legal profession for many decades after the Civil War—one of many reasons blacks had little protection under the law. James Simms was the only black judge during Reconstruction. White attorneys boycotted his McIntosh County court, and the local bar association disqualified him on the charge that he was illiterate—even though he was a newspaper editor. When Democrats retook control of the General Assembly, the legislature abolished his court. To become a black attorney in Georgia was a remarkable achievement. In 1905 there were only twelve black lawyers in the state, and there were only fifteen by 1930. John F. Quarles received legal training in Pennsylvania, returned to Georgia, and was admitted to the state bar in 1870. Judson Lyons was admitted to the bar in Augusta in 1884. Charles H. L. Taylor was a black attorney in Atlanta in 1889. Cassander Woodliff, grandson of Edward Woodliff, was another of the first blacks to practice law in Georgia. Austin Thomas Walden (1885-1965) was the most influential black attorney of his time in Georgia. He completed his foundation work at Fort Valley, graduated from Atlanta University and the University of Michigan and began practice in Macon in 1912. He moved to Atlanta five years later and became involved in many vital civil rights cases. He was a key figure in mobilizing black political strength after the white primary was voided. Like many other professionals, Walden was involved in many efforts outside his field to improve conditions for blacks.

The black press was an extremely significant tool to increase stability and solidity within the black community, to tell whites about blacks, and to protest injustices. The papers had small circulations, and their financial problems were always great. Most were ephemeral, highly personal organs of individual blacks and many disappeared, leaving no traces other than references to them in other writings. The editors were strong and highly individualistic. Owners used their papers primarily to promote the elevation of blacks. At the turn of the century, there were more black newspapers in Georgia (twenty-three) than in any other state. Forty were launched just in Atlanta between 1879 and 1947. Victoria Earle Matthews (1861-1907) was born a slave in Fort Valley and became the most popular female writer in the black press. She often wrote for the *New York Times*.

One motive for founding black-edited newspapers was to counter and challenge the white press's false pictures of "contented darkies" and constant insults. One objectionable white custom reflected in its press was the failure to use "Dr.," "Mr.," "Mrs.," or "Miss," when speaking about blacks. Deeper disrespect was often expressed by using such terms as "Sambo," "Rastus," or worse. These gratuitous insults were a manifestation of the low esteem in which blacks were held by whites. Du Bois said in 1914 that "more injury is done the Negro race through insulting terms than through direct attack." Black editors fought back and used their columns to combat all aspects of second-class citizenship: lynching, peonage, Jim Crow, disfranchisement, unequal distribution of school funds, and corrupt, violent elections. The editors had long memories for past wrongs. In discussing individuals, they often would bring positions or actions of decades past to hold against them.

At the end of the Civil War, the *Colored American* was founded in

Augusta "to be a vehicle for the diffusion of religious, political and general intelligence." Some of the earliest newspapers written for blacks in Georgia were published by white Republicans. In 1866, John E. Bryant, the white Republican leader, along with a black, Simeon Beaird, purchased the dying *Colored American* and transformed it into the *Loyal Georgian*, a weekly devoted to encouraging blacks to think Republican. Bryant later edited the *Atlanta Republican*. Other short-lived, white-financed Republican journals aimed at blacks were the *Augusta Daily Press*, the *Savannah Daily Republican*, and the *Griffin American Union*.

The strongest member of Georgia's early black press was the *Savannah Tribune* (originally called the *Colored Tribune*), edited by John H. Deveaux (1848-1909), long a member of the Savannah black elite. Its first issue was dated December 4, 1875, and was available for purchase in five locations in the city's newsstands and stores. Deveaux's announced purpose was to defend and elevate black people, break down prejudice, and establish friendly relations with whites. Sol C. Johnson became editor in 1889.

Black newspapers cropped up all over Georgia. Prominent Republican William Pledger and William H. Heard, later A.M.E. bishop and minister to Liberia, started the *Athens Blade* in 1879 with the credo: "The Arm of Justice Cannot—Will not Sleep." Only twelve issues of this newspaper are extant. Pledger also founded in Atlanta the *Weekly Defiance*, the *Reporter*, and the *Age*. Like most black editors, Pledger was militant in demanding more rights for blacks. B. T. Harvey edited the *Columbus Messenger* around 1888, and C. E. Yarboro was responsible for the *Atlanta Southern Appeal*. John H. Sengstacke, an able minister, published the *Woodville Times* in 1880 and taught the business to his stepson, Robert Abbott, who edited the most influential black newspaper of all during World War I, the *Chicago Defender*.

William Jefferson White became editor of the *Augusta Georgia Baptist* in 1880 and soon acquired it. With a circulation of four thousand, it was on a strong financial footing and at one time was "probably the most universally read Negro paper in the South," according to Du Bois. White tried to make his print shop all-black, and several future editors got their start with him. His outspoken editorials put him in danger from lynch mobs on more than one occasion. The *Georgia Baptist* continued under White's direction until his death in 1913.

Following the national trend of forming state and national professional and group-interest organizations, on December 26, 1892, at the call of Silas X. Floyd, editor of the *Augusta Sentinel*, thirty-four men representing twelve newspapers met in Augusta and formed the Negro Press Association of Georgia. One of the 1892 resolutions of Georgia's black editors was to spell "Negro" with a capital "N" and to stop using the word "Colored." (As late as 1934, few white Georgia papers used the capital letter.) In 1893, the National Afro-American Press Association was formed in Chicago. Black editors exchanged their papers and publicized each other's causes, news, and gossip.

Benjamin J. Davis, Sr. (1870–1945), began publishing the *Atlanta Independent* in 1903 with the help of subsidies from his fraternal order, the Odd Fellows. Ahead of his time in many ways, he was one of the first blacks to own an automobile in Atlanta. Davis was elected president of the Associated Negro Press in the 1920s. The paper was one of the longer-lived ones in Georgia and became more militant after 1905. It continued publication until 1938. It failed when the fraternal order was no longer able to subsidize it. Davis also edited the *National Baptist Review.*

The *Voice of the Negro* was a unique publication. The high-quality monthly, produced by blacks in Atlanta, began in 1904 with John W. E. Bowen, then professor at Gammon Seminary, as its first editor. Jesse Max Barber, a young black college graduate, was managing editor, and Emmett Jay Scott was associate editor. Scott had been sent to Atlanta by Booker T. Washington to ensure that the *Voice* did not reflect any opposition to the Tuskegee machine. Scott soon resigned, and Barber joined Du Bois's Niagara Movement in opposition to Washington. Washington then used his considerable influence to get advertisers and the rest of the black press to ignore the *Voice*, which Barber dominated. Barber retaliated by running a cartoon showing Washington's lips sealed by white supremacy. Barber fled Atlanta after he was threatened with the chain gang if he did not retract his exposure of white involvement in the Atlanta riot of 1906. Thus, the Atlanta white power brokers, with Washington's help, managed to silence a high-quality, effective protest organ.

W. A. Scott, Sr., started a newspaper in Mississippi in 1901 and taught the trade to all of his sons. One son, William Alexander Scott II, became Georgia's first newspaper tycoon. He attended Morehouse and helped pay his expenses by hiring other students to sell hosiery and umbrellas and bought an old printing plant from Heman Perry. In 1928 he acquired the *Atlanta World*, which became a daily in 1932 with sixty full-time employees. He was an energetic, tireless organizer and began or acquired many other newspapers. In 1933, there were fifty in his Scott Newspaper Syndicate, one of the largest black-owned businesses in the nation. That year, the *Daily World* had a circulation of eighty thousand.

By the 1930s, the total black newspaper circulation in the U.S. was 1,250,000. Two-thirds of the typical paper's income was from subscriptions, which usually cost more than those for white papers. Black papers were more free from pressures from advertisers. (Unfortunately for their balance sheets, they were also more free of advertisements.)

* * *

Arts and entertainment were other paths to recognition and material success for blacks. Because black artists and entertainers did not threaten white supremacy, they often could succeed without arousing white resentment. As Du Bois said in 1917, the *Macon Telegraph*, which "can so seldom mention the Negro decently," had praise for Negro music. When Joseph Douglass, an accomplished black violinist, had his instrument repaired in Atlanta, his playing in the shop attracted a considerable crowd. The *Atlanta Journal* advised readers to attend his concert.

Bob Cole (1863–1911) was born in Athens and became a very successful writer and producer of musicals in New York. Hall Johnson was born in Athens, where he received piano lessons as a child. His mother and grandmother, ex-slaves, gave him a remarkable grasp of slave music that he used later as musical director of *Green Pastures* and producer of *Run Little Chillun*, which played 126 performances on Broadway. Fletcher Henderson, Sr. (1857–1943), an early Atlanta University graduate, became president of Howard Normal School in Cuthbert, one of the AMA's leading schools in Georgia. There his son Fletcher Henderson, Jr., began to learn music at the age of five. A sought-after accompanist, he played for the very first recorded blues songs. Nearly every important jazz instrumentalist from 1923 to 1937 played in his orchestra at one time, and he pioneered in the development of swing. Roland Hayes (1887–1977), a great Georgia-born tenor, began singing before World War I, but he was not well received in the United States before he went to Europe in 1920. He sang for the king and queen of England, and his talents were greatly admired. With this recognition, when he returned to the United States in 1923, he was generally acclaimed. In addition, he promoted Negro folk music and made it more acceptable to white audiences.

Musical genius Thomas "Blind Tom" Bethune (1849–1908) was born a slave near Columbus, his mother's twentieth child. He composed over a hundred pieces for the piano and could memorize and play any piece he heard once, including the classics. Professional pianists were hired to play for him, and he learned some five thousand compositions this way. Unfortunately, even after the Civil War he was kept in thrall to white guardians, who grew rich exploiting his talents. He died penniless.

While several black painters spent time in Georgia, their stays were not necessarily long or happy. The most famous to live in Georgia was Henry O. Tanner (1859–1937), who, when discouraged about the progress of his career, came to Atlanta in 1888 to open a photographic studio. This failed, but Bishop Joseph C. Hartzell, a trustee of Clark University, obtained a teaching post for him there and bought his paintings. In 1891, Tanner left for Europe and gained international acclaim. Atlanta-born artist James L. Wells won the Harmon Gold Medal for his work in 1931 when he was twenty-eight years old. Hale Woodruff studied painting in the North and Europe, and then came to Atlanta to teach at Morehouse.

* * *

Social organizations improved the quality of life of blacks, and their growth was closely related to the rise of the black middle class. These included fraternal groups, social clubs, volunteer fire and "militia" units, music groups, self-improvement associations, secret societies, civil rights organizations, and charitable institutions. Lodges offered direct financial assistance to members through their insurance and banking functions. Rural lodges and clubs were formed to help blacks buy land. As a result of their work, rural lodges were sometimes targets for arsonists. In Early County, seven lodges were bombed in one week.

Black uniformed fire companies, in addition to putting out fires, were social clubs for parades, dances, picnics, and excursions. Most larger cities had at least one such company. Savannah had six, one of which was organized in 1854, and Athens had four. Social organizations provided a variety of entertainments and services. Savannah alone had 193 clubs and mutual aid societies in 1880. The Savannah Pleasure Club held festivals, parades, and concerts. Some organizations chartered excursion trains to fairs, competitions, and other special events. Sometimes a car or two would be set aside for white friends. On these trains, liquor flowed freely, and fights were frequent. Five were killed in a drunken fight on an excursion from Atlanta to Columbus in 1905, and at least seven more died jumping out of windows. One black editor deplored all excursions, which attracted the "worst elements." Atlanta's Gate City Club and the Laboring Man's Pleasure Club served as places to gamble and drink.

Music and drama societies were very important. Black musicians played for their own galas and were also hired by whites. One such group performed during the 1870 annual tour of Confederate graves in Columbus. Savannah blacks produced works in the seven-hundred-seat Peking Theater from 1908 until it was destroyed by fire ten years later. The annual Music Festival Association of Atlanta produced operas, sponsored the Fisk Jubilee Singers, and hosted famous performers of the time. Du Bois's pageant, "Star of Ethiopia," was well received in Atlanta in 1915. Mrs. E. A. Hackley held folk-song festivals in Augusta and Atlanta that attracted audiences of over 1,000 during World War I.

Self-improvement clubs were formed for debates, readings, and lectures. Macon had the Art and Social Club for young married women. Savannah's blacks established their own library in 1906 and in 1912 received a gift of $12,000 from the Carnegie Fund. This, along with some city and federal support, enabled them to have a respectable, for the time, 2,656 volumes in circulation by 1915.

Blacks in Georgia founded several eleemosynary institutions. The first orphanage for blacks in Georgia was established in Atlanta in 1888 by Carrie Steele, an ex-slave who was employed by the railroads for thirty-six years as a depot matron to shepherd women and children safely from train to train. She wrote an autobiography that sold well enough to net her the money to buy a four-acre site for an orphanage. She continued on the job at the Atlanta depot and put all of her money into her dream. She was helped by Mrs. Gussie Logan, who, with her husband, put all of their assets into the orphanage, which they viewed as a tool to keep parentless black children off the chain gang.

Leading the fraternal groups were the Elks, Odd Fellows, Knights of Pythias, True Reformers, and Masons. Savannah had seven such groups by 1880. The True Reformers had eight thousand members in Georgia in the late 1870s, when William Pledger was grand master. There were four hundred members of the Odd Fellows in the state in 1889. The Black Elks were founded in 1898 by B. F. Howard. Like the other black fraternal organizations, the Elks ran into trouble with their white counterpart over the use of the group's name, emblems, and regalia. In 1906, the white Elks of Macon obtained a permanent injunction against the operation of the parallel black organization, which evaded dissolution by slightly altering its name and regalia. That same year in Fulton County, the Negro Knights of Pythias, founded in 1892, were similarly enjoined. The injunction was upheld by the state Supreme Court. However, the U. S. Supreme Court overturned this decision in 1912. In 1919, the Supreme Court refused to review the Georgia ruling against blacks using the Shriner name.

The Grand United Order of Odd Fellows was founded by Peter Ogden, a Northern black, in 1843. By 1912 it had almost 500,000 members and held its national convention in Atlanta, where the city gave it permission to hold a parade "without guns." The segregated public parks were opened to the Odd Fellows for the occasion. Atlanta was chosen as the convention site largely due to the work of *Independent* publisher Davis, whose dynamic and aggressive leadership eventually helped make the Odd Fellows the wealthiest Negro fraternal organization in the South. In 1912, the order bought an entire block on Auburn Avenue and built a six-story office building on it at a cost of $250,000. The following year, they added an annex, an auditorium seating two thousand, for an additional $180,000. This "Odd Fellows' Block" on Auburn Avenue became a center for black business and professional men. In 1912 the order had an income of $20,000 a month in Georgia and was worth $750,000. The Odd Fellows loaned members money for business and farming.

Black Masons, who organized as the Prince Hall Masons, had chapters in Georgia in the nineteenth century. W. E. Terry and J. W. Campbell were Georgia grand masters in the late 1880s. *Savannah Tribune* editors John H. Deveaux and Sol C. Johnson were active Masons. John Wesley Dobbs, who was born in Cobb County in 1882, became interested in the Masons when he started work as a railroad mail clerk in 1903 and rose to become grand master of the Prince Hall Masons of Georgia from 1932 until his death in 1961. He made them a force to be reckoned with. Under Dobbs, the Masons actively promoted black voting, and he was a principal organizer of the 1935 Georgia Voters League, the forerunner of the post-World War II effective political organization of blacks in Georgia.

Many black community leaders belonged to several organizations, and these men and women fought for and supported civil rights advances. A respected minister might also be a power in a local lodge and a pioneer in civil rights activism. A businessman might head a fraternal or cultural group, belong to the NAACP, and be a church official. A lodge leader might lead a petition drive to get congressional support for some progressive bill and at the same time be an important member of half a dozen other organizations. Negro business associations funded investigations of mistreatment of convicts and petitioned for better schools.

In the main, Georgia's black middle class and its organizations fulfilled the role Du Bois envisaged for the Talented Tenth. Some may have used their income and positions merely for personal gratification, but the majority were interested in advancing the status of blacks generally and were willing to make sacrifices to that end.

Religion in Black and White

As Georgia's freed people gained control of their own churches after emancipation, religion became an even more vital force in their lives. Along with education, religion was the most important force for black advancement during the first two generations after slavery. Black churches led the struggle for education, providing classrooms and establishing schools. They financed political campaigns, mobilized voters, hosted rallies, and produced the bulk of black political leaders. Many churches and ministers were attacked by whites for their political and educational work. In an all-too-common occurrence, a black minister was shot near Macon in 1868 for leading congregants to a political rally.

For their part, Georgia's white churches became a main bulwark of the caste system, a sturdy column supporting the edifice of white supremacy. White churches welcomed members who joined lynch mobs, practiced peonage and enforced Jim Crow customs and laws. White churchmen often condoned mob murder. This was a grievous blow to the hopes of blacks for justice. "Worst of all," Booker T. Washington said of lynchings in 1904, "These outrages take place in communities where there are Christian churches, in the midst of people who have their Sunday Schools, their Christian Endeavor Societies and Young Men's Christian Associations."

In addition to serving as a force for education and political advancement, the black church was a shelter against white hostility and a salve for egos bruised by mistreatment. The black church patronized the arts and fostered cultural activities, such as literary and music societies and reading and discussion seminars. They were social institutions, and revivals were the social events of the year. Churches sponsored and organized fairs, suppers, concerts, picnics, spelling bees, and children's programs. They also sponsored special memorial events, such as observances of Emancipation Proclamation anniversaries. The church also functioned as a social control by castigating and or expelling the drunk, dishonest, or immoral. The church was a powerful force for advancement because many black clergymen were relatively independent of white control, compared to black teachers, politicians, businessmen, and most others. However, ministers with small rural congregations were less independent, for they were more likely to depend on other jobs for their livelihood.

The church provided high status in the community for its leaders. Consequently, the ministry attracted many of the most able, at first in part because other avenues were not open to them. To Du Bois, the preacher was "the most unique personality developed by the Negro on American soil. A leader, a politician, an orator, a 'boss,' an intriguer, an idealist. . . . " The best remembered, most famous black clergy were also writers. They edited newspapers and wrote articles and books that spread their influence beyond their congregations.

Many black ministers, like their white brethren, had narrow backgrounds and little understanding of the world or political realities. This was a source of both humor and despair to more sophisticated black leaders. Booker T. Washington joked about the sharecropper who was plowing hard ground on a hot summer day and stopped in the middle of a furrow to announce: "This mule is so cantankerous, the dirt is so hard, and the sun is so hot, that I feel a call to preach," implying it was a way to escape hard work.

Northern missionaries were aghast to find that so many black ministers were completely illiterate. They also were disturbed by emotional services and revivals that took precedence over the classroom. Du Bois reported in 1903 that in scores of Thomas County churches, most ministers were "unlettered or ignorant," with no better than "average" morals. In the 1920s perhaps 20 percent of urban black ministers were college graduates but only 3 percent of rural preachers were. Around the Sea Islands, black Baptist and Methodist ministers openly believed in ghosts and witches as late as the 1930s.

Slaves often rejected white doctrines that called for humility and obedience on earth, with heaven as the reward. Instead, they found inspiration for resistance and revolt in Christianity. The conflicting themes of acquiescence versus resistance developed in black churches after the Civil War. A historical argument has developed: Was the

Southern black religious establishment sufficiently militant? Did it, by preaching otherworldly values, weaken the struggle for increased civil rights, or did it, by advising patience, hold off even greater white attacks? One scholar concludes that Georgia's black leadership during Reconstruction, made up largely of preachers, was conservative and compromising; its "domination of black politics proved costly" and helped lead to Reconstruction's early demise in the state. Others argue that the church risked attack for protesting in the years shortly after the Civil War, but later it went out of its way to accommodate white supremacy. Benjamin Mays surveyed 118 people about their recollections of sermons and ministers around the turn of the century. Only four said their ministers taught them to demand their rights. Benjamin J. Davis, Sr., publisher of the militant *Atlanta Independent*, criticized black ministers who went to the segregated evangelical revival in Atlanta in 1905 conducted by Billy Sunday, the most famous evangelist of his time. Davis said, "There is no need of kicking about Jim Crow conditions, so long as we have Jim Crow Negroes."

Most black ministers, from militant to accommodationist, held a providential view of history and saw the hand of God directing all activities. Their belief that God was just and that the wicked would be punished led to prophecies that God would send avenging angels with fire and sword to punish those who mistreated blacks. Often the misfortunes that befell whites were attributed to God's displeasure. Henry McNeal Turner spoke of an angry God who chose Lincoln "to hurl the thunderbolt of emancipation." The Fifteenth Amendment was God's "chariot of fire" that would carry blacks to safety. Such religious thought held that the Civil War and the Reconstruction amendments were evidence of God's plan, which would lead eventually to the millennium.

Accommodationists certainly did not represent the whole of Georgia's black clergy, which can be divided into three groups: the conservative and often poorly educated fundamentalist shepherds of small congregations of poor, rural blacks; the better-educated but still conservative leaders who rose to control the religious and educational institutions of their denominations; and the more cosmopolitan, liberal, urban clergy who preached the social gospel and had the greatest influence on mobilizing resources for progress.

The first group, isolated in the rural areas where the planters and the courthouse rings ruled with iron fists, were in no position to lead open attacks on injustices because they might be lynched and their churches burned if they did. Indeed, personal and institutional survival often required that they ingratiate themselves with powerful local whites. Rural pastors relied on the fear of everlasting fire and brimstone to keep their parishioners on the straight and narrow path. The more vividly they could depict hell's tortures and the smell of the burning sulphur, the better they could save souls. They did not simply preach resignation to life's woes, however. Usually the faith and hope they preached referred to better days that were coming after death, when the servant would be in the big house and the master would be in the cabin.

Baptist minister Charles T. Walker of Augusta represented the second group of clergy. Walker had a national career and was the most popular black preacher of his time, sometimes outdrawing even Dwight Moody and Sam Jones, the two most popular white evangelists in that age of revivalism. Walker believed that attacks on whites were counterproductive and consistently defended the goodness of whites. When blacks held the first National Baptist Convention in St. Louis in 1886, he defeated attempts to label white Southern Baptists as unchristian. Walker said that the $10,000 they spent on missionary work among blacks proved their Christianity. But Walker was not a complete accommodationist. He spoke out for black education and taught that blacks should not indulge in self-pity but at the same time contended that blacks should receive equal justice and whites should abandon lynching and other abuses.

The Social Gospel of the third group furnished the drive to make religion an effective force for social reforms. Channing Tobias (1882-1962) was an outstanding member of this group. Born in Augusta, he graduated from Paine College in 1902, where he taught biblical literature for six years and became a Methodist minister. He went on to have international influence. He later worked with the YMCA from 1911 to 1946 in Washington, D.C., where he became the first black director of the Phelps-Stokes Fund. A lifetime civil rights activist, he attacked segregation within the YMCA, the church, and the United States. He was chairman of the NAACP for six years.

Such ministers greatly influenced those around them. Congregationalist minister John H. H. Sengstacke of Woodville, stepfather of *Chicago Defender* editor Robert Abbott, would take young Robert to the courthouse in Savannah to watch justice being meted out to black defendants by white judges determined to keep blacks in "their place." When the court permitted, Sengstacke would often intervene in behalf of inarticulate blacks. He protested discrimination and saw his job being not only to lead his parishioners to heaven, but also to help them understand the world so that they could more intelligently work to improve it. He was a "book preacher" who informed his congregation about the world, read newspapers aloud at prayer meetings, and encouraged discussion of current events and world problems.

During Reconstruction, blacks were eager to have their own churches, and whites often cooperated by turning over buildings and physical equipment to remove blacks from the balconies of white churches. The process of dividing up congregations went on all over the state. In other instances when congregations divided, there were struggles over churches and property and concerns over Northern influence, along with fears that "black worshippers freed from white surveillance might fall into the vices of heathenism."

The struggles were especially noticeable in the Methodist church, which had split over the slavery issue in 1844 into Northern and Southern branches. Blacks called the Southern church the "old slavery church" and left it in droves. The Methodist Episcopal North (M.E. North) and African Methodist Episcopal (A.M.E.) churches competed for these parishioners. The smaller M.E. North church had less interest in maintaining the caste system than did the M.E. South. It supported black suffrage and an integrated church in 1865. It was labeled the "miscegenation church" by most Southern whites, and 68 percent of its ten thousand Georgian members were blacks. Fearing radical Northern influences, the M.E. South advised its black members that if they were determined to leave, it would be better for them to join the A.M.E. church than the M.E. North.

The A.M.E. church was born in Philadelphia after Richard Allen and Absalom Jones were pulled from their knees during prayer at a white Methodist church in 1786. The A.M.E. church grew rapidly in Georgia starting with the final days of the Civil War. The Rev. James Lynch crossed the "Rubicon," as he referred to the Potomac River in 1861, and followed black troops and civilians, preaching as he went. The day after Sherman took Savannah, Lynch converted the Methodist congregation of St. Andrews Chapel to his A.M.E. faith after the white minister fled the city.

The M.E. South lost well over half its black members. To stop the massive defections, the church split into a white organization that retained the old name and the Colored Methodist Episcopal (C.M.E.) church (later the Christian Methodist Episcopal church). The C.M.E. and A.M.E. churches were similarly organized, and competition between the two denominations was keen. Both grew as blacks continued to drift away from white churches. The M.E. North also fell prey to Southern thinking and was unable to keep from discriminating against its black members. To keep its black members, the M.E. North set up a separate conference for them in 1875. Lucius Henry Holsey (1842-1920) did much to build the C.M.E. church in Georgia. He was born a slave near Columbus and in 1858 had a chance to hear the powerful preaching of Henry McNeal Turner. In 1871 Holsey became the pastor of the Trinity C.M.E. church in Augusta, then considered the denomination's leading church in Georgia. Two years later, he became a bishop and was instrumental in founding Paine Institute in Augusta. He was one of the first blacks to call for a separate political state for African-Americans.

The A.M.E. church was the most influential black denomination in

Georgia after the Civil War, not because its membership was largest—there were many more black Baptists—but because of its hierarchical organization, which placed the church under a governing board of bishops and gave the church a monolithic quality that Baptists lacked. Because of its centralization, the A.M.E. church could more nearly speak with one voice, which carried more weight than the cacophony arising from Baptists. The A.M.E. church's publications also gave it great influence.

Henry McNeal Turner (1834–1915) was the most effective A.M.E. recruiter in Georgia. He emphasized the blackness of the A.M.E. and taunted freed people who attended white churches. Turner won over many black Methodists throughout the state. White Methodists disliked him for his proselytizing and his militant Republican politics. At one conference, he laid two revolvers atop his Bible and said, "My life depends on the will of God and these two guns." Turner licensed many others to preach, and they in turn spread A.M.E. influence. Aaron Robinson was brought to Georgia by his master in 1847. After the war he met Turner and was licensed to preach in 1868. By the time he retired two decades later, he had organized seventeen A.M.E. churches. Following the overthrow of Reconstruction, Turner left politics in 1876 to manage A.M.E. publications in Philadelphia. He returned to Georgia in 1880 as a bishop and served as chancellor of Morris Brown College. Turner founded three periodicals that he used to attack white supremacy, promote his back-to-Africa movement, and castigate his enemies.

Next to Turner, the best-known A.M.E. bishops in Georgia were Joseph S. Flipper (1859–1944) and Wesley J. Gaines. After studying at Atlanta University, Flipper became a teacher and preacher. He worked his way up to bishop by 1908 and held this position until his death in 1944. He was more conservative than Turner, and instead of fulminating against outrages, he would emphasize the positive. Like many prominent black churchmen, Flipper had business interests and enjoyed an income far above those of his parishioners. He was elected president of the Atlanta Savings Bank while still a bishop. Wesley J. Gaines was born a slave of Robert Toombs in Wilkes County. Although Toombs was an implacable foe of emancipation, he looked the other way when young Gaines learned to read. Gaines helped found Morris Brown College and several churches and was an effective preacher who believed it was not good to dwell on the great wrongs of the past. He was sometimes invited to preach to white congregations.

The M.E. South and the C.M.E. churches continued to work together, mainly in the field of education. M.E. South Bishop Atticus Haygood was a strong ally of C.M.E. schools. He had opposition within his church, for some members did not believe blacks had any right to an education, and certainly not one funded by whites. The M.E. South helped establish

Paine Institute, continued to support it, and often paid one-third of the salaries of white ministers who worked there as teachers and administrators.

Aside from its modest contribution to black education, the nineteenth-century M.E. South church had very little interest in helping blacks advance. This general attitude changed later, and Methodists led Southern white Protestant efforts to improve the status of blacks. In the early 1920s, they elected their first black bishops—after having repeatedly passed over the eminently qualified John Wesley E. Bowen, the first black president of Gammon Theological Seminary.

One point many white and black Methodists agreed upon was the need to train black missionaries for service in Africa, especially in the 1870s, when many churches were swept with "African fever" due to the publicity given the continent by H. M. Stanley, the American journalist who "found" David Livingston. One black missionary, John Wesley Gilbert (1865–1923), was born in Georgia and graduated in Paine's first class. Later, after graduating as a classical scholar from Brown University and doing archaeological work in Greece, he became Paine's first black faculty member. In 1911 he traveled as a C.M.E. missionary to the Belgian Congo (now Zaire) in Central Africa. Turner led in propagating a back-to-Africa movement. A.M.E. minister William H. Heard, born a slave in Elbert County in 1850, actively raised funds for blacks to go to Africa around 1900 before he was anointed a bishop.

Along with Methodism, the Baptist faith was dominant in the South. Ninety-four percent of all Georgians were Baptists or Methodists in the 1880s. At the turn of the century over half of Atlanta's fifty-four black churches were Baptist. After the Civil War, blacks left white Baptist churches and went their segregated ways for the same reasons they left white Methodist churches. They kept the Baptist name and often maintained loose ties with their old churches. While competition among Baptists for positions led to schisms, withdrawals, and reorganizations, this autonomy also allowed each minister more freedom because he was responsible only to his own congregation. This lack of a central organization meant they had more difficulty speaking in one voice than did Methodists. Baptist policy led to rapid growth of independent churches, but it reduced the number of leaders who could achieve prominence at the state and national level. The Georgia Negro Baptist Convention was organized in the 1870s. Generally speaking, Baptist ministers were less politically active than the Methodist clergymen. Despite the denomination's organizational weaknesses, some black Baptists had statewide and even national influence. William Jefferson White, the noted educator and editor of the *Georgia Baptist*, was one of the leading Baptists in Georgia before World War I. Emanuel K. Love (1850–1900) was another prominent clergyman and editor. He was born a slave and began preaching when he was eighteen. He became pastor of the historic First African Baptist Church of Savannah in 1885. He filled several state and national posts and edited two newspapers. White Georgia Baptists led the fight to remove Love and two other blacks from the American Baptist Publication Board in 1889. Later, he helped found a similar organization for the black National Baptist Convention. As president of the Missionary Baptist Convention of Georgia, Love was instrumental in founding Central City College in Macon.

The Rev. Edward R. Carter (1858–1944) pastored the Friendship Baptist Church in Atlanta, which competed with the First Congregational Church to provide for the spiritual needs of the city's black elite. He helped found Spelman College; some of its first classes were held in his church basement. He also was a writer and editor. Ebenezer Baptist Church in Atlanta is now the most famous black Baptist church in the nation because of its association with Martin Luther King, Jr. When the Rev. Adam Daniel Williams (1863–1931) took it over in 1894, it had only thirteen members and no building. Williams was an activist who admired Du Bois and was a charter member of the NAACP. Under his leadership the church grew, and when he died in 1931, his son-in-law, Martin Luther King, Sr., took over the pastorate and served until his death in 1984.

Just as the American Missionary Association (AMA) introduced New England's educational ideals into its black schools, it tried to introduce its religious concepts to blacks through the Congregational church. The AMA was the first to respond when Sherman issued a call for relief supplies when he captured Savannah, and the area became home to several black Congregational churches. The AMA hoped to put a church beside each school, but it did not have great success organizing black churches. The denomination's strong stand for prohibition and Puritan morality plus its cold, unemotional Calvinist services—"four bare walls and a sermon"—did not have the appeal of the music-filled, shouting, handclapping, emotional services of other churches. Although the AMA fought the Southern caste system, most Congregational churches in Georgia had succumbed to segregation by 1890.

There were three major black Congregational churches in Georgia. The First Congregational Church of Atlanta, organized by the AMA in 1867, was the most truly integrated church in Georgia. In 1891, it had 351 members, mostly teachers and students from Atlanta University and the city's growing black elite. Savannah's First Congregational Church was founded in 1869, and by 1916, under the leadership of the Rev. W. L. Cash, it was second only to Atlanta's in size. The Midway Church in Liberty County was one of only two Congregational churches in the antebellum Deep South. It welcomed blacks, both slave and free, but they had to sit in the balcony and could hold no offices in the church.

After the war it had a black preacher, the Rev. Floyd G. Snelson (1845–1905), the first student to complete Atlanta University's theological program. (President Edmund Asa Ware closed the program in 1876 to show that Atlanta University was nonsectarian.) The handful of other black Congregational churches each had fewer than a hundred members.

Henry Hugh Proctor (1868–1933) had a remarkable career as minister at the Atlanta First Congregational Church for twenty-five years beginning in 1892. Educated at Fisk and Yale, he was a pioneer in improving race relations. In 1909 he dedicated a new $250,000 institution that served the spiritual, social and physical needs of the community. It had a gymnasium, a YMCA, a YWCA, a home for young black women, an employment bureau, a clinic, a prison mission, and even an unsegregated water fountain. Such facilities for blacks existed nowhere else in the city. In 1917, James Bond, father of Horace Mann Bond, became minister at Rush Memorial Congregational Church in Atlanta, founded by John Rush, a black minister. Both ministers were leaders in the struggle for black advances.

Presbyterians also divided into Southern and Northern segments before the Civil War. During Reconstruction, three black Presbyterian ministers were ordained by the Southern branch. Seeking equality, they left and joined the Northern branch, which remained small in Georgia. Presbyterians had a spotted record when it came to supporting blacks. In 1899 its General Assembly condemned lynching, but later it blamed blacks for the Atlanta riot. It supported the Dyer antilynching bill in 1923 but did nothing more than pass a resolution.

The Roman Catholic church was not strong in Georgia during the nineteenth century, but it did have some influence and did interact with blacks a little. From 1889 through 1894 it sponsored Negro Catholic congresses. The first one convened in Washington during the final days of the Cleveland Administration. The eighty-nine delegates from Georgia were all received at the White House. When black desires for equality clashed with the conservatism of the Catholic church, the conference movement died. In 1918, a congregation for Negro women was founded in Savannah by one of the orders, the Handmaidens of the Most Pure Heart of Mary. Three black Catholics from Georgia achieved fame in the North. James Augustine Healy (1830–1900), the first black bishop in the Catholic church, was the first son of Jones County planter Michael Morris Healy and his slave wife, Eliza. James Healy was educated in the North, ordained a priest in 1854, and named bishop of Portland, Maine in 1875. Healy's brother, Patrick, was the first black Jesuit and served as president of Georgetown University, a Catholic institution. Their sister, Eliza (Sister Mary Magdalen), also achieved prominence in the church as a teacher and convent superior.

The Protestant Episcopal (P.E.) church, the American offshoot of the

Church of England, had few black members after the Civil War. Some of Georgia's black leaders condemned the Episcopal church as the one that did the least for blacks. Traditionally the church of the most wealthy, it ministered to Southern planters and rich Northerners.

Several black sects were originated by Georgians. Father Divine (ca. 1880–1965) was born George Baker near Savannah. In 1897 he received a sixty-day jail sentence for sitting in the part of a streetcar reserved for whites. He called himself "the Son of Righteousness" and opened a meetinghouse in Savannah. He had to leave the city when whites demanded he prove his claim of divinity by walking across the Savannah River. In 1914 he proclaimed himself God at Valdosta, where his followers were so noisy at street meetings that he was convicted of being a public menace. Given the choice of jail or leaving, he went to New York with twelve disciples. There he developed a large and loyal following that was about 25 percent white and did much to alleviate the misery of the poor in his interracial "peace missions" or "heavens." The growth of his movement was not hurt when the judge who sentenced him to a year in jail (later reversed) in 1931 dropped dead of a heart attack a few days after the sentencing and Father Divine said from his cell, "I hated to do it." After he died, his work was continued by his Canadian-born wife, "Mother Divine."

There were some tremors of change in the early 1900s. At the turn of the century, Atlanta was reputed to be the most liberal of Southern metropolises concerning race relations. In 1902, the Young People's Christian and Education Conference was held there. This was the largest meeting of blacks in U. S. history up to then, and its proceedings were reported in a thousand religious and secular periodicals. Some six thousand delegates representing forty denominations and four thousand visitors, many of them white, attended the sessions.

After World War I, white churches softened their opposition to blacks and became more responsive to black suggestions for Christian brotherhood. Antilynching reform was the main area of cooperation in the 1920s. In 1922, the Methodist Church-South Quadrennial Conference resolved that lynching "has discredited our nation in the eyes of other civilized nations and brought undying obloquy upon many of the states of the Union." When the Rev. P. N. Henningham, pastor of Bush's Chapel A.M.E. Zion Church at Winder, was beaten by the Klan in 1922, a delegation of Atlanta's white Methodist ministers took the then-unusual action of calling on Gov. Thomas W. Hardwick in protest. Hardwick promised to direct the sheriff to protect Henningham, with a posse if necessary, and if that was insufficient, he would declare martial law there.

The governor's unusual response was a product of the concern about the migration of blacks out of Georgia and the growing black middle class. Both functioned to make the white church more humane, as did the increasing influence of the better-educated, urban, and militant black ministers.

In the 1930s the overriding economic problems of the Great Depression sometimes brought blacks and whites closer together. The 1932 Quadrennial M.E. South Conference resolved never again to meet where the color line was drawn. The delegates were far ahead of the rank-and-file membership, however. Much of this advance was due to the influence of the Rev. Ernest J. Tittle, a white who willed his library to Gammon Seminary.

In 1939, the Baptist World Alliance held its Fifth Quadrennial Convention in Atlanta with delegates of all races from all over the world. The Rev. L. K. Williams, a black, presided over one session. Blacks and whites worked side by side registering delegates. Boy Scouts from both groups passed out ice water. Dr. C. D. Hubert of Morehouse College represented all Georgia Baptists at one event, something that would have been unthinkable even five years earlier. When the chairman ordered all Jim Crow signs removed, the applause was thunderous.

7

The Search for a Decent Living and a Better Life

Urban Labor

While most Georgia blacks still worked the land, the freed people who moved from plantations to towns and cities after the Civil War pursued a wide variety of occupations. Blacks in Savannah were involved in fifty-eight different occupations in 1870. In a partial listing, the 1872 Atlanta city directory identified 207 blacks in fifteen occupations. In Athens, blacks pursued at least forty-two different types of work. In Macon, there were thirty-two black carpenters and fifteen draymen in 1870. This diversification continued, and the 1900 census listed 110,000 Georgia blacks—10 percent of the population—working at skilled positions ranging from civil engineering to dressmaking.

Shortly after the Civil War blacks were more apt to receive the same wages as whites. However, a trend was already under way forcing blacks out of the higher-paying, skilled jobs into lower-paying, unskilled jobs. This was one motive for the formation of the original Ku Klux Klan. By 1870 cities had begun to enact ordinances requiring licenses and fees for draymen and vendors and used them selectively to drive blacks from these occupations.

An 1880s survey of three hundred leading Southern manufacturers who employed nine thousand blacks showed that blacks and whites received about equal pay for the same skills. While blacks were concentrated at the unskilled level, they received the same $1.10 a day whites did for equal work. In a Columbus brick plant, the majority of workers were black in 1883. One of the plant's white engineers testified before Congress that year that he employed a hundred masons of both races; they were paid equally and worked side by side in harmony if each worker was on his own. However, he could not mix them in gangs, for then the whites would try to make the blacks do all the work.

After 1890, a wage differential appeared when legalized Jim Crow descended on the land and the status of blacks in industry declined. The increase in discrimination also brought a force-out of blacks from many skilled, better-paying jobs. This displacement by whites was considered a greater problem than low wages. As the twentieth century arrived, life for the skilled black became increasingly difficult. During the 1893 depression white workers' objections to black skilled workers was intense. Continued pressure by whites brought results. In 1897 the *Atlanta Journal* replaced all of its Negro carriers with whites. A decade later, Atlanta's white cabdrivers organized to drive blacks out of the taxi business. By 1913, black motion picture projectionists could not get licenses to work in Atlanta. That same year, when Richard Cain, a skilled blacksmith, moved to Dublin, he was sent a mock coffin with the message that he would be killed if he stayed. White unions in Savannah condemned the mayor for employing blacks at all in 1916. Two years later, Atlanta's black couriers were replaced by whites.

Unfortunately, the industrial education Booker T. Washington advocated was rapidly becoming obsolete. In addition, discrimination, segregation, disfranchisement, violence, and poor educational opportunities combined to suppress black workers' hopes for a better life during the nadir of U. S. race relations. "The black artisan had proven his ability, and a growing urban economy should have brought him prosperity. Instead, the twentieth century marked the decline of Georgia's black craftsmen," stated historian John Dittmer. "Almost as blacks were displaced from skilled jobs, the myth that they were incapable of doing skilled work was born, and took root in the American consciousness, among whites and even among some blacks," wrote another scholar.

Those who made it most difficult for blacks to obtain gainful employment were often the first to condemn them as lazy and unwilling to work. As segregation strengthened, and blacks grew weaker politically, Georgia's leaders could openly advocate their economic and political degradation as a way to achieve "progress." For employers, white supremacy had an additional benefit: It helped them obtain cheap labor by dividing the work force into mutually hostile black and white segments, each willing to undermine the other's standard of living. "So long as white labor must compete with black labor," W. E. B. Du Bois once pointed out, "it must approximate the black labor conditions—long hours, small wages, child labor, labor of women, and even peonage."

White workers generally agreed that blacks were inferior and therefore worth less money, but they were bitter when blacks took their jobs for less than the white wage. In 1875, when there were a thousand skilled white mechanics out of work in Atlanta, blacks were hired at pay rates under those prevailing for whites. This resulted in a white boycott of the employers. The employer policy of replacing white strikers with black "scabs" lowered the wages of both groups and made them despise each other. Blacks saw the employer who used them against white workers as their benefactor and poor whites as their enemies.

Low wages made Georgia textiles very profitable. Starting with a small cotton mill in 1810, textiles became Georgia's main nineteenth-century manufacturing industry. By 1848 there were thirty-two mills employing six thousand workers, some of whom were slaves. Production soon doubled, and the industry tripled in size from 1860 to 1880. It relied heavily on the poorly paid labor of women and children. Many children started out as unpaid "helpers" at the age of four or five, and some worked as long as fourteen hours and staggered home by the light of their lanterns late at night. Georgia had an extremely primitive attitude toward child labor legislation. In 1911, it was the only state allowing children under the age of twelve to work as long as sixty-six hours a week; in 1920 Georgia led the nation in the employment of ten- to fifteen-year-olds in factories.

Stockholders and executives were richly rewarded. The average profit for Southern cotton mills in 1882 was 22 percent; during this time, Georgia textile plants were paying 14 percent dividends and also accumulating healthy cash reserves. Not wanting to see profits fall, mill owners successfully resisted efforts to improve working conditions. A report of the Bureau of Commerce and Labor on conditions for workers in Atlanta cotton mills disclosed poor, overcrowded housing, no social or cultural life for the workers, and wages well below poverty level. Mill owners ignored such criticism and liked to claim they performed a humanitarian service for their workers by elevating poor whites above blacks; they told white workers they were better than blacks and proved it by doing jobs blacks were incapable of doing.

White workers often responded aggressively against the employment of blacks, hurting themselves in the process. In 1897, the Fulton Bag and Cotton Mill in Atlanta hired twenty black women, and all fourteen hundred white workers struck in protest. The blacks were fired after the whites promised to work overtime without extra pay. Similar events occurred in different industries all over Georgia: in Rome and Atlanta in 1896, Barnesville in 1899, Savannah in 1905, and Moultrie in 1906.

Jim Crow and white workers' refusal to work alongside blacks in the factories reduced black employment in the mills sharply. Most blacks who worked in textile plants were custodial workers, but there were several notable exceptions. In 1889, the *Savannah Tribune* reported that so many blacks worked in Columbus's mills that there was a shortage of domestic servants; later, Columbus blacks created a stir when they stayed away from their mill jobs after the 1906 Atlanta riot. There had been a force-out between 1890 and 1900, when Georgia's black cotton-mill operatives fell from 20 percent to 3 percent of the work force. Ten years later, this figure was cut in half.

In 1921 black women constituted 2.2 percent of the textile-mill work force. Their average earnings were $6.20 a week, one-half the white average. A higher ratio, 7.7 percent, of Georgia's garment workers were black—they were more popular because they received only one-third the pay whites got. Part of the wage differential is explained by the fact that blacks were usually excluded from higher-paying jobs. There were instances of white women being replaced by blacks in the garment industry at the lower rate. Managers said the blacks were "most satisfactory," because they worked cheaper and "did not complain about extra, unpaid work."

Blacks were counted on to perform hard physical labor and filled many of the lower-paying, unskilled positions in foundries, ceramic plants, and the lumber and turpentine industries. They also worked as stevedores, longshoremen, and construction laborers. Hundreds of coastal blacks worked in the shrimp- and oyster-canning industries. They were also expected to serve whites. Nearly one-third of Georgia's black labor force worked in the domestic and personal-service industries in the early twentieth century, and many black women worked in laundries.

In Georgia, opposition to labor unions was always strong. This attitude, reflecting employers' economic interests, was intensified in the South due to the legacy of slavery, when any organization of blacks was viewed by whites as an insurrectionary threat. This attitude extended to all workers after the Civil War. Early union movements also were frustrated in Georgia largely by the prejudice of white workers against blacks. Despite these obstacles, workers made many efforts to organize and to improve wages and working conditions.

Reconstruction Republican leaders made some of the first efforts to organize workers. When Albany blacks were holding out for higher wages during the 1867-68 Constitutional Convention, Philip Joiner of Dougherty County and several other black delegates visited and encouraged them. At about the same time, Jefferson Long, Henry McNeal Turner, and J. E. Bryant organized the Negro Labor Union, which asked for fifteen dollars a month for domestic servants, thirty dollars a month for field hands, and higher wages for mechanics. It organized a small strike in Macon and a larger one in Dougherty County, but this attempt to form rural unions achieved little. One of the nine blacks who attended the 1869 National Convention of the Colored National Labor Union was from Georgia. This first national union of black workers had developed enough in Georgia by 1871 to hold a state convention in Atlanta, but it faded shortly thereafter.

The best-organized black workers in Georgia before 1900 were the Savannah and Brunswick longshoremen. Savannah workers struck in 1867 to force the city council to repeal a two-dollar increase in the stevedore badge fee when the jobs paid only twenty-five cents an hour. The city gave in, but not without a struggle: Strike leaders were arrested, whipped, fined fifty dollars each, and sent to the chain gang for ninety days. In 1881, four blacks were killed in a strike for two dollars a day for ten hours' work. In 1889 they struck again in Savannah when nonunion labor was hired to load and unload a British steamer whose captain refused to use union labor.

The late 1880s and early 1890s was a period of labor unrest throughout the nation. There were ninety-nine strikes in Georgia, twenty-two in 1891 alone. The largest 1891 strike by Georgia blacks came when the Savannah Negro Laborers' Union responded to threats to cut their pay to eleven cents an hour. The union claimed up to two thousand members and knew that a picket line would be attacked by well-armed police, so strike organizers used the pulpits and leaflets to beg others not to be scabs. Initially, this tactic worked well. So much cotton piled up on the docks that insurance companies threatened to cancel coverage due to the fire hazard. The railroad sidetracked fourteen hundred cars between Macon and Savannah rather than clog the port further. When the union turned down a 2½ cent raise, the company brought in private troops and a thousand scabs, many of whom were out-of-state blacks, who were paid more than the union asked for. This broke the strike and was perhaps the first use in Georgia by an employer of a private army to break a union. In the 1890s, the Knights of Labor and the International Longshoreman's Association entered the picture and what had been a black near-monopoly became about 50 percent white. Black scabs broke an interracial strike in 1894. Later, the union was rebuilt, and by 1910, blacks had about 95 percent of the less desirable waterfront jobs.

The Knights of Labor were the first national union to try to organize Southern workers on a large scale. Founded in Philadelphia in 1869, the Knights' motto was "An Injury to One Is the Concern of All." National leaders said they welcomed women and blacks on an equal basis, and local unions appeared in Georgia in the 1870s and early 1880s. The Knights succeeded in organizing approximately five thousand Georgia workers, of whom probably over 25 percent were black. Blacks made up 10 percent of the national membership and an even larger portion, perhaps as much as one-third to one-half, of Southern Knights. While they tried to avoid direct attacks on the Southern caste system (local unions were segregated), the Knights stressed land reform, education, and cooperatives. These measures appealed especially to impoverished rural black workers. The Knights opposed the convict-lease system and appointed Andrew Allen as the Negro organizer for Georgia in 1886.

Terence Powderly, head of the Knights, dismissed white Knight organizers in Georgia for the misuse of funds collected from blacks. While the Knights were a progressive force, the union never resolved the antagonism between black and white workers, and after 1886, it became increasingly less responsive to blacks. Poor working conditions and wages in Augusta's textile mills led to a strike organized by the Knights in 1886. Workers were forced back to work without making any gains after a lockout by the employers, who threatened to replace the strikers with blacks. White Knights had their racism reinforced by such incidents. Black membership fell off sharply; by 1891 most black Knights had left the union.

In 1889 the Knights of Labor tried to organize the Northwest Georgia coal mines at LaFayette, but the effort collapsed when union men were all fired. The job of organizing coal miners was taken over by the United Mine Workers (UMW), another union that attracted blacks. It was founded in 1890 and absorbed the Knight-organized miners' locals. A black, Richard L. Davis, sat on its first executive board. It had few Georgia members because so much mining was done by leased convicts. Later, under the leadership of John L. Lewis, the UMW became the foremost advocate of black-white labor solidarity.

The American Federation of Labor (AFL), founded in 1881 by Samuel Gompers, did not start out as antiblack. Some Georgia AFL officials realized that low wages for blacks held down white wages. Around 1900, the white business agent of the Carpenters and Joiners Union, an AFL affiliate, said that if contractors wanted to exclude blacks, that was reason enough for the union to include them, and a Savannah black was made a state organizer. Some black carpenters in Savannah were organized by the AFL in 1913. A black Georgia delegate to the 1905 AFL national convention got an Indiana local fined for discrimination.

In 1900, the Tobacco Workers International Union, an AFL affiliate, gave up trying to organize integrated locals and started segregated ones. Another AFL union, the bricklayers, had an integrated local in Atlanta from 1899 to 1921, when the whites withdrew, but a new mixed local was formed in 1928. Augusta also had an integrated local. Savannah, Augusta, and Atlanta had integrated plasterers' and cement finishers' unions. This "integration" tended to be nominal; blacks had a separate group that, though under the supervision of a white local, was actually apart. Blacks did not ordinarily attend whites' meetings or participate in union business. In 1912 there was only one black AFL local union that was not under the direct supervision of a white local.

Any sign of racial solidarity within unions was one too many for employers, who would accuse white unions of trying to force "social equality" on Georgia. After 1920, discrimination by white unions increased, which led to the development of independent black unions. They grew in the 1920s, but most disappeared during the Great Depression.

As the Augusta mill owners had learned many years before, one way to ensure that black and white workers regarded each other as the enemy was to replace white strikers with black scabs. At times, employers also pitted one group of blacks against another, as when black strikebreakers were used in the 1891 Savannah Negro Laborers' Union strike. In 1906, Macon fired its all-black street-cleaning crews when they struck for more money and hired other blacks at the old wage. In 1919, striking black construction workers in Atlanta were replaced by other blacks.

Georgia's white railroad workers had been among the most militantly antiblack. As a result, Georgia's railroads were the scene of intense, often violent, racial conflict over jobs. When railroads first came to Georgia, putting wood, and later, coal, into the fireboxes of the steam locomotives was a hard, dirty job sometimes done by slaves and later by black firemen. As technological advances made the job more desirable, whites began to replace black firemen.

For whites, the fireman's job was considered a stepping-stone to the position of engineer. The Brotherhood of Locomotive Firemen and Enginemen (BLFE) would not admit blacks, and all engineers had to be union members. Not content with merely excluding blacks from the top union job, in 1898 and 1907 white Georgia railroad workers went on strike, demanding the removal of all Negro firemen and brakemen. They lost both times. Blacks formed their own organization in Georgia, the Colored Locomotive Firemen's Union, but it was little more than a benefit society.

In 1908, the BLFE tried again to force out black firemen. Nearly half of the firemen on the Georgia Railroad were blacks, and they were paid significantly less than white firemen. Railroad owners wanted to maintain the status quo in order to hold down all wages. In the spring of 1909, when the Georgia Railroad replaced ten white hostlers with blacks in Atlanta in an effort to intimidate whites from making demands for higher pay, white firemen, but not engineers, went on strike. The company replaced sixty white firemen with blacks. The firemen retaliated by raising mobs in towns the railroad went through. The mobs attacked and whipped black trainmen, who were forced to give up their jobs. In some instances trains were stopped, and the blacks were taken off and beaten.

After a month of violence, arbitration hearings were held. Both the union and the railroad used racist arguments: The union claimed that blacks were too stupid to be firemen, while the company said blacks could stand the heat from the open fire door better than whites and admitted it hired blacks to depress white wages. The arbitrators decided that blacks and whites should be paid equally. This decision removed the economic incentive to hire blacks and led to many losing their jobs.

The strike was on the minds of the NAACP's founders during the organization's first convention in 1909. One speaker said, "Certain vocations which belonged almost exclusively to the Negroes ever since the days of slavery are fast being closed against them. The present railroad strike in Georgia illustrates the point." Militant black editor William Trotter of Boston said, "The strike in Georgia has opened our eyes. It has been the boast of the South that while they have denied the Colored man political rights, they have given him industrial freedom and liberty." The strike proved this false.

A strike of whites was averted in 1911 when the Southern Railroad agreed to pay blacks 35 percent less than whites and limit their numbers. World War I accelerated the growth of railroads, and blacks occupied more and more jobs as firemen, hostlers, brakemen, switchmen, flagmen, and yardmen. In 1919, a national organization of black trainmen, the International Railroadmen's Benevolent Industrial Aid Association, was formed, with its headquarters in Chicago. There were black locals in Augusta, Macon, and Savannah. By 1926, there were five independent black railroad union locals in Georgia.

The depression of the early 1920s led to renewed efforts by whites to replace blacks on the job. Georgia was one of several states in which black trainmen were lynched so that whites could obtain their jobs. In 1921, James Speed, a black veteran of twenty years of railroad work, had his home blown up because he ignored messages to give up his job, "as white men need work," reported the *Atlanta Constitution*. That year, nine black trainmen were killed and fourteen wounded. The bullet-riddled body of Edgar Stokes of Norcross, a brakeman on the Atlantic Coast Line, was found by schoolchildren in January 1922. He had received threats signed "KKK." According to one account, "The mystery of his death was solved by everyone except the police." In two Atlanta incidents, black railroad workers who were accused of strikebreaking killed their attackers. Marion Richardson was charged with murder in 1922 after he shot into a mob of striking white workers who assaulted him. Charlie Hunt was almost lynched after he used the gun the yardmaster gave him to shoot into a white mob, killing one white attacker and wounding two others.

The intensity of the conflict for jobs decreased in the mid-1920s when economic activity picked up. By 1925, railroads had their peak employment. Then there were almost 11,000 black railroad workers in Georgia, more than in any other state. The Great Depression weakened the position of black railroad workers and led to more racial conflict over jobs. There was another peak in violence in 1932, when six black firemen were killed. The Brotherhood of Locomotive Firemen continued to exclude blacks and oppose their employment on railroads. When it finally dropped its color bar in 1963, it was the last AFL-CIO affiliate to do so.

Black government workers also suffered force-outs in the 1890s and early 1900s. There were many attacks on black post office employees, which naturally tended to drive them from their jobs. Isaac A. Loften, postmaster at Hogansville, Georgia, was shot three times and was forced to relocate. Before the attack, Hogansville whites had arranged to pick up mail directly from the train and take it to a store where a white woman distributed it, leaving Loften to while away his time at the official post office.

In 1909, President William Howard Taft announced a policy of not naming any black to a federal position "against the wishes of whites." Taft then removed most black officeholders, including Henry A. Rucker, who held the top appointment among blacks in Georgia. Rucker was appointed collector of revenue for Georgia by McKinley in 1897. This job of great responsibility required the supervision of over a hundred employees, of whom 90 percent were white.

Many college-educated blacks sought civil service jobs in the post office because so many other areas of employment were closed to them. These jobs did not pay enough to attract college-educated whites. Blacks did well on the examinations compared to white applicants, who often had only a grade-school education. In 1911, 75 percent of clerks in the Atlanta Post Office were blacks. White Southerners were opposed to this situation. In 1912, to freeze out blacks, the Civil Service Commission began recommending three people for each postal job, a strategy that permitted the hiring of whites over better-qualified blacks.

Georgia lawmakers were at the forefront of a movement to limit merit examinations and spare white job applicants the humiliation of being bested by blacks. They found an ally in President Woodrow Wilson, who succeeded Taft in 1913. Wilson's two-term Democratic administration was generally disastrous for blacks. The administration was critical of the civil service system because it was one of the few areas in which blacks competed with whites with any degree of fairness. With Wilson's full backing, the trickle of segregation that had already started in the federal offices became a torrent, and the policy of removing blacks from government jobs went forward rapidly.

Federal officials were given a free rein to demote or discharge black employees. In 1913, Atlanta Postmaster B. H. Jones started segregation in the post office and later discharged thirty-five blacks. Rucker's replacement as Georgia's federal tax collector announced, "There are no government positions for Negroes in the South. A Negro's place is in the corn field." He fired blacks and replaced them with less-qualified whites.

In 1914 the civil service started requiring photographs of applicants. This enabled officials to identify most of the black applicants and avoid the "mistake" of hiring them. There were several purges of Georgia's black postal employees that year. All black postal employees in Americus were dismissed from their jobs. James Tilley, a veteran clerk in the Dublin post office, was the only black postal employee in his congressional district. He was removed in 1914 at the insistence of his congressman. Some black mail carriers were framed with deliberately misaddressed decoy letters, then fired for their alleged incompetence. In response to this egregious discrimination, the National Alliance of Postal Employees was formed by blacks in Chattanooga in 1914. Many blacks survived the purges in the postal service, just as they did in other occupations. In 1915, there were still ninety black postal employees based in Atlanta earning an average of $1,444 a year.

Migrations: The Search for a Better Life

No matter how hard and cheaply blacks worked, some whites actively promoted a black exodus from Georgia and discouraged blacks from relocating there. This effort to replace blacks began immediately after the Civil War and lasted until the 1920s. In 1865, the Georgia legislature considered bills "to prevent persons of African descent from coming into this state." However, since many blacks were then leaving the state, whites also had to deal with an impending labor shortage. The Georgia Land and Immigration Company was formed in 1865 to encourage white immigration. Planters sought to use foreign labor to change the slogan "Forty Acres and a Mule" to "Work Nigger, or starve." The company's representative in Europe failed because prospective immigrants wanted more pay than blacks received. A group of Northern workers was hired but disappointed sponsors by immediately striking for higher wages. Foreign labor turned out to be a major disappointment by 1869 because the few who came wanted the same things the freed people wanted: decent wages and a chance to work up to landownership.

From 1865 to 1868 there was a craze to obtain laborers from China. Chinese were initially described as "docile, sober, frugal, industrious, teachable and always respectful, contented, and jovial." They were purported not to strike or vote, took few holidays, and were content to remain servants and laborers. Planters hoped to hire Chinese for four dollars a month—less even than blacks received. Interest in the "panacea" declined due to the "improved character and estimate of the freedmen, as farm laborers," the *Macon Telegraph* explained. Also, Chinese societies in San Francisco refused to recommend Georgia due to its low wages. Northern fears of "the yellow peril" and anti-Chinese mob violence in the West also helped to kill the movement.

Although efforts to import labor were unsuccessful, Georgia politicians and businessmen kept trying. Georgia appointed a commissioner of land and immigration in 1877 and joined thirteen other states to form the Southern Immigration Association in 1882. In "An Appeal to European Immigrants to Come to the South," delivered at the 1883 convention, the group's president declared, "The Negro is foreordained to the cotton field," whereas European immigrants could raise food and develop industry. Whites believed black land ownership would discourage white immigration, and this attitude created yet another impediment to black hopes for economic independence.

Blacks were not the only victims of intolerance. In the 1890s, religious and political prejudice verged on alarm against Catholics and Jews from southern and eastern Europe. The distaste was mutual; Georgia planters usually did not want to provide any more opportunities for foreigners than for blacks. Since few immigrants wanted to compete with black agricultural workers, only a trickle of settlers came. Of the almost 600,000 immigrants who arrived in the United States in 1892, only 390 registered a desire to settle in Georgia. By 1900, there were only twelve thousand foreign-born whites in Georgia, about 0.5 percent of the population. One group of Germans who came to Georgia complained when they received one dollar a day after they had been promised five dollars a day. They were whipped for complaining. Efforts to import cheap white labor to replace blacks continued into the twentieth century, with no great success. The nativism of Georgia's rural whites made such efforts unpopular.

Blacks quite naturally saw immigrants as a club held over their heads to frighten them into "staying in their place." When Griffin planters imported seventy-five Italian laborers in 1905, the *Voice of the Negro* was pleased that the Italians struck for more pay and were driven off. The *Voice* said, "Negro labor never strikes...we are sure the practice is wise and makes for the peace of the community." The *Voice* tried to link white Georgians' fear of foreigners with a plea for justice for blacks: "Murder, lynching, peonage, white caps, chain gangs, and forced ignorance" were driving blacks away from rural areas; either whites would treat blacks properly, or they would see a land filled "with bomb throwing anarchists from Europe."

* * *

Historically, white Georgians were ambivalent toward the out-migration of blacks. The ambivalence was obvious when antebellum planters were glad to see free blacks leave but expended great effort to catch runaway slaves. This vacillation continued after slavery, because whites wanted blacks' labor but not their company. While blacks endured numerous attempts to drive them from the state, the desire among them to leave Georgia was always greater than the desire among whites to force them out. The hope of owning land, escaping persecution, and living better lives—and their inability to achieve those goals in Georgia—motivated blacks to leave.

During the optimism of Reconstruction, many who had gone North earlier returned. After the Civil War, some left for Florida in search of homesteads from 1865 to 1868. In the late 1860s Mississippi delta planters sent agents to Georgia who promised to double blacks' wages and respect their civil rights. Some twenty-five thousand Georgia blacks, including one thousand from Atlanta, left for Mississippi and Florida shortly after blacks were expelled from the legislature in 1868. Some went to Florida turpentine camps; others sought homesteads and higher wages.

More went to Alabama, Louisiana, Mississippi, Texas, and Arkansas in the 1870s. The *Constitution* estimated that twenty thousand left in 1873 alone. Planters, fearful of losing their labor force, resisted these efforts to get away and spread rumors that the migrants would be sold to Cuba, which still had slavery. If blacks persisted in trying to leave, planters vowed they would "make the woods stink with their carcasses."

The labor agent was the bane of Georgia employers, and the treatment of agents reflected the basic hypocrisy toward black labor. White leaders often explained the poverty of blacks by saying they were shiftless and improvident and claimed that Georgia would be better off if they would all depart. Meanwhile, whites were doing everything they could to handicap efforts of blacks to leave. In 1870, newspapers asked the legislature for laws prohibiting the railroads from recruiting blacks. Labor agents from out of state were heavily taxed—not to raise revenue but to prohibit their operations. In 1876 a fee of $100 for labor agents was adopted. The next year it was raised to $500 for each county where the agent operated. The harassment would continue for more than fifty years.

After Reconstruction, most blacks were too shackled by poverty, ignorance, and oppression to leave. Despite this, some moved to the developing cattle and mining frontiers of the West, with their opportunities for higher wages and more freedom. Few blacks were as fortunate as "Negro Jim," who went from Georgia to Georgetown, Colorado, and hit it rich with a large mining strike in 1880. Much of the western movement funneled through Columbus, to the great annoyance of whites there. Specific local outrages often stimulated a desire to leave. When whites were determined to execute Nie Thompson for killing a white in self-defense in Brooks County in late 1875, the *Savannah Tribune* said that Negroes "are very dissatisfied and are emigrating rapidly." In January 1876, a letter to the editor from Lowndes County said that the annual crop settlement swindle was increasing interest in migration.

There was some interest among both blacks and whites in moving American blacks to foreign colonies. President Lincoln repeatedly proposed colonization as a solution to what he saw as the problem of dealing with emancipated slaves. The American Colonization Society (ACS) continued its work after the Civil War, and most blacks continued to oppose its mission. Whites who wanted to displace blacks with European labor were sympathetic to the ACS's aims.

The most prominent black supporting the "Back to Africa" movement was A.M.E. Bishop Henry McNeal Turner, who declared in the 1880s that there was no future for blacks in the United States. Turner set a figure of $40 billion on the value of the unpaid labor of slaves and asked for $500 million of this for colonization. He said this would be cheaper than the price whites would have to pay for the continual suppression of blacks. By 1900 he had lowered his request to $100 million. Colonization made strange bedfellows. Both Turner and Colored National Emigration and Commercial Association president William H. Heard supported white racist newspaper editor John Temple Graves, who also advocated black colonization. Like African-Americans elsewhere, most Georgia blacks opposed the Back to Africa solution, and several black leaders worked to counter Turner and the lecture he delivered around the state extolling Africa. He was always disappointed by the failure of blacks to support him. He moved to Canada, where he died in 1915.

The climate of increasing racism in 1890s Georgia swelled the ranks of prospective emigrants and made them easy victims of swindlers. Several hundred from Haralson County were left in Atlanta waiting for transportation to Africa by a "Liberian agent" who swindled them out of $5,000. A similar fraud was perpetuated by the United States and Congo Emigration Steamship Company. These disappointing ventures contributed to a decline of interest in the Back to Africa movement, which peaked in Georgia in 1892. However, the interest in leaving Georgia for foreign lands did not die down completely. Three more ships loaded with black passengers left Savannah for Liberia in 1895 and 1896, and in 1899, a hundred Maconites petitioned Congress seeking funding to emigrate to Liberia. In 1903, fifty-four blacks left from Irwin County with the backing of the International Migration Society.

In 1895, eight hundred Georgia and Alabama blacks who were fed up with the "indignities of discrimination" left for Mexico under the leadership of W. H. Ellis. They found conditions in Durango even worse than in their home states. One-quarter of them died, and Congress appropriated money to bring the rest back. Only Texas and Louisiana furnished more black migrants to Latin America than Georgia. World War I brought an abrupt halt to schemes to send black colonists to Africa, Latin America, the Caribbean, and U.S. territories overseas.

During the exodus of 1879, Kansas fever pushed Liberia into the background. Hopeful of finding a better life, forty thousand blacks left the South for Kansas and the Midwest in a largely disorganized folk movement. Former slave Benjamin "Pap" Singleton is largely credited with leading the greatest migration of blacks before 1915. Singleton's promotional materials extolling Kansas circulated in Georgia, and several hundred blacks went directly from Georgia to Kansas. Many of the migrants to Kansas from Mississippi were originally from Georgia. Southern droughts in 1877 and 1878, yellow fever scares and epidemics in Columbus and Savannah, and promotional efforts by labor-hungry railroads encouraged this migration. Those who left made an arduous journey, only to find deplorable conditions and severe winter weather in Kansas. Facing a lack of capital, racism, and stiff competition for jobs from European immigrants, about two-thirds of those who joined in the exodus of 1879 either died on the plains or returned to the South.

Despite this setback, many blacks saw the migration as a brave escape attempt that fulfilled the best frontier traditions. The exodus focused some attention on Southern conditions, gave credence to accounts of Southern outrages, and led to some improvements. Historians Carter G. Woodson and Nell Painter said that the 1879 exodus improved conditions for blacks who stayed in the South because it made whites realize that blacks could protest effectively and hurt the economy—and the whites who benefited from it. U. S. Sen. Joshua Hill of Georgia told the Senate on December 18, 1879, that white Georgians did not want blacks to leave because they needed the labor. The next month, there were meetings of blacks around the state to discuss the exodus. White newspapers countered with stories about prosperous Georgia blacks and horror stories about migrants. Western lands were described as a "burying ground" for blacks.

However, Georgia blacks who supported migration had their own horror stories. They pointed to disfranchisement, poor educational facilities, the convict-lease system, difficulties acquiring land, being cheated at settlement time, and the constant menace of the lynch mob. In 1889, the white *Savannah News* was concerned about the out-migration of blacks and concluded that poor treatment made black laborers "fall for the glib (labor) agent."

In the 1890s, labor agents representing Mississippi delta cotton planters promised one dollar a day wages to Georgia blacks. Enough responded to cause labor shortages in Coweta and Cobb counties. Several hundred left Clarke County for Arkansas in March 1890, and hundreds more were prevented by enforcement of vagrancy laws. R. A. "Pegleg" Williams, a black labor agent working for the Choctaw, Oklahoma and Gulf Railroad was asked by whites in Greensboro to relieve them of some of their excess blacks. He did too well. When he got two thousand blacks to agree to leave, he was prosecuted for failure to pay the $500 labor-agent fee. He lost his case, paid his fees and moved to nearby Morgan County and signed up three thousand more in 1902. Sometimes more than simple court action was used to deal with labor agents. A white in North Georgia was almost lynched in early 1900 for getting blacks to leave.

The movement of blacks out of Georgia was not overwhelming before 1915, but their relative population did decline slightly. In 1880, Georgia was 47 percent black; in 1910 it was 45 percent black. Those who did leave in this period tended to be young males age fifteen to thirty-four. In the 1870s, 4.6 percent of this age group left; in the 1880s, 3 percent; and in the 1890s, 8 percent. The percentage declined in the 1880s during a period of relative interracial harmony between blacks and poor whites, brought about partly by Independent and early Populist protestations of brotherhood. This optimism quickly died in the early 1890s as a wall of segregation crashed down. The increase came with the maturation of the first generation born in freedom; greater literacy, higher expectations, and a sense of injustice also provided reasons to leave.

Some blacks tried to discourage out-migration. The Rev. Emanuel K. Love of Savannah said in 1892 that it would be a mistake for blacks to go North—Jim Crow and bread in Georgia were better than no segregation but starvation elsewhere. Besides, a Southern black could be a greater power among his people. Certainly, the departure by independent, adventurous, and better-educated blacks tended to deprive Southern blacks of those who, had they remained, would most likely have been protest or economic leaders. Carter G. Woodson said that the white South bought off or, failing that, drove out potential black leaders who were most likely to draw the lightning of white wrath. Blacks who went about their daily routines without protest were seldom bothered. For example, Lewis Matthew Blodgett, once reported to be the richest black in the nation, helped build the black community in California after he was driven from Georgia. His father, Albert Foster Blodgett, had a slave mother and a planter father. With freedom, Albert and his wife acquired a house that they traded for a five-hundred-acre plantation during Reconstruction. When Albert was nominated to the Georgia legislature, bitter whites drove him from the state. He returned to live in Augusta, where his son, Lewis, was raised. In 1906, Lewis was forced to flee after he struck a streetcar conductor in an argument over seating. He went to California and built the Los Angeles Liberty Savings and Loan Company from a small, struggling institution worth $16,000 to its 1962 worth of $20 million.

Blodgett was not the only black Georgian to head for the Golden State. A harbinger of the World War II flood of immigrants to California came when some blacks departed for that state in 1907 from Americus. Some whites blamed this on the adoption of Prohibition, but the black press said that disfranchisement, unequal education, taxation of blacks for the education of whites, and Confederate pensions were to blame. Disfranchisement speeded the very thing white supremacists did not want, an exodus of blacks from farms.

The United States was becoming an urban nation, and blacks migrated not only from Georgia farms to farms in other states but from rural areas to cities. Between 1865 and 1915, blacks left the land at the same rate as whites, and after 1900, Georgia blacks moved to cities more than to other rural areas. At first, most went to Southern cities. So did poor Southern whites, and job shortages heightened economic competition and racial tensions. Although blacks fled rural areas to avoid mob murder, nearly half of the sixty-seven lynchings in 1915 came within the corporate limits of Southern towns.

Migrants moved to Northern cities to find a better life, better treatment in the courts, less lynching, and security in their property. The *Voice* said, "Not a month passes without recording that certain quiet and steady, worthy families of the race were whipped and driven out from their possessions." Black Sea Islanders often would go first to Savannah, and when they found the city disappointing, they headed north. Twenty-five percent of those born on St. Helena Island who were in New York City in 1928 had gone to Savannah first.

The rate of migration from Georgia continued to accelerate in the twentieth century, driven by the same proscriptions that started the movement in the first place. The *Chicago Defender* ran an item from Savannah in January 1911:

> Owing to the posting of anonymous placards threatening them with unforeseen dangers and lynching, the Negroes of Turner County have left by the hundreds and are still leaving. This condition of affairs will have serious results at this time of the year for planters who employ Negroes to work their lands.

Many blacks who went to Northern cities arrived penniless, and some young black women were tricked into prostitution. The National League for the Protection of Colored Women (later a part of the Urban League) was organized in New York in 1905 to help safeguard them. From 1900 to 1905, fifteen thousand Southern blacks went to Chicago, but Philadelphia and New York were more popular destinations. One Georgia town lost three hundred to Northern cities in just the first half of 1905. Desperate Southern whites tried some bizarre tactics to discourage the loss of labor. Rumors circulated that physicians and students would kidnap city blacks for dissection. Some Southern landlords disguised themselves as "night doctors" and circulated among the cabins in an effort to give credence to the rumors.

However, a far stronger statement was being made by whites who sought to drive blacks out of Georgia and seize their property. Nightriding and whitecapping in Georgia peaked in Forsyth County in 1912 and neighboring counties in 1913. The push of such persecution and the pull of better-paying jobs in the North helped to foster the Great Migration, a mass exodus of blacks from Georgia and other states that would profoundly influence Southern race relations.

The Great Migration began in Georgia when five Pennsylvania Railroad trains left Savannah in early 1914, each packed with black laborers who had been promised jobs with the railroad in the North. World War I also created opportunities for industrial employment of blacks in the North. After overcoming their initial apprehensions, Northern employers quickly came to like black laborers from the South and embarked on extensive efforts to recruit them. The North presented more opportunities to blacks for educating their children and provided a better chance for accumulating property. The "pull" of opportunity was not enough by itself to cause the mass migration, however. While jobs in the North paid five to ten times the amount blacks received in Southern agriculture, relatively few blacks would have left Georgia without the "push" of oppression. Hundreds of thousands of blacks were finding life not only unprofitable but too dangerous to continue in the South. As Langston Hughes put it, "As long as what *is* is, and Georgia is Georgia—I will take Harlem for mine. At least, if trouble comes, I will have *my own window* to shoot from."

Apologists for the caste system blamed the migration on economic conditions produced by poor crop prices, floods, and the boll weevil. However, the migration began before the price of cotton dropped to five cents a pound in the fall of 1914, and the migration increased after the price recovered; the weather was normal in Georgia from 1914 through 1916; and the boll weevil did little damage to the Georgia cotton crop in the first years of the Great Migration. The boll weevil damaged 3 percent of the Georgia cotton crop in 1916, 10 percent in 1918, and 40 percent in 1923, the year migration slacked off considerably.

These apologists refused to admit that the economic problems of blacks were caused mainly by a system that robbed them of the fruits of their labor. Oppression, not factors beyond human control, provided the "push" for migration and accelerated it. The most lurid manifestation of oppression was lynching, and the North was viewed as a refuge from the lynch mob. R. R. Wright, Sr., wrote in the white *Savannah News*, "There is scarcely a Negro mother who does not live in dread and fear that her husband or son may come in unfriendly contact with some white person so as to bring the lynchers...which may result in the wiping out of her entire family." A study committee of the 1919 A.M.E. conference in Atlanta reported, "Lynching and mob violence...have sent from the South in the last three or four years more than a million...and they continue to go." As with earlier migrations, specific outrages caused blacks to leave. The *Atlanta Constitution* stated: "The heaviest migration of Negroes has been from those counties in which there have been the worst outbreaks against Negroes." A mass migration from Greene County followed a lynching there in 1920. Observers noted relatively few blacks left Dougherty County, where lynchings were rare.

Some blacks opposed the migration. Pastors did not want to lose their congregations. Merchants, professionals, and other businessmen did not want to lose their clients and customers. However, sometimes so many of the rank and file left that black leaders were forced to go also or stay in Georgia with no followers.

This time, whites were much more united in their opposition to the exodus. Businessmen told civic clubs that the migration must be checked. Northern labor agents clearly were unwelcome, and harassment of them intensified: In 1918, the labor agent fee was increased to $1,000, and many cities charged prohibitive fees in addition. Macon charged $25,000 in 1917 and required the agent to have recommendations from ten local ministers and thirty-five local businessmen. Newspapers called for a campaign to halt the migration and the state labor commission urged the press not to print recruiting advertisements of Northern industry. The *Macon Telegraph* said if black labor was lost, "we go bankrupt." Therefore, labor agents should be jailed, it stated.

Law officers harassed blacks trying to leave Georgia. They patrolled railroad stations and sometimes confiscated tickets of blacks waiting for the "freedom-bound" train. Suspected migrants faced loitering and vagrancy charges. Macon police prevented one thousand from boarding a special train bound for Michigan in 1916. Not surprisingly, the newspaper reported, "Surliness now exists among a certain class of negroes." In a crackdown that year Savannah police arrested two hundred blacks at the railroad station. A local judge criticized police for jailing blacks without charging them with a crime, yet the practice continued. Eighteen men were sentenced in Savannah in 1918 for vagrancy although they had jobs. Du Bois concluded that these efforts met only with "trivial and local success."

Although the more enlightened white press in Georgia recognized that lynching was a cause of the migration, less enlightened whites used murder as a tool to keep blacks from improving their lives. In 1916, a black worker was killed near Macon for changing landlords. Three years later, James Waters was lynched near Dublin after he served notice that he was going to leave the farm where he had been working for several years. A white farmer killed three blacks in 1920 because he thought they were enticing his workers to leave.

Just as white Georgians blamed blacks' economic problems on forces beyond human control, they also blamed black discontent on outside sources. During the Great Migration, Southern whites believed that the greatest single source of the "outside agitation" was the *Chicago Defender*, published by ex-Georgian Robert Sengstacke Abbott. Abbott was born on St. Simons Island in 1870 and served an apprenticeship on the *Savannah News* from 1890 to 1896, then moved to Chicago, founded the *Defender* in 1905, and built its circulation to 230,000 during World War I. One newspaper called the *Defender* "the greatest disturbing element that had yet entered Georgia." Fearing for his life, Abbott traveled under an assumed name when he went to Savannah to visit his mother.

Two typical *Defender* headlines read: "*Georgia Brutes Again Lynch United States Citizen*" and "*Child Murdered by Georgia Police.*" Georgia and Mississippi lawmakers responded by making possession of copies of the paper a crime. Throughout the South, its sales agents and correspondents were driven from their homes. Two were murdered while distributing the paper. Two men were convicted in Georgia and served thirty days for "inciting riot" because they possessed copies of a poem the *Defender* had reprinted. One stanza was:

> Why should I remain longer South
> To be kicked and dogged around?
> Crackers to knock me in the mouth
> And shoot my brother down.
> I would rather the cold to snatch my breath
> And die from natural cause
> Than to stay down South and be beat to death
> Under cracker laws.

While its tone was strident, the *Defender* was not alone. Du Bois echoed these sentiments in the *Crisis*. Go North, he said, "as the most effective protest against Southern lynching, lawlessness, and general deviltry."

The Northward migration was so massive that it seriously affected Georgia's economy. Ten thousand blacks left Georgia late in 1916; up to fifty thousand left in 1916 and 1917. Hundreds left the Hinesville area, but the five dollars a week many sent back to their families made the town prosper. In the first six months of 1917, 3,000 each left Savannah, Americus, and Macon, 5,000 left Southwest Georgia, 1,550 left Dawson,

500 Columbus, 800 West Point, and another 500 left Arlington. So it went around the state.

The loss of labor was first felt in the fields. The *Macon Telegraph* tried to alert the state in 1915: "Everybody seems to be asleep about what is going on under our noses, that is everybody but those farmers who have wakened up on mornings recently to find every male Negro over 21 on (the) place gone—to Cleveland, to Pittsburgh, to Chicago, to Indianapolis." In 1917, an Atlanta fertilizer factory had to reduce production because it could get only 35 of the 125 black workers it needed. The Central of Georgia Railroad hired black women to lay ties due to the shortage of black men. They reportedly quit after one day. Du Bois reported gleefully in 1919 that women of some of Georgia's "first families" had to do field work.

The Georgia commissioner of commerce and labor reported that the labor shortage was "acute" in 1917 and 20 percent of jobs were unfilled. This migration-induced labor shortage raised wages. The average 1910 wage for Georgia's black farmhands was $13.00 a month plus board or $18.00 if food was not furnished; by 1918 it had almost doubled to $23.00 and $32.60. Clarke County wages increased 72 percent for general farm work from 1915 to 1919 and 100 percent for cotton choppers, pickers, and female domestics. Sharecroppers and independent landowners profited from higher cotton prices. As an indication of the newfound prosperity, three hundred blacks opened accounts in an Albany bank during one week in September 1916. Labor historian James O'Neal stated that white wages in the South doubled during the exodus.

These economic effects created a climate in which white Georgians were more willing to heed black complaints, which had not changed over the past fifty years. However, the price of ignoring them had risen. White, black, and interracial groups worked to stem the migration. For the first time since the exodus of 1879, whites sat down with blacks to try to understand what blacks were going through. Coercion had failed, so worried businessmen and planters turned to conciliation and persuasion in an effort to stem the migration. Liberal Southern friends of blacks found their task suddenly eased by economic imperatives. However, the caste system was not yet ready to crumble.

As migration proceeded, more newspapers condemned lynching and slacked off their denigration of blacks. One admonished its readers: "Black labor is the best labor the South can get, no other would work long under the same conditions." The *Tifton Gazette* commented on the causes of migration:

> They have allowed Negroes to be lynched, five at a time, on nothing stronger than suspicion; they have allowed whole sections to be depopulated of them... they have allowed them to be whitecapped

and to be whipped, and their homes burned, with only the weakest and most spasmodic efforts to apprehend or punish those guilty— when any efforts were made at all.

The *Constitution* said, "The loss of her best labor is another penalty Georgia is paying for indifference in suppressing mob law," and it began to print white protests to lynching and ascribed low wages as a motive for migration. The racial climate improved sufficiently so that the NAACP could send board member Joel E. Spingarn on a lecture tour of Southern universities in 1917. That same year, the all-white Georgia Federation of Women's Clubs condemned *all* lynching.

Interracial meetings, almost unheard of earlier, were called on both black and white initiatives. Waycross black leaders I. D. Davis and J. B. Ellis met for three days with local whites in 1917 to discuss their need for equal justice, better schools, and more white interest in the general welfare of blacks. There were interracial meetings at Thomasville and Rome that year. Whites called on black leaders to use their good offices with the field hands. The more astute black leaders used the opportunity to wring promises of more schools, better treatment, higher wages, and other reforms "from men who a year before would have scorned to confer with 'Niggers.'" Sheriffs and other law enforcement officials suddenly found themselves under pressure to enforce the law more equitably.

Whites began to realize what blacks had long known: If lynchings were not tolerated by white leaders, they would become far less frequent. Sixteen Georgia blacks were lynched in 1916, but this number was reduced to seven in the following year. Part of this reduction was due to the actions of top officials. When Hugh Dorsey was elected governor in 1917, he inferred he would improve Negro education to stem the migration. He met with seventy-five black leaders and federal and state labor officials in 1918 to discuss the labor shortage. One result of this was the governor's appointment of Henry Alexander Hunt, principal of the Fort Valley Normal and Industrial School, as supervisor of Negro economics in Georgia. Interracial efforts and apparently conciliatory new attitudes of white leaders and employers led to many overly optimistic predictions of a new day for Georgia's blacks. For many, the effort was too little and too late, and the migration continued. Du Bois reported in the fall of 1919 that South Georgia blacks were steadily moving away.

The North was no heaven; poverty, unemployment, and discrimination were endemic. These factors led to the concentrations of blacks in the slums. There was some reverse migration during this period, for not all blacks who went North stayed there. However, attempts by Southern whites to get blacks to return were not very successful. The *Chicago Defender* reported that the Golden Star Employment Agency, operating in Chicago on behalf of Southern employers, waited until there was an unusually cold day and then distributed leaflets urging blacks to accept jobs that were allegedly waiting for them in Dixie. When the agency tried this in January 1920, the two hundred families who came to the meeting did not show up the following Monday to board the train; they had learned that there was also a record cold wave in the South. The temperature went down to zero degrees in Atlanta, and the *Defender* reported at least twelve blacks froze to death in Georgia.

The postwar recession that slowed the northbound migration of blacks bottomed out in 1921. During the downturn, a few blacks returned to Georgia after losing jobs in the North to returning white soldiers or European immigrants, although Congress soon curtailed this supply of cheap labor. As the economy picked up in 1922, black migration resumed and in 1923 peaked at a level not exceeded until World War II. The migration continued because the "push" of violence, injustice, and lack of opportunities remained. In 1923, the *Athens Herald* blamed the exodus in some localities on the terrorism of nightriders. Proponents of national antilynching legislation charged that failure to enact such laws had speeded the exodus by proving that the white South intended to keep on lynching. Meanwhile, cotton growers viewed the efforts of Northern industries to recruit blacks with alarm, and Georgia officials continued their futile harassment of labor agents. Fort Valley's 1926 License Tax Ordinance provided for a tax of ten dollars to seventy-five dollars for each of 162 types of business except "Immigration Agents," whose license fee was set at $26,000.

During the 1920s, Georgia's black population *declined* by 135,233, while the white population increased by 147,907. In 1930, blacks comprised 37 percent of the state's total population, the smallest percentage shown by any census taken since the first one in 1790. Between 1920 and 1922, 151,438 blacks left Georgia, and there were seventy thousand jobs unfilled. The next year, the flow continued at the rate of fifteen hundred a week. In July 1923, the United States Department of Agriculture (USDA) said that 60 percent of the blacks who were leaving were skilled workers. From 1920 to 1925, the number of black farmers in Georgia declined 35.4 percent, from 130,000 to 84,000, which meant that forty-six thousand farms were abandoned. A survey showed that 13 percent of black farm workers had moved north in 1922 and reported that "the situation in Georgia is much worse than is generally realized."

Georgia's businessmen, bankers, and planters watched investments in cropland slowly being swallowed up in weeds. In 1925, thirty-two counties were on the verge of financial ruin, according to statistics forwarded to President Coolidge by congressman Thomas Bell, who asked for emergency federal relief of $500,000. As the number of black-operated farms fell by one-third, the value of the remaining farms fell by two-thirds, in part due to the boll weevil, which cut cotton yields by 50 percent. Those who remained got poorer. This catastrophic attack on the cotton crop helped to erode the old patterns of monoculture, tenancy, and liens.

Blacks continued to use the migration to press for gains. In July 1923, there was a large meeting of black leaders in Atlanta that directed an address to whites pointing out that the injustices blacks suffered were the basic cause of the migration. Some white leaders also called for change. Later that year, James S. Peters, president of the Georgia Bankers Association, urged better wages, schools, and treatment of blacks by law enforcement officials. The City Club of Atlanta took a similar position. In his study of race relations in Georgia, John M. Matthews concluded, "Migration and the economic pressure it generated... did more to help the Negro than vocal protests and agitation."

Robert Russa Moton, Booker T. Washington's successor at Tuskegee, said in 1923 that the migration had cost Georgia $27 million. He tried to show the ruling whites that they hurt themselves in the pocketbook when they treated blacks poorly. Moton predicted, as many had earlier, that conditions would improve for those who remained, as whites would be "activated by economic conditions and justice" to treat blacks better.

The Great Migration had three notable salutary results. It increased the black presence in the North; black voters there began to influence national politics and applied pressure on the federal government to act in behalf of those remaining in the South; in addition, the white South, increasingly concerned about the worsening labor shortage, moved to modify some of the caste system's more harshly repressive measures— albeit in a halting, irresolute way that took several decades to yield major results.

The thirty years between the Great Migration and the end of World War II would mark the long beginning of the destruction of Georgia's caste society. Black initiatives increased during this period, and as militancy and determination rose among blacks, so did the number of white allies and the level of their support. Lynching eventually would go out of style as a popular community recreation.

8

The "New Negro"

Blacks in the Military and World War I

Although blacks felt aggrieved by events in Georgia and the rest of the nation, they were ready to answer their country's call in times of war. African-American soldiers fought valiantly in the American Revolution, the War of 1812, and the Civil War. They continued this tradition in the Indian Wars, during the Spanish-American War, and World War I. Throughout the nation's history, black soldiers have had to prove their mettle, for whites did not naturally assume that black soldiers were brave.

As a result of frontier pressures and the excellent record made by black troops in the Civil War, Congress in 1868 authorized the creation of four black regiments in the regular army. These units, the Twenty-fourth and Twenty-fifth Infantry regiments and the Ninth and Tenth Cavalry regiments, saw action in the Indian Wars from 1869 to 1890. They had the army's lowest desertion rate, and their members won fourteen Medals of Honor. Indians named them "Buffalo Soldiers" because of their physical hardiness and the resemblance of their curly hair to a buffalo's mane. They were considered among the best troops in the West.

Henry O. Flipper was probably the best-known black in the U. S. Army in the late nineteenth century. The first black graduate from West Point and Tenth Cavalry officer was born a slave in Thomasville, Georgia, in 1856. His father, Festus, was a skilled slave shoemaker and carriage trimmer. After the family moved to Atlanta with owner Ephraim Ponder, young Henry began his education at a school for black children that opened in 1864. As Sherman approached Atlanta, the slaves were moved to Macon. With freedom, the Flipper family returned to Atlanta, and Festus opened a shoe shop on Decatur Avenue. Henry's father paid for his son's tutoring by the wife of an ex-Confederate captain. Henry then attended Storrs Academy and entered Atlanta University as a college freshman in 1869, when he was recommended for appointment to West Point by U. S. Rep. J. C. Freeman.

The *Savannah Tribune* reported in 1876 that whites ate, drilled, and stood guard with Flipper but did not associate with or speak to him otherwise. It concluded, "He is smart, they say, and will undoubtedly graduate." Meanwhile, Georgia's white newspapers often wrote abusive reports about Flipper. While Flipper praised West Point's staff and faculty and said they always graded him fairly, he declared, "The white people of Georgia can claim no credit for any part of my education."

Flipper's 1877 graduation was a national event. All of black and some of white Macon turned out to honor him when he returned to Georgia following his commissioning as a second lieutenant, and he reviewed three black militia companies: the Lincoln Guard, the Bibb County Blues, and the Central City Light Infantry. A large crowd watched the eighty men march past Flipper in the first review of black Macon troopers. "The uniforms were tasty and well gotten up," the *Macon Telegraph and Messenger* reported. In 1878, Flipper's autobiographical account, *The Colored Cadet at West Point*, was published.

Flipper was assigned to the Tenth Cavalry, where he served in the Indian Wars from 1877 to 1882. His unit and the Ninth Cavalry campaigned against the Cheyenne and Apache Indians of the Southwest. Flipper's military career was cut short by a court-martial, which acquitted him of embezzlement but convicted him of "conduct unbecoming an officer and a gentlemen." The charges grew out of white prejudice aggravated by his riding horseback with a white woman.

After his discharge, Flipper made good use of his West Point training and became a mining engineer, consultant, and translator of Spanish land grants and laws. In 1919, Flipper went to Washington to work for Albert Fall, then a senator and later secretary of the interior. Fall wrote the secretary of war in 1922 in a vain effort to get Flipper's name cleared. In 1922, Flipper went to Latin America as an engineer until 1931, when he returned to Atlanta and lived the rest of his life with his brother, A. M. E. Bishop Joseph S. Flipper, and devoted himself to clearing his name through one of the many bills introduced in Congress. He did not succeed mainly because the army would not release his trial record. Flipper died in 1940 in Atlanta.

He was exonerated posthumously by the army thirty-six years later due mainly to three years of research and work by Valdosta State College graduate student Ray McColl. His body was then moved from an unmarked grave in Atlanta's South View Cemetery to Thomasville, where he was interred with full military honors beside his parents in the

Magnolia Cemetery. West Point now gives the Flipper Award to the most outstanding black cadet.

Most officers did not want to command black troops on the frontier: They had the worst, most isolated stations, promotions in the units were slow, and they did not get glamorous assignments. In 1889, black soldiers from Georgia in the four regular army units served at Fort Sill, Oklahoma; Reno, Nevada, which was still Indian Territory; and in five Texas military installations. Their stations were segregated, and all officers were white, with the earlier exception of Flipper. Readic Comer enlisted in the Tenth Cavalry in 1912. Comer was born in East Macon in 1894, where his father, Makey Comer, was pastor of St. Luke's Baptist Church. Comer did border duty in Arizona for fifteen dollars a month and was on the futile 1916 Pershing expedition that chased Pancho Villa in Mexico. He retired as a captain in 1944. Jelester Linton, another veteran of the Tenth who served on the frontier, was honored by the Fort Valley State College ROTC in 1979.

Black soldiers in Georgia, not those on the distant frontier, most worried white Georgians. State leaders objected to the presence of black federal troops shortly after Lee surrendered, and because they were a strong symbol of political power, these troops were the primary target of white supremacists. The soldiers were removed, but black militia units were established in major cities during Reconstruction. All officers in these units were black. Men usually had to provide their own uniforms and donate their time for drills, exercises, parades, and musters of these volunteer outfits, which served mainly as social organizations that performed on ceremonial occasions. Five Savannah units paraded in the January 1 Emancipation Proclamation ceremonies in 1876, and seven marched that spring in celebration of the adoption of the Fifteenth Amendment. In 1880, Savannah had one state-supported and seven unofficial black militia units.

Black militia units faced several obstacles, including white units, which were composed mainly of Confederate veterans who went out of their way to show their prejudice. The white press constantly tried to stir up antagonism against black companies as part of the sustained drive to get rid of them. Whites did approve of one function of black militia units: guarding condemned black prisoners on their way to execution to ensure that other blacks did not attempt to rescue them.

As late as 1892, blacks comprised half the state militia units, but the legislature refused to provide any money for their encampments. The legislature knew that black units symbolized resistance to oppression and threatened white supremacy; blacks knew they were not completely beaten down when their soldiers marched, and the black militia units did not mind reminding everyone of this. One can admire the intestinal fortitude, if not the discretion, of the Savannah militia band that played a stirring rendition of "Marching Through Georgia" at the conclusion of Savannah's 1893 Emancipation Proclamation celebration.

An 1885 law required what custom already dictated, the segregation of militia units. Indicative of the increasing Jim Crow, some white militia companies from Savannah and Atlanta refused to march in an 1887 Washington, D.C., parade because Negro troops would also march. Georgia militia units went on annual encampments to sharpen their military skills. In 1891, whites went to Chickamauga, and the blacks went to Piedmont Park in Atlanta.

By 1892, only South Carolina had more black militia units than Georgia, and Savannah had the only black artillery company in the United States. The 1893 legislature authorized seventy-two white and twenty black companies, but only the white units had machine guns, signal corps, and medical departments with hospital and ambulance corps. Black units fell victim to increasing racism, especially after disturbances involving black soldiers at Southern military installations during the Spanish-American War. In 1899, the legislature disbanded five black companies for "inefficiency" and reduced the number of black units to seven. Since its 1878 organization, John H. Deveaux of Savannah was a member of the First Battalion, Georgia State Troops, Colored. When the state militia was reorganized in 1899, Deveaux commanded all Georgia's black companies but was demoted to major. However, in 1901, Deveaux's rank of lieutenant colonel was restored by the legislature.

Because the black militia meant survival of the Negro's right to vote and hold elective office, whites were determined to eliminate this threat. As a precursor to disfranchisement, black units were forced to disband by an act of the 1905 Georgia General Assembly.

By the 1890s, the United States had grown into an industrial giant that was increasingly dependent on imports and exports. As the western frontier closed, Americans were concerned about the country's continued growth and prosperity. Business leaders were shaken by the 1893 depression and wanted to develop overseas markets. American industry was also becoming increasingly dependent on cheap raw materials from the colonial world. Sentiment grew that we, too, should have colonies for our national prestige and to ensure raw material supplies and markets for surplus production. These attitudes, combined with sympathy for the Cubans who revolted against Spain, converged when the U. S. battleship *Maine* blew up in Havana's harbor. The United States immediately assumed this was an act of aggression by Spain and declared war on the fading imperial power. Most blacks supported the war.

In Cuba, the most publicized battle involving black troops, or "smoked

Yankees," as the Spaniards called them, came when Theodore Roosevelt's Rough Riders charged up San Juan Heights on July 1, 1898. They were ably supported by the Ninth and Tenth cavalries. Five days earlier, the Tenth saved the Rough Riders at Las Guasimas when they were pinned down by enemy fire. The Twenty-Fourth Infantry charged the blockhouse at El Caney and snatched victory for the American forces. "They knew no such word as fear, but swept up the hill like a legion of demons," one white soldier recounted. Roosevelt was extravagant in his praise of black valor at the time, but later he found it politically expedient to defame the black troops he had earlier commended.

Most of Georgia's fifteen hundred black militiamen wanted to volunteer for the war, so a recruiting office was opened in Atlanta. In July 1898, a black Atlantan raised a company and was made its first lieutenant. This company was incorporated into the Tenth Regiment of Colored Volunteers, one of the new regiments of black enlisted men authorized by Congress. In response to political pressure by blacks, about one hundred blacks were commissioned officers, mostly as first or second lieutenants. Among Georgian officers were the Rev. Charles T. Walker, chaplain, and Richard R. Wright, Sr., who was appointed paymaster with the rank of major. Lt. Colonel Deveaux and his company volunteered but were rejected.

Most black volunteers remained stateside during the war. At Camp Haskell, near Macon, there were four black units, composed mainly of soldiers from other states. The camp was segregated and many of the white soldiers and nearby civilians were overtly racist. The Macon police made a point of harassing black soldiers when they were in town, and the black troops grew more militant. Four black soldiers were killed by groups of whites, and three others were killed by streetcar conductors when they refused to ride in the Jim Crow trailer. Soldiers of another black unit at Camp Haskell, the Sixth Virginia Volunteers, chopped down a tree in a segregated park that had been used in past lynchings, and black soldiers from another unit broke into the jail and freed some buddies to foil an anticipated lynching. On their way back to camp, this group knocked down and disarmed some whites who stood in their way. As a result, Gov. Allen Candler called for eliminating the black militia units.

The Spanish-American War was also fought in the Far East. With U. S. help, Filipino nationalists started a war of liberation against Spain. After the American victory, the Filipinos were outraged to find they had only exchanged one conqueror for another, and they conducted a guerrilla war against American invaders. Black soldiers were used to suppress the Filipinos just as Buffalo Soldiers were used earlier against Native Americans. Filipinos distributed communiqués among their own people reporting on the treatment of blacks in the South and said it would be better to die fighting than to submit to the United States and risk such abuse. Posters distributed among black U. S. troops by Filipino leader Emilio Aguinaldo's forces called on them to desert and join the islanders to avenge the widely publicized lynching of Sam Hose near Atlanta in 1899.

As racism increased after the Spanish-American War, so did antipathy toward black soldiers, whose bravery inspired more fear than admiration. Although mistreatment of black soldiers and veterans continued, notably in the Brownsville affair of 1906, African-Americans continued to volunteer to serve the nation. In Atlanta more blacks volunteered for duty in the Philippines in 1911 than the army could accept. That year, three black veterans attending a Grand Army of the Republic (GAR) convention in Fitzgerald were taken from their hotel room and whipped in the streets. The GAR buttons were cut off their coats, and they were chased out of town.

Soon after World War I broke out in Europe in July 1914, Georgia congressman Frank Pace introduced a bill to ban all black military officers. In the 1916 debate on the National Defense Act, Southern congressmen tried to exclude blacks from the military altogether. Ironically, after the United States declared war on Germany and the Central Powers on April 6, 1917, black troops were used to protect the White House and other federal buildings from possible German sabotage and spying despite newspaper stories disputing black loyalty. These stories told of German plots aimed at subverting blacks and alleged that federal agents had uncovered German-directed conspiracies among blacks in Georgia. One white said that Germany, with Mexican help, planned to seize Savannah for a base of operations and that the blacks there would rise up and help them. The furor over the Zimmerman note, an intercepted message outlining a German-Mexican alliance, lent credibility to such nonsense. Black leaders in Georgia knocked themselves out disavowing rumors that German agents were active in their midst. Meetings were held in Augusta, Macon, and Thomasville to deny any German influence or sympathy.

Blacks put aside their special grievances, and in the first burst of patriotic enthusiasm, many of them volunteered for the armed forces. In Georgia, blacks comprised 44 percent of the total population but supplied half the initial volunteers. To fill most of the army's needs, however, the draft was necessary. From June 1917 until the war ended in November 1918, 34,303 blacks and 32,538 whites were drafted from Georgia. At the start of the war black soldiers were welcomed into the army and were cheered by white crowds. On Labor Day, 1917, hundreds of Savannah blacks, in an unprecedented show of unity with whites, marched with Confederate flags and units of the Sons of the Confederacy. In April 1918,

Gov. Hugh M. Dorsey and Atlanta's mayor reviewed a parade of ten thousand black soldiers and war workers. Although the crowd applauded, the *Macon Telegraph*—echoing longstanding white sentiment—said that whites viewed blacks in uniform with mixed emotions.

After Southern congressmen failed to keep blacks out of the military, many Southern draft boards went to the other extreme of inducting black registrants whether they were fit or not. To fill quotas without taking many whites, 65 percent of white and less than 3 percent of black registrants in Fulton County were exempted. This was so outrageous that national officials replaced the entire draft board. The chairman and clerk of the Taliaferro County draft board were also removed for extreme prejudice. Georgia's draft boards, composed of local whites, would often take black landowners and exempt blacks who sharecropped for whites. This practice helped reverse the fifty-year trend of increasing black landownership.

The draft law provided that draft evaders would, when caught, have fifty dollars taken from their military pay, which would be given as a reward to the person who apprehended the delinquent. Some whites could not resist the temptation to withhold the draft notice until the black was delinquent and then turn him in to collect the money. Army investigations revealed that Georgia sheriffs in at least five counties reaped bounties "by fraudulently arresting colored men and turning them over to the local boards as slackers, for the sole purpose of getting the reward...." In one case, the black draftee was held incommunicado in the local jail until past his reporting time and then taken to Camp Gordon, where the fifty dollars was collected by a mercenary white.

Many black soldiers were trained at Camp Gordon near Augusta, where they quickly became excellent soldiers and won praise from officers. Camp Gordon's only black officer was Chaplain H. A. Rogers. One unit that trained there, the 514th Engineer Service Battalion, one of the army's 135 black labor battalions, did not even have any black noncommissioned officers. Following long-standing prejudice, most whites believed that black troops, to be successful, needed white officers. This prejudice prevailed, and black troops were handicapped as a result.

As the first burst of initial patriotic fervor died away, all the old discriminations reappeared. The army assigned blacks disproportionately to labor battalions; usually they got the dirtiest jobs and the worst facilities and often were put under racist white officers who treated them with contempt and hostility. Under these circumstances blackk troop performance did not always shine. Black soldiers probably would have done better if there had been more black officers like the twenty-five Atlanta University students who volunteered for the segregated officer candidate school (OCS) at Des Moines, Iowa. Surgeon Louis Wright and

A. T. Walden, an attorney, were two Georgians at the Des Moines facility, which was established with the blessing of the NAACP, although it was for blacks only. The alternative was no OCS for blacks.

In Europe, one of the first Georgians to see action was Eugene Jacques Bullard of Macon. Bullard was born in Columbus but fled in 1894 when nightriders tried to lynch his father. He eventually found his way to France and enlisted in the French Foreign Legion. He was wounded at Verdun and then was assigned to the Lafayette Escadrille, where he became the first black combat flier. The French called him "the Black Swallow of Death." White Americans in the Escadrille were all transferred to the U. S. Air Corps when it was organized in France, but Bullard's application for transfer was denied. After the war, Bullard remained in Paris as an expatriate and married into the French nobility. He amazed many with his daring stunt flying. He served in World War II and won fifteen French decorations and then returned to the United States. Adolphus Webb, another black flier, brought his airplane to Macon after the war and used to taxi around a field behind Mercer University, but authorities would not give him permission to fly.

Only about 42,000 of the 380,000 black soldiers during the war were assigned to combat duty. About 200,000 blacks went overseas, with the vast majority of them serving as military laborers and support personnel. Many of Georgia's black combat soldiers were in the 371st Regiment of the Ninety-third Division. Some of them trained at Camp Gordon before being sent to Camp Jackson, South Carolina, prior to embarking in April 1918 for France, where the 371st was attached to the French army. General John J. Pershing, commander-in-chief of the American Expeditionary Force (AEF), inspected the unit and was pleased with its military bearing and spirit. (Pershing had earned the sobriquet of "Black Jack" as commander of the Tenth Cavalry.) The black doughboys who were attached to French outfits found the French to be relatively free of racial prejudice, and they were treated better than they were treated at home. Echoing a common sentiment, Lt. Charles A. Shaw of Atlanta wrote from France that, unlike the United States, France was a real democracy.

In June 1918, the 371st was sent to Verdun, scene of some of the war's fiercest battles. In September, it saw heavy action in the Champagne area, where 109 were killed and 13 died later of wounds received. The Croix de Guerre was given the unit, and 124 of its members received the Distinguished Service Cross. Other black Georgians were scattered in various units. Lt. Gary C. Clark, an Atlanta University graduate, was killed in action with the 336th Infantry Regiment. Thomas Kane was more fortunate. He taught French cooks how to make pies for the AEF. Eddie Cooper, a native of Screven County and a member of the Ninth Cavalry, trained at Camp Wheeler in Macon and saw combat near Brest, France, where he lost an eye and had his hearing impaired by bombs.

The U. S. Army did its best to export the country's racism along with the AEF. Black troops were often restricted from contact with French civilians, especially women. French officers were told to respect the mores of white supremacy. The French government took offense. After all, the French relied heavily on black American and African troops and were grateful a million African soldiers were fighting for France, not African independence.

Sensing a potential weakness, the Germans kept track of lynchings, racial strife, and oppression in the United States. They tried to capitalize on black resentments by dropping leaflets on black troops, inviting them to surrender. The leaflets said there was no lynching in Germany and asked blacks whether they really wanted to fight and die for the United States. Leaflets dropped on the 371st asked if the soldiers were really fighting for democracy when they fought for Georgia and promised good treatment if they would surrender. The soldiers only laughed at the invitation, however.

Some of Georgia's black troops were retained to work after most whites had been discharged. Some ten thousand soldiers were held over in France to move the thousands of bodies of American soldiers to permanent cemeteries, such as Flanders Fields. When they returned to the United States, soldiers were forced to return to their induction centers to be discharged. This meant that blacks who joined the army in Georgia had to return there whether they wanted to or not. Georgia was not prepared to give black soldiers a hero's welcome.

On the home front, Georgia blacks supported the war effort to the limit of their ability and received some white recognition for this. However, "the wartime flurry of interracial toleration was of course temporary and affected only a small fraction of the population," historian John Matthews noted. Retired Gammon Seminary President Dr. J. W. E. Bowen addressed patriotic meetings in several states. Morehouse President John Hope served in France as a YMCA worker. In 1917, the *Savannah Morning News* suggested that in return for blacks' war work, lynching should end. However, at least seven blacks were lynched in Georgia in 1917; nineteen, the next year. The *Macon Telegraph* said that in Jasper County, a scene of past racial conflicts, white women pinned a tribute on the lapel of every man—black and white—who registered for the draft. Not all communities were so enlightened. In Albany, white women made a flag with a star only for each *white* native son in service.

In 1918, the all-white Georgia division of the Women's Committee of the Council of National Defense praised the state's blacks for their war work, which included buying the bonds that helped finance the war. Black leaders encouraged this financial sacrifice. Mr. and Mrs. C. H. Douglass, owners of the famous Douglass Theater in Macon, bought

$20,000 worth of bonds in 1918. Blacks in Chatham County bought $200,000 in bonds, including $20,000 by the First Bryan Baptist Church and $5,000 by the Wage Earners Bank. The largest single purchase was of $55,500 by the Standard Life Insurance Company of Atlanta and its employees. So it went in black communities throughout Georgia. These efforts did not go completely unnoticed. The white *Augusta Chronicle* compared the valor of Georgia's black soldiers with the sacrifices of blacks on the home front and starkly contrasted these with a recent lynching of a black man who was dragged behind an automobile until he died.

Georgia's blacks contributed to the war effort in other ways. Black girls and women formed patriotic clubs. Julius Hart of Columbus invented three types of aerial bombs for which the government paid him $15,000. Over five thousand blacks heard the governor speak at a food-conservation rally at the Atlanta Civic Auditorium, the first time blacks had been permitted to use that building. Blacks throughout the state cultivated victory gardens and produced larger crops to help overcome the food shortages that existed during the war.

The outbreak of war had an immediate effect on farmers. Cotton prices plummeted in late 1914 due to the German and British blockades of each other. When this happened, Asa Candler, Atlanta millionaire and Coca-Cola director, offered low-interest loans to white planters and stored 250,000 bales of cotton in his warehouses in the fall of 1914. Black farmers received no such support, and thousands had to sell their land at a fraction of its value. By 1916 conditions improved, and cotton farmers experienced relative prosperity. The next year, some independent black farmers increased their livestock holdings and cut back on cotton as the boll weevil made more serious inroads.

During the war, repression was often practiced under the guise of "patriotism." The *Columbus Ledger* editorialized in late 1917 that legislation was needed to force blacks into the army or into the field and stop them from going to the North or becoming "troublemakers." This "work or fight" controversy erupted when U. S. Army Provost Marshal Enoch Crowder ordered, on May 24, 1918, that all able-bodied men of draft age must be employed in an essential job if they were not in the military. Thus encouraged, Georgia whites attempted to keep black men working for low wages, drive black women into domestic service, and stem the Great Migration. The General Assembly passed a law that applied to men through age fifty-five, ten years past the draft age. Atlanta's black community had put up a vigorous fight to prevent the "work or fight" law from being applied to women.

In Georgia's smaller towns, local officials passed "work or fight" ordinances that also applied to women and enforced them with extreme prejudice. In Macon, a black woman who kept busy with her home and children and whose husband made enough to support his family was fined twenty-five dollars for refusing to take a job as a domestic. A Wrightsville ordinance said that all blacks had to work at least fifty hours a week or be jailed. In Pelham, Rufus G. McCrary, an agency director of the Standard Life Insurance Company supervising twenty-five agents, was told by the town marshal that he would have to get another job. Frank McCoy, also of Pelham, was ordered to give up his insurance job in order to work at the local fertilizer factory. Bainbridge passed a city ordinance stating that black housewives must take work as domestics. Some were arrested and fined fifteen dollars each. Then black residents held an indignation meeting and informed city authorities that if arrests continued they would resist "to the last drop of blood in their bodies." There were no more arrests. When several black women were arrested in Augusta for leaving their jobs as domestics for better jobs, the judge dismissed the case when he saw that his courtroom was filled with influential NAACP members.

White Georgians grew extremely apprehensive about the returning black soldiers. U. S. Sen. Thomas W. Hardwick of Georgia said that such a veteran was to be feared. Will Alexander, a racially moderate white Methodist leader, said he was amazed how much fear of the returning soldiers mounted within forty-eight hours of the armistice. Whites were horrified that black soldiers had learned "social equality" from the French and would expect better treatment. When Capt. James A. Scott, one of Georgia's few black officers, led his battalion in the Atlanta victory parade, he was cheered by some of the white onlookers, but the white press did not mention his battalion or the other three thousand blacks in the parade. If blacks thought fighting for their country meant that the caste system would be abolished, they were mistaken. Discrimination against black troops did not let up after the fighting stopped—if anything, it increased. The press spoke of "French women-ruined soldiers" and how they would need to be taught a lesson when they returned. There were some brutal lessons ahead.

Georgia led the lynching parade by a wide margin in 1919. At least ten black soldiers were lynched that year, half of them in Georgia. Many of the demobilized black veterans continued to wear their uniforms, sometimes because they had no other clothes and sometimes because they were proud of their service. Many whites reacted savagely to this practice. In May 1919, a black Georgia veteran who had gone into a drugstore for a soda was hit with a baseball bat for being in uniform. In Sylvester, Daniel Mack, still in uniform, was dragged from the local jail by a mob and beaten to death. His crime—for which he received a thirty-day sentence—had been to announce that since he had fought in France, he would no longer accept mistreatment from white people. When Wilbur Little returned from the army, several whites at the Blakely railroad station forced him to take off his uniform and walk home in his underwear. He continued to wear his uniform and paid with his life.

Other black soldiers died for not quickly stepping back into "their place." Ex-soldier Charles Kelly was killed in Cochran because he failed to show sufficient deference to whites by yielding the right of way. A former private named Elles was beaten to death in Spalding County because he told a white he had just gotten out of the army and was not ready to go back to work. A fifth veteran, James Grant, was lynched in Cordele in 1919. Following this last lynching, four local black churches and three lodge buildings were burned to drive home the point that nothing had changed for blacks in Georgia.

Veterans groups also treated black soldiers without honor. The main organization of World War I veterans, the American Legion, was formed in 1919. It was intensely racist, especially in the South, where blacks were barred from joining. The Georgia American Legion refused to charter even the segregated black posts organized by C. C. Middleton of Savannah. At the Legion's first national convention at Minneapolis in November 1919, Georgia threatened to withdraw from the national organization if blacks were admitted. The American Legion would remain "white as a lily" in the South.

Although there were many criticisms of black soldiers in World War I, they did remarkably well when one considers the obstacles that were placed in their path. Many whites believed so fully in the stereotypes of the "cowardly and childlike black" that they argued that blacks would fail in combat. Yet there was truth to Du Bois's charge that "Southern Bourbons and Northern Copperheads feared Negro soldiers" not because they would not fight but because "they will fight and fight bravely and well." In recognition of the black soldiers' contributions, in 1925 Congress authorized monuments in France to honor them.

Although black civilians and soldiers received a scant measure of justice and opportunity, they made great sacrifices to contribute to victory. Black leaders, such as Henry H. Proctor and Du Bois, had believed that the war's outcome would be more democracy at home and blacks' support of the war would help improve their condition. Events proved this hope false, and Du Bois was quick to admit it when the war ended in a fury of antiblack violence.

World War I did create conditions for change, however. Wartime opportunities encouraged migration. Some 200,000 black troops had gone overseas and met a white population in France that appeared relatively uninfected with racism. About seventeen thousand black Georgians, half of the thirty-four thousand draftees, got a glimpse of what life might be like and resented the situation back home all the more. They returned with higher expectations and ideas on how to realize those goals.

The "New Negro" and the New Klan

Migration, urbanization, and military life combined with the democratic rhetoric of World War I to intensify a new spirit of self-esteem among African-Americans; along with the belief that their situation was intolerable, a more militant resolve to resist wrongs was reborn. In the North, these forces led to the rise of both black nationalism and interracial cooperation, produced the Universal Negro Improvement Association, the Harlem Renaissance, greater political activity, and the militancy of the "New Negro." These developments contributed to change in Georgia, where the new spirit posed a threat to white supremacy. Before it had run its course, it had hammered a few cracks in the caste system despite frenzied counterattacks by the armies of its defenders mobilized by the new Ku Klux Klan.

The increased security of urban life, a decline in religious fervor, and better education in the cities helped make the goals of success for blacks more like those of whites. Urbanized and northward-migrating blacks were less likely to concentrate on going to heaven and held a greater desire for a better life here on earth—immediately, if possible. As rural folk abandoned their guise of humility, so necessary for survival in rural Georgia, and began to compete in the cities, they adopted the more aggressive characteristics that were necessary to survive in the modern urban world.

A vital manifestation of the "New Negro" was the flood of literary creativity of black writers, who rejected the image of blacks as martyrs and embraced the more earthy aspects of black culture. Although this movement is called the Harlem Renaissance, it had many roots in Georgia. W. E. B. Du Bois lived in Georgia when the Renaissance began. In addition to being one of the nation's preeminent social scientists, he was a poet, essayist, and novelist. He contributed to the Renaissance with many writings and opened the pages of the *Crisis* to encourage others.

Perhaps the movement's opening work was Atlanta University graduate James Weldon Johnson's 1912 *Autobiography of an Ex-Colored Man*—actually a novel with a Georgia-born protagonst who leaves for New York City and Europe. He returns to Georgia and witnesses a black burned alive at the stake and is then ashamed of being black. He marries a white woman and disappears into white society but does not find peace in that, either. Georgia and lynching figure in other works by Johnson.

Jean Toomer (1894–1967) was a major figure of the Harlem Renaissance. His classic, *Cane*, was largely set in Georgia, where Toomer's distinguished grandfather, P. B. S. Pinchback, was born. In 1921, Toomer took a job as a temporary superintendent of the Georgia Normal and Industrial Institute in Sparta. The return trip to Georgia unleashed his creative impulse. Toomer said, "I heard folk songs come from the lips of Negro peasants. I saw the rich dark beauty that I had heard many false reports about.... And a deep part of my nature, a part that I had repressed, sprang suddenly to life and responded to them." Most of the sketches in *Cane* have Georgia settings, with Georgia blacks as their main characters. *Cane* also reflected Toomer's ambiguity about his racial identity. He was light enough to pass and later did as he retreated into mysticism.

Georgia Douglas Johnson (1886–1966) was another Georgian who became a significant writer of the Renaissance. She was born in Atlanta, graduated from Atlanta University in 1893, and studied further at Oberlin. She is considered to be Georgia's most significant black literary figure before Alice Walker. Her three volumes of published poetry reflect the life and psyche of black women. She exemplified the spirit of the "New Negro" in her poem "The Octoroon," first published in 1919. She married Henry Lincoln Johnson, a major black Republican political figure, and spent most of her adult life in Washington. She wrote a number of antilynching plays; two promoted the Dyer antilynching bill in the 1920s.

Native Atlantan Walter White wrote two novels, *The Fire in the Flint* and *Flight*, that dealt with lynching and passing, but he is remembered mainly for his work with the National Association for the Advancement of Colored People (NAACP). White was born in Atlanta to middle-class parents in 1893. His mother was one-sixteenth black, and his father, who was one-quarter black, worked for the post office. After graduation, he worked for Standard Life Insurance Company and helped found the NAACP's Atlanta branch. The light-skinned, blue-eyed White went on to a lifetime career with the NAACP, first as an investigator of lynchings, using his ability to pass as a white Southerner. In 1929 he published a nonfiction indictment of lynching, *Rope and Faggot*. He filled the NAACP's top post of executive secretary from 1931 until his death in 1955.

The new mood among blacks made the NAACP's growth in Georgia possible, although it was very slow at first. The organization's founding had marked a change in civil rights organizations. Since most early civil rights efforts were all black, they were virtually ignored by whites. The NAACP was interracial from its beginning and absorbed a number of other protest organizations, such as the Constitution League and the Niagara Movement, whose leaders were the NAACP's staunchest supporters. Its early growth was mainly in the North, where a black who joined did not necessarily risk life and limb by doing so. Atlanta University professor Du Bois was the only black director of the original NAACP, but his main contribution came as editor of the *Crisis*, the NAACP's official organ. The magazine's circulation in Georgia was greater than in any other ex-slave state except Texas, but the NAACP did not take deep root in the state before several Atlanta school crises established the local branch as an effective organization.

Several earlier attempts to establish branches had failed, but in 1917, NAACP field secretary James Weldon Johnson's organizing trip to Georgia bore fruit, and branches were opened in Athens, Atlanta, Augusta, Macon, and Savannah. Standard Life executive Harry Pace was elected president of the Atlanta branch, and Walter White became its secretary. By the end of March, it had 393 members, with 139 paid-up memberships.

The Atlanta Board of Education had eliminated the eighth grade from all its public schools in 1915, and whites graduating from the seventh grade then went directly to high school. Since there were no high schools for blacks in Atlanta (and only three in the state), they would suffer more from this change. In 1917, the school board went further and planned to eliminate the seventh grade for blacks. The fledgling NAACP chapter sent a six-man committee to protest the plan and gained the support of board member James L. Key (later mayor), and the board backed down.

The NAACP went on to push a letter-writing campaign to the school board, asking for the elimination of the double shift, a common practice in all fourteen of Atlanta's black schools and many others in the state. Some Atlanta teachers taught sixty pupils from 8:30 A.M. until noon and sixty more from 12:30 P.M. to 4 P.M. The old, dilapidated wooden buildings still could not accommodate all who wanted to attend. The aroused blacks also demanded better buildings, a junior high school for industrial education, and a high school. Blacks pointed out that they made up one-third of Atlanta's population and paid taxes on $1.5 million worth of property.

Johnson came to Atlanta during the school crisis and heard White speak to a full house at the Odd Fellows' two-thousand-seat auditorium. He was so impressed that he invited White to come to New York City and work for the NAACP at $100 a month. Although White had higher pay and excellent prospects at Standard Life, he accepted. White's January 1918 departure from Atlanta hurt the local branch. By June there were only forty-nine paid members and Harry Pace had resigned as president. However, because of the NAACP's leadership during the school crisis in Atlanta, membership in other Georgia chapters began to rise. Additional NAACP branches were established in Waycross, Columbus, Brunswick, Rome, and Thomasville in 1918. An Albany branch was also formed around this time.

It took another school struggle to make the Atlanta branch a powerful organization. Atlantans wanted to finance city improvements by selling bonds. City leaders had betrayed black supporters of bond issues twice before, in 1903 and 1910, and in 1918 would not make any commitments to improve black schools. All the requests, petitions, and letters asking for more educational opportunities for black children evoked no response until pressure was applied in another way. In Atlanta two-thirds of the registered voters were needed to approve a bond issue. The NAACP set out to defeat the bond issue and increased its membership to two thousand. It organized a voter-registration campaign, a formidable task in the era of disfranchisement. To register, a would-be voter had to pay all back poll taxes. Blacks were encouraged to do so and vote against the bond issue, or not vote, which had the same effect under the rules. Blacks paid up to thirty-two years' worth of accumulated poll taxes. In a bribery attempt, black teachers were told that the bonds included money for salary increases for them. On election day, city factories shut down to encourage whites to vote. Black voters turned out in sufficient numbers at the polls to defeat the measure in 1918 and 1919, and the city's bid was stymied. Adam Daniel Williams, pastor of Ebenezer Baptist Church and president of the Atlanta NAACP, organized a boycott of advertisers in the white *Atlanta Georgian*, which had labeled the bond issue's black opponents "dirty and ignorant."

Atlanta NAACP membership skyrocketed to three thousand by the end of 1920 under the presidency of the Rev. R. H. Singleton, pastor of Big Bethel A.M.E. Church. City leaders realized they would have to share a little with blacks. Resistance to the black demand for a high school collapsed, and a deal was made to give blacks a fairer share of school monies in exchange for support on the next bond issue. In 1921, 20 percent of the city's vote was black, and this segment voted 99 percent in favor of the bond issue in exchange for five new schools, including a combined junior-senior high school (ironically named after the accommodationist Booker T. Washington), which initially went through grade ten when it opened in 1924. This great effort by no means ended educational disparities in Atlanta, however. Separate and unequal education continued.

Georgia sent fifteen delegates to the Cleveland NAACP national convention in 1919. In 1920, in a rather daring move, the NAACP held its national convention in Atlanta in response to an invitation signed by Gov. Hugh Dorsey, Mayor James Key (its ally during the school crisis), chamber of commerce officials, and a committee of white ministers. "We go to Atlanta," Du Bois said, "to say to the South that we want to vote, stop lynching, improve schools, end Jim Crow and peonage, and obtain decent wages and treatment." The association then had eighty thousand black and eighteen thousand white members nationally. Of the fifteen thousand who attended, less than fifty were Southern whites.

The successful convention stimulated the formation of branches in Americus, Cordele, Dublin, Hawkinsville, Milledgeville, and Valdosta in 1920. By then there were sixteen Georgia branches. However, the

Thomasville branch disbanded that year after whites threatened to kill its president, who had already lost his mail-carrier job due to his civil-rights activities. Black physician Percy S. Richardson struggled against black timidity in Thomasville when he tried to revive it in 1924. The Macon branch had similar problems. President Frank J. Hutchins recruited about a dozen members by 1923, but most he approached were too frightened to join. Faced with such harsh opposition, membership in Georgia's smaller branches declined during the 1920s.

The more conservative National Urban League also established a presence in Georgia during this period. The league was founded in New York City in 1910 to help blacks adjust to the problems of city life. A local branch was established in Savannah in 1913, with *Tribune* editor Sol C. Johnson as president. This ensured that the branch got a lot of publicity in his newspaper, but the chapter declined in the 1920s. The Urban League's Southern regional headquarters was set up in Atlanta in 1919, and a local branch was organized in 1920. John Hope became the Atlanta chairman in 1922.

The new militancy was not confined to Atlanta politics. In 1915, the *Macon Telegraph* spotted a disturbing trend and said blacks were beginning to think themselves superior. The newspaper complained about the lack of "outward signs of deference" among blacks. In 1917, Wilson Jefferson of Augusta wrote James Weldon Johnson, "Did you ever know a race to awake as our race has awakened in the last year or so? Augusta is almost another town. The old spirit of humble satisfaction or let-well-enough alone, is fast dying out."

In light of the lofty wartime rhetoric, antiblack outrages became more reprehensible and enraging than before. "I believe my people should defend their homes and families," proclaimed A.M.E. Bishop George C. Clement in 1919. When Du Bois went to Milledgeville that year to speak at a school commencement, he found the town in an uproar. The black school had the same colors as the white school, and whites had been tearing the colors off black students for days. Blacks went to Macon for arms and ammunition, and a hundred armed men guarded the exercises; there were no further incidents. Not all Georgia blacks were infused with this new spirit, however. In Lexington, six blacks signed an open letter to a mob that burned "only" Obe Cox at the stake, saying, "We certainly thank you for handling the case so nice, for it could have been worse for us."

The heightened black militancy produced an alarmed counterattack in defense of white supremacy. When John Hope returned to Georgia from overseas duty with the YMCA during World War I, he was surprised by the number of rumors about armed bands of radical blacks. Whites were responding by driving blacks from their homes. Much of the white alarm stemmed from surprise. Insulated by segregation, most whites were unaware of the long-standing bitterness that blacks felt. When it was expressed more openly in the black press, whites saw a great new menace. James Calloway of the *Macon Telegraph* blamed the *Crisis* and other publications for "scattering all over Georgia" cartoons derogatory toward whites. The lynching of black soldiers was one prong of the attack. Others involved an ideological campaign aimed at showing that the "New Negro" was a menace to the American way of life—a subversive force that should be stamped out. White Georgians, loath to admit that race relations were poor, blamed the new militancy on outside influences. In the fall of 1917, Lenin led the Bolshevik party of Russia to victory in a socialist revolution, and fearful reactionaries in the United States began to see Reds everywhere. Black protest that was misperceived as pro-German during the war was misperceived as pro-Communist afterward. W. J. Wingate said that Georgia's sheriffs needed legal jurisdiction over the Negro fraternal lodges because they were "hotbeds of Bolshevism."

These white flights of paranoia about subversive blacks came despite the fact that most blacks were generally so conservative that they were considered "the despair of radicals, even of liberals." Blacks wanted enforcement of existing laws, not sweeping legislative changes. As James Weldon Johnson told a congressional committee in 1920, "Practically every single thing in which the Colored people are accused of sedition is a thing which every law-abiding citizen should get behind them and fight for."

In Georgia, there was an increase in lynching in a vain effort to suppress the spirit of the New Negro. A major element in this attempt was the resurgence of the Ku Klux Klan. This "Second" Klan was born on Stone Mountain on Thanksgiving night, 1915. It is no coincidence that the Klan was reborn in Georgia. William H. Skaggs, a Southern progressive, said, "In no state could such a diabolical and lawless organization more securely carry on its wicked and proscriptive practices." Clark scholar William Henry Crogman noted the Klan leaders' "keen sense of propriety exhibited in the selection of Atlanta for their headquarters, Atlanta, capital of Georgia, banner lynching state of the South!"

Klan-type violence, with lynching as its ultimate manifestation, symbolized the determination to maintain the threefold economic, sexual, and psychological exploitation of blacks. Most white Georgians continued to view lynching as "regrettable," but necessary. A signed letter to the *Atlanta Journal* encouraging lynching explained the reasons behind the reign of terror:

How many of us would have put up with, five or six years ago, things we have to submit to from Negroes in our daily lives now? They are becoming more impudent, arrogant, and independent all the time....Unless something is done to put a check on the wave of Negro arrogance that is sweeping the country, we will soon be at their mercy.

Several factors contributed to the Klan's resurgence, notably the lynching of Leo Frank and the release of *The Birth of a Nation*, the filmed version of Thomas Dixon's racist play, *The Clansman*. Walter White said *The Birth of a Nation* "did more than anything else to make successful the revival of the Ku Klux Klan." It opened in Atlanta on December 6, 1915 and broke the city's movie attendance records. By this time, the federal government itself actively promoted segregation and other discrimination. The New South's mythology about lynching and the lack of protest for even the most barbaric ones also encouraged the Klan mentality.

The lynching of Leo Frank was the most publicized mob murder in the nation's history and called attention to the fact that not only blacks were lynched. Frank was a white Jewish manufacturer who moved to Atlanta to manage a pencil factory that employed child labor. The body of thirteen-year-old Mary Phagan was found in the basement of the factory on April 27, 1913. After some uncertainty whether to charge Frank or a black janitor, James Conley, with the crime, Frank was indicted, tried in a climate of mob hysteria, and sentenced to die. "One juror stated that he wasn't sure of anything except that unless they convicted Frank, they would never get home alive," stated one account of the trial. After Gov. John M. Slaton commuted the sentence to life imprisonment, Frank was hauled from prison in Milledgeville and lynched at Marietta, the home of Mary Phagan, on August 17, 1915.

The final chapter on the Frank case was not written until seventy years after the lynching. Frank's office boy, Alonzo Mann, told reporters in 1982 that he saw Conley carrying Mary Phagan's body to the factory basement and that Conley told Mann that he would kill him if he said anything. Mann believed that Conley killed Mary Phagan for the pay she had just picked up. Conley had confessed to the murder three times, but he was ignored and then was coached to be a key witness against Frank. Prosecuting attorney Hugh Dorsey did not permit the grand jury to consider the case against Conley because the conviction of a black man would not bring him the publicity that Frank's conviction would. (Dorsey was later elected governor.) Conley died in 1962 and Mann in 1985. Based on Mann's statement and other considerations, Frank was pardoned posthumously in 1986 by the State Board of Pardons and Paroles, which reversed its 1983 refusal to grant a pardon.

Many blacks noticed that the Frank lynching attracted far more attention and protest than it would have had he been black. A black, John Riggens, was lynched in Bainbridge the same day Leo Frank was killed, but his death went largely unnoticed. Frank's lynching broadened the base of the antilynching movement and led directly to the formation of the Anti-Defamation Society of B'nai B'rith, which became an effective supporter of the rights of blacks and an opponent of all lynching.

The lurid and sensational coverage of the Frank case inflamed racist feelings, and Frank's death left a void for the Knights of Mary Phagan that William Joseph Simmons filled when he took thirty-three members of the vigilante group to Stone Mountain to revive the Klan. Unlike the original, rural-based Klan, the revived Klan took root first in the cities. Starting in Atlanta, it spread to Mobile, Birmingham, and Montgomery, but not much elsewhere before 1920. Despite occasional attacks on Jews and Catholics, in Georgia the Klan saw its main task as the maintenance of white supremacy, not Protestant fundamentalism. In Atlanta, Simmons would open meetings by bringing out two revolvers and shouting, "Bring on your Niggers."

Among the thirteen blacks lynched in Georgia in 1915 were a father, Samuel Baker, his son, and two married daughters killed at Monticello in Jasper County for successfully resisting arrest over an incident that began when a policeman struck Samuel's wife. Among the sixteen blacks lynched in Georgia in 1916 were five from Sylvester, in Worth County, charged with the murder of the Lee County sheriff, who was leading a mob intent on returning blacks to peonage. A picture showing all five bodies hanging from the same tree was "borrowed" by a black servant of prominent whites long enough to be copied and sent to the *Crisis*. This mass lynching was followed by a mob rampage in nearby Early County that resulted in the burning of black churches and lodges because they were suspected gathering places of blacks plotting massacres of whites.

Lynchings continued to occur after trivial incidents, and in 1917, the NAACP was unable to find even an alleged reason for the lynching of Joe Nowling at Pelham, one of the seven blacks lynched in Georgia that year. Two others, D. C. and Collins Johnson, were lynched in Mitchell County for disputing a white man's word.

The decline in mob murders in 1916 and 1917 was largely due to white Georgians' fear of economic loss resulting from migration. The number, however, went back up to nineteen in 1918 as white Georgians decided that the New Negro was a far greater threat than the temporary migration-induced economic loss. Therefore, attacks on whites were met with bloodcurdling vengeance. The murder of Hampton Smith, described as "a particularly bestial operator of a peonage plantation" and "a white farmer with a reputation of cruelty toward tenants," led to a five-day reign of terror in Brooks and Lowndes counties in 1918. Hayes Turner was one of several blacks who were lynched for complicity in the murder. His wife, Mary Turner, eight months pregnant, said that her husband was innocent and that she was going to swear out warrants against the lynchers. She was hung upside down by her ankles, soaked with gasoline, and set afire. According to one account of the gruesome deed, "After her clothes burned off, and while she was yet alive, a man slit open her abdomen and her unborn child fell from her womb, gave two cries, and was stamped to death by one of the mob."

Based on investigations of Walter White, NAACP Secretary John R. Shillady sent the names of two ringleaders and fifteen mob members to Gov. Hugh M. Dorsey and received in return a letter with a rubber-stamp signature saying that all efforts to apprehend the guilty had been futile. Mary Turner's brutal death by torture became the year's single most-discussed lynching. It was written about in the nation's press, commented on from the pulpit, introduced as evidence of the oppression of blacks in congressional hearings, and was the subject of many letters to the White House. In 1919, Sidney Johnson was executed by police for suspected complicity in the death of Smith.

Under these circumstances, lynch mobs, even those exacting vengeance for "the usual crime," were easily provoked. In September 1918, Sandy Reeves was taken from peace officers and lynched near Waycross for "assaulting a white girl," according to the white newspapers. Reeves had been picking grapes for an employer and accidentally dropped a nickel. His employer's three-year-old daughter, who had been watching him work, picked it up and started to cry when he took it back.

The "Red Summer" of 1919 was the greatest wave of terror and murder against blacks since the Klan put down Reconstruction fifty years earlier. Nationally, there were twenty-six urban race riots, and more than seventy lynchings, of which nearly a third were reported in Georgia. That year, Eli Cooper, an elderly black working on the plantation of A. P. Petway near Eastman, was burned to death for organizing black field workers and for saying that the "Negro had been run over for fifty years, but it must stop now, and that pistols and shotguns were the only ways to stop a mob." Several local black churches and lodges were also burned in connection with the lynching. When John Dowdy and another white man attempted to rape two black girls, the daughters of Emma McCollers, a widow in Milan, Berry Washington, a seventy-two-year-old black, came to their rescue. He killed Dowdy and turned himself in to the police. He was burned at the stake. The county commissioner asked local editors to suppress the story. After the NAACP exposed this lynching, Governor Dorsey admitted that it was true.

During the Red Summer, Jack Gordon allegedly shot a white and was burned to death near Washington along with Will Brown and Moses Freeman, who were trying to aid Gordon's escape by throwing the mob off his trail. In a case of mistaken identity, four white vigilantes shot and killed Cleveland Butler in Twiggs County. A mob near Gray, in Jones

County, came to the jail to lynch four blacks, but the sheriff had outsmarted them and they found the jail empty, with every door open. The mob vented its frustration by burning two Negro churches and a lodge hall also used as a schoolhouse. In Putnam County, when a Negro spoke up about whites always being served first in public places, arsonists burned five black churches and three schools. Other whites, concerned about the effects of such terrorism, posted a $1,000 reward and started a fund for rebuilding. In Baker, Calhoun, and Miller counties, nightriders burned thirteen black churches and schoolhouses. Ernest Glenwood was lynched for organizing blacks in Dooly County. In Millen, five blacks were killed, and several churches and lodges were burned after two white lawmen were killed after a church disturbance.

Klan-type violence subsided only slightly in 1920. As a lesson to blacks seeking to migrate, Jim Waters was lynched near Dublin. At Waycross, a white passing through a Jim Crow train coach flipped a burning cigarette onto the lap of a black woman. When her husband protested, he was shot dead, and his body was left at the next station. No effort was made to arrest the murderer. Philip Gathers, a black accused of murder, was tortured, castrated, and burned alive by a crowd of thousands near Rincon. The militia was called out from Savannah but arrived too late. Near Dewitt, Curley McKelvey was hanged from a tree and riddled with bullets by a mob looking for his brother, who had allegedly shot a white in a quarrel over the use of a road. Another black was lynched in Greene County after being accused of sheltering a friend who had wounded a local planter in a quarrel.

Klan attacks were not always lethal. Joseph Jackson, a prosperous Elberton black, was visited by a party of six or eight prominent whites; they shot up his house, broke the windows and doors, and wounded some of his family for no apparent reason other than that they resented his prosperity. Fletcher Perdue, a black living in Griffin, was severely beaten for hiring another black away from a white. John Brown, Dough Stahl, and Oscar Amie were among other Griffin blacks taken out and whipped. Tom Allen was beaten for disputing the word of a white storekeeper. Tom Miller was whipped for failing to open his door at night to strangers. Tragedy was sometimes averted. Bessie Revere of Quitman, after being assaulted by a white man, regained consciousness just in time to identify him and thus prevented a mob from lynching a black who had been accused of her rape.

As the Klan grew rapidly in 1921, lynchings and racial attacks drew little white protest. Jim Roland, a prosperous black farmer near Camilla, was ordered at pistol point by Jason I. Harvel, a white farmer, to dance for the amusement of a crowd of whites. Roland scuffled with Harvel, who was shot by his own gun. Roland also refused to dance for the mob that lynched him. In Colquitt County, John Henry Williams was sentenced to hang for murder. He was taken by an impatient mob and burned alive. The following week, the Associated Negro Press reported that the unidentified body of a black, killed by nightriders, was found near Columbus. In Athens, Lee Eberhardt was immolated after the sheriff "placidly" handed over the keys to the jail that had been designed to resist mobs. In November, Jesse Willingham, a black tenant of Hamilton Abelhart, angered his landlord by trying to sell his own cotton rather than turn it over to his landlord for less money. Abelhart beat him unconscious and locked him in his barn and set it on fire, but Willingham escaped. In December, Leroy Graves, Webster Hale, and Aaron Birdsong were lynched in Georgia. In Augusta, a race riot in which three blacks died began when one black resisted arrest and ended with a mob attacking the black section of town.

Mob law continued in the name of "justice." In May 1922, Charles Atkins, aged fifteen, was roasted alive over a slow fire. After shrieking in agony for fifteen minutes, he "confessed" to killing a white. He was then shot; the undertaker said he had two hundred bullet holes in his body. In another case, James Harvey and Joe Jordan received death sentences in court, but Gov. Thomas Hardwick granted a thirty-day stay of execution to consider new evidence gathered by the NAACP in their case. On July 1, the day after the stay was granted, a mob lynched both men. Although Hardwick had said there would be no mob actions while he was in office, he ignored the NAACP demand that he take action against Wayne County Sheriff J. R. Tyre, who let it be known that he would offer no resistance to any mob—and also took the prisoners to the lynching site, as prearranged with the mob's leaders. (The mob was late but the sheriff was patient.)

By 1920, the Klan was sufficiently respectable to participate in Atlanta's Confederate reunion, and during the early 1920s, public opposition to the Klan in Atlanta was rare. In 1922 the Klan helped elect three councilmen and Walter Sims as mayor. Sims introduced an ordinance forbidding interracial church services, a move probably aimed at the Commission for Interracial Cooperation (CIC), which had formed in 1919 in Atlanta to improve race relations. While the Klan controlled Fulton County, court records on the immorality of Klan leaders "disappeared" forever. By 1923 there were fifteen thousand members in Atlanta klaverns. The Klan claimed a national membership of 5 million in 1924, but its membership was more in the range of 2 million, still an impressive figure. Between 1915 and 1944, sixty-five thousand Georgians, including twenty thousand Atlantans, were inducted into the Klan, more than any other Southern state except Texas. Although Imperial Wizard Hiram

Evans said the Klan stood for Americanism, Protestantism, and white people, the Klan was also a moneymaking scheme, thanks to membership fees and the sale of robes, regalia, and other supplies.

The Klan also became a power in Georgia politics, and open Klan membership was no obstacle to political advancement. Governor Hardwick, while an opponent of black political rights, had ended flogging in the prisons and called on the Klan to unmask and stop its violence. When he sought reelection in 1922, he was defeated in the Democratic primary by Klan-backed Clifford Walker. Georgia Supreme Court Chief Justice Richard B. Russell, Sr., was associated with the Klan in 1923, and the Klan enjoyed an extremely close relationship with Georgia's Fifth District congressman, William D. Upshaw, in 1924.

Most of the Klan's influence rested on its ability to punish its opponents. The Klan whipped public officials and schoolteachers and intimidated newspaper editors. In 1923, a large "flogging league" near Macon had both black and white victims. When the mayor of Columbus refused a Klan demand that he remove the city manager, the mayor's home was dynamited. If these "warnings" were not enough, there was always the lynch mob.

During the Klan's heyday, the leading black nationalist came to Atlanta to meet with the Klan. Marcus Garvey founded the Universal Negro Improvement Association (UNIA) to promote racial pride and self-help. By 1922, there were about a hundred UNIA branches in the South. They avoided problems with the Klan and lynchers by voicing their distaste for integration and "social equality." Although the UNIA maintained a low profile in the South, the Klan began to harass it. Garvey went to Atlanta, which had a UNIA headquarters, in the summer of 1922 to explain the UNIA to the Klan. This Atlanta trip was misconstrued and led to erroneous charges that Garvey was in league with lynchers. Later, after Garvey was convicted on federal charges of mail fraud, he served his sentence in the Atlanta penitentiary.

In 1924, Klan backing was tantamount to election, but the Klan collapsed rather suddenly. In 1926, all candidates it backed in Georgia, including Richard Russell, Sr., who was running for the U.S. Senate, were defeated. The sordid scandal involving Imperial Wizard Evans's violation of the Mann Act, which provided penalties for transporting women across state lines for immoral purposes, and the death of his white secretary following a rape helped expose the hypocrisy of the Klan's position on protecting white womanhood. The Klan moved its national headquarters from Atlanta to Washington, D.C., in 1925 in the heady period when it hoped to become a national pressure group. In 1929 it moved back to Atlanta. Short of funds in 1936, it sold its Peachtree Street mansion. Ironically, the building passed on to the Catholic church and became the archbishop's residence. While the Klan died as an organized political force, sympathy for the Klan's ideas continued, and past membership was not a political liability in Georgia for decades. When E. D. Rivers was elected governor in 1936, it was common knowledge he had been a local Klan official in 1928.

However, the South was not completely dominated by the Klan mentality. Mob violence and Klan activity produced a reaction. Blacks more militantly resisted their oppression, and as they did, more whites joined in the struggle for justice. While open criticism of the Klan by whites was rare in 1920s Georgia, not all white Georgians approved of the Ku Klux Klan or the obstacles that degraded life for blacks. The straitjacket blacks were wearing was fraying at the seams as the more decent white elements of the state joined in an interracial attack on the Klan's ideals.

Antilynching Reform

From its beginning, the NAACP recognized that lynching was the number-one problem for blacks: There could be no improvement in race relations while black lives meant so little. Black advances and more militant attitudes combined with other forces to fuel protest against lynching. Many of the South's disfranchised blacks became Northern voters. Also, more whites became aware of their responsibility and enlisted in the reform movement; the realization that the overt racism that led to the Red Summer of 1919 could endanger the entire society led to a large increase in the activities of antilynching reformers. While lynchings were often intended to enforce economic subservience by blacks, mob violence helped to fuel the Great Migration and deprived the Southern oligarchy of the cheap labor it prized. Therefore, Southern whites who might have overlooked the problem earlier were forced to face it.

The Commission on Interracial Cooperation (CIC) was the most important interracial organization in Georgia and the South in the decade following World War I. It was organized in Atlanta in 1919 by white liberals. The CIC's foundations included the interracial committee formed in the wake of the Atlanta riot, the YMCA, the War Work Councils, the Southern Sociological Congress, the University Commission, and several law-and-order leagues. Within a year, the CIC had established five hundred state, county, and local interracial councils throughout the South. By 1921, there were eight hundred, although many only existed on paper. Methodist minister and YMCA worker Will W. Alexander was executive director of the CIC from its beginning until 1944, when it merged with the Southern Regional Council.

While the CIC's methods were similar to those of the NAACP, its goals were different. The CIC did not attack the caste system and opposed federal antilynching legislation until 1935. The CIC's dominant white leaders sanctioned segregation and did not work to change the South fundamentally. They opposed lynching and some other symptoms of racism, but not its causes. Black participation in the CIC was never great and declined after the first few years. The first Georgia black invited to join, John Hope, was pessimistic about the CIC when he returned from France in 1919. Later, Atlanta A.M.E. Bishop Joseph S. Flipper and George C. Clement, father of future Atlanta University President Rufus Clement, were among the seventeen black and fifty-eight white members of the CIC's governing board.

Benjamin Mays was one of many Georgia blacks who worked with the CIC, but he became disillusioned when he went to Will Alexander for some help. Alexander advised Mays to drop a suit he brought against a railroad because he had been forced at gunpoint by whites out of a Pullman car and into the Jim Crow car even though he had paid for the higher-priced Pullman ticket. Mays ignored the advice, hired a Chicago lawyer, and won damages from the company.

The CIC issued press releases, lobbied legislatures, and pinned medals on brave sheriffs. It published *Southern Frontier* and numerous pamphlets, including "Burnt Cork and Crime," which described some twenty-five incidents when whites had blackened their faces and committed crimes, including rape, for which blacks were initially accused. Even though Alexander worried about the "aggressive impatience" of blacks, the CIC was considered radical by most Southern whites in the 1920s. Although composed mainly of ministers, it could find few white churches where it could hold interracial meetings and consequently usually met on black school campuses.

One of the CIC's significant accomplishments was its development of a women's auxiliary. In 1920, Will Alexander asked Lugenia D. Burns Hope, wife of John Hope, to organize a group of black women to meet with the white women of the Methodist Missionary Commission. The meeting was successful, and the auxiliary, headed by Carrie Parks Johnson and later by Jessie Daniel Ames, worked for the CIC's goals. This was important because the stand white women took against lynching helped to undermine the myth that lynching protected white womanhood. However, increasingly, the CIC was regarded by most Georgia blacks as too conservative.

In the 1920s, the NAACP intensified its efforts to secure the passage of an antilynching bill sponsored by Rep. Leonidas Dyer (R-Mo.). The bill provided for fines against the county where the lynching occurred. Some of the fine money would be used to support dependents of the lynched breadwinner. Amazingly, opponents of this provision claimed that the bill's passage would encourage blacks to provide for their families by committing heinous crimes that would incite mobs to lynch them.

Georgia blacks supported the Dyer Bill. Seven black ministers from LaGrange sent President Warren G. Harding a letter saying, "Should the United States fail to blot out this deadly evil of lynching, Babylon, Nineveh, Sodom and Gomorrah will rise up in the judgment and condemn us before God." Black leaders met with President Harding in November 1922 to argue for the Dyer Bill and presented petitions signed by hundreds of Georgians supporting it.

White churchmen of Georgia generally opposed antilynching legislation or remained silent. Meanwhile, Southern politicians fought the Dyer Bill tooth and nail. Still, it passed the House of Representatives, 231-119, in January 1922. In December, the bill was defeated in the Senate by a combination of Republican apathy and a Democratic filibuster. The Dyer Bill was reintroduced in each session of Congress until Dyer was defeated in the Democratic sweep of 1934. Though the measure was defeated, the campaign for the Dyer Bill helped reduce lynchings partly due to fears of federal intervention in Southern race relations and further attacks on the caste system.

Charles Kellogg, historian of the early NAACP, credited both fear of federal interference and the economic effects of the Great Migration for the decline in lynching. Another factor was the increased militancy of Southern blacks. In December 1921, a committee from Oconee County applied to Judge W. C. Cornett in Athens for a federal investigation of lynchings in the area, and members said they would testify concerning the deaths of many blacks over a long period. In July, a group of militant blacks met in Atlanta and loudly protested mob violence and numerous other proscriptions. No doubt in response to such pressures, the oligarchy did increase its efforts to prevent lynchings.

In an effort to give credibility to the argument that the Dyer Bill was unnecessary, the CIC urged greater state action against lynching and found a willing ally in Gov. Hugh M. Dorsey. Leo Frank's prosecutor was elected governor in 1916 with the backing of Tom Watson, a move the race-baiting Watson later regretted. During Dorsey's two 2-year terms, there was increasing pressure on him to act against lynchers. One of the pressures was the wide circulation of an NAACP booklet on Walter White's investigations of the lynchings in Brooks and Lowndes counties in 1918. While Dorsey did nothing about that case, he asked the General Assembly for legislation in 1919 that would provide that juries in the trials of lynchers come from outside the county where the lynching occurred. This would have undermined the practice of filling juries with mob members, which led to the usual verdict "came to death in the hands of persons unknown." Dorsey also called a state conference in 1920 to discuss lynching following the receipt of an antilynching petition prepared by the CIC and signed by sixty-seven college presidents and professors. In January 1921, five prominent blacks charged that the Klan was behind an effort to drive out black farmers and gave Dorsey affidavits charging whites with a series of crimes ranging from "petty cheating to deliberate and plotted murder" of blacks in five counties in one week.

In 1921, the sensational murder-peonage trial of Jasper County plantation owner John S. Williams grabbed national headlines. Shortly after Williams's conviction, on April 22, Dorsey issued a pamphlet that rocked the state. *A Statement from Governor Hugh M. Dorsey as to the Negro in Georgia* detailed 135 cases of lynching, peonage, and other outrages against blacks: "In some counties the negro is being driven out as though he were a wild beast. In others, he is being held as a slave. In others no negroes remain." Dorsey called for several reforms: a state constabulary that could be sent into any county to quell disorders, even if local officials did not request aid; fines against counties where lynchings occurred; and judicial investigations of lynchings. Dorsey reiterated the need for jurors in lynching trials to come from outside the county where the lynching occurred, and he also sought legislation that would allow the governor to set the trial site.

Although he had support from the NAACP and the CIC, Dorsey was bitterly attacked. Cordele Mayor J. Gordon Jones wanted Dorsey impeached and Governor-elect Thomas Hardwick called the CIC the "Amalgamation Mongrel Association" and said Dorsey's booklet was a false slander on the fair name of Georgia. The Guardians of Liberty organized a mass meeting in Atlanta where one thousand people heard more calls for Dorsey's impeachment and resolved that "Georgia—our mother—is being defiled before the world." Klan national chaplain Caleb Ridley denounced Dorsey, and the Klan organized the Dixie Defense Committee, which issued a countering pamphlet that stated blacks were cannibals when they were brought to the United States. Dorsey did not retreat. He issued a statement in his defense that said:

> Since 1885, mobs in Georgia have shot, hanged, burned, or drowned 415 Negroes, some of them women. Since these figures were compiled, in the last sixty days a mob has taken a helpless old Negro woman from her home and drowned her by night.... (In no case) has a member of the lynching mob been punished in Georgia.

As he stepped down from office, Dorsey pointed out that there were fifty-eight lynchings during his term, reiterated his call for antilynching reforms, and requested legislation empowering the governor to remove derelict sheriffs. "I have concluded that there is little reason to expect county grand juries and local officers to adequately deal with the mob murders of their communities. They are too numerous," Dorsey said in his farewell address to the legislature. None of his proposals were enacted, and Hardwick, the incoming governor, continued to brand Dorsey's charges as "slanderous."

Dorsey helped to create a climate of criticism of lynching, and this contributed to change. In 1922 twenty-two indictments and four convictions for lynchings resulted in one- to four-year sentences on the chain gang. This compared to one indictment but no convictions in connection with Georgia's four hundred-plus lynchings between 1885 and 1921. The CIC took credit for obtaining evidence used in the convictions, though in many cases it probably relayed information obtained from independent black sources.

One noteworthy 1922 case involved Will Jones, who was lynched near Ellaville in February after he shot a white who came into his yard. Three whites who took part in the lynching were convicted and sentenced to the chain gang for one to four years. When they were tried in Americus, the jury recommended they be found guilty of a misdemeanor, but the judge overruled the call for leniency. In summing up the case, a black newspaper editor credited the Dyer Bill: "It has taken the most determined federal action to frighten white Georgians into some semblance of respect for human life that is not white."

In another 1922 case, John Glover was accused of killing a Macon deputy sheriff who walked into a poolroom brawl. Glover fled from a mob for several days and then turned himself in to the police in Bibb County, who turned him over to a mob of two hundred that lynched him in Monroe County following a county-line discussion over where he should be strung up. When Bibb County officials agreed to pay the seventy-seven dollar burial bill, the mob decided to kill Glover in Monroe County, in part because there was less chance of effective investigation there. Glover's body was dumped at the Douglass Theater in Macon. This moved Judge Henry A. Mathews to charge a Bibb County grand jury to "active and everlasting opposition to outrages on the law in all cases of whitecapping and murderous lynching." The jury heeded him and voted to investigate the Glover lynching. Later, it indicted five whites, but they escaped conviction.

In 1922, the Klan renewed its active efforts to intimidate black landowners into selling out cheaply, but the migration-induced loss of black labor prompted some whites to take a more active role against the Klan. Willie Peters and his wife, who was expecting their fifth child, were doing fairly well on their own seventy-five-acre farm in the old Klan stronghold of Oconee County until two whites, Henry Hardy and Frank Rouden, tried to buy their farm in 1922. Because Peters refused to sell, his home was attacked. Two assailants were killed. Peters was wounded but escaped to Atlanta, where he was hospitalized. He was tried for murder, and his wife had to sign the farm over to lawyers to get them to defend her husband. That fall, two hundred black and fifty white farmers of Oconee County met to discuss Klan attempts to scare off blacks with warnings to leave or face lynching. In a case with more positive results, when one prosperous black farmer received threatening letters from the Klan and had his home shot into, he filed a suit for $50,000 in damages and obtained a restraining order from an Atlanta court against "certain white men." This official support was virtually unprecedented.

These limited efforts obviously did not solve a deep-seated problem, but lynchings did decline in 1923 primarily due to the continued threat of the Dyer Bill's passage and the heavy out-migration of blacks, which was encouraged by the Dyer Bill's repeated defeats. The bill hung like a sword of Damocles over the entire South. After its 1922 defeat, it was the first bill introduced in 1923, but this effort was less successful than the previous year's attempt. None of the eight hundred plus anti-lynching bills introduced in the sixty years following the first one in 1901 were passed, though efforts in the 1930s came close to success.

These efforts were not in vain. The publicity they gave to lynching focused public opinion against lynchers and encouraged law officers to stand up to mobs. In Savannah, a mob unsuccessfully tried to storm the jail where a nineteen-year-old black rape suspect was being held on June 20, 1923. Chatham County Sheriff Merritt Dixon was given credit for single-handedly holding off the lynch mob, but the militia was also involved, and Governor Hardwick declared a state of martial law. One white was killed, several were injured, and the police reported that forty-nine whites were arrested as a result of the attempted lynching. The arrests helped to undermine the argument for the Dyer Bill that lynchers went unpunished. This incident confirmed many observers' long-held belief that "the valor of mobs has always been in ratio to the complacency of sheriffs," a point Mark Twain made when he praised the sheriff of Carroll County, Georgia, when he stood off a turn-of-the century mob. (Discouragingly but predictably, the lawman was voted out of office in the next election.)

Public tolerance for mobs seemed to be declining. In July 1924, a jury indicted several members of the mob that shot into the Westmoreland home at Griffin and killed Mrs. Westmoreland and wounded her husband and son. Nine of the sixteen who lynched Dave Walker (a white) at Douglas were indicted in August 1926. The CIC reported a lynching prevented in Columbus that year. This crackdown on open mobs, while not always producing convictions, forced some lynchers to make the absurd claim they killed in self-defense.

Some Georgia newspaper editors contributed to the change, most notably Julian Harris, editor of the *Columbus Enquirer-Sun* and son of folklorist Joel Chandler Harris. He received a Pulitzer Prize in 1925 for exposing the Klan, pointing out mistreatment of blacks, and for opposing a state law that would ban the teaching of evolution. Although the *Macon Telegraph* had previously sanctioned lynching, it editorialized against mob murder after the lynching of the American vice consul at Teheran by a Persian mob in 1924. Other Georgia newspapers continued to condone lynching, and even newspapers that opposed lynching in editorials often promoted it on their front pages with false and sensational stories. As one black writer of the time pointed out, Georgia's white newspapers showed "an unhealthy unity" on many points and continued their support of the caste system even if they opposed the worst forms of oppression.

During the prosperity of 1924–29, the black migration northward decreased, and the "New Negro" was considered less of a threat. Due to these and other factors, lynching continued to decline and the antilynching movement moved into the background on the political stage. In 1930, Will Alexander announced, "Lynching is almost galloping to extinction. Ten years from now we will be wondering how it really happened."

Despite Alexander's optimism, 1930 saw Georgia return to lead the nation in lynching with the deaths of five blacks. In April, Pullman porter J. W. Wilkins was taken from a train and lynched near Locust Grove. In early September, two blacks were suspected of intending to rob a bank in Darien because they were "loitering around" outside it. One suspect, George Grant, later killed a police officer before he was captured by a search party. Grant was shot by a mob at the jail. Before dying, he told police he had been with a man named Bryan at the bank. Vigilantes responded by rounding up several blacks named Bryan, and Willie Bryan was shot twice *in the chest* as he "attempted to flee." Police later announced they were looking for Fred, not Willie, Bryan. A later investigation showed that Grant was lynched because he shot a white for "running with his woman." At about the same time, Atlanta police protected Robert Glaze from a lynch mob while he was being held at Grady Hospital under suspicion of murder. Later in September, prison trusty Willie Kirkland was taken from the sheriff in Thomasville and hanged by a mob of seventy-five who had heard that he had tried to assault a white girl. The warden later said that Kirkland was locked up the day of the alleged assault. The next week, John Will Clark was lynched at Cartersville. A picture of the mob, with its smiling members arranged around the body, was printed in the black press.

Deteriorating economic conditions brought more cause for alarm. As the Great Depression settled in on the nation and the number of unemployed whites grew in the cities, organizations developed that were dedicated to the proposition that no black should have a job as long as any whites were unemployed. The most serious manifestation of this in Georgia was the organization, by active Klansmen, of the American Facisti, Order of the Black Shirts. Their leaders promised jobs, much as Hitler was promising jobs to the various "shirt" organizations in Germany. Like Klan leaders, organizers profited from the sale of regalia. A member could buy a black shirt for $1.10 that cost the organization forty-eight cents. By the summer of 1930, the secret organization claimed a wildly inflated membership of forty thousand in Atlanta, and the police and mayor, Isaac N. Ragsdale, a prosperous merchant, helped them hold their parades on Peachtree Street where they carried signs reading: "Niggers, Back to the Cotton Fields—City Jobs are for White Folks." One of the few Black Shirt victories came when women, planted in hotels by police, made false rape and alcohol-sale charges against black bellhops. When the blacks were replaced by whites, charges against them were dropped.

The Black Shirts held their first mass rally on July 10, 1930, and five days later lynched John Hope's driver, Morehouse sophomore Dennis Hubert, son of the respected minister G. J. Hubert. The young Hubert was falsely accused of raping a white girl. When blacks organized a protest to the murder, the Reverend Hubert's home was burned to the ground, and two whites tried to invade the home of the lynching victim's uncle, where they were held at bay until neighbors arrived to help. Hope despairingly asked, "Must Morehouse students, must all the colored youth of Atlanta, of Georgia, forever go about in terror of their lives?" Churches collecting funds for the prosecution of the lynchers were teargassed.

A grand jury investigated the Black Shirts, and Austin T. Walden, pioneer activist black attorney, helped convict the men who killed Dennis Hubert. This was probably the first time a black attorney helped prosecute white men in Georgia. The conviction led Will Alexander to say, "So far as I can see, the Black Shirts and Colonel (William J.) Simmons need not give us any more concern," but blacks thought otherwise. NAACP official William Pickens wrote Walter White, "Will Alexander is entirely too optimistic and cocksure about the influence of the 'good' South."

Indeed, racist groups continued to spring up. The Secret Six, a white supremacist fraternal organization also patterned after the Klan, called for the displacement of all black workers with whites. Men of Justice, a sort of elite group of Black Shirts, lobbied *against* Atlanta University and jobs for blacks and *for* sending blacks back to Africa. These groups were small and soon forgotten. Other militant white supremacist organizations, such as the Silver Shirts of William Dudley Pelley, the Caucasian Crusaders, and the White Band proliferated and made blacks scapegoats for the poor economy.

The 1930 increase in lynching motivated the CIC to form the Southern Commission for the Study of Lynching, chaired by *Chattanooga News* editor George Fort Milton. It included John Hope, Savannah educator Benjamin F. Hubert, and Julian Harris, then news editor of the *Atlanta Constitution*. The commission hired two sociologists to head the investigative work: Walter Chivers of Morehouse and Arthur Raper, a white CIC researcher. In 1931, the commission published *Lynchings and What*

They Mean and distributed thousands of copies to officials, editors, and other interested parties. It also prepared a manual for investigating lynchings. Subsequent investigations of lynching based on this manual indicated that younger blacks tended to leave communities where lynchings occurred and the older ones became "stubborn." When bodies of mob victims were left hanging, only whites came to view them. With lynchings, contempt for the law increased, and whites feared black retaliation. Some black landowners sold their land and dropped down to tenant status because they knew this would decrease their chance of becoming a mob target. In 1933 the commission published *The Tragedy of Lynching.*

The CIC was still far from developing a white consensus opposing lynching. Although lynching was on the decline, Milton believed that opposing lynching meant "few sales if a merchant, fewer patients if a doctor, and fewer worshippers if a preacher." The local press might protest the lynching at first, but if outsiders joined the protest, it would close ranks with the mob leaders and join in the defense of the "Southern way of life," he concluded. He believed the community then would turn on lynching opponents, especially if they were black, and attempt to bring about their ruin. Because of this, some blacks would tell whites what they wanted to hear, namely, that a specific lynching was necessary and justified.

Another response to the 1930 increase in lynching was the formation of the white Association of Southern Women for the Prevention of Lynching (ASWPL) in 1930. It absorbed and expanded the Women's Work Department of the CIC. Under its executive director, Jessie Daniel Ames of Atlanta, the ASWPL grew rapidly. Two years after its founding, it had seven thousand members. By 1935, it had thirty-five thousand members and continued to add a thousand members a year for the next seven years; in addition, hundreds of peace officers signed up to support its work. The ASWPL lobbied state capitals, its members visited and wrote sheriffs, and it conducted an active "Letters to the Editor" campaign. It set up a card file of every white woman in every county who could be depended on to go out and confront mobs, along with a telephone-calling system to alert volunteers to emergencies. Benjamin Mays believed the ASWPL, not the churches, provided the main Southern white voice against lynching. As an example of its work, in 1934 Ames called a local supporter in Schley County when she learned of an impending lynching there. The supporter called the sheriff and others, who, thus bolstered, prevented the lynching.

The ASWPL, like the CIC, was progressive when originally formed. However, neither changed with time, and consequently both grew relatively more conservative. They helped organize limited concessions to stem migration and relieve the South of the unfavorable publicity that lynching brought, but they did not believe in racial equality. Neither Jessie Ames and the ASWPL nor Will Alexander and the CIC would advocate enforcement of the Constitution for blacks, and Southern white women were not able to view their black sisters as equals. One black CIC spokeswoman was asked to speak to a white Baptist women's group "about the work of the niggers" and to come in by the back door. Both groups viewed the NAACP as too radical—an organization that demanded the impossible. In 1935, the NAACP pled with the ASWPL to support the current federal antilynching bill. It refused, to the great disappointment of Lugenia Hope.

Jessie Daniel Ames developed a peculiar idea called the "one-step, two-step" plan that held that funds for education should continue to be unequally divided because blacks would profit in the long run if white children advanced two steps for every one black children were allowed to advance. This was an educational "trickle down" theory that, like other "trickle down" plans, contained the flaw that the "trickle" seldom got "down."

Others thought the ASWPL went too far. The Women's National Association for the Preservation of the White Race was formed in Atlanta in 1931, with Mrs. J. E. Andrews as national president. Although it quickly passed from the scene, it showed the South's ability to set up organizations that mirrored Klan attitudes. This organization attacked the Southern Commission for the Study of Lynching for questioning the guilt of mob victims and, in what must have brought a smile to the poor and puritan NAACP leaders, linked the "incredibly wealthy" NAACP with Tammany liquor interests. Andrews's organization said the NAACP was dedicated to promoting the ruin of the "pure white race." Andrews, acting as though she had never heard of the Klan, wrote a pamphlet in which she expressed regret that there was no militant organization to protect whites. She concluded, "All we need to do is to insist that the Negro get back in line." Her organization was mainly limited to printing propaganda through its periodical, *Georgia Women's World*, which described CIC members as "Communist vultures."

Georgia officials tended to regard antilynching activity as subversive and arrested four people at an antilynching meeting in Atlanta in May 1930 on the grounds that they were "inciting insurrection" under an old slave law. The main evidence that the labor organizers and Negro rights workers were subversive was a leaflet illustrated by a drawing showing a black and white worker shaking hands. Such repression did not stop the reform movement, however. In 1933 the Writers' League Against Lynching was formed and included over a hundred well-known writers, including Georgians Joseph H. Jenkins, Jr., of Atlanta University, Julian Harris, Walter White, Du Bois, Georgia Douglas Johnson, and Jean Toomer.

Increasingly, lynchings were prevented. Jessie Daniel Ames reported that there were no lynchings in Georgia in 1931 and 1932. In 1931, National Guard Major Elbert P. Tuttle dressed John Downer, the target of a fifteen-hundred-person mob, in a Guard uniform and marched him to safety in a company of infantrymen one midnight. The Guard had a chance to intervene because Baptist minister Henry Brookshire held off the mob with passionate eloquence long enough to give the Guard time to arrive. Downer was later tried and executed. Austin T. Walden appealed Downer's conviction on the basis of a Supreme Court dissent in the Leo Frank case, maintaining that a mob-dominated trial was not "due process of law." Downer, though most likely innocent, was again convicted in his second trial. He was executed to "explain" the loss of a white girl's virginity to her boyfriend. Later, as judge on the U. S. Fifth Circuit Court, Tuttle would hand down key decisions supporting the civil rights movement of the 1960s.

In 1933, Georgia had four lynchings of blacks: Will Kinsey, a tenant farmer near Warrenton; T. J. Thomas, of Newton, later proved innocent of any charge; Richard Marshall, also of Newton, lynched as "an example"; and Cephus Davis, of Lumpkin, beaten to death for resisting arrest while drunk. Congressional testimony noted that since the passage of Georgia's 1893 antilynching law, there had been over four hundred lynchings by mobs totaling thousands of people but only five convictions and none since 1922. In Georgia, the governor's hands were tied because the state could not wrest prosecution of mob members from local governments. Clearly, federal action was necessary. Walter White wanted to start the campaign for federal antilynching legislation with a statement from President Franklin D. Roosevelt, then at the little White House in Warm Springs, Georgia. However, Roosevelt could not go out of his way to antagonize Southern supporters, so White would wait until Roosevelt returned to Washington. The president did speak out against lynching in one of his "fireside chats" after California's governor publicly defended the 1933 lynching of two whites in San Jose. This official approval of the mob upset so many people that Roosevelt knew he could issue a statement without weakening his political power.

In 1934, the Costigan-Wagner Bill replaced the Dyer Bill as the main NAACP antilynching effort. To support the new bill, the NAACP made a thorough study of all state legislation. In Atlanta its contacts were Austin T. Walden and A. W. Ricks. In an advance from the 1920s position of the Southern Methodist General Conference, which refused to pass Will Alexander's resolution against the Klan, the women of the Methodist Episcopal church-South supported this bill. Neither the CIC nor the ASWPL supported it directly, although the ASWPL did undercut opposition to the bill by warning that Southern white women would repudiate any argument that lynching was to protect them. Lynching could no longer be defended as chivalry, the ladies said. The Costigan-Wagner Bill failed due to a Southern filibuster in which Georgia's U. S. senators Richard Russell and Walter George played key roles. (George started his senatorial career blasting the Dyer Bill in the 1920s.)

The struggle over the Costigan-Wagner Bill in 1934 produced the same results as the one for the earlier Dyer Bill. Lynchings declined as public discussion of the issue rose. When it became apparent that Congress was not going to act that year, lynchings resumed, with twelve occurring before the end of December. The NAACP and the National Urban League pointed to recent lynchings in Georgia to suggest that more militant self-defense by blacks might be necessary.

Hearings were held on the Costigan-Wagner Bill again in 1935. Charles Houston, dean of Howard University Law School, used the lynching of James Curtis at Darien on October 4, 1934, as an example of what the bill would prevent. One petition in its support had the signatures of eight hundred black Georgians. The highly publicized torture-lynching of Claude Neal in Florida three weeks later did much to increase the nation's growing revulsion from lynching. Neal was forced to eat his own genitals, and the press was given eighteen hours' advance notice of the event. In 1935, Lewis Harris was lynched near Vienna for resisting arrest, and "Bo" Bronson was killed by a mob near Moultrie that was hunting for another man but apparently did not want to go home empty-handed.

The inevitable Southern filibuster against the Costigan-Wagner Bill was led by Russell and George. Strains over the 1935 debate began the breakup of the New Deal coalition, even though many historians have blamed the later court-packing plan as the culprit. While Southerners in Congress could not attack the popular New Deal measures they privately despised, the antilynching bill gave them an opportunity to wail away at Roosevelt.

Though the bill failed to pass in 1935, it was a big public issue. A Gallup Poll in 1936 indicated that 72 percent of the nation and even 63 percent of Southerners favored federal legislation. That year, six of the eight U. S. lynchings of blacks were in Georgia. Lint Shaw was lynched near Colbert on April 28. When he was first arrested, a mob tried to break into the Danielsville jail, but they had been dissuaded by seventy-four-year-old judge Berry T. Moseley, who left his sickbed to delay the mob until the National Guard, then on emergency tornado duty at Gainesville, Florida, could arrive. The sheriff then took Shaw to Atlanta, but when he was returned to Danielsville, the mob was still threatening, so he was moved to the Royston jail. The mob followed and completed its work. Other blacks lynched in Georgia that year include Philip Baker, John Rushin, Tom Finch, Mack Henry Brown and A. L. McCamey.

Brutal lynchings kept the flames of reform hot through 1937. Gallup

Polls taken in January and November showed that Northern support for federal antilynching legislation increased but Southern support declined from 65 percent to 57 percent during the year. The Gallup Poll also reflected a growing belief that lynchings reduced the region's appeal to industry. In one incident, Willie Reid, accused of rape and murder at Bainbridge, was shot by police "while trying to escape" after he was in custody. The disappointed mob broke into the funeral home, carried the body to the ballpark, and burned it on a pyre built from the park fence. Photographers were invited, and many young women were in the pictures of the mob.

The antilynching effort in 1937 and 1938 centered around the NAACP-backed Gavagan Bill. It passed the House of Representatives, although every Georgian (and all Southerners save one) voted against it and the ASWPL lobbied against it by promoting a far weaker bill as an alternative. Despite the poll showing most Southerners favored federal antilynching legislation, Southern leaders continued to claim that state laws were adequate—a disingenuous claim, since no lynchers were punished. The Senate postponed consideration of the bill until the next session.

Antilynching legislation became an even greater issue in 1938. Walter White was on the cover of *Time* on January 24, and in February he tried to get President Roosevelt to speak out in favor of the Gavagan bill. Roosevelt believed he needed Southern support for other legislation too much to alienate Southern congressmen and remained publicly silent on the issue during debate. The filibuster lasted for six weeks, and Southerners expressed more Negrophobia than in 1935. Senator Russell claimed that the legislation was Communist inspired and marked the first step toward federal interference in segregated schools, public transportation, and even state antimiscegenation laws. (As a matter of political principle, Communists supported all antilynching bills; however, it was lynching, not Bolshevism, that inspired the measures.) Once again, the bill was defeated by a filibuster. In March, the president issued a general statement deploring lynching as he left for Warm Springs—after the bill was dead. Still, these battles brought national publicity to the civil rights cause and taught the intricacies of modern public relations, fund-raising, and lobbying to civil rights organizations. They also brought in more allies who stayed to help in future voting and desegregation movements.

In the small town of Arabi in South Central Georgia in July 1938, the sheriff had done nothing to stop a mob that was preparing to burn John Dukes, a turpentine worker, to death because the lynchers voted but blacks did not. The sheriff

walked off and left the Negro to be burned (because) he looked the mob over and saw back of them voters, and he saw back of that dying Negro nothing. . . . Back of that mob was his bread and his butter and the shoes and clothes and schooling for his children, and back of that Negro nothing.

When Sen. Robert Wagner asked the attorney general, Homer Cummings, to investigate this lynching, he refused.

Threats of federal intervention helped to reduce lynching from a depression high of twenty-eight in 1933 to less than ten a year in the late 1930s. In Georgia, 1939 came and went without a lynching, in part because potential mob members believed that such action would increase the chances of federal legislation. In 1939, newly appointed Attorney General Frank Murphy established a Civil Rights Division in the Department of Justice so that lynching and other violations of civil liberties might receive more attention. The new division received eight thousand to fourteen thousand complaints a year and took little action at first, but its presence was a deterrent. Meanwhile, in Congress, the La Follette Civil Liberties Committee began its own investigation of lynching. In the 1940 hearings on proposed federal legislation, Walter White said that the number of lynchings varied inversely with the intensity of the campaign for federal legislation. The NAACP was also campaigning against voting restrictions on blacks, and White tied the two together: "If the Negro can't vote, the sheriff won't protect him."

Although Congress never passed antilynching legislation, as a consensus developed against lynching and lynchers, the practice was driven underground. Lynchings were fewer and increasingly carried out by small bands in secluded places, such as the back rooms of police stations, rather than publicly in the town square. In 1940, Georgia had two lynchings: Ike Gaston, a white, was flogged to death by masked men on March 7, and Austin Callaway, a black, was lynched in LaGrange on September 8. One black, Robert Sapp, was lynched in 1941. The outbreak of World War II and the entry of the United States into it created a need for national unity that lynchings could only disrupt. Lynchings did not end then, but the public mob and advance notice to newspapers to guarantee a big crowd at the "festivities" disappeared.

Politics: Turning Lincoln's Picture to the Wall

Georgia blacks continued the often-disheartening struggle on the political front after World War I. When Martin Luther King, Sr., turned twenty-one in 1920, he tried to register to vote. This required going to the second floor of the courthouse, but the "colored" freight elevator was not working, and the stairs and front elevator were for whites only. He had to try repeatedly over a period of days before he was permitted to go upstairs.

Although the disfranchisement of blacks in Georgia was 90 percent effective, some blacks did vote and directly affected elections, especially in the cities. Atlanta's 1919 municipal-bond referendum is one example. In 1923, independent reform judge Paul E. Seabrook ran for mayor of Savannah and helped hundreds of blacks register. Thanks to black support, he won despite charges that he was endangering white supremacy. In 1929, Savannah's blacks again voted heavily against regular Democrats. However, most white opinion had not changed since 1915, when the *Augusta Chronicle* proclaimed, "Politics is the greatest danger to the Negro."

Many Georgia whites believed that blacks simply didn't want to vote. Feeding the alleged lack of desire were terror and intimidation, the county unit system, the poll tax, the white primary, and literacy and residence requirements. In a move that further disfranchised blacks, Georgia passed the Neill Primary Act of 1917, which gave the entire county unit vote to the candidate with the most votes. This ensured rural dominance and helped further disfranchise urban minorities especially.

Because the main goal of Georgia's rulers was to keep the status quo in race relations, the continuance of white supremacy meant that dissent, new ideas, and progress had to be rejected if blacks might also benefit. Georgia's disfranchised blacks determined the state's position on the Nineteenth Amendment, which granted women the right to vote. During debate over this issue, support for any extension of voting rights was considered an attack on black disfranchisement. The first nine states to consider the Susan B. Anthony amendment ratified it. Georgia, the tenth, took pride in being the first state to reject it. Georgia did not allow women to vote in the 1920 presidential election although enough states had ratified the amendment so that it was adopted on August 26, 1920, in sufficient time to let Republican women elsewhere vote for the handsome Warren G. Harding.

Although the effort turned out to be fruitless, black clubwomen all over the state had worked to register women to vote in the 1920 presidential election. Antilynching leader Mrs. George S. Williams of Savannah said black women "should storm the polls on election day." In Atlanta, four black women registered for every white woman. The legislature did not agree to allow women to vote until 1921, though some cities in Georgia already permitted women to vote on local issues earlier: Waycross in 1917, Atlanta in 1919.

The adoption of the Susan B. Anthony amendment did not change the political standing of Georgia's blacks. The oligarchy's fear of publicly discussing issues and having controversies decided at the polls continued, as did apprehensions that whites might divide on an issue with different factions appealing to blacks for support. Blacks could not be sealed off from the future or separated from the rest of the world, however, and certain advances were inevitable.

* * *

In addition to enforcing the South's exclusionary politics, Democrats on the national level were associated with the extension of Jim Crow and federal apathy toward all black problems. Therefore, the 1920 election to replace the retiring Woodrow Wilson held more than usual interest to blacks. Georgia's black Republicans tried to influence the Republican party to consider the needs of blacks, but Republican presidents during the 1920s would give African-Americans little to cheer.

There were many black Republican political bosses in the South between 1901 and 1935, men who held considerable power over patronage appointments. Henry Lincoln Johnson, known as "Linc," was the era's main black Republican patronage dispenser in Georgia and the only black Georgia Republican on the Republican National Committee in 1920. He was born in Augusta in 1865, graduated from Atlanta University in 1888, and obtained a law degree from the University of Michigan in 1892. As an Atlanta attorney he became active in Republican politics and was a delegate to every national convention from 1896 through 1924.

A major dispute in Georgia's Republican party erupted in 1904 between the old-line powerful faction that included John Deveaux, Henry Rucker, and Judson Lyons and the rival group headed by Linc Johnson and *Atlanta Independent* editor Benjamin Davis. In 1908, Johnson engineered Lyons's defeat as a Republican national committeeman and was rewarded with the Washington, D.C., position as recorder of deeds by President Taft. Johnson campaigned for the Democrats and continued in his position under Wilson until he fell victim to the administration's purge of black officials. Johnson's and Davis's politics, described as "unscrupulous" by historian John Dittmer, would keep them on top of the Republican heap for many years. Booker T. Washington once feared Johnson would replace him as the nation's primary black power broker. The black socialist *Messenger*, known for its vitriol, characterized Johnson as a hog at the trough, one of the "sleek, fat, potbellied Negro politicians who have been trafficking for half a century in the sweat and blood and tears of toiling Negro washerwomen, cotton pickers, miners, and factory hands."

The infighting continued. At the Republican National Conventions in 1916 and 1920, Georgia Republicans split into the two factions, and Johnson won control of the delegates' seats both times. In 1920, top black Republicans met in Chicago to organize the Lincoln League to get out the vote and pressure the Republican party toward greater opposition to lynching, Jim Crow, disfranchisement, and other racial handicaps. Johnson and R. R. Wright, Sr., of Savannah were active in this effort. National Republicans, concerned that black voters would think the party was not sufficiently committed to antilynching legislation, gave Johnson assurances from Harding of improvements if Harding won. Johnson said a Republican victory meant "death to mob law and disfranchisement" because he had Harding's promise that a federal antilynching law would be enacted. Another reason black hopes rose with Harding's election was "the secret of Blooming Grove," the report (put out by an ardent Democrat) that Harding was part black.

Harding turned out to be a disappointment to blacks and just about everyone else. His administration—duly noted in history books as among the most corrupt—continued Jim Crow in federal offices, and Johnson's hopeful proclamation on lynching turned out to be wrong. Harding knew virtually nothing about racial problems. He never spoke out against lynching, disfranchisement, or segregation before the 1920 campaign. Afterward, he spoke out occasionally against lynching and promised to sign the Dyer Bill, but he never attempted to help its passage.

Benjamin Davis editorialized that Harding should appoint more blacks and prosecute the lynchers if a mob killed any of his appointees, but Harding had quite different ideas. Encouraged by Republican gains in the border states, Harding wanted to make the GOP the South's majority party and did little to antagonize white supremacists. "I am not going to appoint any colored men to public office in the South," he proclaimed. "This thing called race prejudice you can not down by battling it. . . . The colored man . . . can, acting through Southern legislators, work out his destiny." This was small comfort to blacks, who knew only too well what "destiny" Southern legislators had in mind. Despite Linc Johnson's advice to the contrary, at Birmingham, on October 26, 1921, Harding said that the black's role was to perform manual labor; blacks would vote when they were fit to do so; and that neither whites nor blacks desired "social equality"—all statements that condoned the Southern caste system.

Harding died of illness in 1923 and was replaced by the taciturn, acerbic Calvin Coolidge just as the Harding administration's scandals were surfacing. Coolidge was even more unfeeling toward the problems of blacks than his predecessor, although he did tell Congress in December 1923 that it should act on lynching, and the 1924 Republican platform supported federal antilynching legislation. Democrats' failure to denounce the Klan during the height of its influence kept most blacks in the Republican fold, even though Coolidge also remained silent on the Klan.

The Georgia lynching record was used in the 1924 election by the black women's clubs, which distributed a map prepared by the NAACP that showed the number of lynchings in each state. Georgia led the way with 429, twenty-four ahead of second-place Mississippi. Leonidas Dyer told blacks that failing to vote for Coolidge would amount to voting for lynching, peonage, the chain gang, Jim Crow, and disfranchisement. The deeply divided Democrats were no match for unified Republicans. After Coolidge's victory, Republicans quickly forgot their campaign rhetoric, for they still hoped to gain more Southern white support. Concerned

Democrats would soon foresee a split of the white vote, and that threatened to open up opportunities for blacks. Georgia congressman Charles R. Crisp said in 1928 that if whites were divided, "our social and political civilization is in danger." Crisp worried needlessly, because the standard disfranchisement practices would continue to prevent any change for decades to come.

Dissatisfaction with the Republican party grew among blacks during the 1920s, although Republicans continued to pay lip service to black hopes for several reasons. Black migrant voters were increasingly tilting the balance of power in several Northern urban political machines. Moreover, some Southern blacks continued to vote despite all the proscriptions they faced. The National Republican party had to have at least a skeleton organization in the South, if only to select delegates for the national conventions. The Republican party in Georgia shrank to a small nucleus of federal appointees and their supporters. Their power lay in their authority to reward the faithful with jobs, and politicians competed among themselves for the spoils. Many of them, both black and white, were political hacks in the mold of Linc Johnson, content with their sinecures and apprehensive of change.

Benjamin J. Davis, Sr., became the party's patronage boss for Georgia upon Johnson's death in 1925. His son said later, "I used to view with sardonic pleasure the small-time postmasters beating a path to my father's door—perhaps a Southern Klan-minded white seeking favors of a Negro political boss." Davis was accused of selling jobs in 1924 and 1928 by Northern white Republican leaders whose primary motive was not reform but a desire to drive blacks from leadership positions in the party because they could not "get out the vote," even though Davis had worked hard organizing the Georgia Suffrage League. Davis was challenged for his seat on the National Republican Committee at the 1928 Republican Convention in Kansas City by Joseph Watson, an Albany black. Blacks dominated the Republican party organization in Georgia then with twelve of the state's sixteen seats on the national committee in 1924 and 1928.

Herbert Hoover was the last Republican president to receive a majority of the black vote, and he did little or nothing to earn it. As secretary of commerce, Hoover had advocated policies which contributed to black alienation. In 1927 there was a major flood in the Mississippi Valley and Hoover was placed in charge of relief work. Blacks were impressed into levee work, herded into concentration camps, and reduced to peonage by the government's policies. Republicans made inroads into the solid Democratic ranks of white Georgians in 1928. The Democratic presidential candidate, Roman Catholic Alfred E. Smith, was depicted as a Northern "city slicker" who opposed prohibition. The victorious Hoover did not carry Georgia, but enough whites joined blacks in supporting him that he received 44 percent of the state's popular vote.

Hoover did not like being associated in the public mind with blacks. His continued support of white Georgians who wanted to seize control of the state Republican party helped precipitate a lynching. S. S. Mincey, the seventy-year-old black leader of Montgomery County, had long been active in politics; he had been a delegate to the Republican National Convention four times and had recently been reelected over white opposition to the post of county chairman, which carried control of some patronage. Mincey was taken from his home late in the night of July 29, 1930, by a hooded mob that beat him senseless and left him with mortal wounds. Although the grand jury investigating this lynching failed to return any indictments, the investigative report by the Commission of Interracial Cooperation, the white Democratic press, and Georgia blacks confirmed Mincey's dying statement: The mob told him to resign as chairman of the county Republican Committee so that a white could have the job. This lynching aroused more indignation than usual among white Democrats because they feared a white Republican party might become a real threat to the entrenched Democratic courthouse rings. Benjamin Davis declared that the lynching was a direct result of the demand from Washington for a completely white Republican organization in Georgia.

Meanwhile, the worst economic collapse in U.S. history was taking place. The Great Depression began in 1929, shortly after Hoover took office. He was unwilling and unable to provide effective leadership, and a dense pall of misery descended over the land. Hoover was a staunch advocate of the "trickle down" theory, which held that if the rich continued to prosper, they would keep the economy sound and the benefits would trickle down to the middle class and the poor. The theory did not work. Hoover was also criticized for job discrimination on the public works programs he advocated. The largest of these was Boulder Dam (now Hoover Dam), on the Colorado River.

As the 1932 elections approached, Hoover realized he was in big trouble, mainly because the economy was in such a mess. His advisers realized better than he did that the black vote could make or break him, and the White House was barraged with suggestions on how black support could be solidified. Hoover had built an abysmal record, however. With such a man at the head of the ticket, black Republican politicians grew desperate as the 1932 election approached. If the Republicans lost, many of them would lose their jobs—not a pleasant prospect as the Great Depression gripped the land. That year, *Pittsburgh Courier* editor Robert Vann voiced his disgust for the Republican party when he said: "It's time to turn Lincoln's picture to the wall." Although

Hoover got the majority of blacks' votes in 1932, 23 percent of blacks nationally voted for the winner, Franklin Delano Roosevelt—the highest percentage for a Democratic presidential candidate up to that time.

Meanwhile, the national Democratic party was changing; it was no longer so dominated by the Southern cabal. The party of Lincoln had lost much of its appeal to blacks, and in Georgia whites moved to solidify their hold on the state GOP, although Benjamin Davis remained prominent in the party until his death in 1945. In the North, the Democratic party was growing, and it needed black support. This change, due in part to the migrants from the South, blew back winds of change toward Georgia. Black hopes were fulfilled by the new administration more than past experience had led them to expect. Blacks everywhere deserted the Republicans en masse in subsequent elections. Young blacks today are surprised to learn that in the past, failure by their forebears to vote Republican was considered a sin.

9

The Depression, New Deal, and World War II

The Great Depression and the New Deal

The Great Depression was hard on all Georgians, but blacks, traditionally "last hired and first fired," were devastated. Domestic servants were especially hard-hit. In May 1934, 62 percent of Atlanta's 16,541 adult blacks on relief were in domestic services. By 1935, 66 percent of employable persons on relief in Atlanta were black, double their percentage of the city's population. This number included scores of college graduates—mostly teachers but also physicians and dentists who were working on relief projects. Half of all black retail merchants failed in the 1930s.

The dismal situation weakened caste lines, and the pinch of hunger overcame prejudice. Whites took "Negro" jobs, such as collecting garbage, even in black neighborhoods. Some Georgia churches replaced black janitors with jobless white parishioners. White storekeepers in need of business began saying, "Mister," and "Yes, sir," to black customers.

The problems of the depression were so great that some blacks and many whites, dissatisfied with the pace of reform, sought radical solutions. The Communist party competed with the NAACP for black support. Although relatively few blacks actually became party members (nationwide, black membership rose from about two hundred in the 1920s to more than two thousand in the 1930s), American Communists waged militant attacks on both the country's capitalist system and the racial caste system. The two organizations had different philosophies concerning lynching. The Communists attacked the NAACP for considering lynching "an isolated phenomenon, the terrible sport of lawless uneducated whites." Communists called lynching "one of the weapons with which the white ruling class enforces its national oppression of the Negro people and tries to maintain division between white workers and Negro toilers." Ironically, "a consuming fear of Communism" was cited as a reason behind some lynchings, and lynchers in turn blamed the party for causing blacks to get out of line. Meanwhile, Communists opposed the 1934 congressional antilynching bill because it did not go far enough and impose the death penalty on mob leaders.

Communists mounted a more radical attack on the Southern criminal justice system's racism than did the NAACP. The 1931 Scottsboro (Alabama) case was the most widely publicized civil rights case of its time. Nine black youths ranging in age from thirteen to seventeen were pulled off a freight train by police after fighting with some hoboing white youths. Two white girls, who were riding in a different car from either group, were found on the train and claimed the blacks had raped them. The "Scottsboro Boys" were given a quick trial and sentenced to death. The case was marked by disputes between the NAACP and the Communist party's legal arm, the International Labor Defense (ILD). The NAACP and other groups joined in the defense, but the Communist party gave the case worldwide publicity. The ILD appealed the verdict all the way to the Supreme Court, prevented the executions, and made the Scottsboro case an international cause célèbre.

Five of the nine Scottsboro boys were from Georgia: Charley Weems, Ozzie Powell, Clarence Norris, Olen Montgomery, and Haywood Patterson. Montgomery was one of four who were released from prison in 1937. He was nearly blind, could barely read, had no skills, was often fired from jobs, and was in need of help. Once, while in Atlanta in the 1940s, a policeman recognized him and said that he might yet be lynched. Walter White's brother-in-law, Eugene Martin, got Montgomery out of town quickly. Montgomery finally returned to his home in Monroe, Georgia. In 1950, the last Scottsboro "boy" was freed, shortly after Patterson escaped from the Alabama prison and went to Michigan, where officials refused to extradite him. He wrote his story, *Scottsboro Boy*, which told of the South's horrible prison conditions.

In another cause célèbre, Angelo Herndon was sentenced to twenty years on a Georgia chain gang in 1932. Herndon was a nineteen-year-old black Communist who came to Atlanta to organize the unemployed. His organization, the Unemployment Council, had a simple goal: relief for the hungry. It used the hunger march as a tactic. After twenty-three thousand families were dropped from Atlanta's relief rolls, an integrated crowd of a thousand, led by Herndon, marched on city hall; it was purportedly "the biggest biracial demonstration in the South in several decades." It was effective. The next day, officials approved $6,000 for additional emergency relief.

The size of the demonstration and its interracial composition frightened local officials, who were determined to destroy the radical movement. When the police searched Herndon and his living quarters, they found several pamphlets. One, *Self-Determination in the Black Belt*, called for confiscation of white-owned land tilled by blacks and the formation of a new "49th state" that would include two-thirds of Georgia and other parts of the South where blacks were in the majority. A Georgia law originally passed in 1833—in response to the slave-insurrection scare brought on by *David Walker's Appeal* and Nat Turner's revolt—was still on the books. Herndon was charged under the anachronistic law, which carried the death penalty for anyone possessing written material calculated to incite rebellion.

Herndon's attorney was Benjamin J. Davis, Jr., a Harvard Law School graduate who had once been suspended from Morehouse for leading a student strike. Davis, son and namesake of the Republican stalwart and *Independent* editor, was appointed by the ILD to defend Herndon in the Fulton County court, where the prosecutor referred to him as "Nigger" and "darky lawyer" in open court with no protest from the judge. Elbert Tuttle was also on the Herndon defense team. Davis appealed the sentence to the Supreme Court and obtained a reversal and an invalidation of the state law under which Herndon was convicted.

By this time, Georgia's prison system had become a national issue. As part of the publicity campaign mounted to defend Herndon, a reproduction of a Georgia chain gang went on tour, and 2 million signatures were obtained in a petition drive sponsored by hundreds of organizations, from the Communist party to the YWCA. Herndon got an unwitting assist in shaping public opinion against chain gangs with the 1932 publication of the story of a white victim of Georgia justice, entitled, appropriately enough, *I Am a Fugitive from a Georgia Chain Gang!* That same year, the book was made into a movie starring Paul Muni and George Raft. Jesse Crawford was a black fugitive who also brought more disrepute to Georgia's chain gangs by telling his story to anyone who would listen. Crawford was sentenced to a chain gang in Atlanta for theft in 1931 and had to eat rotten food, march three miles to work in leg-cutting iron shackles, and break rocks for twelve or more hours a day. After two months, he escaped to Detroit, where officials refused to extradite him back to Georgia.

Herndon's case continued to twist through the courts. In 1935, the

U. S. Supreme Court voted 6–3 against a review of the case, but shortly after Roosevelt announced his court-packing plan, the court ruled 5–4 to overturn Herndon's conviction in 1937, and Herndon was freed after five years as a prisoner. Herndon then coedited the short-lived *Negro Quarterly* with Ralph Ellison and published an autobiography, *Let Me Live*. Like most Communist party members who joined during the radical 1930s, he later left the party. He moved to the Midwest, where he lived quietly as an insurance salesman. Davis later moved to New York City and was elected to the city council as a Communist in 1943 and 1945. He was sentenced to five years in prison under the Smith Act, which made membership in the Communist party a crime, until the Supreme Court ruled the law unconstitutional. Davis spent the rest of his life as a party functionary and died in 1962.

The depressed economy that encouraged the growth of both Klanlike organizations and the Communist party also brought a new political order, Franklin Delano Roosevelt's New Deal. When Roosevelt took office in March 1933, the economy was prostrate and the country's mood was desperate because the outgoing Hoover administration was doing nothing. Humorist Will Rogers said if Roosevelt had burned down the White House, people would have applauded because something was happening.

Roosevelt had a special tie with Georgia that began when he first came to Warm Springs in 1921 for polio treatments. He observed the state's poverty and backwardness and reflected on the narrow bigotry of its leaders. He knew that the success of his national and international programs depended on keeping the support of the white supremacists who made up the Democratic party's backbone in the South. Therefore, he did not attack the caste system head-on. However, he wanted to build a base of support in the South that would be independent of racist demagogues, amd many of the policies he advocated did much to help blacks.

Roosevelt encouraged an open climate in Washington that led to promotion of unorthodox ideas and innovations in government programs. Harold Ickes, secretary of the interior, had been president of the Chicago branch of the NAACP before going to Washington. In 1933, he selected white Atlantan Clark Foreman, who had worked with the Commission for Interracial Cooperation, as a special assistant on the economic status of blacks. The black press howled at the appointment, and Ickes compromised by pairing Foreman with Robert C. Weaver, who later became the first black presidential cabinet member as secretary of housing and urban development under Lyndon Johnson. Top-flight black leaders went to Washington to serve in important administrative posts. This group came to be known as the "black cabinet," and by 1936, 243 additional blacks worked under Ickes. Frank S. Horne, who worked with Henry A. Hunt at

Fort Valley in the 1920s, later became an assistant to Mary McLeod Bethune in the National Youth Administration (NYA), which was a part of the Works Progress Administration (WPA). Hunt became an adviser in the Department of Agriculture. The black cabinet raised the consciousness of Washington officials concerning race relations.

Stagnation during the Hoover years made the country willing to try many new things—direct federal relief, for example. Inadequate private, municipal, and state relief programs quickly exhausted their resources after the depression hit. Some religious and charitable organizations, North and South, excluded blacks from their soup kitchens. Roosevelt's New Deal was fairer to blacks than preceding administrations, but it also was biased. When federal relief began in May 1933, whites received more relief money, and they received it with less opposition; some whites resented *any* relief for blacks. One study of rural areas showed that only 18 percent of black families (compared to 35 percent of white families) received the more desirable work relief. This paid an average of thirteen dollars a month to whites and seven dollars to black families. In Georgia, the discrepancy was wider, with a "wage" of nine cents an hour for whites and four cents for blacks.

The inequities continued as the depression wore on. In 1940, 38 percent of Georgia's children were black; only 12 percent of those receiving welfare were black between 1937 and 1940. One Georgia study of Federal Emergency Relief Act (FERA) aid indicated that the average black families' income without the federal aid was only 34-50 percent of the average white family income, yet a greater percentage of whites received federal relief than blacks. Of Georgia's fifty-five rural counties with a black majority, fifty had more whites than blacks on relief between 1933 and 1935.

One of the first New Deal programs was the National Industrial Recovery Act (NIRA), enforced through the National Recovery Administration (NRA). The NIRA permitted business representatives to gather in Washington and write the codes and regulations that would cover their particular industries. These codes fixed prices, set wages, and regulated hours of work. The first code approved was for cotton textiles. It provided for wages of twelve dollars a week in the South and thirteen dollars in the North. In the South, three-fourths of the industry's fourteen thousand cleaners, outside crewmen, and yardsmen were black. The codes did not cover these jobs; therefore, they were paid even less. Many thought the NRA minimum wage was too much for blacks and if it had to be paid, whites should get it. Consequently, many blacks in covered jobs who held their positions thanks to the wage differential lost their jobs to whites. In Georgia, the greatest displacement was in Columbus.

The NRA came to be known as the "Negro Removal Act," "Negro Run Around," "Negroes Ruined Again," "Negroes Rarely Allowed," "Negro

Robbed Again," and even "No Roosevelt Again." Southern industries dominated by blacks, such as lumber and coal mining, had minimum NRA wages lower than other regions. The Southern lumber industry paid 23 cents an hour; elsewhere workers got 40 cents. The NRA set 42.5 cents an hour for Georgia miners, most of whom were black, but in areas where most miners were white, the wage was set at 60 cents. Most of Georgia's laundry workers were black, and their code wage was 14 cents an hour. The D. Nachman Company of Augusta appealed the 1935 cotton pickery code wage of 25 cents for men and 18 cents an hour for women. Nachman thought 10 cents an hour was sufficient.

Blacks argued that the wage differentials were unfair, perpetuated discrimination and poverty, and undermined white wages. Those who supported the differential claimed that blacks were accustomed to a lower standard of living, were less efficient, and that lower wages for them were traditional. The *Macon Telegraph* favored equal wages "not so much for the benefit of the Negro... but for the benefit of Macon and Georgia." There was little chance for effective protest, however. Lawrence Oxley, chief of the Negro division of the NRA, investigated pay differentials in Georgia and said there was no recourse for a black who was fired for organizing a protest against differentials.

Several federal work relief programs, such as the Civil Works Administration (CWA), Public Works Administration (PWA), and the Works Progress Administration (WPA), helped blacks far more than any state relief programs did, even if they fell short of complete equality. The PWA was headed by Ickes, who was sympathetic to the problems of blacks, and started out paying up to fifty cents an hour in the South until state pressure forced it down to the twelve-to-twenty-cent range.

Atlanta's University Homes, begun in 1933, was the first federal public housing project for blacks in the nation. This $2.5 million project provided homes for 675 families, who paid an average of $5.87 monthly rent. John Hope was instrumental in obtaining initial approval for the project. The Techwood Development in Atlanta was the first federal public housing project that required a hiring quota of skilled black workers. More than 24 percent of skilled construction workers were black. At Techwood, 13 percent of the payroll for skilled construction work went to blacks during the project's first two months, and by the time the project was completed, blacks got about 20 percent of the better Techwood jobs. In 1937, 88 percent of Atlanta's unskilled construction workers were black, and they received 78 percent of the work on PWA housing projects in Georgia.

The WPA became the main federal program that provided work relief. It was responsible for the construction of many schools, post offices, and parks. The first black school it built was in Georgia. In 1938, of the fifty-three thousand heads of families on WPA relief in Georgia, 40 percent were black. Even though the problems of the depression were still acute in the late 1930s, the WPA, as with other New Deal agencies, had its funds cut by political enemies. Anyone on a WPA job could not turn down private employment. When the war-induced boom in construction came to Georgia in 1939, the WPA in Bibb County removed all blacks from its rolls so that they would be forced into private construction jobs. Some had to wait in bullpens, sometimes for days, before going on the private jobs that paid less.

When the Silver Shirts protested that there were no separate drinking fountains for blacks and whites in the WPA's Atlanta headquarters, the state administrator pointed out that there were none such in the Capitol or the Fulton County Courthouse, either. The WPA's position was unusual, for even on street projects in Atlanta, while there might be only one barrel of drinking water for workers, it had a "white" and a "colored" side, each with its own dipper.

The WPA Writers Project salvaged part of the history of slavery by interviewing all the ex-slaves it could find. It found several hundred, and their personal narratives comprise a twenty-volume account of slave life. Two volumes are about Georgia slaves. The oldest ex-slave then was Liverpool, born in 1829. He had been a slave of Pierce Butler's and received a small pension from Henry Ford. A living legend, he charged admission to those who wanted to see him. He died at the age of 110 in 1939.

The Civilian Conservation Corps (CCC) took idle youths off the streets and put them in outdoor camps where they received good food, fresh air, and useful work. Young men, ages eighteen to twenty-four, were paid thirty dollars a month. They kept five dollars for spending money, and the rest went home to their families. The CCC did some much-needed tree planting and other conservation work. Its top administrators did not actively promote discrimination, but because programs were locally controlled, blacks suffered. At first, Georgia's CCC administrators were reluctant to recruit blacks at all. In the first month of operation, although Georgia was 36 percent black, only 0.5 percent of the enrollees were. Clarke and Washington counties were 60 percent black, with no black enrollees in the CCC. The agency did not try to break down segregation, and all Southern installations were Jim Crow, but the CCC did establish 265 camps for blacks.

Other New Deal programs failed to avoid discrimination. The Social Security system, one of the Roosevelt era's major reforms, originally did not include agricultural, domestic, and other occupations many blacks pursued. In 1939, when the national-average old-age assistance check was $19.47, it was $8.12 in Georgia, reflecting the state's general poverty and low wages. Only Arkansas and Mississippi had lower average benefits. Coverage was subsequently extended to most job categories. Like many

New Deal agencies, the U. S. Employment Service was not discriminatory in theory, but local practice made it so. The Atlanta office reported in
1942 that only whites had been referred to professional and managerial
positions and only blacks had been referred to agricultural jobs. The
Federal Housing Administration (FHA) encouraged residential
segregation.

Because most blacks lived off the land in Georgia during the depression, the collapse of agricultural prices affected them most. Cotton,
which sold for eighteen cents a pound in 1929, dropped to six cents in
1933. The federal government tried to cope with depressed commodity
prices by restricting production and paying farmers to let the land lie
idle. In the Cotton Belt, tenant farmers often received short notice from
the landlord that the land was being idled.

Having no alternative, the evicted tenants went to the cities and
applied for relief. At the beginning of the depression, the Red Cross
supplied relief. Planters said blacks would not work if "on the Cross" and
wanted relief cut off during harvest time. They complained that relief
programs made it impossible to get cheap black labor. The planters got
their way. Landlords paid fifty cents per hundred pounds for hand-
picking cotton. If the crop was poor due to erosion, stinting on fertilizer,
insect infestations, or bad weather, cotton pickers could not make a living
wage. If the workers objected, nightriders might show up on their
doorsteps.

The federal agricultural program, the Agricultural Adjustment Administration (AAA), was administered by local boards consisting of county
agents and planters who had always worked closely together. These
boards discriminated assiduously. Under 1934 revisions in the AAA law,
tenants were to receive half of the government payments when cotton
fields were plowed up, but one study showed that landlords used force on
22 percent of the white and 58 percent of the black tenants to get them to
give up their share. Often force was not necessary, for there were many
ways the landlord could apply pressure. One landlord refused to supply
fertilizer because the tenant's son had taken a job in a quarry rather than
stay and help work the land. In accordance with the "company store"
tradition, government checks intended for tenants were often confiscated
by landlords to pay "debts" inflated by usurious interest rates. Black
farmers seldom received any cash. Overall, 90 percent of government
payments went to landlords.

The big landlords got bigger while the average black-owned farm stayed
the same size, usually about a hundred acres. Many black landowners lost
their land due to the difficult economic circumstances, aggravated by
unfair administration of federal programs, and blacks were bumped back
down the economic ladder they had worked so hard to climb. Owners

became tenants, and cash renters became sharecroppers. Those who remained continued to live primitive lives. As late as 1940, less than 20 percent of rural homes had electricity and inside toilets, and 10 percent of black families and 2 percent of white families did not even have outdoor privies.

Old ways died hard. One of Georgia's most shameful traditions was peonage. Howard Kester, a white liberal, gathered information on peonage in Warren County for the NAACP, the American Civil Liberties Union, and the Worker's Defense League in 1937. That year, armed planters and their hired guards mobilized to prevent blacks from leaving Warren County at cotton-picking time. They also forced some to return to the fields from cities.

William T. Cunningham owned three large Oglethorpe County plantations and enslaved scores of blacks, who were forced to work fourteen- to seventeen-hour days; they were underfed, paid no wages, and beaten for attempting to escape. In 1939, Cunningham pursued four escaped peons to Chicago and tried to gain their extradition to Georgia, but he was exposed. The Committee to Abolish Peonage was established by the ILD, which sent full details of the Oglethorpe County peonage to the FBI in 1940, but the bureau ignored the matter. Herbert Aptheker, pioneer scholar in black history, traveled to Georgia that year and set up a "modern version of the underground railroad" to help about thirty of Cunningham's peons to escape.

Continual political pressure forced the Justice Department to investigate. In 1941, a federal grand jury in Chicago indicted Cunningham for conspiring to retain and hold blacks in a condition of peonage and slavery. However, a federal judge in Georgia refused to extradite him. Georgia's contract law was not overturned by the U. S. Supreme Court until 1942, but the practice of debt slavery continued for many years after that.

In efforts that were somewhat reminiscent of the 1880s Alliance Movement, blacks revived their interest in cooperatives in hopes of escaping rural poverty. These efforts were short-lived, however. In the rural South there were steps toward interracial cooperation to solve economic problems also reminiscent of the Populist Movement—except that some of the efforts of the 1930s were more committed to racial equality. The Southern Policy Conference, a distinguished group of white liberals, met in Atlanta in 1935 to recommend the abolition of tenancy.

The most progressive agricultural program of the New Deal was the Resettlement Administration (RA). In 1936, it planned the Fort Valley Farms in Peach County to help urban blacks return to the land. Local white opposition prevented the project's implementation. The project was relocated to Macon County, where local opposition was not so vociferous, and emerged as the 10,653-acre Flint River Farms. Each of the 106 black families settling there was provided with about one hundred acres. They prospered under federal guidance at first and almost quadrupled their average net worth the first year. They developed good kitchen gardens, preserved and canned food, diversified their crops, and developed cooperative marketing, a health center, and a school under the management of Cozy L. Ellison, later chairman of the Agricultural Division of Fort Valley State College. According to historian Michael S. Holmes, the Flint River project proved that blacks' "former positions as tenants and croppers were not the result of some innate inferiority, but the product of the state's economy and certain definite attitudes about their color." Flint River Farms was the RA's most successful project and the first to be attacked by Georgia's congressmen and senators.

Despite discrimination within its ranks, the New Deal did much to benefit blacks. Historian Lerone Bennett said the New Deal marked a major turning point in Negro fortunes by starting a revolution in rising expectations. Blacks pointed to low-cost housing, the CCC, NYA, WPA, federal relief, encouragement of trade unions, the Farm Security Administration, the RA, and the appointment of many blacks to high office as some of the New Deal's positive accomplishments.

To the extent the New Deal benefited blacks, it incurred the wrath of Georgia's leading white supremacists. Such people would give up the new programs in order to keep the caste system. Longtime Georgia congressman Eugene "Goober" Cox had more relatives on the federal payroll than any of his colleagues but inveighed against the growth of the bureaucracy and programs benefiting blacks. Another "rabid" opponent of the New Deal was the Georgia Women's Democratic Club, which accused the WPA in 1936 of all manner of wrongdoing, including letting black and white women sit side by side in a sewing program.

Southern leaders regarded the New Deal as dangerously radical. Sen. Richard Russell said in 1934, "We have all but been completely Russianized." The new programs, which increased people's financial dependence on the federal government, undermined the courthouse rings as the main political force. "Slowly the race issue came out of the bag," stated New Deal historian Harvard Sitkoff. "The growth of federal power was pictured as a dagger pointed at the heart of the state's right to regulate its own racial affairs." Despite Roosevelt's efforts to step lightly around white Southerners' sensitivities, his support of efforts to abolish the poll tax—in order to unseat the anti-New Deal, anti-Semitic, antilabor, and racist Southerners elected thanks partly to the tax—was the last straw.

Throughout the New Deal, Georgia officials worked to keep down the black vote and funnel New Deal benefits to whites. Gov. Eugene Talmadge (1933–37 and 1941–43) was a leader of the anti-New Deal forces. An opponent of civil rights and founder of a political dynasty, he was one of the last Georgian demagogues to ride the horse of unadulterated white supremacy into the governor's mansion. His record in office hurt the state, and his antigovernment program helped big business more than the poor whites he claimed to champion.

Ol' Gene, as his friends called him, opposed old-age pensions, free textbooks, extension of the school term, slum clearance, child-labor legislation, and unemployment insurance. Once, when asked what he would do for the unemployed, Talmadge roared, "Let 'em starve." He absolutely refused to follow Washington's guidelines for equal pay for blacks and whites and made this an issue in his 1934 political campaign. Blacks constituted half the highway department's labor force, but they never received NRA code wages. Ickes referred to Talmadge as "his chain gang excellency." Then again, Georgia was known as "the Chain Gang State," and Talmadge praised the gangs, which "kept men out of doors in God's open country where they could enjoy the singing of the birds and the beautiful sunrises and sunsets."

Talmadge's racial attitudes have been described as typical for the time, and they provide an unappealing picture of early-twentieth-century Georgia. When Talmadge was growing up, local blacks called him "mean Lugene." Talmadge paid the standard low wages to the blacks who worked on his farm. Talmadge biographer William Anderson wrote that Talmadge believed blacks were "childlike, basically stupid, barely removed from a savage ancestry, and should be closely controlled. He did not hate the race, but he had very little respect for blacks as human beings." Talmadge beat and flogged black workers. He once grabbed an ax handle and chased the black chauffeur of a Northern white couple when the chauffeur was walking on a McRae street beside his employer's wife. "We in the South love the Negro in his place—but his place is at the back door with his hat in his hand," Talmadge proclaimed.

Talmadge was sympathetic to the Klan and toured the South with leaders of antiblack and anti-Semitic groups, such as Silver Shirt leader Gerald L. K. Smith and Thomas Dixon, the Klan-glorifying writer. Talmadge had a penchant for martial law and big military staffs and admired Hitler. When First Lady Eleanor Roosevelt hosted a garden party for black students and socialized with Howard University ROTC cadets, Talmadge's followers attacked her by popularizing a ditty:

> You kiss the Negroes
> I'll kiss the Jews,
> We'll stay in the White House
> As long as we choose.

Walter George was a more effective opponent of the New Deal than Talmadge, who challenged the state's senior U. S. senator in the 1938 election. Roosevelt tried to prevent George's reelection in 1938, particularly because the senator, while supporting some New Deal legislation, had opposed the president's "court-packing plan," an attempt to add judges to the Supreme Court and create a federal judiciary more sympathetic to New Deal legislation. Southerners claimed the plan was the first step toward destruction of white supremacy and the poll tax. In a speech at Gainesville, Roosevelt said that the Georgia oligarchy was feudal and compared its members to European Fascists. George responded by condemning Roosevelt for seeking Northern black votes. While the administration was pumping money into Georgia to aid Roosevelt's hand-picked candidate, Lawrence Camp, a report surfaced that Georgia's Democratic leaders were trying to displace all blacks on the federal payroll with whites. Roosevelt's attacks on George stirred resentment among Georgians and benefited the senator, who compared Roosevelt's involvement in the campaign with the horrors of Reconstruction. George waged a race-baiting campaign and denounced federal antilynching legislation. Thanks to the county unit vote, George beat both Talmadge and Camp. He served until 1956, remaining a consistent opponent of equal rights for Georgia's blacks.

In Georgia's larger cities black political organizations were developing. In Atlanta, the Civic and Political League, established on Lincoln's birthday in 1936, was able to double the vote by the next election. In Savannah, the Young Men's Civic Club organized in 1938 for the same purpose. The importance of voting was brought home to the Rev. M. E. Moon of Macon in the 1930s, when he tried to get a liberal white attorney to take a case involving police brutality but was refused. The attorney planned to run for office, and blacks did not vote in sufficient numbers to help him get elected. The black vote outside the urban centers was virtually a cipher. In 1939, the political boss of Hall County said, "Niggers have been ruled out; it's our private affair, and we don't invite them in, and that's that." All over the Deep South, only 2.5 percent of the potential black voters cast ballots in the 1940 presidential election.

The poll tax was just one of the obstacles that kept blacks from voting in Georgia. Another one was the declining influence of blacks in the Republican party. In 1932, only 20 percent of delegates to the Georgia state convention were black. Black influence was reduced further in 1936. "The white people are 100 percent in control of the Georgia Republican Party," a state GOP official exaggerated slightly in 1936, "and we want to keep it that way." Meanwhile, the Democratic party became increasingly attractive to blacks. Prodded by his wife, Eleanor, Roosevelt became more sensitive to racial problems as his years in office passed by. Much of this was due to the increase in black officials that the New Deal had encouraged and the need for national unity. In 1936, 76 percent of Northern blacks voted for Roosevelt and the ditty "Let Jesus lead you and Roosevelt feed you" became popular.

The problem of poor public education for all of Georgia's children persisted during the depression. Under Gov. Eurith D. Rivers, who supported New Deal programs, the state for the first time began to provide free textbooks in public schools and guaranteed, in theory at least, a minimum term of seven months. Racial disparities remained, and classroom space for blacks was severely limited. In 1940, 83 percent of Atlanta's black schoolchildren still were double-shifted, a practice that remained peculiar to black schools. There was an average of seventy-six black students per class compared to thirty white children per class. In Macon, the physical plant was so deficient that the L. H. Williams Elementary School for blacks lacked electricity until the mid-1930s.

Higher education for blacks in Georgia had improved in 1929 with the formation of the Atlanta University Center, with Morehouse and Spelman concentrating on undergraduate work and Atlanta University developing as a graduate school exclusively. John Hope became Atlanta University's first black president in 1929. In 1932, Morris Brown joined the center. Later Gammon and the Atlanta School for Social Work joined. Following a policy dispute over segregation with Walter White, W. E. B. Du Bois (who advocated economic separatism in the face of segregation) resigned from the NAACP in August 1934 and returned to Atlanta University as chairman of the sociology department. Hope died in 1936, and Rufus Early Clement was named to replace him. Benjamin Mays was named president of Morehouse in 1940.

Improvements were made in the black colleges outside of Atlanta also. Savannah's Georgia State Industrial College for Colored Youths became part of the University System of Georgia in 1932, and its name was changed to Georgia State College. Fort Valley High and Industrial School grew from a primary school into a junior college and enjoyed good relations with many of the local whites. When, in the mid-1930s, a student was suspected of the rape of a white women and local ruffians were on their way to attack the college, President Henry A. Hunt contacted Fort Valley's leaders and whites came out to guard the campus. The college grew rapidly under Horace Mann Bond, a distinguished scholar who was named president in 1939 after Hunt's death. That same year the college joined the university system as a four-year college.

In 1938, when the Georgia State Department of Education was calling for "the extension to every individual, regardless of birth, class, race, religion, or economic status, the opportunity for the fullest development of his capacities," blacks were forbidden to enter any white units of the university system. However, the bitterest foes of school segregation were not found at black colleges. The students, faculty, and especially administrators had vested interests in segregation and were often the despair of those who wanted real change.

*   *   *

Georgia's white workers were slow to fight for equal wages for blacks and slow to realize that as long as black workers received less, whites also would be in a weak position to demand more. Consequently, pay scales remained low. In 1938, Georgia's average weekly wage for industrial and manufacturing workers was $13.71, the nation's lowest. The "cheap and docile" Southern white labor attracted New England textile manufacturers, whose labor costs had been raised through collective bargaining by their employees.

Georgia's white supremacist leaders were also fiercely antiunion. "Goober" Cox had led the fight against the Wagner Act, which upheld the right of workers to join labor unions and bargain collectively for better wages and working conditions. Georgia workers, black and white, received harsh treatment when they challenged low wages and poor working conditions. Federal officials reported that black women in Georgia lost their jobs for simply showing interest in a union in 1934. In 1934 and 1935, there were eighty-eight deaths and countless beatings of labor organizers in the United States; in the South, nineteen of the forty-two killed were black.

During the 1934 national textile strike, Governor Talmadge vowed, "I will never use troops to break a strike." He soon broke his promise and helped textile baron Cason Callaway with four thousand troops to break strikes in Newnan and Covington. Soldiers took 128 white strikers from Newnan to Fort McPherson, where they were put into a stockade surrounded by barbed wire until the strike was broken.

The formation of the Congress of Industrial Organizations (CIO) in 1935 marked a startling change in labor-union policies. CIO leader John L. Lewis's experience as president of the relatively nondiscriminatory United Mine Workers fortified his resolve to include blacks as equals in the CIO. Because it organized all workers, not just skilled workers, as the AFL did, the CIO had no color line. It gave hope to millions of blacks who had been shut out by employers and AFL unions, most of which continued their short-sighted policies. The Steel Workers Organizing Committee-CIO ended segregated union meetings in Atlanta in 1936. In 1939, black union miners in Georgia were involved in a national coal strike that the union won because it was integrated. As late as 1942, ten international AFL unions had color bars and others, such as the Brotherhood of Railroad Clerks, had separate segregated locals for blacks who paid dues but did not vote. The CIO was a double threat to the Southern way of life: It undermined cheap labor and the caste system. It was common for people working for the Textile Workers Organizing Committee-CIO to be kidnapped and beaten with the cooperation and in the presence of police. In 1937, Macon's mayor offered rewards for the identification of CIO workers distributing material.

The Klan, ever protective of Southern mores, found a new enemy.

Imperial Wizard Hiram Evans announced in early 1939 that the Klan would drop racial and religious issues and concentrate on fighting labor organizations. Actually, the Klan did not drop its old targets, although it did take on the new one. In 1938 scores of blacks, along with several white union organizers, were kidnapped and flogged by hooded Klansmen. An outbreak of floggings in and around East Point in 1939 and 1940 resulted in at least three deaths. The Klan was linked to at least fifty of the attacks. When twenty men, including three deputy sheriffs, were indicted for this, some were found guilty of misdemeanors, and eight were sent to prison but soon were released by Governor Talmadge.

Although attempts by the legislature and the Atlanta City Council to pass antimask regulations were unsuccessful, public opinion was beginning to turn against the Klan, and its fortunes soon declined. Its links to the German-American Bund, an organization of Hitler's sympathizers, made it appear unpatriotic. By the time the United States entered World War II, there were only five hundred active Klansmen in Atlanta. The Klan officially dissolved at its 1944 Atlanta convention after the IRS demanded $685,305 in back taxes, but it would soon reappear in another of its various incarnations.

World War II

Adolf Hitler's rise to power in Germany profoundly influenced race relations in the United States. People were horrified by Nazi cruelties and tortures following his ascendancy in 1933. Hitler showed the world that an ideology of racial supremacy, carried to its ultimate of genocide, did not spare whites. Opposition to Nazis eventually grew into powerful support for the civil rights movement. Antilynching reformers compared Nazi anti-Semitism and barbarism with American lynching and racism. Mussolini's brutal conquest of Ethiopia in 1935 was compared to the treatment of Southern blacks.

As history's first truly global conflict loomed on the horizon, the United States grew more sensitive to world opinion regarding race relations. Americans abroad were called on to explain why the nation tolerated lynching. Americans also grew more sensitive to the opinions of blacks because the coming war would require great national unity. Many white Americans joined the civil rights struggle during the 1930s and 1940s. Realizing that racism hurt the nation's entire social fabric, they spoke out for improved race relations.

When the Southern Conference on Human Welfare (SCHW) was founded in Birmingham in 1938, Eleanor Roosevelt and Supreme Court Justice Hugo Black addressed the nine hundred white and three hundred black delegates. The SCHW, which contained both liberals and radicals, began as an active opponent of segregation and disfranchisement and marked the high point of Southern liberalism during the New Deal. The SCHW fathered the 1940 National Committee to Abolish the Poll Tax, which solidified the anti-New Deal stance of Georgia's politicians.

In 1943, the Commission on Interracial Cooperation (CIC) sponsored a conference in Atlanta of 113 white business, professional, and religious leaders who endorsed the Durham Statement, issued by black leaders at a 1942 conference in North Carolina. The Durham Statement called for an immediate end to discrimination. While approving the statement, whites cautioned blacks to go slow. Some of them believed segregation was proper if it was "fair" and simply favored making "separate but equal" more equal. After an interracial group of representatives from Durham and Atlanta met at Richmond, the Southern Regional Council (SRC) was chartered in Atlanta in 1944. Atlanta University President Rufus Clement and *Atlanta Constitution* editor Ralph McGill were among the SRC's organizers. The SRC took over the work of the CIC and the Association of Southern Women for the Prevention of Lynching. The SRC moved more boldly than either of the earlier organizations. By 1955, Georgia Attorney General Eugene Cook included it with the NAACP on his list of "Communist" organizations. Such labeling was a common, though inaccurate, accusation made by segregationists. Despite such pronouncements, the SRC endured.

The 1940 election campaign pushed Roosevelt into more support of black advances because his Republican opponent, Wendell Willkie, was a very outspoken champion of black progress. Willkie called for federal antilynching legislation and promised to end discrimination in the federal government and the military. To prevent greater black defections from the Democratic party, Roosevelt made some key appointments of blacks to high-level positions. Benjamin O. Davis, Sr., became the first black American general in October 1940—just before the election—and William H. Hastie, later the nation's first black federal judge, was assigned to the secretary of war as a top adviser. Roosevelt won, but his share of the popular vote dropped significantly.

Only 16 percent of Georgia's voting-age population cast ballots in the 1940 election, and Eugene Talmadge moved back to the governor's mansion following a four-year absence. His racist-inspired attacks on the University of Georgia in 1941, known as the "Cocking affair," cost him his job, however. Dr. Walter Dewey Cocking, the university's dean of the College of Education, was concerned about the status of education for blacks in Georgia. Among Cocking's political sins was his authorship of a report showing that Georgia supported Negro higher education less than any other Southern state. At the time, the university was cleaning house by firing incompetent teachers. These teachers and some others bypassed for promotion went to Talmadge with charges that Cocking wanted to start an integrated teacher-training school near Athens.

In the ensuing controversy the governor demanded the dismissal of Cocking and President Marvin S. Pittman of Georgia Teachers College at Statesboro (now Georgia Southern University), who had welcomed visiting black faculty from Tuskegee Institute. When the regents voted 8–7 to keep Cocking, Talmadge forced three regents to resign. After a staged hearing, the new board did his bidding and voted to fire Cocking along with ten other "foreign (out-of-state) professors trying to destroy the sacred traditions of the South," as Talmadge put it. Pittman was also dismissed. "The whole affair had been like a bad movie about Southern demagogues," Talmadge's biographer wrote. The politicized university and ten other Georgia colleges lost their accreditation. Students, faculty, alumni, parents, and everyone else who valued higher education were furious.

Talmadge also opposed federal funding for education on the grounds that it would lead to desegregation. He used the state's Department of Revenue to harass the CIC and branded its leaders as Communists. Talmadge used the Cocking affair to encourage a witch hunt against "subversive" books that might encourage racial equality and integration. The Statesboro library was searched for "Communism or anything else except Americanism."

Contributing to Talmadge's ire was the university's acceptance of funds from the Rosenwald Fund, known for its encouragement of black education: "Jew money for niggers" was the way Talmadge put it. Talmadge convinced his supporters that Rosenwald was part of a "Jewish-Communist-mongrelizing" conspiracy, although the Rosenwald fund actually helped perpetuate segregation by making it more palatable. (The Peabody Fund, through its Southern agents, played an even greater role in promoting the continuance of segregation.)

Contrary to Talmadge's ravings, Georgia educators still practiced segregation and failed to acknowledge its ingrained hypocrisy. In January 1942, one month after the United States entered World War II, Georgia educators heard a keynote address, "Moral Obligations of a Democracy," in a meeting that excluded black educators. However, Talmadge had simply gone too far, and his actions became a major issue in the 1942 gubernatorial campaign. State Attorney General Ellis G. Arnall hailed from Coweta County and used the issue of academic freedom to defeat Talmadge in the 1942 governor's race. For Arnall, a former Talmadge ally, the issue was not integration, and he was not above Negro baiting. "If a nigger ever tried to get into a white school in my part of the state, the sun would never set on his head," he proclaimed. Arnall depoliticized the Board of Regents, and Georgia schools regained their accreditation. Pittman was rehired. Cocking was offered his job back, but he refused to accept it.

Talmadge's most prominent black supporter was Joseph W. Holley, the extremely accommodationist president of Albany State College (once described as a "noted member of the Uncle Tom school of Negro college presidents"). Holley resented Rosenwald money going to Fort Valley State College, which graduated its first four-year class in 1941. Fort Valley State President Horace Mann Bond believed that Holley had convinced Talmadge of the fund's evil effects. Bond defended the fund by inviting Talmadge during his 1942 campaign to address the festivities commemorating the merger with the Forsyth-based State Teachers and Agricultural College. Talmadge came, knowing white voters would be there. Bond made sure he got photographs of Talmadge smiling and shaking hands with blacks—photos that, if publicized among his constituency, could ruin him. Bond was offered $5,000 for the photos but instead used them to "persuade" Talmadge to cease his attacks on the Rosenwald Fund and to consider getting blacks included in the next salary increase for college faculty. With the election of Arnall, Holley was eased out of his position.

As a result of a constitutional amendment passed in 1941, Arnall was the first modern governor to serve a four-year term. Georgia's youngest governor pushed through some progressive measures. His administration repealed the poll tax in 1945 and lowered the voting age to eighteen, two measures tending to increase the black vote. He forced the Interstate Commerce Commission to equalize freight rates by taking his "Northern Railroad Conspiracy" case against discriminatory freight rates to the Supreme Court. Railroads charged Georgia shippers 39 percent more to move the same weight the same distance as a Northeastern shipper would pay. Arnall argued that removing this bar to industrialization would increase Georgia's prosperity and thus help the race problem, which fed on the poverty of both blacks and whites. His 1946 court victory made the nation a true common market.

When war with both Germany and Japan seemed imminent, the United States was tooling up to become, in President Roosevelt's words, "the Arsenal for Democracy." By 1940 employment was increasing rapidly as defense plants opened up and unemployment largely disappeared—except among blacks. As depressed industries revived, many of the unemployed went back to white-only jobs. In 1940 the national jobless rate for blacks was 29 percent (19 percent for men and 36 percent for women), twice that of white unemployment. Ten years earlier, the black rate was only 50 percent higher. This widening gap reflected the growth in job discrimination during the depression. Blacks grew increasingly restive; equal opportunity in the workplace became a top priority on the black agenda.

Reacting to the threat of a massive march on Washington by 100,000 blacks led by A. Philip Randolph, president of the Brotherhood of

Sleeping Car Porters, President Roosevelt signed Executive Order No. 8802 on June 25, 1941. It was intended to end racial discrimination by businesses working on government contracts. The Fair Employment Practices Commission was created to enforce the order. However, the FEPC had little immediate influence in Georgia. In December 1941, there were no facilities to train blacks in Georgia for defense work. Two months later, the U. S. Employment Service listed fifty-two hundred blacks actively seeking employment in Atlanta and thirty-one hundred in Savannah, where two-thirds of the unemployed were black. To put pressure on the state, the National Urban League publicized some glaring examples of discrimination in defense industries. The Bell Aircraft Company was erecting a new defense plant in Marietta in 1942 after city fathers had exacted a promise from the company that there would be no equal hiring of blacks. As an inducement to get the plant located there, the Atlanta school system started training future employees. Bell promised to hire blacks if they received the training. Over five thousand blacks registered for the training, but as of June 1942, there were no classes they could attend. There were fifteen classes in session for whites.

Events during the war disrupted the fabric of race relations and planted the seeds for more progress in the decades to come. Racial violence became less tolerable because the war required an unprecedented degree of national unity. Lynchings jeopardized this goal because they could diminish the loyalty of blacks. Lynchings, though fewer, continued during the war, and the Axis powers made the most of them by claiming the United States lied when it said its aims were democratic. Radio Tokyo and Radio Berlin quickly reported U. S. racial incidents to the world. A photograph of Georgia lynching victim Son Jones was reportedly used in Germany as anti-United States propaganda. Axis criticism of U. S. race relations struck a sensitive nerve, and some official efforts were made to counteract enemy propaganda.

Everyone was needed to work or fight as the military's needs grew and industry fully converted to war production. This induced the greatest migration ever of blacks out of Georgia during the war years. For the first time, great numbers went to the West Coast. They found jobs there, although the pay was not great. In 1941, 80 percent of defense workers averaged less than thirty dollars a week—but it beat picking cotton for fifty cents a day. As new opportunities opened up, blacks left their positions as menials, underpaid domestics, and agricultural serfs. As this occurred, white anger grew, and Georgia saw a repeat of the World War I atmosphere of white resentment and fear of blacks' newfound economic independence and increased militancy.

Word spread in Atlanta and other cities that blacks were buying up weapons to prepare for a military uprising and wanted an Axis victory to help them succeed. Stories about blacks calling whites by their first names were evidence of nefarious plots. Domestic servants reportedly formed Eleanor Clubs, named after the First Lady. Members were supposed to refuse low pay and heavy work. Evidence of "revolt" consisted of black women quitting ten-cent-an-hour domestic jobs to earn forty cents an hour in army laundries.

Just as the World War I migration lead to a more reasonable attitude on the part of some whites, World War II changes in Georgia led eventually to even more progress. In 1943, Georgia saw the first convictions of lynchers since the early 1920s. Baker County Sheriff Claude Screws and two local lawmen, Jim Bob Kelly and Frank Jones, were sentenced in federal court to three years and fined $1,000 for beating to death black prisoner Robert Hall while he was handcuffed in January 1943. The U. S. Supreme Court upheld the conviction in 1945. This case required federal action because many Georgia officials still retained the attitude of the Oglethorpe County lawman who responded to a black woman's request to arrest an abusive white storekeeper by saying, "I will not give any nigger a warrant for a white person."

The case of "Georgia justice" during the war that aroused the most national and worldwide attention was the beating of Roland Hayes, internationally famous concert tenor. Even a man of international repute could not escape the petty viciousness of white Georgia. After a triumphant tour of Europe, Hayes returned to the United States and bought a six hundred-acre Georgia plantation twelve miles north of Rome that he named "Angel Mo" in honor of his mother. He spent much of his time there when he was off the concert circuit. On July 23, 1942, his wife entered a shoe store in Rome and protested when she was asked to wait in the back while the clerk served white customers who came in later. Roland came to her support; the clerk called the police and claimed that Mrs. Hayes had cursed him. When her husband denied the charge, he was beaten by an unidentified man who accompanied the police, and the officers then dragged Hayes off to jail. There was a storm of pro-Hayes protest all over the nation. The news of Hayes's beating was scissored out of periodicals by U. S. censors before delivery abroad. Hayes sold his Georgia property and never returned to the state.

Governor Talmadge, whom journalists called "the Fuehrer of Sugar Creek," made the baseless charge that Hayes, then fifty-five, had attacked the police. He responded to criticism of the Hayes beating by warning blacks who did not like the state's segregation laws "to stay out of Georgia." By then, Talmadge was bitter because enforcement of federal FEPC rules caused Georgia textile manufacturers to lose some government war orders. After his 1942 defeat, Talmadge moved even further to the right and accused President Roosevelt of using the war to promote equality for blacks.

During World War II, white Southerners feared race riots if many black soldiers were stationed in the South, especially if they were from the North. Officers at Camp Wheeler, Georgia, wanted no black officers, and the Southern Governors' Conference asked the War Department to send no Northern blacks to the South and to refrain from placing black soldiers where they might mingle with white soldiers. The army, more concerned with the war effort than local protest, spread blacks all over the nation but avoided placing them in large concentrations.

More than a million black Americans entered the military during the war. At first, many black volunteers were turned away, and contrary to the World War I experience, blacks were disproportionately rejected by local draft boards. Manpower shortages caused a reversal of these policies. Blacks comprised 5 percent of the army in the summer of 1941; by the end of 1942, 10.3 percent of the army was black, close to their proportion of the total population. The great wartime increase of black soldiers had no influence on breaking down patterns of discrimination. The military was completely segregated in jobs, dining, and living quarters, and black soldiers' duties had not changed much from World War I. Throughout the war, one-third to one half of all quartermaster, medical corps, sanitary units, and other service units were composed of blacks. At Camp Gordon Johnson in Florida, black GIs did housekeeping work for German prisoners while the Nazis played volleyball.

The army's Ninety-third Division was activated in 1941 for black troops, and a number of black college graduates were sent to Fort Benning in Columbus for officers' training. Although black enlisted men were segregated there, black officer candidates ate in the same mess halls, slept in the same barracks, and attended the same classrooms as white candidates. However, when they were assigned to the division under white senior officers, they were segregated even from white officers of the same rank.

The black Twenty-fourth Regiment had been transferred to Fort Benning in 1922 over the objections of blacks nationwide, who feared the worst for the soldiers. At Fort Benning, they were disarmed, insulted, and stripped of their sympathetic commander, and their mail was censored. Just prior to World War II, most of the Twenty-fourth worked as truck drivers, stable boys, and cooks. In 1941, Pvt. Felix Hall of the division's Company E died under mysterious circumstances and some evidence indicated he had been lynched by white military policemen.

The black sense of grievance was heightened by the contrast between actual events and the nation's rhetoric that called for a world in which everyone could enjoy the "Four Freedoms": freedom of speech and worship and freedom from want and fear. Violent incidents at or near Georgia military posts created much resentment among black soldiers. In 1943, Howard Daniels, a black soldier at Camp Gordon, was mauled by a white officer; the latter received the minor punishment of a transfer. A false rumor that Hinesville police fatally beat a black soldier's wife set off a riot at Camp Stewart on June 3, 1943, in which several died. There were similar riots at military bases throughout the nation. The army tried to minimize black resentment by suppressing facts and opinions that might disturb black soldiers. The military banned works on civil rights and a 1943 pamphlet, *Races of Mankind*, that attacked pseudoscientific racial theories and prejudices.

Despite the proscriptions, blacks were eager, as usual, to prove their patriotism and gloried in the heroism of those in combat. The greatest source of pride was the Ninety-ninth Pursuit Squadron, formed at Tuskegee Institute for black pilots in 1940 after Howard University student Yancey Williams sued when the army air corps turned him down due to his race. The air corps was then calling for thirty thousand pilots a year. The Ninety-ninth became part of the 332d Fighter Group under the command of Benjamin O. Davis, Jr., who later became the nation's first black lieutenant general. Several pilots, including David "Lucky" Lester, were from Georgia. Their superb record (the squadron never lost a bomber it was protecting) helped lead to the quick integration of the air force after President Truman ordered the desegregation of the armed forces in 1948. This goal took years in the other branches of the service.

Many of the forces that were at work in 1919 were still active in 1945. Half a million blacks had been overseas in World War II, over twice as many as in the earlier war. Black GIs brought back the same favorable impressions of France that World War I soldiers had.

Wartime advances led to rising expectations and an intense unwillingness to return to the old ways in Georgia. The more militant New Negro that appeared in the North during World War I appeared in Georgia after World War II. Dr. Harry F. Richardson of Gammon Theological Seminary said that the goal of blacks in Georgia was the end of Jim Crow, job discrimination, and disfranchisement. The open expression of this attitude was something of a shock to whites.

When the war ended, many people believed the country was moving toward racial harmony. While there was some progress, most customs and racial attitudes remained strong. A white chief railroad mechanic in Macon explained, "We feel toward them (blacks) like the affection one has for a dog, we love 'em in their place. . . . Sometimes we have to keep them there." For some whites, "keeping them there" meant it was time to revive the Klan. Claiming more than twenty thousand members in Georgia, a group of Klansmen burned a cross atop Stone Mountain in October 1945, just a year after its second incarnation had purportedly expired.

A similar organization appeared in Atlanta after the war. The Columbians wore brown shirts with armbands bearing a drunken thunderbolt design. Their professed aim was to exterminate the Jews and send all blacks back to Africa. While they frightened blacks from moving into the "wrong" neighborhoods, they also developed a peculiar way to raise money. They teamed up with certain Atlanta real estate agents who sold homes to blacks in white neighborhoods. Then, as the black family started to move in, a menacing group of uniformed Columbians would appear and threaten the blacks, who would be frightened into selling the house back to the agent at a much reduced price. The Columbians and agents then split the profits—until the police ended the brutal scam.

As before, crimes against blacks were rarely punished, schools for blacks were overcrowded and underfunded, and Jim Crow was as strong as ever. Georgia's municipal, county, and state officials could ignore the minuscule black vote and concentrate on catering to their white constituencies. This façade of white supremacy was beginning to crack, however. Both the poll tax and the white primary were on their way out.

Most blacks could not see paying for the right to vote, especially when they had so little money and the vote had so little meaning. Many counties were worse than Bibb County in 1944, when there were 9,000 potential black voters but only 785 had paid the poll tax; nearly 8,000 whites had. The poll tax had become a symbol of racial discrimination and black powerlessness to prevent lynching. Although the U. S. Supreme Court upheld Georgia's poll tax in 1937, Governor Arnall ended it in 1945.

Georgia's white primary, another long-standing tool of white supremacy, ended with the Primus King case. The Rev. Primus King (1900–1986), a black Baptist and barber in Columbus, sued the Muscogee County registrar for denying him the right to vote in the Democratic primary election on July 4, 1944. King won his suit in federal court and on appeal. On April 1, 1946, the U.S. Supreme Court refused to review the case. When Governor Arnall refused to call a special legislative session to try to subvert the court decision, Georgia was forced to end the white primary. Columbus observed Primus King Day in 1973. The $100 that the Democratic party was ordered to compensate King was not paid until 1977.

10

Postwar Progress

Opening the Door of Politics

The Primus King case had a dramatic effect on Georgia politics. Black political influence, which had begun during Reconstruction and was snuffed out by the New South of Henry Grady and Hoke Smith, revived in the 1940s. In Atlanta, only three hundred blacks had voted in the 1940 white primary. In 1946, black registration there jumped from three thousand to twenty-one thousand—from 4 percent to 27 percent of the electorate. In 1946, the All Citizens Registration Committee helped thousands of blacks to register. The local chapter of the NAACP, the Atlanta Urban League under Grace Towns Hamilton, the *Atlanta World*, and black college faculty helped make the drive so successful that blacks soon held the balance of power in Atlanta. Consequently, Mayor William B. Hartsfield moved away quickly from the philosophy of segregation.

There were gains throughout the state; Georgia's black voter registration surged to 135,000. However, that amounted to only 18 percent of eligible blacks. In 1946, Eugene Talmadge ran again for the state's highest office. Although his candidacy was dismissed by many observers early on, he took advantage of the increasing black voter registration by becoming the only gubernatorial candidate to *emphasize* opposition to black voting. He promised to restore the white primary, and as a bonus to his rural white constituency, he announced his plan to thwart a recent federal ruling against segregation in interstate transportation by requiring all passengers to get off buses fifty feet from the Georgia line and then buy a ticket good only in the state. "If I get a Negro vote, it will be an accident," he declared.

Talmadge succeeded in making white supremacy the campaign's only issue, and white voters more than countered growing black political strength. Approximately seven whites registered for every black voter. Voting lists were so padded that there were more registered white voters than white people in thirty counties, according to a University of Georgia study. The black vote was large enough to throw fear into whites but not large enough to be courted, which encouraged Georgia's politics of negativism. The Talmadge machine also moved to purge the rolls of blacks before the primary. Talmadge supporters were urged to take advantage of an obscure law that let any citizen challenge any other citizen's right to vote for any of several reasons. Thousands of challenge forms were mailed to white rural voters. Officials also challenged and tested black voters. Many blacks were struck from the rolls when they could not name all the federal government's departments or define "ex-post facto" and "bill of attainder."

Primus King and his wife enjoyed an incident-free trip to the polls in 1946, but many blacks were not so fortunate. More than sixteen thousand blacks were purged from the rolls, and far more were kept from the polls by intimidation. Less than a week before the election, Talmadge warned blacks not to vote: "Wise Negroes will stay away from the white folks' ballot boxes on July 17.... We are the true friends of the Negroes... and always will be as long as they stay in the definite place we have provided for them." A black church was burned at Soperton, and the Klan burned crosses several other places. Gun-firing whites drove through a black section of Grady County. In Manchester, whites picketed the polls and warned blacks not to vote. Similar reports came from counties throughout the state. Because the hard core of white supremacy lay in the rural areas where the black population was concentrated, obstacles to black voting were greatest there. In several counties, blacks were not permitted to register.

Remarkably, 85,000–100,000 Georgia blacks defied the custom of white-only politics and cast ballots in the primary, and 98 percent of them supported reform candidate James V. Carmichael. The purges and intimidation, when coupled with fraud and chicanery, enabled Talmadge to carry many of Georgia's rural counties. In Talmadge's home county of Telfair, for example, only four of seventy-six eligible blacks were permitted to vote. Carmichael won the popular vote by sixteen thousand votes, but Talmadge won the tainted election thanks to Georgia's county unit system, which had replaced the white primary as the chief weapon in the denial of black political rights. It gave disproportionate weight to rural counties and awarded the candidate who carried a county all its votes. Since Talmadge carried 105 of Georgia's 159 counties, he received 242 county unit votes to Carmichael's 146. Despite their triumph, white supremacists saw that their worst fears were being fulfilled by the increased black vote.

The climate generated by Eugene Talmadge's campaign was reminiscent of Hoke Smith's Negro-baiting campaign forty years earlier. All but one of the blacks lynched in the nation that year died in Georgia within days of the primary. Macio Snipes, a veteran and the only black to vote in Taylor County, was shot and killed while sitting on his porch on July 20, 1946. A sign posted on a black church said: "The First Nigger to Vote Will Never Vote Again." Five days later, a mob of twenty men shot to death George Dorsey, a recently discharged soldier, and his friend Roger Malcolm in Walton County near Monroe. The two men had recently married sisters and were dragged from an automobile in which they were riding with their brides. When the unmasked mob members realized that the women could identify them, they lynched them too. Shortly after that, a black union organizer was murdered near Gordon.

Local blacks were so terrified that friends and relatives were afraid to come to the funeral services of the Walton County victims. Although Georgia was pilloried in the national press for the Walton outrages, the local sheriff said that he could do nothing. The NAACP investigated the quadruple lynching and forwarded its findings to the FBI, to no avail. No one stepped forward to claim the NAACP's $10,000 reward.

Benjamin Mays persuaded the General Missionary Convention of the black Baptists in Georgia to declare Talmadge's inauguration day a day of prayer, "asking God to make of him a good, just, democratic and Christian governor." However, Talmadge died of cirrhosis of the liver before taking office. Talmadge had been in poor health, so his machine had arranged for write-in votes for his son Herman in the November general election in hopes that the contest then could be decided in the General Assembly. The legislature, led by Speaker Roy Harris, militant segregationist and later head of the White Citizens' Council, named Herman Talmadge as governor after fifty-six more late, fraudulent write-in ballots were "discovered" in Herman's home county. As one reporter put it, "They rose from the dead in Telfair County and marched in alphabetical order to the polls, cast their votes for Herman Talmadge and went back to their last repose." When Ellis Arnall refused to give up the governor's office to a "pretender," Herman's followers seized control of the office by force and changed the locks. After two bitter and confusing months, the Georgia Supreme Court overturned the legislature and named Lt. Gov. Melvin Ernest Thompson acting governor.

The Talmadge machine pushed its plan to restore the white primary through the legislature during Herman Talmadge's bogus term in 1947. The disfranchising legislation met with a storm of protest, however. Black opposition was led by Austin T. Walden and the black Georgia Association of Citizen Democratic Clubs, which had 100,000 members in seventy branches in 1947. White opposition to Talmadge's plan came from the Atlanta, Macon, and Columbus ministerial alliances, which called the plan "contrary to the teachings of Jesus Christ." After Thompson took office, he vetoed the white primary bill.

Meanwhile, attitudes were changing on the national level. Walter White met with President Harry Truman in the White House in 1946 to discuss Southern racial violence. White told Truman about Isaac Woodward, a black soldier whose eyes were gouged out by a South Carolina policeman after he was discharged from Camp Gordon, Georgia. Truman listened with clenched fists and said, "My God, I had no idea that things were as terrible as that. We've got to do something."

Truman, who had grown increasingly sensitive to the problems faced by blacks, began the most vigorous presidential leadership for civil rights the nation had yet seen. In December 1946, he appointed the President's Committee on Civil Rights. Its 1947 report, *To Secure These Rights*, condemned lynching, police brutality, disfranchisement, and employment discrimination. Truman included some of its recommendations in his 1948 Civil Rights Message to Congress. Truman's actions led angry Southern delegates to walk out of the 1948 Democratic convention and form a third party, the "Dixiecrats."

Another split in Democratic ranks occurred when Henry Wallace, Roosevelt's third-term vice-president and an outspoken proponent of civil rights, became the Progressive party's standard-bearer. The Klan warned Atlanta's mayor and police chief to enforce segregation when Wallace and his supporters spoke at black churches. At Atlanta's Wheat Street Baptist Church, police forced blacks and whites to sit on separate sides of the aisle. Larkin Marshall, a fearless black civil rights activist of Macon, ran on the Progressive ticket against Richard Russell for his Senate seat. A huge majority of blacks voted Democratic, however.

Republican Thomas Dewey was expected to win the November presidential election in a landslide, but Truman scored one of history's great upsets. He won largely due to black support in several key Northern states. More than ever before, white power in the South was balanced by black power in the North. It was a good augury for the future of race relations in Georgia.

Terror and intimidation against black voters, often organized by the Klan, figured prominently in the 1948 gubernatorial campaign. Georgians saw a preview of this in Wrightsville, the Johnson County seat. Over three hundred hooded and robed Klansmen, led by Grand Dragon Samuel Green in his jeep with a lighted cross on its hood, paraded in town on the eve of the March 3 local elections. Green predicted "blood would flow in the streets" if the federal government tried to protect black voting rights. The Klan burned a fifteen-foot cross on the courthouse lawn. Of the county's forty-five hundred blacks, four hundred were registered voters, but none dared vote the next day.

Blacks prepared for the 1948 governor's contest by registering in record numbers to vote for Thompson. The Klan openly entered the race in support of Herman Talmadge after he pledged to continue the fight for white supremacy and to battle Truman's civil rights program. The Klan issued threats to black leaders and worked to further purge blacks from election rolls.

Herman Talmadge was elected governor in 1948 because many of the 200,000 blacks who would have cast their votes for Thompson in a peaceful election climate were kept from the polls. Much of the election-year violence was centered in East Georgia, in the heart of Talmadge country. Miniature coffins were left on the doorsteps of black political leaders in Swainsboro in March. The Klan mailed threatening leaflets to potential black voters from Mount Vernon in Montgomery County. Isaiah Nixon, a black Montgomery County sharecropper, was shot in front of his wife and six children for ignoring warnings not to vote in the September 8 primary. His killers, though known, were never brought to trial. In November, NAACP President D. V. Carter was beaten by Montgomery County whites for escorting blacks to the polls. In nearby Toombs County, Robert Mallard was lynched for voting after he had been warned not to. National NAACP official Roy Wilkins blamed the Talmadges for encouraging race bias, discrimination, and terror in Georgia.

Antiblack brutality and intimidation continued after the election. Three male students from Spencer High School in Columbus were abducted, taken over the Alabama line to Phenix City, and beaten for participating in an NAACP-sponsored brotherhood week in February 1949. Macon was the national headquarters of one Klan group after World War II. Local Exalted Cyclops Herman Lavender and Grand Dragon Green tried to organize a women's auxiliary in March 1949. Two months later, Green got in his jeep and led a mile-long Klan motorcade through Warner Robins. The caravan, including school buses from Twiggs and Baldwin counties, went through the black section of town, and many blacks stayed home from work the next day. Caleb Hill, an Irwinton black, resisted arrest for "creating a disturbance" and was taken from the jail by whites and beaten to death in May. That year, a black farmer near Bainbridge was lynched because he objected to a group of whites fishing in his farm pond. The next year, near Swainsboro, a mob of two to three hundred men burned a cross at the home of black tenant farmer Otis Jordan and severely beat him. The Klan wanted to drive all blacks out of the county. A month later, near Dublin, Willie Lee Brinson and his wife suffered critical injuries when flogged by robed men who ordered them out of the county.

In January 1949, Governor Talmadge presented his "Four-Point White Supremacy Program" to the legislature. He hoped to bar 80 percent of

Georgia's blacks from voting by reinstating the poll tax to prevent Negro "bloc voting"; strengthening the county unit system; requiring all 1,200,000 registered voters, including 150,000 blacks, to reregister every two years; and demanding that voters "explain" sections of the federal or state constitution.

The "30 Questions" test was adopted by the 1949 legislature. To qualify as a voter, a person was expected to answer questions such as:

How many congressional districts are in Georgia?
How long has your representative served?
Does the Constitution require a Supreme Court?
Name three Supreme Court justices.
Name the chief justice of the Court of Appeals of Georgia.
Do all counties have the same number of representatives?

Both the *Atlanta Journal* and *Constitution* opposed the test, which several state legislators flunked. Registrars often did not confine their questioning of black voters to the official list of questions, but made up others in no way related to government—such as the Telfair County requirement to count the drops in a glass of water.

The more the black vote was limited in Georgia, the more politicians vied against each other to appear the most racist. In a slap at federal civil rights legislation, Senator Russell introduced a bill in 1949 to provide over $4 billion to send Southern blacks north and bring whites south. Talmadge made Samuel Green an honorary lieutenant colonel and aide de camp and branded Truman's civil rights program a Communist plot. Such insults to blacks would be rewarded as long as Georgia's election laws remained in effect. In 1950, the U. S. Supreme Court refused to review Georgia's county unit system by a 7-2 vote. Shortly after that, the court also refused to review Georgia's infamous literacy requirements. Talmadge was reelected to a four-year governorship in 1950, defeating Thompson, whom he blasted for vetoing the white primary bill and supporting the Fair Employment Practices Commission.

Despite the cloud of Talmadgism that hung over it, many observers considered Georgia the Deep South state that offered the most voting rights to blacks. While blacks had relatively little effect—except perhaps a negative one—on the General Assembly and statewide politics, in Georgia's larger cities blacks were making advances that were directly attributable to voting. In 1947, black voters in Macon helped elect the mayor. Savannah blacks, who had been well organized for many years, got swimming pools, recreation centers, and new schools. Atlanta, Macon, and Savannah had black police officers by the late 1940s.

Atlanta had become a major center for black political, economic, and cultural development. Besides helping to keep Mayor Hartsfield in power, blacks voted to put progressive candidate Helen Douglas Mankin in Congress in 1946. The Talmadge machine found a way to negate her support in subsequent elections, thanks to the county unit system. In 1949, Austin T. Walden joined Atlanta's black Democrats with John Wesley Dobbs's Republicans to form the Atlanta Negro Voters League, which became the most potent black political force in the South. As a result, Atlanta University President Rufus Clement in 1953 was elected to an at-large post on the Atlanta School Board, where he served fourteen years.

Due mainly to black initiatives, the climate of opinion in Georgia was slowly changing. In Atlanta, more whites supported some black advances; for example, political consultant Helen Bullard, the architect of Atlanta's reputation as "the city too busy to hate"; *Atlanta Constitution* editor Ralph McGill; and Dorothy Tilly, a crusader for equality. There also was increasing interest in interracial organizations dedicated to change. Tilly organized the interracial Fellowship of the Concerned. Its members accompanied blacks to the polls and attended civil rights trials in hopes that prominent white women in the courtrooms would lead to more responsible judicial behavior. She received numerous awards for her work, as well as scorn and threats from white supremacists. There was even some progress in the legislature. In 1951, lawmakers enacted anti-Klan measures to outlaw cross burning and wearing masks, indicating that the Klan was losing its clout. While Talmadge signed the laws, he continued his race baiting in 1952 by attacking radio and television personalities who hosted blacks on their shows and criticized Eisenhower when Ike said he might name a black cabinet member.

Tensions arose during the 1954 governor's race amid more appeals for white solidarity. When Ernest Davis of Ocilla filed for a city council post, two uniformed policemen took the black man for a ride and fired a shot at him as a warning against running. Twenty-two blacks were deprived of their voting rights in Cuthbert. However, when they sued the three registrars who violated their rights, they won $880 in damages, which the registrars had to pay. The officials promptly resigned their posts. More suits around the state were threatened, which gave pause to other voting officials. Eight of the nine Democratic gubernatorial candidates called for continued segregation. The ninth got only 1 percent of the vote. Blacks voted for a moderate segregationist and placed improved black education above integration. Marvin Griffin, the most extreme segregationist, won. Griffin practiced the "old ways of segregation, cronyism, and outright corruption," according to historian Robert Dubay.

In 1955, Talmadge published *You and Segregation*, a book that would later embarrass him after Jim Crow was overturned and discredited. In 1956, he won a U. S. Senate seat. In the polling, thousands of qualified black voters were denied the vote by the White Citizens' Council, which examined registration certificates. Despite the great obstacles and hazards they faced, the number of black registered voters in Georgia rose from 145,000 in 1952 to 163,000 in 1956.

The all-white state legislature continued to look for ways to keep blacks away from the polls. In 1958, the "30 Questions" literacy requirement was toughened. In 1957, Georgia had twenty-seven counties in which blacks outnumbered whites. In these counties, the percentage of black votes was lowest because the more fearful white power structures fought change more adamantly. These were also the areas of poorest education; black registration was higher where the opportunities for education and economic status were greater. Early, Miller, Seminole, Decatur, Clay, Calhoun, Baker, Dougherty, Quitman, Randolph, Terrell, Lee, Sumter, Webster, and Stewart counties in Southwest Georgia were notorious for extreme resistance to black advances.

In 1957, majority leader Lyndon Johnson (D-Tex.), in part to develop a national base of support, maneuvered a civil rights bill through the U. S. Senate that improved black voting rights and established a Commission on Civil Rights. It was the first civil rights bill since 1875. After the bill's enforcement provisions were weakened, it passed the Senate 72–18, with both Georgia senators voting against it. Russell claimed it was "a cunningly devised scheme to put black heels on white necks."

The first test of the new law originated in Terrell County, where registrars refused to register qualified blacks. Only 48 of the county's 5,034 blacks, compared to 2,679 of 3,233 whites, were registered to vote. On April 7, 1958, five blacks, including four Dawson teachers, all college graduates—Edna Mae Lowe, Janie Breedlove, David Gibson, and Grace Boyd Gibson—tried to register. The teachers were disqualified on flimsy excuses. The four sued, and the case went to court on September 7. When FBI agents asked for voting records, federal judge Walter I. Greer of Colquitt threatened to jail them and ordered the registrars to refuse to hand over records. Governor Griffin announced that he backed Greer up with "the entire resources of the state." Greer also threatened to jail any NAACP officials who came within his jurisdiction. A week after the trial opened, Love was fired from her job at Carver High School and declared illiterate. She held a master's degree from New York University. The case was appealed. Two years later federal district judge T. Hoyt Davis in Macon upheld Greer and voided the applicable section of the 1957 civil rights law. The Justice Department then bypassed the appeals court and took the matter straight to the Supreme Court, which ruled 9–0 against Judge Greer and in favor of the blacks. In the first appearance of an attorney general before the Supreme Court in thirteen years, William Rogers said, "Georgia has refused to register teachers of her own schools who were graduates of her own colleges on the grounds that they were illiterate." Federal district judge William Bootle then enjoined the registrars from administering different tests for blacks and whites.

Even though Georgia was becoming increasingly urbanized, the steadily shrinking rural vote still held control of the state Capitol. The county unit system remained an obstacle to political progress and fair representation. In 1958, Fulton County had one unit for each 21,666 voters, while Chattahoochee County had one unit for each 155 voters— this gave a Chattahoochee resident over two hundred times the voting power of an Atlantan in a statewide election. In 1958, Atlanta's Mayor Hartsfield challenged the system's validity, but the courts upheld the plan. By 1960, the thirty-eight most populous counties with two-thirds of the state's population elected only about 40 percent of the legislators.

The demise of Georgia's county unit system began with an Alabama reapportionment case, when Tuskegee Institute and all but five black voters were gerrymandered out of the city. Charles G. Gomillon, chairman of the Social Science Division of Tuskegee, sued Tuskegee Mayor Philip Lightfoot and won in the Supreme Court in 1960. Two years later, the Supreme Court ordered the reapportionment of state legislatures on the basis of "one man, one vote." Within hours after this decision was announced, Atlanta attorneys filed against Georgia's county unit system. The decision in *Gray v. Sanders* said that the system was unconstitutional; a related case, *Toombs v. Fortson*, required reapportionment of the legislature. In 1965, *Wesberry v. Sanders* applied the one man, one vote rule to Georgia's congressional districts. The door was at last opened to effective black political participation in Georgia. By then, Senator Talmadge was already busy building a "Negro machine."

"Separate but Equal" Flunks in Court

After World War II, Georgia's blacks had no better chance to get a decent public education than they did previously. In 1949, the median number of years in school for blacks was four; for whites it was eight. Less than a third of Georgia counties had high schools blacks could attend. Investment in land, buildings, and equipment to teach black children was less than one-quarter of that allocated to whites.

The NAACP had long pursued a plan to change this. In 1929 the Garland Fund gave the NAACP $100,000 to mount an attack on segregation. In 1934 the NAACP sent Howard Law School head Charles Houston, mastermind of the school desegregation movement, on a fact-finding tour of the South, which included a stop in Augusta. The NAACP decided to begin its assault at the postgraduate level, where opportunities were especially sparse. The first Supreme Court victory came in 1938, when the University of Missouri was required to admit blacks if equal educational facilities were not otherwise available. This ruling was an ominous sign for the status quo. Nevertheless, when three blacks applied for admission to the University of Georgia in 1939, President Harmon W. Caldwell said that Georgia was not ready "just now" to admit them.

The court continued to rule that black graduate students should be admitted to state institutions because the separate education offered to blacks was unequal, hence unconstitutional. In an attempt to undermine the NAACP's position, fourteen Southern governors met in 1947 to discuss developing a regional university for blacks. There were no blacks at this meeting, but Rufus Clement of Atlanta University was one of three black college presidents invited to a follow-up meeting to work out details. None of them supported the idea of a segregated university, so the plan was dropped.

Until the contract plan was adopted in 1943, Georgia remained one of nine Southern states with no provisions for graduate school or professional training for blacks. Under this plan to forestall integration, Southern states that barred blacks from their colleges would pay schools elsewhere to accept them. Georgia paid the difference between out-of-state tuition and Georgia tuition and also funded two round trips per year between the student's home and school. Some black graduate students were grateful for the superior educations they got in out-of-state schools. Up to 2,700 black students took advantage of the state's program during its heyday in the 1950s, when the state spent nearly $300,000 a year to keep black graduate students out of state schools. The contract program was discontinued in 1967, but those who had already started graduate work were allowed to continue. By 1970, Georgia had paid over $4 million under the plan.

Meanwhile, Georgia's black colleges grew and changed. Atlanta University, the flagship of black education in the South, continued to mature. In 1945, Horace Mann Bond left Fort Valley State College to become the first black president of his alma mater, Lincoln University, in Pennsylvania. By 1947, Georgia State College (renamed Savannah State College in 1950) had a budget of $343,000, 885 students, and fifteen thousand books in the library. By upgrading Georgia's three public black colleges, Georgia hoped to thwart the NAACP's plans. A $3,715,000 campus building program for black colleges was launched while Herman Talmadge was governor.

By 1950 it was apparent that the Supreme Court would eventually rule against all unequal educational opportunities for blacks. In a futile attempt to forestall the inevitable, Southern states also tried to make facilities and conditions more equal for black elementary and high school students. Black initiatives provided a helpful push. One of the first victories in the battle to improve public schools for blacks was equal pay for black teachers.

In 1936, Martin Luther King, Sr., helped organize teachers who wanted to protest unequal pay. They were afraid of losing their jobs by protesting or even voting. In 1944 the Atlanta School Board started the "Track and Step" plan for teacher pay. Most blacks were stuck in the lowest level, Track I, which started at $175 a month and could "step" up to $250 after sixteen years of service. In 1946, black principals averaged $240 a month, $100 less than their white counterparts. With Austin T. Walden as his attorney, high school principal William H. Reeves sued in 1947 to receive the same pay a white principal would receive. Reeves knew he would be fired quickly for "making trouble." By arrangement, he was hired by Atlanta Life Insurance Company, whose leaders supported the suit. "We had to guarantee this job security before anyone would become involved with the court case," Daddy King explained. The suit was ultimately successful. In 1951 the average starting pay for black teachers was $1,655 a year, 77 percent of the white salary. The equalization provision was applied in 1952, with $2,400 as the average annual pay. With increased pay came higher educational qualifications among black teachers, and by 1952, the per capita expenditures per black student had gone from one-third to two-thirds of that for whites.

In 1951, Georgia enacted a Minimum Foundation Program for Education financed by a 3 percent sales tax. Over half the new money was slated for black schools, although the school population was only one-third black. For the first time in some Georgia towns, black students went to the new school, while whites went to a separate but older building.

The NAACP's 1951 national convention was held in Atlanta, where delegates received Mayor Hartsfield's official greeting. Hartsfield shook hands with blacks and called them "Mister" when he was campaigning and said that Atlanta was "the city too busy to hate," but city hall water fountains, restrooms, and other public accommodations remained segregated. UN official and Nobel Peace Prize winner Dr. Ralph Bunche addressed the convention. While he was the first black to receive a police escort through the city, he could not stay in a downtown hotel. Meanwhile, plans were being laid. At the convention, NAACP attorney Thurgood Marshall met with colleagues "for the final rush on Jim Crow."

Georgia's leaders were fearful of an adverse decision by the Supreme Court and continued efforts to upgrade black schools so they could claim they were equal. At the same time, they lashed out at anyone with opposing views. The Board of Regents fired Albany State College President Aaron Brown for participating in an NAACP voter registration drive. In 1953, as the likelihood of a legal defeat on school segregation appeared strong, Talmadge, Lt. Gov. Marvin Griffin, and Attorney General Eugene Cook promoted a voucher plan to finance private schools that they hoped would be beyond the court's reach. Talmadge said that state payments to private schools were the only way to prevent "strife and bloodshed" if the court ruled to strike down segregated schools.

Several desegregation cases are now known collectively as *Brown v. the*

Board of Education of Topeka. Linda Brown was a Kansas schoolgirl who had to walk across town to a black school when there was a better white school only three blocks from her home. As a result of the NAACP suit filed on her behalf, the U. S. Supreme Court ruled unanimously on May 17, 1954, that school segregation was unconstitutional because "separate educational facilities are inherently unequal." Although it was a landmark decision, *Brown* did not sharply veer away from precedent. For fifteen years, the Supreme Court had been unanimously ruling against segregation in higher education. During this time, foreign and domestic pressures pushed the nation toward greater racial equality.

Georgia and Georgians provided important contributions to the case. Horace Mann Bond helped prove that state constitutions in the South after the Civil War did not include provisions for racial segregation, which indicated that the Fourteenth Amendment had outlawed this practice. John Julian Brooks was the NAACP's first expert witness. His testimony, based on nine years as an Atlanta teacher, detailed how blacks were disadvantaged in segregated schools.

There was much optimism in *Brown's* immediate aftermath. Georgia NAACP members were ecstatic. Less than a week after the decision, NAACP representatives from seventeen segregationist states met in Atlanta and declared that local branches should petition their school boards for immediate implementation of the decision. Articles in the national press said there would be little resistance. The *Atlanta Constitution* advised moderation: "It is no time to indulge demagogues on either side or those who are always ready to incite violence and hatred. . . . It is a time for Georgians to think clearly."

However, the progressives were overly optimistic; they seriously underestimated the forces of reaction. Six Georgia NAACP branches unsuccessfully petitioned school boards for an end to segregation; few white Georgians shared the NAACP position. Others, while disagreeing with the court, took the position that however disagreeable, the court's ruling was the law of the land. Many more white Georgians thought desegregation might be inevitable in the long run but 1954 was too soon; therefore, implementation must be delayed. For some, "too soon" was a euphemism for "never." Extreme segregationists, headed by Talmadge, did not bother with euphemisms. They said "never" loudly and often, labeled May 17 "Black Monday," and vowed to fight desegregation to the death. Within hours of the decision, Talmadge vowed that Georgia would never desegregate its schools and predicted that enforcement of the ruling would bring violence.

Because extreme segregationists held power then, Georgia led the way in resisting *Brown.* In Georgia it seemed that any position short of shooting or jailing integrationists was moderate in the 1950s. One 1954 gubernatorial candidate proposed a "three-school" plan: one for whites, one for blacks, and one for those crazy enough to want to integrate. Six weeks after the *Brown* decision, six people in Augusta asked the superior court for a charter for their new organization, the National Association for the Preservation of the White Race.

Although demagogues stood out, the problem lay in the prejudices of the many, not just with a few officials and a fringe of extreme white supremacists. Marvin Griffin, winner of the 1954 gubernatorial race, proclaimed, "Come hell or high water, races will not be mixed in Georgia's schools." He also promised to protect the state "from outside NAACP agitators." When Georgia voters elected Griffin, they also approved a constitutional amendment authorizing the expenditure of public money for private schools. This patently unconstitutional plan was intended to destroy the public school system in case of integration. It would not be Georgia's only show of contempt for the U. S. Constitution.

In the aftermath of *Brown*, Georgia passed several segregation laws and intensified its persecution of integrationists. Lawmakers proposed making teachers in private schools eligible for state pensions and made it a felony to teach a mixed class or use tax money for integrated schools. The Georgia Education Commission, created by statute, became the state's pro-segregation "steering body" to plot strategy and spy on "subversives." Some schoolteachers, both black and white, did not have their contracts renewed because of their stand on the race issue. The state school board resolved to revoke the license of any teacher who taught in an integrated classroom or who was a member of the NAACP, although it later rescinded its order. Dr. Guy H. Wells, president emeritus of the Georgia State College for Women at Milledgeville, was stripped of his title and almost lost his pension over the issue after he spoke at the private black Paine College against segregation in 1956. The state school board banned a song book because "brothers" had been substituted for "darkies" in two of Stephen Foster's songs.

For their part, state officials despised the NAACP. Talmadge had been concerned for some time that it was sneaking "subversive" books into school libraries. In 1955, the state attorney general labeled the group subversive because, he said, integration was "Communist inspired." A 1956 barratry law was designed to punish the NAACP for its lawsuits. (Barratry is the "offense" of being overly litigious.) Also that year, the NAACP's Atlanta branch president was jailed and the organization fined $25,000 for not turning over tax records to investigators. Then it was charged $17,000 for back state taxes that, as a non-profit organization, it did not owe.

The NAACP had long endured harassment in Georgia. In 1942, John Jenkins and Dr. E. M. Calhoun ran an advertisement in the *Macon Telegraph* asking blacks to join the NAACP and "fight for your rights." Before the newspaper was printed, they were questioned by a grand jury about "outside influences" and asked to abandon the effort. It required courage to openly support the NAACP in Georgia in the 1950s. During one period, the NAACP sent its fund-appeal letters to Georgia in plain envelopes with no return address to protect the recipients' identities. Although racial violence had subsided somewhat—1952 was the first year since Tuskegee Institute began keeping records in 1881 of U. S. lynchings that it reported none—there always had been danger involved in civil rights work. Dr. Thomas A. Brewer of Columbus, a leader in the Primus King voting rights case, was shot to death in 1956. Many people believed it was due to his civil rights advocacy. He had integrated the Columbus golf course and had several suits pending when he was killed. Only thirty brave souls attended the 1955 annual Emancipation Proclamation celebration in McRae, the home of the Talmadges. Despite the harassment, the NAACP grew in Georgia.

Facing growing delay and outright sabotage in the implementation of its decision, the Supreme Court felt compelled to strengthen the original *Brown* decision in 1955 with *Brown II*, which ordered compliance with "all deliberate speed." The year's delay had given opponents time to organize a campaign of "massive resistance" to subvert the Constitution. Walter George led the U. S. Senate fight to discredit *Brown*; meanwhile, the Georgia legislature called for the impeachment of Supreme Court justices.

In 1955, Governor Griffin said, "No matter how much the Supreme Court seeks to coat its bitter pill of tyranny, the people of Georgia and the South will not swallow it." He vowed, "If we have to choose between integrated schools and no schools at all, then we will have no schools at all." Southern segregationists were getting at least tacit encouragement from high places. The Eisenhower administration failed to provide proper support for the *Brown* ruling. Blacks were greatly disappointed in the president's failure to speak out for justice and equality. Instead, Eisenhower told Southern governors that he opposed the *Brown* decision. An avid golfer, Eisenhower often played at the segregated Augusta National Golf Course, home of the Masters.

Eisenhower ignored calls to act against persecution and terrorism directed toward Koinonia. An integrated communal farm run on Christian principles near Americus, Koinonia was founded in 1942 by Clarence Jordan and his wife, Florence, on 440 acres eight miles southwest of Americus. Except for a 1943 visit from the Klan, which objected to blacks and whites sitting down together to eat, Koinonia was generally ignored and did not make headlines until hysteria erupted over school integration. In 1956 some blacks tried to enter Georgia State College but were rejected because they had no alumni references (a new ploy colleges adopted to keep out blacks). When Jordan, a University of Georgia graduate, tried to help them, a Sumter County grand jury declared

Koinonia a Communist front. Banks refused further credit to Koinonia, and local merchants and suppliers started a boycott of the cooperative. The roadside stand where the farm sold its products was bombed three times starting in July 1956, and its insurance was canceled. The next year, nightriders shot up buildings, cut fences, and destroyed three hundred fruit trees. When Americus High School barred the children of Koinonia's partners (as the members of the commune were called), it took a lawsuit filed by the ACLU to get them reinstated.

Resistance to desegregation was encouraged by federal apathy and bolstered by Georgia politicians. In 1955, between stints in the governor's office and the U. S. Senate, Herman Talmadge published *You and Segregation*. Continuing to urge defiance to *Brown*, he wrote, "The citizens of the sovereign states are the court of last resort." White defiance was permanently symbolized on July 1, 1956, when Georgia's state flag was changed to include the battle flag of the Confederacy. It signified that white Georgians, once willing to die to protect slavery, were also willing to die to protect segregation. That year, ninety-six Southern congressmen, including the entire Georgia delegation, signed what became known as the Southern Manifesto, a vow to resist the "illegal" *Brown* decision.

White Citizens' Councils and similar groups like the Georgia States' Rights Council were organized to nullify the *Brown* decision and intimidate white and black integrationists. Roy V. Harris, publisher of the *Augusta Courier* and four-time speaker of the Georgia House of Representatives, helped organize the first statewide meeting of the council in Augusta in December 1954. The organization forced the cancellation of the thirteenth annual Soap Box Derby in July 1955 because two contestants were black. Georgia's council never developed the strength that others in the Deep South did. It originally hoped for 150,000 members, but in its peak year of 1958, it had only 10,000. While the council was nicknamed "the white collar Klan," with some justification, the middle-class segregationists in councils shied away from Klan terrorism.

In 1956, the legislature enacted five laws to lay the groundwork for a private school system and seven to reinforce segregation on state property and in public accommodations. It also approved a resolution, with only one dissenting vote, declaring the *Brown* decision "null and void." One law denied state funds to any school board permitting integration. The University of Georgia also tightened entrance requirements in the face of black applicants.

In 1957, the state board of education outlawed all interracial meetings and organizations and the legislature memorialized Congress to repeal the Fourteenth and Fifteenth amendments. It also gave the governor power to suspend compulsory school attendance laws, first enacted in 1916, for any child forced to attend school with a child of another race.

Ernest Vandiver was elected Georgia governor in 1958 with the campaign slogan "No, Not One," which referred to the number of black children he wanted to see in white schools. He was stamped from the same mold as his predecessors, Talmadge and Griffin, the "Never, Never" boys. While campaigning Vandiver said, "There is not enough money in the federal treasury or enough federal troops to force us to mix the races in the classrooms of Georgia while I am your governor."

Under Vandiver, the legislature passed several more laws against school integration that authorized the governor to close any school ordered to integrate, allowed state income tax credit for contributions to private schools, and let the state pay the legal expenses of any school system taken to court for its failure to abide by integration orders.

While some Georgians may have believed they had successfully warded off school integration, these efforts were only delaying tactics. Black leaders, with little white support, had been whittling away at segregation patterns for some time. In 1955, a lower court's sanction of the exclusion of blacks from an Atlanta golf course was overturned by the Supreme Court, which used *Brown* as a precedent.

Despite the massive resistance of Georgia's leaders, Atlanta led the way in public school desegregation in the Deep South. In 1957, a group of eighty Atlanta ministers issued a statement condemning intolerance and urging obedience to the law. The States' Rights Council attacked the ministers as enemies of Christ. The following year, a larger group of 312 ministers and rabbis, including all but five of the city's prominent white clergymen, reaffirmed the earlier group's stand.

In 1958, the NAACP filed suit on behalf of ten black parents seeking the admission of their children into all-white Atlanta public schools. Constance Baker Motley was the lead attorney for the plaintiffs. State efforts to make "separate" become "equal" by building several new schools in black neighborhoods fell short of the people's needs. The schools lacked books, and the notorious practice of double-shifting was still going on in black schools, most of which were old, unattractive, and rundown. When one white school was converted to black use, the front door was bricked up so that students could use only the rear entrance. In November, Herman Talmadge said that the state might close its public schools if the NAACP won the suit. Senator Russell echoed by saying that "the fight to preserve the white race in Georgia" had not even started. Vandiver pledged to tighten segregation laws.

The NAACP won its case. In 1959, U. S. District Court Judge Frank Hooper ordered the Atlanta school board to come up with a desegregation plan. The board approved a "stair step" plan that would desegregate the twelfth grade in the fall of 1960 and one additional grade in descending order each year; by 1973 the entire system would be desegregated. Because the plan's implementation was postponed for a year, the two top grades were scheduled for desegregation in the fall of 1961. One reason for the delay was the legislature's threat to cut off Atlanta's school funds.

In January 1960, Vandiver told legislators, "Let us hope the NAACP will not force the closing of a single school," and was greeted with a storm of applause and rebel yells. Meanwhile, prominent white businessmen and leaders were warning politicians to move away from their obstructionist stance. Manchester banker James S. Peters, chairman of the state board of education and elder statesman in the Talmadge segregation plans, wrote a letter to Roy Harris stating that integration was inevitable and that closing the schools would destroy Talmadge politically. W. R. Bowdoin, vice president of the Trust Company of Georgia, noted that many national companies with Georgia branches were concerned about the level of education of their workers. Mills B. Lane, Jr., president of the Citizens and Southern Bank, said that the state could lose one industrial plant for every day schools were closed.

The legislature adjourned in February after appointing the Sibley Commission to study school desegregation. Judge Hooper delayed his final ruling while the nineteen-member panel held hearings in all the state's congressional districts and heard 1,620 witnesses. The hearings gave segregationists an opportunity to vent their feelings. Chairman John T. Sibley was sympathetic but reminded the public that the law must be obeyed. In all, the majority of witnesses in five districts favored school closings, four districts favored local option, and one district was divided on the issue. In heavily black South Georgia, there was more white sentiment for closing schools. The nation had an opportunity to follow along through the media. The May 27, 1960, "CBS Reports" was based on the commission's work. One film clip showed *Albany Herald* publisher James H. Gray, the force behind local resistance to desegregation, testifying angrily. Ultimately, the commission voted eleven for local option and eight for closing the schools if necessary to prevent integration. "Local option" was the bridge to ending state laws requiring segregation. Support for desegregation developed with time. In May 1960, the president of the Georgia Bar Association called for the repeal of segregation laws. And at the 1960 fall meeting of the Georgia Baptist Convention representing nearly a million communicants, a resolution was passed against closing the schools.

During this time, Atlanta was the scene of a multifaceted protest. In addition to the drive for desegregating schools, many blacks were involved in the sit-in protests demanding desegregation of the lunch counters and added a boycott of downtown stores to force them to hire blacks. In mid-December 1960 the black English Avenue Elementary School was bombed. Feeling this combination of pressures, the chamber of commerce headed a drive to get businesses to oppose school closing. Mayor Hartsfield said, "It is time for the substantial citizens of Atlanta, the people who own its great stores, office buildings, plants, and factories, to assert themselves."

Segregation at the University of Georgia had ended under court order in January 1961. Under mounting pressure to be reasonable, Governor Vandiver reversed his position and came out for local option. He warned the state legislature:

> Failure to resolve (the school crisis) will blight our state. Like a cancerous growth, it will devour progress, consuming all in its path, pitting friend against friend, demoralizing all that is good, stifling the economic growth of the state and denying the youth of Georgia their proper educational opportunity.

Although Roy Harris denounced him, the legislature voted to wipe out all public school segregation laws. However, it also voted to provide money to parents wishing to send their children to private schools. Catholic church leaders made plans to desegregate parochial schools when the public schools did in the fall. Downtown merchants also agreed to desegregate stores in the fall. Diehard Herman Talmadge fought on, but he was beginning to feel pressure from constituents to moderate his stand.

Atlanta's news media, church leaders, civic clubs, and other groups and individuals worked to make school desegregation peaceful and orderly. HOPE (Help Our Public Education, founded in 1959) merged with twenty-six other organizations in April 1961 to form OASIS (Organization Assisting Schools in September). The new umbrella group organized a speakers bureau, distributed literature, and succeeded in bringing white and black students together. Robert Woodruff, head of the Coca-Cola Company, worked behind the scenes to promote progress, as did longtime civil rights leader Dorothy Tilly. When the Klan threatened to bomb her home, Mayor Hartsfield provided police protection.

In May 1961, the school board began accepting applications from blacks seeking to transfer to white schools. More than 135 of the 3,500 blacks in the eleventh and twelfth grades wanted to transfer. Based on grades and personal interviews, ten were selected. They all tested higher academically than the average white students in the schools they were integrating. One of the black students then decided to go to Spelman instead.

Atlanta was tense as dawn broke on August 30. Although city officials had learned the lessons of Little Rock and New Orleans, there was the very real prospect of Klan bombs. Nazi George Lincoln Rockwell had threatened demonstrations. The ubiquitous racist J. B. Stoner was scurrying around the fringes of the scene. To encourage intimidation of the handful of pioneering black students, the Klan had issued a leaflet with their names, addresses, and pictures. The police geared up for trouble and had armored cars ready to quell any disturbances.

Unlike Little Rock and New Orleans, there were no howling mobs in Atlanta. When the nine black students, accompanied by black policemen in civilian dress, entered Brown, Grady, Northside and Murphy high schools, there were no especially notable incidents, although four white youths were arrested for disturbing the peace and later exchanged Nazi salutes in court. President Kennedy began his August 30 press conference by congratulating the city for its "responsible, law-abiding manner." Security was relaxed the next day. The Southern Regional Council sent Harvard psychiatrist Robert Coles to counsel the black students and monitor the schools they attended. This experience later became part of the background of Coles's five-volume, Pulitzer Prize-winning *Children of Crisis.*

Integration proceeded so well that the "stair step" plan was accelerated in 1964 and scrapped in 1965; all grades were integrated by 1967. Gradually less attention was paid to a teacher's color when positions were assigned. In 1965, West Fulton High School got its first black counselor. Half the teachers in the Head Start program were black, and Atlanta's school superintendent received only one complaint that year from a white mother about her child being taught by a black.

With the exception of a few freedmen who tried to enter the University of Georgia during Reconstruction and the three 1939 applicants, the first black to challenge segregation in the university was Horace Ward, a black teacher in Georgia who tried to enter the university's law school in 1950. When he was denied entrance he appealed, but university officials continued to deny him admission. Ward sued, but he was drafted into military service in 1953 before the case could be decided. At that time a graduate student poll showed little opposition to blacks who were already attending graduate schools in eight other Southern states. When Ward completed his military service two years later, the suit was still unresolved so he entered Northwestern University Law School.

The trial started in December 1956. The university claimed Ward was unqualified because his work at Morehouse College and Atlanta University was in schools that were not accredited by the Southern Association of Colleges and Secondary Schools. Of course, the association accredited no black schools then.* The suit was dismissed as moot because Ward had

---

*In 1957, Albany State, Atlanta University, Clark, Fort Valley, and Morehouse were admitted into the association. The Association of Colleges and Secondary Schools for Negroes, founded at Spelman in 1933, was disbanded in 1964.

enrolled in another university. After graduation, Ward returned to Georgia and began a successful career as an attorney. He later served in the state Senate and was appointed a federal district judge in 1979 by President Jimmy Carter.

In another attempt to desegregate the university, Pfc. Winfred Mundle of Fort Benning registered with the University of Georgia in March 1956 for a correspondence course in criminology. Although he had a law degree from Georgetown University, the registrar at Athens said Mundle would have to take an entrance examination to take the course. This was a ploy to discourage him, since the course would close before he could take the test. Mundle advised Harlem's militant black congressman Adam Clayton Powell, Jr., that the only place segregation still existed in army correspondence programs was at the Fort Benning center, where black students were all steered to Albany State College. The NAACP pursued the case, but the army sidestepped the issue by transferring Mundle to Fort Belvoir. The army then issued a directive that segregation in Fort Benning's educational activities must cease. The university responded by moving its extension facility to Baker High School in Columbus, where state laws required segregation.

Charlayne Hunter and Hamilton Holmes broke the color line at the University of Georgia several months before Atlanta began its desegregation. Both Hunter and Holmes applied to the university after their 1959 graduation with honors from Atlanta's Turner High School. They were denied admission purportedly because they had applied too late, so Hunter entered Wayne State University and Holmes enrolled in Morehouse College, and they continued their attempts to enroll at Georgia. Holmes's mother, an Atlanta schoolteacher, received harassing phone calls when he applied for transfer and admission at Athens. Federal judge William Bootle ordered their admission on January 10, 1961, ruling in a case in which they were represented by Horace Ward and his partner Donald L. Hollowell, with assistance from veteran civil rights attorney Constance Baker Motley. Bootle then stayed his order; appeals judge Elbert Tuttle reversed the stay, and the Supreme Court backed Tuttle.

When Hunter and Holmes arrived on campus Vandiver moved to cut off state funds (and to change the laws that required the cutoff). Judge Bootle enjoined the governor from denying state funds to the university, however. Hundreds of the school's seventy-four hundred students signed a petition against closing the university. Other students, augmented by part of the crowd coming from a January 11 Georgia-Georgia Tech basketball game, joined Klan leader Calvin Craig and his minions in rioting outside Charlayne Hunter's dormitory. Windows were broken and rocks were thrown at the Athens police and university personnel headed by William Tate, dean of men, who "stood like a wall" against the rioters, according to Hunter. Fire hoses and tear gas finally dispersed the mob of two thousand.

Hunter and Holmes were suspended the following day and taken to their Atlanta homes by the state police. That evening, the local chapter of the American Association of University Professors called a faculty meeting to protest the expulsion, and half of the six hundred faculty came. History professor Horace Montgomery prepared a resolution supporting the readmission of the two that eventually four hundred faculty signed. On January 16, Judge Bootle ordered Hamilton and Holmes readmitted. Two students and eight Klansmen involved in the riots were indicted, and thirteen students were suspended from the university for their part in the disturbances. Despite widespread support for Hunter and Holmes and condemnation of the rioters, the Georgia legislature passed a resolution praising the faculty who refused to sign the faculty petition and urged reinstatement of the expelled troublemaking students.

The two pioneers had to endure considerable harassment before they earned their degrees. Holmes found the faculty basically decent, but some of his classmates, while civil in the classroom, would turn their heads to avoid greeting him on campus. Holmes drove home every weekend and often hated the prospect of returning on Mondays. His tires were punctured several times. When he was hassled by members of Kappa Alpha, a fraternity that venerated the Confederacy and flew its flag, he made them think he carried a gun. Harold Black, another early black student at Georgia, had bricks and firecrackers thrown into his dormitory room.

Holmes and Hunter became two of the university's most celebrated graduates. Hamilton Holmes graduated cum laude, with a Phi Beta Kappa key and a $1,200 scholarship to Emory Medical School. (Although theology and graduate students had called for Emory to begin admitting qualified black students in the mid-1950s, the school did not admit its first black student until 1962.) Holmes graduated from Emory in 1967 and became a respected orthopedic surgeon, with offices in Atlanta and Conyers, and a trustee of the University of Georgia Foundation. Charlayne Hunter received a journalism degree. She worked for the *New York Times* and the *New Yorker* before joining public television's "MacNeil-Lehrer Report" in 1977. She was appointed to the advisory board of the University of Georgia School of Journalism. The university instituted a Hunter-Holmes lectureship in 1985. In 1988, Charlayne Hunter-Gault became the first black to deliver the University of Georgia's commencement address. She did not sugarcoat her message. She recalled that her often unpleasant college days were spent "amid misunderstanding, confusion—and hate," and told graduates that the school "has not prepared you for the real world... one in which people of color are on the ascendancy." While she praised university President Charles Knapp's attempts to increase black faculty, she pointed out that the Confederate flag still flew on campus and that blacks made up less than 5 percent of that year's graduating class.

Barriers fell in other Georgia colleges soon after Holmes and Hunter matriculated at Athens. Ignoring a minor Klan demonstration, three blacks entered the Georgia Institute of Technology (Georgia Tech) the following fall, after the school voluntarily removed the color bar. A poll of Georgia Tech students—when emotions regarding Hamilton and Holmes were at a fever pitch—showed that 75 percent favored integration over closing. Georgia Tech already had nonwhite students from foreign lands.

Macon's private Mercer University admitted two blacks in 1963. One, Bennie M. Stephens, a graduate of Macon's Appling High School, was no stranger to discrimination. The other, Sam Oni, had just arrived from Nigeria, where an alumnus missionary had recommended Mercer. Oni had difficulty coping with the insults and abuse. He is the subject of a book, *Ashes for Breakfast*, by Thomas J. Holmes, pastor of Oni's church. Oni worked in the civil rights movement, and after graduation he founded Project Ploughshare to encourage self-sufficiency in Africa. Cecil Dewberry transferred from Fort Valley State College to become Mercer's first black graduate in 1965.

Atlanta's civic leaders would point with pride to the fact that the city had desegregated its schools peacefully. While the first steps toward integration had been taken, the vast majority of Georgia's schoolchildren continued to go to segregated schools. Residential segregation would continue to play a key role in most school districts, and smaller cities and towns were still years away from compliance with the 1954 Supreme Court decision. Although the "separate but equal" education afforded blacks in Georgia became less separate and more equal in the twenty years after World War II, there was far to go before truly equal opportunities would be available. More than just schools were involved. Inequality in income and medical care and discrimination throughout society would remain significant obstacles.

11

The Civil Rights Movement

"The South in Miniature"

Racial repression, injustice, and brutality in Georgia and elsewhere had not gone completely unnoticed and unprotested. Although it was sometimes difficult to appreciate at the time, during the 1950s the nation gradually awakened to at least part of the black experience. As Cold War tensions intensified after World War II, the Soviet Union and the United States vied for the support of Third World nations in disputes before the United Nations. Both superpowers wanted to be known as the one true champion of the world's downtrodden and tried to undermine each other's claims. Potential allies judged the United States partly on how its darker-skinned people were treated. A propaganda war was on. *Pravda*, official newspaper of the Soviet Communist Party, greatly exaggerated U. S. lynchings in 1948, although many blacks in Georgia would have agreed with the description in the *Great Soviet Encyclopedia* of the American Georgia as an "economically backward, agrarian state with strong remnants of slavery."

There was a wave of racial violence in the South triggered by the bombing murder of Florida NAACP president Harry Moore and his wife near the end of 1951. U. S. and Soviet Communists claimed Moore's killing showed that the United States was willing to commit genocide on blacks. "The Bomb Heard Round the World," as Moore's killing was called, "demonstrated conclusively that U. S. racists must answer to a new judge and jury—world opinion." Soon afterward a black social club in Rome, Georgia, was bombed while a party was in progress. Although

Tuskegee Institute reported no lynchings in 1952, the NAACP called 1952 "The Year of the Hate Bomb." In 1953, whites threw a tear-gas bomb on a bus filled with Augusta blacks, injuring six. Following another year with no reported lynchings, Tuskegee announced in 1954 that it was abandoning its annual lynching report. The next year, there were three in Mississippi, including the killing of Emmett Till. The Associated Press reported 530 racially motivated killings, beatings, and bombings in the South from 1955 to 1959.

Oppression tarnished the nation's reputation. American travelers abroad were embarrassed by questions on the race problem and Soviet bloc UN delegates increased their taunting of the United States for its treatment of blacks. Georgia was singled out for contempt. The intense criticism of American race relations emanating from the Soviet bloc was an important reason why the situation in the United States began to improve.

Some American blacks associated with the Civil Rights Congress—perhaps hoping to force change at a faster rate—helped load Soviet propaganda weapons by presenting a petition to the UN General Assembly in 1951. "We Charge Genocide" listed hundreds of acts of violence against blacks in the United States between 1945 and 1951—murder, rape, bombings, peonage, and other violations of civil liberties, including 140 acts of terrorism in Georgia. The petition also used statistics on the poor life expectancy, infant mortality, education, health care, and diet of blacks. It declared that the white power structure, if left to itself, would wipe out blacks as a people.

The United Nations had adopted an antigenocide treaty that member nations were expected to ratify. Even though President Truman signed it in 1949, the U. S. Senate refused to ratify the treaty amid concerns that lynching might be construed as a genocidal practice. Finally, in 1986, the United States joined ninety-six other nations in ratifying the Genocide Treaty, but only after adding a provision that the World Court rulings would not be binding on the United States.

Truman, in part responding to Cold War pressures, signed an executive order desegregating the armed forces in July 1948. Blacks organized to support the order, and A. Philip Randolph threatened organized draft resistance and civil disobedience by blacks if it were not put into effect. Also, the Korean War experience of black and white fighting men softened the views somewhat of Rep. Carl Vinson of Georgia and Sen. Richard Russell, both chairmen of their respective Armed Services Committees, at least toward military segregation. In 1953, Fort Benning was the only post in the nation that still had segregated facilities. When it was desegregated that September, Governor Talmadge branded it a mistake, explaining that neither whites nor blacks wanted desegregation.

As African-Americans watched black Africans strike off the restrictive shackles of colonialism and independent African states emerge after World War II, their desire for more freedom here was increased, and their will to struggle was encouraged by every step toward freedom that Africans took. When the twenty-seven-year-old leader of the Kenyan independence movement, Tom Mboya, visited Georgia in 1957, he met an equally youthful Andrew Young, who was so impressed by Mboya's commitment to the cause of freedom for his people that Young vowed to commit himself to the freedom of American blacks.

Black hopes of a more just society, uplifted on May 17, 1954, and reinforced the next year by *Brown II*, had been dashed by a wave of massive resistance to desegregation led by Georgia politicians. The Supreme Court's ruling looked like another empty vow in a long series of broken promises that stretched back nearly two hundred years to the Declaration of Independence. Rather than despair, blacks grew angry at white defiance of the law of the land. The anger led to bravery, and something resembling a revolution erupted—not out of hopelessness but in expectation of a better future. When militant Harlem congressman Adam Clayton Powell, Jr., spoke in Atlanta to a black audience, reporter Pat Watters was surprised "not so much at his wild insistence that Negroes had the same rights as white people, but at the fervent response, the glad assent of all those Negro Atlantans, those faceless, familiar black people in such unfamiliar behavior."

Even though blacks were ready for change, most Southern whites were not. Although in 1949 representatives of fifteen Protestant denominations in ten Southern states met in Atlanta and labeled most white racial attitudes "un-Christian" and called for white Christians to take the initiative to change them, the vast majority of white churchgoers remained intransigent. Most white Christians who might have disagreed with ardent white supremacists were cowed into silence. In 1957, the Rev. Robert B. McNeill, after over six years as pastor, was ousted from a white Presbyterian church in then 30-percent black Columbus for advocating in a national magazine not desegregation but only "creative contact" with blacks to take the indignity out of segregation. The successful ouster was started by a small minority of fifty of the twelve hundred members of the church.

The black church continued to provide much of the leadership for the revolt against the stifling status quo. In the mid-1950s, the nation's attention shifted to Montgomery, Alabama, where a black Baptist minister from Atlanta rose to prominence. The Montgomery Movement is generally considered the opening battle of the black revolution, a revolution that brought ten years of Southern brutality.

Martin Luther King, Jr., a third-generation activist minister, was born in his parents' home in Atlanta on January 15, 1929. He grew up in a literate family and considered a life of service to humanity at an early age. In the 1930s, he endured the shattering experiences that were ingrained in the experience of all blacks who lived then. His white preschool playmates abandoned him at their parents' insistence when they reached school age. When, in the eleventh grade, he was forced to give up his seat on a bus to a white, "It was the angriest I have ever been in my life," he recalled. He vividly remembered his father being called "boy" by a policeman and learned a lesson in dignity when his father told the officer that young Martin was the only boy in the car. He sometimes despaired of getting shoes because his father refused to sit with him in the back of shoe stores.

Martin Luther King, Sr., well understood the many forms of white retaliation that immobilized black protest. When he was not able to get other ministers to join him in protesting Jim Crow at Atlanta's city hall, he went alone and, despite threats of arrest, was able to end segregation on the elevators and at the water fountains. He also understood the role of white paternalism in coopting blacks. When his daughter Christine, who had a double master's degree from Spelman, applied to teach in Atlanta, she was turned down because the school board did not approve of her father's activities. A phone call from "Daddy" to Mayor Hartsfield got her the job, but the idea was troubling that connections, not merit, were what counted.

After high school, Martin Jr. entered Morehouse at age fifteen and worked during the summers in Connecticut tobacco fields. At Morehouse, under the influence of Benjamin Mays, he abandoned his earlier ambition to become an attorney and opted for theology. He graduated number one from the Crozier Theological Seminary in 1951 and received his Ph.D. degree from Boston University in 1955. In Boston he met Coretta Scott, an Alabama native who was studying at the New England Conservatory of Music. Despite some initial objections from his father, they were married in 1953 and decided to come south the following year when he received the call from the Montgomery, Alabama, Dexter Avenue Baptist Church. There he put his evolving philosophy of social justice into practice.

Montgomery's blacks had long chafed under the strictures of Jim Crow. They seized an opportunity when Rosa Parks was arrested for refusing to give up her seat to a white man on December 1, 1955. A meeting of Montgomery ministers the Monday after Parks's arrest revealed much timidity and fear. When King said he was not afraid to take action, he was nominated to head what history now calls the Montgomery Movement. The 381-day bus boycott succeeded due to the strength, determination, and dedication of Montgomery's blacks, who wore out their shoes walking, and the three hundred autos volunteered for the car pools. The Montgomery bus boycott catapulted the little-known King to national fame. Montgomery's blacks also prevailed in court. The NAACP filed suit, and the U. S. Supreme Court ruled on December 19, 1956, that segregated bus seating in Montgomery was unconstitutional.

Many activist ministers had become involved in the struggle and organized the Southern Christian Leadership Conference (SCLC) in Atlanta in 1957 to enlarge the arena of the civil rights movement. Veteran civil rights activist Ella Baker was named executive director. (She was later replaced by Wyatt T. Walker.) The first SCLC campaign, "Crusade for Citizenship" was held throughout the South to register voters. King said, "If Atlanta succeeds, the South will succeed. If Atlanta fails, the South will fail, for Atlanta is the South in miniature." The Crusade for Citizenship did not prove to be very successful, but the battle had just begun.

With segregated seating on city buses declared unconstitutional in Montgomery, Atlantans would have to change also. Atlanta's leaders, both black and white, chose an orderly process. White leaders did not want to appear to be giving in to black pressure that a boycott would represent but would abide by a court decree. Therefore, the courts would be provided with a test case. In January 1957, six black Atlanta ministers (William Holmes Borders, A. Franklin Fisher, Robert H. Shorts, Howard Bussy, R. H. Williams, and B. J. Johnson) got on a bus and sat in the front. The driver pulled to the curb with "mechanical trouble," which was fixed as soon as the six got off. Governor Griffin put the militia on standby, and all six ministers were indicted for violating Jim Crow laws. It was a civilized event. According to the *Atlanta Constitution*, the ministers "spent a day convincing a reluctant police chief (Herbert Jenkins) to arrest them, and in a telling symbol of civil rights warfare Atlanta-style, the cell door was never closed."

Another suit was filed by two other ministers, King's associate John Porter and local NAACP president Sam Williams. On January 9, 1959, federal U. S. District Court Judge Frank A. Hooper ruled on the Porter-Williams suit and outlawed Atlanta's segregated seating on public transportation but refused to grant injunctive relief to the plaintiffs. Bus integration began on January 22, 1959, after a rally at which black leaders told the men not to sit by white women but otherwise to sit where they pleased.

Despite the change in bus seating, Atlanta was still a thoroughly segregated city, although it had become the South's center for black political, economic, and cultural development and enjoyed a progressive image. John Howard Griffin, a Georgia-born white who dyed his skin dark and traveled through the South in 1959 to see what it was like to be a black in Dixie, wrote *Black Like Me*. He concluded that Atlanta was a progressive community for blacks because of a large educated Negro population. That year, the *New York Times* labeled Atlanta the most moderate Southern city on segregation and Birmingham the least. Yet in Atlanta, Paschal's Restaurant, a landmark founded in 1959, for several years would be one of the few places whites and blacks could eat together.

King had survived bombing attempts in Alabama and a near-fatal stabbing in New York by the time he moved to Atlanta on February 1, 1960, to devote more time to the SCLC. When he said blacks should break any state law not in harmony with federal statutes, Governor Vandiver promptly attacked King and kept him under constant surveillance. He joined his father as copastor of the Ebenezer Baptist Church at a salary of $6,000 a year. The SCLC, which had little money, paid him one dollar a year, and King gave to the movement everything over $5,000 a year from his book royalties and honoraria. At their peak, they ran as high as $230,000 a year.

The black revolt entered a new phase on the day King moved back to Atlanta, when four students of the black North Carolina Agricultural and Technical College went downtown in Greensboro, North Carolina, to perform the simple, revolutionary act of sitting down at the Woolworth lunch counter and ordering food. To most whites, this was an outrage. Service was refused, so the students just sat, and the "sit-in" was born.

Lonnie King, a navy veteran and Morehouse football player, read of the Greensboro events in the *Atlanta Daily World* and with Julian Bond organized a meeting of students three days later that formed the Atlanta Committee on Appeal for Human Rights. This group favored immediate action, but President Clement of Atlanta University and other more conservative blacks counseled delay and helped get money for the committee to buy newspaper space to publish their "Appeal for Human Rights." The appeal criticized both black and white leaders. Georgia officials quickly recognized the threat to white supremacy. On February 18, 1960, the legislature passed an antitrespassing law that made it a crime to refuse to leave a business when requested to do so. Vandiver described the students' demand to end segregation as "un-American" and Communist inspired.

The students considered boycotts the most effective tactic, while more conservative blacks favored the ballot. (Whitney Young, dean of Atlanta University's School of Social Work since 1954, was one of the few Atlanta University Center faculty to work closely with student protesters. He became director of the National Urban League in 1961.) The sit-ins began a week after the "Appeal" ran when it became clear there would be no immediate positive white response. The *Atlanta Daily World* criticized the students; they were in turn disgusted with the *World* and founded a new newspaper, the *Inquirer*, with Julian Bond as the managing editor. Bond's wife, Alice, worked as office manager, receptionist, and makeup editor.

What one journalist called "the Second Battle of Atlanta" began on

March 15 when two hundred students sat in at ten downtown lunch counters. They struck the state Capitol restaurant when six students went through the serving line. Instead of taking their money, the cashier called the lieutenant governor, who told them to leave. They refused and were arrested and taken to Fulton County Jail. Seventy-seven were arrested under the new antitrespass law. All through 1960, Atlanta had the South's largest and best organized sit-ins. Variations on the sit-in included "wade-ins" to desegregate public swimming pools, "read-ins" at libraries, "kneel-ins" at churches, and "stand-ins" at voter registration offices. The protests put Georgians on edge. When black youths accused white youths of molesting black girls, a fight broke out at the Marietta town square resulting in some injuries and fourteen arrests.

In April 1960, the Student Nonviolent Coordinating Committee (SNCC) was formed in Raleigh, North Carolina. Committee members came to Atlanta in May to meet with King, and an office was opened to raise money and to coordinate all the demonstrations in the South. The established civil rights organizations—NAACP, SCLC, and the Congress of Racial Equality (CORE)—each wanted the students as a youth division. The students wanted independence. Ella Baker encouraged the students to remain independent despite King's wish that they become part of the SCLC. The youths in Nashville and Atlanta each wanted control of SNCC, so a compromise was reached. Marion Berry of Nashville, later mayor of Washington, D.C., was chairman. Headquarters were in Atlanta in an office shared with the SCLC. John Lewis, later to be a Georgia congressman, became chairman in 1963.

Early attempts to bring local white college students in on the protests met with less than resounding success. The Field Foundation furnished $60,000 to bring black and white students together for seminars on race relations under the auspices of the National Student Alliance (NSA). Agnes Scott College graduate Connie Curry ran the local NSA office. Present at SNCC's founding, she was the only white on the SNCC executive committee at the time. She tried to recruit students from Atlanta's white colleges to join the sit-ins. Six white college students attended just one meeting "because they were terrified," Curry said. "Oh, it was just hysterical... they took one look at Lonnie King and all those students and never said a word and went home that night and we never heard of 'em again."

Many of the sit-in leaders received training and encouragement at the Highlander Folk School established in 1932 at Monteagle, Tennessee, by Myles Horton with the encouragement of Eleanor Roosevelt and Will Alexander, director of the Commission on Interracial Cooperation. It was integrated from the beginning and helped to train trade-union leaders, especially in the textile industries in the 1940s. In 1953 it began to hold classes in race relations and by 1960 was the foremost meeting place for civil rights activists. John Lewis and Julian Bond came to Highlander for training in the practice and tactics of nonviolence; here, for the first time, Lewis sat down and ate with whites. At Highlander, black students learned the song that became the movement hymn, "We Shall Overcome," perhaps the most influential song since the "Marseillaise" or "The Battle Hymn of the Republic." Georgia's leaders called Highlander a Communist training school and spied on it. In 1961, Tennessee shut down Highlander because it was interracial and confiscated all of Horton's property, leaving him broke and convicted of violating the state's Jim Crow laws. Highlander soon reopened near Knoxville and continued to support the civil rights movement. King realized that many of the young leaders who were emerging would need training, and the SCLC held joint programs with Highlander to do this. The SCLC also opened a training center to teach the theory and tactics of peaceful protest at the Dorchester Community Center in Liberty County, Georgia. By 1963, six hundred militant, nonviolent activists had graduated from it.

The first lunch-counter desegregation suit to go to the federal courts came on August 3, 1960, when Austin T. Walden filed class-action suits against the state, Fulton County, and the city of Atlanta for maintaining segregated eating facilities. Governor Vandiver reacted by closing the state Capitol cafeteria on August 8. Mayor Hartsfield then closed the city hall cafeteria to the general public but allowed the twenty-two black employees to eat with those of the 582 white employees who cared to stay.

Dr. King was one of dozens of protesters arrested when he went with a group of students on October 19 to sit in at the Magnolia Room of Rich's Department Store, then one of Atlanta's fancier dining places. King and fourteen of the students refused bond. The day after the arrests at Rich's, there were twenty-two more arrests. There were protests against the arrests; one group, the Jewish Labor Council, asked presidential candidates Richard Nixon and John Kennedy to intervene on behalf of the students. The students added "fair employment" to their demands. Hartsfield appealed to old-line black leaders for a sixty- to ninety-day cooling-off period. They agreed on thirty days. The twenty-two students were released. King stayed in jail.

King endured legal trouble as well as threats to his life. When he moved to Atlanta from Montgomery, he did not obtain a Georgia driver's license. In May 1960 he was driving in DeKalb County with well-known author Lillian Smith and was stopped by police, who disliked seeing an integrated automobile. He was cited for not having a Georgia license and on September 23 was fined twenty-five dollars and put on probation for a year. King paid the fine, but apparently his lawyer failed to inform him that he had been put on probation. After his October sit-in arrest, King was charged with violating probation. He was sentenced to four months at hard labor and taken to the state prison at Reidsville in handcuffs during the dead of night on October 26. Amid great fear that he would be murdered by racists in the jail, many people protested King's incarceration, which became a major event in the climaxing presidential election.

King had asked Kennedy earlier to come to Georgia to speak on civil rights, but the two men were unable to come to terms on issues and logistics. However, when Kennedy learned that King was deep in the bowels of "Georgia justice," he called Coretta King to express his sympathy and offer his assistance. Campaign director Robert Kennedy also called the judge to protest his denial of bail to King. Some accounts credit John Kennedy with arranging King's release through Governor Vandiver, who reportedly contacted sentencing judge Oscar Mitchell to obtain King's release. However, the release came on October 27, after Mitchell ruled during a scheduled hearing on a motion by attorney Donald Hollowell to release King on $2,000 bond. Mitchell said the release was mandatory under Georgia law.

Daddy King switched his considerable support to Kennedy, as did many traditionally Republican blacks throughout the nation. The Kennedy campaign, which had been initially skittish about becoming involved in the case, decided to contrast Kennedy's concern with Nixon's apathy—without alienating white voters. The Democrats distributed a million copies of a leaflet that contained glowing statements by the Kings to black churches across the nation on the weekend before the election. Although Republican officials were aware of the case and considered doing something, they took no action. At the time, Nixon believed that his loss of black votes from doing nothing would be more than offset by Kennedy's loss of white votes for speaking out. If the decision had been left only to whites, Nixon would have been elected president in 1960. However, Kennedy won the presidency by history's narrowest margin after receiving overwhelming black support.

In Atlanta, 33,163 blacks voted in the 1960 election, the vast majority for Kennedy. (He carried Georgia with 63 percent of the vote.) Although a stronger civil rights bill was enacted in 1960, Georgia still had several counties, dominated by the rural courthouse rings, where no blacks were allowed to vote. A foreign observer did not have to travel far from Atlanta to see the "other" Georgia. On Election Day, a diplomat of the Ghanian embassy, escorted by a U. S. Commerce Department guide, was sent to Georgia to observe electoral procedures, only to be roughed up by the police in Mableton, near Atlanta, and ejected from the polling place. White voters apparently resented his presence.

The Kennedys understood the implications of such incidents and the need to counter them. The following May, when Robert Kennedy spoke at the University of Georgia on Law Day, the attorney general delivered a "resolute" speech on civil rights to a crowd in which state politicians were noticeably absent. "In the worldwide struggle, the graduation at this university of Charlayne Hunter and Hamilton Holmes will without question aid and assist the fight against Communist political infiltration," Kennedy said. "Burmese and Congolese will see before their eyes Americans living by the rule of law." His comments were greeted by polite silence from the sixteen hundred members in the audience. Outside, five fundamentalist preachers paraded with signs stating, "The Bible teaches segregation" on sidewalks that had "Yankee Go Home" painted on them.

Martin Luther King, Jr., believed that Kennedy was an improvement over Eisenhower, but the new president was somewhat paralyzed on the subject of civil rights due to his slim margin of victory and his perceived dependence on the Southern wing of the Democratic party. Vandiver claimed in 1961 that he had made a deal with Kennedy. He would support Kennedy in exchange for a promise that Kennedy would never send troops to Georgia, as Eisenhower had at Little Rock. As it turned out, events in Georgia did not require such action. Although Kennedy planned to appoint Benjamin Mays to the Civil Rights Commission, he changed his mind when senators Russell and Talmadge objected.

By October 1960, four national chains had integrated lunch counters in 150 of their stores in 112 cities, but none of them were in Georgia. Still, there were heartening successes in the state: H. D. Coke, a black insurance executive from Birmingham, won his suit to prevent Dobbs House from putting blacks behind screens at its Atlanta airport restaurants, which led the Columbus airport to desegregate its facilities voluntarily in October. Even arrests provided opportunities. After his arrest, CORE member Charles H. Seniors filed suit to desegregate Atlanta's misdemeanor courts.

White merchants refused to negotiate, and the thirty-day cooling-off period ended on November 25. The protests were stepped up. Picketing resumed at thirteen stores, with white students from Emory and Agnes Scott joining the black students. They added a boycott of downtown merchants that refused to hire blacks but welcomed black customers and their money. Pickets wore signs reading "Wear Old Clothes and New Dignity"; "The Presence of Segregation Is the Absence of Democracy"; and "Close Your Charge Account with Segregation and Open Up Your Account with Freedom." There were no arrests. However, downtown lunch counters were closed except at the YWCA, which served five blacks along with white diners on November 30.

The city "too busy to hate" was having trouble living up to its motto, for the *Brown* decision and the civil rights movement brought an upsurge of Klan activity. H. J. Jones of Jonesboro, Georgia, announced the formation of another splinter group, the Knights of the Ku Klux Klan, which, he said, planned for an eventual membership of 10 million. In October, the Klan was implicated in the flogging of two blacks in Carroll County.

The student protest brought a counterdemonstration of a hundred robed and hooded picketing Klansmen at Rich's. Georgia KKK Grand Dragon Calvin Craig passed out leaflets. Lester Maddox, head of another pro-segregation group, Georgians Unwilling To Surrender (GUTS), persuaded the Klan pickets to leave, perhaps because, as Lonnie King said, they kept the customers out better than the students. Six Klansmen picketed the *Journal-Constitution* building because they considered the newspaper soft on segregation. White supremacists had long referred to Ralph McGill, its progressive editor, as Rastus, a derogatory nickname similar to "Sambo." (McGill won a 1958 Pulitzer Prize for editorials against racial and religious intolerance.)

Atlanta was becoming a focus of national interest, and the protesters were gaining strength and sympathy from near and far. The Rev. William Holmes Borders, chairman of the Student-Adult Liaison Committee, continued to try to negotiate with merchants, who still refused to make concessions. On December 3, seventy-five people picketed Macy's department store in New York City because its Atlanta branch, Davison's, did not integrate. On December 11, eight thousand blacks attended a prayer meeting at Atlanta's Herndon Stadium, and two thousand of them marched downtown to support desegregation and to bolster the sit-in demonstrators. On December 15, the chamber of commerce refused to meet with black leaders to seek an end to the demonstrations.

By February 1, 1961, the first anniversary of the sit-in movement, there were few results to show for the protests other than the arrest of many demonstrators. The frustrated students became more militant in the face of white merchants' refusal to end Jim Crow and intensified the boycott, which was nearly total on the part of Atlanta blacks. The anniversary was marked by a march of two thousand from Morris Brown College to the Capitol. Then the sit-in movement adopted the "jail—no bail" policy, first used in Rock Hill, South Carolina, when SNCC activists served out their full thirty-day sentences. Atlanta saw many more arrests, and the students refused to come out on bail. In jail, they studied for exams. On February 7, seventeen students were arrested in a cafeteria that served federal employees. Twenty more were arrested on February 8, thirty-nine the following day, and ten the next as the "jail—no bail" policy spread. On February 15 seven black ministers and one white minister were arrested for demonstrating on behalf of the jailed students. The white was the Rev. R. W. Anderson, who was then doing missionary work for Koinonia.

Rich's was the main holdout, though it had in the past contributed generously to Negro causes and was one of the first stores where blacks were addressed as "Mr." or "Mrs." Economic pressure worked, however.

Downtown business was off 14 percent during one week in February, and the city's merchants were forced to concede that the boycott had been almost 100 percent effective. The militant students might thrive on the antagonism of whites, but to obtain concessions, conservative blacks had to step in and negotiate. Negotiations between Walden and chamber of commerce head Ivan Allen and Robert B. Troutman, Rich's attorney, yielded results. Black and white leaders met with sit-in leaders Lonnie King and Herschelle Sullivan and told them on March 6 that the lunch counters would be desegregated the following fall, when the schools were. Demonstrations would end. Trespassing charges against the students would be dropped. Some six hundred black workers who had lost their jobs in downtown stores during the demonstrations would be rehired.

Walden and Daddy King favored accepting the proposal, since it was a far greater concession than the white power structure had ever offered before. The younger people, impatient and wanting more immediate results for their efforts in the sit-ins, were not ready to accept it. At a stormy March 10 meeting of fifteen hundred blacks at the Warren Memorial Methodist Church, students almost repudiated the agreement and attacked Daddy King and others for selling out, booing and hissing them as they took to the pulpit to defend the agreement. Martin Luther King, Jr., deeply embarrassed for his father, then spoke eloquently to reconcile the young and the old. The agreement held.

Atlanta quietly awaited school and public accommodations desegregation, which came in the fall. The desegregation agreement catapulted Ivan Allen into the mayor's office. On the day of the agreement, the Georgia Court of Appeals ruled that Judge Mitchell's one-year probation on King's traffic conviction was excessive and voided his prison sentence.

The South, which had previously refused to serve black customers on equal terms, was forced to begin to change its ways. From the first sit-in in February 1960 until August 1961, over seventy thousand black and white demonstrators were involved in twenty states. Almost ten thousand were arrested, and 141 students and 58 faculty were dismissed from various schools, but eating places were desegregated in 108 cities, including three in Georgia.

This did not mean the end of segregation in Atlanta. A year later, the state legislature, that bastion of the status quo, still maintained segregated seating in its gallery. This had been challenged by students beginning in 1958, when an integrated group from Spelman was ejected. In 1961, Dr. Ovid Futch, a white Morehouse College professor, and two students, William Anderson and Alton Hornsby, Jr., sat together in the Negro side of the gallery. House members cheered when the doorkeeper ejected them. In 1962, when groups led by CORE leader James Forman and Julian Bond tried to sit together, they were refused admission, as was

Howard Zinn, a white Spelman professor, when he tried to join his black friends on their side of the gallery. Blacks were also arrested for picketing the legislature and for trying to desegregate the white clinic at Grady Hospital.

The protest movement continued to draw strength from the black church. Students engaged in the sit-ins went to the churches to speak and win support throughout Georgia; many ministers encouraged their rebellion. Despite minor concessions and noble-sounding pronouncements and resolutions by governing officials, Georgia's white churches nearly unanimously turned a deaf ear to the just grievances of blacks. To be a moderate white Christian in Georgia during the 1960s generally meant remaining silent on racial matters, and that meant consent to the status quo of white supremacy. This was especially true of rural Georgia.

In 1959, Atlanta's Druid Hills Presbyterian Church voted to admit blacks during church services. They were required to sit in segregated pews. Because they were among the last institutions to integrate, churches were also targets of the Atlanta sit-in movement, with mixed results. Blacks were admitted to four of the six churches they visited on August 7, 1960. The following Sunday, small student groups held "kneel-ins" at six white Atlanta churches without incident, while groups were turned away at four other services. The next Sunday, all "kneel-iners" were turned away.

In 1961, Paine College students were denied admission to Augusta's white Methodist and Baptist churches. That year, three Atlanta black Presbyterian churches were scheduled for admission into the Atlanta presbytery if black Presbyterians would agree to restrict their activities and not "unwisely" attempt to mingle. White feelings about the occasional black worshipper in a white church changed from open hostility to apparent toleration when it became obvious that blacks did not particularly want to attend the white services and would come only to test the point that they would not be excluded.

As with other denominations, there was a great contradiction between official Southern Baptist Convention (SBC) theories on race relations and the actual practice of the members. The SBC seminaries officially desegregated and enrolled a black student in 1951, three years before the Supreme Court ruled in the Brown case. In 1956, Georgia white Baptists approved incorporating Negro congregations into white conferences. Yet rank-and-file white Baptists manned the barricades against integration.

The civil rights movement created a strain not only between white and black churches but also within the black Baptist community. The Progressive National Baptist Convention was formed by the more trained and forward looking clergy following a schism within the National Baptist Convention USA in 1961. Progressives favored a limited-tenure presidency and supported Dr. Martin Luther King, Jr., more than the older group, which was headed by an avowed enemy of King's, the Rev. Joseph H. Jackson of Chicago's Mount Olive Baptist Church. King's efforts to influence the National Baptist Convention failed, and Jackson, an entrenched conservative, did not support the civil rights movement.

Jews, long victims of prejudice, needed less prodding than white Christians to help blacks. A 1958 *Time* survey indicated that 50 percent of Southern Protestant and Catholic clergy opposed desegregation, whereas 75 percent of Southern Jews, who were less than 1 percent of the total population, were sympathetic to the idea of more rights for blacks, although their small number and desire to get along with the white majority led many of them to keep silent.

White church leaders most opposed to black advances were the same ones most inclined to be anti-Semitic. As violence rose against blacks, Jews also became more frequent terrorist targets. Rabbi Jacob M. Rothschild, who came to Atlanta in 1946, expressed his shame at race hatred, chided the Rotary Club for its racism, and called on Jews to act more forthrightly to combat race discrimination. He publicly supported and worked for school desegregation, and his synagogue, the Atlanta Temple, was bombed on October 11, 1958. A wave of anti-Jewish violence forced Southern Jewish leaders, who had been silent on race relations since the Leo Frank lynching, to speak out as Rothschild urged them to. Jews marched side by side with blacks throughout the freedom movement of the 1960s.

Although there was much more work to be done, Atlanta's civil rights struggle disappeared from the headlines after the March 7 agreement. Then the freedom rides, organized by CORE, the nonviolent Chicago-based civil rights organization, to test court rulings desegregating interstate transportation, hit the South like a thunderbolt in the spring of 1961.

Although the U. S. Supreme Court ruled against segregated interstate public transportation in 1946, its decision had been ignored (except by Eugene Talmadge, who used it in his race-baiting 1946 gubernatorial campaign). Georgia first became involved in the issue in 1951, when James L. P. Rumble of New York City asked a U. S. District Court to rule against Georgia's segregation laws in public transportation because his business required him to travel to Georgia. The following year, when Rosalynd C. Richardson, a West Virginia college teacher, was arrested in Athens for not sitting in the back of a Greyhound bus, the judge instructed the jury to find in her behalf. The ruling had little effect. When James White returned from Korea and got on a Milledgeville-bound bus in Atlanta, the white driver said, "All you niggers get in back."

In December 1960, the Supreme Court had extended the 1946 ruling to include terminal accommodations and trains. The freedom rides began on May 4, 1961, when a group of seven black and six white CORE members left Washington. When they reached Atlanta on May 13, they found the restaurant at the Greyhound terminal closed but were able to eat at the Trailways terminal without incident. This was in contrast to the violence that was perpetrated on freedom riders in Alabama and Mississippi and the arrests that followed. Soon there were more than 360 freedom riders in Mississippi jails under the "jail—no bail" policy.

Media exposure and public pressure forced the federal government to act. Although the trials and appeals continued for years (the U. S. Supreme Court overturned the protesters' convictions in 1965), the freedom rides soon proved successful. On May 29, the U. S. attorney general called on the ICC to abolish segregation. On September 22, the ICC issued an order abolishing Jim Crow in interstate transportation, and the order went into effect on November 1.

Although victory in the civil rights struggle in Atlanta was far from complete, in September 1961, 254 establishments, some of which had been closed since the preceding Thanksgiving, agreed to serve blacks. Although similar gains had been won in more than a hundred Southern and border communities earlier, Atlanta was the largest city up to then to accede to the demands of the protesters. Atlanta became a model for other cities, such as New Orleans. Rich's Magnolia Room was desegregated by four well-dressed, white-gloved black women on September 28, shortly after the lunch rush hour had ended.

The students' great victory did not signal the death of Jim Crow in Atlanta. The NAACP held its annual convention there in July 1962. When UN undersecretary Ralph Bunche attended the convention, he was refused accommodations in a downtown hotel, just as he had been eleven years before. Most of the forty-eight main hotels and seventy motels refused to desegregate even for the convention; delegates were served food in some places and turned away at others. The Defensive League of Registered Americans, a tiny group of segregationists, joined with a few Nazis and Klansmen on Stone Mountain on July 4 to protest the NAACP convention. About a hundred showed up for this hate rally, and a few robed Klansmen wandered downtown to the bemusement of passersby. For these and other reasons, King thought that the NAACP convention slogan commemorating the centenary of the Emancipation Proclamation,

"Free by '63," was overly optimistic and picked the year 2000 as a more realistic date.

Albany and Other Places

A month after the first student lunch-counter sit-in, Senator Russell organized one of history's longest filibusters against the 1960 civil rights bill. It passed in May—after sections designed to ease school and employment discrimination were removed. The new federal law made it a criminal offense to interfere with voters in federal elections, provided for federal poll referees, and abolished literacy tests. Along with black initiatives such as the sit-ins, freedom rides, and the work of the SCLC, the NAACP, and SNCC, the new law threatened Georgia's oligarchic political system, whose leaders felt besieged and fought back, especially outside Atlanta. Voting rights were the key to victory in the struggle, which had all the elements of a morality play.

The federal government took action against segregation of blacks and whites in polling places—a practice that was not only demeaning but held the potential for corruption, since counting ballots separately did not necessarily mean counting them equally. The Clinch County town of Homerville abolished separate voting lines and boxes when local officials received a letter from the Justice Department in April 1962 stating that Judge William Bootle had ruled the custom unconstitutional. Macon chose to defy Judge Bootle. In the federal government's first attempt to challenge physical segregation in the election process, the Justice Department sued Macon. Judge Bootle ordered half the polling places desegregated by September and the rest within a year. The FBI also investigated segregation at the polls in Fayette and Peach counties, where people voted separately but dropped ballots into one box. Fayette County had 1,255 voting-age blacks but only 25 were registered; nearly all 3,500 whites were ready to vote.

In Atlanta, beyond the reach of courthouse rings, 41 percent of eligible blacks voted in 1960, but of Georgia's thirty-six counties with a black majority, only Liberty County had majority black registration. Liberty, with its Congregationalist heritage, also was home to the SCLC training center at Dorchester. Nearby McIntosh County had regularly elected black legislators until disfranchisement went into effect in 1908, and in 1961, Darien High School Principal Chester A. Devillars became the first black to sit on a voter registration board in modern Georgia. In many Georgia localities, whites put up strong resistance when an active black community pushed for voting rights, desegregation, and equal opportunity. There were fights between white and black youths in many places.

One in the Gwinnett County town of Buford resulted in the arrest of forty-two in August 1961. In many cases sheriffs led the fight to maintain white supremacy and insisted blacks behave subserviently. Dr. King described one Georgia sheriff as meaner than Jim Clark, Selma, Alabama's infamous sheriff. "Something about a Negro wearing a hat drove him crazy," King said. "He would yell, 'take off that hat, boy.'"

Problems were especially great in Southwest Georgia, which drew federal attention in 1960 because it was home to one of the nation's four "cipher" counties, where not a single black voted. In Webster County, not one of thirteen hundred voting-age blacks was even *registered*, whereas 934 of 949 whites were. This feat was accomplished by the use of a "voucher" system, where two registered voters had to "vouch" for each new voter, much as Georgia's colleges required alumni references so that they could exclude black applicants in the 1950s. Early County was also investigated.

In 1961, Albany, Southwest Georgia's largest city, would take center stage in the civil rights struggle. Located near Plains, in the heart of Georgia's peanut, pecan, and watermelon country, Albany had done little since World War II to draw much attention. Blacks constituted 80 percent of Dougherty County's population in 1900, but due to migrations, by 1960 they were outnumbered forty thousand to twenty-six thousand.

The lethargy was broken slightly in the 1950s when Albany State College President Aaron Brown was dismissed by the regents for joining the NAACP. However, the town had been relatively unaffected by the sit-in movement and the freedom rides, although a small group of blacks circulated a modest petition for change early that year. The segregationist *Albany Herald* condemned the call for reform, and the city commission rejected it. More hints of unrest came when white hoodlums drove through the black college campus throwing eggs, firing shots, and allegedly trying to run down students. Also, white men were sexually harassing women students in their dormitories. Students protested the attacks, but the conservative black college administration was disinclined to help.

SNCC's Atlanta leaders decided they needed to work in South Georgia. They believed a voter registration drive would draw the least white backlash. Then, no longer afraid of white retaliation, blacks throughout the South would troop to the polls and begin to exert more control over their lives. Albany, with its large black population, would serve as a center of operations. Historian Howard Zinn wrote that Albany was picked because black students

> wanted to return...to the source of their people's agony, to that area which was the heart of the plantation system...to cleanse it once and for all time. Albany was...surrounded by the past. In the

counties around Albany blacks outnumbered whites; they worked the land and lived in shacks and didn't dare to raise a single cry against the rutted order of their lives.

Charles Sherrod and Cordell Reagon, SNCC veterans of Mississippi and the freedom rides, arrived in Albany in the early fall of 1961 with twelve dollars between them. They were later joined by Charles Jones. Sherrod was SNCC's field director for voter registration. In addition to his voting rights work, the young black Baptist preacher also planned to test the ICC's desegregation decree. Such plans seemed dangerously radical to some fearful blacks, who crossed the street to avoid Sherrod. When SNCC workers went to the Albany State campus, they were ordered to leave by college officials, who wanted very much to get along with the white power structure. The two activists stayed with Emanuel and Goldie Jackson, who were later fired from their jobs. She was a college librarian and he was a circulation manager for the *Albany Herald*. Blacks considered *Herald* publisher James H. Gray their most formidable enemy, with good reason. As chairman of the state Democratic party, he was guardian of Georgia's soon-to-be-outlawed county unit system, "the white man's best friend."

Sherrod and Reagon recruited students, gained support from local black churches, and conducted workshops in nonviolent protest. When the ICC ruling went into effect on November 1, the local NAACP Youth Council planned, but canceled, its test of railroad-terminal segregation. Sherrod and Reagon hastily put together a SNCC effort. They rode a bus from Atlanta to Albany, but their attempt to test the new rule was prevented by a dozen city police officers who blocked the riders from the white waiting room at the Trailways station. Later that day, nine students who went into the station's white waiting room were ordered out by police. They complied—it was not time for jail yet—and filed affidavits with the ICC. This was the beginning of a long struggle against Albany officials, led by Police Chief Laurie Pritchett, who was both adamant and cunningly nonviolent in enforcing segregation.

Whites were so out of touch with attitudes in the black community that they were shocked and angry when long-simmering discontent boiled to the surface. Albany soon became a center of black protest, and events there became front-page news. Albany began as a local movement as black youths insistently demanded their rights. Black townspeople followed their lead. To coordinate protests, the NAACP Youth Council, the Black Ministers Alliance, and other groups formed the Albany Movement on November 17, 1961. "Those kids were going to do it anyway. We didn't want them to have to do it alone," said movement president Dr. William G. Anderson. Real estate broker Slater King was vice president.

On November 22, three black high school students and Albany State students Bertha Gober and Blanton Hall were arrested for standing in the "white" line to buy Trailways tickets. Albany State dean Charles Minor went out of his way to cooperate with law officials; he had gone to the station and preached obedience to Jim Crow laws, then suspended Gober and Hall. At Mount Zion Baptist Church on November 25, movement leaders addressed a packed auditorium. Tensions heightened on Monday, when the five students went on trial. About five hundred blacks gathered outside the courthouse to protest. The students were found guilty, and Charles Jones led a protest march to Albany State. Not only did college president William H. Dennis, Jr., refuse to meet with protesters; he also swore out warrants for the arrest of the three SNCC activists. Only Sherrod spent a night in jail, because state authorities told Dennis to withdraw the warrants before Reagon and Jones could be apprehended— they probably planned to prosecute the SNCC workers themselves. Some students involved in the protests were fired from part-time campus jobs. Protests and retaliation continued. Soon forty-eight more students were suspended or expelled. They received offers from Atlanta colleges to complete the year.

On December 10, eleven freedom riders (including James Forman, formerly of CORE, now SNCC's executive secretary, and white activist Tom Hayden) rode from Atlanta to Albany. They were arrested after leaving the railroad terminal's white waiting room and charged with "obstructing traffic." The arrests fired up the protest movement. Mayor Asa Kelley later said, "We never should have arrested those freedom riders. That's what started all our troubles." The police chief called a news conference to announce that four freedom riders had criminal records, failing to mention that the arrests had come in nonviolent civil rights protests. Pritchett did say, "We can't tolerate the NAACP or the SNCC or any other nigger organization to take over this town with mass demonstrations." As the freedom riders' trial began on December 12, nearly three hundred black students marched on city hall and were arrested en masse. The next day, Slater King and seventy others were arrested in another protest. That night, another two hundred protesters were arrested. King was charged with contempt of court and sentenced to five days in the city jail, where a jailer roughed him up. Sherrod was sent to the Terrell County Jail, where he was slapped for not saying "sir" to a white man. Over five hundred arrests had been made. Pritchett said the arrests would continue "if I have to put them in jails all over Georgia." Gov. Ernest Vandiver dispatched the National Guard to Albany.

While there were some behind-the-scenes (and fruitless) biracial negotiations going on, the movement entered a new phase on December 13 at Shiloh Baptist Church with a call for a boycott of white merchants. Dr. Anderson asked old college friend Martin Luther King, Jr., to come to Albany and lend his considerable support. (Anderson had helped King organize a NAACP branch at Morehouse.) King intended to come, speak, and quickly return to Atlanta. Once again, he was drawn into leadership he did not originally seek. Nevertheless, there he was, on the night of December 15, telling an overflow crowd at Shiloh, "We will wear them down with our capacity to suffer." King was so moved by the people's enthusiasm and determination that he committed himself to the Albany Movement and promised to lead a march the next day.

King's presence, the mass arrests, and heightened tensions brought television news coverage, which in turn developed nationwide support for the Albany Movement and brought activists trekking to the city. On December 16, Dr. King, Ralph David Abernathy, 263 blacks, and one white University of Georgia student were arrested when they knelt in prayer on the city hall steps in protest against the city's refusal to release jailed demonstrators. By then the police had made more than 750 arrests, which created a crisis for the movement. Where were its lawyers and bail money, since the city refused to release demonstrators without bond? White lawyers were often unwilling to help, with the exception of those sent by the ACLU and the National Lawyers Guild. The NAACP sent some attorneys. Local black lawyer C. B. King (Slater's brother) and Atlanta's Donald Hollowell and partner Howard Moore also worked steadfastly with the Albany Movement.

C. B. King and Hollowell arranged a truce with Pritchett that provided for release of jailed demonstrators on bond, a thirty-day cooling-off period with no demonstrations and no boycotts, and an end to segregation in railroad and bus terminals. The city commission also would consider forming a biracial committee to discuss other grievances. With the crisis apparently resolved, Martin Luther King allowed himself to be bailed out of jail. The last of the jailed demonstrators were released on December 19. The city's promise to discuss reforms sapped the movement during the Christmas season. Unfortunately, the agreement turned out to be a sham. The only part implemented was the desegregation of the Trailways bus terminal. Critics questioned King's sincerity, for he had promised to stay in jail until conditions were remedied. City officials denied making any concessions.

Already, internal divisions within the Albany Movement were causing problems. The most serious split came between the SCLC and SNCC. Albany Movement secretary Marion Page said that the SCLC seemed to be trying to take over what SNCC had started. SNCC students derisively referred to Martin Luther King, Jr., as "De Lawd" and SCLC as "SLICK." They resented King's media attention and his perceived lack of militancy, and they were willing to claim credit for his defeats. When SNCC was originally formed, King viewed it as a child of SCLC and was very supportive, but Atlanta students were distrustful of the older leaders' conservatism. The SCLC-SNCC split opened in Albany. SNCC did most of the work, while the SCLC received the attention and the money. When the SCLC called a meeting in Albany, SNCC would call a countermeeting. There were other schisms. Local NAACP president E. D. Hamilton told SNCC students to leave Albany, and Sherrod told the NAACP youth that they needed new leadership. When Vernon Jordan, then an NAACP field secretary, and Ruby Hurley came to Albany, they castigated SNCC for trying to steal NAACP members. SNCC organized direct action, which meant they needed people to march, and SNCC had little patience with the NAACP's slower, legalistic approach. Forman was attacked by the NAACP as a Communist, a charge that was also leveled at SNCC as a whole. Later, Julian Bond expressed one of SNCC's objections to the SCLC when he said King "sold the idea that one man will come to your town and save you." This was an unfair criticism, as were many of the criticisms that were traded around. The SCLC was not above the fray. It was notorious for pirating employees from other organizations, and some of its staffers referred to the NAACP as the "Black Bourgeoisie Club." Recriminations were nasty, and Dr. King admitted this when he told the 1962 NAACP national convention, "We are enticed into self-serving statements and borderline slander about others to furnish gossip and colorful copy."

Forman objected to King's presence in Albany because the movement had enough local support to grow on its own. After all, it was attracting adults and getting media coverage. Forman believed that the rank and file needed the experience of maintaining a protest without the help of a charismatic national leader. One reason for the feud was that publicity meant money. Whoever got the most media attention would collect the most contributions. (In February, King started a fund-raising effort for the Albany Movement.) To King, Albany presented an opportunity to try out the plan that later worked at Birmingham and Selma: "Select as a target a community dominated by racist officials likely to employ severe repression; mount a well-organized campaign galvanizing thousands of blacks into action; and supply detailed information to cooperative mass media."

On January 12, black student Ola Mae Quarterman was arrested for not sitting at the back of a city bus and using obscene language when ordered to the back. She said, "I paid my damned twenty cents, and I can sit where I want." The arrest started a bus boycott and signaled a shift from mass demonstrations to "selective buying," the euphemism for a black boycott of white merchants. One grievance was that only Belk's Department Store and Silver's Ten Cent Store had restrooms that blacks could use. Eighty percent of the bus business was black, and a black car pool took its place. On January 23, 1962, Dr. Anderson and Marion Page appeared before the Albany City Commission and asked city leaders to reaffirm their oral agreement to desegregate public facilities, refund cash bonds for demonstrators in exchange for property bonds, and form a biracial commission to look at race problems. Despite the city's earlier pledge to discuss the issues, immediately after the two black leaders made their appearance, the meeting was abruptly adjourned. There was no good faith on the part of city leaders. Hard-line segregationists controlled the commission and were willing to concede nothing to the movement, even though the bus boycott was so successful that the bus company's daily revenue was cut from $400 to $100. While the company was willing to desegregate, city officials would not permit it. The boycott forced the bus company to shut down operations.

Trials of hundreds of arrested demonstrators started February 27. King and Abernathy were defended by C. B. King and Hollowell in a three-hour trial before Recorder A. N. Durden, who delayed his verdict until July. The trial of the freedom riders was held in March. Charles Sherrod was knocked to the floor by a deputy when he tried to sit in the white section of the courtroom. Early in April, Dr. Anderson and three others were convicted of disorderly conduct for picketing a downtown store. Later that month, twenty-six more were arrested for sitting in, and twenty-nine were arrested while protesting the death of Walter Harris, a black café operator who was killed by police. In June, nine more protesters were arrested for picketing stores.

On July 10, 1962, King and Abernathy returned to face Durden, who found them guilty of unlawful assembly and sentenced them to forty-five days in jail or a $178 fine. They both said they would stay in jail and work on the street-repair gang with other prisoners, in accordance with the civil rights movement's "jail—no bail" policy. This revitalized the Albany Movement, which was once again in the headlines, thanks to King.

The next day, thirty-two marchers protested King's conviction. They were arrested, and there were violent clashes between the police and brick-throwing black youths. King's jailing made national news, and President Kennedy asked for a report on his case. Evidence that many of the foot soldiers in this battle for justice were suffering from battle fatigue came when only fifteen people at that night's Shiloh rally said they were willing to go to jail.

There was great consternation when King and Abernathy were expelled from jail after less than two days. The SCLC had returned the bail money sent by a group of New York state legislators. However, "an anonymous, well-dressed black man" paid the fines over King's objection. The money probably had been put up by a coalition of conservative whites and blacks who wanted to discredit the movement so that Albany could return to "the good old days." King was embarrassed, since he had promised to stay in for the full term of his sentence. Abernathy remarked ruefully, "I've been thrown out of a lot of places in my day, but never before have I been thrown out of a jail."

Demonstrations continued as protesters attempted to desegregate the Carnegie Library and ten other places in July. The efforts failed, but they quickened black interest; there were a thousand blacks at the nightly Shiloh meetings, five times the number that had been turning out just a few days before. One of the movement's strengths—the enthusiasm of ordinary people—came from the music. Singing brought people together. Many of Albany's older blacks came to early rallies to hear the music, then stayed to march. Albany native and movement leader Bernice Reagon called it a "singing movement," and its emotional fervor and depth of feeling "would take the roof off." Charles Jones believed there would have been no Albany Movement without the music. Police Chief Pritchett said, "Their singing incites them."

Not since the early days of the CIO had there been such an outpouring of protest songs. Many lyrics from spirituals, folk songs, and labor union songs were adapted to the local situation. In addition to singing the civil rights anthem, "We Shall Overcome," protesters converted the old slave song from "Gonna be free my Lord, come by here" to "They're bombing our houses Lord, come by here." The standard movement song "Ain't Gonna Let Nobody Turn Me Around" had lines adapted to Albany: "Ain't gonna let Pritchett turn me around...I'm on my way to freedom land...If you don't go don't hinder me...." SNCC realized their inspirational power and taught the songs in training sessions. Songs from Albany were used in countless later SNCC meetings.

Although many of Albany's white businessmen were willing to negotiate with the Albany Movement, conservatives on the city commission continued to dictate policy. Georgia's leaders backed the segregationists, even though Jim Crow was beginning to crumble in the state's larger cities. Governor Vandiver sent Freeman Leverett, deputy assistant attorney general, to plan Albany's strategy to maintain segregation. Vandiver applauded federal judge J. Robert Elliott, an avowed segregationist, when he handed down an injunction on July 20 against King and five other leaders that prohibited them from attending white churches or demonstrating. King denounced Elliott for engaging "in a conspiracy...to maintain the evil systems of segregation." However, King respected the injunction—to his later regret. The next day at Shiloh, the Rev. Samuel Wells of the Williams Springs Baptist Church led a group of two hundred, mostly teenagers, in a march defying the injunction while King remained in the church study. The protesters were all arrested. A heartened King said, "They can stop the leaders, but they can't stop the people."

After some quick maneuvering by movement attorneys, on July 24 the

Fifth Circuit Court of Appeals in Atlanta overturned Elliott's decision. There had been some previous clashes between rock-throwing black youths and police, and tensions erupted in Albany on the day of the ruling. Word was spreading that Slater King's pregnant wife had been beaten severely at the nearby Camilla jail. (She later miscarried.) Members of a crowd of about two thousand blacks went on a rampage after police arrested forty demonstrators that evening. One officer had two teeth knocked out. Pritchett yelled at reporters, "You see them nonviolent rocks?" Forty-one were arrested, and Vandiver offered to send twelve thousand National Guardsmen to quell disturbances. SCLC negotiator Andrew Young bawled out one group of violence-prone blacks: "You're too yellow to march. But you stand over there and throw things and give us a bad name." King called for a day of penance and spent the next day in shops, pool halls, and taverns urging everyone to remain cool. Raising funds and attracting sympathy depended on preserving the aura of moral superiority to the segregationists. Those who threw rocks at their tormentors hurt the cause.

On July 27, after two futile weeks of trying to meet with the recalcitrant city commission after he had been expelled from jail, King went with Abernathy, Anderson, and seven others to city hall. Pritchett refused to let them enter the building, so they knelt in prayer on the steps outside and were arrested. King and Abernathy went to jail for the third time. Two hours later, eighteen black youths were also arrested when they knelt in prayer outside city hall. William Hansen, a white SNCC worker with the group, had his jaw broken and was beaten unconscious in jail. The next day, when C. B. King came to check on Hansen's condition, he was clubbed with a heavy cane by Dougherty Sheriff Cull Campbell. The sheriff said, "I wanted him to know that I'm a white man and he's a damn nigger."

On August 1, President Kennedy urged a settlement and called Albany's refusal to negotiate "inexplicable." Mayor Kelley responded that this remark was "inappropriate" and that Albany would never negotiate with "outside agitators," even though he had tried to negotiate, only to be criticized by other city officials. Senator Russell charged that Kennedy was being "political."

City leaders sensed that the movement was faltering and believed tensions would ease if King left. King said he would gladly go if the officials would negotiate in good faith. King did go, the city did *not* negotiate in good faith, and a lack of results contributed to the relative apathy that settled in. The only thing to show for the massive effort that resulted in over twelve hundred arrests by August was the Trailways terminal desegregation. Schools and lunch counters remained segregated. The city had contended in court that there was no segregation in Albany, and to prevent a test, it temporarily closed its public facilities, including Tift Park. It sold the swimming pool to a private group, the better to maintain segregation. Pritchett bragged that the city was as segregated as ever. King then realized that obeying Elliott's injunction had been a mistake, because he had missed the chance to force the city's hand on Jim Crow. On August 10, Judge Durden found King and his fellow defendants guilty but suspended their sentences. Albany officials were determined to keep him *out* of jail.

Albany marked the most sustained, concentrated effort by civil rights groups in the country. On Sunday, August 12, St. Teresa's Roman Catholic Church and St. Paul's Protestant Episcopal Church admitted blacks for the first time. The next day, two whites and three blacks were convicted of loitering after they tried to integrate the local Holiday Inn. King returned to Albany that night and announced "segregation is on its deathbed in Albany," and the only question was how expensive the city would make the funeral. The next Sunday, three blacks were arrested for trying to attend the First Baptist Church. One local white minister publicly deplored the arrests. Efforts to integrate six of Albany's fifty white churches were repulsed that day.

The movement continued to draw sympathetic protests and support in Northern cities. Dr. King called on the nation's religious leaders to come to Albany after Robert Kennedy refused to send federal marshals there to protect blacks' civil rights. Kennedy believed there was no violence to stop. On August 28, fifty-four white and twenty-one black religious leaders from outside Georgia and five Georgia clergymen who had heeded King's call "congregated" on the sidewalk and did not disperse upon Pritchett's request. They were all jailed. For the record, the white Albany ministerial alliance opposed this invasion by "outside agitators." Fifteen of the men began a fast in the jail. King called attention to this and urged presidential mediation of the crisis. Five days into their fast they sent a letter via Andrew Young to President Kennedy urging him to speak out. They were released from jail on September 4, the eighth day of their fast. James Gray called the clergy's demonstration a "publicity stunt" and accused them of "practicing blasphemy." Mayor Kelley said Kennedy had made a mistake by calling on the city to negotiate with "outside agitators." However, Kelley had welcomed outside help from the state attorney general and state police. While Dr. King was the most famous "outsider" involved in Albany, there were as many as 150 outsiders on the scene, including federal agents, segregationist politicians, the Klan, and American Nazi leader George Lincoln Rockwell, who offered to send storm troopers to Albany to assist segregationists.

Despite Kelley's claims, local blacks were not happy. However, they were tired of protest. On September 4, local white schools refused to admit nineteen black students. Parents were stopped by police barricades. Near the entrance to the high school, a sign read: "No Niggers

Please." The failure of the visiting clergy to influence events led to a decline in movement morale to its lowest ebb, despite an appearance by baseball great Jackie Robinson, who came to Albany on September 9 and encouraged the freedom fighters. King came back to Albany, but the enthusiasm and exuberance were gone. Despair and disillusionment prevailed, and the movement collapsed without bringing any significant changes at the time. On November 1, 1962, the Albany Recorder's Court started sentencing the seventy-five clergy each to a fine of $200 or thirty days in jail. Demonstrations became rarer, and the civil rights emphasis shifted from protests to voter registration.

In March 1963, the city commission rescinded its segregation ordinances. Although the library had opened to blacks on March 11 after a seven-month shutdown, all tables and chairs had been removed, so there was no chance that blacks and whites might sit down together. By late 1963, the Albany Movement appeared to have been defeated, and journalists wrote it off as a loss. The *New York Herald Tribune* declared Albany "a stunning defeat" for King, one of the worst in his career as a civil rights leader.

In a long-term view, Albany was not a failure. It brought together the freedom-ride impulse, the SCLC's spiritual power, and SNCC's non-violent guerrilla warriors for voter registration and grass-roots community organization. Although the immediate gains seemed hardly worth the effort, Albany showed that rural blacks could be activated and, once on the move, would never go back to "their place." The struggle eroded class lines between the black bourgeoisie and the masses. Albany served as a training ground for many future leaders, although Andrew Young later confessed, "There wasn't any real strategy in Albany." However, the SCLC learned how to mobilize masses of people and put together the staff team in Albany that went on to win victories in Birmingham and other places.

While the Albany Movement against segregation was revolutionary, help from the federal government was paltry at best, and the outsiders who came to help were too few to matter. In 1960s Albany, whites remained united. With few exceptions, even those who were sympathetic to blacks' demands remained silent. Albany segregationists could stand firm because local businesses were not branches of national firms that might pressure local stores to help protect the corporate image.

Many of the Albany Movement's lessons came the hard way. Even though local businessmen had at times been willing to negotiate with the Albany Movement, the protest had focused on city officials, who, as politicians catering to a white clientele, could safely reject its demands. The movement was also handicapped by a lack of support from the federal government, which refused to back effectively the rights of blacks to protest and ignored continued violations of the ICC ruling. Pritchett had impressed federal officials and disappointed movement leaders by acting contrary to expectations. He bowed his head when the demonstrators prayed, then arrested them. He provided a police car and a chauffeur for King. He also expressed belief in nonviolence, and the nation did not see televised brutality against peaceful, prayerful blacks as it would later in Birmingham and Selma. Police brutality in Albany came behind closed doors or in nearby counties. Also, the "jail—no bail" tactic failed because the movement was unable to overload the jails. Pritchett had arranged for jail space in all towns within a hundred miles of Albany, sometimes cramming over fifty prisoners in cells built for six. No matter how many protesters there were in jail, Pritchett always found room for more. The Albany Movement ran out of bodies before Pritchett ran out of jail space. The city held up to $600,000-$800,000 of protesters' bond money at a time, which created a financial drain on the movement.

On July 17, 1962, six FBI agents joined the half-dozen already in Albany; Justice also filed a brief with Judge Elliott arguing that Albany blacks had a right to protest. Despite these actions, Attorney General Robert Kennedy accepted the word of Albany officials and the FBI that no federal help was needed. The presence of nearly a dozen federal agents was a misleading signal of greater federal vigilance. Dr. King urged blacks to report incidents to the FBI, but he was dismayed at the bureau's lack of response and criticized the FBI's role in Albany, along with President Kennedy's appointments to the federal bench. The FBI took dozens of affidavits from blacks whose civil rights had been violated but did nothing about the complaints. Robert Kennedy may not have known what was really going on. The FBI agent in charge of the Albany office was considered a racist, sided with city officials, and did not send accurate reports back to Washington. On August 2, 1962, when movement representatives and attorneys met with Robert Kennedy and Justice officials, Kennedy said the Justice Department had done all it could. He failed to mention the widespread wiretapping of movement officials.

On August 9, 1963, the Justice Department obtained federal indictments against Dr. Anderson, Samuel Wells, Slater King and seven others on charges of obstruction of justice and perjury. The case of the "Albany Nine" grew out of the picketing of the supermarket of an Albany grocer, Carl Smith, who had been on a jury in a civil suit of a black claiming to have been beaten and shot by Baker County Sheriff L. Warren Johnson. The jury exonerated Johnson, and the government claimed the picketing was in retaliation for this and not because, as the picketers stated, Smith would not upgrade any of his black employees—even though most of his clientele was black. Scores of FBI agents (estimates range from thirty-five to eighty-six) were assigned to investigate this allegation. Of the thirty-six thousand pages of documents and messages that passed in and out of the Albany FBI office from 1961 to 1963, most concerned this case. Civil rights leaders felt betrayed. One student of the Albany Movement called the prosecution "grotesquely unjust—the last straw," for it proved to many blacks that the federal government was against them.

However, the Albany Movement did not stop in 1963. Weekly meetings were held for the next five years. Pritchett left Albany to accept the post of police chief at High Point, North Carolina, and change came as old customs gradually eroded. By 1970, Albany had a new bus terminal, and its air-conditioned restaurant served blacks, but the swimming pool, sold to private interests, still would not admit them. Ten black civil rights workers were sentenced for attempting a "swim-in" on July 5, 1964, although that year saw the beginning of local school desegregation. Charles Sherrod, one of Albany's many heroes, was still occasionally getting beat up in Southwest Georgia for voter registration work. The archfoe of desegregation, James H. Gray, ran fourth in the 1966 gubernatorial primary that Lester Maddox won. Gray stopped fighting progress and worked to benefit Albany. He was elected mayor in 1973 and kept this job until his death in 1986.

Thirty years after the Albany Movement began, the city had a black police chief, two black judges, and over a dozen black lawyers. Three blacks, including Sherrod, sat on the seven-member city commission.

After 1963, there was a change in emphasis in Southwest Georgia from demonstrations to voter registration. Even before the Albany Movement reached its zenith, SNCC activists had fanned out from that town to other Southwest Georgia communities, many of which had a long record of brutality toward blacks. In Terrell County, James Brazier was beaten to death by local police in 1958. The county seat of Dawson and nearby Sasser were considered two of the most brutal places in Georgia. Soon after they arrived, SNCC workers began to call the county "Terrible Terrell." Ralph Allen, one of the first white SNCC workers to come to Albany, was beaten and terrorized repeatedly in Terrell County, then charged with insurrection and attempted murder.

When the voter registration drive started in October 1961, Terrell County was home to 8,209 blacks and 4,533 whites. Fifty-three blacks and 2,894 whites were registered to vote despite federal civil rights cases that had been initiated under the 1957 and 1960 civil rights bills. Whites were furious at the prospect of a black voter registration drive. Sheriff Zeke Mathews, three deputies, and twelve other whites invaded a voter registration rally in the Mount Olive Church in Sasser on July 25, 1962. "We want our colored people to go on living like they have for the past 100 years," Mathews explained. To prevent panic, Sherrod led blacks in the Lord's Prayer; then they sang "Jacob's Ladder." Mathews interrupted, took the names of those present, and said whites were "a little fed up with this registering business," and muttered threats about what "disturbed white citizens might do." Blacks began to hum "We Shall Overcome," and the intruders left. A few days later, Allen and Sherrod were arrested for vagrancy after they escorted blacks to the Terrell County courthouse to register to vote. The Justice Department filed a lawsuit on August 13 to stop intimidation of Terrell's black voters.

Then came the nightriders. Mount Olive Church was burned to the ground as part of a wave of white terrorism. Several black churches in Leesburg, Sasser, and Dawson were burned. Four homes of Lee County blacks active in registration were fired on with shotguns and rifles, and three voting-rights workers were injured by a shotgun blast in Dawson on September 5. SNCC called on Kennedy "to stop this Nazi-like reign of terror." Kennedy called the church arson "cowardly as well as outrageous." Jackie Robinson visited Mount Olive's smoking ruins and headed up a drive to raise funds for rebuilding the churches.

Although the Kennedy administration was not terribly fond of freedom rides and mass demonstrations, it expressed support for voter registration efforts. SNCC workers were bitter that the federal government did nothing to stop the harassment and violence that was directed at them. After a Sasser lawman was acquitted by an all-white jury of charges he had chased SNCC workers out of town by firing shots at their vehicle, Sherrod asked, "Must we die before the federal government stops compromising with the bigots?" There were already signs of change, however. Three white men had pleaded guilty to church arson and were given seven-year sentences in a Terrell County court.

Americus also became a center of SNCC activity. In July 1963, the Americus voter registration drive broadened to include desegregation demonstrations at the theater and other public facilities. Local officials counterattacked viciously by dusting off an 1871 anti-insurrection statute still on the books, even though the U. S. Supreme Court had voided it thirty years earlier in the Angelo Herndon case. One black and two white SNCC field workers were arrested for violating the unconstitutional law and were denied bail. Sallie Mae Durham, a black fourteen-year-old Americus resident, was arrested and denied bail. C. B. King had acid poured on the front seat of his car while visiting prisoners in Sumter County. In November 1963, at the request of Morris B. Abram of the National Lawyers Guild, the Fifth Circuit Court of Appeals ordered the immediate release of the SNCC workers, who by then had spent two months in jail. When Allen's insurrection charge was thrown out, local authorities charged him with assault with intent to murder a policeman and gained a conviction. It, too, was thrown out.

Despite the terror, arrests, and intimidation, voter registration workers continued their efforts. After less than a year's work, there were sixty blacks registered in Terrell for every one registered when the drive began. The newfound black political power began to take the "terrible" out of Terrell and surrounding counties. Eventually, Judge Elliott, that old Talmadge politician, issued a permanent injunction against officials of Terrell County, Dawson, Sasser, and eight white residents and ordered them to stop intimidating workers in the voter registration drive.

Georgia's larger cities were forced to deal with the civil rights movement. Macon, like Albany, was an antebellum center of cotton and slavery. Although Macon's black voters helped elect an anti-Talmadge mayor in 1947, they were unable to achieve the level of political respect Atlanta blacks had won. Although Macon hired its first black police officer in the late 1940s, white law enforcement officials seemed determined to enforce racial mores to an unreasonable degree. In 1951, two black soldiers were sentenced to sixty days and a fine of twenty-five dollars for disorderly conduct and resisting arrest when they protested being called "nigger." In 1954, a young white Mercer graduate and his black friend were arrested for allegedly violating segregation laws when the white visited the black's home. Only afterward did police discover that there was no law against such visits. Local blacks used the ballot in 1956 to help elect James I. Woods, a fair-minded white, as sheriff. Three years later, Ed Wilson received 81 percent of the black vote and became mayor. Blacks were so well organized that charges of vote-selling surfaced. After several attempts, Macon blacks finally built a strong NAACP branch in the early 1960s.

William P. Randall, Sr., was Macon's most influential black political leader then. He inherited his militancy from his father, who returned from the Spanish-American War determined to fight for the vote. In 1952 he had an experience that sharpened his determination to fight segregation when his six-year old son, William P. Randall, Jr., was ordered off of a drugstore-fountain stool. He gave up his building contracting business in the early 1960s, in part because his activism made him a target for retribution.

Even before the freedom rides, a federal judge in Macon fined Trailways Bus Company and its driver for forcing Marguerite Edwards to move to the back of a bus in September 1960. Municipal buses remained segregated, however. In 1961, William Randall, Jr., his twelve-year old sister, Jackie, and Harold Wilson were among the 15 members of the 350-member NAACP Youth Council that decided to attack segregation by refusing to sit at the back of the city buses. The young protesters were jailed for a few hours, and their release was enthusiastically greeted by a large crowd of blacks. This sparked a systematic attack on segregation.

Encouraged by the youths, blacks demanded an end to segregation in downtown stores. In June 1961, demonstrators arrived to sit in, only to find all lunch counters closed. These were integrated in October following a conference of black and white leaders. The attack on bus segregation continued. H. R. Rancifer and three other ministers were arrested on February 9, 1962, for not sitting in the back of a municipal bus. Blacks quickly organized a citywide bus boycott. The bus company responded by appealing to whites to "ride a bus and help break the boycott." The boycott did not last long. On March 1, Judge William Bootle struck down segregation on the city's buses. Macon's downtown merchants were willing to integrate because they wanted to avoid a Savannah-style boycott. Although there had been sporadic outbreaks of violence in Macon, the city was calm in comparison to Georgia's oldest city.

Savannah was a center of conflict during the American Revolution and renewed that role during the early 1960s. It was the home of Georgia's strongest free Negro community before the Civil War and of a large, educated, and respectable black middle class afterward. As evidence of the political importance of black Savannah in the 1950s, black Republican Louis B. Toomer was appointed register of the treasury by President Eisenhower. The city had thirteen thousand black voters in 1960.

In some respects Savannah's home-grown civil rights movement was unique in Georgia. It did not need outside personalities to inspire it. Local leaders mobilized Savannah and ended up being pushed by their followers. The struggle was more violent in Savannah than in Atlanta or Albany, and demonstrations were larger—thousands of protesters at a time took to the streets. Unlike Albany's Pritchett, Savannah's police chief ran out of jail space long before the movement ran out of bodies.

One reason for the militant civil rights movement in Savannah was its leader, Hosea Williams. While Andrew Young represented the conservative wing of the SCLC, Williams led the militant faction. Both went on to achieve prominence in the civil rights movement and in politics. Williams was tough. Young once said, "Hosea could scare the sheet off a Klansman." Williams, an injured World War II combat veteran, was roughed up on his way home to Attapulgus, near the Florida line in Decatur County in deep Southwest Georgia, after he drank from a "white" water fountain in a bus station. His home was on the plantation next to archsegregationist Marvin Griffin's spread. Griffin's brother, Cheney, became Williams's friend and early partner in hustling and financed his way through Morris Brown College.

Williams went to work for the U. S. Department of Agriculture as a chemist in Savannah. There he had an experience similar to that of the Randalls in Macon. One day when Williams took his two sons to a drugstore, he had to tell them that they could not sit on the stools at the soda fountain and have a Coke. He promised that someday he would bring them back when they could. Williams said that the incident was the spark to his involvement in the civil rights struggle. He became active in the NAACP and led the Savannah protests.

Savannah's sit-ins started in mid-March 1960, at the same time as Atlanta's. Seven stores were targeted, and three students were arrested during the protests. The next day, state police were called in when fighting broke out at the Saint Patrick's Day parade after white and black spectators traded insults. In a savage battle between black and white youths in a park two days later, members of each group were jailed, and others were hospitalized. Savannah saw the first court test of Georgia's antitrespass law on May 5, 1960, when thirty-two blacks were convicted for sitting in and sentenced to a $100 fine or five months in jail.

The Savannah sit-ins and boycott caused some predictable reactions, including arrests and Klan cross burnings. Twelve blacks were jailed in a wade-in at a city swimming pool that summer. When seven blacks were arrested in January 1961 for playing basketball in a white playground, the Justice Department said it would investigate. To avoid such incidents— and to keep blacks out of Wells Park—the city closed it down.

Soon the city's rigid segregation began to crack. One break came in the spring of 1961, when the city golf course was completely desegregated. This was no great concession, because only a few middle-class blacks played golf. Then the Rev. Oliver C. Holmes, a black, was appointed to the Bacon Park Commission by Mayor Malcolm McLean, who took a moderate stand during Savannah's desegregation struggles.

Violence and turmoil continued. Benjamin West, a member of the NAACP Youth Council, was beaten by eight whites at a Woolworth's sit-in. All 914 students walked out of the black Sol C. Johnson High School, and twenty-three were arrested for picketing the school board when their principal, Al Cheatham, was fired for his work with the Crusade for Voters movement. Fights between blacks and whites continued when they met in the segregated parks.

The sit-ins were well organized. Ten thousand pieces of literature were sent out to churches, which coupled desegregation with voting rights. As the NAACP became more active, its membership doubled to one thousand. In fact, the local NAACP was too active for some black leaders' tastes. Williams left the NAACP in 1962 because Roy Wilkins vetoed his candidacy for its national board of directors at the Atlanta convention, believing that Hosea was too militant. Williams then became active in the SCLC. Williams considered himself a field general for King and said that his job "was to go out among black people who were scared to death and get them jumping up, marching around, and filling up the jails." He was very successful. By his count he was jailed over a hundred times.

Although freedom rides through Savannah were incident-free and downtown merchants agreed to desegregate lunch counters in June 1961, hotels, motels, theaters, and restaurants remained segregated. Adding to tensions was an announcement by the White Citizens' Council and the Association of Southern Patriots that they would boycott the desegregated eating establishments. Protests climaxed in the summer of 1963 with demonstrations by the Williams-led, SCLC-affiliated Chatham County Crusade for Voters, which mounted a final push for desegregation. City police allowed the demonstrations, and thousands marched. On July 9, Hosea Williams was arrested on a warrant sworn out by a white women who declared that the demonstrations made her fear for her life. She also complained that demonstrators kept her awake at night. Other whites stepped forward to press charges against Williams, who remained in custody under a slew of peace warrants that carried a collective $30,000 bond. Williams would spend sixty-five days in jail, the longest continuous stretch of any movement leader. Subsequent demonstrations staged to gain his release broke down into rioting and brick throwing by demonstrators and spectators, who were teargassed by local and state police. At least three blacks were shot. After the Sears, Roebuck and Firestone stores were burned, Citizens and Southern Bank President Mills B. Lane, Jr., stepped in as a mediator and made it possible for Williams to get out of jail. Williams told him he would be back in jail the next day if protesters' demands were not met.

In response to the demonstrations, Savannah's most influential whites formed a "Committee of 100" and accompanied blacks to integrate white-only establishments. When a manager at the Union Camp paper mill, Savannah's largest employer, went with his wife and Williams to a theater, Klan demonstrators across the street fled quickly when they saw their boss. Savannah began integrating its schools that fall. In August 1964, when seven-eighths of all Southern public accommodations were still segregated, King declared Savannah the most desegregated city in the South. When the battle was over, Hosea took his sons back to the drug store to get their Cokes. "That was one of the happiest days of my life," he said.

Augusta saw less racial strife than Savannah during the early 1960s, but the river town had its share of upheaval. By 1960, the area's white residents had grown accustomed to federal desegregation at nearby Fort Gordon. However, black soldiers were often unwilling to accept local practices. Pvt. George Johnson, influenced by the sit-ins in Atlanta and elsewhere, was arrested for refusing to leave the white-only restaurant at the Trailways bus depot in the spring of 1960. Meanwhile, black attorneys Horace Ward and Donald Hollowell filed suit on behalf of five black students who were arrested for refusing to move to the back of a city bus.

As in Macon, a federal judge ruled against Augusta's bus segregation in 1962.

White leaders in Augusta, like those in Columbus, watched events in Atlanta, Savannah, and Macon and saw that some desegregation was inevitable. Columbus was probably the most peaceful of Georgia's larger cities in the early 1960s. There a biracial agreement on December 11, 1961, to desegregate some eating places beginning in 1962 signaled the beginning of the end of de jure segregation. In Augusta, an interracial conference similarly agreed that all lunch counters would be desegregated early in 1962.

When Augusta whites showed little inclination to implement the agreement, black leaders announced on March 25, 1962, that daily desegregation rallies, accompanied by a boycott of the *Augusta Herald* and *Chronicle*, would begin the following week. The newspaper had fired three reporters for providing stories of racial unrest to outside media— stories the Augusta paper would not print. The demonstrators were assured the maximum national publicity, as the rallies were timed to coincide with the opening of the Masters Golf Tournament, held at Augusta's world-famous National Golf Course.

To forestall adverse publicity during the Masters, lunch counters in five stores were quietly desegregated before the rallies began. More places were desegregated in the following few days. Blacks added a policy of "don't buy where you can't work," and the NAACP Youth Council began a boycott of businesses that practiced unfair employment. Demonstrations turned ugly. At one supermarket, a crowd of 250 blacks attacked a black shopper with rocks and destroyed the groceries she had purchased. Six were arrested. Meanwhile, white youths drove through black neighborhoods throwing rocks and bottles and tried to run down black youths. The police intervened and arrested forty white youths who had weapons in their cars. Tensions rose as blacks struck back, and one white youth was killed. The next day, local NAACP leader the Rev. C. S. Hamilton obtained an agreement with the supermarket owner to hire blacks.

Frank Dumas, Jr., was tried for the murder of the white youth and sentenced to life imprisonment, while five of the other nine indicted received up to ten-year sentences from an all-white jury. By August, the demonstrations plus court orders resulted in desegregation of public accommodations in Augusta, and the city disappeared from the headlines as a center of racial turmoil.

Although the national media concentrated on one subject at a time— usually Martin Luther King, Jr.—the struggle by blacks to achieve basic civil rights occurred throughout the South. Although the early 1960s struggle bypassed many of Georgia's smaller towns and rural areas, the fight for freedom went on in many places, often led by men, women, and even children whose work has never been adequately recognized. Many significant battles never received much more than local attention, and their stories still wait to be told.

Shattered Dreams

As champion of "Georgia's two greatest traditions—segregation and the county unit system," Marvin Griffin in 1962 sought his old job and faced off against State Sen. Carl Sanders of Augusta. Griffin had the backing of the Klan, citizens' councils, and Albany city officials. He threatened to put King so far into jail "that air would have to be piped to him." Sanders was a "racially moderate" segregationist who attacked both hard-liners like Griffin and Roy Harris *and* civil rights leaders. Sanders said he would obey court orders and work to maintain peaceful race relations. Sanders also ran against the corruption during Griffin's mid-1950s administration.

Two major factors heavily influenced the election, which Sanders won by 156,000 votes. Sanders had successfully challenged the county unit system in court. Now each urban voters' ballot would count as much as a rural vote. Also, due to voting-rights drives, there were now 200,000 black voters, about 15 percent of the total—still only about half their proportion of the state's population. During the campaign Sanders said he would never put a lock on the schoolhouse door, and blacks overwhelmingly supported him in the September 12 primary. Sanders's pitch for economic development also brought support from most of the state's business leaders and major newspapers.

Atlanta's black voting strength was almost double what it was statewide. In 1962, approximately 28 percent of the city's 144,600 voters were black. With their support, Ivan Allen, Jr., had defeated segregationist Lester Maddox in the 1961 mayoral race. After Allen took office, the "Colored" signs at city hall came down, the city fire department and transit system began hiring blacks, and black police officers were authorized to arrest whites. Atlanta's white leaders and businessmen still clung to the vestiges of apartheid, however. Many restaurants and hotels remained segregated. After Allen signed an ordinance creating a racial "buffer zone," the city erected barricades on December 18, 1962, on Peyton and Harlan roads in a futile attempt to enforce residential segregation between predominantly black Collier Heights and white Cascade Heights.

Georgia seemed to be pulling free from the stranglehold of the Democratic party's racist right wing, although Georgia would remain a one-party state. Republicans failed to field a gubernatorial candidate in

1962. (They tried, but the state requirement that they back up their candidate with a seventy thousand-signature petition proved insurmountable.) By then, blacks were a diminishing factor in Republican politics. Although Republicans drew a majority of votes in Atlanta's black precincts during the 1950s, black voters gravitated toward the national Democratic ticket after the Kennedys became involved when Martin Luther King, Jr., was incarcerated at the Georgia State Prison at Reidsville. In 1962, Atlanta's triumphant candidate for Congress, Charles Weltner, abandoned the state party's traditional anti-civil rights position and captured 70 percent of the black vote. He was one of only two Southern Democrats to vote for the 1964 Civil Rights Act.

The court-ordered redistricting of the state Senate gave Atlanta two predominantly black districts. In 1962, thirty-four-year-old Leroy Johnson defeated four whites in the primary and triumphed over his Republican opponent, black insurance executive T. M. Alexander. Johnson became the first black to serve in the Georgia Senate since 1870, and the first black in any Deep South legislature for over fifty years. Johnson, a Morehouse graduate with a law degree, had been a criminal investigator on the Fulton County solicitor's staff. His election was broadcast to the world over the Voice of America radio network as evidence that the U. S. system of democracy worked. Senator Talmadge sent him a "Dear Leroy" letter signed "Herman" inviting him to Lovejoy, the family homestead. Other white politicians scurried to make the same move. Taking a less than charitable view of such turnabouts, Ralph McGill would write, "The politicians who lied and incited riots are now seeking Negro votes."

Georgians and events in Georgia, especially during the early 1960s, were crucial to dramatic changes in race relations. Atlanta became the headquarters of the civil rights movement because Martin Luther King, Jr., lived there and the SCLC's offices were headquartered in "the city too busy to hate," which had been improved by its concessions to black demands for progress. While the civil rights movement was developing in Georgia and segregation was crumbling, events elsewhere also propelled the nation toward greater democracy. Federal laws and court decisions, plus growing black protest in other states, helped create a climate of rising expectations that appeared to foreshadow King's "beloved community." Many reformers believed a truly just society could be achieved—if only the pressure for change could be maintained. King had his doubts, however. After the Albany Movement, King endured criticism of his leadership for failing to win a clear-cut victory. He was so despondent that he considered quitting the civil rights struggle and became more active at Ebenezer Baptist Church. Then he got an offer of

$100,000 from impresario Sol Hurok to lecture around the world. Andrew Young said the offer forced King to make a decision. By turning down the offer, King committed himself irrevocably to the struggle.

In 1963, King focused his attention on Birmingham and the SCLC planned massive desegregation demonstrations during April and May. The city's police commissioner, brutal Eugene "Bull" Connor, failed to learn the lessons of Albany's police chief and brought out nightsticks, dogs, and fire hoses to attack demonstrators. The police brutality was on the national TV news daily. This aroused the nation's conscience and increased sympathy for the freedom struggle. King readily exploited white guilt feelings and was able to gain concessions after twenty-four hundred arrests and many injuries. Klan-led violence resulted in riots by blacks that threatened to tear the city apart. Then Birmingham's establishment became serious about enforcing a desegregation agreement.

To push for further reform, King, along with Bayard Rustin and A. Philip Randolph, planned a March on Washington for Jobs and Freedom to rivet the nation's attention on the unfinished business of providing equal opportunities for all its people. The event was a great success. Whites made up about a quarter of the more than 250,000 people who gathered on the mall facing the Lincoln Memorial on August 28, 1963, to hear movement leaders articulate their hopes and dreams. King's "I Have a Dream" speech will live long in the annals of eloquence.

One of the march's goals was to help persuade Congress to pass a far-reaching civil rights act that President Kennedy had introduced in June 1963. Kennedy did not live to see the bill pass. He was assassinated on November 22, 1963, in Dallas, Texas. President Lyndon Johnson supported the civil rights movement and secured passage of the legislation, the Civil Rights Act of 1964.

In Atlanta, segregation was dying, but not without a struggle. On January 6, 1964, John Lewis led 150 high school students in an anti-segregation demonstration at the mayor's office. At Mayor Allen's urging, the city council repealed the city's segregation ordinances. On January 11, fourteen major hotels agreed to abandon Jim Crow. A week after that there were confrontations between demonstrators and robed Klansmen outside several eating places that had not desegregated. Mayor Allen then met two hundred white and black leaders who agreed to a thirty-day truce if the city would push desegregation and fair employment practices. However, it would take more federal legislation to break down the barriers of Jim Crow.

On July 2, President Johnson signed the Civil Rights Act of 1964, which forbade discrimination in employment and public accommodations and authorized the attorney general to implement the law's provisions.

Senator Talmadge particularly objected to the section on public accommodations but had been unable to include a provision that would provide federal compensation to business owners who closed down facilities rather than desegregate them. Lester Maddox attracted the nation's attention on July 3 when he used a pistol and an ax handle to stop three blacks from entering his Pickrick restaurant in Atlanta. Maddox closed his restaurant in August rather than integrate. One Atlanta motel unsuccessfully challenged the new law all the way to the U. S. Supreme Court in *Heart of Atlanta v. U. S.*

Outside Atlanta, in the "other" Georgia, resistance to civil rights continued. Americus remained a center of strife into the mid-1960s. Klan attacks also continued. Lemuel Penn, a black army reserve officer, was gunned down on July 11, 1964, near Colbert in Northeast Georgia by a shotgun blast from a passing car as he was returning to his Washington, D.C., home from training duty at Fort Benning. Two Klansmen, Howard Sims and Cecil Myers, were tried in a local court for Penn's murder. Despite a signed confession by the car's driver, the two shooters were acquitted by twelve white men. In 1966, a federal jury convicted Sims and Myers of violating Penn's civil rights, and they served about six years each for the crime, which was probably triggered when they saw black men in a car with a Washington, D.C., license plate.

Although there had been gains in Georgia, by the end of 1964 most blacks there and throughout the South still could not vote. Most blacks saw the 1964 presidential election as a contest between the mostly good Lyndon Johnson and the mostly bad Republican Sen. Barry Goldwater of Arizona, who opposed the 1964 Civil Rights Act. Goldwater heralded a conservative white backlash to the civil rights movement and became the first Republican presidential candidate to take Georgia's electoral votes. Many Southern segregationists deserted the national Democratic party. James Gray, nemesis of the Albany civil rights movement, headed Democrats for Goldwater in 1964. With overwhelming black support, Johnson was elected president. Republicans won sixteen seats in the Georgia General Assembly, and Goldwater supporter Howard "Bo" Callaway, a wealthy textile heir, became the first Republican congressman from Georgia in nearly a century. Horace Ward became Georgia's second black state senator.

King's stature and influence continued to rise. He was *Time* magazine's "Man of the Year" for 1963. His second major book, *Why We Can't Wait*, was published in 1964. It contained proposals for redistributing wealth and raising the poor from their poverty with a domestic Marshall Plan, based on the principle that America owed a debt to the poor and disadvantaged who had built the nation. *Why We Can't Wait* sold several hundred thousand copies in a few months and was quickly translated into ten foreign languages.

In 1964, King became the third black man to receive the Nobel Peace Prize. The prestigious award incensed FBI Director J. Edgar Hoover, whose attitudes were spiked by racism and paranoia over communism and "moral degeneracy." King's criticism of the FBI and growing prominence led Hoover to increase his efforts to discredit the civil rights leader. These efforts had been ongoing for several years and included widespread wiretapping and sending reports on King's private life and alleged Communist connections to the White House and top government officials. A month after the award was announced, Hoover took his hatred of King public, calling King "the most notorious liar in the country," for remarks King had made in 1962. King had said that FBI agents in Albany were Southerners who favored segregation and failed to properly investigate beatings and intimidation of blacks. Hoover seized on the fact that some of the Albany agents were Northerners to dispute King's word, but he ignored the more important charge that they had failed to do their duty.

Coretta King once noted, "The FBI treated the civil rights movement as if it were an alien enemy attack on the United States." Hoover and the FBI were self-proclaimed guardians of an established social order that felt threatened by the movement. In April 1964, Hoover publicly stated that Communists were exploiting the civil rights movement. The charge was in line with his longtime personal crusade.

After King's statement about Albany FBI agents, the bureau's focus shifted from trying to find a Communist under King's bed to finding a woman other than Coretta in it. In October 1961, the FBI began the expensive practice of manning several taps on SCLC telephones twenty-four hours a day, seven days a week. The FBI also bugged hotel rooms over a six-year period in an effort to find evidence of subversive or sexual activities that could be used to discredit and replace the civil rights leader with someone more to Hoover's liking. The FBI tried to get many editors, including *Atlanta Constitution* editor Eugene Patterson, to publish rumors on King's sex life. They all refused, even Lou Harris of the then-segregationist *Augusta Chronicle*. The FBI's harassment of King reached sordid depths when a top bureau official wrote an anonymous letter to King threatening to expose him if he did not commit suicide before he accepted the Nobel Prize. Top FBI officials were bitter that their scandalous tidbits about "burrhead" (Hoover's favorite nickname for King) were not published and King's stature was undiminished.

At least in Atlanta, attitudes had improved. Some of the city's more progressive white leaders thought that the Nobel winner should be honored by his hometown. A testimonial dinner was arranged, largely due to the efforts of Helen Bullard. It was sponsored by Catholic

Archbishop Paul Hallinan, Rabbi Jacob Rothschild, Ralph McGill, and Benjamin Mays. Protestant ministers and many business leaders did not support the January 27, 1965, biracial banquet at the Dinkler Hotel. One banker, whose social conscience was matched by his grammar, said, "We ain't gonna have no dinner for no nigger." More importantly, Coca-Cola magnate Robert Woodruff supported the event, which helped ensure its success. Some, such as department-store owner Richard Rich, would not purchase tickets at first, then found that they had all been sold. Four hundred waited in the lobby hoping that they could take the place of "no-shows." The banquet was a huge success, and it was remarkable because, in Helen Bullard's words, "It was the first thing Atlanta had done that they didn't have to do. Everything else had been the threat of a court order."

Neither Atlanta nor Georgia was the center of demonstrations during the last half of the 1960s. As this period began, King was at the height of his power and influence. He had influenced millions to think that something could be done to improve their status, and he had led the way in achieving surface concessions. This result may not have been so much a tribute to his nonviolent tactics as it was a sign of the fears of whites that if nonviolence did not work, more militant blacks without any philosophy of nonviolence would take over the movement.

In 1965, movement leaders planned a voter registration drive at Selma, Alabama, and a Selma-to-Montgomery march. In a historic confrontation at Selma's Edmund Pettus Bridge on March 7, marchers led by Hosea Williams and John Lewis met an army of Alabama state troopers and local lawmen led by Sheriff Jim Clark. The lawmen used tear gas and clubs to drive back the demonstrators, scores of whom were wounded. Lewis was severely injured by a blow to the head from a police truncheon. To prevent the recurrence of violence during a rescheduled march two weeks later, the president federalized the Alabama National Guard to protect marchers, led by Lewis and King.

Events in Selma helped trigger quick approval of the 1965 Voting Rights Act, which helped further to break down barriers that stood between blacks and the ballot box. It suspended literacy and other tests in locales where 50 percent of the voting-age population failed to vote. The law produced a dramatic increase in the number of registered black voters and black political power. In 1965, there were fewer than a hundred elected black officials in the South; fifteen years later there were over two thousand.

Despite the new laws, many blacks in rural Georgia were afraid to stand up for their rights, with good reason. In Lincolnton, near the South Carolina line, SCLC marchers were beaten on October 22, 1965. A march planned for the next day was turned back by state troopers, who claimed that the entire town was armed and lying in wait for the marchers. Six days later, the Rev. Charlie Brown, Willie Bolden and Edward Bedford led fifty pulp-mill workers in a march that lacked support of the town's blacks. Bolden accused the local black leaders of "selling their souls to feed their families." Successful marches were held the last two days of the month, and then blacks lined up at the courthouse to register to vote.

The Selma-to-Montgomery march and passage of the Voting Rights Act probably mark the high point of the civil rights movement and King's influence. When he tried to broaden his efforts in the North, he did not meet with much success. Frustration among inner-city blacks was turning to rage in Northern ghettos, where riots broke out in 1964 and during the "long hot summers" of 1965, 1966, and 1967. Five months after Selma, a pall of smoke hung over the Los Angeles suburb of Watts in the aftermath of a massive five-day riot. When King went to Watts, he found that few young blacks had heard of him. King tried to take his movement to Chicago in 1966, a city that had been the scene of three nights of rioting in 1965. Despite police protection, white supremacists stoned and wounded him in the suburb of Cicero.

In the South, violence against peaceable demonstrations for simple justice continued. When James Meredith was shot in the back during a voter registration march in Mississippi on June 6, 1966, the movement, long hampered by internal disputes, was on the verge of disarray. Civil rights groups united one last time to continue Meredith's march. The Meredith march was the last link in a chain of events leading to raising the slogan "Black Power." John Lewis, SNCC chairman since 1963, had been replaced a few weeks earlier by Stokely Carmichael. Carmichael and H. Rap Brown were disillusioned with King's tactics of nonviolence and began to speak of Black Power in a way that alienated white supporters and scared Southern white supremacists into increasing their resistance. Carmichael's leadership of SNCC heralded its domination by Northern students centered at Howard University, and SNCC became less accepted in the South, where blacks earlier had felt more comfortable with the student leaders from Fisk and the Atlanta University Center. With the rise of Black Power ideology, militants viewed whites in the movement as a handicap. The young militants rejected nonviolence and called for "an eye for an eye" retaliation against attacks on them. By then, white America was tired of confronting its conscience.

Many young blacks admired the black nationalism of the Nation of Islam, led by Elijah Muhammad, who was originally from Sandersville, Georgia. Eloquent Muslim evangelist Malcolm X was also greatly admired. He became a "threatening counterpoint to the nonviolent, assimilationist movement...of King," wrote biographer Peter Goldman. Malcolm X had split with Muhammad in 1963 and was assassinated, most likely by rival Muslims, in February 1965.

Atlanta was not immune from the urban riots of the late 1960s. Tensions erupted in the Summerhill section of Atlanta in the late summer of 1966. The day after Labor Day, Atlanta police shot and wounded a fleeing black auto theft suspect. When angry blacks began to congregate to protest, Mayor Allen came to the scene and spoke to the crowd while standing on an automobile roof. The crowd was in an ugly mood from the exhortations of Carmichael, who sent a sound truck and ten SNCC workers to tell the residents to ignore the mayor. The result was a riot that required 750 police using tear gas to suppress. Allen was toppled off the car, two white police and two blacks were shot, many were arrested, and fourteen blacks, including Carmichael, were indicted. Four nights later, a smaller disturbance in Atlanta followed the murder of Herbert Vorner, a four-teen-year-old black. Black Power advocates attended the next city council meeting and announced, "We're going to put every Georgia cracker in Atlanta on his knees." Carmichael was charged under the same statute that was overturned when used against Angelo Herndon in the 1930s and in 1963 against Sumter County civil rights workers. Again, the Supreme Court threw out the charge.

The Georgia General Assembly's lower house districts were redrawn in 1965, and Atlanta had several new posts in majority-black districts. John Lewis and SNCC workers persuaded Julian Bond to run in the 136th against two other blacks: the Rev. Howard Creecy, a Democrat, and Republican Malcolm Dean, an Atlanta University administrator. Bond energetically hit the streets campaigning for a two-dollar minimum hourly wage, repeal of the state right-to-work law, abolition of the death penalty (when Georgia had the highest execution rate in the country), and other proposals geared for a district with 50 percent male unemploy-ment. Bond took 70 percent of the May 5 primary vote and over 80 percent of the general-election total. Five other blacks had won House seats, and the two black incumbent senators kept theirs. Bond prepared to take his seat on January 10 under the Gold Dome, where he had been ejected in 1961 for trying to integrate the visitors' gallery. The twenty-five-year-old freshman was blissfully unaware that the state assembly would react to his antiwar sentiments with one of its most drastically repressive acts since the ouster of all black legislators in 1868.

In November, SNCC drew up a position paper opposing the war in Vietnam. On January 6, SNCC publicly suggested that potential military draftees should be allowed the alternative of civil rights work—to fight for democracy in the United States rather than fight for an undemocratic Asian regime. When news spread that SNCC member Bond agreed with that position, all hell broke loose for him. Pro-war patriotism played well politically in Georgia then. Most blacks disagreed with Bond's position, for that matter. Although blacks sat in the legislature, they were supposed to "behave themselves," not speak out. The local media sensationalized the story and goaded politicians to react.

Bond became the victim of accumulated white resentment against the gains made by the civil rights movement over the past four years. White legislators felt a need to strike back at a genuine civil rights activist. Even moderates wanted Bond to apologize and recant in order to take his seat. "This boy has got to come before us humbly, recant and just plain beg a little," privately explained one legislator. Bond could not and would not do this. When the legislature convened, a group led by James "Sloppy" Floyd moved to deny Bond his seat. One South Georgia lawmaker, a leader of the rural bloc, was practically in tears as he declared,

> Blood runs down the trenches in a far-off land, causing tears to run down widows' cheeks and husbands' and children's faces. . . . The legislature has been invaded by one whose thinking pursues not freedom for us but victory for our enemies. . . . The infamous Mr. Bond.

As sole judge of the fitness of its members, the legislators voted to refuse Bond his seat on opening day, 184-12. Five black representatives and seven whites from metropolitan Atlanta supported him. Although Bond's treatment was reminiscent of that accorded Georgia's black legislators in 1868, white lawmakers claimed their action was not racially motivated.

Bond became a cause célèbre. Over the objections of Atlanta NAACP President Samuel Williams, one thousand SCLC and SNCC protesters, led by King, marched to the Capitol to object to Bond's expulsion. Dr. Williams wanted to do the impossible and keep civil rights and Vietnam issues separate. Meanwhile, Bond's case went to court. The U. S. District Court's ruling against Bond was appealed to the Supreme Court, which ruled unanimously in *Bond v. Floyd* on December 5, 1966, that Bond had to be seated. In the meantime, Bond won two special elections called to fill the "vacancy" from his district. He also went on a national speaking tour. One year after he was denied admission, he took his seat at the Capitol.

The governor then was one of Georgia's most interesting, and he arrived in office following a curious race. In 1966, James Gray ran in the Democratic primary as the country club's segregation candidate. He came in fourth, behind third-place finisher Jimmy Carter, a little-known state senator from Plains. Lester Maddox, who had run unsuccessfully for mayor of Atlanta and lieutenant governor, won a runoff with Ellis Arnall. Maddox was a folksy, overt racist whose campaign played on white fears that were heightened by federal civil rights programs. Maddox suggested that Martin Luther King, Jr., be jailed or deported and equated school desegregation with communism. He passed out ax handles to his followers to remind voters of his stance on segregation; the ax handle became a symbol of the state's more unregenerate racists. Many who approved of his attitudes on race also admired his ability to ride a bicycle backward. Maddox's public career would always exhibit a certain side-show quality.

Charles Weltner quit Congress rather than pledge loyalty to a Democratic ticket with Maddox at the head. "I cannot compromise with hate," said the future state Supreme Court justice. Republican candidate "Bo" Callaway opposed federal desegregation efforts and received more votes than Maddox, but he did not have a majority, for many Georgians could not bring themselves to vote for either candidate. Instead, they wrote in Arnall's name in November. The decision was thrown into the Democratic-dominated legislature, where Maddox triumphed, to no one's surprise. Most of Georgia's 290,000 registered black voters were dismayed. Georgia had taken a giant step backward, it seemed. Maddox was widely considered an embarrassment to the state.

Once in power, Maddox was forced to conform and dropped some of his worst "redneck" attributes, however. He became a prime example of a "crumbled cracker," one who changed as blacks began to vote more. He desegregated state facilities, stopped state troopers from referring to blacks as "niggers," and initiated federal food programs and prison reforms. He closed no schools, increased the budget for education, and helped raise teachers' salaries by one-fourth. While he appointed no blacks to higher offices, he did name twenty-two to serve on draft boards. While Maddox was governor, Atlanta public relations executive Wayman Scott Wright became the first black president of the Georgia Young Democrats. Later, when Maddox was lieutenant governor, he named Leroy Johnson as chairman of the Senate Judiciary Committee after Johnson helped Maddox beat off some attempts to strip him of part of his power. This gave Johnson more power than any of Georgia's black Reconstruction legislators were able to achieve.

Dr. King was the most prominent black Georgian to oppose the war in Vietnam, speaking openly against it in 1964. His wife, Coretta, active in the Women's International League for Peace and Freedom, had already opposed it. King had access to the president and high officials in the Kennedy administration. This was curtailed during the Johnson administration, especially after King began to put the struggle for freedom on a worldwide scale.

In February 1967, Dr. King stepped up his criticism with his first speech devoted entirely to Vietnam. "We are taking the young black men who have been crippled by our society and sending them eight thousand miles away to guarantee the liberties in Southeast Asia which they have not found in Southwest Georgia and East Harlem," he said, and sadly concluded his own government was "the greatest purveyor of violence in the world today." After King's February speech, a Harris Poll reported that 75 percent of whites and 48 percent of blacks disagreed with his position.

The FBI considered King's stance "revolutionary" and began to categorize the SCLC as a "Black Nationalist Hate Group." Perhaps Hoover reflected Johnson's fear that King would run as a peace candidate for the presidency in 1968 and siphon off Democratic votes. The civil rights movement's collapse accelerated when Johnson withdrew his support of King and began to look upon the movement as an enemy. Before long, Northern antiriot troops in training at Fort Gordon, Georgia, were practicing crowd control on a "mob" whose leaders were identified by their signs, which said not "Stop the War," but "We Shall Overcome."

King saw how society gave precedence to the demands of the militaristic conflict in Vietnam over the one at home against poverty. He wanted to reverse Johnson's agenda and give the highest priority to feeding America and rescuing the nation's poor from their plight. To achieve this, he proposed a Poor People's March on Washington—because, he said, "Something is wrong with capitalism."

King's concern with economic issues led to his support of sanitation workers in Memphis when they went on strike against discrimination and low pay. While he was preparing for the Poor People's March on Washington, King responded to a call to come to Memphis and support the strikers. While King was leading a Memphis march of six thousand, black youths started smashing store windows and looting, and four thousand National Guardsmen were called in. One black youth was killed, 62 were injured, and 280 were arrested. King left greatly disturbed by this outbreak of violence but promised to return from Atlanta the following week and lead a nonviolent demonstration. While standing on the balcony of his room at the Lorraine Motel in Memphis, King was struck down by a sniper's bullet on April 4, 1968.

Four days after the assassination, Coretta Scott King led forty-two thousand marchers, and eventually the workers won union recognition, a dues checkoff, and the fifteen-cent raise they sought, double what the city originally offered. President Johnson used King's death to push harder for passage of a civil rights bill with controversial fair housing provisions. It sailed through Congress just six days after King's death.

King's murder sparked angry riots in more than a hundred cities in twenty-eight states. Forty blacks and five whites were killed. In addition to the riots, there were countless peaceful protests, marches, rallies, and meetings. Only a few of these were accompanied by small disturbances. Several store windows were broken in Macon, and there was minor violence in smaller towns such as Fort Valley and Cordele.

At King's nationally televised funeral at Ebenezer Baptist Church, many dignitaries and top-ranking officials were among the 800 who crowded into the church while 100,000 stood outside to hear the moving eulogies. Governor Maddox did not attend. He protested the lowering of flags to half-mast and refused to permit schools to close on the day of the funeral.

Two months after the assassination, James Earl Ray was arrested in London and charged with King's murder. Although various conspiracy theories had developed, Ray eventually pleaded guilty to the crime, and there was no trial. Ray was sentenced to life imprisonment.

By the time of King's death, the movement was already in disorder. King began by bridging the gap between old and young, between conservative and radical blacks, but eventually the cleavage became too great, and the movement split apart. The parts fragmented, and white liberal support drifted away. Perhaps the greatest tragedy of King's life is that his developing vision in the last five years of his life was so quickly forgotten. He believed that the promoters of imperialism were also responsible for poverty; consequently, racism's economic basis had to be attacked. This vision has been replaced in the American consciousness by the 1963 view of his dream for brotherhood. In truth, King was approaching disillusionment when he died. One month before his murder, he said, "We are constantly trying to finish that which is unfinishable.... Life is a continual story of shattered dreams." A week before he died, he told Williams, "Truly America is much, much sicker, Hosea, than I realized when I first began working in 1955." King died disappointed in America.

With time, King's role has been reevaluated. The charismatic, eloquent leader is no longer viewed as the "indispensable man" who was responsible for the civil rights movement's existence. As former SCLC staffer Ella Baker said, "The movement made Martin rather than Martin making the movement." Another part of the reevaluation of King relates to the halo his followers and the media placed on his brow. Initially, supporters ridiculed charges of King's extramarital sex life for fear that the truth would be used by Hoover and other enemies of black progress. Gradually, the realization has grown that the affairs existed but did not detract from his love of his family nor from his contribution to society. By one account, King's greatest contribution came when "he taught blacks how to confront those who oppressed them and how to take pride in their race and their history." Hosea Williams put it more succinctly: King "not only talked that talk; he walked that walk." In a touch of poetic justice, after Hoover died, a picture of King was hung in Hoover's old office.

King had indicated that Ralph David Abernathy was to be his successor. Abernathy, one of the Montgomery ministers who founded the SCLC, had moved to Atlanta as pastor of the West Hunter Baptist Church in 1961 to continue to work closely with King. Abernathy was not alone in thinking he could not replace King, but he tried manfully to go ahead with the Poor People's March. King had said that its goal was to achieve "40 acres and a mule" with interest. The march, headed by a mule train, began on May 2, 1968.

The FBI had fretted and watched over the Poor People's March, which turned into a disaster. Originally there were 2,650 people staying in the specially designed and donated plywood A-frames that served as tents. By June 19 there were only eight hundred remaining at the protest site. The rest had left its squalor, drugs, and crime, along with the militancy of some Black Power disciples. Disorganization and malaise displaced optimism. The police closed it down, and the A-frames were quickly whisked away on June 24 as cleanup crews emptied the site and replanted sod. In ninety minutes all evidence of the ill-fated endeavor was erased. The original Southern mule train arrived at about the time the encampment closed.

President Johnson presided over an increasingly divided country and decided not to seek reelection in 1968. Despite party admonitions to make delegations more representative, Maddox, as Georgia's governors were wont to do, handpicked the state delegation to the Democratic National Convention and included Leroy Johnson. There were four voting blacks, each with a black alternate, in the 107-person delegation. This delegation was challenged by one assembled by the Georgia Democratic Forum, an interracial coalition of liberals originally formed to support Ellis Arnall in the 1966 governor's race. The Credentials Committee voted to seat half of each delegation. Several of the unseated Maddox delegates switched to the Republican party in protest.

Bond was spokesman for Georgia's dissidents. As a well-known war opponent since the uproar at the Gold Dome in 1966, Bond became a national figure during the Chicago convention. He was nominated for vice president so that speakers supporting him could criticize the war and the police riot against antiwar protesters that was going on in the streets outside the convention hall. Bond withdrew his name, since he was several years short of meeting the age requirement. Nevertheless, he was the first black nominated for vice president at a major party's national convention.

Hubert H. Humphrey, Johnson's vice president, won the Democratic party's nomination, while Richard Nixon was the Republican candidate. The South yielded a third-party candidate, Alabama's segregationist governor George Wallace. Wallace announced his candidacy in Atlanta at a rally where three blacks were beaten with metal folding chairs. Richard Nixon won the election, although Wallace received the most votes in Georgia, thanks mainly to Talmadge's followers. Atlanta's blacks voted 80 percent for Humphrey, who got 22 percent of the white vote. Four new black legislators were elected that year, including the first from DeKalb County.

Blacks did not consider Nixon a good leader. Some resented Nixon's presence at Dr. King's funeral and complained of "crocodile tears." Nixon's top black appointment was Atlanta University graduate Elizabeth Duncan Koontz, who was named director of the Women's Bureau of the Department of Labor. His appointments to the Supreme Court did not sit so well with blacks. The Senate rejected two of them in part because they were so averse to civil rights. One of those rejected was G. Harrold Carswell, a native of Irwinton in Middle Georgia and "former" segregationist. Nixon's presidency, which ended in disgrace, was a cause of general dissatisfaction to blacks and yielded the terms "Southern Strategy" and "Benign Neglect" to describe methods of countering blacks' votes and ignoring their needs, respectively.

The March on Washington and King's "I Have a Dream" speech may have been exhilarating, but the fundamental status of most blacks did not change. The struggle to end Jim Crow in public places was mostly won in the 1960s, but achievements during that decade no longer seem revolutionary. The modest opening of society the movement brought about let relatively few blacks in, and this occurred without much assistance from Southern whites.

While Atlanta's largest white Baptist church voted to allow blacks to be seated in the main sanctuary in the mid 1960s, Mrs. King reminded the 1978 Southern Baptist Convention that its members had not helped in the civil rights struggle. Although individual churchmen spoke up for social justice, the majority who shied away from racial and social justice issues then continued to avoid them. Mrs. King told the Baptists that the next battle would be for full employment, a battle that had not been won as the nation entered the last decade of the century. The most significant measure of black progress—income—yielded disillusioning, even chilling, results. The median black income was 56 percent that of whites when the Montgomery bus boycott began. During the next twenty-five years it rose to 62 percent but dropped back down to 56 percent by 1985. Instead of making progress toward economic equality, blacks had come full circle, largely due to job discrimination and continued unequal education.

12

Modern Politics

The Quest for Empowerment

Since the mid-1960s, blacks have increasingly relied on the ballot box rather than street confrontations to seek change. As black voters' ranks increased and the legal system of segregation collapsed, politicians' overtly racist public rhetoric diminished and in most cases disappeared. The Republican party continued its mostly vain efforts to attract black voters. The bedrock conservatism of Georgia's white voters and politicians remained a political constant. Feelings of powerlessness and disillusionment persisted among many potential black voters, and "informed apathy" replaced "enforced apathy."

Black leaders increased their call for coalition politics, while Black Power advocates, with their appeal to "vote for someone who looks like you," were disregarded. Hancock County was a notable exception to this rule. The community was unique in the state, and probably the nation, due to the intensity of its racial polarization in the early 1970s. Blacks outnumbered whites four to one in the rural East Georgia county of ten thousand residents. However, whites received most of the benefits provided by local government in the impoverished county, which had never recovered from a 1920 boll-weevil infestation. The county seat of Sparta treated local blacks as ancient Sparta had treated its Helots. Total segregation was the rule. Blacks were barred from courthouse restrooms. Poverty and discrimination in the majority black county provided the combustible materials, and charismatic black activist John McCown lit the match. When the change came, it was furious. Hancock became a center of fear and anger after blacks wrested political control from the county's white courthouse ring.

The spark had come in 1966, when the SCLC started a voter registration drive. Blacks began to vote en masse and elected a majority of county commissioners in 1968. McCown established the East Central Committee for Opportunity Inc. (ECCO), which obtained huge sums of money—up to $10 million in federal and Ford Foundation grants—over the next several years. Black officials' demands for school desegregation brought race relations to an all-time low. The ECCO, based in Mayfield, began several projects for economic development—without any help from local whites.

Sparta bristled with small arms in the early 1970s as both blacks and whites prepared for armed warfare after McCown had risen to become the county's undisputed political boss. Whites, fearing blacks would open competing businesses, reacted to black militancy and store boycotts by arming. White Sparta Mayor T. M. "Buck" Patterson used city money to buy ten submachine guns. McCown then further armed his followers, and racial polarization became almost complete as mysterious fires and gunshots disturbed the peace. Between 1970 and 1974 virtually all white Hancock officials had lost their jobs. By 1974, public schools were 99 percent black, the private John Hancock Academy was 100 percent white, and McCown often led armed demonstrations on Sparta. The ECCO collapsed amid federal investigations of improprieties and McCown died in a January 1976 airplane crash. While a measure of calm returned, McCown's legacy of black political power remained. Over time, black officials gained a measure of acceptance by whites and often ran unopposed. Edith Ingram Grant became Georgia's first black probate judge in 1985. By 1986, racial tensions had eased to the point that Patterson pledged his support to Betty Hill, the first black woman to head a county commission in Georgia.

In 1970, there were fourteen black state legislators, including senators Leroy Johnson and Horace Ward and a dozen representatives: William Alexander, Julian Bond, Benjamin Brown, Julius C. Daugherty, James E. Dean, Clarence G. Ezzard, Grace Towns Hamilton (Georgia's first black woman legislator), John Hood, and E. J. Shepherd, all from metropolitan Atlanta, and Richard A. Dent of Augusta, Bobby Hill of Savannah, and Albert W. Thompson of Columbus.

That year, Albany attorney C. B. King, who ran for Congress in 1964, became the first black to seek the governor's office. Blacks also ran for lieutenant governor and secretary of state. King received seventy thousand votes, about 9 percent of the total. Leroy Johnson, the most politically powerful black in the state, did not support King because he thought King's chances of winning were nonexistent. Johnson supported racially moderate former governor Carl Sanders, who was running for his old job. Sanders got twice as many black votes as King, but the winner, a man named Jimmy Carter, received less than 10 percent of the black vote.

There were tinges of racism to his campaign, but Carter would later surprise supporters and foes alike. In 1966, Carter ran in the gubernatorial primary as a moderate and lost. Apparently unwilling to make that mistake again, in 1970 he identified with George Wallace and visited segregated schools. Carter announced he was proud to be running on the ticket with Lester Maddox, who could not succeed himself as governor and was running for lieutenant governor. Reports of dirty tricks surfaced. A photo of Sanders getting doused with victory champagne by black Atlanta Hawks basketball players was mysteriously distributed throughout South Georgia. Julian Bond maintained that the Carter campaign had helped to finance King's gubernatorial effort in order to pull black votes away from Carter's more liberal opponent, Sanders. Carter was labeled "an ignorant and bigoted redneck peanut farmer" by the Atlanta media. Carter's mother, "Miss Lillian," a Peace Corps volunteer at age seventy, and Carter's later actions helped to soften his image.

Carter, a Naval Academy graduate, had returned to his Southwest Georgia home in 1954 to manage the family farm and peanut warehouse. Before he took a seat on the Sumter County school board, Carter said he did not realize that white children rode buses to school while black children walked. He ran for the state Senate following the 1962 reapportionment. Quitman County boss Joe Hurst almost stole the election from him. Hurst arranged for the dead to vote, and since there was no secret ballot in Quitman, Hurst watched how the live people voted. There were 433 ballots cast in one 300-voter precinct. The primary results were overruled, and Carter got on the ballot and won the fall general election. One wag told him there should be an ethical standard for South Georgia elections: No one should be allowed to vote who had been dead over three years. Carter represented probably the most conservative district in the state during a time when voting-rights activists were being jailed in Americus, the Sumter County seat. His first Senate speech attacked the "30 Questions" test for black voters, which was applied to every black would-be voter in his home county. Though he was fearful for his political future, he was reelected in 1964. As governor, Carter told assembled judges and lawyers at the 1974 University of Georgia Law Day that none of them could have answered all the questions in that test.

Maddox also won his race. Although Carter had declared he was "proud to have Lester Maddox as a running mate," they became enemies, and Carter said the bickering with Maddox was his greatest problem while governor. Maddox disliked much of what Carter was doing, mainly because Carter was Georgia's most progressive chief executive yet regarding race relations. Carter said in his inaugural address that "no poor, weak, or black person should ever have to bear the additional burden of being deprived of the opportunity of an education, a job, or simply justice," and "the time for racial discrimination is over." He appointed dozens of blacks to key positions, including state Sen. Horace Ward to Fulton County Civil Court, thus making him the state's only black judge. Over Maddox's hysterical protests, Carter hung pictures of Martin Luther King, Jr., black educator Lucy Laney, and Henry McNeal Turner in the state Capitol on February 17, 1974. Although he had courted archsegregationist Roy Harris during the campaign, Carter did not reappoint Harris to the Board of Regents.

While Leroy Johnson was Georgia's most powerful black politician in 1970, Julian Bond was the most famous. A national poll of blacks that year put him at the top of the "most-admired" list. Although he received offers of support in 1970 to run for the Fifth District seat in Congress, Bond decided not to enter the campaign. Former King aide and Congregationalist minister Andrew Young did run in 1970 and lost to a Republican incumbent. In 1971, the legislature had gerrymandered the district to cut black voter strength from 40 percent to 35 percent, but the Justice Department disapproved of the plan under Section 5 of the Voting Rights Act. In 1972, Young ran again. He enjoyed a good reputation among whites, who appreciated his moderation as much as his dedication during the previous decade's civil rights struggles. The son of a New Orleans dentist became the first black to represent Georgia in Washington since Jefferson Long a century earlier. He was easily reelected in 1974.

The 1970s marked the maturation of black political power in Atlanta. In 1965, Q. V. Williamson was the first black elected to Atlanta's city council since Reconstruction. A thirty-year-old lawyer named Maynard Jackson, Jr., made a name for himself when he ran against entrenched U. S. Senator Herman Talmadge in 1968. The next year, he was elected vice mayor of Atlanta. Born of a long line of preachers, professors, doctors, and political activists in 1938, Jackson became Atlanta's first black mayor in 1973. Jackson was not Georgia's first black mayor, however. That distinction belonged to Richmond Hill of Greenville, who was elected earlier in 1973 and drew a fifteen-dollar-a-month-salary for the job.

While mayor, Jackson angered the city's white business leaders (the so-called Big Mules) by promoting minority set-asides on city contracts. The hallmark of his administration was the new Hartsfield International Airport, completed in 1980. Carl Ware served alongside Jackson. Ware was elected to the city council in 1973 and served as council president from 1976 to 1979. Jackson was barred by the city charter from serving a third consecutive term and went back to a lucrative law practice. By that time, Atlanta was solidly under black political control, although the city's powerful white business leaders wanted to see a friendlier face at city hall.

In part, Jackson had Leroy Johnson's shrewd machinations to thank for his rise. Johnson got half of black Atlanta to vote for Sam Massell for mayor in the 1969 election, although most black leaders supported black candidate Dr. Horace E. Tate. Johnson did not think Tate could win, and if Massell won, he would carry Maynard Jackson into the vice mayor's post. Johnson made the mistake of running against Jackson in 1973 and was soundly defeated. At one time the Deep South's only black lawmaker, Johnson was able to command high lecture fees; he made $40,000 in two years at up to $1,000 per speech. He had developed a lucrative private law practice that was worth $50,000 a year by 1970, when his net worth was half a million dollars. He represented soul singer James Brown in a divorce proceeding and a paternity suit. Johnson lived the high life. Much of his wealth came from his work as a boxing promoter. From 1967 to 1970, many different promoters had tried to put together a match between Muhammad Ali and Jerry Quarles. The government resented Muhammad Ali's refusal to be drafted on the grounds that he was a Muslim minister. Ali had gone to jail for his beliefs and was stripped of his heavyweight title. Johnson pulled off the coup and got $175,000 for setting up the match, which marked Ali's return to the ring.

Soon Johnson's fortunes would decline. The Internal Revenue Service started investigating Johnson two days after the fight. Johnson claimed the IRS was out to get him for organizing the match. In 1974, he was charged with tax evasion. After Johnson lost his Senate seat to Horace Tate in 1974, the tax-evasion charges were dropped, but he was convicted on a lesser charge of filing a false affidavit, one Johnson said he did not submit. The conviction came despite testimony from character witnesses Carl Sanders, Daddy King, and Benjamin Mays. Johnson finally received a sentence of sixty days and a year's probation, but his political career was shattered. The case raised questions about a double standard for politicians, one that was deliberately set higher for black officials in order to trip them up. As blacks continued to gain elective offices, those questions would persist.

Julian Bond continued to speak out on the issues and served as a national spokesman for black interests. He published *A Time to Speak, A Time to Act: The Movement in Politics* in 1972. In 1974, *Time* named Bond one of "200 faces for the future." That year he replaced Horace Ward in the state Senate following Ward's appointment to the bench. The state Senate seat would be the highest prize in a political career that disappointed Bond's many admirers, for they hoped he would go much further. While Bond continued to get media coverage, other blacks got power. In 1973, Carter advisers picked State Rep. Ben Brown over Bond for a seat on the exclusive and influential twenty-five-member National Democratic Election Committee.

In 1974, with the support of Brown, head of the legislature's fourteen-member Black Caucus, George Busbee defeated Maddox in a primary election runoff. Maddox had pledged to remove King's picture from the Capitol and claimed Busbee would use the state's highest office to advance Bond's presidential aspirations. That year, Zell Miller, who opposed the 1964 Civil Rights Act but had since moderated his views, won the lieutenant governor's race. Busbee's election marked the advent of pro-business "Chamber of Commerce" governors who promoted racial moderation and economic growth throughout the 1970s and 1980s.

Blacks continued to make advances. Hosea Williams was elected to the Georgia House in 1974 from DeKalb County. In 1975, Bond's brother James was elected to the Atlanta City Council. Reps. Richard A. Dent of Augusta and Albert Thompson of Columbus became the first black chairmen of House committees. Black Georgians were more successful in attaining state and local offices in 1976 than any year previously. John Lewis of the Voter Education Project reported that seventy-three blacks were voted into office in 1976 in Georgia, more than in any other Southern state.

Although Carter had received mixed reviews as governor, he was ambitious and burst onto the national scene in 1976 with his presidential campaign. Unelected Republican President Gerald Ford was vulnerable because he had pardoned Richard Nixon quickly after the disgraced president left office as a result of the Watergate scandal. Alabama Governor George Wallace opened up the Democratic campaign in the lead (only 1 percent of Democrats polled in March 1976 said they supported Jimmy Carter), but Wallace faltered during the primaries. Carter owed Daddy King a huge debt after the candidate got in trouble for saying he would fight federal attempts to dilute "the ethnic purity" of neighborhoods. A well-publicized meeting with King helped Carter deflect criticism that the comment was racist. Andrew Young also played a major role in the campaign. Carter's volunteer "Peanut Brigade," with several black members, helped him obtain the Democratic nomination. The brigade traveled the nation knocking on doors and helped Carter gain key victories in the New Hampshire, Florida and Wisconsin primaries.

Bond also harbored presidential aspirations. He began to campaign in 1975 on a populist platform of controlling multinational corporations, instituting national health insurance, and reducing the defense budget. Lack of financial support forced him to withdraw before the race developed. Bond was unenthusiastic about the man from Plains. He once said that Carter was not his first choice, or even his tenth. He campaigned for Carter in Florida mainly as a way to campaign against Wallace. Bond claimed that Carter was a cynical politician who could not honestly claim liberal principles; after all, Carter had identified with George Wallace in his 1970 campaign. Bond traveled the country warning blacks "to be wary of the smiling Georgian who sang their hymns." Bond also expressed interest in succeeding Roy Wilkins as NAACP executive secretary. Bond called the post "the most powerful job a black American could hold." At the time, Wilkins denied rumors he would retire. When he did step down later, Benjamin Hooks got the job.

Even though many blacks stayed home on Election Day in 1976, Georgia's favorite son defeated Ford, who was linked to Nixon's policies in the minds of many blacks. Carter garnered upwards of 90 percent of the black vote, which enabled him to capture several Southern states. On the morning of Carter's inaugural, Daddy King preached an old-time Southern camp-meeting sermon at the Lincoln Memorial, and the 120-voice Atlanta University five-college choir under the direction of Morehouse's Dr. Wendell Whalum sang "The Battle Hymn of the Republic."

President Carter appointed more blacks to high office than any previous chief executive. In his first three weeks he appointed seventeen blacks to cabinet and subcabinet positions, more than any other president. His appointment of thirty-seven black judges exceeded the total of all previous presidents combined. Carter's appointment of Griffin Bell as attorney general was generally popular with Georgia's blacks, for Bell had consistently supported civil rights as a federal judge. Bell and Carter both supported the extension and expansion of the Civil Rights Commission. Carter's highest appointment of a black came when Andrew Young was named ambassador to the United Nations. "Of all the people I have known in public service, Andy Young is the best," Carter said. Young had sympathy for and understanding of Third World problems that went beyond the administration's, and he often found himself in trouble for his candid, off-the-cuff comments. Young was forced to resign when, contrary to U. S. policy, he met with representatives of the Palestine Liberation Organization.

By the mid-1970s, Bond expressed concern that Southern black politics had been "a tremendous success in winning elections and putting black faces in high places, but a failure in having an ideology that would make all the effort and suffering of the past meaningful." The root problems of the black experience remained. In a speech at Fort Valley State College in 1977, Bond said, "Prayer, protest, and politics have not done it. Elections, riots, and demonstrations have not changed the relationship of the haves and the have-nots. . . . We are ignorant despite integrated schools. . . . The struggle now is for economic democracy." At that year's meeting of the Georgia Association of Black Elected Officials held in Americus, State Rep. David Scott took a more conciliatory tone and called on blacks to stop being "destructive and jealous" of each other and to "start building alliances with the many good and decent white people of the state."

The Republican party tried to counter the massive black support for Carter in Georgia and renewed its efforts to recruit minority voters. The Fulton County Republican Club even quoted Jesse Jackson: "Don't put all your political eggs in one basket." However, the GOP's discouragement of federal activism, which blacks knew they needed to make progress, made the party's efforts to attract blacks in Georgia difficult. Fort Valley A.M.E. minister James Webb won an upset victory to the post of first vice chairman of the state's Republican party in 1977. In 1978, he was unopposed for lieutenant governor in the Republican primary but was defeated by Democratic incumbent Zell Miller in the fall. Like his fellow statewide Republican candidates, Webb was only able to gain 18 percent of the vote. The party was weak, and Webb, running as a traditional Republican, was unable to get black voters to cross over.

In 1978, J. B. Stoner raised his sights, though not his outlook, and ran for governor against George Busbee, who, thanks to a change in the law, could seek a second term. Stoner condemned the moderate incumbent as "one of the worst race-mixing governors in the history of Georgia" and blasted Georgia's Fair Employment Practices Act, a law Stoner denounced as the first civil rights bill in the history of modern Georgia. One of Stoner's campaign leaflets said, "We cannot have law and order...and niggers too!" The Atlanta chapter of the NAACP, headed by Bond, sued unsuccessfully to force the Federal Communications Commission to censor Stoner's use of his favorite racial epithet in paid TV advertisements. Busbee won; Stoner received 5 percent of the Democratic vote in the primary.

In 1980, there were 249 black elected officials in Georgia. The state's population was 27 percent black, but blacks made up only 3.7 percent of the state's 6,660 elected officeholders—this was the most dismal showing in the Deep South. Nine of the states' twenty majority-black counties had no black elected officials. Eighty of the 107 counties that were at least 20 percent black had no black elected officials. Georgia also had the South's worst showing on this score. In many towns it was extremely difficult for blacks to gain elective office, yet this was necessary to achieve equal treatment. For example, when black plumber Roosevelt Arnold was elected to the Fort Valley Utility Commission in 1970, he was able to change the practice of cutting the electricity off for nonpayment by blacks ten days earlier than if the delinquent account belonged to a white.

There were several reasons why whites maintained political power out of proportion to their numbers. Black voter apathy and failure to register, at-large voting, white bloc voting, interference and intimidation, and/or absentee-ballot abuses often played a role in thwarting black political empowerment.

In 1980, although Taliaferro County in East Georgia was 72 percent black, no black county commission candidates ever won, due largely to the misuse of absentee ballots. White candidates or their helpers would go to illiterate or easily intimidated black voters and get them to apply for an absentee ballot. Officials would send the ballot to the white "helper," who would then take it back to the black voter and "help" fill it out. More than one-third of the votes cast there in 1980 were absentee. Blacks in Clay County in South Georgia on the Alabama line were particularly disheartened that year when black farmer Arnett Richardson was defeated for a county commission post. Richardson had gone to bed on the night of the Democratic primary thinking he had won the race, only to find out the next morning that he had been defeated by seven votes, thanks to white bloc voting through absentee ballots. Nearly a third of the white candidate's 140 votes had come from absentee ballots. Only 5 of Richardson's 133 votes were absentee.

One abuse the 1965 Voting Rights Act helped correct was at-large voting, a common practice in Georgia that often hurt the chances of black office seekers. Candidates would be elected on a countywide or citywide basis rather than from districts, some of which would have a black majority. This ensured the election of whites by diluting black voting strength. Black candidates were usually overwhelmed by white bloc voting in at-large elections. This induced voter apathy among blacks, who reasoned they had no influence on local politics. Some Georgia counties implemented at-large voting after the Voting Rights Act was in force without notifying the Justice Department, a practice that was a clear violation of both the spirit and the letter of the federal law.

Where blacks were in a minority, a smaller percentage of blacks than whites voted. In 1980, when 20 percent of Houston County's potential voters were black, only 12 percent of the registered voters were, and less than 10 percent actually voted. Black Warner Robins educator Houston Porter overcame these odds to defeat a white commissioner from Perry in 1980 for an at-large seat on the Houston County Commission. However, at-large elections in the county seat of Perry continued to keep blacks off the city council, although they made up 35 percent of the population. Under the Voting Rights Act, election-law changes in Georgia and other Southern states had to be approved by the Department of Justice. When Perry's city charter was redrawn in 1983, its authors were careful not to alter the election code. By avoiding changes, they also avoided review by the Justice Department.

By the mid-1970s the American Civil Liberties Union's Atlanta office was inundated with requests to challenge at-large voting under provisions of the Voting Rights Act. The ACLU's Voter Law Project began systematically challenging at-large elections and winning the suits. There were also many suits against at-large voting by black voters, candidates, civil rights groups such as the NAACP, and the Atlanta-based Voter Education Project, headed by John Lewis. Wherever blacks constituted at least 20 percent of the population, they had a decent chance to gain representation if single-member districts were adopted. Such suits were long, drawn-out, expensive affairs. A 1976 suit against Putnam County and Eatonton took five years to resolve. Blacks were a 51 percent majority there but lost every opposed election. U. S. District Court Judge Wilbur Owens, Jr., of Macon found that Eatonton was a "racially polarized community" where officials had been and continued to be "unresponsive to their black constituency." Owens ordered the city and county to abandon their at-large voting system. Two blacks were elected while the suit was in progress, and others have gained office since.

Few counties dropped at-large voting without a fight, especially in the Black Belt that stretched across Georgia's old plantation country. Twenty-two suits were filed against at-large voting in 1980, and 156 federal election observers monitored balloting in eight Georgia counties: Bulloch, Calhoun, Early, Johnson, Mitchell, Sumter, Telfair, and Tift. An ACLU suit against Dooly County charged that at-large voting for the school board and county commission had been adopted two years after the Voting Rights Act but had not been cleared with the Justice Department. When it was submitted (over a decade late), Justice objected. The county signed a consent decree, the General Assembly established single-member districts, and the first black was elected to the Dooly Board of Education in 1981. The struggle to implement the Voting Rights Act required long-term vigilance. The district boundaries for county commission and school-board elections were based on the 1970 census. By 1986, because of demographic changes, these boundaries failed to meet federal guidelines for black voter registration and black voters filed suit again.

In 1982, the Voting Rights Act was extended for twenty-five years. Changes in the law removed the requirement that plaintiffs prove intent to discriminate; from then on they only had to show that the system's effects were discriminatory. This and a U. S. Supreme Court decision that year involving Burke County put more pressure on counties to reform their at-large systems or face the likelihood of defeat in court.

Successful lawsuits did not erase white contempt for blacks' political aspirations. Baldwin County was the target of a successful 1982 voting-rights suit, and the county commission was converted to single-member districts for the 1984 election. Baldwin was the only Georgia county to have federal poll watchers at a fall 1984 runoff election, after black candidate Clarence "Smokey" Simmons successfully challenged his white opponent on the basis of voting irregularities. Simmons and Oscar Davis became Baldwin's first black commissioners, but they quickly ran into a problem countless black politicians have faced before and since: They were outnumbered and ignored on the five-member panel. Although the city of Milledgeville had avoided the 1982 lawsuit by adopting district city council seats, controversy surrounded the 1985 election after a black candidate lost a race by a twelve-vote margin after absentee ballots were counted. The victorious white candidate summed up his racial attitudes and disgust with federal law in one breath when he told a reporter, "Gonna have to beat niggers two or three times, looks like now." Outraged blacks called for his resignation, and he fell back on the time-honored political tradition of denying he made the statement.

Many Georgia counties elected their first black officials in the mid-1980s as a result of legal challenges. In 1983 the Justice Department sued to overturn Lowndes County's at-large election system. Although the county was 30 percent black and Valdosta, the county seat, was 39 percent black, the county's electoral process was so discriminatory that no black had ever tried to run for office. In the first half of 1984, four at-large systems were overturned in court, and another four were broken up as a result of settlements. Successful suits came in Clay and Morgan counties, the town of Cochran in Bleckley County, and Dawson in "Terrible Terrell." Carroll County agreed to changes to avoid suits, and Soperton and Treutlen, Monroe, and Calhoun counties signed consent decrees after suits was filed. A 1980 consent decree changed Calhoun County's at-large system. A black county commissioner was appointed in Bulloch County as a result of an out-of-court settlement. A similar suit was filed against Crawford County, which was about 40 percent black. In 1985, Judge Owens ordered Crawford County to divide into five single-member districts. Two of the new districts were 72 percent black. In counties throughout Georgia, local blacks, the Voter Education Project, and other groups continued the pressure for reform.

Perhaps the most dramatic and positive results from these struggles came in Burke County, a 60 percent black county near Augusta on the South Carolina line. Before blacks took their case all the way to the Supreme Court, there had never been a black county commissioner. As a result, the county was clearly unresponsive to the needs of blacks and supported a private school for whites that had been set up to circumvent integration, hired only token blacks, and paid them less than whites for the same work. The county also kept blacks off grand juries and interfered with their voting rights. It was still the custom in 1980 for white creditors to stand conspicuously near polls on Election Day to ensure that poor blacks voted "right."

In 1976, blacks challenged the practice of electing five commissioners by countywide vote and asked in a federal lawsuit that the county be divided into five districts to end at-large voting for the county commission. White officials battled the case all the way to the Supreme Court. In July 1982 the Supreme Court used the Fourteenth Amendment to rule that Burke County had illegally discriminated against blacks and held that district commission elections should replace at-large contests. The county was ordered to divide into five districts, each of which would elect one commissioner, and to pay the black plaintiffs $300,000 for legal fees. Burke County was the only county in the state to have federal monitors that year. To ensure honesty at the polls, the Justice Department dispatched thirty-six observers to watch the fall elections. Two blacks were elected to the commission. In 1984, a third was elected from a predominantly white district, giving blacks a majority on the board.

The rise of blacks to political power meant a better deal for both black and white residents. The health budget quadrupled, and the recreation budget increased thirty times from the minuscule figure it was earlier. Nutrition programs for senior citizens were installed. That Burke County was enjoying a construction boom did not hurt. In an otherwise depressed rural Georgia, Burke became an island of prosperity because of the construction of Georgia Power Company's $9-billion-plus nuclear Plant Vogtle, which injected jobs, money, and taxes into the local economy. Long-range plans for water and sewerage development were formulated to attract industry, for after Plant Vogtle was completed, nearly ten thousand construction workers would be terminated. Some white observers admitted that the black commissioners were more professional and service-oriented than the white farmers who had preceded them. Black faces appeared behind desks in the courthouse and in the sheriff's department. (After all, the commission set the sheriff's budget.) Although most whites accepted the changes, Burke County was not spared from racial turmoil. On August 18, 1984, a rumor that a black had been beaten to death by police set off a demonstration that was quelled by a hundred law officers. The Georgia State Crime Laboratory concluded that the man had died of heat exhaustion aggravated by the presence of the sickle cell trait. In 1985, legislation was passed to make the school board an elective body. Black leaders blamed themselves for a low black voter turnout in 1986, when whites maintained a 4–1 majority on the school board.

Perhaps nowhere in Georgia was the struggle to gain representation more significant than in the northwest Burke County community of Keysville. In 1985, Keysville had no police or fire department or other city services; in fact, it had no government since 1933, even though the city charter was still valid. Whites had responded to a potential black majority by allowing the city government to lapse. In 1985, Keysville was 80 percent black, and the white minority did not want *any* government installed or to pay the taxes that would be required to establish city services. Nevertheless, local blacks called a town meeting in 1985 and scheduled elections. Unopposed blacks qualified to run for mayor and a five-member city council. Whites refused to participate and filed a suit contending that the procedures were illegal. A judge in Augusta threw out the election results because the town's boundaries were not properly fixed. Eventually, the boundaries were fixed, and more elections were held in 1988, resulting in the election of a black mayor and a 4-1 black majority on the city council. The last suits were thrown out in 1990, and Keysville Mayor Emma Gresham turned to the everyday matters of providing city services and redrawing the outdated city charter.

Another form of at-large voting involved sole commissioners, who were invariably white. In 1984, Georgia was the only state with counties under one-man rule. Twenty-four sole commissioners could (and often did) ignore the law requiring calling meetings before making decisions. Perry Usher ran majority black Stewart County as he pleased; blacks feared reprisals if they voted. (Usher's wife issued the county's allotment of food stamps.) Voter Education Project complaints to the Justice Department led to a probe of this practice in 1984, but one-man rule remained a significant factor in Georgia politics. A 1986 lawsuit by the NAACP and the Voter Education Project failed to overturn one-man rule in Carroll County. Dodge and Bleckley counties also survived legal challenges. By 1990 the number of sole commissioner counties had fallen to nineteen, due to local referenda. Although most one-member commissions existed in North Georgia counties with relatively few black voters, one-person rule still applied in several South Georgia counties with significant black populations: Wheeler, Dodge, Bleckley, Pulaski, and Stewart. State Rep. Tyrone Brooks of Atlanta pushed unsuccessfully in 1989 and 1991 for legislation to outlaw all one-person commissions in the state.

District voting did not ensure the election of blacks. If districts were drawn with white majorities, virtually all blacks who bothered to run would be defeated. Although Savannah, Augusta, and Columbus had black legislators in 1970, Macon and Bibb County had to be redistricted before William Randall, Jr., and David Lucas could become the first black legislators to represent Macon since Henry McNeal Turner. Change bred more change. Randall in turn introduced legislation to redistrict the local water and sewerage authority, which then got its first black members, Booker W. Chambers and Herbert Dennard, in 1980. Randall and Lucas also pushed successfully for majority-black Macon City Council and Bibb County Commission districts.

Gaining power was one thing; keeping it was another matter. Blacks struggled for many years to gain empowerment in Fort Valley, about a half hour's drive south of Macon, then lost their voting majority on city council in the next election. Majority-black Peach County was formed in 1924 from Houston and Macon County and named after the county's most famous agricultural commodity. Home to a family-owned bus-manufacturing company and the state's most rural predominantly black college, Fort Valley seemed like a typical Middle Georgia small town in the early 1960s. The local NAACP branch had withered away a decade before that, and black physician Otis W. Smith had been run out of town for violating racial mores in 1957. Many blacks were afraid to vote because they had no faith that the ballot was secret, since voting was segregated. Unlike Georgia's other black colleges, Fort Valley State College had been quiet during the early days of the civil rights movement. There were awakenings in 1963, after a handcuffed black prisoner was shot to death by a state trooper. Blacks organized the Citizens Education Committee and staged a successful boycott of local merchants to protest employment discrimination. Blacks began to seek office in 1964. The next year, Peach county moved from a plurality to a runoff election system—yet another method whites used to keep blacks from gaining office. Even if a black came out of a primary as the top vote getter, white voters could rally to the polls in the runoff and make sure the white candidate won.

In 1970, black mortician Claybon Edwards ran for the Fort Valley City Council. The city charter disallowed those who owed property taxes from voting. A group of blacks recently purged from the rolls due to this requirement got an injunction against the city and were allowed to vote on a separate machine. Edwards was ahead when the machine votes, not counting the "injunction machine's" were tallied, but lost initially by eleven votes when numerous absentee votes mysteriously appeared and were counted; those from the "injunction machine" were not. Edwards took his case to court, and Superior Court Judge George Culpepper ruled against Edwards, as did the federal District Court. However, Judge Griffin Bell on the Fifth Circuit Court of Appeals reversed the lower courts, and Edwards was seated fifteen months after the election. Bell later cited this ruling to President Carter as proof he was fit to be attorney general.

In 1972, the Georgia General Assembly passed a law allowing college students to vote where they went to school. This—and the fact that a full slate of black candidates were up for election that year—alarmed local whites, who registered and turned out in record numbers to beat back the challenge. Rumors that the town's largest employer, Blue Bird Body Company, had threatened to pull out of town in response to a "black takeover" helped suppress and intimidate the black vote. Several lawsuits came out of the election. An unprecedented lawsuit was filed by whites against the Board of Regents demanding the integration of Fort Valley State College. Although the suit assailed the quality of education at the school, its main purpose was to attack the college as a political power base. The suit was originally filed not by prospective white students, who in all likelihood would have been admitted, but by Fort Valley's voter registrar. The county school superintendent fired several black teachers for supporting Dr. Robert Threatt, a college education professor running for the school superintendent's job. The teachers won their suit and were reinstated. In the April 1972 city elections, three blacks, Dr. Clinton Dixon, William Arnold, and Claude M. Lawson, were running for city posts and were beaten, thanks to absentee ballots. They sued the county election commission. In 1973, the Justice Department filed a similar suit against city officials. The court ordered city officials to quit handing out absentee ballots to nonresidents. Although there had been voting abuses, the court refused to throw out the election results. The three defeated candidates wanted to push the issue, but they could not afford the legal fees—a problem for many frustrated black candidates. Peach County adopted single-member county commission districts in 1979 in response to a suit filed by Fort Valley State College faculty member H. W. Berry and others that went to the U. S. Supreme Court. Berry also filed a successful suit that challenged the county's discriminatory jury-selection methods. This was especially important because Peach County's school board members were selected by the grand jury, not by election.

Blacks continued to work for political gains, and Fort Valley got its first black mayor, Rudolph Carson, in 1980. Carson was one of six black mayors in Georgia's 551 municipalities. In a strange twist, white businesses had banded together behind Carson to prevent a former mayor who was popular with blacks from winning. While this challenge never materialized, Carson barely defeated another white candidate, who blamed his defeat on a low white turnout. With the 1980 elections, blacks held eight elective offices and a voting majority on the city council and the utility commission—quite a change from 1970. Blacks were unable to hold on to their gains, however. Once elected, Carson downplayed racial politics and promoted himself as a "colorless" mayor. In his study of Peach County, Lawrence Hanks stated that Carson may have committed "political suicide" in a local newspaper interview after his first year in office. Carson said he did not want to see Fort Valley become a black town, and he resolved that since he was mayor of all the people, he would never attend a conference of black mayors. Many blacks resented his refusal to identify with his core constituency. To compound his problems, Carson's white support faded when he was challenged by a white pharmacist in 1982. Due to a low black turnout, Carson, two black council members, and a black utility commissioner—all of the black candidates up for re-election—lost their posts. Race would continue to be the dominant political factor in the majority-black county throughout the 1980s.

Despite the litigation, voter organization, and political campaigning by blacks going on all over Georgia, the white establishment in some communities refused to recognize that blacks had more rights than they did a generation before. In Wrightsville (home of Heisman Trophy winner Herschel Walker), a small town of 2,000 fifty miles east of Macon, this attitude caused trouble to flare up in 1980, when black leaders used the time-honored tools of the civil rights movement. Johnson County was one of Georgia's most rural, backward, and impoverished counties. Although its population was about one-third black, only one black (a justice of the peace elected from a militia district) had held elective office there since Reconstruction.

Sheriff Roland Attaway ran Johnson County from 1960 to 1985 as his fiefdom from his office in the courthouse in Wrightsville, where the honor roll saluted only the county's white Vietnam veterans. The local American Legion maintained an all-white park, Little League, and swimming pool. The city cemetery was for whites only. Tension had long existed because of employment discrimination against blacks, who occupied only menial positions with the county government and were shut out of the better private-sector jobs. The Rev. E. J. Wilson, pastor of the Neeler Chapel A.M.E. Church, began to organize local blacks to gain their rights shortly after he came there in 1979 from Albany. Earlier Wilson had worked with controversial black activist John McCown in Hancock County. The local supermarket relented and hired its first black cashier following two months of picketing.

As in many rural counties, the sheriff was the most powerful politician. Because Attaway's grip on the town was so complete, black leaders directed their demands to him, not to the city council, county commission, or school board. After the protests began, tensions built up, and the U. S. Justice Department sent two black mediators to Wrightsville, a development that local whites resented. On April 8, Attaway swore out warrants charging local SCLC leader John Martin and Wilson with "interfering with a law officer" after the two refused to leave his office. Violence erupted the next night, when Wilson led seventy-five marchers to the courthouse to protest the warrants and an alleged death threat to Martin by Police Chief Linton Smith. Black protesters were attacked by a mob of two hundred whites armed with clubs and chains. Meanwhile, local law enforcement officers either encouraged or participated in the attack. During the melee, federal mediator Fred Crawford tried to telephone the Justice Department in Washington about the conflict but was attacked by mob members. "You Justice Department people get out of this town," Attaway said. Another federal mediator was struck in the face by a chain-wielding mob member after being called a "nigger lover." Two newspaper reporters were also beaten by the white mob. At least nine people were injured.

The rallies and demonstrations continued through the week. Schools closed the following day, and riot-equipped police dispersed groups of whites and blacks the following night after black demonstrators read a list

of their grievances in front of the sheriff's office. The state patrol was
called in to ensure peace. Reporters covering events in town were
amazed at their resemblance to the civil rights struggles of nearly two
decades before. Attaway liked to view the protest as an alien-led invasion
and refused to recognize Martin and Wilson as Johnson County residents,
even though Martin had lived in Wrightsville since 1969. The sheriff
called Martin "a transplant from Dublin" (a larger town about twenty
miles away) and used that charge to deny the legitimacy of all protests.
Attaway had a simple solution: The county's problems would be solved
"when the good black people get rid of the bad black people." Smelling
strife, J. B. Stoner and the Klan descended on the town in hopes of
inciting violence. On Saturday, April 12, about three hundred protesters,
organized by SCLC leader Joseph Lowery, came to Wrightsville and
faced Stoner and Imperial Wizard Bill Wilkinson along with about one
hundred whites, some in white sheets calling for "White Power." Over a
hundred state troopers kept the two groups apart. The SCLC held
marches and demonstrations at Wrightsville every Saturday for the next
nine weeks. Stoner also made regular visits, and the state patrol
maintained its presence.

The white power structure gave no hint of concessions, and blacks
became more apprehensive and militantly defensive. Tensions continued
to build; in mid-May, they were punctuated by sporadic gunfire and
suspicious fires. Attaway tried to intimidate blacks into submission.
Martin and Wilson were arrested on May 19 on the warrants Attaway had
sworn in April. That day, the Rev. Fred Taylor, an SCLC official from
Atlanta, was beaten severely and had ribs broken by a mob of seventy-five
to one hundred whites as he came out of Attaway's office. Taylor was taken
to the county line by a deputy and told to stay out. That night, following
fires and shootings that the sheriff blamed on a conspiracy by blacks,
Attaway and his men arrested between thirty-eight and fifty blacks in an
indiscriminate roundup that was conducted without warrants or probable
cause. Some were held several days and were denied permission to
contact lawyers. Blacks continued to demonstrate. Leading a May 24
protest, Wilson said, "We will not be satisfied until all our brothers are
behind bars or free."

Attaway either failed to gauge the depth of blacks' resentment, or he
did not care. Blacks increased their activities with a voter registration
drive and picketed stores that did not hire blacks. Faced with a growing
protest movement that had not been cowed by violence, whites sat down
with blacks to seriously discuss the issues. In June, a biracial committee
was established, a contract was signed to pave three streets in black
neighborhoods, and two black deputy voting registrars and one black
deputy sheriff were appointed.

The violence and tension subsided, but Wrightsville's problems were not solved. Wrightsville was the scene of demonstrations for the next several years. Attaway and fifteen other whites faced civil suits filed by civil rights organizations seeking $21.3 million in damages in connection with the April 8 attack on demonstrators and the mass arrests in May. Curiously, the Justice Department (now under the Reagan Administration) refused to let black mediator Robert Ensley testify. He had written a report stating that Attaway and his chief deputy "led a group of armed white men in an attack on a group of blacks who were peacefully protesting on the courthouse grounds" on April 8, 1980. An all-white federal jury in Dublin ruled against the plaintiffs in February 1983. In August 1984, the SCLC appealed the verdict on behalf of eight of the arrested blacks. In 1986, a federal appeals court partially reversed the decision and ruled that two black victims, Dearest Davis and Cassandra Linder, should collect damages.

Due to unrelenting pressure by blacks in the form of federal suits and demonstrations, conditions in Wrightsville slowly improved. In October 1983, black candidate Willie Linder was elected to the Wrightsville City Council after the at-large system was cut up into three districts, one of which was 75 percent black. Sheriff Attaway suffered a stroke at a fish fry at the time of the appeal and was partially paralyzed only one week after he was reelected to his seventh term as sheriff in August 1984. On June 17, 1985, Attaway was removed from office because of his physical condition, and an election to replace him was scheduled for August 13. The Justice Department sent nineteen observers to this election, since observers at earlier elections had reported irregularities. Chief Deputy Russell Tanner defeated other whites and became the next sheriff. By then, blacks also had been elected to the county commission and the school board. In January 1986, the Reverend Wilson died of a heart attack at the age of forty-three. Black mourners held a memorial rally for him— in front of the courthouse.

Throughout the 1970s, Atlanta's increasing crime rate—largely the function of a growing black underclass—drew more and more negative attention to the city. Additionally, the Atlanta Police Department had suffered through a police-promotion scandal. By 1979, Atlanta had been named "the Murder Capital of the United States." The city was just beginning a two-year nightmare of missing and murdered black children. Atlanta police arrested Wayne Williams on June 21, 1981, in that case. Whites, fearing that no black would act effectively against crime, vigorously opposed Andrew Young's mayoral candidacy in 1981. A record number of black voters turned out that fall to elect Young as mayor (in nonpartisan elections) over white state legislator Sidney Marcus. The new mayor, calling himself "a law and order man," immediately acted against crime, restored the morale of the police department, and gave blacks a much larger role in law enforcement. In his first year as mayor, the Atlanta crime rate dropped 6 percent, the first decline in five years. Atlanta lost its ranking as the nation's murder capital. Unfortunately, the improvement was only temporary.

White business leaders and Mayor Maynard Jackson had endured an antagonistic relationship; Young changed that. Young's role in the civil rights movement had been as a conciliator, and he patched up the relationship between the white business community and the black political power structure. There was no doubt that Young was pro-business. "My agenda for the first year and the business community's were almost identical," he said. His critics agreed, charging that white business interests continued to run the city even though blacks occupied the key political positions. To his admirers, Young was continuing the brand of coalition politics that had marked the pre-Jackson administrations. Young was an international figure, and he wanted Atlanta to be an international city. The globetrotting mayor used his international contacts gained as UN ambassador to get a hundred foreign companies to locate their U. S. headquarters in Atlanta. Atlanta Chamber of Commerce President Gerald Bartels called Young's administration "the golden years for Atlanta." Young's critics accused him of being a weak manager and an absentee mayor, due largely to his out-of-town trade missions.

Critics also faulted him for promoting development over neighborhood preservation and for "presiding over the widening gap between the haves and the have-nots." Some of Young's former civil rights comrades in arms opposed his adoption of the business community's agenda, which included a one-cent sales-tax increase to lower property taxes. This led some to label Atlanta "the Oreo City," black on the outside but white on the inside. Young's support for the Presidential Parkway, a road that would connect downtown Atlanta with the Carter Library but would also serve as a major traffic corridor through some of Atlanta's most politically active neighborhoods, also drew fire. One neighborhood preservationist said, "He never met a building permit he didn't like." Some of Young's old colleagues resented his coolness toward Jesse Jackson's presidential ambitions. A Walter Mondale supporter in 1984, Young was booed at the Democratic Convention that year by Jackson delegates. Despite the criticism, Young, like Maynard Jackson, was a popular mayor. He was reelected in 1985 with 80 percent of the vote in a three-man race.

Young had to deal with "white flight"—the movement by white middle-class residents away from Atlanta to the surrounding suburbs. This was a problem for many large cities, whose centers were becoming dangerous deserts after working hours as the people who worked there went back to their suburban homes at the end of the workday. This left the areas hostage to the desperate poor, unemployed youth gangs, and criminal elements that increasingly drove out people who could afford to leave. In 1986, Young hoped to reverse this trend of inner-city deterioration with the development of fourteen thousand new housing units inside Atlanta, especially in the downtown area, for middle-class families with incomes of at least $26,000. With the same goal in mind, Young pushed the $142 million development of Underground Atlanta, an entertainment, dining and shopping complex just south of Five Points in the city's center. Completed in 1989, Underground's first years were very successful. The complex drew hundreds of thousands of tourists and suburb dwellers back downtown at night and on weekends, providing additional sales-tax revenues and an estimated two thousand jobs.

The interconnected problems of unemployment, poverty, and crime continued. In the late 1980s, Atlanta had the nation's second-highest poverty rate. In his last year in office, Young brought up a $3.75 billion proposal to build 42,500 housing units and rehabilitate 36,400 others over fifteen years, mostly for low-income families. The proposal "came so late in his tenure that it only served as a reminder that he never took the issue very seriously," wrote *Atlanta Constitution* columnist Cynthia Tucker. Young had always hoped that the economic development he had promoted would benefit all the city's citizens, and he was quick to point out that he had been elected "mayor, not messiah." As his legacy he could point to $4.3 billion in economic development: Foreign-bank branches had climbed from eleven to thirty-one, and one thousand foreign firms and twenty-six trade offices that accounted for about $3 billion in foreign investments and fifty thousand jobs had located in the city. Young left office at the end of 1989 and planned to use this record in his campaign to become Georgia's first black governor.

Atlanta had become a bastion of black power and a major player on the international scene. It was a leading business, transportation, and convention center, host to the 1988 Democratic National Convention, and designated host to the 1994 Super Bowl and the 1996 Olympics. (Young received a large measure of credit for helping Atlanta secure the Olympics.) Atlanta had "the most powerful black leaders in the United States," according to one expert, who also believed that the city's black businessmen were the single most influential group in the city. The city's politics had grown more sophisticated, and the old politics of race had undergone some unusual transformations. In 1986, Atlanta City Council President Marvin Arrington sounded an increasingly common warning to his colleagues: Being black would not save them from an angry constituency if they failed to do their jobs effectively. Despite a 51 percent white majority in Fulton County, blacks gained a 5-2 majority of commission seats with the 1986 elections, which were highlighted by Martin Luther King III's election.

In 1989, black Fulton County Commission Chairman Michael Lomax, a literature professor, geared up to run against Maynard Jackson in the Atlanta mayor's race. Lomax was accused of racism after he appealed to white voters by using whites in television advertisements that criticized Jackson's crime-fighting record. Jackson appeared unbeatable, and Lomax bowed out, however. Atlanta city councilman and former state representative Hosea Williams challenged Jackson, but Jackson *was* unbeatable. When Jackson entered his third term of office in 1990, thirteen of the eighteen city council members were black, and eight were women. Jackson pledged to fight drugs and crime, work to house the homeless, and maintain the city's economic growth. He also wanted to reconcile any differences with the white business leadership that lingered from his first two terms of office.

In 1937, the Negro Voters League could command 90 percent of the black vote in Atlanta with its recommendations. This power continued for decades. In 1990, the so-called black slates containing lists of endorsements still were considered an important part of Georgia's political life. As politicians tried harder to gain black votes, the choices were not so clear anymore, especially since more than one candidate for an office might have an appealing record. Because politicians had to pay a "distribution fee" to some slate authors and competing slates proliferated, there was always a chance that some suspect endorsements would crop up. In 1990, Mayor Jackson, Martin Luther King III, Ralph David Abernathy III, the Shrine of the Black Madonna, and the Kennedy-King Democratic Club all put out competing Atlanta-area slates. Increasingly complicated political alliances between black and white politicians have raised questions about the slates' value. Similarly, the black church's role in politics, while still powerful, was diminishing in an increasingly complicated political scene.

The political maneuvering surrounding the Fifth Congressional District illustrates these complexities. While Young represented a majority white district in Congress, due to changing population trends, his successor, Wyche Fowler, represented a majority black district. Although it was 51 percent black, it held a majority of white registered voters in 1980. Fowler had beaten challengers John Lewis, Clint Deveaux, State Rep. Billy McKinney, and State Rep. Hosea Williams in succession between 1978 and 1984, even though a reapportionment battle had resulted in a supposedly "safe" black district in 1982. As a result of the 1980 census, state legislators had drawn a 57 percent black Fifth District, which left a majority of white registered voters and placed thousands of blacks in the predominantly white Fourth District, centered in DeKalb County. Almost immediately, black legislators, who had been excluded from key redistricting planning sessions, asked the Justice Department to force Georgia to create a congressional district that recognized Atlanta's contiguous black population and where a black candidate would stand a reasonable chance of winning. The Justice Department asked the courts to reject the redistricting plan because it was calculated to prevent the election of a black congressman; it fragmented Fulton County just as the black population there was growing rapidly. The Supreme Court upheld a lower court ruling that invalidated the boundaries because they were drawn for illegal racial motives.

The pursuit of a black district caused an alliance of convenience between blacks and Republicans. A largely black district would by necessity leave a largely white Fourth District and increase the chances for a Republican victory there. In a court-mandated special legislative session in August 1982, state lawmakers finally put most of Atlanta as well as some Fulton County suburbs into the Fifth District, making it 65 percent black while reducing the Fourth District's black population and increasing its Republican strength, which resulted in the 1984 election of Pat Swindall, a candidate who appealed almost exclusively to the religious right.

Congressional elections had to be postponed during the 1982 controversy, and uncertainty over district boundaries hampered black candidates. Fowler easily won reelection. In 1984 the power of the incumbency proved mightier than the black establishment's support of Hosea Williams, whose reputation was damaged by numerous run-ins with the police over his driving habits. Although Fowler had been an effective representative, by 1986, it was time for him to give up his seat—largely in deference to black desires to recapture the Fifth District and certainly because he saw the chance to move to the U. S. Senate. He survived a Democratic race in which the term "liberal" carried racial connotations and went on to defeat Republican incumbent Mack Mattingly in the fall.

Mattingly had scored a stunning upset over Herman Talmadge in 1980, thanks to the odd combination of suburban white Republican votes and black votes. Mattingly received 33 percent of the black vote in 1980—an amount so high it would have been inexplicable had he not been running against a Talmadge. Talmadge had certainly softened his racial views since *You and Segregation* was published. He had helped develop the school-lunch and food-stamp programs, both of which also increased markets for his agricultural constituency. However, he still favored the term "welfare cheaters," which carried racist connotations for many blacks. Of course, they may have voted against "Hummon" in 1980 for the same reasons other voters did: Talmadge had been denounced by his colleagues for "reprehensible conduct" involving large amounts of cash, he had gone through a very messy divorce, and he was no longer able to conceal his alcoholism. On Senator Mattingly's recommendation, Larry Thompson was appointed the first black U. S. attorney in Georgia history.

Julian Bond, who had tried to get a 69 percent black Fifth District, hoped to replace Fowler in the House. Fellow civil rights veteran and old friend John Lewis was the other main contender in a crowded field. Like Bond, Lewis was named by *Time* in 1974 as one of two hundred likely future leaders of the country. In 1977, President Carter appointed Lewis as a deputy director of ACTION, the domestic equivalent of the Peace Corps. In 1980 he returned to Atlanta and was elected in 1981 to an at-large seat on the city council, where he gained a reputation for high ethics. (His was often the only voice favoring ethics legislation.) He worked for jobs and housing for the poor and often sided with neighborhoods against developers.

The black establishment in Atlanta had a history of working to avoid dividing the black vote. Once, when a black minister announced his intention to run against Benjamin Mays for a seat on the Atlanta Board of Education, he was quickly transferred to a Florida parish following a meeting at Paschal's restaurant. In 1984, Alveda King Beal, daughter of Martin Luther King, Jr., charged that Andrew Young and Hosea Williams tried to get her to drop out of the Fifth District race in exchange for a job running Williams's office if he won the election. In 1986, there were rumors of finding some reward for Lewis to get him to drop out of the race. Lewis was unswayed by any offers that might have been made. Bond, the son of a noted black educator, who came in first, and Lewis, the son of an Alabama sharecropper, who finished second in the primary, faced each other in the runoff. The race pitted the thinker against the foot soldier. Lewis was clearly the underdog. Bond, who stood up to the white establishment and was denied his House seat in 1966, was the darling of the black political establishment. He was witty, urbane, and articulate. However, he was also criticized as an ineffective legislator who was aloof from the people. Lewis was perceived by many as a plodding, earnest man, but no one ever accused him of being aloof. The race between two old friends turned bitter. Lewis ran as an antiestablishment populist candidate and outpolled Bond among whites by a 4–1 margin. Bond won 3–2 in majority-black precincts, but Lewis won the runoff with 52 percent of the vote.

The next year, Julian Bond would become a political "dead duck." In March 1987, Bond's estranged wife, Alice, went to the police and told them that Bond—then president of the Atlanta NAACP chapter—was a regular cocaine user. Bond denied the allegations, but the damage had been done. Exposed was his close relationship with a woman who would later be convicted on drug-trafficking charges. A scandal erupted as allegations were aired of widespread cocaine use among Atlanta's black leaders, and countercharges of a media "witch hunt" were made. Mayor Young felt compelled to call a news conference to say he did not use cocaine. Young was exonerated, and although Bond was not accused of any crimes, his political career was over. Nevertheless, he survived the revelations and has continued as a popular writer, lecturer, and television personality.

Although there had been steady advances by the mid-1980s, to many black leaders the issue was not how far they had come but how far they had yet to go to achieve proportional representation—and real power. After the 1982 elections, black legislators said they would request the Justice Department to force the state to promote more blacks. Although 28 percent of the state employees were black, in line with their ratio in the general population, the vast majority were in nonsupervisory jobs. Although blacks held 32 percent of state jobs in 1986, they continued to be concentrated at the lower levels. In 1986, State Rep. Tyrone Brooks bemoaned the fact that "we are letting real power slip right through our hands." He had just released a study showing that blacks accounted for only 6.5 percent of Georgia's elected officials (about four hundred). Just over 60 percent of the state's eligible blacks had even registered to vote. State NAACP President Robert Flanagan laid blame on the black clergy who did not mobilize their congregations to vote and to middle-class blacks "who are now only concerned about themselves and have no conception of the civil rights movement."

In 1986, the agenda of Georgia's twenty-four-member legislative Black Caucus included hopes for funding Morehouse Medical School, help for financially distressed farmers, reduction of the infant death rate, an increase in Medicaid and support for hospitals that accepted indigents, grants to homeless persons, limiting the police use of deadly force, and improving workfare with better day care, insurance, and transportation. Later that year, black legislators protested when the Business Council of Georgia scheduled prelegislative forums at all-white country clubs.

While the General Assembly was not interested in adopting the Black Caucus's agenda, some black legislators had risen to leadership positions. Some of the new leaders, such as Columbus banker and political insider Rep. Calvin Smyre and Sen. Al Scott of Savannah, were conservative and business-oriented. Smyre was appointed Gov. Joe Frank Harris's assistant floor leader in 1983 and House floor leader for the 1987 legislative session; Sen. Eugene Walker of DeKalb County became Democratic whip. Smyre had been named the top elected black official in America for 1985 by the National Black Caucus of State Legislators. After a dozen years in the House, Smyre's rise to prominence revealed a rift among black legislators who had "walked the walk and talked the talk" of the civil rights movement and relative newcomers who were now, twenty years later, coming into power as a result of the movement's successes. There clearly was a changing of the guard. Rep. William Randall, Jr., had replaced defeated Rep. J. C. Daugherty as chairman of the House Special

Judiciary Committee. In 1986, the year Martin Luther King III was elected to the Fulton County Commission, Ralph David Abernathy III gained a seat in the House.

A true test of black political power would come in statewide races. Governor Harris made a historic appointment in 1984 when he named black Cartersville attorney Robert Benham as a judge on the Court of Appeals. With a heavy dose of political help from the state's top official, Benham was elected to a full term in a low-key, nonpartisan contest. In December 1989, Harris appointed Benham to the Georgia Supreme Court and named Fulton County Superior Court Judge Clarence Cooper, a black, to the Court of Appeals as Benham's successor. Both men were reelected in 1990. Their success at the polls was not an accurate measure of black candidates' political strength statewide, however. They did not gain office by election, and they did not have to run in partisan, high-profile races. Many voters did not know they were black, even though Cooper's opponent advertised the fact.

Jesse Jackson's ground-breaking presidential campaigns in 1984 and 1988 encouraged blacks like Otis A. Smith of Augusta to seek statewide office. Smith, a Presbyterian minister and retired army colonel, ran for a seat on the Public Service Commission (the utility regulatory commission) in 1988 and received 33 percent of the vote against an established incumbent. In 1990, Al Scott ran as the state's establishment candidate for an open seat on the commission and came in second with 22 percent of the vote. Smith, running in a crowded field that year, was unable to match his 1988 effort.

In 1990, Andrew Young hoped that he would gain enough white crossover votes to become Georgia's first black governor. Young came in second in the primary, in which Zell Miller's call for a lottery was the main issue. Miller had substantial black support, and there was cross-racial voting. Young's advisers admitted they failed to turn out blacks and liberal whites in sufficient numbers to win. While Young ran a strong race, the vote tallies pointed out an embarrassing weakness. He received a much higher percentage of black votes in Columbus, Macon, and Dougherty counties than he did in Atlanta, where people were most familiar with him. Young also had to deal with the fact that candidates from Atlanta traditionally do poorly out in the state. Young received 45 percent of the white votes in central Atlanta, less than 20 percent in suburbs, and under 10 percent in rural areas. Young's efforts to court rural white voters probably backfired, causing him to lose black votes while failing to pick up white ones. In addition, Jesse Jackson's supporters remembered that Young never supported their man's bids for the presidency. While the two men had publicly mended fences, there were still misgivings in the Jackson camp about Young.

In the July 17 primary, Miller finished with a twelve-percentage-point lead over Young. In the August 8 runoff, racial voting was more pronounced. Miller won easily with 62 percent of the vote and went on to defeat Republican State Rep. Johnny Isakson in November. After the election, Miller announced he would make appointments in line with the state's population and named Al Scott to the elective post of Georgia labor commissioner, where Scott would try, and fail, to become the first black official to win a partisan statewide contest in 1992.

While blacks had gained a measure of political power in the twenty-five years since the Voting Rights Act passed, it was by no means a full measure. In 1991, the Georgia General Assembly's Black Caucus was the nation's largest, with thirty-five members. Yet voting-rights lawsuits continued and Georgia continued to rank near the bottom in voter turnout. In 1990, a class-action lawsuit failed to overturn the grand jury appointment of local school boards, a practice that still existed in nearly thirty counties. Brooks and other black activists pushed lawsuits challenging the state's runoff system and circuitwide method of electing superior court judges.

Blacks continued to make election gains. In 1990, the coastal city of Brunswick joined the local governments with black majorities on their governing bodies. In most communities where blacks gained power, initial white fears were allayed and biracial politics made local governments more efficient and responsive.

Political maturation brought new dilemmas. More black politicians spoke of broadening their agendas to address the problems that plagued their constituents. In Georgia, too many children, black and white, faced lives of poverty, ignorance, and disease. In 1986, Brooks pointed out that blacks made up 60 percent of the prison population in Georgia; unemployment for blacks was three times as high as that for whites; and the infant mortality rate for black babies was nearly 2 percent, twice the rate for white infants. Blacks hoped to match political gains of the past three decades with economic gains. Unfortunately, the gap between the haves and the have-nots had grown wider.

As Georgia entered the 1990s, the state faced a recession. During a time of budgetary cutbacks, the state's top priority was building more prisons to house mostly black inmates. Meanwhile, spending on schools faltered. Most Georgia lawmakers made sure the voters saw that they were "getting tough on crime." They did not point out that the state had failed miserably to curtail the poverty, unemployment, inadequate education, and other factors that bred crime. In such a political climate, the prospects for justice seemed grim.

13

The Struggle for Economic Advancement

A Tale of Several Georgias

There was much debate during the 1980s over the "two Georgias." One was the thriving economic powerhouse of metropolitan Atlanta, so the conventional wisdom held, and the other was a rural desert of poverty, joblessness, and economic despair. Like the notion that there were two Americas, black and white, the notion of two Georgias was an oversimplification. If there ever was one Georgia, it died with Oglethorpe's dream of a colony populated by yeoman farmers. Modern Georgia was a combination of black, white, rich, poor, rural, urban, and suburban entities, to name a few. There were pockets of prosperity in rural Georgia, and there was widespread urban poverty in Atlanta.

In Georgia, as elsewhere, the gap between rich and poor grew wider. Although many blacks made progress since the 1964 Civil Rights Act, many blacks did not, and income disparities between blacks and whites continued. Throughout the 1980s, the median net worth—the accumulated wealth—of black families was less than one-tenth that of whites. In Georgia, black income rose from 37 percent of white family income in 1960 to 52 percent in 1970 and to 56 percent in 1980. There it stayed for the rest of the decade. Nationally, black per capita income creeped toward 60 percent of white income as the 1980s closed out. Even so, the dollar-income disparity widened between the two groups. In the mid-1980s, the Southern Policy Board predicted a relative decline in the black economy in Georgia because of the large in-migration of whites and the decline of the percentage of blacks in school.

460

Due to several factors, the percentage of blacks living in poverty was disproportionately high. In 1980, 55 percent of Georgians in poverty were black, over twice their representation in the total population. Then one in six Georgians lived below the poverty line, and only seven states had a higher poverty rate. In 1980, when 14 percent of the nation lived in poverty, Atlanta's 27.5 percent poverty rate was the second worst among the nation's larger cities. Macon's 22.9 percent poverty rate was the ninth worst, and Savannah's 22.3 percent placed it tenth. No other state had three cities ranked in the bottom ten. Among Bibb County blacks, 36 percent lived below the poverty line.

Between 1968 and 1978, a million new industrial jobs came to the South's economy. As industry did trickle into some of Georgia's poorer rural areas in the 1970s and 1980s as a part of the overall economic development of the Sunbelt, it brought disproportionate benefits to whites. In a 32 percent black ten-county area of South-Central Georgia, employment in the better professional and technical jobs increased 28 percent for white residents but only 1 percent for blacks from 1976 to 1981. White in-migrants received an even larger share of the jobs.

Looking at Georgia as a whole, the economic picture in the mid-1980s was bright. In 1986, Georgia was fifth in the nation in attracting new and expanded industry. However, most of this growth came in (or more precisely, around) Atlanta. Between 1982 and 1986, the area's economy added nearly 227,000 jobs. In 1986, residents of twenty-two urban and suburban counties accounted for two-thirds of Georgia's personal income. "Without Atlanta, Georgia is poorer than Mississippi," declared University of Georgia College of Business Dean Albert Niemi, Jr.

For those who promoted the concept of the other Georgia, there was no better place to start their argument than with Georgia's Black Belt, mainly in East-Central and Southwest Georgia. "They say we're the second Georgia down here," said a Clay County official. "It feels like the fifth or sixth to me." These old cotton-belt counties had some of the state's worst housing, highest poverty rates, lowest educational attainments, and lowest manufacturing employment. Racial discrimination still played a key role in the location of new plants and was "especially prevalent in majority-black counties," according to the *Atlanta Journal and Constitution*, which in 1986 published an extensive series on the South's Black Belt. Businessmen feared that Southern black workers were "militant, unpredictable, and untrained." They also feared that black political power meant instability—often because whites were struggling vigorously to hold on to the power they had. Superstitions that blacks would flock to unions kept manufacturers from locating in Black Belt counties. The newspaper concluded that while much of the rural South was caught in an economic vise, "Only the Black Belt has lost jobs because of racial apprehension."

The most severe poverty in Georgia was in fifty-two rural counties south of the fall line that ran from Augusta through Macon to Columbus—a band of rural Black Belt counties with severely high poverty rates that stretched across the old cotton country in the middle of the state. Peach County, with over 25 percent of its residents below the poverty line, was the only metropolitan county in the "severe" category. A Ford Foundation-sponsored study reported in 1986 that eight of the poorest counties in the nation were in rural Georgia. All eight had a high percentage of blacks: Clay, Dooly, Hancock, Jenkins, Quitman, Randolph, Screven, and Stewart. The 1990 census reported that Georgia's five poorest counties were Stewart, Hancock, Quitman, Wheeler, and Atkinson.

The rural poor were older and less educated than their urban counterparts and—contrary to popular opinion—were generally in two-parent families. Many rural blacks had been agricultural laborers but were forced out of even this meager income by automation and other changes. Between 1945 and 1959, the use of tractors, mechanical harvesters, and chemical weed control depleted the ranks of tenant farmers by 70 percent. The first year in which over half of the crop was picked by machines was 1960. By 1972, all of it was. As agricultural laborers lost their marginal living, they moved to urban centers and compounded city problems. Only after World War II were the state's blacks more likely to live in an urban setting than down on the farm. By 1990, only one in ten of Georgia's rural residents was a farmer.

The most disturbing trend throughout the rural South was the loss of land by black farmers. In 1920, there were 130,000 black farmers who owned their own land in Georgia; in 1978, there were fewer than 3,000. That number declined to 2,068 by 1982, and the decline continued. Black farmers suffered both from problems that affected agriculture generally and from discrimination. Due to longtime white dominance, most black-owned farms were small. Usually lacking capital, black farmers were unable to buy larger holdings or effectively use labor-saving technology. They often were barred from buying more land. In the 1950s some Georgia land auctions began with the auctioneer's announcement that only whites could bid. Between 1959 and 1969, 84.1 percent of Southern black commercial farmers went out of business. Over the next five years, Georgia blacks lost title to 230,000 acres.

In 1982, blacks owned 4.2 percent of Georgia's farms—less than one-sixth of their share of the state's population. The average size of Georgia's black-operated farms was 135 acres, and the average black farmer raised $17,000 worth of crops for market, less than a third of the statewide average. Black farmers usually needed an outside job to help them hang on to their small farms. With the rural economy suffering, this presented additional problems.

In the late 1980s, there were some minor attempts by the federal government to ease the plight of black farmers. By then, government policies had already succeeded in helping to keep black farmers economically weak by denying them a fair share of technical support and loans—most large university agricultural research and federal farm commodity programs benefited large operators, even though they were not necessarily more efficient. The Farmers Home Administration (FmHA) grew out of the New Deal's Resettlement Administration and provided loans to farmers who could not get them elsewhere. Loan decisions were made by committees of local, mostly white, farmers. Racism and discrimination were rampant in local FmHA offices. Georgia had only sixty-one black FmHA committee members in 1979; in 1980 this small number was reduced to twenty-four. In 1981 the number of farm-operating loans dropped, and blacks got a smaller piece of a smaller pie. Georgia's black farmers also were unable to benefit fairly from housing and special "limited resource" loans. The agricultural crisis of the 1980s brought mass foreclosures. At the beginning of 1986 about 490 of the 665 black farmers in Georgia who had FmHA loans were delinquent. Overall, Georgia farmers had a 55.3 percent delinquency rate that year. It shot up to 73.4 percent the next year, making it one of the worst in the nation.

One black Cochran farmer became a symbol of the American farmers' plight and received national attention on November 15, 1985. On that day, armed supporters prevented the Bleckley County sheriff from evicting sixty-six-year-old Oscar Lorick and his wife from their seventy-nine-acre farm, which had been in the family for 119 years. Lorick had worked full-time on the farm since his father died when he was five years old. He never had a chance to go to school and remained illiterate. Troubles accumulated in the 1980s. The bank seized and auctioned off $150,000 worth of Lorick's farm equipment in 1984. In March 1985 the bank foreclosed on the farm, and the sheriff held an eviction notice in November. The NAACP advised the sheriff that a suit had been filed to prevent the eviction, and the lawman was happy to postpone action. He had come unarmed, hoping to avoid confronting Lorick's militant supporters, some of whom cradled automatic rifles in their arms while fifty curious well-wishers looked on. The heart of the armed resistance consisted of four heavily armed men from the Oklahoma-based Heritage Library, an extreme right wing organization that opposed taxation.

Lorick received a number of small financial contributions and a few invalid offers to buy his farm and let him remain living on it. Black attorney Alvin McDougald of Fort Valley represented Lorick. Independent Atlanta businessman Frank Argenbright gave Lorick an $8,000 Rolex watch and then headed up a fund-raising effort. By the next spring the fund neared $60,000. On March 28, 1986, the day his benefactor's option to buy the farm was due to run out, the Kroger Company donated the $18,590 needed to buy the farm. On April 12, five hundred supporters gathered at Lorick's farm and watched him burn his mortgage and accept the gift of a rebuilt tractor. He planned to return to his lifelong occupation of growing crops. After the crowds left, however, the tractor broke down, and Lorick was unable to farm his land. He still lived there in 1990, tending hogs for his son and living on Social Security.

Lorick was the exception. Most black farmers were ignored as they went under. It was unlikely that Georgia's black farmers—generally beyond middle age, with small holdings, lack of descendants interested in farming, and limited resources—would be able to enlarge and modernize their farms enough to pass on holdings sufficient to support their heirs. Lack of education made unsophisticated black landowners easy prey to trickery by lawyers, land speculators, and officials operating through tax sales, partition sales, and foreclosures to gain title to land. The historical distrust of the legal system kept nine out of ten Southern black landowners from drawing up wills, the Emergency Land Fund (ELF) reported in 1981. The result was often a partition sale that was forced when any heir asked for his or her share of the estate.

Even with a valid will, owners could still lose the property through ignorance of legal procedures. Often there were dozens of heirs, none of whom wanted to pay taxes on property they would not use. In the case of missing heirs, the land's title was too clouded to permit a sale. Often an heir could not be located because he or she was the child or grandchild of a family member who migrated north decades ago and had lost contact with Georgia relatives.

Real estate development also has been the enemy of continued black land ownership. While one solution to the problem of multiple heirs was "shared ownership," its weakness allowed a developer to purchase one heir's share and then demand that interest be partitioned from the rest. That usually meant the sale of all the land. The developer got not only the one share but a chance to buy it all. Many blacks on St. Simons Island were pressured to sell out by high land prices and property taxes that followed the island's development into a resort area and retirement haven for the wealthy.

High-handed government confiscation also wreaked havoc. In 1943 the federal government confiscated 2,687 acres of land belonging to seventy black families in a small fishing and farming community near Eulonia in McIntosh County. They were paid seven dollars an acre for the land, which was to be made into an airstrip as part of the World War II effort. The blacks were told that the land was only being "borrowed" and would be returned after the war. No airport was built. Instead of returning the land, the government incorporated it into the Harris Neck National Wildlife Refuge. In 1978, the SCLC, the NAACP, and the ELF mounted protests and began legal action. Protesters camping out on the disputed land were ordered to leave. Four men were convicted of contempt and given thirty-day jail sentences. In 1980, the courts ruled that the black families had no right to buy back their land.

In the 1960s and 1970s, several organizations were created to help black landowners avoid the pitfalls to which they were especially vulnerable and halt or reverse the trend of declining black landownership. Although there were some successes, the forces they battled were unstoppable. The ELF was organized in 1971 to help black farmers with technical, legal, and financial assistance. The National Association of Landowners (NAL) was established in 1976 by the ELF to help black farmers expand their holdings, use land more efficiently, and prevent them from losing their land.

In 1973, the ELF came to the rescue of New Communities Inc., a fifty-seven-hundred-acre cooperative in Lee County, probably the largest piece of land in the nation owned by blacks. It was founded in 1969, twenty miles north of Albany, by minister and civil rights activist Charles Sherrod, one of the Albany Movement's founders. The land was purchased from white farmers for $1.3 million with funds furnished by the Prudential Insurance Company, the United Church of Christ, and philanthropic organizations. In its early days, the cooperative was subject to harassing gunshots and mysterious fires. Governor Maddox killed one federal grant channeled through the state. The technical and financial assistance furnished by the ELF contributed to good crops in 1973 and a renewed lease on life for the cooperative. In 1974, Sherrod hoped to see New Communities develop a better school, a day care center, a health center, and freezing and canning plants, all of which would be available to the wider community. He also hoped that black families, by developing management abilities, would be more able to manage the cooperative and to control their own destinies. Unfortunately, the 1980s brought drought and financial hardship, and the cooperative's mortgage was foreclosed in 1985.

Some blacks banded together to form cooperatives. Black Georgia educator Benjamin E. Mays was president of the Rural Advancement Fund (RAF). One of its projects, the Eastern Georgia Farmers Cooperative, in Burke County, was established in the late 1960s on the initiative of local black farmers. In West Georgia, seventy black families formed a cooperative in rural Harris County near Columbus. The integrated Koinonia commune in Sumter County persevered despite terrorism and harassment. When founder Clarence Jordan died in 1969, his wife continued the operation with the help of blacks such as Slater King. By 1986, the original 440 acres had increased to 1,100, and its promotion of interracial understanding had branched out through Habitat for Humanity, which used volunteer labor to build low-cost homes to be sold to the poor on long-term loans at no interest. The Nation of Islam (Black Muslims) acquired some land in Georgia as part of the forty-two hundred acres it owned in the South in 1970. The products went to self-help Muslim groups in the North.

Southern Rural Action Inc. (SRA) represented a noteworthy attempt at black economic self-help in rural Georgia. SRA was founded in 1966 by Randolph T. Blackwell, who had been director of the Atlanta-based Voter Education Project and program director of the SCLC. SRA spurred blacks to create new rural industries and provide alternatives to flight to the cities. One of the first SRA projects was in the Black Belt town of Crawfordville in Taliaferro County, where the average income in 1960 was $700. Bitter white reprisals for court-ordered school desegregation cost black leaders their jobs; their installment purchases were repossessed, and mortgaged property was scheduled for foreclosure. These actions further weakened the local economy. The SRA used donations from the SCLC and the United Presbyterian Church to start a silk screen printing factory to provide jobs. Although the plant was successful, SRA was forced to break ties with it following a long battle with the U. S. Office of Equal Opportunity. Two spinoff projects folded, and the garment factory passed over to private ownership. The SRA also left its mark in Lincolnton and in Sumter County, where it built a roof truss plant, a brick plant, a community center constructed by local teenagers, a day care center, and a housing subdivision, Africana Village, where mortgage payments were thirty-five to sixty-five dollars a month in 1974, depending on income. Blackwell was awarded the Martin Luther King Prize in 1976.

Blacks who were not able to succeed as independent farmers had two main choices. They could go to some city where they often lacked marketable skills, or they could stay and become day laborers in agriculture. Two generations ago agricultural laborers in Georgia earned little more than nineteenth-century wages. In the 1960s black children were paid as little as three dollars a week for field work chopping cotton, shaking peanuts, and weeding. In 1984, Georgia had the lowest pay for agricultural field workers of all fifty states. The average then was $3.56 per hour, an amount that would earn a worker, fully employed throughout the year, all of $7,120—before taxes. Seasonal layoffs, weather interruptions, and the expenses of moving from job to job meant that even when the children worked it was difficult for a family to bring its income up to the poverty line. Between 30,000 and 50,000 migrant farm workers passed through Georgia annually during the 1980s. Increasingly, Hispanic workers satisfied the agricultural industry's need for cheap labor.

*   *   *

The percentage of unemployment and underemployment among blacks has traditionally been twice that of whites, although recent data indicated that black unemployment was over three times the white rate. In 1988, when Georgia's overall jobless rate was 5.8 percent, the unemployment rate for whites was 3.5 percent, and the black rate was 11.8 percent. For black teenagers, it was nearly 33 percent. These figures marked an improvement. In 1986, 39 percent of black teenagers were jobless, and in 1985 the overall black unemployment rate was 12.5 percent.

Georgia, because of its low percentage of organized workers (14.5 percent in 1980), few strikes, and low wages, taxes, unemployment compensation costs, and energy costs, had a good climate for low-paying, low-technology, nonunion industries, such as textiles—which later fled to foreign shores to exploit even cheaper wages. Georgia's wage advantage meant less as a skilled, educated work force became more important, and even hourly manufacturing jobs required computer operation. Unfortunately, low wages and taxes also meant that the state neglected to adequately fulfill its duty to educate its citizens. As service industries grew more dominant in the economy, development experts advised local leaders to stop "smokestack chasing" and concentrate on homegrown economic opportunities, preferably involving high technology.

Georgians' prejudice against labor unions and blacks, especially those suspected of union activities, helped to keep them poor. The anti-union climate helped account for the relative poverty and lower pay scales in rural Georgia and the attractiveness of cities for blacks. One study showed that a job in Southwest Georgia paid only 61 percent of a comparable job in Atlanta. Although earlier unionists were concerned about alienating Southern segregationists, gradually the unions became more progressive, largely due to pressure from northern affiliates and their black members. In 1965 the AFL-CIO Civil Rights division opened a special Atlanta office to end discrimination in trade unions. The inclusion of blacks undeniably strengthened the trade union movement. A Georgia Teamsters local abandoned discrimination in 1952 and grew from fifteen hundred to nine thousand members. Progress was far from uniform, however. In 1966, the Brotherhood of Railway Clerks still maintained separate black and white locals.

The fear that blacks would unionize was probably a tacit recognition that unorganized black workers were often exploited. Stirred by a 1961 story in the fledgling *Atlanta Inquirer*, the NAACP branded the Lockheed aircraft plant at Marietta "most rigidly segregated." Blacks had the most menial jobs, no chance for advancement, separate restroom and lunch facilities, and separate time clocks—even the time cards for black and white workers were different colors. Despite blatant discrimination, Lockheed had just received a $1 billion defense contract when President

Kennedy appointed Vice President Lyndon Johnson to head up the President's Committee on Equal Employment Opportunity. Within a year, fifty-nine blacks were promoted, two hundred more were hired, and all dual facilities were eliminated.

Even in the absence of unions, there were many efforts to negotiate with employers or take them to court over discriminatory conditions. In 1983 the Blue Bird Body Company, the world's largest manufacturer of school buses and Fort Valley's largest employer, settled a suit brought against it by black employees in 1981 by agreeing to increase the percentage of blacks in higher positions. One of the largest discrimination settlements in state history was reached in 1990, when Westinghouse Electric Company agreed to pay $5.3 million to about eight hundred current and former workers at its Athens transformer plant. The settlement occurred four years after U. S. District Judge Wilbur Owens, Jr., ruled that the company had deliberately discriminated against black employees. Some workers had waited for a resolution to the case since 1969, when twenty black workers sent a complaint to the Equal Employment Opportunity Commission (EEOC). A class-action suit had been filed in 1977 accusing Westinghouse of, among other things, putting new black workers in low-paying jobs, failing to promote or train black workers, and disciplining them unfairly.

Domestics were among the most intensely exploited black female workers in Atlanta. Dorothy Bolton organized the National Domestic Workers Union there in the early 1970s. Union members won wage increases and the right to refuse to get down on their hands and knees to scrub floors. With the improvements, some domestics began to think of sending their children to college. Of the 3 million American workers who received less than the $4.25 minimum wage in 1991, many were black domestic workers. Like other occupations, domestic service changed with time. Higher wages and required Social Security contributions meant many families could no longer afford housekeepers. Also, more whites worked in the home-cleaning franchises that supplanted many full-time domestics.

Black unemployment would have been worse if not for affirmative action programs that were installed at many Georgia institutions. The programs were designed to provide more jobs and better education for minorities and women. They were mandated by Section 7 of the 1964 Civil Rights Act and enforced by the EEOC and the courts. In 1978 Georgia enacted a law forbidding discrimination in the workplace and set up the Office of Fair Employment Practices to enforce it. No longer could an advertisement of employment be labeled "white only." Usually litigation was required to start compliance.

Georgia's state and local governments struggled with discrimination lawsuits and affirmative action plans throughout the 1970s and 1980s. In 1967, only 5.7 percent of state employees in Atlanta were black, although they comprised 38 percent of the city's population. Tokenism was the rule. More than half the seventeen state agencies that employed Atlanta blacks as white collar workers employed *only one* black. Women faced similar discrimination. In 1974, the EEOC put together a case that charged widespread discrimination in state hiring and promotions. "It was a blockbuster," said one EEOC employee. "There were all kinds of civil rights violations—people being passed over for promotions, jobs being given to friends and relatives of department officials. The case just reeked." While the state had adopted more progressive employment standards and blacks filled 29 percent of merit system jobs in 1982, they held less than 4 percent of top administrative positions. That year, the Office of Fair Employment Practices charged that most state agencies had "forgotten or ignored" affirmative action goals. The next year, Gov. Joe Frank Harris appointed a task force to investigate charges of discrimination. Not only were all its members white males: they were also the heads of the departments that had been accused of wrongdoing. In 1984, the case was settled, and the state agreed to set aside $1.9 million and 243 jobs to compensate blacks and women who had been denied jobs or promotions during the 1980s. The Legislative Black Caucus, which had put pressure on the state to mend its ways, endorsed the settlement "with some hesitation."

Through the years, at Central State Hospital in Milledgeville over three thousand employees were confined to low-paying, menial jobs and barred from advancement simply because they were not white. James White went to work at Central State in 1952 as a medical records clerk but also had to function as a janitor. Blacks and whites ate separately then, of course. According to White, black workers had to pay a fee to maintain their separate eating facilities. White was one of three black workers who filed a bias suit in 1977. In 1982, Judge Owens ordered the state to pay the workers at the facility $3 million in back wages. The state agreed to settle the suit the next year. Over twenty-four hundred blacks who worked at Central State between May 1972 and April 1979 were eligible to share in the largest race discrimination settlement paid by the state up to that time.

Many of Georgia's local governments instituted affirmative action programs in response to lawsuits. The city of Macon was sued in 1976 over police and fire department hiring practices and in 1978 over citywide hiring. Bibb County was sued in 1977 over job discrimination in the sheriff's department. In a scene reminiscent of the 1960s, hundreds of protesters marched downtown on November 18, 1978, moving past the county jail, the Water and Sewerage Authority, and several businesses they singled out for alleged discrimination before reaching the Bibb

County Courthouse, where the Rev. Joseph Lowery of the SCLC addressed the crowd. The suits against the city were merged, and a 1981 consent decree set down minority hiring goals. The city agreed to make its work force 31 percent black. Before affirmative action, 23 percent of Bibb County's employees were black. This rose to 33 percent in 1985 on the way to the goal of 38 percent. Despite affirmative action, black employment in higher positions still lagged.

As blacks achieved political empowerment, they gained more control over public-sector jobs. An interesting reverse-discrimination case that occurred in Andrew Young's first term as Atlanta mayor showed that black politicians were not necessarily above using the tactics they had once decried. A federal jury found city officials guilty of discriminating against several whites. Civil War buff Dennis A. Walters, Jr., was awarded $165,000 for being passed over several times for promotion to the directorship of the Cyclorama, the museum that features a huge circular painting depicting the 1864 Battle of Atlanta.

Private industry did not do as well as government in implementing affirmative action, although many larger firms put plans into effect. There were large gains in Georgia from 1970 to 1980 in the numbers employed, but the new opportunities for blacks were mostly at the bottom level. Macon ratios were fairly typical for the state in 1982, when the labor force was 26 percent black but only 9 percent of the managers, administrators, and executives were black. Statewide black employment increases during the 1970s varied from 13 percent in construction to 142 percent in banking, finance, and insurance. Increases were much smaller at the management level, where blacks comprised 2 percent in construction and 14 percent in financial categories in 1980, although the latter figure represented a 461 percent increase. In 1988, slightly less than 12 percent of the state's black workers were classified as managers and professional specialists, while over 27 percent of whites were.

While the military was commonly regarded as a relative stronghold of equal opportunity, black civilian workers at Robins Air Force Base told a different story. At Robins, Middle Georgia's largest employer, the higher up the pay scale, the lower the percentage of blacks. In 1984, 18 percent of the 15,695 civilian employees were black, but they held only 10 percent of the white collar jobs and less than 1 percent of the upper-management jobs. Black civilian employees had formed the Georgia Association of Public Employees Inc. in 1975 to seek corrections for discriminatory treatment. A class-action lawsuit was settled by consent decree in 1984 and provided that $3.75 million would be distributed to up to twenty-five hundred black civil service employees who were hired at Robins between March 24, 1973, and November 19, 1983. The average settlement was about $1,500 per aggrieved black employee. The settlement also set aside

240 of the next 480 job promotions for blacks. This was the largest discrimination settlement in air force history.

Public support of affirmative action, never overwhelmingly strong, eroded as its opponents raised the cry of "reverse discrimination." Affirmative action turned into a racially polarizing issue mainly because conservative white politicians used the specter of racial quotas in race-baiting campaigns. Some black opponents of affirmative action argued that preferential treatment was racist because it assumed blacks were inferior. As blatant discrimination declined somewhat and the increasingly conservative U. S. Supreme Court's decisions grew more favorable to employers, it grew increasingly difficult for plaintiffs to win race-discrimination suits. By 1991, there was only one law firm in the state that handled discrimination lawsuits on a contingency basis.

In 1988, there were 454,000 black women in the Georgia labor force, an increase of nearly 50 percent since 1983. During that time, the state's population of black women had increased about 39 percent. A 1987 study suggested that Atlanta's black women were able to gain management positions in private industry more readily than their counterparts in other cities, perhaps due to the influence of Atlanta's black colleges and Atlanta's healthy economy. Nevertheless, well over half of black professional women in Atlanta worked in the public sector in the mid-1980s; among white women, 60.2 percent worked for private business. One reason black women chose government work was the desire to avoid discrimination. Unfortunately for them, the high salaries were in business.

While job growth during this "boom time" generally outstripped population growth, white males continued to dominate top management jobs and women and minorities who thought they were on the fast track to success discovered the "glass ceiling." They could not see the barrier to their upward mobility until they crashed into it. Women and minorities hired under affirmative action programs were often the first victims when companies made personnel reductions, since seniority counted heavily in layoff decisions.

The Institute of Southern Studies reported in 1990 that due to Atlanta's influence, black men filled a bigger share of professional jobs in Georgia than in any other state in the region—yet they comprised only 3.4 percent of the total. Black men held only 5.3 percent of Georgia's managerial jobs, although they represented 13 percent of the labor force. Still, this was a threefold increase over the previous 20 years. In 1988, 20 percent of black women held managerial positions, up from 8 percent in 1969. Black women still held less than 5 percent of all managerial jobs.

Some things did not change. White males still held more than half of the managerial jobs and 95 percent of the top executive jobs.

Several black women challenged the glass ceiling. In 1990, Ryland McClendon became the first black, the first woman, *and* the first public transportation official to chair the MARTA board of directors. *Ebony's* January 1991 issue honored five Atlantans among "the 100 Most Promising Black Corporate Women in America": Henrietta Phillips Antoinin, public relations director for Atlanta Life; Vicki G. Roman of Coca-Cola Enterprises; Xernona Clayton, vice president for urban affairs with Turner Broadcasting System; Hannah Brown, regional manager for Delta Air Lines, and Geri P. Thomas, senior vice president of Citizens and Southern Corp.

Georgia was the eighth-fastest growing state during the 1980s, when its population grew from 5,463,105 to 6,478,216, an increase of 18.6 percent. The state gained an eleventh U. S. House district—with a black majority. Growth in Asian and Hispanic populations added diversity. Cities and rural areas both lost population as suburbs grew. The racial makeup of rural Georgia did not seem to change much during the 1980s, though most of the counties that lost population contained high percentages of blacks.

In 1920, 1.2 million blacks lived in Georgia but due to migration from rural terror, discrimination, and poverty, their numbers declined and did not again reach this level until the 1970s. Since World War II, the search for economic opportunity has been the prime motivating factor impelling Georgia's blacks to move. In Georgia, the black population increased from 26 percent in 1970 to 27 percent in 1980 and 1990. This black in-migration was one of the reasons Georgia grew by 19 percent in the 1970s and 18.6 percent in the 1980s.

Whites also moved, mainly from Atlanta to the suburbs. Atlanta, with 38 percent, had the second-highest percentage of blacks among major cities in 1960. By 1980 Atlanta was 68 percent black, while the suburbs were 85 percent white. Similar patterns developed elsewhere. In 1983, Macon was 53 percent black. By 2000 it is expected to be 62 percent black; by 2010, 70 percent black. While Atlanta became more black, neighboring Cobb, Fayette, and Gwinnett counties became more white. If a high percentage of whites in the suburbs as contrasted to a low percentage in the city is a measure of racial polarization, Atlanta is the fourth-most-polarized urban area of over 1 million in the nation, based on population shifts between 1960 and 1980. Due to suburban growth both from in-migration and "white flight," more than 40 percent of Georgians lived in metropolitan Atlanta in 1990, which had increased its population during the 1980s 32.5 percent to 2,833,511, making it the sixteenth-largest metropolitan area in the nation.

Though a high percentage of Georgia's rural blacks were poor, due to increasing urbanization, most poor blacks lived in the state's cities. One reason Atlanta's poorer blacks were unable to improve their condition was that whites also moved, and the jobs followed them. As Atlanta proper in Fulton and DeKalb counties became more black, the counties became relatively poorer, and the counties to which whites moved became relatively more wealthy. Corporate offices moved away from downtown, and Rich's Five Points store closed in July 1991, although construction at Underground Atlanta, the Georgia Dome, and 1996 Olympics-related projects provided a measure of hope for the city. Nevertheless, Atlanta's inner-city core grew poorer and blacker as white flight fed the expanding suburban "doughnut" around it. In 1990, Atlanta was one of the nation's three blackest cities.

Because only DeKalb and Fulton counties belonged to the Metropolitan Atlanta Rapid Transit Authority (MARTA), blacks who lacked transportation were effectively locked out of the booming suburban Cobb and Gwinnett job markets. Gwinnett voters' refusal in 1990 to join MARTA meant that most poor urban blacks would remain locked out for the foreseeable future. Until Cobb County set up a bus system to connect with MARTA, it was the largest county in the United States with no public transportation.

Many blacks with the means to do so also moved away from the city and settled down into suburban life. According to census figures (which city officials disputed), Atlanta lost ninety thousand residents between 1960 and 1990. Cobb, Gwinnett, and Clayton counties showed 238, 344, and 314 percent increases in black population, respectively. Gwinnett was still 95 percent white; Cobb, 90 percent white. While Atlanta shrank, suburban Fulton County grew. DeKalb County's black population jumped from 27 percent to 42 percent, while the white population of DeKalb and Clayton counties declined. Muscogee and Bibb experienced similar population shifts. While DeKalb County had the most ethnic diversity of any Georgia county in 1990, Dawson and Forsyth counties remained lily-white.

Atlanta has enjoyed a dazzling reputation as a mecca for black economic success. Its black business community received considerable attention and the city's reputation as a civil rights stronghold, its highly visible black political leadership, and the prestigious Atlanta University Center all served to beckon blacks. However, the city did not live up to its reputation for economic opportunity for all its blacks, and many who succeeded did so against the odds. Nevertheless, Atlanta remained a top destination for ambitious African-Americans and continued to blossom as a center of black culture.

Atlanta, long considered the best city for blacks in Georgia, was rated one of the ten best in the nation in 1973, thus proving a city did not have to be very good to be the "best." It was then just over half black, and 16 percent of black wage earners were rated "high salary" by the U. S. Department of Labor as compared to 53 percent of the whites. This was an improvement; a decade earlier, 65 percent of white Atlantans earned over $5,000, while only 22 percent of Atlanta's blacks did. In 1967, the EEOC reported that while blacks represented 23 percent of all workers, they constituted only 2.3 percent of white-collar employees.

In 1986, a study shocked conventional wisdom when it placed Augusta well ahead of Atlanta as far as black economic power was concerned. Five years later, black *Atlanta Constitution* columnist Ernest Holsendolph wrote, "Atlanta has a favorable reputation as a place to work and get ahead but largely fails to live up to it." Recent studies had shown that Atlanta lagged behind other cities in developing a large black middle class. By one account, Atlanta's black middle class was "politically empowered yet relatively small and lacking economic clout. It is more suburban than urban, and still largely segregated from its white counterpart." Atlanta also served as a magnet for the state's rural poor, and an extremely bleak picture of the city's growing black underclass was developing.

For those who "made it," Atlanta was a very nice place, but there were different ways to view the city's ability to live up to its image as a black mecca. In a study commissioned by *Georgia Trend* in 1987, University of Georgia sociologist Everett Lee found that Atlanta's black middle class had grown more rapidly than those in New York, Chicago, Detroit, New Orleans, or Washington, D.C., between 1959 and 1979. In 1959, only 13 percent of black families fell into the top 60 percent of all households, ranked by income. By 1979, 43 percent did. Atlanta also had the second-highest percentage of black college graduates, behind Washington. According to Lee, a relatively high proportion of Atlanta blacks made their living in private-sector business. Clearly, Atlanta was a mecca for Georgia blacks, because more than 80 percent of Atlanta's black middle class was from Georgia. However, the percentage of Georgia-born blacks decreased toward the top end of the economic scale. Preliminary 1990 census figures gave a different picture: Atlanta had the smallest black middle class among the nation's ten largest metropolitan black populations. About 33 percent of metropolitan Atlanta black households had incomes of $24,000-$60,000. About 9 percent had incomes above $60,000, ranking the area seventh among the ten.

Another fissure in the black community developed between suburban middle-class blacks and those within the city. "The thing about Atlanta... is that you've got two black middle classes who don't talk to each other," said demographer Joel Garreau. "The downtown middle class refuses to believe the suburban middle class exists. The majority of blacks who make money in Atlanta don't live within the city limits." Sociologist

Lee considered this largely a split between older and younger, upper-income blacks. Not only could a case be made for several Georgias, but for at least three black Atlantas as well.

Figures for 1980 showed that approximately 15 percent of blacks in Atlanta held either managerial or professional jobs. As a more informal measure of the business climate for Atlanta blacks, *SuccessGuide 1991* for Atlanta contained thirty-eight hundred listings for black professionals and entrepreneurs. Since the demise of segregation and due to affirmative action and civil rights gains, many blacks tried to make it to the top of corporate Atlanta—and encountered the "glass ceiling" that halted their advances just as effectively as it did elsewhere. Though some Atlanta blacks sat on boards of directors of major companies, they were not chief executive officers. Coca-Cola's highest-ranking black executive in 1991 was former Atlanta City Council President Carl Ware, who was named deputy group president, overseeing operations in Africa. (A consummate insider, Ware also served on the board of directors of Georgia Power Company.)

Georgia Trend listed eleven blacks among the one hundred most influential Georgians in 1991. While such a list was subjective, it showed which blacks observers *thought* had the most clout—a large part of the power game. All eleven were based in Atlanta and were part of the civil rights, education, or political establishment. Six were politicians: Marvin Arrington, state representative and civil rights activist Tyrone Brooks, Fulton County Commission Chairman Michael Lomax, Atlanta Aviation Commissioner Ira Jackson, Maynard Jackson, and Andrew Young. Only three were businessmen: Jesse Hill, Herman J. Russell, and Felker Ward. Johnnetta Cole and the Rev. Joseph Lowery also made the list. Attorney and investor Ward, a mediator during racial disputes, served on the state's Judicial Nominating Commission. He was chairman of Georgia's Human Relations Commission and in 1981 was the first black board chairman of the Department of Natural Resources.

Black political empowerment brought some minority business advances. Black businesses received a big push when Maynard Jackson took office in 1974. Before then, black firms had city contracts amounting to only $40,000, less than 1 percent of the total. Jackson took on the white business establishment over the issue of minority business contracts, and the main battleground was the new Hartsfield International Airport, the crowning achievement of Jackson's first administration. The mayor insisted that blacks receive 25 percent of the construction and terminal-operation business at the new, expanded facility. (The city's goals were later increased to 35 percent.) Seventy-one of the two hundred construction firms involved were black owned; eight hundred of the eighteen hundred construction workers were black. Minority contracts on the project reportedly made millionaires of twenty-one blacks. The facility opened in September 1980 on schedule and under budget and became one of the world's busiest. During his first two terms, minority companies got contracts totaling more than $188 million. Jackson's successes had drawn national attention. Between terms in office, Jackson worked as a municipal-bond attorney and shared his expertise with black mayors who wanted similar results.

Getting a piece of the public works pie was important. Atlanta's minority contractors got about 93 percent of their business from public projects, while white contractors got 80 percent of their business from the larger and more lucrative private sector.

Mayor Andrew Young's administration continued Jackson's initiatives. In 1988, Atlanta awarded more than $29 million in business to minority-owned and operated companies, more than 36 percent of the city's business. Between 1975 and 1988, $300 million had gone to minority firms, and the set-asides were widely credited for black business advances. While Hartsfield was Jackson's biggest achievement, Young could point to Underground Atlanta, which was rebuilt to far surpass its former glory. The Atlanta Economic Development Corporation, established during Maynard Jackson's first stint as mayor, packaged city loans totaling $1.9 million to minority businesses that opened up in Underground Atlanta. The city also helped locate other public financing in the form of SBA-backed bank loans. In all, twenty-seven minority-owned businesses had space when Underground Atlanta opened in 1989.

In Middle Georgia, efforts were also under way during the 1980s to increase minority business participation. Macon and Bibb County had limited results and no set goals to meet. It was different at Robins Air Force Base, which had the area's largest procurement budget. Congress had mandated federal agencies to award 5 percent of their 1987 contract amounts to minority contractors, which forced the huge air base to actively seek minority suppliers. In 1982, minority businesses got $12.6 million in contracts, less than 0.5 percent of the nearly $3 billion Robins contracted out. By 1986, minority contracts had climbed to $35 million, or 1.4 percent. The next year, base procurement officials were scrambling to locate minority suppliers.

It was more difficult for minority businesses to land state contracts. In 1975, black contractors in Atlanta protested their exclusion from the construction of the World Congress Center and sued the state of Georgia and the principal builder. In 1982 the 292 minority-owned companies that were registered with the state got 1 percent of its business in service contracts. During the 1980s, the Legislative Black Caucus unsuccessfully pushed for a law to change state bidding procedures by setting aside a percentage of state business for minorities. In lieu of a set-aside program, the General Assembly approved a 10 percent tax credit for general contractors who subcontracted with minority businessmen. By 1986, minority firms were fulfilling 4 percent of the state's government service contracts, or about $17 million in business. State officials declared themselves pleased with the results. Federal regulations required that 10 percent of road work using federal funds be directed to minority contractors, and in Georgia $95 million worth of federal highway jobs went to minority contractors from 1982 through 1985.

Black economic gains drew opposition from some white businessmen. In late 1984 the white Associated General Contractors of Georgia filed a suit against Atlanta's new requirements for minority participation in city contracts after the state Supreme Court invalidated the city's previous plan. White businesses found allies in Washington. Both the Reagan Justice Department and the U. S. Commission on Civil Rights came out against set-asides. The big blow came in January 1989, when the U. S. Supreme Court overturned a Richmond, Virginia, minority-participation program. Atlanta's leaders had deemed the case so important that Mayor Andrew Young hosted a $100-a-plate fund-raiser that raised $50,000 for Richmond's legal defense. In March, the Georgia Supreme Court quickly followed the high court's lead and struck down the city of Atlanta's Minority Business Enterprise (MBE) program. During 1989, minority firms' share of city contracts dropped to 28.7 percent and declined to 23.5 percent during the first half of 1990.

Affirmative action was not dead yet. Significantly, the nation's black leaders gathered in Atlanta in April 1989 to map a strategy to preserve affirmative action programs. City leaders encouraged white-owned firms to voluntarily form partnerships with minority firms when they sought city business. A group of Atlanta contractors announced the Atlanta Minority Assistance Partnership for this purpose. The city commissioned a study that documented past discrimination in awarding public contracts and found the local pattern of bias "ongoing and pervasive." Such evidence that an MBE program was needed to correct discrimination, along with a legislative mandate, would be necessary to support a set-aside program that would withstand a legal challenge. The city revamped its policy. In June 1991, the U. S. Supreme Court upheld Fulton County's use of federally funded contracts to boost minority-owned businesses, believing such federally mandated programs were on a surer legal footing than local ones. During 1988, 1989, and the first half of 1990, Fulton County was able to surpass the 20 percent minority-participation goal it set. MARTA and DeKalb and Gwinnett counties also had affirmative action programs, although DeKalb had problems meeting its goals.

There were several initiatives to increase minority contracts in the private sector. Georgia Power Company encouraged blacks to bid on subcontracts at Plant Scherer near Macon and awarded some thirty black contractors a total of $20 million in contracts. It also assigned some contracts to black-owned businesses during construction of the problem-plagued nuclear Plant Vogtle near Augusta. The NAACP's Operation Fair Share Program led to agreements to increase business with minority and female-owned firms by more than forty major corporations in the state. In 1985, U.S. Sen. Sam Nunn cosponsored a procurement conference for black entrepreneurs in Macon. Members of the Georgia Minority Supplier Development Council reported an 85 percent increase in private-sector sales between 1985 and 1990. In August 1991, Billy Payne, head of the Atlanta Committee for the Olympic Games (ACOG), held out a tantalizing prospect of minority involvement in 1996 Olympics projects. The ACOG announced it would adopt federal guidelines and review prospective contractors for their affirmative action and equal opportunity plans. Despite these efforts, several hundred black contractors remained concerned that they would not get a fair share of work on future projects.

Atlanta's MBE program was subject to criticism, including accusations that white contractors used minority "front" firms that were not bona fide contractors. There were also charges of sweetheart concession deals and favored treatment for well-connected black contractors at Hartsfield. In one instance, Mayor Young extended the bid clock by three minutes to allow Herman J. Russell's firm to enter a bid. The contract went to Russell's firm, and the city was sued by a losing bidder and its minority partner, R. Mitchell Construction Company. Such incidents led to charges of a new "old-boy" network which did not benefit the vast majority of blacks. Despite the criticisms, minority set-asides helped bolster the black middle class and reduce black unemployment.

Public-sector construction work helped build H. J. Russell and Company into a banking, real estate, and broadcasting conglomerate—the largest black-owned company in Atlanta and the fourth-largest such company in the United States with $143 million in sales in 1990. Next to Jesse Hill, Herman Russell was considered the most influential black businessman in Georgia, and following Hill, Russell served as Atlanta Chamber of Commerce president in 1981. Russell became a well-known developer, and by arrangement with the city, H. J. Russell subsidiary Gibraltar Land built the 188-unit 330 McGill Place, a condominium designed to fill the need for downtown housing. In 1987, McGill Place was shaping up as a model of integration, with 65 percent of buyers white. Other noteworthy black construction entrepreneurs included E. R. Mitchell, Sr., and Jr., C. David Moody of Atlanta, Albert Billingslea of Macon, and Edgar Roberts of Valdosta. In 1990, the Thacker Organization of Decatur was the fifteenth-largest black-owned firm in the nation.

Before they were able to capitalize on set-asides, most black builders operated in the residential market. During the 1950s and 1960s, blacks in Atlanta made up 40 percent of the population, yet lived on only 15 percent of the land. Black Atlanta was described as "bursting at the seams." The prime area for construction of black middle-class housing during the 1950s was Collier Heights, an area fifteen minutes west of downtown. By 1961, about six thousand people lived in the upscale black neighborhood. Around that time, blacks began to move into Cascade Heights, a prosperous neighborhood in Southwest Atlanta south of Interstate 20, which precipitated white flight from the area. In more recent years, South DeKalb was the main market for upscale housing for blacks. Much of the DeKalb development was done by white-owned companies. In the late 1980s black developers like Thomas Cordy, owner of AMC Mechanical Contractors, were building subdivisions on Atlanta's south side.

While Atlanta was a bastion of black empowerment, it was less than a paradise for black attorneys. There were some very high profile, powerful black lawyers, notably black Republican Larry Thompson, the U. S. Attorney for the Northern District of Georgia, who quit to join King and Spalding. As a black partner in a major Atlanta law firm, Thompson was a rarity. While spokesmen for major firms claimed they went out of their way to hire black attorneys, blacks' experiences in major law firms paralleled their experiences in the corporate world. Few rose to the top. A state bar survey released in 1990 found that while more than 27 percent of white male attorneys had salaries above $100,000, only 12.5 percent of black male attorneys did. Of black women lawyers, only 3.4 percent made more than $100,000 annually.

Most black attorneys worked alone or in small, very young partnerships. Many of them longed to compete head-to-head with the old boys at the silk-stocking firms. By 1990, several black firms were appealing to white clients and major corporations by specializing and diversifying. Thomas, Kennedy, Sampson, Edwards, and Patterson marked twenty years in business in 1991 and handled pro football players' business and medical malpractice litigation as well as corporate work. That year, Marvin Arrington's law firm formed a partnership with five other minority law firms across the nation to form Arnell, Fitch, Lewis, Sanchez, Arrington and Alexander, a "multilingual and multicultural" partnership designed to woo large corporate clients that might be reluctant to give their business to one small minority firm.

Blacks also had difficulties scaling the upper ranks of management of the white-owned media. Despite high-profile personalties such as long-time WSB-TV news anchor Monica Kaufman, blacks remained under-represented in the mainstream media, especially at the top. The *Atlanta Journal and Constitution* probably was outperforming the field in 1990 when 19 percent of its newsroom employees and 13 percent of supervisors were minorities. In 1991, Al Johnson became executive editor of the *Columbus Ledger-Enquirer*, Georgia's third largest newspaper. He was the first black to hold such a position in the South.

The *Atlanta Daily World*, which became a daily in 1932, was one of the nation's major black papers. *Daily World* reporter Harry McAlpin was the first black newsperson accredited by the White House in 1944 and helped pave the way for others. Although the *Daily World* advocated some reforms, the generally conservative, "rock-ribbed Republican" paper under C. A. Scott did not support the 1960 student sit-ins. To back the movement, Jesse Hill, J. Lowell Ware, and others launched the *Atlanta Inquirer* in July 1960, and many advertisers switched to it from the *World*. Lonnie King, Julian Bond, and others joined their talents in getting out the first issues. Martin Luther King, Jr., was a charter stockholder in the paper. Carl Holman, who later joined the Civil Rights Commission, was the first editor. Between 1963 and 1969 the *World*'s circulation dropped 15 percent due to Scott's conservatism and because blacks moved to neighborhoods where the carrier system did not function well. Ware left the *Inquirer* in 1966 to work with Ed Clayton on a new paper, the progressive *Atlanta Voice*. Clayton suffered a heart attack soon after the paper's first issue came out; Ware took over the shoestring operation and stayed at the helm of the paper until his death in 1991.

Atlanta was probably the nation's most competitive black newspaper market. As the *Journal and Constitution* condensed and combined, black papers multiplied: The *People's Crusader* was founded in 1970; the monthly *Atlanta Tribune*, in 1987; the *Atlanta Metro*, in 1988; and the *Atlanta Weekly*, in 1990. These publications faced the same problems the newspaper industry generally faced, such as declining circulation and advertising revenue, except that in the case of black newspapers, they were more intense. Undercapitalization often meant they had outdated equipment and small news budgets. They also continued to lose readers and news sources to mainstream news media. Across Georgia, papers like the *Savannah Tribune*, the *Augusta Focus*, the *Columbus Times*, the *Albany Southwest Georgia* and the *Macon Courier* served the black communities. Sometimes even newspapers in smaller cities faced competition. Black newspapers sprang up in towns as small as Fort Valley, but they invariably operated on a tight budget and suffered a tenuous, short-lived existence.

WERD in Atlanta was the nation's first black owned and oriented radio station when it started broadcasting at sunrise on October 3, 1949. It was owned by Jesse B. Blayton, who came to Atlanta in 1922 as an auditor for the Standard Life Insurance Company and by 1929 was one of the few black certified public accountants in the United States. WERD paid its personalities $100 a week in the 1960s and lost many in a "brain drain" to the North. Black businesses failed to support it, and the station was sold to white owners in 1969 and closed in the 1970s. Augusta's WRDW was founded by the James Brown Broadcasting Company in 1969. Since then, blacks have started or purchased several radio stations across Georgia, from Savannah to Columbus. Television-station ownership came much more slowly. Dr. Carl Gordon, Albany's first black physician, founded WTSG-TV, but the station was sold to nonminority owners in 1987. Part of Herman Russell's business empire included partnership in Russell-Rowe Communications, Inc., which possessed Georgia's only black-owned network affiliate, Macon's WGXA-TV (ABC).

In Atlanta, Auburn Avenue was thriving at the turn of the twentieth century, and the city was home to several venerable black business and professional organizations: the Atlanta Business League, founded in 1933; the Empire Real Estate Board (1939); and the Gate City Bar Association (1948). There have been many individual success stories throughout Georgia. Macon's oldest black-owned business was Paul Duval and Son, a furniture upholstering and refinishing business founded in 1883. William Duval, grandson of the founder, was named Georgia's Minority Small Business Person of the Year in 1985, and two of his sons continued the tradition.

For many decades, the white businesses that did not serve blacks at all, such as restaurants, hotels, and some retail stores, left opportunities for black entrepreneurs. Throughout Jim Crow Georgia, black businesspeople and professionals took advantage of the color line and catered to a black clientele, especially in personal-services businesses. Attorneys, physicians, newspaper publishers, and funeral-home operators were among the most prosperous and influential members of the black community. In the 1950s, Freddye Scarborough Henderson founded Henderson Travel Service, the first black travel agency in the nation to handle domestic, international, and steamship travel. She was the first travel agent—black or white—to organize cultural tours to Africa. By the 1970s, her volume had reached $2 million a year, twice the average of all travel agencies. There were several Atlantans on *Ebony's* 1962 "100 Wealthiest" list: Walter Aiken, Atlanta builder and real estate broker; Clayton B. Yates, co-owner of the Yates & Milton drugstore chain; Jesse B. Blayton; and three physicians—F. Earl McLendon, Richard Hackney, and J. B. Harris.

The funeral business, due to strong cultural and religious traditions, has not been affected by desegregation. Black funeral-home operators were often the wealthiest blacks in a town and branched out into other areas. Macon's two largest black businessmen owned mortuaries: William S. Hutchings and William Randall, Sr., who, with his other interests, grossed over $1 million in 1979. Hutchings Funeral Home was founded in 1900. William Hutchings gave up medical school to help his father and later inherited the business. It grew to handle a majority of the black funerals in Macon and employed eleven people in 1985. Randall acquired Central City Funeral Home from Ruth Hartley Mosely in 1967 for $100,000 and renamed it the Randall Memorial Mortuary.

In the United States, insurance has traditionally been the largest black business. The Pilgrim Health and Life Insurance Company of Augusta was founded in 1898 as the Pilgrim Benevolent Aid Association. Savannah was home to Guaranty Mutual Insurance Company. *Ebony's* 1962 list of America's one hundred wealthiest blacks started with Norris Herndon, due to his ownership of about 75 percent of the stock of Atlanta Life Insurance Company, founded by his father, Alonzo, in 1905. Pilgrim owners Hattie B. and Walter Hornsby followed.

Atlanta Life Insurance Company was the largest black stockholder-owned insurance company in the world. (North Carolina Mutual was the largest overall.) Atlanta Life continued to grow under the leadership of Chief Executive Officer Jesse Hill, Jr., who began with the company in 1949 and worked his way up to take charge in 1973. Assets increased to $108 million in 1980, when the new Herndon Plaza headquarters was dedicated at Auburn Avenue and Courtland Street. Throughout its history, Atlanta Life bought other black-owned insurance companies. It purchased Savannah's Guaranty Life in 1962 and absorbed its operations ten years later. Pilgrim was large enough to be on *Black Enterprise's* 1985 list of the nation's top 100 black businesses. By the end of the decade, Pilgrim was ailing, however, and it, too, was purchased by Atlanta Life, which then had assets of $134 million and 850 employees. Atlanta Life also purchased minority-owned insurance companies in Kentucky, Florida, Chicago, and Virginia. Its $31 million in capital and surplus made it more sound than many companies, but it was beginning to experience troubles.

When Norris Herndon died in 1977, his stock went into a trust fund, and profits from the trust were used to fund scholarships for blacks and to maintain the Herndon Home, a museum in Atlanta's West End. While Atlanta Life was strongly capitalized entering the 1990s, it had lost money steadily since 1986. "Revenue is flat, expenses are rising, and the product line is dated," reported *Georgia Trend*. The company was still tied strongly to its bread-and-butter policy of burial insurance for poor blacks, serviced by door-to-door salesmen who made paltry salaries. Hill needed to update the product line, appeal to upscale black customers, and also modernize company operations. He was approaching retirement and faced the daunting prospect of changing the company's way of doing business in order to survive into the next century. In a move to save the company, Hill ousted the entire board of directors and replaced them with outside directors, including Spelman College President Johnnetta

Cole, construction magnate H. J. Russell, and Dr. Edward Irons, dean of Clark-Atlanta University's School of Business.

Throughout his career, Hill continued the commitment to civil rights that the Herndons established. One of Atlanta's most respected business and community leaders, he served on MARTA's board of directors and those of major corporations, including Delta Air Lines and Knight-Ridder Newspapers. He served as chairman of the Martin Luther King, Jr., Center for Social Change and chaired Maynard Jackson's 1973 mayoralty campaign and Andrew Young's 1972 congressional campaign. Gov. Jimmy Carter appointed him to the Board of Regents in 1973, and in 1977 he was the first black elected to lead the Atlanta Chamber of Commerce. Always the social activist, Hill was critical of prosperous blacks who ignored their social responsibilities. The black bourgeoisie, he said, "should push away from their bridge tables and help those in the ghetto."

Like the insurance companies, black-owned banks also filled an economic niche. Citizens Trust Bank in Atlanta and Carver Savings Bank of Savannah were among the fourteen U. S. banks owned by blacks in 1955. Citizens Trust was the largest black-owned bank during that era, but it hit hard times later, losing money in 1974. Under the leadership of Chief Executive Officer I. Owen Funderburg, Citizens Trust returned to profitability and prominence, moving up to become the nation's second-largest black-owned bank by 1991, with assets of $115 million. Carver Savings and Mutual Federal Savings and Loan of Atlanta remained among the top black-owned financial institutions during the 1980s.

According to the Small Business Administration, the average minority-owned business lasted only five years. Many lasted less than a year. Black businesses often faced deep-seated problems, including lack of capital and the unwillingness of many whites to patronize a minority business. The buying habits of black consumers, who spent most of their money outside the black community, posed the biggest problem for black businesses. Booker T. Washington inveighed against the failure of blacks to patronize their own at the turn of the century and African-American leaders decried it nearly a hundred years later. In the days of Jim Crow, a black going into a white-owned business had to be prepared to be insulted and demeaned. Ironically, many blacks believed that changes since 1960 hurt them economically. When blacks were more free to shop where they pleased, many black-owned businesses, especially retail and service firms, began to experience difficulties. Blacks were much more likely to patronize a white-owned business than vice versa, a fact that brought frustration and despair to the black business community.

In 1991, black journalist Tony Brown reported that blacks spent only 5 percent of their income in the black community, compared to 13.5

percent before segregation ended. While other ethnic groups recycled money five to twelve times within their own group, blacks did so less than once. Brown said more than white prejudice was to blame for blacks' failure to make economic advances, and he pointed to the many West Indians and Africans who came to America and soon exceeded the living standard of American blacks. Black leaders pointed out that if their people were a nation, they would be the tenth-richest in the world, but their buying habits were self-defeating. They did not see their consumerism as a "sleeping giant," according to Alex Habersham, publisher of the weekly *Macon Courier*, who said in 1980 that if blacks patronized black establishments, 40 percent of Macon's white firms would fail within six months.

Although black incomes lagged behind white earnings, in 1990 black buying power in Georgia reached nearly $16 billion and was expected to pass that mark in 1991. Nationally, black consumer spending was estimated at $264 billion that year. Corporations increasingly targeted this lucrative market with marketing efforts. More than forty thousand consumers attended Black Expo USA '90 at Georgia's World Congress Center in March. The successful consumer-oriented trade show became an annual event. In 1990, the *Metro Atlanta Black Pages*, a business directory for minority concerns, published its thirteenth annual edition. Publisher Ken Reid pleaded, "We must...make a concerted effort to patronize the businesses within our community whenever and wherever possible, as often as we possibly can."

Blacks in Macon, Atlanta, and other cities tried various ideas to demonstrate their "green power" and win respect from merchants. In 1985, the local NAACP participated in a week-long "Black Dollar Days" in Macon and asked blacks to make their purchases with two-dollar bills or Susan B. Anthony one-dollar coins so their purchases would be noticed. Although Macon banks stocked about $50,000 of the special currency for use in the demonstration, the effort fizzled due to apathy and lack of knowledge of the campaign within the black community. Similar efforts continued into the 1990s with less than spectacular results. The NAACP also tried to negotiate with merchants for more and better jobs for blacks. Where demonstrations of black economic clout or negotiations did not bring gains, the boycott or the euphemistic "selective buying campaign" was used. In 1981 such a campaign was instituted against the Atlanta-based Coca-Cola Company by Jesse Jackson's Operation PUSH, which called on the soft-drink giant to place more advertising through black advertising agencies and to increase the number of black-owned bottling companies and franchises.

Just as black home buyers had trouble getting loans, so did black entrepreneurs who wanted to start or expand a business. Lack of contacts at banks, knowledge of the banking system, and a dearth of collateral hurt them. There was also the issue of discrimination. Irvin Betts started in

1981 with $14 and built a $3-million-a-year produce business in seven years. Betts operated his business without a loan because he could not get one, a problem that he believed kept his business from reaching potential annual revenues of $10–$15 million. City Council President Marvin Arrington said he had been unable to get banks interested in making loans to businesses along Auburn Avenue, which had undergone a decline since its heyday. One Fulton County official charged, "Redlining is worse on the commercial side than in housing." The *Atlanta Journal-Constitution* conducted an analysis of all SBA loans made in Georgia between 1982 and 1987. It found that no Atlanta financial institution made more than 20 percent of SBA-backed loan amounts to minority or female-owned businesses. Exposure of the situation, which embarrassed Atlanta's banks, may have loosened some purse strings and pushed financial institutions toward compliance with the spirit of the Community Reinvestment Act. Time would tell.

Despite the odds, many black entrepreneurs ventured out on their own, and Georgia experienced fairly rapid growth in black businesses. From 1969 through 1972 the number of black-owned businesses in Atlanta rose from 870 to 1,600. Most were small retail stores, and many were on such shaky financial footing that they did not survive the next recession. In ten years, this rose to 7,077, when Atlanta was home to about half the state's black businesses. In Georgia, the number of black businesses increased from 9,716 in 1977 to 14,652 in 1982. In 1987, Atlanta was the nation's sixth-ranked city in terms of black-owned businesses, with 11,804 with revenues of $747 million.

Automobile manufacturers offered franchise opportunities for black entrepreneurs. Juanita Powell Baranco, along with her husband, Gregory, ran the nation's largest black-owned automobile dealership. Mrs. Baranco also served on the Board of Regents and several community service groups. Several other black Georgia auto dealers made the *Black Enterprise* "top 100" list during the 1980s: William Huff Ford Inc. of Manchester; J. Mac Olds-Cadillac of Warner Robins; Robinson Cadillac-Pontiac of Atlanta; Spalding Ford-Lincoln-Mercury of Griffin; Sim Fryson Buick-Saab of Smyrna; and Quality Ford Sales of Columbus.

The billion-dollar-plus black cosmetics field offered major opportunities. M & M Products Company was founded in 1973 by two Georgia-born Fort Valley State College graduates, Cornell McBride and Therman McKenzie. It grew to be the eleventh largest black-owned company in the United States by 1985, an international company marketing more than fifty products in the United States, Canada, England, Europe, Africa, and the Caribbean. It was sold to a Boston firm in 1989. Bronner Brothers, founded by Morehouse graduate Nathaniel Bronner, was another successful black cosmetics firm, with $18 million in sales in 1990, ranking it fifty-sixth on the *Black Enterprise* list. Bronner Brothers sponsored an annual Mid-Summer International Beauty show in Atlanta that drew tens of thousands of cosmetologists, exhibitors, and students. Another Atlanta-based black cosmetics company, Frankie Jennings Cosmetics, Inc., started in 1976 when Jennings, an Albany State College graduate, combined a bubble-bath product with good advice on relaxation for black women. Her company grew into a multi-million-dollar operation that manufactured and distributed over thirty products.

Some of Atlanta's black entrepreneurs competed in the fields of high technology and international finance. In 1989, when Lance Herndon was thirty-three, his ACCESS Inc. employed forty-nine people and had annual revenues of $2.4 million. The computer consulting firm had more than fifty clients, including IBM and Coca-Cola. The next year, Herndon's firm had sixty-five employees and more than $4 million in revenues, and he was planning to compete for 1996 Olympics business. Joseph Profit, president and chief executive officer of Communications International Inc., announced in 1991 that his firm had won a $50 million contract for reconstruction of Kuwait's oil-field telecommunications system. Financial wizard George Hand moved in the realm of billion-dollar deals. He started his own firm, HK International, in 1989 and put together what was regarded as Georgia's most creative transaction in 1990—a $150 million international acquisition to help form Deutz-Allis, the fourth largest farm-equipment manufacturer in the United States. Perhaps no one set their sights higher than Michael Hollis, who founded the first black-owned airline, Air Atlanta, in 1984. The airline catered to business customers but was unable to grow fast enough to survive and went bankrupt in 1987.

The food-service industry offered many opportunities. One of Atlanta's most successful black businessmen was Nathaniel Goldston III, who founded The Gourmet Companies and turned the business into the nation's largest minority-owned food-service firm, with $30 million in sales in 1990. Helen Willinsky, cofounder of Gourmet Concepts International in Atlanta, was another successful black businesswoman. The ex-Jamaican and her husband founded the company in 1978. By 1987, the food-service firm had $4 million in sales.

Some black businesses prospered under both the old and the new way of doing things. The Paschal brothers, James and Robert, started a sandwich shop on Hunter Street (now Martin Luther King, Jr., Drive) in 1947 with James's savings as a Pullman porter and Robert's from a pharmacy job. In 1959 they obtained a $1 million loan to open a restaurant and La Carrousel nightclub across the street from their original location. Although the nightclub was licensed for "Colored Only," up to 60 percent of the clientele was white on some nights, attracted by performers like Ramsey Lewis, Lou Rawls, and Aretha Franklin. The restaurant became a meeting place for Atlanta's black establishment and civil rights activists in the 1960s and remained a center of black political life. It was considered a required stop on the presidential campaign trail, and Jesse Jackson was almost a regular. In 1967, the Paschals opened Atlanta's first black-owned hotel at the same location.

The Paschals were able to profit under the city's MBE program and get in on the action at Hartsfield. In 1978 they signed a contract with Dobbs House, the world's largest airport terminal operators, and became 25 percent partners of Dobbs-Paschal Midfield Corporation, which leased space in the airport to concessionaires, many of them also minority owned and operated. The Paschals also operated snack bars and cocktail lounges at Hartsfield. The arrangement between the city and Dobbs-Paschal was so good for the company that it was considered a "sweetheart deal." In the mid-1980s, the Paschals' share of airport business was estimated to be $13 million a year, ten times the amount they pulled in from their older enterprises. On the downside, airport tenants complained about high rents and seven of eleven minority vendors failed during the 1980s.

Despite numerous success stories, the overall statistics on the economic and social welfare of black Georgians have been grim. In recent years, the average black family income failed to keep pace with inflation, and the number of blacks below the poverty line increased. Atlanta was regarded as a haven for middle-class blacks, yet those grim statistics showed that, overall, things were getting worse, not better for blacks in the city. While it was true that well-educated black married couples moved toward economic equality with whites and many black women were making advances in education and income, less than 40 percent of Atlanta's black households were headed by both parents in 1980. Half of Atlanta's black female-headed households were poor in 1980, and Georgia's poor blacks lived disproportionately in female-headed, one-parent households that began with a teenage pregnancy or an early divorce or separation.

In 1980, Georgia's poverty rate was 16.5 percent, higher than both national and Southern averages. Only seven states had higher poverty rates. Among blacks, poverty rates were often more than twice the overall rate. The poverty rate among black Atlanta families climbed from 25.1 percent in 1970 to 31.4 percent in 1980. The Reagan years saw a massive transfer of funds from less wealthy Americans to the rich. Taxes were cut, especially on businesses and upper-income brackets, while social programs benefiting the disadvantaged were reduced. Black Georgians especially were hit hard by these changes.

Georgia, like most states, taxed its poor more heavily than its wealthier citizens, due mainly to regressive sales taxes. According to one study, the poorest 20 percent of Georgians, with an average income of $11,900, paid an average 13 percent of their income in state taxes. The richest 20 percent paid only 9.2 percent. In 1989 the General Assembly raised the state sales tax from 3 to 4 percent. While Governor Zell Miller promised to exempt food from the sales tax and provide tax credits to the working poor, he backed down from his pledges in the face of a state revenue shortfall.

14

Social Problems

Health, Welfare, and Housing

In the past, Georgia's attitude toward relief efforts to the poor seemed sometimes to vary between indifference and contempt. During the Great Depression relief offices closed down when workers were needed in the cotton fields; that way, the poor who had been driven to the cities by lack of work in agriculture would be driven back for the short time they were needed. In the 1950s and 1960s welfare was denied Georgia mothers when field work was available if their children were over three years old, no matter how low the wages were. Later, the same practice was routinely applied to food-stamp recipients. When Lester Maddox became governor in 1967, sixty-nine counties had no food-assistance programs. Under Maddox, food stamps and commodity distribution programs were extended to all counties except one in which officials refused to accept them. The state's methods have become more professional and compassionate, although the programs remained insufficient and often suffered bureaucratic lapses.

In 1991, Georgia officials offered the nation's smallest package to participants in the supplemental food program for Women, Infants and Children (WIC)—$24.46 a month, compared to a national average of $30.44. That year, Georgia would return $2 million in WIC aid because it had failed to enroll enough participants in the program—at a time when more than 175,000 women and children in the state were going hungry. Georgia food stamp applications increased from 168,100 to 213,800 from 1988 to 1990. During 1990, Georgia had the nation's second-highest error rate in its food-stamp program. As a result, the state faced a $9 million fine.

489

While rural and urban areas were subject to widespread poverty, the suburbs were being introduced to the "new poor" as suburban workers lost their jobs during the recession and their families plummeted into poverty. In 1987, Clayton County's food-stamp office had no lines of people waiting to see officials. Three years later, the line formed an hour before the office opened, and the waiting room was jammed with people. Suburban Atlanta in 1990 experienced a 40 percent increase in the number of people getting food stamps or Aid to Families with Dependent Children, while Fulton County experienced just a 15 percent increase. Statewide, the increase was about 12 percent.

The high teenage and out-of-wedlock birthrate constantly increased the ranks of the poor. The problem, which had reached an epidemic level, cut across racial lines but was more intense among blacks than whites. In Bibb County in 1983, there were 13 births to unwed whites age fifteen to seventeen and 131 to unwed blacks in the same age group. In 1989, 63.7 percent of black babies and 14 percent of white babies in Georgia were born out of wedlock, figures that were not quite as dismal as the nation's statistics. Of the 9,419 black Georgia teenagers who had babies in 1989, 93 percent were unmarried. While Georgia's rate dropped to eighth by 1988, and statewide black teenage pregnancies stabilized, pregnancies among black teenagers in metropolitan Atlanta shot up from 69 per 1,000 to 95 per 1,000. In Clayton County that year, over 20 percent of black girls aged fifteen to seventeen were pregnant. Reasons for the rise in pregnancies were increased sexual activity and the interrelated factors of lack of education, low self-esteem, and poverty. School dropout rates among teenage mothers approached 80 percent. To keep young mothers in school, some Georgia school systems began providing day care and special counseling, beginning with Savannah-Chatham schools in 1985.

For many of these single-parent households, Aid to Families with Dependent Children (AFDC) was vital. This program began with the New Deal and included assistance to the blind, disabled, and elderly. In 1972, the other programs were combined and called Supplementary Security Income (SSI) and only AFDC remained separate and continued to be known as "welfare." Contrary to popular belief, the average stay on AFDC was relatively brief, usually only a couple of years. Eighty percent of AFDC recipients were black and—also contrary to the popular conceptions about large welfare families—the average mother receiving AFDC had less than two children. These families were concentrated in the poorer rural counties and in the inner cities. In Atlanta, the number of AFDC recipients increased from 3,064 families in 1965 to 21,052 in 1974. In 1980, there were 219,306 recipients statewide. Welfare payments in Georgia were among the lowest in the nation: During the mid-1970s, Georgia cut AFDC payments, and in 1978, Georgia ranked forty-eighth among the states with payments of $148 a month for a family of four. It had improved its rank to forty-first by 1987.

Job training was clearly needed to help the poor improve their condition. In the Atlanta region, 39 percent of the total adult population lacked the skills needed to get and keep a job. The Comprehensive Employment and Training Act (CETA) of 1973 was one program that tried to help but it was cut early on in the Reagan administration. Sen. Dan Quayle's most famous legislative handiwork, the Job Training Partnership Act (JTPA), was approved in 1982 and was intended to replace CETA. It was supposed to work more closely with employers and was to be more closely geared to local business needs. In Atlanta, at least, it ended up being mainly a federal subsidy to private businesses and failed to help many of the truly disadvantaged workers. The JTPA may have had better local implementation in Middle Georgia, where the Georgia Coalition of Black Women used JTPA funding for the Jobs Club, a project that provided nurse's assistant classes in Lamar, Hancock, Upson, Monroe, Washington, and Treutlen counties. Perhaps due to the JTPA's focus—to provide not education and training, but cheap labor—prominent black groups, like the Atlanta Urban League and Economic Opportunity Atlanta (EOA), did not participate fully in the program. The Urban League operated the Career Opportunities Project through funding from the Rockefeller Foundation. The embattled EOA closed down in July 1990 after operating for 26 years and was replaced the next year by the Fulton-Atlanta Community Action Agency.

The Positive Employment and Community Help (PEACH) program, introduced by Tyrone Brooks and passed by the legislature in 1986, provided child-care centers, vocational training, and transportation to places of employment for those receiving public assistance. Such a program represented progress over the older workfare programs that had required those receiving public assistance to work at public-service jobs but did not lead to graduation into real jobs—and were considered as punishment by many recipients. PEACH was geared to the development of marketable skills, and by 1988 was operating in twenty Georgia counties through local Departments of Family and Children Services and had provided assistance to five thousand families. The program continued to operate into the 1990s.

Nonsupport by fathers has been a tremendous problem, especially for poorer women and children. Forty percent of all fathers ordered to pay child support had never made a single payment, and 35 percent defaulted in less than a year. Georgia established a child-support recovery office in 1978 to track the fathers of children on welfare and have them reimburse the state for AFDC payments made to the child's mother. To comply with a 1985 federal law, this was extended to cover fathers of children who were not on welfare—to keep them from going on welfare.

Besides neglect, unemployment and health problems among black males were cited as reasons for failure to pay child support. The black male's long-standing plight drew increased public attention in the late 1980s and early 1990s. He had become an endangered species, according to many black leaders. Joblessness, low educational achievement, black-on-black violence, drug abuse, teenage pregnancy, alcoholism, and other problems had taken their toll. With the flight of the black middle class away from the inner city, drug dealers and pimps were often the role models for young children there.

The need for positive role models within the black community was partially filled by 100 Black Men of Atlanta. Concerned Black Clergy, representing more than a hundred churches, sponsored a salute to black fathers in June 1990 that drew about two thousand people to the Georgia World Congress Center. Proceeds from the event went to fund summer programs for kids in Atlanta's housing projects. On May 12, 1991, Mayor Jackson, Joseph Lowery, and five thousand black men and boys summoned up the spirit of the civil rights movement and marched from Morehouse College to the King Center to show support for young black males. Lowery spoke about "a new kind of slavery in America, the new KKK—Killer, Krack, and Koke." Unfortunately, neither the state nor the nation appeared ready to tackle the problem.

Putting the problems of Georgia blacks in terms of survival was not far-fetched, for poverty directly affected health and longevity. Poor diets and living conditions and lack of medical care have been part of the black experience in Georgia since the beginning and have made blacks more susceptible to a variety of diseases. Impoverished Black Belt counties had the same life expectancy rates as Third World countries like Guatemala, Iraq, and Zimbabwe. The average black male born in 96 of Georgia's 159 counties in the 1980s could expect to live less than sixty years, five years less than the national average for black men, and more than twelve years less than that of the average white man. Of the South's ten "most deadly" counties, five were in Georgia: Long (1), Talbot (2), Chattahoochee (5), Clinch (6), and Marion (10).

From the beginning of life, blacks were at higher risk. In Atlanta in 1936, more than one in ten black babies died before they were a year old; this was cut in half by 1946. With improvements in neonatal centers, high-risk babies had a greater chance of survival, though the infants' chances varied inversely with parents' income. Georgia still had one of the nation's worst infant death rates in the 1980s, and the state's black infant mortality rate was nearly double the white rate. The problem was especially bad in heavily black Southwest Georgia, where the infant death rate was 20.3 per 1,000 live births in 1981. Among blacks, infant mortality rates fell from 24 per 1,000 live births in 1980 to under 19 per 1,000 in 1985, when the statewide rate was 12. The state made no significant progress in the late 1980s and remained near the bottom of the rankings.

As black children grew up, they faced additional health risks. Because health problems were largely a function of poverty, they were more acute among blacks than whites. Unhealthy lifestyles, lack of access to medical services and higher incidences of heart disease, stroke, cancer, homicide, and AIDS yielded a higher death rate among blacks. Georgia's blacks often lacked resources or insurance for private clinics and also lacked access to self-help treatment programs such as Alcoholics Anonymous, Narcotics Anonymous, and Cocaine Anonymous. In 1990, about $60 million in taxpayer funds was spent on drug treatment in Georgia, but the demand for it far outstripped the supply, especially in black neighborhoods.

Blacks have always faced a shortage of medical care in Georgia due to poverty, discrimination, and the shortage of black doctors. Health-care costs continued to outstrip inflation and more than 40 percent of people without insurance lived in the South. Ironically, perhaps, free health care was one of jail's benefits. Medicaid, the federal program established in 1965, was intended to improve poor patients' access to health care. Despite recent funding improvements in Georgia, the program did not measure up to its goals of fostering a healthier public because it was not set up to help prevent illness. Patients had to be acutely ill before Medicaid would pay their bills. Health checkups, screenings and preventive care were not covered. Many doctors did not take routine Medicaid patients because of the paperwork and low fees. Also, the program was underfunded and subject to abuse. Some patients saw their doctors when they did not need to, and a few concealed their assets to qualify for Medicaid, but much more fraud was committed by bill-padding doctors and hospitals.

Black doctors were often the only ones in the community willing to handle the large volume of Medicare and Medicaid business that came with treating the poor. Unfortunately, these medical professionals were too few and far between. Problems were intensified in the 1980s by federal funding cuts for health insurance, aid to education, research, and welfare.

Historically, many white doctors in Georgia did not have black patients because of their unwillingness to treat blacks, the blacks' inability to pay, and the desire on the part of blacks to be treated by black doctors. Segregation ensured that Georgia's few black doctors would have much work—if not much income—from their poor patients. It also meant that the less capable white practitioners were often the only ones willing to take on black patients. Since many communities had no black doctors or dentists, blacks were sometimes victimized by the most incompetent or uncaring white medical personnel. When she was a young girl, Charlayne Hunter was the victim of a dentist who pulled eight of her teeth one afternoon without checking with her parents or offering any alternative.

Segregation in hospitals posed a variety of problems for black medical professionals and patients. Practitioners were barred from county medical societies. Sometimes they were not permitted to use the local white hospital facilities for their patients and, to get them admitted, would have to turn them over to a white doctor. This situation existed even in Atlanta as late as 1967. In 1979, local residents and employees of Newnan Hospital charged that it refused routinely to admit or treat black patients except in certain emergencies, even though it received $220,000 in federal funds that year.

Not until 1952 did the Medical Association of Georgia admit black doctors to its scientific sessions, though they could not then vote or hold office. Due to this discrimination, Georgia's black doctors formed their own medical organization, the Georgia State Medical Association. In 1961, eight black Atlanta physicians attending a medical conference became the first medical professionals in the nation to be arrested for protesting discrimination. When they were excluded from eating with other participants at Atlanta's Biltmore Hotel, they conducted a "stand-in." The Atlanta NAACP and a group of black doctors later sued and won the right to practice at Grady Hospital.

In 1985, Dr. Edgar Proctor of Atlanta, president of the Georgia State Medical Association, said that black physicians trying to get established in communities that had no black doctors previously were subject to hostility and denial of hospital privileges and loan applications and had difficulties finding suitable housing. In addition to racism, established doctors may not have wanted competition. Few black doctors were subjected to more white hostility than Otis Wesley Smith of Fort Valley. In connection with a June 1957 medical emergency, Dr. Smith telephoned Atlanta, and when the operator disconnected him to make circuits available for a white, he swore at her. Charged with using obscene language in the presence of a white woman, he was sentenced to eight months in a prison camp. The sentence was suspended on the condition that he pack up and leave Fort Valley for good. He did, and prospered in Atlanta, where he also became a civil rights leader.

When Dr. George A. Johnson, Sr., began to practice in Macon in 1951, there were about nine black doctors there who took care of about one-fourth of the black population. They worked out of the old St. Luke

Hospital on Tattnall Street, a facility that was torn down in the 1960s. They were denied use of other hospital facilities, medical libraries, and access to research and could not join the local medical society. This discrimination encouraged blacks to view them as "less of a doctor," and the lack of faith hurt. Dr. Johnson eventually joined the medical society and was allowed to practice at Macon Hospital, later named the Medical Center of Central Georgia. Although he had no white patients in 1983, two of his sons, also Macon physicians, did. Perry got its first black doctor, Luther Vance, in 1978. Dr. Carl Gordon became Albany's first black doctor in 1968. Seventeen years later, the city had nine.

Great credit goes to Grace Towns Hamilton (who was also Georgia's first black female legislator) for pioneering improvements in heath care for blacks in Atlanta. Before 1952, Grady Hospital accepted only indigent blacks, which meant there were virtually no local facilities for those who could pay. This meant they had to plead poverty and endure the indignities meted out to black charity patients or leave Atlanta to obtain hospitalization elsewhere. As executive director of the Atlanta Urban League, Hamilton worked to change that. In 1947 she published a report, "Hospital Care of the Negro Population in Atlanta," stating that there were less than two-thirds the number of hospital beds for blacks than the U. S. Public Health Service considered the minimum acceptable level and that there were few black doctors or opportunities for them. The report recommended a Negro hospital that could train black doctors. She prevailed on Chairman Hughes Spalding of the Fulton-DeKalb Hospital Authority to appoint her to the board, which planned a 116-bed annex to Grady Hospital for blacks named the Hughes Spalding Pavilion, which opened in 1952. Spalding called Hamilton "the instigator and moving force of the project." Despite this improvement, medical care for blacks in the city lagged, and in 1960, only 680 of the city's 4,000 hospital beds were available to blacks.

The training of black doctors was supposed to start at Grady Hospital in 1948, the fruit of an agreement between Grady and Emory. Emory did not fulfill its part of the bargain, so the actual graduate and postgraduate training did not start until 1960, with black doctors treating black patients in black wards. Dr. Alvin Johnson, a Meharry graduate, was the first to intern there. In June 1965, Grady was desegregated by court order, but de facto integration occurred earlier every time poor whites were dumped into the Negro wards. In 1966, black doctors and dentists in Atlanta charged that the federal government violated its own laws by giving Medicare funds to segregated hospitals.

The first black medical school founded in the twentieth century was started at Morehouse College in the fall of 1978, with a charter class of twenty-four students under Dean Louis W. Sullivan (later President George Bush's secretary of Health and Human Services) and with initial state support of $2.1 million. Before this, the only other black medical schools were at Howard University, in Washington D.C., and Meharry Medical School, in Nashville. Initial plans were for a two-year medical program, with students then transferring to Emory, Howard, or Meharry. The first four-year graduates received their diplomas in 1984. When Morehouse Medical School opened, less than 2 percent of the nation's doctors were black and the percentage of blacks in the first-year classes of other medical schools was declining, from 6.3 percent in 1974, the heyday of affirmative action, to 5.6 percent in 1983. It continued downward after that as the Reagan administration made "affirmative action" a dirty phrase and financial aid to students dried up.

In 1985, only 3 percent of Georgia's more than eight thousand doctors were black. There were 271 black physicians, or one for each 5,408 blacks, and one white doctor for each 498 whites. Atlanta had 60 percent of the black physicians, while forty-one of the fifty-two counties in the Black Belt from Columbus to Augusta had no black doctors, even though ten of them had ten thousand or more blacks. Of the forty-nine black doctors in this area, thirty-five were in Columbus, Macon, or Augusta. In 1985, Floyd County had about fifteen thousand blacks, mostly in Rome, and the all-white doctors' corps was charged by the local biracial Council on Human Relations with failure to see the need to recruit a black doctor.

In January 1989, Dr. Hamilton Holmes, one of the University of Georgia's first black students, became the medical director of Grady Hospital and shifted some of his attention from a successful orthopedic surgery practice to dealing with the funding and staffing problems of one of the nation's largest indigent health-care facilities. Grady's primary task was to treat poor patients from Fulton and DeKalb counties, whose governments provided a large share of the hospital's funding. Grady served as a magnet to the poor elsewhere who came to Atlanta in hopes of getting health care. Grady moved into the 1990s with a $300 million renovation that required changing the original H-shaped floor plan that was built in deference to Jim Crow. With integration, Hughes Spalding increasingly was viewed as an anachronism. Eventually, it was absorbed into Grady's operations.

Georgia blacks had to endure much more than their share of substandard housing and fell victim to widespread housing discrimination, lending bias, outright rip-offs, and federal policies that ignored their problems. After World War II, both the quality of housing and home-ownership levels increased, reaching a peak during the 1970s. However, in the 1990s, many blacks still lived in slum housing. While defective housing in urban areas has received the most attention, rural Georgia— with its legacy of unpainted shacks with dirt yards and no indoor plumbing—also had its problems. In 1990, about 40 percent of rural blacks still lived in substandard housing. As a measure of the power of the vote, blacks in Dublin and Spalding County finally got sewer lines installed after whites split into political factions and appealed for their support.

The major push for improvement came during the War on Poverty in the 1960s. The federal Fair Housing Act of 1968 was drawn up to end discrimination in 80 percent of the sales and rental of apartments and homes. The first housing-desegregation suit filed in Atlanta involved the Sahara Apartments in 1972. While there was progress toward the goal of fair housing during the 1970s, there were declines in the 1980s. Top Housing and Urban Development (HUD) officials since Kennedy approved segregated projects, and Reagan's secretary of HUD, Samuel Pierce, denied that the federal government had any role to play in ending racial discrimination. Of all the budget cuts during the Reagan years, no programs were affected more heavily than construction of housing for the poor. Between 1983 and 1987, Atlanta's federal housing and community-development money fell from $8 million to $4 million.

Housing discrimination was widespread in Atlanta. A city-sponsored study of rental housing discrimination conducted by Metro Fair Housing Services Inc. in 1988-89 proved this conclusively. A similar HUD study conducted in 1979 also surveyed suburban complexes. It found that whites received preferential treatment 45 percent of the time, blacks received preferential treatment 29 percent of the time, and in only 27 percent of cases was no discrimination encountered.

Like black doctors and lawyers who were kept out of the mainstream of their professions, Atlanta's black real estate brokers founded their own organization, the Empire Real Estate Board, in 1939. Black real estate agents and brokers were still denied access to real estate listings for white areas in 1990. In the early 1970s, whites were complaining that black agents were acting as "blockbusters" in the Flat Shoals area of South DeKalb County. When the first black families moved there in 1971, there was a white flight that opened up more housing for blacks. By 1973 the neighborhood stabilized at about half white and half black. Then black real estate agents began to hound remaining whites to sell and move. An interracial community group of nine hundred families, the Flat Shoals Alliance, was formed to counteract this.

The myth that the movement of blacks into a neighborhood caused property values to fall fitted readily in with the prejudices of many whites. One result was the criminal harassment of blacks who moved into white neighborhoods. In May 1975, when Mrs. Virginia Coley moved into a one-story brick home in a then-white neighborhood in Southeast Atlanta, a cross was burned on her front lawn and a sign reading "Niggers, get off this block" was nailed to a tree. After ten years of saving for a "dream house," the Allen Cater family found one in a white neighborhood in Mableton. After they moved in, shotgun blasts were fired into the home. Similar incidents occurred fairly regularly into the 1990s, notably in Clayton and Gwinnett counties, where there were rapidly increasing black populations.

White attitudes on having blacks for neighbors did change somewhat. Whereas 45 percent said in 1963 that they would relocate if a black family moved in next door, by 1978 only 16 percent said they would move. If a large number of blacks moved into the neighborhood, white reactions showed the same trend but were more extreme. In 1963, 78 percent said they would move under such circumstances, and by 1978 the number had fallen to 45 percent.

While most middle-class blacks moved into previously all-white neighborhoods without incident, there was not much social mingling between the races in the suburbs. Even neighborhoods that statistically appeared perfectly integrated were usually black at one end and white on the other. In 1990, only 10 percent of white Georgians lived in a neighborhood that was less than 90 percent white, and nearly half of black Georgians lived in neighborhoods that were 90 percent or more black.

In 1989, the Fair Housing Act was strengthened by an amendment that provided for prompt judicial action for HUD complaints and stiff fines for violations. One of its first tests came in DeKalb County. On June 11, 1989, a white Sandy Springs real estate broker signed a contract to sell a Stone Mountain house he owned to Terryl and Janella Herron of Decatur. When Gordon Blackwell found out they were black, he broke the contract and leased the house to a white couple. The Herrons filed a complaint with HUD. A federal judge on August 2 ordered Blackwell to sell the house to the Herrons and slapped a restraining order on Blackwell to keep him from selling the house to anyone else while the complaint was resolved. Real estate agent Donald Wainwright, who handled the sale, also filed a complaint with the Georgia Real Estate Commission over Blackwell's conduct. In a landmark ruling, the administrative law judge ordered Blackwell to pay $75,000 in fines and damages in the case—$40,000 to the Herrons, $20,000 to the white couple forced to move out of the house, as well as $5,000 in compensatory damages and the maximum $10,000 penalty under the new provisions of the Housing Act. Under the old law, Blackwell only could have been fined $1,000 and been "asked" to sell the house to the Herrons. After they discovered a defect in the house, the Herrons decided against buying it.

In May 1988, the *Atlanta Journal and Constitution* exposed the practice of racial "redlining" by the city's leading mortgage lenders. The newspaper's series, entitled "The Color of Money," won a Pulitzer Prize for detailing pervasive racial discrimination in lending practices among Atlanta's banks. Reporter Bill Dedman showed that Atlanta's financial institutions rarely made home loans in black and integrated areas, even in high-income neighborhoods. "Race—not home value or household in-come—consistently determines the lending patterns of metro Atlanta's largest financial institutions," Dedman wrote. Black-owned Citizens Trust Bank and Mutual Federal Savings and Loan had the best records for lending to blacks, and Citizens Trust, which loaned almost exclusively to blacks, had the lowest default rate on real estate loans of any bank its size in the country in 1986.

One reason for the discrimination was that federal bank regulators were lax in enforcing the Community Reinvestment Act (CRA) of 1977, which required financial institutions to help meet the credit needs of their local communities, including low- and moderate-income neighborhoods. However, community activists began to use the CRA to challenge the banks' discrimination by attempting to block their expansions and mergers. "The Color of Money" had a similar effect, stunning the image-conscious banking community, which had consistently maintained that it was a progressive force in the city's life. Shell-shocked and defensive—and facing boycotts by angry blacks—the city's chastened financial wizards agreed to create the Atlanta Mortgage Consortium, pooling $20 million to set aside mortgage money on "attractive terms" in black neighborhoods. By early 1991, the consortium had made 633 loans averaging $50,000.

Dedman found that several banks closed branches in areas that went from white to black. The absence of banks from Atlanta's black neighbor-hoods created a market for unregulated check-cashing services and mortgage and finance companies, which almost always charged much higher rates and frequently engaged in unscrupulous practices. Often, desperate homeowners who needed home repairs or faced foreclosure were taken in by lenders who promised to help them avoid a desperate fate—only to find out a worse fate awaited them. In what one attorney called "the dirtiest business in Georgia," unlicensed mortgage companies would charge high interest rates and hidden fees. One black Americus woman who wanted home repairs took a loan of $9,745 and had to pay $2,150 in fees and 23 percent interest. When she fell behind in her payments, the company foreclosed.

Stiff terms also might include hidden charges such as a onetime "balloon payment" of thousands of dollars that the homeowner could not afford. Georgia's usury law did not provide much help. It only limited the interest a lender could charge to a rather hefty annual rate of 60 percent. In one Atlanta case, Brown Realty Associates agreed to pay $2.74 million to twelve former homeowners who allegedly had been tricked into selling their property. The victims of these schemes did not realize until too late that they were not borrowing money on the house. They were selling the house without recovering the equity they had invested in it. Some home repair firms had the owners take out a second mortgage, then performed shoddy work and sold the mortgage. The homeowner had no recourse to get the work done properly—but could lose the house for failing to pay the bill.

In the first fifteen years after World War II, almost 9,000 new housing units were made available to blacks in Atlanta. Only about 10 percent of newly constructed housing for the poor in Atlanta from 1975 to 1979 went to blacks, according to the Southern Regional Council. During the 1980s, rent went up and housing quality declined. About 17 percent of Atlanta's poor blacks lived in inadequate housing in 1978, and that figure did not change much over the next four years. Poor whites living in substandard housing went from 6 percent to 10 percent during that period. Meanwhile, black suburban renters living in substandard housing doubled from 13 percent to 27 percent, while whites in a similar predicament declined from 5 percent to 3 percent. The average poor Atlantan paid more than two-thirds of his or her income for rent and utilities in 1982.

The problem of homelessness worsened during the late 1980s, when estimates on the total number of homeless persons in Atlanta ranged from ten thousand to fifteen thousand. Between 1986 and 1989, apartment evictions in Fulton climbed 60 percent, from 4,063 to 6,500. During that time, DeKalb evictions also rose 60 percent, from 2,357 to 3,587. Property managers blamed misplaced priorities and frequently cited drug abuse. But the near-absolute poverty behind homelessness had a variety of causes, including job loss, mental illness, and abandonment. During the last half of 1989, Atlanta's homeless were 72 percent black, half of them were under thirty years old, and 41 percent were women with children, according to the Task Force for the Homeless.

There were severe problems in Atlanta's public housing projects and in the Atlanta Housing Authority (AHA) that ran them. The AHA was the fifth-largest in the nation, with an $85 million budget in 1990. It oversaw twenty thousand units of public housing and subsidized housing with fifty thousand tenants, the vast majority of them black. Single mothers headed 98 percent of the households with children. Only about 5 percent of the residents had jobs. The AHA was considered one of the worst-run housing authorities in the nation. It was plagued by high vacancy rates, especially among the larger four, five, and six-bedroom units at a time when the city desperately needed single-room occupancy (SRO) units for the homeless. It had shoddy maintenance, poor inspections, and problems collecting rent. In November 1990, for the second time in eleven years, the AHA was declared a "troubled" authority and placed under close HUD monitoring. The AHA board, appointed by the mayor, was accused of being passive. (Even its chairman admitted it often served only as a rubber stamp.)

In 1988 and 1989, fifty people were victims of drug-related killings in the projects. This violence brought attention to the residents' plight. In December 1988, the U. S. Postal Service, MARTA, and Southern Bell Telephone Company temporarily curtailed service to the five hundred-unit Bankhead Courts, citing drug-related violence. The phone company's decision came after workers were harassed and threatened. (Some Bankhead residents thought the telephone company vans were set up to perform drug surveillance for the Georgia Bureau of Investigation.) Both the telephone company and the Postal Service reversed the policies following sharp criticism by city officials who had not been consulted about the cutbacks before they were made. An angry Mayor Andrew Young accused them of using violence in the projects as a cover to avoid serving poor people.

One positive sign was increased activism among public housing tenants. Susie LaBord of Grady Homes was the first tenant to be a full-fledged voting member of the AHA board in 1972, and the tenants' champion served until her death in 1991. Other residents on the AHA board were nonvoting members until 1989, when a state law gave them voting power. In 1990, public housing advocates grew more insistent in demanding their rights. After they called on Governor Harris to declare a state of emergency and bring in the National Guard to patrol drug-infested areas, the city put more police patrols in housing projects in a sixty-day experiment. Tenant leaders increasingly used the media to convey their message, pushed voter registration, and lobbied legislators. More than thirty lawmakers attended one reception cosponsored by the AHA and tenants. They were clearly gaining political savvy. In 1989, twenty-four-year-old Perry Homes resident Jared Samples defeated long-time incumbent Archie Byron for a seat on the Atlanta City Council.

There were some short-term signs of improvement, but then again, the AHA was under severe pressure to make changes. University Homes—completed in 1937 next to Spelman College as the first public housing project for blacks—underwent a $17.3 million renovation that was completed in 1991. It was difficult to see how Atlanta's poorer communities would change dramatically, but residents increasingly demanded a voice in any process that would lead to change. Since the federal government was no longer a major source of funding, community leaders increasingly looked to local and private funding for redevelopment in Atlanta's blighted areas. There was much hope that there would be such redevelopment in areas near venues for the 1996 Olympics, but community leaders were concerned that the coming of the Olympics might herald the destruction, not the salvation, of places like Summerhill, near the site of the planned eighty-five-thousand-seat Olympic Stadium, and

Techwood Homes and Clark Howell Homes, near the proposed Olympic Village. (Techwood was the first federally funded housing project in 1936 and housed only white tenants until the 1960s.)

Atlanta remained a largely segregated city. Generally speaking, blacks who left the inner city moved south, while suburban whites and the majority of new growth were in the north. In 1962, Mayor Ivan Allen tried to halt residential integration by placing a wall on a street in Southwest Atlanta. Thirty years later, that area was 98 percent black. In 1991, *Georgia Trend* writer Paul Thiel noted, "The area's residential streets are as well-kept as those in the leafy neighborhoods of Dunwoody or Sandy Springs, but the business district is blighted." The lack of economic development in Southwest Atlanta, where many of Atlanta's wealthiest and most powerful blacks lived, pointed to their relative powerlessness to overcome the racism that kept investors from developing the area. While Michael Lomax might have wanted upscale Lord and Taylor or Neiman-Marcus stores to locate in his neighborhood, he could not get the folks at Kmart to return his calls.

In *The Closing Door*, Gary Orfield and Carole Ashkinaze pointed out that housing opportunities grew increasingly more limited in Atlanta, and housing was growing less affordable for poor blacks during the 1980s. They also found that blacks were becoming more unlikely to own their own homes and saw little cause for optimism. Much of their study of the economic status of blacks refutes the idea that housing disparities are purely the result of color-blind economic forces. They found that race explained much of these differences and stated, "Unequal housing for those blacks who are fully able to pay is one of the most serious aspects of contemporary discrimination, helping maintain self-perpetuating black and white societies within metropolitan Atlanta."

Crime and Criminal Justice

Throughout its history, Georgia's criminal justice system failed blacks, other minorities, and the poor generally. For them, Georgia had much crime but little justice: "Law and order" really meant that laws were enforced to keep the poor and minorities in order. While Georgia provided work for blacks inside prisons, there was no work for many of them outside, before they committed crimes. Politicians were more interested in appearing "tough on crime" to voters than in trying to remedy its causes. As a result, punitive sentences and social neglect packed the prisons, often with inmates sentenced for economically motivated, nonviolent crimes.

As the crime rate increased in the 1980s, largely fueled by an increase in cocaine use, the already widespread problem of prison overcrowding grew even worse throughout the nation. Georgia imprisoned a larger percentage of its population than any other state or nation, more even than South Africa or the Soviet Union. The annual cost in 1982 was $7,288 per prisoner, a figure that doubled by 1990. In May 1987 there were 18,000 state prisoners in a system built for 16,400, plus a backlog of 3,000 prisoners in the 145 municipal and county jails waiting to go to state facilities; local officials complained when the state only paid a third of the cost of their maintenance. The state went on a prison-building spree in the late 1980s, but many experts considered this a misguided tactic.

Almost half of those sent to prison in 1981 were first offenders who committed nonviolent crimes; 13 percent were for misdemeanors. Reformers recommended more emphasis on alternatives to imprisonment. It only cost $2,000 a year per person in one of the state's twelve restitution centers and even less to put them under intensive probation, while keeping a person in prison cost several times as much. A prison-reform group warned Southern legislators in 1983 that building more prisons to cope with the rapidly growing number of inmates was throwing money "down a rat hole."

It seemed that the most highly publicized crimes involved black perpetrators and white victims. This helped perpetuate the stereotype of the black man as the burly brute that the New South had used to justify lynching. Following the death sentence imposed on Emmanuel Hammond, a black, in March 1990 for the brutal rape and murder of a white teacher, Julie Love, white women in news interviews admitted what black men already knew—all black strangers were suspect. The Hammond case was a rarity in Fulton County in that prosecutors sought and obtained the death penalty. Later that year, suburban Gwinnett County voters overwhelmingly voted down a referendum to join the Metropolitan Atlanta Rapid Transit Authority (MARTA). Many of MARTA's opponents claimed that the public transit system would bring crime to the 94 percent white county; to many African-Americans, "crime" was a code word for blacks.

It certainly was true that most of Georgia's prison inmates were black. In 1976, Georgia was 26 percent black, but blacks made up 60 percent of the prison population and 15 percent of the guards. At the end of the 1980s, one in six black men in Georgia was in prison, on probation, or on parole, and 65 percent of Georgia's eighteen thousand prison inmates were black. However, most crime is intraracial, not interracial. About 80 percent of crimes by both blacks and whites involve victims of their own race. Besides the obvious factor of proximity to the victim, Atlanta Public Safety Commissioner George Napper said in 1984 that the reasons for black-on-black crime included racism, poor education, few job opportunities, and overcrowded housing. Blacks often turned on those closest to them to vent their frustration and rage; similarly, drug addiction caused black addicts to victimize their families, friends, and neighbors in order to satisfy their needs. Crime statistics added to the negative image because they were weighted heavily toward street crime (homicide, rape, robbery, aggravated assault, burglary, larceny, and auto theft), which made it appear that blacks were disproportionately criminal. Napper pointed out that if white-collar crimes, such as embezzlement, were included in the statistics, the share of crimes committed by blacks would be sharply less.

Another reason blacks were jailed out of proportion to their numbers was inadequate legal counsel and discriminatory sentencing in the courts. Poor blacks were often dependent on court-appointed attorneys who were often apathetic about their clients' fate. Georgia's criminal justice system was white-administered, and this made the system even more unfair: Poor blacks were often brutalized and victimized, especially in the rural areas of the state.

The most notorious criminal case in Georgia since the Leo Frank trial and lynching involved black-on-black crime. In June 1979 black children and youths began to disappear from Atlanta streets while they were out playing, running errands, or returning home from school. Their bodies showed up in isolated places, covered with brush or slightly hidden in the woods. Later, bodies were usually recovered from streams and rivers. This went on for a year before the separate crimes were connected in the minds of the public or city police. Then a special task force was set up to solve the murders. In all, twenty-eight bodies were found from June 1979 to May 1981.

When Atlantans realized that there appeared to be a systematic effort to kill the children of poor blacks, fear and panic spread through the city and to other communities in Georgia. Children were cautioned to avoid strangers. Later, when it became known that there appeared to be no signs of struggle on the victims' part, children were warned to beware of friends and acquaintances. A miasma of suspicion and dread settled over Atlanta. Many blacks believed that some demented white had to be responsible for the ghastly crimes; whites hoped that the criminal would be black, or at least nonwhite.

After task-force members spoke of the unique fibers that were found on the victims, the bodies began to show up in streams and rivers. The task force then staked out various bridges. One team, parked at the Jackson Parkway Bridge at the Chattahoochee River, heard a splash late one night and identified Wayne Williams, a black free-lance photographer and self-styled talent scout, as having just driven on the bridge. Two days later, the body of Nathaniel Cater was found downstream from the bridge.

Williams was charged with the murders of Cater, age twenty-eight, and Jimmy Ray Payne, age twenty-one. Many whites breathed a sigh of relief when the suspect was black. Though they were hardly children, the case continued to be known as the Missing and Murdered Children case.

Williams's conviction at the end of a nationally publicized nine-week trial in 1982 hinged heavily on the fiber evidence. The eighteen different fibers found on the bodies of Cater and Payne were identical to those found in Williams's cars and in his parents' home, where he lived. The same type of fiber was found on ten other bodies, and though Williams was charged with only two murders, police said he was responsible for all the deaths. Williams was sentenced to two consecutive life sentences, and the police blamed him for twenty-two other murders and disbanded the task force. On December 5, 1983, the Georgia Supreme Court upheld the conviction. The FBI participated in the investigation under the direction of John Glover, who headed the Atlanta office. Glover was promoted and became one of the bureau's eleven assistant directors later that year and thus became the FBI's highest-ranking black. The case did not die, however. A sensational CBS television docudrama was based on a book that challenged official accounts of the crime. It aired in February 1985 and showed Williams as an innocent scapegoat and depicted city officials as incompetent. Williams continued to deny his guilt; his lawyers pressed for a new trial into the 1990s.

A new series of murders in Atlanta brought a sense of déjà vu and rekindled earlier apprehensions. From March 1 through April 9, 1986, four poor, elderly black women were raped and murdered when their homes were broken into in the same neighborhood as the child murders. The Guardian Angels—a controversial civilian crime patrol group from New York City—made a reappearance. George Napper asked the group to leave, as did his predecessor, Lee Brown, during the Missing and Murdered Children case. The crimes were soon solved, however. Police announced the arrest of Louis Hunter, a black, in late April and his indictment for the four murders spared the city its earlier trauma. Officials said Hunter had a drug habit and that robbery was the motive in the murders.

Atlanta's frequent appearances at the top of national crime rankings worried image-conscious city officials, who feared that bad publicity might hurt the city's 1996 Olympics bid and cut down convention business and tourist traffic at Underground Atlanta. In 1990, Atlanta had the highest crime rate in the nation. Even so, it had dropped 7 percent from 1989, and it was not the nation's murder capital. (It was third.) Although crime statistics soared in the latter half of the 1980s, Atlanta's murder record of 263 was set in 1973. Atlanta had 252 murders in 1989, up from 217 in 1988. The state's overall crime showed the largest increase in the nation from 1984 to 1985 and climbed 45.8 percent from 1985 to

1989. The Georgia Bureau of Investigation (GBI) reported that murders in the state climbed from 705 in 1988 to 809 in 1989, an increase of 14.8 percent. Statewide, crime was up 10 percent in 1989 from the previous year. The rise was fueled by an increase in cocaine trafficking. Reports of drug transactions climbed a phenomenal 37 percent from 1988 to 1989 largely because "people are so blatant with the sale of crack cocaine," said a GBI spokesman. Cocaine-related arrests increased by more than 800 percent in the latter half of the 1980s. On the positive side, under Mayor Jackson, Atlanta was responding to its problems by putting more money and effort into law enforcement, and metropolitan Atlanta area counties showed some declines in their crime rates at the end of the 1980s.

Other Georgia cities were also affected by rising crime rates. Police in Brunswick got a taste of inner-city gang activity in 1986. In 1989, when Atlanta's crime rate ranked first, Macon's was ranked number 40, Savannah's number 64, and Columbus's number 127 among the nation's larger cities. Albany got the often-misleading tag of National Murder Capital following a very bad year, 1988, when there were twenty-nine murders in the area. Police found that most of the killings involved domestic violence. The city took action by making arrests in domestic cases before the killing occurred and relieved itself of the ignominious title.

By 1990, Atlanta was beginning to experience gang warfare, often associated with the crack-cocaine trade and imported from other cities, notably Miami and Los Angeles. Inner-city youths joined the gangs in order to be feared and respected and to make money dealing drugs. In 1990, the Georgia Organized Crime Prevention Council estimated that there were thirty gangs in the state, most of them operating in public housing projects. A dispute between the Crips and Bloods, Los Angeles-based gangs, allegedly broke out in a fatal shooting at Underground Atlanta on August 10, 1990. Police had downplayed or even denied gang activity before this. Four adults and one juvenile were charged in the case, and city officials quickly called for drastic solutions. Jackson wanted to have gang members summarily arrested on criminal conspiracy charges, a prospect that caused civil libertarians to shudder. Within two months, police reported that drug-dealing gangs were operating in a dozen Atlanta locations. Among the identified gangs in Georgia were Down by Law, Ladies Down by Law, the Herndon Home Boys, the Miami Boys, Fried Heads Gang, Pimps on Duty, Skull Crushers, Eight Ball Posse, and Homicide Boys. Asian youth gangs also began to pose a problem to their neighborhoods and to the police.

Under Jackson, Atlanta tried a variety of crime-prevention tactics, including a nighttime curfew for youths under seventeen years of age. The curfew, reinstituted in November 1990 after a decade of disuse, was applied almost exclusively to black youths and was intended to curb youth violence, which had reached alarming proportions in the city's poorer sections. Within three months of the curfew's institution, police had detained seventy youths and reported some success with the crackdown. Proposals to fight crime often included crackdowns on the city's large homeless population centered in downtown; critics charged that this was a problem of cosmetics, not crime, although increasingly insistent panhandlers intimidated downtown office workers and there were frequent complaints by women of sexual harassment. In early 1990, city officials denied they had created a vagrant-free "hospitality zone" for the benefit of conventioneers and tourists, but the police began arresting more than a hundred panhandlers and street people on charges of public drunkenness or blocking traffic.

Isolated incidents at MARTA stations and Underground Atlanta drew much publicity, but those places were relatively safe, thanks to a heavy police presence. Most of the violence was in the city's poorer sections, although no individual or place was immune from a sudden attack. Georgia, like many other states, lacked uniform handgun restrictions and licensing procedures. Atlanta officials believed the easy access to guns hampered their efforts to curtail violent crime. Some of the newer automatic weapons out on the streets—such as Uzi submachine guns, assault rifles, and armor-piercing bullets—left police officers feeling outgunned and vulnerable. Even though Atlanta, Fulton County, and DeKalb County had waiting periods for prospective handgun buyers, surrounding counties had no such restrictions. This lack of a standard law was highlighted when James Calvin Brady walked into Perimeter Mall on April 24, 1990, with a newly purchased handgun and opened fire, killing one person and wounding four others. Brady was a recently released black mental patient who believed a device installed in his body ordered him to kill people. (Like the prison system, the state's mental health system was badly overburdened.)

Nationwide polls showed that drugs were the number one domestic problem, and that blacks were more concerned about them than any other group. Even while drug use declined overall in the late 1980s, crack cocaine wreaked havoc on the inner city. Crack is a powerful, highly addictive cocaine derivative that users smoke for a few dollars a hit. Selling crack was a lure for young men to make money when there were no other jobs available. The drug problem spread to rural Georgia. In 1990, police in Claxton, the "Fruitcake Capital of the World," reported that crack users had resorted to cattle rustling to support their habit. Clearly, the growing drug-fueled crime wave was everyone's problem, yet blacks were victimized out of proportion to their numbers. Black politicians were in an uneasy position of combating the problem without appearing to fight their own people.

Cocaine was well known to spark aggression, irrationality, and violence. Nearly half of all Fulton County homicide victims were cocaine users in 1989, up from an estimated 20 percent in 1985. Also, the economics of the drug trade led to robberies of dealers and buyers, revenge for unpaid debts, or retribution for being sold fake drugs. Innocent bystanders were also gunned down. Atlanta police estimated that perhaps as many as 40 percent of all killings were related to drugs. Young children who watched the slaughter grew hardened and indifferent to the violence. The most horrifying result of the influx of drugs and guns to the inner city was the increase in violent black-on-black crime. By the end of the 1980s, the leading cause of death among young black males was... young black males.

Poverty and desire for status figured into a new crime wave. Black youths who wore expensive basketball shoes and athletic jackets were being robbed of their trendy clothing in Atlanta in 1990 at the rate of one a day. Brenda Muhammad, the mother of a boy who was killed in a dispute over a New England Patriots jacket, formed Mothers of Murdered Sons (MOMS) to seek tougher penalties for blacks convicted of violent crimes against blacks. The youth who killed her son was acquitted.

Repeated studies backed MOMS's contention that the state's white-dominated justice system was unmoved by black-on-black crime. There was similar outrage from victims' families following eighteen-month sentences after plea bargains by the killers in drug-related slayings in the Red Oak housing project in 1990. Black civil rights and religious leaders in Atlanta, Savannah, and other cities called for tougher penalties and sought ways to reduce black-on-black crime. While blacks had previously avoided advocating stiffer penalties, that sent the wrong message to criminals—"that black life is cheaper," according to the Rev. Timothy McDonald III, executive director of Concerned Black Clergy.

To many blacks, Georgia's unequal justice system began with the police. Unfortunately, police brutality against blacks was an accepted part of Georgia's way of life for so long that it was difficult to begin to eradicate or even publicize it. *Atlanta Journal* editor Wright Bryan said in 1940 that he could not print stories of police brutality or the police would attack his reporters. During World War II, a teenager named Pat Watters saw an Atlanta policeman "grimly and mechanically clubbing the life out of a giant of a drunken black man on a downtown Atlanta sidewalk." Later, as a chronicler of the civil rights movement, Watters wrote that while he was at the time expecting to go fight the Nazis, "No account I had read of the gas chambers (and) the concentration camp horrors was as real to me... as that scene." Interracial organizations such as the Commission for Interracial Cooperation and the growing black vote began to bring improvements.

In the vast majority of Georgia's 159 counties, the sheriff is the key law enforcement official. His traditional role in the century after the Civil War was to defend the establishment against attacks on white supremacy. After World War II many Georgia counties continued to be run by "courthouse rings," little cliques of powerful men who had little or no respect for the rights of blacks. Too many law officers and political insiders considered themselves above the law and took it upon themselves to mete out judgment and punishment without due process, often without consideration of constitutional restrictions against cruel and inhuman punishment.

Meriwether County was such a place in 1948 when John Wallace, a member of the ruling clique, killed Wilson Turner, a Negro sharecropper who had worked for Wallace for over two years and was turned off the farm without his pay. Turner returned and "stole" a cow in lieu of the wages denied him. Wallace tracked him to Coweta County, killed him, burned the body, and thought no more about it. After all, no one had questioned his earlier actions, when he had tortured and killed other blacks. Wallace knew the Meriwether sheriff would do as he was told. Unfortunately for Wallace, Coweta County Sheriff Lamar Potts upheld his oath and saw that Wallace was arrested and tried for his crime. Wallace was convicted on the testimony of blacks—a rare occurrence— and was executed in 1950. Potts was an uncommon individual. Not many law officers would have sought justice when a powerful white man killed a black. In fact, many sheriffs during this time were Klan members.

Although times were changing, the older generation had difficulties accepting it. Dade County Sheriff John W. Lynch and three deputies were indicted for turning seven blacks over to a Klan mob for flogging in 1949. A Harris County deputy sheriff and seven others were indicted by a federal grand jury in Macon for beating Willie Capers the year before. Three law officers were indicted in Americus in 1952 for taking blacks to the jail and beating them. In 1975, Lumber City Police Chief Ray Cook and a patrolman were suspended and charged with beating a black, Fletcher King, whom they suspected of informing on their moonshining operation. Bloody, cut, and permanently injured, King was dumped half naked on the highway out of town and told never to come back.

Like justices of the peace, sheriffs were paid according to the fee system. The more they could extract from the people who passed through the system, the greater their incomes. Under the fee system, many poor, powerless black victims were legally robbed by fines and unjustly imprisoned. In 1951, except for Bibb, Chatham, Richmond, and Fulton counties, all sheriffs were paid by fees. The fee system ended in 1965, but this did not end dishonesty among sheriffs. Later, the rigid salary structure was cited when sheriffs turned bad and took bribes from drug traffickers. Between 1980 and 1990, more than two dozen Georgia sheriffs were indicted on corruption charges.

Since sheriffs are elected, the increase in black voting did much to attenuate the traditional racism at this level in the justice system. However, blacks continued to be underrepresented among the state's sheriffs. Georgia's first black sheriff since Reconstruction was Richard Lankford, elected in 1984 in Fulton County, where he supervised a staff of 350 and a budget of $8 million. Unfortunately, like many of his white counterparts, Lankford ran afoul of the law. He was convicted in March 1990 of two counts of extortion and two of tax evasion in connection with payments received from a county vendor. In 1992, his conviction was overturned, however. His replacement, Robert McMichael, was also black.

As it became more apparent that law officers required extensive training, Georgia's 1863 "posse law," which permitted a sheriff to recruit volunteers into a posse, had become an anachronism. It was passed when the problem of slave control intensified during the Civil War. In Vienna on January 21, 1985, an inexperienced volunteer posse recruit killed an unarmed black suspect by twice shooting him in the back with a shotgun. To prevent this problem from recurring, black State Reps. William C. Randall and David Lucas of Macon introduced legislation early in 1985 to prohibit sheriffs from organizing posses. Their bill failed, and the posses rode on. Four years later, black legislator Billy McKinney (a former Atlanta policeman) called members of Fulton County's sheriff's posse "citizen cowboys" and attacked the county's attempts to officially sanction the posse as part of county government. Fulton officials responded to criticism by renaming the group the Fulton County Sheriff's Reserve. In June 1990, only half of its 280 members were state-certified police officers. While modern state law requires that sworn law enforcement officers undergo training and certification, police recruits and deputies can work up to a year before they take the 240-hour course, which is the second shortest in the nation. In 1990, the *Atlanta Constitution* noted that Georgia had tougher training standards for its barbers than for its police.

When blacks perceived that police violence was racially motivated, they were more likely to protest militantly after 1960 than they had before. When the Augusta police were charged with beating a black man to death in 1970, six more blacks were killed during a protest demonstration. In 1976, when a twenty-one-year-old black man involved in a dispute with his grandparents was killed by police in Savannah, several nights of demonstrations resulted. There were similar incidents in Eatonton and Brunswick. Ashburn experienced a night of protests following the death of a prisoner shot by a Turner County deputy sheriff in 1985. This and similar cases led the General Assembly in 1986 to approve limitations on police use of deadly force. The NAACP had lobbied for years for this.

Richmond County Sheriff J. B. Dykes admitted in 1982 that police brutality was a major problem in his department when Willie Albert Fludd was wounded by a police bullet while observing the arrest of another man. There was an interesting development in the lawsuit Fludd filed over the shooting. While a jury found in favor of the defendants, the case went to the U. S. Supreme Court, which ruled that attorneys in civil cases could not strike prospective jurors due to their race. Filing suits alleging police brutality was practically unheard of before World War II. More recently, litigation has served as a curb on police brutality.

Many blacks believed that the inclusion of African-Americans in law enforcement agencies would help alleviate white police brutality against blacks. Such inclusion on a fair basis was not easy. Like many other civil rights gains, it involved increased voting power by blacks along with litigation by the affected parties. Then police brutality, once intense, diminished. The first two black policemen in Rome were hired in 1956, when nearly half of the city's blacks were registered to vote. Woodbury in Meriwether County had the state's first black police chief when Gary Kendrick took the job in 1976.

That year also marked the beginning of major change in Macon. Although blacks had served on the Macon force for years, the Afro-American Law Enforcement League brought suit against the city in 1976 charging that no black patrolmen had been promoted, that they were assigned to black neighborhoods only, were disciplined for minor infractions of the rules more severely than white officers, and, adding insult to injury, were the targets of white officers' racial epithets. In 1981, Macon agreed to hire and promote blacks to fill 40 percent of the vacancies until they constituted 31 percent of the force and held 31 percent of the positions of sergeant and above, in line with the city's racial makeup. In 1983 the Federal District Court ordered the city to pay $853,000 in attorney's fees and damages in this case. The suit had a salutary effect: In 1981 Macon had three black police sergeants; in 1985 it had twenty. With the favorable verdict, the racial slurs almost completely disappeared, according to league president Sgt. Willie May. Furthermore, in 1985 the U. S. District Court ordered Macon to pay $150,000 to eighty-eight blacks whose applications with the police department from 1974 to 1981 had been rejected. In 1986, one of the original complainants was named Macon's Officer of the Year. Similar litigation resulted in advances by blacks in the Bibb County Sheriff's Department.

In 1984, Columbus lost a suit filed in 1971 protesting the dismissal of six black officers for removing the American flags from their uniforms in protest against departmental discrimination. This action followed the arrest of a black policeman on contempt-of-court charges after he called in sick and asked officials to reschedule his court appearances. The dismissals prompted four nights of violence and fire bombings. While pleased with the outcome of the case, which went all the way to the U. S. Supreme Court, Melvin Cooper, founder of the Afro-American Patrolman's League, noted that racial prejudice still impeded the careers of black police in the city. In 1992, the city of Columbus agreed to pay each of the ex-officers $120,000 to settle the case.

Savannah's first black policemen since Reconstruction started patrolling in 1947, a year ahead of Atlanta. Of the original nine, three were college graduates, others had some college work, and all were high school graduates. They began at $170 a month under the same restrictions that operated in Atlanta about wearing uniforms and arresting whites.

It was a struggle for blacks to become members of the Georgia State Patrol, a bastion of white male power and political cronyism. After they were hired, black troopers had to endure racial insults and discrimination. It was not until 1983 that the first black woman was hired as a trooper. The patrol's sordid past of harassment against black and female employees was well documented. It was the target of a dozen discrimination lawsuits in the 1980s, including one filed by the U. S. Justice Department that resulted in more than $1 million in damages. In 1991, only one black was among the forty-eight post commanders, and no black woman held a rank above trooper. Times change, if slowly. One would-be trooper named Eddie Smith had to file a discrimination complaint when he was trying to join the patrol. Fifteen years later, he was the patrol's spokesman.

Atlanta may be the "city too busy to hate," but in the past blacks often saw its police as the enemy due to the controversial deaths of suspects while in police custody and the perception that the white police force was "out to get them." Herbert Jenkins, a reformed Klansman, did much to begin to change this. In 1948 he was police chief under Mayor Hartsfield when the first black officers were hired. (The hirings were delayed for a year due to a 1947 restraining order obtained by the leader of the anti-Semitic, anti-black Columbians.) Eight new black police started training in March; five had attended college, and seven were army veterans. The work entailed many humiliations, according to black officer Robert McKibbons, who stayed on the job until he retired in 1980 with the rank of detective. Their segregated roll call was in a local YMCA; black officers could only patrol black areas and could not arrest whites or wear their uniforms in court or off duty. Jenkins asked the city council to drop the prohibition against arresting whites; it was removed in 1962.

More recently, Atlanta police improved relations with the community, although there continued to be complaints about excessive force. In the mid-1970s, Atlanta was able to reduce the crime rate thanks partly to the efforts of Reginald Eaves, director of public safety under Maynard

Jackson. Eaves, a former activist Morehouse student and Boston-trained attorney, shook up the police department and greatly increased the training time for new officers. Under Eaves, arrests went up 50 percent, and the burglary rate in the Model Cities area, the city's most crime-prone district, went down 42 percent from 1975 to 1976. Unfortunately, Eaves was another lawman turned criminal. He was later elected to the Fulton County Commission and convicted in May 1988 of selling his votes in a zoning case following a federal investigation into local corruption.

Another black, Lee Brown, was Atlanta police chief during the Missing and Murdered Children case, and his presence did much to defuse tensions before the arrest of Wayne Williams, when many blacks thought that the crimes were being committed by whites. Brown moved to a similar job in Houston, Texas, in 1982 and later became New York City police chief under Mayor David Dinkins. Police Chief George Napper, who had a Ph.D. in criminology, became Atlanta's second black director of public safety. In 1990, Napper's position was abolished, and he was forced out. Then the controversial Eldrin Bell became Atlanta's chief of police. The next year, Fulton County Assistant Police Chief Louis Graham moved up to become the county's first black chief.

Problems of unequal justice often started at the time of arrest. The presumption of innocence and the niceties of due process did not always extend to poor black suspects. Police, in their efforts to clear caseloads, might coerce confessions from them. In addition, lack of adequate legal counsel, jury biases, and sentencing disparities in white-dominated courts combined to fuel black grievances against Georgia's judicial system.

Because the poor often have inadequate counsel in court, authorities are often able to suppress evidence, which may result in convictions even though the defendant did not commit the crime. Jerry Banks was a black man who was convicted in rural Henry County of the murder of two whites in 1974 and sentenced to die. Banks, an unemployed truck driver, went hunting with an old single-shot shotgun and came across the bodies of two whites. He promptly reported this and was charged with murder. The police knew of witnesses who would have testified they heard several rapid shots—proving Banks's gun was not the murder weapon—but they suppressed the information. After spending six years on death row Banks was cleared and released. Banks never got his life back together. He later shot his wife and killed himself.

Suppression of evidence and jury bias figured in the May 20, 1975, sentencing of Earl Charles, a black, for the murder of a white furniture store owner and his son in Savannah. Charles was convicted even though he had left Savannah two weeks before the crime and was working in

Tampa. Prosecutors knew this but withheld the evidence and managed to get the death sentence for an innocent man. After three and a half years on death row, Charles was released in 1978 after a Tampa lawman publicly verified his alibi. Charles was awarded $415,000, to be paid by the city of Savannah for the damages that resulted from the city police department's frame job.

The case of the Dawson Five attracted national attention and was compared to the Scottsboro case of 1931 for its potential to become a miscarriage of justice. Five young blacks were charged with the 1976 murder of a white customer in a small grocery store on the outskirts of Dawson in "Terrible Terrell" County. The police arrested the five and threatened one with castration and electrocution while they questioned him and then forged his signature to a waiver of rights. The Dawson Five's defense was headed by Millard Farmer, a prison reformer and civil rights activist who practiced law in Atlanta and headed the Team Defense Project against the death penalty. The five were freed when the confession extracted by torture was deemed inadmissible.

In 1978, 81 percent of Georgia's prison inmates had annual incomes under $3,000 when they were convicted. A 1989 *Atlanta Constitution* survey found that 64 percent of the men in Georgia prisons were unemployed at the time of arrest. Even the idea that the accused has a right to counsel if he or she cannot pay for it is relatively new, a result of the 1963 landmark Supreme Court's *Gideon v. Wainright* decision.

All of the various methods Georgia set up for indigent defense had their shortcomings, notably money. Georgia historically has been stingy when it came to indigent defense. In 1987, Georgia was one of only eleven states that did not provide state funding for the legal defense of the poor. In 1986, when the national average per case was $223, the average indigent defendant in Georgia could count on only $138 to mount a defense. Even then, the quality of defense depended upon the local jurisdiction, which yielded a system of "patchwork justice," according to the *Macon Telegraph*. In 1989, the state's average had risen to $175, but spending in majority-black Taliaferro County was an absurdly low $16.29 per case. The state established the Indigent Defense Council in 1979 but failed to provide it with funds to give counties until ten years later. Then the situation had improved slightly. Georgia contributed $1 million to 119 counties in 1990—still, this was only about 5 percent of what was needed. Counties picked up the rest of the tab. Of the forty states that allocated funds for indigent defense, Georgia provided the least.

In 1985, Georgia Supreme Court Chief Justice Harold Hill said funding legal defense of the poor was "one of the most pressing problems facing the Georgia judiciary." In 1985 the American Civil Liberties Union

(ACLU) filed a federal lawsuit to force Georgia to provide counsel for indigent defendants. Then the state was spending less than half the national average—even less than it spent four years earlier. Ironically, the legislators who called for tougher sentences and refused to adequately fund indigent defense failed to realize that poor defenses can and did result in the overturning of convictions, successful appeals, new trials, and a far greater expense to the taxpayer than if proper defenses had been originally furnished.

Often overworked, underpaid, and overmatched public defenders were employed by some local jurisdictions. In 105 counties, panels of local lawyers selected attorneys for the court to appoint to defend indigents. This often resulted in assigning cases to less experienced attorneys, who also were poorly paid and often presented an inadequate defense. Where public defenders were provided by the county, one attorney might handle over three hundred cases a year, a load far too great to adequately defend any of his or her clients.

In the state's most populous county, one public defender's caseload reached a mind-boggling seven hundred cases in 1990; that year the American Bar Association reported that the Fulton County Public Defender's Office was on the verge of collapse after operating in crisis for several years. It was in the worst shape of any the evaluators had seen. On a typical court day, lawyers were expected to handle thirty clients' cases with no privacy and little time. Lawyer and client met, often for the first time, in the hall for five or ten minutes before a plea was entered. Guilt or innocence might not be the deciding factor in many cases. If the defendant pled guilty and the sentence was reduced to time already served, he or she might choose that option and walk out of the courthouse. A *Constitution* report found prisoners who remained in jail even though the charges against them had been dropped as well as inmates who pleaded guilty to the wrong charges just to get out of jail. Public defenders did not start work on a case until there was an indictment, and in December 1990, nearly a third of the sixteen hundred defendants awaiting trial had been in prison more than thirty days without an indictment.

The situation could be especially bad in rural Georgia, where there was often no guarantee defendants even would get a lawyer. In 1987, reporter Tracy Thompson found a disturbing practice. Color indigent defendants in rural Georgia were convicted of misdemeanors and sent to jail up to a year without a judge even asking them if they wanted a lawyer. Although the Supreme Court declared that practice unconstitutional in 1972, many Georgia judges ignored the ruling. Fifteen years later, a third of the judges surveyed admitted they followed similar practices in their courts.

* * *

While a jury trial is among Americans' basic rights, in Georgia the jury system often has been turned against blacks when officials intentionally excluded them from juries. This was accomplished in two ways: either by striking blacks from juries or by eliminating them from the jury pool. Lawyers could dismiss jurors for cause, or they could use their peremptory challenges to dismiss jurors without giving any reason. Georgia law allowed prosecutors to use their peremptory challenges to exclude up to ten jurors. In one 1984 case, the conviction by an all-white jury of Michael Moore for the murder of his white girlfriend's mother was a source of bitterness among blacks in the small Southeast Georgia town of Claxton. Fifty-four blacks were included in the pool of jurors for the trial. Fifty were dismissed for cause by the prosecution, which then used its peremptory challenges to eliminate the other four.

Although Georgia refused to go along with a growing number of states that abolished peremptory challenges, one improvement in jury selection had been accomplished in 1976 when, for the first time in Georgia, a lower court judge threw out indictments against two blacks when it was shown that blacks were underrepresented in the Decatur County jury pool. Later, other counties were ordered to desegregate jury lists. A more important step was taken in 1986 when the U. S. Supreme Court ruled that blacks could not be excluded from a jury without cause.

The other method of excluding blacks from juries was to avoid putting them into the pool from which jurors' names were drawn. Jasper County was not unique in 1962. Officials there could not recall a single black on a grand or trial jury for thirty years, although the county was 60 percent black. One way to achieve this was to use the "key men" system, in which the community's established white leaders would recommend jurors. In 1982, when blacks averaged 35 percent of the population in eighteen counties covered by the Middle District Court of Georgia, the jury lists were only 7 percent black. This inequity might have been worse except for a 1966 case and the 1968 federal Jury Selection and Service Act, which made rank prejudice in jury selection more difficult. In DeKalb County, the computer-picked jury list was thrown out in 1975 for discrimination against blacks and women.

With all the aforementioned factors coming into play, it should come as no surprise that blacks historically have received heavier sentences than whites for the same crimes. The perception of injustice was nurtured by a white-dominated court system. At the end of 1990, the state had 6 black superior court judges out of 138 and no black district attorneys among forty-five. The state's second-most-populous county, DeKalb, did not have any black superior court judges until 1991, when Michael Hancock and Linda W. Hunter were appointed.

In 1989, the *Atlanta Constitution* published the results of its investigation into sentencing disparities and found that across two-thirds of Georgia, black men were *at least* twice as likely to go to jail as white men convicted of the same crimes, ranging from drug sales to acts of violence. While Superior Court Judge Asa Kelley, Jr., of Albany (the mayor during the Albany Movement) said, "I try not to be race-conscious" and claimed that he used his discretion, there was a certain consistency in his sentencing. He routinely sentenced blacks in burglary cases to ten years—except for one he sentenced to twenty years. Whites, on the other hand, got one to seven years. Kelley did pass out uniform sentences for violent crimes, however. Both white and black defendants got five years for aggravated assault. Black State Sen. Gary Parker of Columbus noted: "For a long period of time, a black was probably in more trouble for stealing from a white than for killing another black." More people went to prison in Georgia between 1985 and 1988 for property crimes (34 percent) than violent crimes (27 percent).

The juvenile justice system was plagued by the same problems that faced the state's adult justice system, including blatant racism. A University of Georgia study released in October 1990 cited the system's "gross racial disparities" and a children's advocate said, "The system picks on black kids.... It's state- and county-sponsored child abuse by race." Of the children in Georgia's four youth prisons, 80 percent were black, and all 110 serving time for drug offenses were black. Parents with money could most likely get their kids into a private treatment center. Meanwhile, poor and black children who were imprisoned for drugs would find that the state had woefully inadequate drug-treatment facilities.

Georgia has never been noted for sparing its children, however. The state's minimum age for execution was seventeen, and Georgia executed more teenage murderers than any other state. In this century, Georgia has executed forty-two people who committed crimes while under the age of eighteen. Of these, thirty-nine were black.

The death penalty was the most controversial aspect of Georgia's criminal justice system. While polls show most Americans favor executions, civil rights groups protest the death penalty because it is used mainly against poor and black defendants. Critics also consider it cruel and unusual punishment and point out that it fails to act as a deterrent to crime. Amnesty International in 1987 called it "a horrifying lottery" that victimized blacks, Southerners, and the poor. Nationally only about 1 percent of all convicted killers ended up on death row in the 1980s. These unfortunate souls tended to be nonwhite, poor, undereducated, and poorly represented in court. Few defendants in capital cases can afford adequate defense, and the court-appointed lawyers tended to be young and inexperienced; some did not care what happened to their clients. An

American Bar Association Task Force singled out Georgia for the poor quality of representation that was offered to defendants facing the death penalty.

Death penalty historian Watt Espy had records back to 1735 showing that Georgia executed 950 persons from then to 1984, more than any other state. U. S. Justice Department records cover from 1930 and also rank Georgia number one, with 369 executions between 1930 and 1984; over 80 percent of those executed were black. Hanging was the state's method for official executions until it was replaced by the electric chair in 1924, a time when Georgia had more than twenty capital crimes on the books. The first man to die in Georgia's electric chair was a black, Howard Hinton, who was executed on September 13, 1924, just twenty days after he was sentenced. Back then, executions took place at the state prison at Milledgeville. The sturdy white-painted wooden chair was housed at Reidsville from 1937 until it was moved to the Georgia Diagnostic and Classification Center near Jackson in 1980. Between 1924 and 1990, Georgia put 429 men and women to death in the electric chair.

Between 1967 and 1977, there were no executions in the United States. In a 1972 case led by the NAACP, the U. S. Supreme Court ruled 5–4 in *Furman v. Georgia* that the death sentence was unconstitutional on the grounds that there was no consistency in sentencing; it held that sentences were imposed "freakishly" and "in a discriminatory fashion." Justice William O. Douglas noted the disproportionate number of blacks receiving the death sentence. The court's ruling led to the temporary suspension of the death penalty nationally. Georgia rewrote the laws on capital offenses in 1973 and specified that a court had to find one of ten specific aggravating circumstances in order to impose the death penalty and further provided that the Georgia Supreme Court would review all death sentences. Troy Leon Gregg was convicted and sentenced to die under the new law for the 1973 murder of two men who had offered him a ride in Gwinnett County. The new law was upheld by the U. S. Supreme Court on July 21, 1976, in *Gregg v. Georgia*. Georgia's new and improved death penalty became a model for other states and led to the reinstatement of the death penalty nationwide and a resumption of executions in 1977 with the death of white murderer Gary Gilmore by a Utah firing squad.

The new death-penalty laws did not remove the bias against blacks. From 1976 to 1986, when 12 percent of the nation was black, 41 percent of the executions were of blacks. In 1976, 62 percent of those on Georgia's death row were black. Over the next ten years, the complexion of Georgia's death row changed somewhat. In October 1986, Georgia had 112 prisoners on death row: fifty-five black men, fifty-five white men, one black woman, and one white woman. The number and racial makeup remained fairly constant through 1990. Only three states had more death-row inmates, and only Florida had more per capita. From the time Georgia resumed executions in 1983 through June 1986 six of the seven men who died in the electric chair were poor blacks. Of the next seven executions, four were of blacks. Of all fourteen, thirteen were executed for crimes against whites. A controversial study by University of Iowa law professor David Baldus of the 2,484 homicides committed in Georgia from 1973 through 1978 indicated that the killer of a white was eleven times as likely to receive a death sentence as the killer of a black and that a black who killed a white was eighteen times more likely to receive the death sentence than a white who killed a black.

In 1985, Patsy Morris of the Georgia ACLU stated that the death penalty was applied in the rural areas of Georgia disproportionately to their populations. In these areas racial bias most affected the criminal justice system. The three judicial districts with the highest per capita use of death sentences are composed of sixteen counties whose average population is under eleven thousand. Columbus was dubbed "the valley of death" due to the eagerness of all-white juries to impose death sentences. A study released in 1991 showed that prosecutors in the Chattahoochee Judicial District around Columbus sought the death penalty in one out of every three murder cases involving a white victim and only one out of seventeen cases with a black victim.

State officials have made some adjustments to make the death penalty seem less harsh. Even death-penalty advocates were uncomfortable when Jerome Bowden, a mentally retarded black Columbus man, was put to death in June 1986. In 1988, the General Assembly banned executions of mentally retarded inmates.

The condition of Georgia's prisons and the degraded lives that convicts lived in them posed some of the most serious long-standing problems in the state's criminal justice system. The publication of *I am a Fugitive from a Georgia Chain Gang!* in 1932, followed by investigations initiated by Eleanor Roosevelt, led to some changes. The main change was the construction of a penitentiary at Reidsville, a town of under two thousand in Tattnall County, sixty miles due west of Savannah. The prison came under attack soon after it was completed in 1937 as a WPA project to replace a 1911 building. Conditions were so bad there in 1957 that forty-one prisoners on the rock pile broke their own legs in protest.

In 1972, reacting to long-existing conditions, inmates led by Arthur S. Guthrie filed a federal suit charging that the penitentiary was unsanitary, unsafe, and inhumane. Federal District Court Judge Anthony Alaimo ordered an investigation, and it confirmed that guards were brutal, medical services and sanitation facilities were extremely inadequate, and that the prison's entire administration was racist. Blacks constituted two-thirds of the inmate population at the overcrowded facility, which had been built for twenty-two hundred prisoners but contained about three thousand. Discrimination was constant and came in the form of more privileges for white prisoners—*some were even supplied with weapons by guards.*

Reidsville nourished the seeds of racial turmoil, and racial clashes increased. Tensions were heightened by the integration of the dormitories in April 1974. There were two major outbreaks of interracial violence in Reidsville, leaving one dead and forty-two injured. Later, three blacks were killed and twenty-three prisoners were injured when white inmates waylaid black prisoners. The inmates formed an integrated unity committee in March 1978 following the killing of another black by whites. Guards objected to the committee, and some of its leaders were placed in the prison "hole" as violence resumed. When yet another black prisoner was killed, the prison was resegregated. By then one guard and five inmates had been killed since the court-ordered desegregation was implemented. Six blacks were charged with murder when a guard and two white convicts were killed.

The public was aware that much was wrong at Reidsville, and protests mounted. In August 1979, Hosea Williams led a week-long march of two hundred people from Savannah to Reidsville, where their numbers swelled to five hundred, to protest the death sentence, conditions at Reidsville, and the murder charges against the six black inmates who had become known as the "Reidsville Brothers." Racial violence continued with a major outbreak on February 17, 1981. In September 1981 guards stood by and watched as a group of white prisoners attacked two blacks in the showers, beating them and stabbing one to death. Four guards were fired, and three white inmates were convicted of murder. Three of the guards were soon reinstated. Judge Alaimo's patience was wearing thin, for he had ordered reforms back in 1975. The latest racial clash impelled the judge to state that there had been no substantial compliance with his previous orders. In 1982, a study by the National Institute of Corrections, a branch of the U. S. Department of Justice, stated that the racial violence existed to the extent it did because officials tolerated it. In October 1982, Judge Alaimo held prison officials in contempt for continued poor treatment of inmates.

The reforms ordered in 1975 in response to the 1972 suit brought on a building program that eventually cost the state $50 million. This program was completed in 1985, and each inmate then had a private cell, thus alleviating overcrowding, a major source of the disturbances. The number of inmates at Reidsville was reduced to less than one thousand in 1985 and more personnel were hired. After thirteen years of litigation, supported by the NAACP and the SCLC, the court order was lifted. In 1987, Reidsville was considered among the best prisons in the nation. Alaimo, who had endured intense pressure to weaken his orders for reform, was pleased that Reidsville had become a model prison for other states to copy.

Reidsville was only one of many correctional institutions in Georgia with intolerable conditions. In 1985, a federal court order was required to stop guards at the Coastal Correctional Institution from using racial slurs and carrying pick handles. The situation also was bad at Georgia's women's prison at Hardwick, where 75 percent of the 330 inmates were black. Early in 1973, a protest was made by some inmates who worked in the Central State Hospital's laundry without pay while others were being paid to learn new skills. In *Hardwick v. Ault* (1979), U. S. District Court Judge Wilbur Owens, Jr., ruled that Hardwick's "behavior modification" program, which put prisoners on bread and water in solitary confinement, where they baked in the summer and froze in the winter, was cruel and inhumane punishment.

In 1985, Georgia had 266 inmate facilities, most of which were local city and county jails. Many of the local communities found their jails under attack by inmate suits in the 1970s and 1980s for failure to meet minimum standards. Dozens of counties then had to upgrade their facilities under court orders, and some fifty new jails were built between 1974 and 1986.

The infamous convict-lease camps became public work camps when the state took over their operation early in the century. Later, they became county correctional institutions. They were known for their miserable living conditions, and whippings were still administered in the 1950s—and perhaps later. Georgia used to have ninety-three such camps. In the late 1960s, under Governor Maddox, twenty-eight of these "rat holes" were closed, and work-release programs were extended. By 1985 their numbers were reduced to twenty-seven, housing 2,965 prisoners, 18 percent of the state's total. State regulations have made life in these camps less brutal, limiting their hours of work and forbidding work outside when the temperature is below twenty-eight degrees. Such restrictions made prisoners less profitable to the counties, and many local governments gave up the camps. Those remaining were the larger ones that profited from the economies of scale.

In the 1980s and early 1990s, the flood of drug arrests, convictions, and tough mandatory sentencing forced the state to begin a "crash" construction program to reduce prison overcrowding. While there were some efforts at reform, Georgia's leaders mainly committed the state to a "build-em and fill-em" policy instead of heeding critics who pointed out that the solutions to the problems of crime in Georgia, as elsewhere, lie in the eradication of its root causes—poverty, unemployment, and lack of education.

"The Negro is coming more and more to look upon law and justice, not as protecting safeguards, but as sources of humiliation and oppression," W. E. B. Du Bois wrote in 1903. Unfortunately, this was still true as the century neared its end. As a result, Georgia's criminal justice system continued to breed disrespect for the law, said James T. Morris, a member of the State Board of Pardons and Paroles, in 1990: "You're dealing with a young black male population with no hope out there, and a slowly evolving, smoldering hostility and hatred for the system."

15

Modern Education and Culture

In the Years Since *Brown*

After the Supreme Court's 1954 *Brown* decision, Georgia lagged behind the South generally in public school integration, and there was little change in the status quo over the next decade. While Gov. Ernest Vandiver signed laws undoing massive resistance in 1961, he had sent a contradictory signal by proposing to end compulsory education, making state grants to private schools, and leaving school desegregation to local option. This helped to continue resistance to integration. By 1964, although 6 percent of Georgia's public school districts were supposedly desegregated, only one-third of 1 percent of the state's black children were in integrated classrooms, with most of them in Atlanta. Three years later, the number had risen to only 8.8 percent. Local systems continued to ignore the law and circumvent court directives. The Georgia Board of Education identified schools as "white" and "colored" well into the 1960s.

The 1964 Civil Rights Act authorized the cutoff of federal funds to segregated schools and encouraged the attorney general to act against those systems that were willing to forgo such funding to maintain segregation. In 1963, local blacks brought suit against the Bibb County school system. Macon's leaders decided to try a gradual desegregation plan two months before the new federal law went into effect. School and NAACP officials selected sixteen top black students to test the waters by entering white schools. The trouble many Maconites expected when schools opened in September did not materialize, but it would be several more years before the lawsuit was settled. Widespread integration in Bibb County schools did not come until 1970. Americus, Augusta, Marietta, and Albany also moved away from total segregation in 1964, but they, too, were far from being truly integrated.

While the Georgia Board of Education signed a desegregation pledge in January 1965 to obtain $55 million in federal aid, less than ten of the state's school systems complied with the federal Office of Education's desegregation guidelines. Whites sometimes avoided desegregation by transferring large numbers of white students out of integrated systems into nearby all-white public schools, a practice that would continue for decades. The Taliaferro County School Board closed the all-white Alexander Stephens Institute in 1965 when eighty-seven blacks attempted to enroll there. All white students transferred out on county school busses to other counties or went to private schools. (Five were started since 1965.) The Ku Klux Klan was on hand to harass black students who attempted to board buses with whites. The system was placed under federal receivership, and Alexander Stephens was re-opened—as an all-black school.

Meanwhile, blacks continued to push for progress and racial tensions ran high. In 1965, three hundred black students at Washington in Wilkes County trashed their school in a protest against its inferiority and sat down in front of the white high school demanding enrollment. All were arrested, but their sentences were suspended. School protests also erupted in Lincolnton. Five months later, three hundred black Cordele students, protesting their poor school, marched on the courthouse, hauled down the United States and Georgia flags and raised a "Freedom Now" banner. This precipitated a Klan rally that five hundred whites attended.

Despite black protests, desegregation in Georgia proceeded at a glacial pace. In 1966, Georgia was ruled in violation of federal rules and funds were cut off at the end of the school year. Senator Russell continued to lead the fight against desegregation. He protested federal guidelines, and in 1967, he proposed an unsuccessful measure that would forbid the cutoff of funds for failure to desegregate. In March 1967, the Fifth Circuit Court of Appeals, in *U.S. v. Jefferson County School Board*, directed Georgia and the other states within its jurisdiction to end their dual school systems. This undercut the "freedom of choice" plans that were considered the ultimate defense against the Supreme Court. This decision was reinforced a year later in *Green v. County School Board*, which declared the freedom of choice plan unconstitutional. Still, not much changed in rural Georgia. That year, Hosea Williams and Tyrone Brooks led a four-day march from Perry to Atlanta to protest Perry's refusal to integrate its schools. White hopes that the Supreme Court would change its mind and overrule lower federal courts were dashed by a unanimous ruling in *Alexander v. Holmes* (1969), a Mississippi case stating that there would be no further delay in desegregation in the South.

In 1969, the Department of Health, Education, and Welfare (HEW) cut off federal funds to Washington County, Georgia, schools because only 1 percent of the black students attended school with whites. In 1970, when Washington County tried to implement a faculty-integration plan sixty-eight white teachers boycotted the classrooms, but forty-eight returned after a week.

Regardless of whites' misgivings, integration was supposedly the law of the land and one way to comply with court orders was by busing. Suddenly white Georgians were dead set against this practice, even though "busing" had been going on in the state since 1914, when the state's first consolidated rural school used horse- and mule-drawn wagons on unpaved roads. As consolidation proceeded, busing increased, and many blacks had childhood memories of watching a bus taking white children to a modern school pass them by while they plodded through the rain to their primitive one-room schoolhouse. In 1979, a Darden Research Poll indicated that although 60 percent of Southern whites believed integration was good, only 11 percent favored busing to achieve it. A major problem with most busing plans was that they involved mainly the movement of blacks to white schools but not the reverse. Upson County blacks protested this in 1983.

When extensive busing was ordered by federal judge Alexander Lawrence in 1972 to integrate Augusta's sixty schools, many white parents organized protests, and over half of the thirty thousand students stayed home on February 14. Conservative local, state, and national leaders encouraged this sort of resistance. The segregationist and white supremacist Richmond school superintendent said the court order "stinks." The protesters had the sympathy of President Nixon, who continued to undercut efforts to use busing to enforce desegregation.

Nevertheless, the court plan was implemented. Richmond whites led a second boycott on February 28 and attempted to make the protest statewide. Although 60 percent of Augusta whites and half of Savannah whites stayed away from school, the absentee rates in Albany, Macon, and Columbus were much lower.

While the state school board in 1968 refused to allow state funds to transport students to other school districts to achieve desegregation, most whites did not object to interdistrict busing to *avoid* integration. The state school board continued its obstructionist policies into the 1970s with resolutions against desegregation plans that assigned students away from their neighborhood schools. (This policy finally was overturned in 1990.) The practice of transferring white students from schools with large percentages of black students to those with white majorities ignored a

1971 federal court ruling; the court had ordered Georgia and some eighty of its school districts to restrict transfers that contributed to racial imbalance.

In 1985, Georgia NAACP President Robert Flanagan charged that the transfer scheme was being used to perpetuate segregation. Burke, Glascock, Hancock, Jefferson, Johnson, Macon, McDuffie, Peach, Schley, Stewart, Warren, Washington, and Webster counties were singled out for criticism. Federal officials later cleared most of these counties despite strong evidence of wrongdoing in some cases. In 1985, the Hancock County school system was 99 percent black because most white children attended private schools or public schools in other counties for "racial reasons," according to Hancock School Superintendent Marvin E. Lewis. The transfer of white students from Twiggs County schools to Bleckley County schools yielded two racially unbalanced systems: Twiggs schools were 69 percent black, and the Bleckley system was 71 percent white.

Faced with federal actions to enforce integration, angry local white establishments also increased the number of all-white private schools, where parents sent their children to avoid putting them in integrated classrooms. These private schools proliferated in the 1970s, when it became almost impossible to further delay public school desegregation. In 1969, there were 151 private schools teaching 34,105 students in grades one through twelve. By 1978 there were 366 such schools in Georgia with 80,686 students. By 1983, Bibb County alone had fifteen private schools below the college level, of which nine were church related. In the Middle Georgia area of Bibb, Baldwin, Houston, Jones, Laurens, Monroe, and Twiggs counties, there were thirty-two private schools below college level enrolling 8,370 students in the 1984-85 academic year. They ranged in enrollment from 5 students to 759, with the average being 260 students. The trend continued throughout the nation. In 1984 over 12 percent of the nation's 46.2 million precollege students were in 24,500 private schools. By 1989, 83,449 students, 8 percent of the state's total, attended 527 private schools in Georgia. Fewer than 20 percent of them had accreditation from either the Southern Association of Colleges and Schools or by the Georgia Accrediting Commission.

Not all private schools were all white, nor did they all foster segregation. Atlanta's Trinity School, founded in 1951 by Trinity Presbyterian Church, admitted several black children in 1963, including two of civil rights activist Andrew Young. (That year, the prestigious Lovett School, affiliated with the Episcopal church, refused to enroll Dr. Martin Luther King, Jr.'s son.) Boggs Academy in Keysville, twenty-two miles southwest of Augusta, in Burke County, was founded in 1907 and became Georgia's first accredited black secondary boarding school. While many private schools accepted minority students and even offered scholarships to some, prohibitive tuition costs kept the vast majority of nonwhite students away. Overall, the trend toward private schools tended to defeat the egalitarian intent of the *Brown* decision to bring blacks and whites together to learn from each other and, by association, to foster mutual toleration, appreciation, and respect.

As private schools grew, so did the number of local school systems with a majority of black students. This was true of twenty-three of Georgia's 188 school systems in 1966. Ten years later, forty-eight systems were majority black. As whites deserted the public schools, there was less support for high-quality education for the remaining children. This often showed up as a refusal to adequately fund the public school system, especially when it was managed by a white school board and superintendent who sent their children to private schools. In 1983, Terrell County blacks demanded that the county school board fire all employees who had children in private schools, including the school superintendent.

Sumter County afforded a malevolent example of this gutting of public schools and was labeled "a blight on the state." For twenty years after the *Brown* decision, Sumter's all-white school board ignored court decisions, protests, boycotts, the U. S. Department of Justice, the ACLU, and individual lawsuits, including one filed by former county school board member Jimmy Carter when he was governor. The local board, composed principally of large landowners who sent their own children and grandchildren to the private white Southland Academy, dropped taxes as whites left the public school system. Southland had eleven hundred white students when it opened in 1970. This left the public schools 80 percent black. Before the 1970 desegregation order, the millage rate for county property taxes was 19.5; by 1983 it had dropped to 7. Deteriorating public school buildings were not being maintained, and only the one in Plains had air conditioning—only because so many tourists came there. The Leslie Elementary School lacked air conditioning and screens, and one teacher said, "Your choice is to burn up or eat bugs." As of 1983, 40 percent of Sumter's students dropped out prior to graduation and 30 percent failed the basic-skills test required for graduation. Of those who did pass, 90 percent barely did so. In 1986, a federal judge broke up Sumter's at-large school board system.

In Atlanta, the neighborhood-school concept meant there was much school segregation due to residential segregation, which had been encouraged by local real estate agents and federal housing policies, especially before 1965. After World War II, the percentage of black students in the Atlanta school system increased due to a rise in the city's black population and the flight of whites to the suburbs and private schools. In 1954, Atlanta's public school population was 33 percent black;

in 1970 it was 70 percent black; in 1972, 80 percent. By 1980 it was 90 percent black. By 1990, Atlanta's public schools were 94 percent nonwhite.

Atlanta's changes were modified somewhat by the greater black input into policy decisions and more involvement of black and interracial organizations. The city's first tentative steps at integration had not settled the 1958 lawsuit filed by the NAACP, however, and the pace of school desegregation was too slow for activists and their allies in the courts. In 1970, federal District Judge Frank Hooper directed Atlanta's school system to transfer some eight hundred black teachers to predominantly white schools and some eight hundred white teachers to predominantly black schools to enforce a federal court order that each school's faculty should reflect the system's racial balance. The order resulted in much greater faculty integration, but it also led to the resignation of hundreds of teachers and an acceleration of white flight. In 1976, about five hundred white children returned to the public schools, thanks largely to the Northside Atlanta Parents for Public Schools.

In the desegregation suit, the NAACP Legal Defense Fund had filed a plan to bus about thirty thousand black students to make every school predominantly black. A rift developed when local NAACP leaders worked on a compromise with local school officials to give up extensive busing in exchange for control of the school system. In 1973, the federal court approved a compromise that provided for a black superintendent, a 50 percent black administrative staff, and a minimum of 30 percent black teachers in majority white schools. This agreement resulted in sixty-four integrated schools and eighty-three segregated schools, with the busing of less than three thousand students. Alonzo Crim became the new black superintendent and held the post until his resignation in 1987. Roy Wilkins, then national head of the NAACP, objected strenuously. Wilkins labeled the agreement an "Atlanta Compromise," referring to Booker T. Washington's 1895 proposal to exchange political and social rights for economic opportunity (which never came). He suspended the Atlanta chapter and its leader, Lonnie King, from the organization.

This "Atlanta Compromise" was challenged in a suit filed by the ACLU on behalf of black Atlanta parents against suburban school systems. The plaintiffs wanted to enroll blacks in suburban schools and thus defeat one of the purposes of white flight. This was in accord with the national policies of the NAACP, which held that each school should reflect the metropolitan area's racial composition, since segregated housing patterns were the product of decades of deliberate actions. In 1980, the Supreme Court, without hearing arguments, upheld the district court's denial of a metropolitan remedy. This sanctioned continued racial imbalance in both Atlanta and suburban schools and, according to the ACLU, reflected the

Burger Court's "callous disregard for the need to remedy the effects of centuries of racial discrimination."

Busing to achieve a "metropolitan solution" had been supported by whites to maintain segregation. For decades, several area school systems cooperated to bus blacks across county, city, and school district boundaries to Atlanta's black Washington and Howard high schools. Even in the late 1960s, black students were bused into Marietta to keep Cobb County schools white. One factor ameliorating the failure to adopt a "metropolitan solution" was the "Majority-to-Minority" program sanctioned by federal courts. This permitted blacks in majority black schools to transfer to majority white schools and vice versa.

The DeKalb County school system, the state's largest, was ordered to desegregate its schools in 1969, and a follow-up order in 1976 required busing. DeKalb County schools were 94 percent white in 1969; ten years later they were 71 percent white. By 1990, DeKalb's population was 40 percent black, but the seventy-three-thousand-student school system was 60 percent black. The desegregation case returned to court in July 1987, when half the black students attended schools that were at least 90 percent black and a fourth of white students attended schools that were 90 percent white. DeKalb was spending $350 more per pupil at predominantly white schools—because the teachers there were better trained and more experienced and therefore commanded higher salaries. On June 30, 1988, U. S. District Judge William C. O'Kelley ordered DeKalb to put more of its better-trained and more experienced teachers from schools on the north side to the south. This was accomplished the next year.

On October 11, 1989, the 11th Circuit Court of Appeals found that DeKalb schools were still segregated and ordered DeKalb to consider busing and redrawing school attendance lines. As an incentive to get white students to attend predominantly black schools, DeKalb designated eight magnet schools with special programs in South DeKalb. The program sparked resentment among black students who were not allowed to enroll in the programs. Meanwhile, a rift over busing developed among blacks.

DeKalb appealed the case to the Supreme Court. On March 30, 1992, the court ruled 8-0 in a landmark decision favoring the school system. DeKalb would not be forced to bus children to achieve integration, and neighborhood schools could reflect the racial composition of their areas. Two years earlier, in August 1990, DeKalb filed suit claiming that the state was responsible for segregated schools, and the state was forced to consider paying millions of dollars to aid the county's desegregation efforts. Similar suits were filed by Savannah-Chatham County schools and school districts in other states.

In 1982, some Augusta blacks came to a similar conclusion that Lonnie King had in Atlanta, namely, that upgrading black education was more important than integration. They were willing to give up busing and integration in exchange for increased funding for the inner-city elementary schools. However, the Rev. Otis Smith, president of the Augusta NAACP, called the plan a throwback to the days of segregation. "My experience with separate education is that it is never, never equal," he stated. "My children have learned to appreciate whites and other people by associating with them. . . . It eliminated a lot of fear. That's education in itself." Another black leader said that the blacks who backed the antibusing plan were a "black elite who see themselves as separate from the masses. They live in the suburbs now. Their kids go to suburban schools. They don't see their interests tied to the inner city."

Although de jure desegregation came to Georgia's public schools in the early 1970s at the latest, litigation continued and as a practical matter, many classrooms were filled with children of one race. White fears of a majority-black high school were at the center of a consolidation struggle in Meriwether County that lasted into the 1990s. In the mid-1980s, the Chatham County NAACP protested a desegregation plan that would shut down black inner-city schools and bus the blacks to the then predominantly white schools. In 1988, Chatham's magnet-school plan was adopted and approved by the courts. That year, the Justice Department began moving to dismiss seventeen Georgia school districts from a 1969 desegregation suit, which brought a challenge from the NAACP. Although Columbus was relatively calm during the early days of desegregation, the NAACP reopened the twenty-year-old Muscogee County case and charged that the school system had never complied with Judge J. Robert Elliott's 1971 order to desegregate. Between 1969 and 1990, Atlanta's school system enrollment fell from 111,906 to 61,378. Two reasons given were a declining birthrate and parents who refused to send their children to public schools. *Atlanta Constitution* writer Jane O. Hansen compared metropolitan Atlanta's school districts to "a giant powdered-sugar jelly doughnut—white on the outside and dark in the center."

While blacks had long fought for desegregation, they often protested the method of integration in the 1970s. They resented the loss of black jobs and the disappearance of the black school's heritage when it was combined with a white school. Trophy cases, viewed with pride for years, were often abandoned, as were athletic-team identities and student organizations. Many black students believed school administrators and teachers held high-handed disregard for their beliefs and traditions. Many other students had conflicts with white students during the initial tense periods of desegregation. Where conflict resulted, it was the black student who was usually blamed and disciplined more severely. Some who were suspended simply dropped out.

A University of Michigan professor's study of black and white Georgia educators in 1978 found that prior to integration, black teachers and principals were the primary role models who prodded, pushed, and cajoled students toward excellence. When the dual system was displaced, many of these role models were laid off or demoted. Where a community had both black and white schools that combined, the black principal lost out. In the 1960s, the number of black principals declined more than 90 percent in Southern states. If there were surplus teachers under the new system, usually black teachers were forced out.

Before 1973, no Georgia county had a black superintendent of schools. That year, Marvin E. Lewis, a black, was elected to the post in Hancock County. The next three years saw this position filled by blacks in only Atlanta and Talbot County, although there were over forty school systems with black student majorities. Women suffered from discrimination, too, as top school positions continued to be dominated by white males.

On the other hand, the Georgia Association of Educators (GAE) adopted a progressive attitude when black and white teachers' associations merged in 1970. The Georgia Teachers and Educators Association (white) and the Georgia Educators Association (black) merged to form the GAE, which had black presidents during the 1970s. The GAE named Andrew H. Griffin—a Harvard doctorate—as its first black executive director in 1987. Norman Thomas was elected the Georgia Parent-Teacher Association's first black president in 1985.

The practice of choosing school boards undemocratically greatly increased the difficulty of obtaining fair treatment for black students, faculty and administrators. The Thomaston School Board, created in 1915, filled its own vacancies and was self-perpetuating. Just before a city school board member's term expired, the board would select a replacement. In 1979, after sixty-four years without a black board member, blacks sued. The city lost and appealed the case all the way to the U. S. Supreme Court, but the court ruled in 1983 that the discrimination was "purposeful" and ordered the board to appoint blacks. Almost as onerous was the practice of having grand jurors appoint school board members. This custom was, interestingly enough, most prevalent in majority black counties and could be used to keep blacks out of power. This system of selection came under increased legal attack after the court abolished it in Johnson County in 1984, but it survived court challenges through 1990. At-large elections posed a similar problem, but many of these systems were abolished by successful voting-rights lawsuits.

After desegregation, social segregation continued, with minimal contact between white and black students. As a general rule blacks and whites sat on separate sides of the classroom, and white teachers often addressed themselves exclusively to the white students. The two groups usually sat at separate tables in lunchrooms and kept their distance from each other in assemblies, athletic contests, and other events. Students who made friendly approaches to those of the other race were often threatened with social ostracism by their peers. Administrators often dealt with these problems by setting racial quotas for student groups, such as cheerleaders and flag girls, by maintaining separate proms for black and white students, and by having separate but equal homecoming queens.

At schools, racial discord was common. Peach County was typical: there were numerous altercations between white and black students that usually resulted in more severe disciplinary action being taken against the black students. Whites resented what they perceived as an intrusion of alien people into their world, and blacks resented this perception. In 1972, black students walked out of the high school and were sprayed with mace. In 1976, four black students filed a suit against the all-white school board protesting their arbitrary suspension. Two decades after desegregation, in 1990, Peach County High School held its first integrated prom.

In many places, school desegregation proceeded during the early 1970s with an unexpected lack of turbulence. When Eatonton desegregated its schools in 1970, there were dire predictions of violence and social turmoil that failed to materialize over the next four years. A biracial volunteer committee allowed everyone to air their grievances. The committee would then contact the persons who could deal with the grievance. Volunteers patrolled the basketball games to maintain order. Others worked within the black community and helped black students having academic or personal problems.

The Klan often made a concerted effort to capitalize on racial tensions in schools throughout the nation and developed a youth corps comprising up to 15 percent of the total Klan membership. Its slogan, "Tomorrow Belongs to Us," was borrowed from the Hitler youth movement. In August 1980, James Venable of Decatur, the aging wizard of the National Knights of the Ku Klux Klan, boasted that his organization had recruited 684 teenagers so far that year. The GAE warned parents, school officials, and students of this resurgence in 1982. The Klan often reacted to reports of interracial dating or sexual activity by demonstrating and recruiting. The Klan handed out literature to students at Rome, Jonesboro, and in Cobb County. Using questionable judgment at best, the Griffin-Spalding County School Board rented the high school auditorium to the Klan for a 1982 meeting, but when the Klan did not pay in advance, the permission was withdrawn. Throughout the 1980s, wherever racial trouble erupted in the schools, the Klan was sure to go: Ludowici, Dublin, and Telfair County in 1985; Madison County in 1986; and Winder in 1987.

Griffin and Valdosta schools were the scenes of racial violence in 1989, and such incidents continued to erupt in Georgia schools into the 1990s. In Gwinnett County, two teenagers who put a cross in a black neighbor's yard later joined the Knights of the Junior Klansmen Alliance at Meadowcreek High School. School officials quickly outlawed the group. Violent racial incidents at Creekside High School in South Fulton County in 1990 were the third in area schools in two weeks. More than seven hundred students stayed away from school after an outbreak of racial fighting. Creekside's administration reacted by adding a black assistant principal and formed biracial committees to promote communication and understanding. By the end of the school year, tensions had eased at the racially mixed school. In January 1991, the Fulton County School Board became the first in the state to approve an antibigotry policy that banned racial slurs and abusive actions by students, school employees, and visitors. School Superintendent James Fox, Jr., said that the policy was a response to a growing attitude during the 1980s that acts of racism were "more acceptable than they were in the '70s and '60s."

In Newton County, where the popular television series "In the Heat of the Night" was filmed, racial tensions erupted into fighting in the fall of 1990. The Governor's Commission on Human Relations blamed school leaders for not knowing what was going on. Problems resurfaced in 1991 when a dispute over whether a black or a white should be declared valedictorian. The school board failed to make a choice between the two, and a federal judge named the white and black students co-valedictorians.

The biggest problems in Georgia's schools did not involve those who competed for valedictory honors, but those who struggled to get by in deficient schools. The entire nation agonized over its educational system, but Georgia's schools scored poorly on virtually every test. There were some improvements during the 1960s, and the state legislative passed the Adequate Program for Education in Georgia (APEG) in 1974, but it was never fully funded or implemented.

A decade later, Gov. Joe Frank Harris pledged that his administration would give education the highest priority. He appointed a forty-four-member Education Review Commission that spent a year and a half drafting a comprehensive plan to improve the public school system. The result was the Quality Basic Education (QBE) Act, which the General Assembly passed unanimously in 1985. The act went into effect on July 1, 1986. It upgraded teacher salaries and set higher requirements for teachers, students, and school systems. It improved teacher-student ratios, infused money into local school systems for improvements, funded new schools, and started a statewide full-day kindergarten program. While the QBE Act attempted to address fully the state's educational deficiencies, it suffered from funding problems and local resistance.

Beginning with faculty integration, teacher competence became a statewide issue in Georgia. Starting in 1978, the state required that teachers must pass the Teacher Certification Test (TCT). Effective in 1987, the QBE Act also mandated that veteran teachers—except those hired before 1974 who had lifetime certificates—take tests to renew their certificates. Some blacks viewed this requirement as racist, since tests were presumed to be culturally biased. The GAE went to court to block testing requirements for veteran teachers, stating that the black failure rate of 42 percent after retesting, as compared to the white failure rate of 6 percent, was proof of discrimination. The test stood, however, producing a disproportionately large failure rate among black teachers. While the TCT was designed to test teachers' subject knowledge, the state had difficulties instituting an effective test of teachers' classroom effectiveness. In 1990, 99.4 percent of the teachers passed state-mandated appraisals by their principals that were required to earn merit raises. The extraordinary passing rate led the *Constitution* to call the test "phony."

The cavalier attitude that cost many black educators their jobs in the 1960s and 1970s was replaced by a fierce recruiting drive in the 1980s and 1990s. Although Georgia probably did not suffer the loss of black teachers that other states did, in the late 1980s, there were few school systems that could boast as high a percentage of black faculty as there were of black students. By then, the state had come to recognize this as a problem and understood the positive role black teachers played in students' lives. In Barnesville in 1986, this issue of black teacher shortages sparked protests by Lamar County blacks. In 1990, a study by Georgia's Professional Standards Commission stunned state educators with its claim that Georgia had an extremely high percentage of black educators: 21 percent, compared to 9 percent for the region and 5 percent for the nation. Then Georgia's public school student population was 38 percent black. Even so, experts said that many of Georgia's black teachers were older and would retire before the year 2000. Blacks represented only 16 percent of the new teachers hired in 1989, and there were further indications that the percentages would decrease. Competition for minority teachers was intense. With the opening up of other professions to college-educated blacks, education majors at traditional black colleges dropped 40 percent from 1977 to 1986. As one solution, Georgia began holding a statewide teacher recruiting fair at the Atlanta University complex.

School systems throughout Georgia were accused of discrimination against blacks in grading, class assignments, testing, and placement. In 1984, the state NAACP charged that thirteen Georgia school districts discriminated against blacks by assigning them to special-education classes before they were tested and evaluated. Unfortunately, many Georgia schools lacked special programs for the gifted. In 1986, the U. S. Department of Education reported that black males, while constituting

38 percent of the male students in Georgia, got 53 percent of the suspensions and 46 percent of the corporal punishment and made up 67 percent of the educable mentally retarded classes and only 8 percent of the gifted and talented student classes. In 1988, the *Atlanta Constitution* found widespread evidence of racial disparities in school discipline in Fulton, DeKalb, Rockdale, and Newton schools.

The QBE Act mandated three types of high school diplomas: college preparatory, vocational, and general. While this was supposed to be an improvement, it encouraged the already too prevalent practice of "tracking" students—that is, segregating them into groups based on school officials' perceptions of their learning abilities. Due to a variety of factors, including rank racial prejudice, school officials often abused the tracking system and assigned capable black children to the lower tracks. In 1991, one-third of Georgia's seniors received general diplomas, which many employers considered to be essentially worthless for all but the most menial jobs. In 1990, convincing evidence surfaced that showed black students were being steered away from seeking college-preparatory diplomas. In another piece of bad news, the Georgia Senate Research Office reported that 45 percent of blacks who got college-preparatory diplomas had to take remedial courses in Georgia's public colleges. (Later research revealed that white students did not do much better.)

The QBE Act was unable to eradicate the differences between good and bad schools that arose from economic disparities between districts. Because much public school funding came from property taxes, poor counties had less money for education than rich ones. The Southern Regional Council reported in 1981 that in Georgia's Black Belt, local resistance to integration was replaced by neglect. Majority-black school districts were among the state's poorest, and in such places, major repairs or investment in new school facilities fell dramatically during the 1970s. This was one of the more subtle aspects of racism, which continued to play a key role in the quality of education. "There are many counties in South Georgia where meager support for the public schools is essentially a matter of race," noted Alan Ahrenhalt in *Georgia Trend*. Local white leaders with children in private academies refused to spend tax money on a system that they considered of no benefit to them. In Burke County, white officials used public money to fund a private school. In rural Georgia, farmers who owned the tax base needed field hands, not scholars. They sat on school boards to keep taxes down and took pride in running systems cheaply.

There were innovations in Georgia, including programs launched in recent years to combat adult illiteracy and deal with the potential problems of "at risk" children from poorer homes. Atlanta, Fulton, and DeKalb school systems set up preschools to prepare children for kindergarten. Much of the innovation has been the result of black initiatives, such as Project Success, which was established by 100 Black Men of Atlanta and guaranteed college tuition to thirty-five students (a home-room class) from Atlanta's Archer High School—one of five such programs in metropolitan Atlanta.

Meanwhile, private schools sprang up to cater to blacks who no longer trusted public schools to educate their children. In 1989, among Atlanta's private schools was all-black International Preparatory Institute, with 135 students and $3,600 tuition. In 1991, Fred Hampton founded Atlanta Preparatory School, Atlanta's first non-church-related college prep school for black students. Tuition was $3,000 a year. The curriculum included stiff academic coursework, including Japanese-language courses, other advanced classes, and African-American studies.

A year before Atlanta's schools were first integrated, Horace Mann Bond wrote:

> Our worst schools are where our best should be; our best, where family circumstance already provides an unequal best chance for the children of the economically favored.... there *is* talent among Negroes, and among the other poor of this nation. To provide for these children, the very best in education opportunity, and inspiration; this is the next great need of American Education.

Over the next thirty years, Georgia and America failed to meet that need. Republican administrations encouraged resistance to integration and advanced proposals to assist segregated private schools. Black reading skills improved dramatically thanks to Head Start programs, then stopped improving during the Reagan years, when funding for this preschool program for disadvantaged children was cut back.

After the QBE Act was implemented, education's share of the state budget declined, while the state was busy at work building more prisons. There had been improvements, but Georgia's educational system was still widely viewed as a failure. As the 1990s began, Georgia had not yet achieved the goal of providing its children with a quality basic education. Its failure to fully desegregate its schools further complicated its educational task. Residential segregation, white flight, and racial and economic disparities all combined to keep education in Georgia largely separate and unequal. Although access by blacks to educational opportunities had increased greatly by 1990 from the blatantly inferior dual system that prevailed for nearly two decades after school segregation was declared unconstitutional, a nonracist environment in the schools did not develop, racial strife continued in schools all over Georgia, and desegregation litigation involving school districts across Georgia continued.

Racially motivated discipline plus downgrading of black faculty and the virtual elimination of black history in public schools led some to feel that integration was a failure. Still others believed it was a mistake to make schools the battleground for integration, and some blacks sought to win improvements for their own neighborhood schools instead. Atlanta abandoned the battle in the 1970s in exchange for power over a system that grew blacker and whose students grew poorer as middle-class blacks joined in the flight from the city. Thirty-six years after *Brown*, metropolitan Atlanta had some of the most intensely segregated schools in the nation. Many local school boards continued to shortchange students in majority-black districts. Despite the problems of the modern educational system, desegregation marked an improvement. Most importantly, blacks could no longer be excluded from the public debate on educational issues or from the goals that the state proclaimed for its children.

Higher Education

In the 1980s, even though more black students were finishing high school, minority college enrollment was stagnating, and black male enrollment was actually declining. The fact that there were more black males in prison than in college was frequently cited. There were several reasons for the decline. Federal student aid during the Reagan years had shifted from grants to loans, which put a heavier financial burden on economically deprived students. There was also a lack of recruiting, competition from the military, and stiffer entrance requirements.

Between 1985 and 1988, black enrollment at the University of Georgia dropped from 1,437 to 1,358—only about 5 percent of the student population. Fierce recruiting drives by Emory University and Georgia Tech yielded slight increases in black enrollment. University of Georgia officials scrambled to recruit minority students, faculty and administrators. In 1989, the school reported a 16 percent increase in black applicants for admission from the previous year. Unfortunately, blacks who graduated from college and went to work in Georgia would earn 18 percent less than their white male counterparts, according to a survey released in 1987 by Georgia State University.

After World War II, the proportion of black college students who attended the nation's predominantly black colleges began to decline. In 1965, 58 percent of black college students attended historically black colleges. As white colleges abandoned segregation, the better black students enrolled in white colleges in increasing numbers. This "brain drain" had an adverse effect on Georgia's three state-supported, predominantly black colleges: Fort Valley State, Savannah State, and Albany State. Fort Valley's enrollment declined more than a thousand from 1971 to 1983. The late 1980s saw a reversal, however. An upsurge of racism on college campuses across the nation and a belief that integration was not working influenced many black students to choose predominantly black colleges. Fort Valley State's enrollment climbed from fourteen hundred to twenty-one hundred by 1990. Between 1989 and 1990, Savannah State saw an increased enrollment from 2,075 to 2,335; Albany State from 2,306 to 2,404.

The University of Georgia recruited minorities because, among other reasons, it had to. As a result of a federal lawsuit filed by the NAACP's Legal Defense Fund, the U. S. Department of Health, Education, and Welfare (HEW) was placed under a 1972 court order to submit desegregation plans for the public university systems of ten states, including Georgia. Several plans were rejected before Georgia finally came up with acceptable proposals in 1983 to desegregate its system, but it was several more years before the state's efforts would satisfy federal education officials. Changes included improving the three predominantly black schools. This led to the construction of a $3.65 million Farm and Community Life Center at Fort Valley and a $3.25 million Criminal Justice Building at Albany, among other things. In 1984, Fort Valley State became the university's Cooperative Extension Service district headquarters for thirty-seven counties in Georgia's Piedmont region.

One of the many problems in the desegregation plan was the use of the Regents Test, instituted as a mandatory requirement for graduation to ensure reading and writing competency. Students at the university system's three traditionally black colleges had special difficulties passing the test. After a complaint was filed by Dr. H. W. Berry of Fort Valley State College in 1975, the Office of Civil Rights of the Department of Justice investigated the test and found that it was discriminatory because the university system continued to use it while failing to remedy the effects of past discrimination in the black schools. In 1984, the state and federal government agreed to put more money into remedial programs to help students at these colleges pass the test. The controversy over the Regents Test revealed another problem: Fort Valley, Albany, and Savannah were widely perceived as diploma mills, and their right to continue as predominantly black colleges was questioned. A proposal to merge Savannah State with predominantly white Armstrong State College failed due to strong protests, especially by friends of Savannah State. Strong black alumni associations vehemently objected to any proposals they believed would destroy their old schools, and they remained distrustful of state officials whom they suspected of wanting to use integration as a weapon to destroy the black colleges. On the other hand, regents stressed a commitment to keep the schools' black heritage intact while improving academic standards.

Many critics of the black colleges misunderstood the schools' role and the severe challenges they faced. Many of their students came from poor families and poor schools, had low SAT scores, and were not prepared to do college-level work. Without these schools, it was likely that these students would not have the chance to advance their education. The colleges were forced by circumstance to provide the education that Georgia's elementary and high schools had failed to provide. It was no great surprise that they were unable to raise student test scores to the systemwide average in four years. Despite the schools' comparatively low academic standing, many students at Fort Valley, Savannah, and Albany went on to postgraduate work and to succeed in business, politics, and other fields.

As part of the desegregation plan, whites were encouraged to attend the traditionally black institutions, or "TBIs," as they were known in desegregation jargon. Whites continued to believe falsely that "black" colleges had no white students or faculty. These schools always had some white faculty and, as all black colleges, welcomed those white students who would attend. This was also true at the Atlanta University Center, where in 1983, 40 percent of the faculty members were white. Whites went in small but increasing numbers to the three public TBIs during the 1970s and 1980s. In fact, the TBIs were more integrated than the state's flagship university, which had roughly 5 percent black enrollment. In 1985, 18 percent of Albany State students, 16.6 percent of Savannah State students, and 7 percent of Fort Valley State students were white. In Fort Valley, there was much local white antagonism toward the college, which was demonstrated by two politically motivated desegregation suits filed against the school by whites who neither wanted nor tried to attend the school. Meanwhile, new programs were instituted, and the college branched out to serve nearby communities. Fort Valley held classes at Robins Air Force Base, where many of the whites enrolled at the school attended classes.

Throughout the system, there was gradual progress. In 1986, Hamilton Holmes, Jr., enrolled at the University of Georgia, where his father, one of the first two blacks to attend the school, was a member of the university's board of trustees. Eldridge W. McMillan, originally appointed to the Board of Regents in 1975, became the regents' first black chairman in June 1986. Black regent Joseph Green of Thomson was chairman during 1988 and 1989.

To many whites, the most prominent black students were the athletes who led their old school to victory on the gridiron and the basketball court. Herschel Walker helped take the University of Georgia Bulldogs to the 1980 national collegiate football championship and won the Heisman Trophy in his junior year in 1982, then left school to play professionally. While Walker's athletic exploits were glorious, there was trouble brewing on campus. Critics of big-time college athletics questioned the exploitation of black athletes, which took the form of keeping players academically qualified until their period of athletic eligibility ran out. Then the university lost interest in them. Between 1975 and 1985, only 17 percent of black football players and 4 percent of black basketball players graduated from the University of Georgia while 50 percent of white football players, 63 percent of white basketball players, and 61 percent of all students finished school. (Georgia Tech had a somewhat better record, though it was not very impressive, either.)

The use of athletes, especially black athletes, to produce revenue for schools where they had little chance of obtaining a degree became a scandal at the University of Georgia in 1986 known popularly as the Jan Kemp case. Kemp, a white instructor in the university's Developmental Studies program, charged that athletes received special treatment. Their grades were raised and they were exited from developmental courses to take regular courses before they mastered the remedial material. When Kemp was demoted and fired, she said it was for objecting to this favoritism. She sued her supervisors for back pay and reinstatement.

The presiding judge in the federal civil trial was Horace Ward, who was refused admission to Georgia as a student in the 1950s. The early 1986 trial turned into a tremendous embarrassment for the school. Three-fourths of four hundred scholarship athletes were in the special studies program, compared to under 2 percent for the entire school. Some black athletes arrived at the university with second- and third-grade academic skills. One had the absolute minimum SAT scores that were possible. Leroy Ervin, the black director of Developmental Studies at Athens, had said that athletes were only "raw material" used to produce income; some could not read or write. The jury awarded Kemp $2.58 million, but Ward ruled that the amount was excessive. Negotiations yielded a $1.08 million award and Kemp's reinstatement under new supervisors. University President Fred C. Davidson lost his job in the trial's aftermath. In subsequent years, the school struggled with reform and went beyond NCAA requirements in the standards it set for recruits.

Far from being an anachronism, black colleges continued to persevere, change, and even thrive. This was especially true of the schools of the Atlanta University Center, which promoted their special tradition to recruit and retain black faculty members who might be lured away by more richly endowed, higher-paying universities. In the generation after Du Bois and John Hope, outstanding scholars and educators Clarence Bacote, Benjamin Mays, and Horace Mann Bond had risen up. After they passed from the scene, a new generation of educational leaders stepped forward. Atlanta became the home of the prestigious, scholarly *Journal of Negro History*, founded in 1916 by Carter G. Woodson, when Alton Hornsby, Jr., head of the Morehouse history department, became its editor. The schools continued to enhance their reputations, and enrollment increased during the late 1980s.

Spelman and Morehouse were recognized as two of the finest liberal arts colleges in the South. At Spelman, Johnnetta Cole became the first black woman president of the historically black woman's college in 1987. Cole's friends Bill and Camille Cosby gave $20 million to Spelman in 1988, then the largest gift ever given to a predominantly black college. Money from the donation was used to build the Camille Olivia Hanks Cosby Academic Center, which contained an African-American art museum, library, and media center. In 1990, the Coca-Cola Foundation gave Spelman a five-year, $1 million grant to support scholarships for Atlanta city high school students. Even with such gifts and an endowment of $50 million, Spelman was still relatively poor compared to its competition.

Historically male Morehouse College was busily turning out a new generation of achievers and could point with pride to Atlanta Mayor Maynard Jackson, federal Secretary of Health and Human Services Louis Sullivan, and controversial, critically acclaimed movie director Spike Lee as "Morehouse Men." An estimated 11 percent of the nation's blacks with doctorates in chemistry have been taught in the classroom of Dr. Henry C. McBay, who had logged forty-five years of teaching at Morehouse by 1991. In 1990, Morehouse President Leroy Keith announced the school's largest private grant—a $3 million donation from the Robert W. Woodruff Foundation. Morehouse Medical School graduated fourteen men and fourteen women in 1990.

Schools within the Atlanta University Center consolidated to share resources and increase their efficiency. Gammon Theological Seminary (Methodist) had merged with the Morehouse School of Religion (Baptist) and Morris Brown's Turner Theological Seminary (African Methodist Episcopal) in 1959 to form the Interdenominational Theological Center under the leadership of Dr. Harry Richardson. It became one of the nation's most respected theological schools.

Atlanta University suffered through a financial crisis in the late 1970s and 1980s, which was one reason Clark College and Atlanta University consolidated to form Clark Atlanta University in September 1989. The school moved forward with several ambitious programs, including increasing its international programs, joining a research consortium with other historically black colleges and seven Midwestern research universities, and working with the surrounding low-income neighborhoods to renovate substandard housing and train graduate students in social work. Clark Atlanta University President Thomas Cole, Jr., was awarded a $100,000 prize by the Knight Foundation in 1990 for exceptional leadership.

Morris Brown, the first black school in Atlanta founded wholly by blacks, joined the Atlanta University Center in 1932. The school came close to closing after President John Middleton withdrew it from the Atlanta University Consortium in 1972 because he believed that the $20 million Ford Foundation grant to the center would undermine Morris

Brown's traditional black control. In 1974, Middleton was forced out and replaced by Robert Threatt, head of Fort Valley State College's Education Department. Under Threatt, Morris Brown's youngest president, the school rejoined the consortium and received $400,000, its first-year share of the Ford grant, and obtained federal grants and loans in the amount of $4.3 million for academic improvement and building construction. Morris Brown hit another low point in 1984, when enrollment fell to less than eleven hundred students. New President Calvert Smith cut staff and directed a three-year fund-raising campaign that brought in $5 million for the school. Its enrollment almost doubled by 1990, thanks largely to the efforts of admissions director Tyrone Fletcher. Financial troubles continued to plague the school, however, and by the end of 1992, Morris Brown faced a deep fiscal crisis.

Entertainment and Culture

The biennial National Black Arts Festival firmly established Atlanta as a black cultural mecca. Largely the brainchild of Fulton County Commission Chairman Michael Lomax (who was also a literature professor), the festival debuted in Atlanta in the summer of 1988. It was a smashing success and quickly became one of the nation's premier artistic events. The proceedings, organized by Stephanie Hughley and Michelle Smith, were cochaired by Harry Belafonte and Cicely Tyson. More than 500,000 people attended the hundred-plus events, many of which paid homage to the Harlem Renaissance. The event also pumped $20 million into the local economy. During the 1990 festival, more than 600,000 people saw 159 events and exhibits at forty locations. Approximately two thousand artists from the United States, Africa, the Caribbean, and Latin America put on music, theater, dance, visual arts, film, literature, and other cultural events under the umbrella theme of "Today's Roots," an exploration of African influence on art. The festival budget climbed from $1 million to more than $2 million.

By 1990, black artists were comparing Atlanta's cultural awakening to the Harlem Renaissance. Thanks largely to black political power, local government funding for the arts was strong. Hammonds House, a renovated 1857 Victorian home on Peeples Street in Atlanta's historic West End, was established as a gallery and resource center of African-American art. In 1986, Fulton County purchased the home along with the late Dr. Otis Hammonds's extensive art collection. Some predominantly white artistic outfits were stunned when their local government stipends were cut due to a "lack of cultural diversity."

The black theater was also growing. Atlanta's first black company, Black Image Theatre, was cofounded in the late 1960s by native Atlantan and Spelman drama student Andrea Frye. Atlanta had two outstanding black theater companies in the 1980s, Just Us, organized in 1979, and Jomandi, organized in 1978. In 1990, Jomandi had a $1 million budget and moved from community theater to major theater status with the Georgia Council of the Arts. In 1990, Kenny Leon was named artistic director of the Alliance Theatre, becoming the second black to hold this position in a major American resident theater.

Throughout Georgia, in towns large and small, blacks worked to preserve their heritage. Macon was home to the Harriet Tubman Historical and Cultural Museum, which opened in the mid-1980s. Macon struggled for decades to save the historic Douglass Theater, where many black performers got their start. Longtime Savannah civil rights leader W. W. Law formed the Beach Institute Historic Neighborhood Association to preserve the city's oldest surviving black community. His biggest achievement in 1989 was the restoration of an 1896 house, the King-Tisdell Cottage, which became a museum of black history. He also conducted tours of the "Negro Heritage Trail."

Auburn Avenue, called by *Fortune* magazine "the richest Negro street in the world" in the 1950s, had begun to decline during the 1960s. The end of Jim Crow and the construction of Atlanta's Downtown Connector overhead contributed to Auburn's fall from grace, although in 1980, Atlanta Life headquarters at Herndon Plaza was dedicated and in that same year, Congress declared portions of the east end of Auburn the Martin Luther King, Jr., National Historic District, which held what some people called "America's only black shrine." Hundreds of thousands of people visited King's birthplace and tomb each year. Between the MLK district and Herndon Plaza were several historic churches and buildings, the SCLC headquarters, and a run-down commercial district.

Auburn's heritage of black commerce and culture was a powerful incentive for revitalization of the area. There was also much feuding over what should be done and who should pay for it. While there were ambitious plans to bring back trolley cars to Auburn and spruce up the area, funding did not exist by mid-1991. Fulton County moved ahead with plans to construct an $11 million non-circulating library across the street from Herndon Plaza. The library was designed for research into black history and culture, especially that of Atlanta, Georgia, and the Southeast. One of Auburn's more recent attractions was the African American Panoramic Experience (APEX), a cultural museum of black American life. Although its beginnings were modest, in 1991, APEX founder Dan Moore had ambitious plans for a 100,000-square-foot museum that would cost $25 million.

The best-known and best-selling black man of letters was Georgia's Frank Yerby, although many who read his works did not realize he was not white, since his publishers conspired to keep his race a secret lest it affect sales. Yerby, born in 1916, graduated from Paine College in Augusta in 1937 and spent most of his writing career in Europe. He did return to his alma mater to speak at the college's ninety-fifth commencement in 1977. His first published short story, "Health Card," won an O. Henry Award in 1944. Two years later, his *The Foxes of Harrow* was a bestseller, and he went on to write prolifically using the same formula. With the advent of Black Power and increased respect for things black, he began to use black themes and characters. *The Dahomian* is representative of this change. Yerby died in 1991.

John Oliver Killens was born and lived his first seventeen years in Macon. In 1933, he left for New York, where he wrote his first major novel, *Youngblood* (1954), about growing up black in Georgia. In this and other works he drew on the tales told him by his paternal great-grandmother, who remembered the days of slavery in Georgia, and on his own memories of growing up in Macon. While Yerby wrote to entertain the world and make money, Killens wrote to change the world and lectured widely on the stereotypical and mistaken images of blacks in the media. He wrote seven other books, numerous plays and articles, and has been translated and published in fifteen other countries. Killens died in 1987.

Many blacks have used Georgia as a setting for their works. Putnam County native Alice Walker, the youngest of eight children of sharecroppers, attended Spelman and Sarah Lawrence colleges. She was the first black woman to win a Pulitzer Prize and the American Book Award for a novel. The awards came in 1983 for *The Color Purple*, the story of Celie, a much-abused black woman, and her African missionary sister. This book, based on experiences of women in her own Putnam County family, was made into a film that received eleven Academy Award nominations (but no Oscars) in 1986. *The Color Purple's* unflattering portrayal of black men sparked controversy and debate, as did the snub on Oscar night. Walker returned to her hometown to attend a premiere of the movie.

Fifty years ago, 80 percent of black actors and actresses played either maids or butlers in Hollywood's major movies. Although actress Hattie McDaniel was able to add some dignity to the role of the black mammy, she was not allowed to attend the 1939 Atlanta premiere of *Gone With the Wind*, even though she later won an Oscar for her performance.

Since then, the black role in movies has advanced somewhat. Morehouse graduate Spike Lee did much to revolutionize the black role in Hollywood with his controversial, critically acclaimed movies. Lee, a 1979 graduate, said Morehouse administrators kicked him off campus in 1987 during the filming of *School Daze*, a movie that dealt with caste and color prejudices at an all-black college. (In 1990, Lee returned to Morehouse to be honored for his work.) Lee was nominated for an Academy Award for his 1989 screenplay of *Do The Right Thing*, a movie that depicted a race riot in the Bronx. Ossie Davis, born in Cogdell, Georgia, in 1917, appeared along with his wife, Ruby Dee, in director Lee's *Do the Right Thing* and *Jungle Fever*. While Davis was known mainly as an actor, he also wrote the musical *Purlie Victorious*, which was set in Georgia.

The Third World Film Festival began in Atlanta in 1980, and Georgia grew popular as a shooting locale for motion pictures and television. Much of the Oscar-winning film *Glory*, which told the story of the black Fifty-fourth Massachusetts Volunteer Infantry during the Civil War, was shot on the Georgia coast.

Black Georgians have made major contributions to music. Due to discrimination, many blacks, such as Roland Hayes, went to Europe to launch their careers. Soprano Mattiwilda Dobbs, daughter of longtime Atlanta community leader John Wesley Dobbs, also made her fame and fortune in Europe. Grand opera in the United States was closed to black singers until Marian Anderson sang with the Metropolitan Opera in 1955. McHenry Boatright, born in Tennille, Georgia, learned spirituals at an early age from his father, who sang them on his railroad job. Young Boatright left home for the New England Conservatory of Music at the age of twelve with only a bus ticket and a sweet potato pie. He became a respected opera singer and appeared on national TV when he sang the Brahms Requiem with Eugene Ormandy and the Philadelphia Orchestra in memoriam for President Kennedy in 1963. Jessye Norman, born in Augusta, was admired in Europe fourteen years before she was able to debut with the Metropolitan Opera in 1983. Allan Evans, a Macon-born black opera singer, also had to make a career in Europe before he was invited to sing with the Metropolitan. While the Atlanta Symphony had low black participation, by 1990 the city had the sixty-piece Atlanta African-American Philharmonic Orchestra and more than a hundred singers in its affiliated chorale.

Blacks were better known for their contributions to popular music than to opera. Gertrude "Ma" Rainey (1886-1939) was born in Columbus and became the first great "classic" blues performer. She influenced Bessie Jones, the singer and folklorist who founded the Sea Island Singers and promoted that area's unique black culture. Several black Georgians made it to the top of the music industry and influenced other performers. Albany native Ray Charles, Macon's "Little Richard" Penniman, and Augusta's James Brown were three of the biggest stars in popular music history and were in the first group of inductees into the Rock and Roll Hall of Fame in 1986. Macon especially was a hotbed of musical talent: Otis Redding, Percy Sledge, and Solomon Burke all hailed from there. Multiple Grammy winner Ray Charles's version of the Hoagie Carmichael tune "Georgia on My Mind" was adopted as the state song in 1979, and Charles performed it at the state Capitol to introduce it. Charles was so versatile he was also a hit as a country and western singer. Little Richard put out a string of hits, including "Tutti Frutti" and "Good Golly Miss Molly" in the 1950s and appeared in the hit movie *Down and Out in Beverly Hills* in 1986. He was honored with a star on Hollywood Boulevard in 1990. James Brown, known as the "Godfather of Soul" and "the hardest working man in show business," also was a multiple Grammy winner. Gladys Knight started out in Atlanta in 1953. At the age of four, she sang at Mount Moriah Baptist Church. She won the $2,000 first prize on "Ted Mack's Amateur Hour" when she was nine years old. Soon she and the Pips (a pip is "a dapper young man," according to Knight) were booked at Atlanta's Royal Peacock supper club on Auburn Avenue. Then they went on the road. Their "Midnight Train to Georgia" was first a hit among blacks and then was number one on the pop charts.

Since desegregation blacks have risen higher, faster, and in greater numbers in professional sports than any other area. Georgia is home to three major professional sports teams and two major universities, and that has increased the visibility of prominent black athletes. The main sport blacks dominated even before the 1954 *Brown* decision was boxing, the first major sport to accept blacks into the mainstream. Atlanta's Evander Holyfield became the world heavyweight champion on October 25, 1990, with a third-round knockout of James "Buster" Douglas in Las Vegas. Like many boxers, Holyfield had a rags-to-riches story. He was raised without a father in Bowen Homes and won the bronze medal in the 1984 Olympics following a controversial disqualification involving a late punch. He had a gentleman's reputation in a cruel sport and waited two years as the sport's number-one contender before he got his chance with Douglas.

The color bar in baseball fell long after blacks perfected the game in the old Negro Leagues. The Negro National League was formed in 1919. Josh Gibson (1911–47), one early baseball star from Georgia, was born in Buena Vista and moved to the North with his family when he was twelve. From age nineteen to thirty-five he was probably the world's best slugger, hitting up to seventy-five home runs a season and with a lifetime batting average of .423. At least as good as Babe Ruth, the most Gibson ever made was $1,200 a season in 1939, compared to Ruth's $80,000. Gibson died just three months before Jackie Robinson broke baseball's color bar. The Atlanta Black Crackers won a Negro American League pennant in 1938. In 1990, several players for that team were honored by the Alliance Theatre in conjunction with the staging of August Wilson's Pulitzer Prize-winning *Fences*. WIGO-Radio sportscaster and *Daily World* columnist Chico Renfroe played for the Crackers and later with Jackie Robinson on the Kansas City Monarchs.

Jack Roosevelt Robinson was born in Cairo, Georgia, and began to play in the majors with the Brooklyn Dodgers in 1947. Two years later, the Dodgers were scheduled for a three-game exhibition series with Atlanta's all-white Georgia Crackers during spring training. Herman Talmadge and Klan Grand Dragon Samuel Green objected to the visitors using Robinson and Roy Campanella. A bill was introduced into the legislature to bar blacks and whites from appearing in the same athletic event, theater or vaudeville performance, or opera, but it was too late. More than one-third of the fifteen thousand who turned out at Ponce de Leon Park were blacks, who were consigned to the left field bleachers and not allowed to buy refreshments. For them, it was probably worth the indignity to see the Crackers go down 6–3 in the first game as Robinson drove in two runs. Robinson's success as a player led other major league teams to sign blacks. By 1960 all of them had black players, and integration meant the demise of the Negro Leagues.

In 1962 the Peachtree Manor Hotel was the first major hostelry in Atlanta to house members of visiting integrated ball teams together. The National League Braves moved from Milwaukee and played their first game in Atlanta in 1966, when Carl Sanders was governor. One former Negro League player on the team was the best slugger in the history of baseball. Henry "Hank" Aaron broke Babe Ruth's home-run record with his 715th on April 8, 1974. He finished his career with 755 home runs and 2,297 runs batted in. Although he was honored by his team, Aaron's on-field successes caused resentment among many white fans. The Braves retired his uniform number "44" at the start of the 1977 season. A ten-foot-high bronze statue of Aaron swinging the bat was placed at Atlanta-Fulton County Stadium in 1982. That year, Aaron was elected to baseball's Hall of Fame by an overwhelming margin in his first year of eligibility.

In baseball, blacks were high achievers on the playing field but were kept away from team management. Ted Turner bought the Braves in 1976 and did much to promote blacks. He named Bill Lucas general manager in 1977, making him then the highest-ranking black in the game. After Lucas's death in 1979, Aaron would have this honor as vice president and director of player personnel. He remained an especially outspoken critic of discrimination in baseball, which was the least integrated of the three major sports forty years after Robinson took the field. In 1986, Tracy Lewis became the first black president of a baseball franchise since the demise of the Negro Leagues after her father bought the minor league Savannah Cardinals.

After the Boston Celtics broke the color barrier in the National Basketball Association in 1950, some of Georgia's outstanding basketball players had an opportunity to play in the NBA. Georgian Walt Bellamy was the center on the 1960 Olympic gold medal team. Jeff Malone grew up on the playgrounds of south Macon and joined the Washington Bullets of the NBA in 1983 and was named to the league's all-rookie team. Another Maconite, Norm Nixon, played for several professional teams, including the Los Angeles Lakers. Pervis Ellison, a graduate of Savannah High School, was named Most Valuable Player when his Louisville team won the NCAA national basketball championship in 1986. Kenny Walker, from rural Crawford County, starred at Kentucky and went on to play with the New York Knicks. For many years, the Atlanta Hawks built their offense around former University of Georgia star Dominique Wilkins.

Since the National Football League was integrated, many stars have come from Georgia. None were brighter than Jim Brown, who was born in 1936 on St. Simons Island. After starring at Syracuse University, Brown was the first-round draft pick of the Cleveland Browns in 1957. One of the pioneer black players in the game, he was named Rookie of the Year and made the all-pro team every year in his Hall of Fame career until he retired in 1965.

Several Georgia blacks won Olympic gold medals. Morehouse graduate Edwin Moses set many hurdling records, and the gold medal winner dominated that sport for many years. Roger Kingdom of Vienna was another great Olympic runner. Several Georgia black female athletes also were prominent in international competition. Wyomia Tyus of Griffin won Olympic gold medals in 1964 and 1968, becoming the first sprinter to win gold medals in consecutive games. University of Georgia basketball stars Teresa Edwards and Katrina McLain led the U. S. women's team to the gold medal in 1988.

The color bar fell sport by sport. The Georgia Women's Bowling Tournament integrated in 1962 when two black teams were allowed to compete. Albert Thomas Wilson, Sr., founded the black Georgia State Tennis Association before the sport integrated. Golf remained the most segregated event because so many tournaments were played at all-white country clubs. In 1975, Lee Elder was the first black golfer to play in the Masters at Augusta National Golf Club, which had no black members until fifteen years later. In 1990, the SCLC's Lowery threatened to boycott the products of advertisers of televised Professional Golfers Association tour events held at racially exclusive clubs. Many clubs were still extremely reluctant to change their membership and admit blacks, but Augusta National was not among them. In September 1990, the home of the Masters got its first black member, Maryland television executive Ron Townsend.

16

Civil Rights and Race Relations

Flying the Rebel Flag on MLK Day

Martin Luther King, Jr.'s influence did not end with an assassin's bullet on April 4, 1968. Shortly after his death, Coretta Scott King led in establishing the Martin Luther King, Jr., Center for Nonviolent Social Change and devoted herself to continuing her husband's dream. Her stature increased, and for many Americans, she served as the representative for his beliefs.

The King family was destined to endure more horror. Dr. King's parents had been honored in 1969 as the "Daddy and Momma" of the civil rights movement. Mrs. Martin Luther King, Sr., "Alberta" to her many friends, was shot to death as she played "The Lord's Prayer" on the Ebenezer Baptist Church organ for Sunday services June 30, 1974. The killer, Marcus Wayne Chenault, a deranged black who was later sentenced to death for the crime, said he had been ordered by God to do it and that Daddy King had also been on his list. A decade later, following a life that had witnessed much tragedy, Martin Luther King, Sr., died on Sunday, November 11, 1984, at the age of eighty-four. Memorial services were held throughout Georgia.

Dr. King's successor at the SCLC, Ralph David Abernathy, had been King's closest confidant in the movement but was unable to gain the attention or respect his friend had commanded. The civil rights movement entered the doldrums of the 1970s, which were marked by schisms within its leadership. Jesse Jackson broke his formal ties with the SCLC and made Chicago's Operation Breadbasket into an independent organization, People United to Serve Humanity (PUSH), in 1971. While King had raised up to $2 million a year for the SCLC through a 208,000-name mailing list that targeted white liberals, by 1973, the SCLC's budget was down 75 percent, it was $50,000 in debt, and the number of chapters and affiliates had declined greatly. Meanwhile, Coretta King was raising considerable funds for the center and would not share money with the SCLC. Hosea Williams joined Abernathy in criticizing her for this. Abernathy announced his resignation as SCLC president in the summer of 1973 as he stood in front of King's tomb and asked the fallen leader to forgive him for his inability to keep the organization together. He later withdrew his resignation but gave up his post for good in 1977 to run for Congress, finishing third behind Wyche Fowler and John Lewis.

In 1977, on the twentieth anniversary of the organization's founding, 150 SCLC delegates met in Atlanta and heard criticism by young militants who said it had grown "too middle class...too satisfied, more interested in talking about poor people's economic problems than in fighting with protests and pickets and boycotts." The Rev. Joseph Lowery, pastor of Atlanta's twenty-three-hundred-member Central United Methodist Church (later he was transferred to Cascade United Methodist Church), succeeded Abernathy as the SCLC's third president in 1977. Abernathy became president emeritus. As a sop to militants, State Rep. Hosea Williams—who liked to be called "Reverend" but was a chemist by trade—was named executive director. Williams and his backers believed that if they hit the streets in protest, the cash would flow in, just like the old days.

While there were hopes and hints of a comeback by the organization, there was also infighting. Lowery, claiming Williams could not do justice to both his SCLC position and the state legislature, fired him in 1979. State Rep. Tyrone Brooks also was relieved as national field director. They did not go quietly. There was a scuffle in front of the SCLC's Atlanta headquarters to see which faction would have possession. Williams remained as head of the Metro Atlanta SCLC chapter and formed a short-lived "Martin Luther King, Jr., National Coalition to Save the SCLC" in response to his ouster. Williams kept a high public persona but was considered an embarrassment by much of Atlanta's civil rights establishment. The fiery populist kept his support among the people despite his constant run-ins with the law—not just for his civil rights activities, but also due to his driving habits. He lost a bid for Congress in 1984, and his wife, Juanita, succeeded him in the state legislature. He would later lose to Maynard Jackson in the 1989 Atlanta mayor's race, then win a seat on the DeKalb County Commission in 1990.

Although President Carter had a good record of including blacks and minorities in his administration, Williams and Abernathy backed Republican Ronald Reagan in 1980. Blacks made up more than 12 percent of Carter's appointments overall and 16 percent of his judicial nominations. Carter's chances for a second term were severely damaged by the hostage crisis in Iran. After condemning uncritical support of Carter by blacks in 1976, Williams endorsed Reagan because he thought Reagan would help him develop black enterprise. Abernathy endorsed Reagan for similar reasons. They were the exceptions, for Reagan appealed almost exclusively to white voters, and his candidacy alarmed many blacks. State Rep. Grace Hamilton of Atlanta said, "The very thought of Reagan makes my blood run cold." Reagan won while getting only 8 percent of the black vote in 1980.

The Reagan era was viewed with horror by the civil rights community. Under Reagan, appointments of blacks to significant policy-making decisions fell dramatically. Lowery criticized the Reagan administration for promoting "reverse Robin Hood economics." He said, "It takes from the poor and gives to the rich" and "beats plowshares into swords." Julian Bond charged that Reagan staged a full retreat from previous civil rights gains. He is "worse than Nixon," Bond declared in disgust. "That's the incredible thing." Reagan did not seem to care what his black critics thought, for that matter. His most prominent black appointees were Clarence Pendleton as chairman of the Civil Rights Commission and Samuel Pierce as secretary of Housing and Urban Development (HUD). Both turned in ignominious performances. The combative Pendleton went out of his way to attack affirmative action programs and became so repugnant to many blacks that black Republicans demanded Pendleton's resignation in April 1986 on the grounds that he was more reactionary than his boss. Pierce's tenure was marred by scandals within HUD.

Black attempts to communicate with the Reagan White House proved futile. Abernathy had learned his lesson when Reagan ignored him after the election. Abernathy underwent surgery for a blocked artery in his head in 1983 and then devoted himself to his pastorate at West Hunter Baptist Church and began to write his autobiography. In 1984, both Williams and Abernathy backed Jesse Jackson, and Abernathy served as honorary chairman of Jackson's Georgia campaign. While Jackson's candidacy energized black voters, white liberal Walter Mondale won the Democratic nomination with the support of many black leaders. In the fall campaign, President Reagan came to Macon and praised Jefferson Davis. If blacks had any doubts about Reagan's feelings, they should have been dispelled when he proclaimed, "The South will rise again," the battle cry of unreconstructed Rebels. Lowery said this was a code for going back to the days of "Yassah Massah." Reagan swept the South in racially polarized voting—90 percent of black voters backed Mondale, and 75 percent of white voters supported Reagan. Williams was surprised to receive an invitation, sent by mistake, to attend Reagan's second inaugural ball.

Even though civil rights organizations had fallen on hard times and the nation seemed far from realizing his goal of justice, Dr. King symbolized something special to the United States. A national holiday to memorialize him came to represent the most fitting tribute and guarantee that his ideas would live on and grow. In 1971, Abernathy brought a 3-million-signature petition favoring a holiday to Congress, where a King holiday bill was introduced every year since King's assassination. Some states and cities made his January 15 birthday a holiday in the 1970s. The King Center sponsored annual marches in Atlanta on King's birthday. Communities, schools, churches, and civil rights groups across the land held annual marches, prayer vigils, voter registration drives, rallies, and special events on that day. Schools, public buildings, streets, and bridges were named after the "drum major of social change" in the United States and in other countries. Paul Winfield played King in a six-hour NBC-TV special that originally aired during Black History Month in 1978. This increased national interest in King, though some in the SCLC felt such a treatment glamorized King too much and ignored the common foot soldiers who made King's successes possible. In 1979, the U. S. Postal Service issued a commemorative fifteen-cent stamp on January 13 depicting King and presented the first copy to his father. In October 1980, President Carter signed legislation establishing the Martin Luther King, Jr., National Historic Site in Atlanta, a four-block area where King was born and raised, later preached, and is now entombed.

King became one of the world's most honored figures. Visitors to his tomb came from all over the world. His books were translated into many languages, including German, Italian, Polish, French, and Spanish. Israel and the Bahamas made his birthday a national holiday. The Martin Luther King, Jr., Forest was established in 1976 by the American Jewish Congress on the hills of Galilee in Israel. Each year it was enlarged by gifts of trees from many lands. By 1983 at least thirty-three nations had issued postage stamps honoring King and bearing his picture. France struck a commemorative medal honoring King, and President François Mitterand said in 1984 that King "left his mark and message on the whole of modern times."

King also had his detractors, Reagan among them. Reagan's record on civil rights legislation was poor, and the president opposed the King holiday. By the summer of 1983, the District of Columbia and thirteen states, but not Georgia, had established a holiday for King. Congress held hearings on such a national holiday over Reagan's objections. That year was marked by a march on Washington for jobs, peace, and freedom to commemorate the twentieth anniversary of the August 1963 event. The Senate approved House Resolution 3706 overwhelmingly on October 11, 1983. Reagan, who had questioned King's loyalty and patriotism, reluctantly signed the bill declaring the third Monday in January a national holiday honoring King beginning in 1986.

Black Georgia legislators labored for ten years before the state recognized the holiday. In 1982 gubernatorial candidate Joe Frank Harris pledged to support a King holiday. However, the 1983 General Assembly refused for the ninth straight time to declare King's birthday a holiday. After Congress approved the holiday, the General Assembly reluctantly agreed to observe all federal holidays and eliminated one Confederate holiday. As a sop to white conservative politicians, the 1984 bill did not mention King's name, and the state observance was put off until sometime in November. The year before the federal holiday law took effect, Georgia's legislature agreed to a January observance, and state recognition of Jefferson Davis's birthday was eliminated.

Congress also created the Martin Luther King, Jr., Federal Holiday Commission to promote its observance. Coretta King was appointed chairperson. Among the other thirty commissioners were King's sister, Christine King Ferris, his daughter, Yolanda, Jesse Hill, Lowery, and Andrew Young. Unfortunately, the holiday did not unify the state's civil rights champions. Gadfly Hosea Williams called the King Center elitist. The $15 million complex, with a $2 million annual budget and sixty-three-person staff, was drawing 500,000 visitors by 1986. Williams charged that it ignored the movement's original leaders and failed to follow King's path and produce leaders to continue the struggle.

Fifty-seven countries sent representatives to Atlanta for the first official observance of the holiday in 1986, which included a national TV extravaganza broadcast live from New York, Washington, and Atlanta. Atlanta budgeted $100,000 to honor King with ten days of events. Sen. Edward Kennedy spoke at Ebenezer Baptist Church and hailed King as the founder of a second American Revolution. Jesse Jackson noted that King was not killed for dreaming but for acting. Anglican Bishop Desmond Tutu, winner of the 1985 Nobel Peace Prize for his work against apartheid in South Africa, spoke. So did Vice President George Bush. This was followed by a march of fifteen thousand people that included representatives from all fifty states. Many other Georgia communities held similar programs, including a march of six hundred to the Macon Coliseum. In October, a bust of King was installed in the U. S. Capitol alongside the busts of presidents. Although Abernathy was honored in Atlanta in November 1985 as the "unsung hero" of the civil rights movement, he was not asked to sit on the holiday commission, and in

1986, he was not invited to participate in the Atlanta observances, slights that deeply wounded him. He spent the first national King holiday 3,500 miles away at observances in Alaska.

By 1987, the holiday's novelty was gone, and the commission had more difficulty raising money. The SCLC held a sit-in outside Governor Harris's office, where members prayed and sang freedom songs. As in 1986, there were dozens of local observances in Georgia, but there was no star-studded national TV extravaganza in 1987. Although thirty-eight states observed the holiday, only ten gave their workers the day off with pay; by 1993, all fifty states observed the holiday.

The most startling event during the 1987 King holiday celebration grew out of a "march for brotherhood" at the Forsyth County seat of Cumming on January 17, when a small group of marchers led by Hosea Williams was attacked. Forsyth, just north of Fulton County, was home to thirty-eight thousand people, all of them white. It had a reputation as a racist enclave ever since whites had driven out virtually all the county's eleven hundred blacks in 1912 after a lynching and orgy of nightriding and whitecapping.*

Blacks were made to feel unwelcome whenever they set foot in Forsyth. Signs posted in the 1960s warned: "Nigger—Don't Let the Sun Set on You in Forsyth County." The signs meant business. After Lake Lanier was created on the east boundary of Forsyth County, it became a popular recreational area and a destination for white flight from Atlanta. Some Atlantans who built cabins there found notes on their doors saying, "Don't bring your maid the next visit." In 1968, ten black boys and their counselors on a camping trip from Atlanta to Lake Lanier were told to leave Forsyth County or be carried out "feet first." In 1976 a cross was burned when one black rented a slip for his boat at the Bald Ridge Marina. Black truck drivers making deliveries to the Tyson chicken-dressing plant in Cumming had to be escorted by Georgia Bureau of Investigation (GBI) agents as late as the 1970s. In 1980 a black Atlanta firefighter was shot and wounded while driving near Lake Lanier. Two years later, another black was shot in a racial incident at the lake; a black couple also was shot and wounded. J. B. Stoner's *Thunderbolt* blamed removal of the warnings for such incidents.

Charles Blackburn, a white karate teacher in Cumming, had the original idea for the 1987 march, but he got so many threats he canceled his plans. Then Dean and Tammy Carter of nearby Gainesville took up plans for the march. They were joined by the crusty Williams, who was

---

*The 1920 census showed a black population of thirty. By 1960, it had shrunk to four. The 1980 census indicated that one black lived in the county, although that person's existence was suspect.

ready to march once more. On Saturday, January 17, they led seventy-five marchers, mostly from Atlanta, to Forsyth County in a "Brotherhood Anti-Intimidation March." They arrived late, and the seventy-five-man police and state-trooper force assigned to protect them was unable to stop a crowd of about five hundred Klansmen and sympathizers from overwhelming the police lines. The counterdemonstrators had been worked up to a fever pitch by hate speeches by J. B. Stoner, who had been released from his Alabama prison sentence for church bombing just two months before. Grand Dragon Dave Holland of the Southern White Knights of the Ku Klux Klan joined Stoner in whipping members of the crowd, waving Confederate battle flags, into a frenzy. Hundreds of jeering, screaming whites broke through the police cordon and threw rocks and bottles at the marchers while shouting racial slurs. Williams said, "In thirty years in the civil rights movement, I haven't seen racism any more sick than here today." The march was called off when police told the marchers that they could not ensure their safety. Officers arrested eight of the most violent Klansmen. All but one were Forsyth County residents.

News of the attack spread quickly. Pictures of hate-contorted faces and flying rocks and bottles were reminiscent of the brutality of Birmingham and Selma in decades past. On Sunday, the Klan attack was discussed throughout the nation; it had come amid concerns about the increasing number of racial incidents in the United States. In marking the King holiday on Monday, Coretta King spoke from the site of her husband's tomb and said, "Match bigotry with courage and resist violent acts with nonviolence." Williams and Dean Carter held a joint news conference that evening to announce another march in Forsyth County the following Saturday.

Forsyth's community leaders were upset, because racial violence was bad for business. After the January 17 Klan riot in Forsyth County, the Mead Corporation canceled any plans it may have had for a five-thousand-worker plant there. The chamber of commerce moved to deemphasize the importance of the attack on the marchers and, in the interests of continued economic development, took out full-page newspaper advertisements declaring that the racists did not represent Forsyth County.

The subsequent march drew national and international attention. More than twenty thousand marchers went to Cumming, some chanting "Forsyth County, have you heard—this is not Johannesburg." About two thousand counterdemonstrators showed up with Confederate flags and hateful banners: "The Great White Hope—Sickle Cell Anemia" and "James Earl Ray—Great American Hero." Fifty-five of the counterdemonstrators were arrested, mainly on assault charges. Over seventeen hundred National Guardsmen and five hundred other lawmen were there to control the white supremacists. The march concluded with speeches.

One by Williams listed six demands that included the formation of a biracial council in Forsyth, fair employment, and the return of property lost by those forced to flee in 1912.

The march was a major media event. There was almost a traffic jam of helicopters overhead as police and media choppers jockeyed for position. In addition, several foreign correspondents covered the event. The largest civil rights demonstration in Georgia history was unique because white participants outnumbered blacks, and those arrested were trying to thwart racial progress, as opposed to the old days, when those seeking to promote it spent time in jail. In 1987, both of Georgia's U. S. senators joined a hundred local church and civic leaders to greet the marchers and wish them well.

The class-action suit filed by Williams and other marchers in March 1987 against the Forsyth County assailants for their activities during the January 17 march went to trial in 1988. A federal jury in Atlanta levied $950,000 in damages against Daniel Carver, Holland, Ed Stephens of Jonesboro, eight other individuals, the Southern White Knights, and the Invisible Empire. Williams announced that he wanted to be dropped from the suit because he did not want "to take away from them their hard-earned possessions simply because they brutalized us in responding to the sicknesses of our capitalistic society." The U. S. Supreme Court upheld the award, and the plaintiffs were partially successful in collecting damages.

Events in Forsyth County indicated how much Georgia had developed since World War II. The brutality that symbolized an earlier era was neither encouraged nor tolerated. Blacks could go most places that whites could, and expressions of belief in racial equality were common. Even the Klan said it was not antiblack; it simply wanted "white rights." There were subsequent marches, both by Williams and the Klan. In other ways, little had changed. In 1990, black workers were employed in Forsyth County, but virtually no African-Americans lived there.

Georgia has long been linked with the Ku Klux Klan in the popular mind. Dick Gregory once joked, "Georgia is to the Ku Klux Klan what the Palace was to vaudeville." Since Reconstruction, the Klan had risen up more than once in an attempt to thwart black political and economic gains. The twentieth-century Klan was born on Stone Mountain, which was subsequently carved up to yield the world's largest Confederate monument. Stone Mountain was once owned by the Venable family, whose patriarch, James Venable, headed the National Knights of the Ku Klux Klan.

The Klan's fortunes certainly had declined since the 1920s, when the organization exerted considerable control over Georgia politics. Nevertheless, fifty years after that high-water mark, J. B. Stoner was still working to stir the latent Klan-like tendencies that lingered in some Georgians. Although he was widely viewed as a pathetic figure, there was some growth in the Klan following his 1974 antiblack, anti-Semitic campaign for lieutenant governor, when he received 2 percent of the vote.

Estimated Klan membership nationwide had declined from seventeen thousand in 1967 to only about fifteen hundred members in 1974. The next year, the Klan held several organizational meetings in Georgia near Macon, Eatonton, and Stone Mountain, where a black journalist was beaten up. Two Atlanta-based civil rights workers were beaten by Klansmen in 1978. Violence worsened the next year, when five leftists were murdered in Greensboro, North Carolina, at an anti-Klan rally and Joseph Lowery's wife, Evelyn, was nearly killed by gunfire in Decatur, Alabama, when Klansmen attacked a civil rights march. The Klan held marches and rallies in Macon and Columbus in 1979.

The Georgia General Assembly was concerned enough about the upsurge of right-wing fringe activity to pass a law forbidding paramilitary training in 1981. A coalition of civil rights groups organized the Atlanta-based National Anti-Klan Network early in 1981 to monitor, publicize, and help prosecute the Klan's illegal activities. (The network's name was later changed to the Center for Democratic Renewal.) In Rome, civil rights leaders formed a Community Action Coalition to counteract Klan demonstrations in Northwest Georgia. That year, Klansmen burned a cross at Pearson, harassed Hispanic workers in Cedartown, painted swastikas on mailboxes of Jewish families in Marietta (the site of Leo Frank's lynching sixty-five years before), and counterdemonstrated against a civil-rights march in Walton County.

The Klan used economic problems in its recruiting drive by blaming blacks for white unemployment. Georgia's Klan membership grew to almost one thousand in 1982, making it one of the few states to register an increase. In May of that year, the Anti-Klan Network reported a 300 percent increase in Klan activity, which included roadblocks, leafletting, nightriding, threats, and/or shootings in thirty-seven Georgia counties. On May 15, about a hundred robed Klansmen marched through LaGrange, and between five hundred and six hundred people attended a Klan rally that night. Encouraged by the turnout in LaGrange, Klan leaders staged rallies at Stockbridge and Carrollton. The Klan also surfaced in Jonesboro, Darien, Millen, Hogansville, and Columbus that year. In Hogansville, Klansmen got into a shoving match with counterprotesters from the Anti-Klan Network. In an attempt to unite the various Klan factions, leaders staged a "Unity Rally" at Stone Mountain on September 5, 1982. About three hundred people attended.

The Spalding County seat of Griffin became a center of Klan activity. The Klan was allowed to enter floats in the 1980 Fourth of July and Christmas parades. In May 1982, law officers broke up a Klan rally near

Griffin led by neo-Nazi New Order KKK leader Edward Fields of Marietta (where crosses had been burned that year). A federal judge later ruled that the county ordinance banning such meetings was unconstitutional. In June, a Spalding grand jury indicted three Klansmen on charges of burning crosses at the homes of a black man and his white attorney.

In 1982, Democratic Georgia gubernatorial candidate Joe Frank Harris angrily rejected a purported Klan endorsement and pledged to form a special investigative unit to help suppress Klan activity. The GBI's antiterrorism squad was organized under a new law shortly after Harris took office in 1983. During the mid-1980s, the Klan was unable to unify its factions and membership declined. Nevertheless, the Klan remained active and exacerbated racial tensions whenever it could. In 1985 open Klan meetings were held in Athens and Canton. That year, Commerce canceled its Christmas parade rather than let the Klan participate, then replaced the traditional parade with an interracial ecumenical religious service to show brotherhood.

In 1986, the GBI estimated the state had only 250 hard-core Klansmen, and they were divided into five factions. In the summer of 1986, Klan activity in the Northeast Georgia towns of Hartwell and Danielsville drew legal sanctions and restraining orders. In November 1986, about seventy-five Klan members marched through Augusta after the city failed to stop the parade. College Park officials also tried to ban a downtown parade by Klansmen to protest the killing of a white boy after four black youths were indicted for the crime. The usual procedure was followed. The Klan applied for a parade permit, which was denied by the city. The Klan, with the legal assistance of the American Civil Liberties Union (ACLU), filed a civil rights lawsuit in federal court, where the Klan prevailed. About two hundred Klan members marched through College Park in February 1987. Later that year, Christian Knights of the KKK rallies in Milledgeville and Macon fizzled when they drew only a handful of participants.

In the late 1980s and early 1990s, Gainesville was a center of Klan activity thanks to local Invisible Empire Grand Titan Daniel Carver. He had disrupted Christmas celebrations in Commerce in 1985, then led a dozen robed marchers through a black neighborhood in Gainesville in March 1986, allegedly to protest drug sales. In 1989, about 280 Klan members were separated from 1,500 counterprotesters by about 250 state and local law enforcement officers. In 1991, Gainesville blacks were angered because they had become victims of an ordinance that was designed to control the Klan by allowing parades only near the city square. They went to court after the city told them they could not hold a

King holiday parade through black neighborhoods—an event they had been holding without incident for twenty years.

Although the Klan was in decline, it seemed that it would never go away. The several Klans and allied paramilitary groups remained a small but troublesome force in the state's race relations. The combination of their fondness for sophisticated weapons and an unsophisticated social philosophy made them dangerous. Some Klan groups used computer networks and "Dial a Hate" telephone recordings to disperse their message. By the mid-1980s, Klan marchers were often outnumbered by counterdemonstrators, although the largest community response to their activities was something between apathy and hostility. Most black leaders urged people to ignore the marchers, and local governments tried to restrict white supremacist protests as much as they could without having their actions overturned in court.

In 1988, the Anti-Defamation League (ADL) said that two of seventeen KKK groups were based in Georgia: the Forsyth County Defense League and the Southern White Knights. Other sources identified the U. S. Klans as Georgia-based; the United Klans of America, one of the most violent factions, was founded near Indian Springs, Georgia, in 1961. Also, the neo-Nazi National States Rights party was in J. B. Stoner's hometown of Marietta. In 1991, nationwide Klan membership was estimated at four thousand, and Georgia was one of the few states to show an increase after a decade of decline, according to Stuart Lewengrub of the ADL.

White supremacist groups kept rallying in opposition to the King holiday. These attempts to disrupt celebrations were largely futile, although one effort to sour the mood succeeded on January 21, 1989, when Mississippian Richard Barrett led a march of eight white supremacists in downtown Atlanta. An estimated one thousand counterdemonstrators turned out, and though the white supremacists were surrounded by nearly two thousand security troops, they were attacked by rock- and bottle-throwing assailants, mostly black youths. There were thirteen injuries and forty arrests. Security costs ran well into the hundreds of thousands of dollars. In 1990, police blocked off access to a protest at the state Capitol and avoided a repeat of the 1989 melee.

The Klan built its reputation over a century ago on its ability to inspire fear through terrorist acts committed by masked men. In May 1990, a Gwinnett County judge ruled that Georgia's thirty-nine-year-old anti-mask law was unconstitutional following a legal challenge by Klansman Shade Miller, Jr., of Calhoun. The local judge ruled that the law, which prevented Klansmen from wearing hoods over their faces in public, violated their right of free speech. The state attorney general's office immediately appealed the ruling. In December, the state Supreme Court voted 6–1 to uphold the antimask law.

The biggest problem in race relations was not the Klan but the fact that its mentality lived on and racism remained imbedded and institutionalized in Georgia, the South, and the nation. In addition, the national mood of conservatism had an ugly side. "The real threat to human rights in America today is not the bedsheet brigade, but the plainclothes 'klux' in the halls of government and black-robe 'klux' on the bench," said Stetson Kennedy, who spent more than a decade infiltrating and exposing the Klan in the 1940s and 1950s.

While a 1979 Darden Research Corp. poll conducted for the *Atlanta Constitution* indicated that there had been some progress in race relations, according to a poll released by the National Opinion Research Center in January 1991, most whites still held a negative image of minorities. They thought blacks were more likely to prefer living on welfare, less hardworking, more violent, and less intelligent. Rank prejudice continued to show up among "the best people." In 1987, Turner Broadcasting executive Xernona Clayton was "disinvited" from an April 28 speaking engagement at the Business and Professional Women's Club in Rome when the ladies in Rome learned she was black. Black University of Georgia pharmacy student Tommie Faye Bateman was dismissed from an internship at a Tifton drugstore that summer because the owner thought he would lose customers due to her presence. Just south of Atlanta, in East Point, Mayor Bruce Bannister and Councilman Cecil Kennedy were taped using a racial slur to describe the black city manager in 1989.

Although racism generally seemed more sophisticated and subtle than in the days of segregation, it also found crudely violent expression. Besides the Klan's activities, there were scores of racial incidents across Georgia in the 1980s and early 1990s. The 1980s closed out with a horrifying series of mail bombings that killed a white federal judge in Alabama and black Savannah civil rights attorney and City Councilman Robert Robinson. A letter to the news media from the bomber, Leroy Moody of Rex, Georgia, justified the killings by citing the rape and murder of a white woman by a black man and special treatment of blacks by the courts. NAACP offices were tempting targets for racial terrorism. Moody sent a mail bomb to the Jacksonville, Florida, NAACP office (it did not explode, however). A teargas bomb exploded at Atlanta NAACP headquarters in West End in August 1989. In July 1990, the son of a Clayton County community leader was one of three youths arrested for the firebombing that gutted the local NAACP headquarters.

Elsewhere in Georgia, racial incidents continued in 1990. In the West Georgia town of Carrollton, the fire chief forced a black fireman to take his bed with him when he transferred so that no white firefighters would be required to sleep in it. The chief later resigned after an investigation. In Cartersville, a woman was evicted from her apartment for having black friends. She filed a complaint and was awarded over $15,000 in damages by a Housing and Urban Development administrative law judge. In the South Georgia town of Cordele, a man was sentenced to four years in prison for violating the civil rights of a black family when he paid someone to burn down their house after they moved into a predominantly white neighborhood.

Atlanta's suburbs were subject to increasing strife as blacks moved out of the inner city and sought a better life. Habitat for Humanity reported "entrenched and occasionally violent resistance" by local residents to its low-cost homes. This included arson and a petition drive to prevent Habitat from operating a homeless shelter in Gwinnett County. Clayton County had the fastest growing black population in the metropolitan Atlanta area (from 7 percent in 1980 to 14.6 percent in 1990) and saw more than its share of trouble. In addition to two firebombings at the local NAACP offices, there were about a dozen racial incidents in 1990, including a firebombing of a black family's home, cross burnings, and spray-painted "KKKs" and racial epithets.

There were attempts to alleviate racial tensions, of course. Through most of this century, Atlanta has had organizations designed to air differences and promote racial harmony dating back to the Commission on Interracial Cooperation and, later, the Southern Regional Council and Atlanta Action Forum. In the late 1980s the state set up a Human Relations Commission. By 1990, Cobb, Gwinnett, and Clayton counties had formed race-relations panels, but civil rights leaders complained that only seventeen out of five hundred members of the citizen advisory groups in the three counties were black. They believed this would prevent minority concerns from reaching county commissioners.

Racial antagonism and other forms of prejudice were complex, fed by both seemingly primitive urges against "outsiders" and also containing a long-standing economic and class basis. It was certainly not restricted to antagonism between blacks and whites. There were also tensions between blacks and the Korean merchants in their neighborhoods. In addition, some blacks were anti-Semitic. Louis Farrakhan, leader of a Black Muslim sect, was outspokenly anti-Semitic during the 1984 presidential campaign of Jesse Jackson. Despite his claims that he did not hate Jews, Farrakhan continued to preach that there was a white-Jewish conspiracy against blacks. More than twelve thousand people came to see him speak at the Omni in Atlanta in April 1990. Other black leaders have denounced Farrakhan's message, but the charismatic preacher continued to find a receptive audience in the black community.

Farrakhan was more closely allied with the beliefs of Elijah Muhammad's Nation of Islam than with the orthodox religion. Elijah Muhammad, under whose leadership the Black Muslims became an important group, was born Elijah Poole in 1897 in Sandersville, Georgia, where his father and grandfather were Baptist ministers. Poole went North with a fourth-grade education in 1913 and succeeded Black Muslim founder W. J. Fard, expanding the sect in the early 1930s in Detroit and later Chicago. Muhammad's message was that of militant separatism: All whites were devils, and blacks must develop separate economies and social and cultural lives based on self-reliance. When Elijah Muhammad died in 1975, there was a struggle for leadership. His son Wallace Muhammad took over the organization. The "devilish" nature of all whites was downplayed and an economic program of self-help and development of pride in self was emphasized, as was a shift from racial militancy to traditional Islamic beliefs and practices.

Black Muslims worked for the elimination of illicit drugs and alcohol in the black community and among prison populations and were often much misunderstood. In 1970, a Black Muslim killed a Cordele police officer who arrested him for selling *Muhammad Speaks*. Whites were frightened by their militant rhetoric, which, if examined more closely, was actually defensive. They much preferred self-help to race war, a fact that Georgia officials acknowledged in 1973, even before the shift to traditional religion. One way Black Muslims tried to implement the principle of self-help was to establish businesses and profitable cooperative farms in the South. In 1970, their efforts fell victim to terroristic attacks. By the 1980s, Georgia prison officials no longer feared Muslims, because their faith, with its strong self-discipline, made them model inmates.

The Muslim faith continued to grow. In the late 1980s, there were an estimated twenty thousand Muslims in Atlanta, and 90 percent of them were black. There was also a growing business class among Muslims. Mosques, with mostly black worshipers, were located in Atlanta, Macon, and other cities. H. Rap Brown, the 1960s radical, converted to Islam and changed his name to Jamil Abdullah al-Amin and served as the imam (officiating priest) of the Community Mosque in Atlanta's West End. Sister Clara Muhammad School, run by Plemon T. El-Amin in East Atlanta, entered its fourteenth year in 1988 with 263 students in classes from prekindergarten to ninth grade.

In Georgia's Christian churches, 11:00 A.M. on Sunday remained the most segregated hour, by mutual choice of blacks and whites. Most of the integration that occurred came when blacks attended white churches. The Colored Methodist Episcopal church changed its first name to Christian in 1954 to show that all ethnic groups were welcome (and to remove any stigma the former name carried). The merger of a black and white church was a newsworthy event; the black Atlanta Metropolitan Church merged with the white Cornerstone Baptist Church in 1986. The Baptist religion remained the predominant faith among Georgia blacks. Many of Georgia's most influential blacks were ministers, including Cameron Alexander, pastor of Antioch Baptist Church; William Holmes Borders of the Wheat Street Baptist Church; and Julius Hope, who revitalized the Brunswick NAACP chapter in the early 1960s and later headed the state NAACP when he was pastor of Macon's First Baptist Church. Through groups such as the SCLC and Concerned Black Clergy, church leaders retained a key civil rights role.

In the mid-1980s, approximately 15,000 of Georgia's 140,000 Catholics were black. In 1988, Pope John Paul II named Eugene Marino as the archbishop of the Atlanta archdiocese, making him the first black American to become an archbishop. Tragically, Marino's pastorate fell apart in a sensationalized sex scandal. He resigned in 1990 and went into seclusion. He was replaced by another black, Archbishop James P. Lyke.

Civil rights leaders faced tough times going into the century's last decade. The twenty-year-old debate over whether civil rights groups had outlived their usefulness continued. While leaders had shifted their emphasis from integration to economic issues, critics charged them with pursuing "middle class" issues and ignoring the needs of their poor constituencies. However, the SCLC, NAACP, Urban League, and King Center continued to be concerned with crime, drugs, education, and affirmative action in the face of a national conservative backlash that also had been ongoing for two decades. Discouragingly, Republican race-baiting campaigns by George Bush, Jesse Helms, and David Duke struck a responsive chord with white voters. Civil rights leaders feared that the nation was regressing and that racism was fashionable again. Against such a depressing backdrop, the King holiday became a rallying point. It was a centerpiece of national life and focused attention on Dr. King's dream of social justice. Each January renewed the debate over whether the dream was closer to being reality.

There were concerns about finding new leadership for a movement whose leaders were growing old, and the Atlanta branch of the NAACP was racked by infighting and declining membership entering the 1990s. Lowery remained a prominent spokesman for the civil rights movement into the 1990s, but he was nearing the age of seventy. Carl Holman died in 1988, and King lieutenant Bernard Lee died in 1991. The King Center, which received major corporate donations, was reexamining its mission. In 1991, Harvard University administrator Dr. Ronald Quincy was named as its first executive director.

The final year of one civil rights giant was marred by controversy and bitterness. For some time, relations had been strained between the Kings and the Abernathys. In 1989, the publication of Ralph David Abernathy's autobiography rocked Atlanta's civil rights community. *And the Walls Came Tumbling Down* would not have been controversial had it not been for a short passage that dealt with Dr. King's last night alive. While charges that King had had extramarital affairs had been repeated countless times in other accounts, Abernathy's book sparked a furor and public condemnation because the allegations came from someone so close to King. No one within the movement had "betrayed" King that way. Abernathy also wrote that King had a violent confrontation with a woman early on the morning of his death, a revelation that contradicted King's philosophy of nonviolence. Atlanta's black leadership railed against the book and its author. The harsh criticism ensured that the book would get widespread publicity. Abernathy was reviled and ostracized. He died on April 17, 1990. Although there was a measure of honor after his death that many people thought was lacking during his lifetime, bitterness remained between the families of two great friends.

As the 1990s began, communism was crumbling in Eastern Europe, and the grip of apartheid was loosening on South Africa. Nelson Mandela, leader of the African National Congress (ANC), was released from prison in February 11, 1990, after serving twenty-seven years and went on a triumphant tour of America. Stoic and dignified, the seventy-one-year-old Mandela received a hero's welcome. Mandela was as much a symbol of the international freedom struggle as King had been. Therefore, his trip to Atlanta on June 27, 1990, took on heightened significance. In a whirlwind tour, he visited the King Center, met with Coretta King, and laid a wreath at Dr. King's tomb. He visited Big Bethel A.M.E. Church and Morehouse College, then spoke to a crowd of fifty thousand at Georgia Tech's Bobby Dodd Stadium and drew on the similarities of America's civil rights movement to his struggle to end apartheid at home. He paid homage to Atlanta's reputation as the center for civil rights in America and echoed Dr. King's 1963 "I Have a Dream" speech. The Shrine of the Black Madonna Church collected a fifty-gallon barrelful of money for the ANC.

As blacks questioned the role of traditional civil rights groups, there was a resurgent interest in Malcolm X and his message of black nationalism and self-help, a message that was embraced by both black conservatives and militants. There was renewed interest by blacks in their African heritage that was highlighted by Atlanta's role as a center of black culture and its ability to draw major exhibits and support the businesses that sprang up to supply the demand for African goods. Some blacks began celebrating Kwanzaa, the seven-day festival that followed Christmas.

By the early 1990s, Georgia had not resolved the contradictions in its character. Georgia gave the world *Gone With the Wind* as well as Dr. Martin Luther King, Jr. The classic romantic novel of a mythologized Old South remained a cultural icon, and many Georgians continued wistfully to remember a past that never was. Georgians continued to wave the Confederate battle flag as they honored dead Confederate veterans. Black attitudes ranged from apathetic to hostile toward Georgia's continued observances of Confederate holidays and the playing of "Dixie." Many saw the continuing celebration of the past as a glorification of slavery and became more willing to take offense and challenge the use of such symbols. Many black high school students walked out on programs when they heard "Dixie." Georgia's leaders tacitly acknowledged the song's offensiveness when site-selection officials for the 1988 Democratic National Convention were not allowed to see the laser show at Stone Mountain because "Dixie" was part of the program.

While officials were sensitive to outside opinion, Georgia's white politicians generally failed to acknowledge the racial symbolism of the state flag, which was changed in 1956 to incorporate the Confederate battle flag to symbolize massive resistance to the Supreme Court's *Brown* decision. Many whites thought that the state flag was a century-old bow to tradition, despite its recent derivation. For blacks, the prominence of the symbol of the fight to defend slavery remained a nettlesome issue, and debate increased during the 1980s as the battle flag showed up more frequently at white supremacists' gatherings. Black legislators tried to change the state flag but lacked support among white legislators, who liked the flag just fine. Governor Harris wished that the entire controversy would go away. His successor, Zell Miller, at first dismissed the importance of changing the state flag, then changed his position and called for a return to the flag's pre-1956 design. While it also carried a Confederate motif, at least it did not carry the Rebel battle flag. On May 28, 1992, he stated, "The Georgia flag is a last remaining vestige of days that not only are gone, but also days that we have no right to be proud of, days that should not be revered as one of the high points in the history of this state." Changing the flag was "the final step Georgia must take to really become a member of the New South," he declared.

Proponents also argued that Georgia should change the flag to avoid negative publicity during the 1996 Summer Olympics, when the world's attention would be focused on the state. Despite Miller's best efforts and widespread media and business support for the change, most white members of the General Assembly—and most white Georgians—wanted to keep the flag the way it was. As the General Assembly adjourned in 1993, a banner that was specifically designed to show the state's hostility toward equality for blacks fluttered over the Gold Dome.

Notes

1
The Formation of Georgia

p. 6: "inhabit or reside": Candler, *Colonial Records*, I:19, 21.

p. 6: "scratch the earth": Wood, *Slavery in Colonial Georgia*, p. 7.

p. 8: Captain Davis incident: Higginbotham, *In the Matter of Color*, pp. 231–32.

p. 8: "denying the use of negroes": Patrick Tailfer et al., *A True and Historical Narrative of the Colony of Georgia* (orig. pub. 1741) (Reprint; Freeport, N.Y.: Books for Libraries Press, 1971), p. 79.

p. 10: "If they should see": Thomas Gamble, Jr., *History of Bethesda* (Spartanburg, S.C.: The Reprint Co., 1972), p. 31.

p. 12: "No regiment may be seen": Philip S. Foner, *History of the Labor Movement in the United States* (New York: International Publishers, 1975) 1:43.

p. 14: "the Negroes have a wonderful art": Williams, *History of the Negro Race*, p. 339.

pp. 16–17: Austin Dabney: See Alton Hornsby, Jr., "Dabney, Austin," *Dictionary of American Negro Biography*, p. 154.

p. 17: Joseph Scipio: National Archives and Records Service, "Special List No. 36" (Washington: GSA, 1974), p. 7.

p. 17: effort...to recapture Savannah: See T. G. Steward, "How the Black Domingo Legion Saved the Patriot Army in the Siege of Savannah," American Negro Academy, *Occasional Papers*, No. 5 (New York: Arno Press and the *New York Times*, 1969), pp. 1–15.

pp. 18–19: One of the major diplomatic problems: See Bergman and McCarroll, *Negro in the Congressional Record* 1:57, 66–74, 86–123 passim.

p. 19: "best disciplined band of marauders": Carter G. Woodson, "In the War for Independence," *Negro History Bulletin* 7 (Nov. 1943) 29.

p. 21: Christian Priber: See Knox Mellon, Jr., "Christian Priber's Cherokee 'Kingdom of Paradise,'" *Georgia Historical Quarterly* 57 (1973) 319–31.

p. 25: "were openly eager for battle": John D. Milligan, "Slave Rebelliousness and the Florida Maroon," *Prologue* 6 (Spring 1974) 8.

p. 25: 1,483 blacks left Cumberland Island: See Mary R. Bullard, *Black Liberation in Cumberland Island in 1815* (DeLeon Springs, Fla.: Ed Painter, 1983).

2
A System of Bondage

p. 28: "Anyone who attacks slavery": Bergman and McCarroll, *Negro in the Congressional Record* 2:21.

p. 29: the David Mitchell case: See Averitt, "Democratic Party in Georgia," pp. 168–70; Royce Singleton, "David Brydie Mitchell and the African Importation Case of 1820," *Journal of Negro History* 48 (July 1973) 327–40.

p. 29: The *Wanderer* and Charles A. L. Lamar: Thomas Henderson Wells, *The Slave Ship Wanderer* (Athens: University of Georgia Press, 1967), p. 84; see also Wells, "Charles Augustus Lafayette Lamar; Gentleman Slave Trader," *Georgia Historical Quarterly* 47 (1963) 158–67.

p. 30: Plantation records show a dependence on muscle power: Genovese, *Political Economy of Slavery*, pp. 59, 61.

p. 30: surprisingly large body of literature: See Rawick, *American Slave*, vols. 12 and 13 for Georgia narratives; see also Brown, *Slave Life in Georgia*, and Blassingame, *Slave Testimony*. For a bibliography of seventy-one slave narratives, see Blassingame, *Slave Community*, pp. 240–42.

p. 30: Mr. Johnson: Blassingame, *Slave Testimony*, pp. 124–28.

p. 31: John Sella Martin: Ibid., pp. 702–35.

p. 31: W. B. Allen: Rawick, *American Slave* 12:12–16.

p. 38: Dimmock Charlton: Blassingame, *Slave Testimony*, pp. 325–38.

pp. 45–46: Two famous runaway slaves: For the Crafts' autobiographical account, see William and Ellen Craft, *Running a Thousand Miles to Freedom* (orig. pub. 1860) (Reprint; Miami: Mnemosyne, 1969); see also "The Flight of William and Ellen Craft," *The Liberator*, Jan. 12, 1849, cited in Aptheker, *Documentary History* 1:277–78.

p. 47: Macon and Savannah advertisements: Katz, *Eyewitness*, pp. 112–13.

p. 48: "There are many cases": Flanders, "Planters' Problems," p. 23.

p. 48: "outrageously impertinent" slave: Letter from Margaret E. Harden to Edward R. Harden, dated Sept. 27, 1863, in Edward Harden Papers, Duke University.

p. 55: slave trials: See Edwards, "Slave Justice"; E. Merton Coulter, "Four Slave Trials in Elbert County, Georgia," *Georgia Historical Quarterly* 41 (1957) 237–46; Robert G. McPherson, "Georgia Slave Trials, 1837–1849," *American Journal of Legal History* 4 (1960) 257–72, 364–77.

p. 55: "exceed the bonds of reason": Catterall, *Judicial Cases* 3:35–36.

p. 56: "The suppressive system": "Legal Basis of American Slavery," *Massachusetts Quarterly Review* 1 (June 1846) 291.

p. 57: "the deep-seated schizophrenia": Herbert Aptheker, *One Continual Cry: David Walker's Appeal to the Colored Citizens of the World* (New York: Humanities Press, 1965), p. 1.

p. 58: catechisms were used to brainwash: See "A Slave Catechism" in Fishel and Quarles, *Black American*, p. 114.

p. 64: "In Georgia": Lawrence M. Friedman, *A History of American Law* (New York: Simon and Schuster, 1973), p. 196. For a general treatment of free blacks, see Berlin, *Slaves Without Masters*.

p. 64: The number of free Negroes: Bureau of the Census, *Negro Population 1790–1915* (Washington: GPO, 1918), Table 6, p. 57.

p. 66: "Generally the free Negroes": Unger, "Free Negroes," p. 39; see also Flanders, "The Free Negro."

p. 70: antebellum Savannah as a bustling, crime-ridden city: Richard H. Haunton, "Law and Order in Savannah: 1850–1860," *Georgia Historical Quarterly* 56 (1972) 1–24.

3
THE CIVIL WAR AND RECONSTRUCTION

p. 77: "The moment any improper interference": Howard, "Georgia Reaction," pp. 49, 55.

p. 80: "propaganda skillfully": Coleman et al., *History of Georgia*, p. 150.

p. 80: "was paper thin" and "Georgians were so equally divided": See Johnson, "New Look at the Popular Vote."

p. 82: "Its cornerstone rests upon the great truth": Mohr, *On the Threshold*, p. 50.

p. 83: "Many were punished": Taylor, *Reminiscences*, pp. 67–68.

p: 84: Impressment, "refugeeing," and the breakdown of the pass and patrol system: See Mohr, *On the Threshold*, for a detailed account of Georgia blacks during the Civil War.

p. 87: "the most pernicious idea": Charles E. Wesley, "The Employment of Negroes as Soldiers in the Confederate Army," *Journal of Negro History* 4 (July 1919) 247. For Brown's thoughts on the issue, see *Georgia House Journal*, Extra Session, 1865, pp. 22–23.

p. 90: This happened at Ebenezer Creek: See James P. Jones, "General Jeff C. Davis, USA, and Sherman's Georgia Campaign," *Georgia Historical Quarterly* 47 (1963) 231–48.

p. 92: Turner and Lynch: Litwack, *Storm*, pp. 184–85.

p. 92: "If we cannot whip": Escott, "Context of Freedom," p. 100.

p. 92: Northern newspaper journalists: See especially J. T. Trowbridge, *The South: A Tour of Its Battlefields and Ruined Cities* (Reprint; New York: Arno Press and the *New York Times*, 1969), pp. 463, 499–500; Sidney Andrews, *The South Since the War* (Reprint; New York: Arno Press and the *New York Times*, 1969), pp. 233, 288–98; and Carl Schurz, *The Reminiscences of Carl Schurz* (London: John Murray, 1909) 3:173, 175–76.

p. 93: apprenticeships: Cimbala, "Reconstruction's Stepchildren," pp. 5, 6, 13, 15, 20.

p. 94: "wise and patriotic": *Georgia Senate Journal*, March 12, 1866, p. 585.

p. 95: race relations were the main order of business: *Georgia Senate Journal*, Dec. 5, 1865, pp. 13–14; Dec. 6, 1865, pp. 17–18; Feb. 15, 1866, p. 264.

p. 96: Turner stated that... terms were misrepresented: "Testimony of Henry M. Turner, Nov. 3, 1871," in Cox and Cox, eds., *Reconstruction*, pp. 279–85; see also Rawick, *American Slave* 12:229.

p. 96: City life held many problems: See Owens, "Negro in Georgia," pp. 88–89, 95–97; Johnson, "Negro in Macon," pp. 12–14.

p. 97: Jenkins proposed... tax on working blacks: *Georgia Senate Journal*, Jan. 16, 1866, pp. 96–97.

p. 97: Mortality rates: Thompson, "Freedmen's Bureau," p. 43; Ransom and Sutch, *One Kind of Freedom*, pp. 53–54.

p. 97: Sutton letter: C. H. Sutton to John S. Dobbins, July 14, 1865, in John S. Dobbins Collection, Emory University Archives.

p. 97: Augusta freedmen's convention: *Proceedings of the Freedmen's Convention of Georgia, Assembled at Augusta, January 10th, 1866, Containing the Speeches of General Tillson, Capt. J. E. Bryant, and Others* (Augusta: The *Loyal Georgian*, 1866), pp. 1–40.

pp. 97–98: "It is essential": *Georgia Senate Journal*, Mar. 12, 1866, pp. 586–87.

p. 99: "shamefully abused their trust": Drago, *Black Politicians*, p. 131.

p. 99: Raushenberg correspondence: Cox and Cox, eds., *Reconstruction*, pp. 339–44.

p. 100: [O]ur towns, cities, and villages: *Georgia Senate Journal*, Feb. 15, 1866, pp. 256–57.

p. 100: black troops in the South: See *Harper's Monthly* 32 (Mar. 1866) 396; Johnson, "Negro in Macon," pp. 6–8; Drago, *Black Politicians*, p. 94.

p. 101: The Ku Klux Klan: For discussion of the original Klan, see Trelease, *White Terror*. Compare to Fitz Simons, "The Ku Klux Klan in Georgia." Fitz Simons saw the Klan as necessary and claimed any abuses were from "low elements" who rode in its name after it was disbanded. For a firsthand account by a Klansman, see Reed, "What I Know."

p. 108: he was "probably arrested": Blassingame, "Before the Ghetto," pp. 477–78.

p. 108: vilification in the white press: For examples, see E. Merton Coulter, "Aaron Alpeoria Bradley, Georgia Negro Politician During Reconstruction," *Georgia Historical Quarterly* 51 (1967) pt. 1, 15–41; pt. 2, 154–74, pt. 3, 264–306. Coulter's views of Bradley and other black leaders during Reconstruction were heavily influenced by prejudiced newspaper accounts at the time. For a more balanced view of Bradley, see Joseph P. Reidy, "Aaron A. Bradley: Voice of Black Labor in the Georgia Low Country," in Rabinowitz, ed., *Southern Black Leaders*.

pp. 108–9: At the convention, Bradley tried to neutralize planters: *Journal of the Constitutional Convention, State of Georgia, 1867–1868*, Jan. 23, 1868, pp. 179–80; Feb. 8, 1868, pp. 271–77; Feb. 12, 1868, pp. 294, 297–98.

pp. 110–11: Tunis G. Campbell, Sr.: Like Bradley, Campbell was the subject of constant vilification in his time and in later historical accounts. See E. Merton Coulter, "Tunis G. Campbell, Negro Reconstructionist in Georgia," *Georgia Historical Quarterly*, pt. 1, 51 (1967) 401–24; pt. 2, 52 (1968) 16–52. For an autobiographical account, see Campbell, *Sufferings*. For an in-depth biography, see Duncan, *Freedom's Shore*.

p. 112: "I charge Mr. Johnson": Litwack, *Storm*, pp. 530–31.

p. 113: the legislature turned on its black members: See *Georgia House Journal*, Sept. 9, 1868, pp. 294–95; *Condition of Affairs in Georgia*, 40th Cong. 3d sess., HR misc. Doc. 52 (Reprint; Freeport, N.Y.: Books for Libraries Press, 1971), pt. 2, p. 6. For the protest of Campbell and Wallace, see Aptheker, *Documentary History* 2:568; and Campbell, *Sufferings*, p. 9.

p. 114: "some of the white members": Coleman et al., *History of Georgia*, p. 213.

p. 115: "We have pioneered": Turner's speech is reprinted in Christler, "Participation of Negroes," pp. 82–96, and Foner, *Voice of Black America*, pp. 358–66.

p. 116: Richard W. White: *White v. Clements*, 39 Ga. 232 (1869) is discussed in Ware, *Constitutional History*, p. 136-85 passim.

p. 117: planters grew bolder. . . . Freedmen's Bureau records: letter from John Leonard to Col. J. R. Lewis, Aug. 26, 1869, p. 266; letter, George R. Ballou to Maj. O. H. Howard, Sept. 1, 1868, pp. 274–75; letter, Ballou to Howard, Oct. 31, 1868, pp. 277–78; letter, W. C. Morrill to Howard, Sept. 30, 1868, p. 270, all in Cox and Cox, eds., *Reconstruction*.

p. 117: worst single incident of violence came at Camilla: See Fitz Simons, "The Camilla Riot."

pp. 117–18: Perry Jeffers: Trelease, *White Terror*, pp. 228–30.

p. 118: fall elections "convinced conservative whites": Matthews, "Race Relations," pp. 26–27.

p. 119: "I have seen men": "Testimony of Henry M. Turner, November 3, 1871," in Cox and Cox, eds., *Reconstruction*, pp. 280, 283.

p. 120: Overall, twenty-one of the sixty-nine blacks: Drago, *Black Politicians*, Appendix.

p. 120: "have no more regard": Ibid., pp. 66–67.

pp. 120–121: Campbell... protested their presence: Campbell, *Sufferings*, pp. 11–12; Duncan, *Freedom's Shore*, pp. 69–70.

p. 121: It is true that divisions: Drago, *Black Politicians*, p. 144.

pp. 123–24: Jefferson Long's speech: *Congressional Globe*, 41st Cong., 2d sess., Feb. 1, 1871, p. 881; also in Aptheker, *Documentary History* 2:607–8.

p. 128: Georgia whites "reacted hysterically": Wingo, "Race Relations," pp. 25–27.

p. 131: "a Democratic machine": Kenneth M. Stampp, *The Era of Reconstruction: 1865–1877* (New York: Random House, 1967), p. 179.

p. 131: William A. Pledger led the revolt: McDaniel, "Black Power." See also articles on Pledger in *Dictionary of Georgia Biography* and *Dictionary of American Negro Biography*.

p. 133: "The Supreme Court is an organized mob": Redkey, *Respect Black*, p. 78. For the significance of the 1883 decision, see Grant, *Anti-Lynching Movement*, p. 21 ff.

p. 134: "One holds": Turner, "Reasons for a New Political Party," in Foner, *Voice of Black America*, p. 506.

p. 135: he and the clerk were burned in effigy: *New York Age*, Aug. 24, 1889, p. 2; coverage of Lewis's appointment of C. C. Penny and the subsequent uproar bears out Fortune's charge. See *Atlanta Constitution*, Aug. 6, 1889, p. 8; Aug. 7, 1889, p. 4; Aug. 8, 1889, p. 4, Aug. 9, 1889, p. 4; an Aug. 13, 1889, editorial complains about Northern press reactions to the effigy-burnings.

pp. 135–36: Afro-American League: See Aptheker, *Documentary History* 2:703–708 and Grant, *Anti-Lynching*, pp. 23–27.

4

POST-RECONSTRUCTION HORRORS

p. 137: "consciously and carefully": W. E. B. Du Bois, *The Negro American Artisan*, No. 17 in the *Atlanta University Publications* (Reprint; New York: Arno Press and the *New York Times*, 1968), p. 135. For a detailed review of blacks' postwar economic condition, see Ransom and Sutch, *One Kind of Freedom*. See also Litwack, *Storm*, and Owens, "Negro in Georgia."

p. 140: "not dead, nor gone": Ransom and Sutch, *One Kind of Freedom*, p. 46.

p. 142: A recent study... concluded that racism: Ibid., p. 177.

p. 142: "In time, sharecropping": Coleman et al., *History of Georgia*, p. 226.

p. 143: "all possibility of dispute": Ransom and Sutch, *One Kind of Freedom*, p. 146.

p. 143: Augusta and Savannah murders: *Savannah Tribune*, Mar. 11, 1876, p. 3.

p. 144: "irresponsible" cropper: "The Negro Contract Jumper," *Atlanta Constitution*, Jan. 31, 1914, p. 4.

p. 145: Du Bois's study of Dougherty County: "The Negro as He Really Is," *World's Work*, June, 1901; reprinted in Du Bois, *The Souls of Black Folk* under chapter heading "Of the Black Belt."

p. 145: "a cynic might have imagined": Frederick Lewis Allen, *The Big Change: American Transforms Itself 1900–1950* (New York: Harper & Row, 1952), p. 178.

p. 146: 32 percent had one tenant: Ransom and Sutch, *One Kind of Freedom*, p. 79.

p. 146: a smaller percentage of blacks owned land in Georgia: Fisher, "Negro Farm Ownership," p. 483.

p. 147: in 75 percent of the cases...where blacks acquired: Ibid., p. 484.

p. 148: "A Georgia Peon Camp": Charles W. Chesnutt, "Peonage, or the New Slavery," *Voice of the Negro* 1 (Sept. 1904) 394–97; for a discussion of the legal aspects of peonage, see Sydney Brodie, "The Federally Secured Right to be Free From Bondage," *Georgetown Law Journal* 40 (Mar. 1952) 367–68; Fred G. Folsom, Jr., "A Slave Trade Law in a Contemporary Setting," *Cornell Law Quarterly* 29 (Nov. 1973) 204; and Harry H. Shapiro, "Involuntary Servitude: The Need for a More Flexible Approach," *Rutgers Law Review* 19 (1964–1965) 71–74.

p. 149: "will occasion practical slavery": *Harper's* 34 (Feb. 1867) 399–400.

pp. 150–51: Clyatt case: *Clyatt v. U. S.* 197 US 207 (1905); see also Daniel, *Shadow of Slavery*, pp. 8–18.

p. 151: McRee case: "Peonage in Georgia," *Independent* 55 (Jan. 24, 1903) 3079.

pp. 152–53: One who told his story: See "A Negro Peon Speaks," in Hamilton Holt, *The Life Stories of Undistinguished Americans as Told by Themselves* (New York: 1906), pp. 183–99, reprinted in Aptheker, *Documentary History* 2:832–38.

p. 153: "a system that left a trail of dishonor": Fletcher M. Green, "Some Aspects of the Southern Convict-Lease System in the Southern States," in *Essays in Southern History Presented to Joseph Gregoire de Roulhac Hamilton*, edited by Fletcher M. Green (Chapel Hill: University of North Carolina Press, 1949), p. 122.

p. 155: "Drive the vagrants": *Atlanta Constitution*, Oct. 3, 1904, p. 4.

p. 155: Maddox and Bartlett: Wingo, "Race Relations," p. 248.

p. 155: "There is no system": W. S. Scarborough, "An Inside View of the Convict-Lease System," *Indianapolis Freeman*, Dec. 7, 1891, p. 5.

p. 156: "Ten years, as the rolls show": George W. Cable, "The Convict Lease System," in Cox and Cox, eds., *Reconstruction*, pp. 384–95; see also Cable, *The Negro Question*.

p. 156: Dade County coal-mining convict camp: Ward, "Bourbon Democrats," pp. 421–22; Adams, "Agrarian Movement," pp. 75–78; *Savannah Tribune*, Dec. 3, 1892, p. 2.

p. 157: "selling the poor": See Rebecca A. Felton, "The Convict System in Georgia," *Forum* 2 (Sept. 1886–Feb. 1887) 484–90.

p. 158: Harry Jamison case: *Voice of the Negro* 1 (Aug. 1904) 300–10.

pp. 158–59: Fulton County convicts: *Crisis* 9 (Feb. 1915) 168.

p. 159: "Until we are free": Redkey, *Respect Black*, p. 159.

p. 159: Amos Bines and Monday Roberts: *Savannah Tribune*, Feb. 26, 1876, p. 2; Mar. 4, 1876, p. 2; Mar. 20, 1876, p. 2.

p. 159: Jerry Hamilton: *New York Globe*, June 2, 1883, p. 2.

p. 160: whites were "usually suspicious": M. A. Majors, "The Illiterate White Man," *Indianapolis Freeman*, Jan. 8, 1898, p. 1.

p. 160: 3,224 recorded lynchings: See NAACP, *Thirty Years of Lynching;* see also White, *Rope and Faggot.*

p. 160: "Men have been lynched": Testimony of Pledger in U.S. Congress, House Report 2194, *Commission to Enquire Into the Condition of the Colored People* to accompany HR 12940, 57th Cong., 1st sess., May 23, 1902 (SS 4406).

pp. 161: "Disfranchisement makes lynching": Cox, *Caste, Class, and Race,* p. 555.

pp. 161–62: Palmetto Five: See Alfred Holt Stone, *Studies in the American Race Problem* (New York: Doubleday Page, 1908), p. 460; *Savannah Tribune,* Mar. 18, 1899.

p. 162: a monster in human form: *Congressional Record,* 56th Cong., 1st sess., Feb. 1, 1900, p. 1414. Hose's name is sometimes given as Holt, and according to some accounts, Cranford was involved in the lynching of the Palmetto Five. For contemporary press accounts of the Hose lynching, see *Atlanta Journal* and *Atlanta Constitution,* Apr. 15, 24, and 25, 1899; *Savannah Tribune,* Apr. 29, 1899; and Ginzburg, *100 Years,* pp. 10–21. For Du Bois's reaction to the lynching, see his *Autobiography,* p. 222.

p. 163: Reverdy Ransom's investigation: *Salt Lake City Broad Ax,* June 6, 1899, p. 1 (this newspaper moved to Chicago for its next issue); *New York Age,* June 20, 1899; for Ida B. Wells's investigative report, see *Richmond Planet,* Oct. 14, 1899.

p. 164: "Whenever an aristocracy": Du Bois, *Correspondence,* I:153.

p. 165: Between 1891 and 1904: *Atlanta Constitution,* Sept. 23, 1891; Sept. 14, 1899; June 20, 1902; Mar. 16, 1904; all cited in Matthews, "Race Relations," p. 162.

p. 165: "The Statesboro tragedies": NAACP, *Thirty Years,* pp. 15–16; Langston Whitley, "The Statesboro Tragedies," *Christian Advocate* 79 (Sept. 1, 1904) 1425–26; *Voice of the Negro* 1 (Sept. 1904) 375–76, 411–12; Kelly Miller, "The Attitude of the Intelligent Negro Toward Lynching," *Voice of the Negro* 2 (May 1905) 307–12.

p. 166–67: "riot" in McIntosh County: See Brundage, "The Darien 'Insurrection' of 1899."

p. 168: "To adopt lynch-law": *Salt Lake City Broad Ax,* May 30, 1899, p. 4.

p. 168: *"Lynching Probable": Atlanta Constitution,* Feb. 7, 1890, p. 2:1.

p. 168: "Must Put Down the Mob": Mark Bauman, "Race and Mastery: The Debate of 1903," in Fraser and Moore, eds., *From the Old South to the New,* pp. 187–88.

5

THE NEW SOUTH AND FURTHER DEGRADATIONS

p. 173: Colored Farmers' Alliance: See Adams, "Agrarian Movement" and Matthews, "Race Relations," for more information on this organization.

p. 174: fundamental conflict of interests... surfaced: *Savannah Tribune,* Dec. 7, 1889, p. 2.

p. 176: "You are kept apart": Thomas Watson, "The Negro Question in the South," *Arena* 4 (1892) 548. For different views of Watson's racial attitudes, compare C. Vann Woodward, "Tom Watson and the Negro in Agrarian Politics," *Journal of Southern History* 4 (Feb. 1938) 15–32, and Crowe, "Watson, Populists, and Blacks."

p. 177: "the Negro as a political force": Henry Grady, *The New South: Writings and Speeches of Henry Grady* (Savannah: Beehive Press, 1971), pp. 140–41.

p. 177: "power which your situation gives you": Matthews, "Race Relations," p. 59.

p. 177: "beer by the barrel": Coleman et al., *History of Georgia*, pp. 299–300.

p. 179: "The notion that the black man...betrayed Populism": Shaw, *Wool Hat Boys*, p. 78.

p. 179: "impossible to trust": Wingo, "Race Relations," p. 92.

p. 181: "Lynch law is a good sign": Allen, *Reluctant Reformers*, p. 80.

p. 184: The Bourbons "worshipped business success": Ward, "Bourbon Democrats," pp. iii–v.

p. 185: "the most extraordinary man": Du Bois, *Black Reconstruction*, pp. 509, 511.

p. 185: "the dollar their god": Bruce Clayton, "Grady, Henry Woodfin," in *Encyclopedia of American Biography*, edited by John A. Garraty (New York: Harper & Row, 1974), p. 443.

p. 185: "Each has his place": Henry Grady, "In Plain Black and White: A Reply to Mr. Cable," *Century Magazine* 29 (Apr. 1885) 909–17.

p. 186: New South speech: See "The New South" in Henry Grady, *The New South: Writings and Speeches of Henry Grady* (Savannah: Beehive Press, 1971).

p. 186: Grady "was either lying or stupid" and "Grady stands up": For the modern view of Grady's speech, see *Atlanta Constitution* Dec. 21, 1986, p. 1–A; Fortune responded to Grady in *New York Freeman*, Jan. 22, 1887, p. 2.

p. 186: Grady "screamed with laughter": *Atlanta Constitution* May 24, 1921; "The Race Problem in the South" is also contained in Grady, *The New South*.

p. 187: J. W. Hood believed that the efforts: See Hood, "The Enfranchisement of the Negro No Blunder," *Independent* 55 (Aug. 27, 1903) 2021–24.

p. 187: reporters..."have excused...mob law": Du Bois, *Correspondence*, I:274.

p. 187: Black journalists were outspoken in rebuttal: See *New York Freeman*, July 30, 1887, p. 2; *Savannah Tribune*, Sept. 21, 1889, p. 2; *Indianapolis Freeman*, Feb. 1, 1890, p. 2.

p. 188: "the most dangerous of the group": Gaines's speech to the Negro Young People's Christian Educational Conference was carried in the *Chicago Broad Ax*, Aug. 6, 1906, p. 1.

p. 188: Graves on lynching: See "A Friend of the Mob," *Nation* 77 (Aug. 20, 1903) 146–47; Mark K. Bauman, "Race and Mastery: The Debate of 1903," in Fraser and Moore, eds., *From the Old South to the New*, p. 183; *Christian Advocate* 78 (Sept. 3, 1903) 1414–17; Hall, *Revolt Against Chivalry*, p. 147.

p. 188: restore the Negro to "a condition of morals and industry": Alexander Hooper, "Race Riots and Lynch Law: The Cause and Cure," *Outlook* 85 (Feb. 2, 1907) 259–63; for an example of articles accepting the New South's mythology, see E. L. Godkin, "The Republican Party and the Negro," *Forum* 7 (Mar.–Aug. 1889) 246–57.

p. 189: 1900 Conference: See Southern Society for the Promotion of the Study of Race Conditions and Problems in the South, *Race Problems of the South* (Reprint of the Society's 1900 *Proceedings*) (New York: Negro Universities Press, 1969), p. 206, "Closing Remarks," and Alexander C. King, "The Punishment of Crimes against Women," p. 165.

p. 190: "God and the Race Problem": Grimké, *The Works of Francis James Grimké*, edited by Carter G. Woodson (Washington: Associated Publishers, 1942), I:364–68.

p. 191: "Perhaps no writings": Mays, *Born to Rebel*, pp. 345–46.

p. 191: giving the vote to blacks..."was a terrible mistake": Atticus G. Haygood, "Black Shadow in the South," *Forum* 16 (Oct. 1893) 167–75.

p. 193: "(T)he most spectacular and exotic development": E. Merton Coulter, *The South During Reconstruction* (Baton Rouge: Louisiana State University Press, 1947), p. 142.

p. 193: "This interpretation": Wharton, "Reconstruction," in Link and Patrick, eds., *Writing Southern History*, p. 298.

p. 194: The New South "proscribes and persecutes": W. S. Scarborough, "The Future of the Negro," *Forum* 7 (Mar.–Aug. 1889) 80–81.

p. 194: "it is the first premise" and "we may reach the moon": Cable, *The Negro Question*, pp. 62–63, 71; Fortune's comment is in *New York Freeman*, Apr. 11, 1885, p. 2.

p. 195: "Our special reason for fear": Fannie Barrier Williams, "The Negro and Public Opinion," *Voice of the Negro* 1 (Jan. 1904) 31–32; see also *Crisis* 3 (Nov. 1911) 9; 3 (Apr. 1912) 243.

p. 195: "For the South": Woodward, *Origins*, p. 140.

p. 195: "First we would vote": *Chicago Broad Ax*, Aug. 25, 1906, p. 1.

p. 197: "the most effective bar": Kousser, *Shaping of Southern Politics*, pp. 64–65.

p. 198: "The merchants of the North": *Atlanta Constitution*, July 1, 1890, p. 1:2; July 20, 1890, p. 14:1.

p. 198: "hope of development": Hoke Smith, "The Disastrous Effects of the Force Bill," *Forum* 13 (Mar.–Aug. 1892) 688.

p. 201: A petition from John Hope: See "Georgia Negroes on the Hardwick Bill, 1899," in Aptheker, *Documentary History* 2:784–86.

·p. 202: "I am almost disgusted": Woodward, *Origins*, pp. 337–38.

p. 202: In the 1904 election, when few blacks voted: *Voice of the Negro* 1 (Dec. 1904) 587–88.

p. 202: "The rich educated white man": June 27, 1902, letter from Watson to Felton cited in Wingo, "Race Relations," p. 102.

pp. 203–4: "Make the ballot the prize": Ibid., p. 110. For accounts of the race, see Adams, "Agrarian Movement," pp. 320–33, and Grantham, "Georgia Politics and Disfranchisement."

p. 204: "out-Nigger each other": See Dittmer, *Black Georgia*, pp. 98–100, and Crowe, "Racial Violence," p. 243.

pp. 204–8: The Atlanta race riot: See Crowe, "Racial Massacre." Crowe gives a compelling account of the Atlanta riot's first night. See also Crowe, "Racial Violence." For a contemporary white journalist's account, see Ray Stannard Baker, "A Race Riot and After," in *Following the Color Line* (orig. pub. 1908) (Reprint; Harper Torchbooks) (New York: Harper & Row, 1964).

p. 206: Walter White: White, *Autobiography*, p. 11.

p. 206: "the respectable colored citizens": Torrence, *John Hope*, p. 153.

p. 229: "Our people must die": Aptheker, *Documentary History* 2:868.

p. 207: The black press was also a riot victim: *Chicago Broad Ax*, Apr. 27, 1907, p. 1; Barber's letter in Aptheker, *Documentary History* 2:866; "Why Mr. Barber Left Atlanta," in the *Voice* 3 (Nov. 1906) 470–71 (the magazine's name was changed with this issue).

p. 208: While Washington publicly praised: See Washington, "We Must Be a Law-Abiding and Law-Respecting People," in Foner, *Voice of Black America*, pp. 652–54.

p. 208: "It is nonsense": Meier, *Negro Thought in America*, pp. 180–81.

p. 211: "in a prison": David Herbert Donald, "A Generation of Defeat," in Fraser and Moore, eds., *From the Old South to the New*, pp. 3–17.

p. 212: "One of the strangest things": Woodward, *Strange Career of Jim Crow*, p. 19.

p. 213: "By 1908, the color line": Wingo, "Race Relations," p. 118.

p. 215: Savannah's...black community resisted: Meier and Rudwick, "A Strange Chapter in the Career of 'Jim Crow,'" in Meier and Rudwick, eds., *The Making of Black America* 2:15.

p. 216: "The failure of the Savannah boycott": Coleman et al., *History of Georgia*, p. 278.

p. 216: racial clashes "almost daily": Matthews, "Race Relations," p. 132.

pp. 217–18: Atlanta received a Carnegie Library: See Du Bois, "The Opening of the Library," *Independent* 50 (Apr. 1902) 809–10.

p. 218: ordinance against black barbers: The court case was *Chaires v. Atlanta* 164 Ga. 755 (1926).

p. 219: Uncle Remus Avenue: *Nation* 154 (Jan. 3, 1942) 14.

p. 221: "the best doctors": White, *Autobiography*, pp. 135–38.

p. 222: education...was the most important factor: Blassingame, "Before the Ghetto," p. 476.

p. 224: "yet it will thrive": Letter from L. Lieberman to J. R. Lewis, Aug. 28, 1869, in Cox and Cox, eds., *Reconstruction*, pp. 267–68;

p. 224: American Missionary Association: For an excellent account of the AMA's activities in Georgia, see Jones, *Soldiers of Light and Love;* see also Drake, "The American Missionary Association."

p. 225: "damned whores": Jones, *Soldiers*, p. 29.

p. 231: *Cumming v. Richmond County Board of Education:* 175 US 528 (1899); see also Kousser, "Separate but Not Equal."

p. 231: "an impossible contradiction": Du Bois, "The Economic Revolution in the South," in *The Negro in the South*, p. 113.

p. 231: "Redeemers"...accused blacks of not paying their share: *Savannah Tribune*, Jan. 30, 1892, p. 2; Aug. 20, 1892, p. 2; Jan. 14, 1893, p. 2; George W. Cable, "Does the Negro Pay for His Education?" *Forum* 13 (Mar.–Aug. 1892) 645; Toppin, "Walter White," p. 6; Ward, "Bourbon Democrats," pp. 461–63.

p. 232: "turned the feelings": Matthews, "Race Relations," p. 93.

p. 232: "nigger colleges": *Indianapolis Freeman*, Dec. 28, 1894, p. 5.

p. 233: The 1877–78 school year in Columbus: Wingo, "Race Relations," p. 211.

p. 234: "the very best books": William E. Dodd, "Some Difficulties of the History Teacher in the South," *South Atlantic Quarterly* 3 (Apr. 1904) 119–21.

pp. 234–35: salaries...and the right to vote were related: Toppin, "Walter White," pp. 3–4.

p. 235: Du Bois noted...Druid Hills: *Crisis* 13 (Apr. 1917) 268.

p. 236: Jeanes teachers: See Sessoms, *Jeanes Supervision.*

6

BLACK INSTITUTIONS AND ADVANCEMENT

p. 240: Atlanta University: See Clarence A. Bacote, *History of Atlanta University* (Atlanta: Atlanta University Press, 1969).

p. 241: Clark University: James P. Brawley, *The Clark College Legacy* (Atlanta: Clark College, 1977), pp. 1–10.

p. 243: "Holley was perhaps more accommodating": *Dictionary of Georgia Biography*, 1:468–70; see also Holley, *You Can't Build a Chimney From the Top* (New York: William-Frederick Press, 1948).

p. 243: "overburdened instructors": Bardolph, *Negro Vanguard*, pp. 162–63.

p. 243: (Du Bois's) vast writings: See Herbert Aptheker, *Annotated Bibliography of the Published Writings of W. E. B. Du Bois* (Millwood, New York: Kraus-Thompson, 1973).

p. 244: American Negro Academy: See Alfred A. Moss, Jr., *The American Negro Academy: Voice of the Talented Tenth* (Baton Rouge: Louisiana State University Press, 1981). Hope's paper is No. 11 and Steward's is No. 5 in American Negro Academy, *Occasional Papers 1–22* (Reprint; New York: Arno Press and the *New York Times*, 1969).

p. 248: Savannah's black community...in 1870: Blassingame, "Before the Ghetto," pp. 466–68.

p. 249: "new men"...old guard: Birmingham, *Certain People*, pp. 223–25. See also Porter, "The Auburn Avenue Residential Community."

p. 251: Georgia's most successful black insurance company: See Henderson, *Atlanta Life Insurance Company*.

p. 252: The rise and fall of Standard Life Insurance Company: Alexa B. Henderson, "Heman E. Perry and the Downfall of Atlanta's Standard Life Insurance Company" (paper presented at Fort Valley State College, May 14, 1982); *Crisis* 7 (Jan. 1914) 142–45; 9 (Feb. 1915) 201; 11 (Dec. 1915) 96; 11 (Apr. 1916) 299.

p. 255: black doctors in Georgia: Matthews, "Race Relations," p. 270.

p. 258: Negro Press Association of Georgia: *Savannah Tribune*, Dec. 10, 1892, p. 2; Dec. 31, 1892, p. 2.

p. 259: Scott had been sent...by Booker T. Washington: See Harlan, "Washington and 'The Voice of the Negro.'"

p. 260: the *Macon Telegraph*, which "can so seldom mention the Negro decently": *Crisis* 13 (Apr. 1917) 289.

pp. 261–62: first orphanage for blacks: *Voice of the Negro* 1 (Nov. 1905) 538–40.

p. 264: "unlettered or ignorant": W. E. B. Du Bois, *The Negro,Church* Atlanta University Publication No. 4 (1903) (Reprint; New York: Arno Press and the *New York Times*, 1968), pp. 57, 61; see also Benjamin Mays, *The Negro's Church* (New York: Negro University Press, 1969), p. 239.

p. 265: "domination of black politics proved costly": Drago, *Splendid Failure*, p. 161.

p. 266: Charles T. Walker: See Silas X. Floyd, *Life of Charles T. Walker* (Nashville: National Baptist Publishing Board, 1902).

p. 267: "black worshippers freed from white surveillance": Litwack, *Storm*, pp. 466–71.

p. 270: Congregational churches...succumbed to segregation: See Richard B. Drake, "The Growth of Segregation in America's Congregational Church in the South," *Negro History Bulletin* 21 (Mar. 1958); see also Cable, "Congregational Unity in Georgia" in the *Congregationalist* (Sept. 26, 1889), reprinted in Cable, *The Negro Question*, pp. 197–203.

p. 272: Father Divine: See John Hosher, *God in a Rolls Royce: The Rise of Father Divine* (New York: Books for Libraries Press, 1971); Claude McKay, " 'There Goes God!' The Story of Father Divine and his Angels," *Nation* 140 (Feb. 6, 1935) 151–53; Federal Writers Project, *Drums and Shadows*, pp. 9–10.

p. 272: "has discredited our nation": *Norfolk Journal and Guide*, May 20, 1922, p. 1.

p. 273: In 1939, the Baptist World Alliance: "A Chronicle of Race Relations, 1939," *Phylon* 1 (1st Quarter 1940) 94.

7
THE SEARCH FOR A DECENT LIVING AND A BETTER LIFE

p. 275: "The black artisan": Dittmer, *Black Georgia*, p. 29.

p. 275: "Almost as blacks were displaced": Herbert Hill, *Race, Work, and the Law*, vol. 1 of *Black Labor and the American Legal System* (Washington: Bureau of National Affairs, 1977), pp. 21–22.

pp. 275–76: "So long as white labor": Du Bois, "The Economic Revolution in the South," in Du Bois, *The Negro in the South*, p. 114.

p. 276: The average profit for Southern cotton mills: Woodward, *Origins*, pp. 131–33.

p. 276: A report... on conditions for workers: cited in March 16, 1912, *Congressional Record*, 48:3496.

p. 277: In 1921 black women constituted 2.2 percent: Women's Bureau, U.S. Dept. of Labor, *Women in Georgia Industries* (Washington: GPO, 1922), pp. 30–31.

pp. 278–79: Knights of Labor: See McLaurin, *Knights of Labor in the South*. For a broader view of blacks in the union movement, see Foner, *Organized Labor and the Black Worker.*

p. 280: employers also pitted one group of blacks against another: For examples, see Matthews, "Race Relations," pp. 214–15.

pp. 280–81: Georgia railroads were the scene of... racial conflict: See Hammett, "Labor and Race"; Matthews, "Race Relations," pp. 219–21.

p. 281: "Certain vocations": *Proceedings of the 1909 National Negro Conference*, pp. 86, 91, 113, 127.

p. 281: black trainmen were lynched so that whites could obtain their jobs: For contemporary accounts of 1920s violence, see *Chicago Defender*, Jan. 18, 1922, p. 1; Jan. 20, 1922, p. 1; Feb. 18, 1922, p. 1; Mar. 4, 1922, p. 15; May 13, 1922, p. 1; *Atlanta Constitution*, May 21, 1921, p. 9; for an account of 1930s violence, see Davis et al., *Deep South*, p. 427.

p. 282: Taft announced a policy: *Crisis* 1 (Nov. 1910) 8; see also Ibid., 2 (Sept. 1911) 184; 3 (Feb. 1912) 141; 5 (Feb. 1913) 176–77.

p. 283: "There are no government positions": Kluger, *Simple Justice* 1:112.

p. 283: bills "to prevent persons of African descent": *Georgia Senate Journal*, Dec. 14, 1865, p. 57; Dec. 15, 1865, p. 73; *Georgia House Journal*, Dec. 8, 1865, p. 26; Dec. 15, 1865, p. 88.

p. 283: Chinese were... "docile, sober, frugal": Ward, "Bourbon Democrats," pp. 276–78; Steven E. Anders, "Chinese Labor for the Reconstruction South: A Post-War Panacea" (paper presented at the Southern Historical Convention, Atlanta, Georgia, Nov. 11, 1983).

p. 284: "The Negro is foreordained": See A. J. McWhirter, "An Appeal to European Immigrants to Come to the South," (address to the Southern Immigration Association, 1883) in *Annals of America* (Chicago: Encyclopedia Britannica, 1968), 10:587–94.

p. 284: only 390 registered a desire: Bert James Loewenburg, "Efforts of the South to Encourage Immigration, 1865–1900," *South Atlantic Quarterly* 33 (1934) 380.

p. 284: Blacks quite naturally: For examples of its coverage of immigration, see *Voice of the Negro* 2 (Apr. 1905) 270; 2 (June 1905) 423; 2 (July 1905) 453; 2 (Sept. 1905) 595–96; 3 (Sept. 1906) 620–21; and *Voice* 4 (Jan.–Feb. 1907) 12.

p. 285: "make the woods stink": Owens, "Negro in Georgia," p. 70.

pp. 285–86: Specific local outrages: *Savannah Tribune*, Dec. 4, 1875, p. 2; Jan. 1, 1876, p. 2.

p. 286: Georgia and Alabama blacks who were fed up: Arnold Shankman, "The Images of Mexico and the Mexican-American in the Black Press: 1890–1935," *Journal of Ethnic Studies* 3 (Summer 1975) 44; see also U.S. Congress, House, *Message of the President re Failure of the Scheme for the Colonization of Negroes in Mexico*, H. Doc. 169, 54th Cong., 1st sess., 1896 (SS 3420); Robert Lewis Williams, Jr., "The Negroes' Migration to Latin America," *Negro History Bulletin* 19 (Feb. 1956) 102.

p. 287: "glib (labor) agent": *Savannah Tribune*, Apr. 6, 1889, p. 2.

p. 288: "Pegleg" Williams: Matthews, "Race Relations," pp. 245–46.

p. 289: "Not a month passes": *Voice of the Negro* 1 (May 1904) 209–10.

p. 289: Owing to the posting: *Chicago Defender*, Jan. 28, 1911, p. 1.

p. 290: "As long as what *is* is": Langston Hughes, "Toast to Harlem," in *The Best of Simple* (New York: Hill and Wang, 1961), p. 23.

p. 291: "There is scarcely a Negro mother": Scott, *Negro Migration*, p. 172; see also Scott, "Letters of Negro Migrants."

p. 291: "Lynching and mob violence": Matthews, "Race Relations," p. 253.

p. 291: "we go bankrupt": *Macon Telegraph* cited in *Crisis* 13 (Nov. 1916) 22; see also Matthews, "Race Relations," p. 256; Henri, *Black Migration*, p. 62.

p. 291: "Surliness now exists": *Crisis* 13 (Dec. 1916) 62, 89.

pp. 292: Why should I remain: Roi Ottley, *The Lonely Warrior: The Life and Times of Robert S. Abbott* (Chicago: University of Chicago Press, 1955), p. 167.

p. 292: Go North... "as the most effective protest": *Crisis* 13 (Jan. 1917) 115.

p. 293: They have allowed...: Ottley, *Lonely Warrior*, pp. 79–80.

p. 294: "from men who a year before": St. Clair Drake and Horace R. Clayton, *Black Metropolis: A Study of Negro Life in a Northern City* (New York: Harcourt, Brace, 1945), p. 59.

p. 295: "the situation in Georgia": *Chicago Defender*, Apr. 28, 1923; Nov. 21, 1925; see also John William Fanning, "Negro Migration," Phelps-Stokes Studies No. 9; *Bulletin of the University of Georgia*, No. 30, June 1930.

p. 296: "Migration and the economic pressure": Matthews, "Race Relations," p. 257.

p. 296: whites would be "activated by economic conditions": *Chicago Broad Ax*, Nov. 24, 1923, p. 1.

8

THE "NEW NEGRO"

pp. 297–98: Henry O. Flipper: See Flipper, *Colored Cadet*, and William P. Vaughn, "West Point and the First Negro Cadet," *Military Affairs* 35 (Oct. 1971) 100–102.

p. 298: "He is smart, they say": *Savannah Tribune*, July 22, 1876, p. 1.

p. 299: In 1889, black soldiers from Georgia: Ibid., July 27, 1889, p. 2.

p. 300: "Marching Through Georgia": Ibid., Jan. 7, 1893, p. 3.

p. 300: Black units fell victim to increasing racism: See Matthews, "Race Relations," pp. 336–37.

p. 301: "They knew no such word as fear": David F. Trask, *The War With Spain in 1898* (New York: Macmillan, 1981), p. 237.

p. 302: black veterans were...whipped in the streets: *Chicago Defender,* Apr. 15, 1911, p. 1; *Crisis* 2 (July 1911) 100.

p. 302: black troops...protect the White House: James Weldon Johnson, *Along This Way* (New York: Viking, 1933), p. 319

p. 302–3: Blacks put aside their special grievances...mixed emotions: Matthews, "Race Relations," pp. 350–53; *Crisis* 16 (Sept. 1918) 231.

p. 303: Fulton and Taliaferro draft boards: Ibid., 15 (Feb. 1918) 192; 16 (May 1918) 33.

p. 305: "by fraudulently arresting colored men": Dittmer, *Black Georgia,* p. 198; see also Barbeau and Henri, *Unknown Soldiers,* p. 37.

p. 305: "the wartime flurry": Matthews, "Race Relations," p. 354.

p. 306: Asa Candler...offered low-interest loans: U.S. Commission on Civil Rights, *Decline of Black Farming,* p. 23.

pp. 306–7: "work or fight" controversy: See Walter F. White, "'Work or Fight' in the South," in Foner, *Voice of Black America,* pp. 724–29; see also Dittmer, *Black Georgia,* pp. 198–99; *Crisis* 15 (Nov. 1917) 32; 17 (Apr. 1919) 281, 283; 18 (June 1919) 97.

p. 307: At least ten black soldiers were lynched: 66th Cong., 2d sess., House Doc. 1027, *Report on the Lynching of Ex-Soldiers,* May 22, 1920; Barbeau and Henri, *Unknown Soldiers,* pp. 175–77; Ginzburg, *100 Years,* pp. 118, 125; Dittmer, *Black Georgia,* p. 204; *Crisis* 18 (July 1919) 155; 18 (Oct. 1919) 309; 19 (Nov. 1919) 349; 20 (Aug. 1920) 167; *Chicago Defender,* April 5, 1919, p. 1; May 17, 1919, p. 1; Sept. 6, 1919, p. 1

p. 308: "Southern Bourbons": *Crisis* 14 (June 1917) 61.

p. 312: "We go to Atlanta": *Crisis* 20 (May 1920) 5.

p. 313: "Did you ever know": correspondence cited in Matthews, "Race Relations," p. 238.

p. 314: "the despair of radicals": Herbert J. Seligmann, *The Negro Faces America* (New York: Harper, 1920), p. 281.

p. 314: "Practically every single thing": James Weldon Johnson, "Statement to the Senate Judiciary Committee," Jan. 29, 1920.

p. 314: "keen sense of propriety": Letter from Crogman to Grimké, Aug. 9, 1927, in Grimké, *The Works of Francis James Grimké,* edited by Carter G. Woodson (Washington: Associated Publishers, 1942) 4:417.

pp. 314–15: "How many of us": Letter from P. N. Pittenger reprinted in *Competitor* 2 (Oct.–Nov. 1920) 192.

p. 317: "After her clothes burned off": Dittmer, *Black Georgia,* p. 201. For a listing of Georgia lynchings in 1918, see *Crisis* 17 (Feb. 1919) 180–81.

p. 317: the "Negro had been run over": *Chicago Defender,* Sept. 6, 1919, p. 1.

p. 322: Alexander advised Mays: Mays, *Born to Rebel,* pp. 93–96.

p. 324: "Georgia—our mother": *Nation* 112 (May 25, 1921) 727; see also *Atlanta Constitution,* May 22, 1921, p. 3–A; *New York Times,* May 16, 1921, p. 15.

p. 327: "an unhealthy unity": William N. Colson, "Bourbonism in the Southern Press," *Messenger,* Aug. 1920, pp. 71–72.

p. 327: "Lynching is almost galloping": *Atlanta Constitution,* Jan. 12, 1930, p. 10–A.

p. 328: "So far as I can see" and "Will Alexander is entirely too optimistic": Letter from Alexander to Walter White, Sept. 8, 1930; memorandum from William Pickens to White dated Oct. 1, 1930, NAACP Files, C–217.

p. 329: "few sales": George Fort Milton, "Reflections on the Vanishing Mob" (unpub. ms., Milton Papers, box 88).

pp. 333–34: The sheriff walked off and left the Negro to be burned: Hall, *Ames,* p. 225.

p. 334: Martin Luther King, Sr.: King, *Daddy King,* p. 65.

p. 335: "storm the polls": *Competitor* 3 (Apr. 1921) 28.

p. 336: "unscrupulous"..."sleek, fat, potbellied Negro politicians": Dittmer, *Black Georgia,* pp. 93–94; Theodore Kornweibel, *No Crystal Stair: Black Life and the Messenger* (Westport, Conn.: Greenwood Press, 1975), p. 241.

p. 336: "death to mob law": *St. Louis Argus,* Nov. 12, 1920, p. 1.

p. 337: "I am not going to appoint": Ibid., Aug. 6, 1921, p. 1.

p. 337: Leonidas Dyer told blacks: Ibid., Oct. 18, 1924, p. 17.

p. 338: "I used to view with sardonic pleasure": Robert H. Brisbane, "Davis, Benjamin J(efferson) Sr.," *Dictionary of American Negro Biography,* p. 159.

p. 339: S. S. Mincey: Grant, *Anti-Lynching,* p. 164.

9

The Depression, New Deal, and World War II

p. 342: "an isolated phenomenon": Susan Brownmiller, *Against Our Will: Men, Women, and Rape* (New York: Simon and Schuster, 1975), p. 227.

p. 343: "the biggest biracial demonstration": See Charles H. Martin, *Herndon Case,* pp. 1–6.

p. 343: Jesse Crawford: Jesse Crawford, "Cheating the Georgia Chain Gang," originally published in *Crisis* (June 1938); reprinted in Aptheker, *Documentary History* 4: 318–24.

p. 349: One of Georgia's most shameful traditions was peonage: See Herbert Aptheker, *Afro-American History: The Modern Era* (New York: Citadel Press, 1971), pp. 192–200; Daniels, *Shadow of Slavery,* pp. 175–81. Georgia's contract law was overturned in *Taylor v. Georgia* 315 US 25 (1942).

p. 350: "former positions as tenants": Holmes, *New Deal in Georgia,* pp. 284–87.

p. 350: "rabid" opponent of the New Deal: Ibid., p. 132.

p. 351: "You kiss the Negroes": Sitkoff, *New Deal,* p. 106.

p. 352: "Niggers have been ruled out": Ibid., p. 98.

p. 353: "the extension to every individual": Georgia State Department of Education, *The Open Road: Program for the Improvement of Instruction in the Public Schools,* cited in Alfonso Elder, "About Negro Education," *Phylon* 2 (1st Qtr. 1941) 74.

pp. 356–57: "The Cocking affair": See Bailes, "Talmadge and the Board of Regents," pp. 409–23; Anderson, *Wild Man,* pp. 197–204; and Walter Cocking, *Report of the Study of Higher Education of Negroes in Georgia* (Athens, 1938).

p. 357: "If a nigger": *Nation* 155 (Sept. 19, 1942) 223.

p. 358: To "persuade" Talmadge: See Williams, *The Bonds,* pp. 139–42.

pp. 359–60: military uprising and... nefarious plots: For examples of whites' fears of black militancy, see Howard W. Odum, *Race and Rumors of Race* (Chapel Hill: University of North Carolina Press, 1943).

p. 360: Claude Screws: See Robert K. Carr, "*Screws v. United States*: The Georgia Police Brutality Case," *Cornell Law Quarterly* 31 (1945) 48–67.

p. 360: the beating of Roland Hayes: *New York Times,* July 17, 1942, p. 9:5; July 24, 1942, p. 33:5; *Pittsburgh Courier,* July 25, 1942, p. 1; *Nation* 155 (Sept. 19, 1942) 238.

p. 363: Columbians: Harold R. Martin, *Ralph McGill, Reporter* (Boston: Little, Brown, 1973), pp. 128–30.

10

POSTWAR PROGRESS

p. 364: "If I get a Negro vote": Belvin, "Georgia Primary of 1946," p. 43; see also Anderson, *Wild Man*, pp. 229–30.

p. 365: more registered white voters than white people: Bernd and Holland, "The Case of Georgia," p. 407; see also Bernd, "White Supremacy and Disfranchisement."

p. 366: "asking God": Mays, *Born to Rebel*, p. 223.

p. 367: "My God": Wilkins, *Standing Fast*, pp. 192–93.

p. 367: "blood would flow in the streets": *New York Times*, Mar. 3, 1948, p. 3:6.

p. 370: Fellowship of the Concerned: See Arnold Shankman, "Dorothy Tilly and the Fellowship of the Concerned," in Fraser and Moore, eds., *From the Old South to the New*, pp. 241–49.

p. 373: Georgia was not ready "just now": *New York Times*, Nov. 12, 1939, IV, p. 10:7.

p. 373: Up to 2,700 black students: Williams, *The Bonds*, pp. 138–39.

p. 374: "We had to guarantee": King, *Daddy King*, p. 125.

p. 374: "final rush on Jim Crow": Wilkins, *Standing Fast*, p. 211.

p. 374: "strife and bloodshed": *New York Times*, Aug. 18, 1953, p. 25:4.

p. 375: Articles in the national press: See Harold C. Fleming, "The South Will Go Along," *New Republic* 130 (May 31, 1954) 6–7; Hodding Carter, "The Court's Decision and the South," *Reader's Digest*, Sept. 1954, pp. 51–56.

p. 376: National Association for the Preservation of the White Race: *New York Times*, July 7, 1954, p. 34:8; see also R. Ray McCain, "Reactions to the United States Supreme Court Decision of 1954," *Georgia Historical Quarterly* 52 (1968) 371–87.

p. 376: state officials despised the NAACP: *New York Times*, Oct. 20, 1955, p. 18:7; Jan. 10, 1956, p. 42:1; Vander Zanden, *Sociology*, p. 140.

p. 377: "No matter how much": Ibid., p. 138.

pp. 377–78: persecution and terrorism directed toward Koinonia: See Lee, *Cotton Patch Evidence*, pp. 99, 121–32; *New York Times*, Feb. 17, 1957, p. 60:1; Mar. 2, 1957, p. 19:2; Mar. 24, 1957, p. 33:3; Apr. 6, 1957, p. 40:5; Apr. 18, 1957, p. 23:3; Apr. 24, 1957, p. 24:6. May 20, 1957, p. 19:1; Sept. 13, 1960, p. 33:1.

p. 379: "There is not enough money": Black, *Southern Governors*, p. 66.

p. 379: Atlanta golf course: *Holmes v. Atlanta*, 350 US 859 (1955).

p. 379: "The fight to preserve the white race": *New York Times*, Nov. 22, 1958, p. 3:1.

p. 380: "Let us hope": Ibid., Jan. 12, 1960, p. 19:1.

p. 381: "It is time": Ibid., Dec. 14, 1960, p. 24:3.

p. 381: Failure to resolve: Ibid., Jan. 19, 1961, p. 1:8.

p. 382–83: Horace Ward case: See Thomas G. Dyer, *The University of Georgia: A Bicentennial History, 1785–1985* (Athens: University of Georgia Press, 1985), pp. 303–13.

p. 383: Pfc. Winfred Mundle: See Ernest L. Mathews, "Trooper Mundle vs. the University of Georgia," *Negro History Bulletin* 20 (Feb. 1957) 23–24.

pp. 383–84: Charlayne Hunter and Hamilton Holmes: See Calvin Trillin, *An Education in Georgia* (Reprint; University of Georgia Press, 1991); see also Horace Montgomery, "Origin of the University of Georgia Faculty Resolution of 1–12–1961," *Negro History Bulletin* 21 (April 1962) 57–158; Alan Wexler, "The Lonely Years of Hamilton Holmes," *Ebony* 19 (Nov. 1963) 101–9.

11

THE CIVIL RIGHTS MOVEMENT

p. 386: Moore's killing... "demonstrated conclusively": "The Bomb Heard Around the World," *Ebony* 31 (Nov. 1975) 63–70 (reprint from April 1952).

p. 387: "We Charge Genocide": See William L. Patterson, ed., *We Charge Genocide* (New York: International Publishers, 1951).

p. 388: "not so much at his wild insistence": Watters, *Down to Now*, p. 45.

p. 388: the Rev. Robert B. McNeill: Robert B. McNeill, "A Georgia Minister Offers a Solution for the South," *Look*, May 28, 1957, pp. 55–58; see also *New York Times*, June 8, 1959, p. 1:2; June 10, 1959, p. 19:4; Sept. 27, 1959, VI, p. 16.

pp. 389–90: Montgomery Movement: see Martin Luther King, Jr., *Stride Toward Freedom: A Leader of His People Tells the Montgomery Story* (New York: Harper and Brothers, 1958).

p. 390: "If Atlanta succeeds": Oates, *Let the Trumpet Sound*, p. 130.

p. 392: "because they were terrified": Raines, *My Soul Is Rested*, pp. 103–6.

p. 394: diplomat of the Ghanaian embassy: *New York Times*, Nov. 10, 1960, p. 5:2.

p. 395: "In the worldwide struggle": Ibid., May 7, 1961, p. 1:3.

p. 395: Vandiver claimed in 1961: Ibid., May 10, 1961, p. 29:7.

p. 399: Jews... needed less prodding: See P. Allen Krause, "Rabbis and Negro Rights in the South," *American Jewish Archives* 21 (1969) 22–23; see also Janice Rothschild Blumberg, *One Voice: Rabbi Jacob M. Rothschild and the Troubled South* (Macon, Ga.: Mercer University Press, 1985).

p. 402: "Something about a Negro wearing a hat": José Yglesias, "Dr. King's March on Washington, Part II," in Meier and Rudwick, eds., *Black Protest in the Sixties*, p. 278.

pp. 402–403: black students wanted to return: Zinn, *New Abolitionists*, p. 124.

p. 403: "Those kids were going to do it": Ibid., p. 128.

p. 404: "We never should have" and "We can't tolerate": Carson, *In Struggle*, pp. 59–60.

p. 406: "We are enticed": *New York Times*, July 16, 1962, p. 47:1.

p. 406: "Select as a target": Meier and Rudwick, *CORE*, p. 168.

p. 406: "I paid my damned twenty cents": *New York Times*, Jan. 28, 1962, p. 65:4.

p. 408: "I've been thrown out": Carson, *In Struggle*, p. 61.

p. 408: outpouring of protest songs: *New York Times*, Aug. 20, 1962, p. 14:2.

p. 408: engaging "in a conspiracy": Lewis, *King*, p. 161.

p. 409: "You're too yellow to march": Watters, *Down to Now*, p. 211.

p. 413: "We want our colored people": *New York Times*, July 27, 1962, p. 1:3; Aug. 1, 1962, p. 63:4; Aug. 14, 1962, pp. 1:1, 16:4; Claude Sitton, "Sheriff Harasses Negroes at a Voting Rally in Georgia," in Meier and Rudwick, eds., *Black Protest in the Sixties*, pp. 48–52; Carson, *In Struggle*, p. 75.

p. 414: "Must we die": Ibid., p. 84.

p. 416: One reason...was its leader, Hosea Williams: See Raines, *My Soul Is Rested*, pp. 435–44.

p. 421: "The politicians who lied": Harold R. Martin, *Ralph McGill, Reporter* (Boston: Little, Brown, 1973), p. 265.

p. 423: Lemuel Penn was gunned down: See Bill Shipp, *Murder at Broad River Bridge* (Atlanta: Peachtree Publishers, 1981).

p. 424: Hoover's longtime personal crusade: See Garrow, *FBI*.

p. 425: "We ain't gonna have no dinner": Raines, *My Soul Is Rested*, pp. 410–15.

p. 428: "Blood runs down the trenches": See Williams, *The Bonds*, pp. 216–34.

p. 428: "Something is wrong with capitalism": Garrow, *Cross*, p. 537.

p. 431: "We are constantly trying" and "Truly America": Garrow, *FBI*, pp. 215, 219.

p. 431: "The movement made Martin": Garrow, *Cross*, p. 625.

p. 431: "he taught blacks": Oates, *Trumpet*, p. 372.

12
MODERN POLITICS

p. 434: Hancock County was a notable exception: See Hanks, *Struggle*, pp. 51–94, 149–50; *Macon Telegraph*, June 9, 1974, pp. 1–A, 2–A (part of a series on Hancock County entitled "A House Divided"); see also John Rozier, *Black Boss* (Athens: University of Georgia Press, 1982).

p. 438: Leroy Johnson's shrewd machinations: See Lesher, "Leroy Johnson."

p. 439: Bond was unenthusiastic about the man from Plains: Julian Bond, "Why I Don't Support Jimmy Carter," *Nation*, April 17, 1976, pp. 454–55.

p. 440: "Prayer, protest, and politics": Bond's speech was given Jan. 15, 1977.

p. 442: Taliaferro and Clay counties: *Atlanta Constitution*, Dec. 8, 1980, p. 1–A; Dec. 9, 1980, p. 1–A (both articles are part of a series entitled "Voting: A Right Still Denied").

p. 444: "Gonna have to beat": *Macon Telegraph*, Sept. 25, 1985, p. 1–B (state editions).

p. 445: a better deal: See *Atlanta Journal*, May 11, 1986, p. 7–C.

p. 445: Black leaders blamed themselves: *Atlanta Constitution*, Sept. 14, 1986, p. 24–A.

p. 446: Perry Usher ran...Stewart County: *Macon Telegraph*, June 4, 1984, p. 2–B; see also *Atlanta Journal and Constitution*, Feb. 23, 1991, p. 3–B.

p. 446–48: Blacks struggled...in Fort Valley: See Hanks, *Struggle*, pp. 96–118.

p. 448: Carson...lost their posts: *Atlanta Journal*, Apr. 8, 1982, p. 2–C.

p. 452: "the golden years for Atlanta": For a review of Young's record as mayor, see *Atlanta Journal and Constitution*, Dec. 31, 1989, pp. 1–A, 6–A.

p. 453: The proposal "came so late in his tenure": *Atlanta Constitution*, Jan. 3, 1990, p. 11–A.

p. 453: "the most powerful black leaders": Ibid., March 13, 1987, p. 5–C.

p. 453: Arrington sounded an increasingly common warning: Ibid., Aug. 8, 1986, p. 17–A.

p. 454: Lomax was accused of racism: Ibid., July 19, 1989, pp. 11–A, 1–C, 4–C; July 21, 1989, p. 1–D.

p. 457: "we are letting real power" and "who are now only concerned": Ibid., Aug. 30, 1986, p. 2–E.

13
THE STRUGGLE FOR ECONOMIC ADVANCEMENT

p. 460: "two Georgias": See Charles Floyd, "The 'Two Georgias' Problem," and "The Two Georgias Revisited," *Georgia Business and Economic Conditions* 45 (Mar.–Apr. 1985) 3–13 and 46 (May–June 1986) 1–5.

p. 460: the dollar-income disparity widened: See Albert W. Niemi, Jr., "Income and Race: The Gap Between Blacks and Whites Is Widening," *Georgia Trend*, Oct. 1989, p. 14.

p. 461: "Without Atlanta": *Atlanta Constitution*, Aug. 3, 1985, p. 1–B; see also Ibid., Feb. 10, 1986, p. 10–C; Feb. 26, 1986, pp. 1–D, 8–D.

p. 461: "They say we're the second Georgia": Ibid., Nov. 16, 1986, pp. 1–A, 12–A, 14–A (the newspaper's series ran Nov. 16–20, 1986).

p. 462: loss of land by black farmers: See U.S. Civil Rights Commission, *The Decline of Black Farming;* Browning, "Erosion"; C. Scott Graber, "A Blight Hits Black Farmers," *Civil Rights Digest* (Spring 1978) 20–29; Fisher, "Negro Farm Ownership."

p. 462: The number declined to 2,068: U.S. Department of Commerce, Bureau of the Census, 1982 *Census of Agriculture*, vol. 1, part 10, *Georgia: State and County Data* (Washington D.C.: GPO: 1982), pp. 3–4; see also Rusty Brooks and Douglas Bachtel, "Georgia's Changing Farm Population," *Issues Facing Georgia* 1 (Apr. 1983) 1–4.

p. 463: 490 of the 665 black farmers... were delinquent: *Atlanta Constitution*, May 25, 1987, p. 1–F.

p. 464: He still lived there in 1990: *Atlanta Journal and Constitution*, Feb. 4, 1990, p. 9–A.

pp. 464–65: Harris Neck: Ibid., June 3, 1979, pp. 18–B, 19–B.

p. 465: New Communities: Emergency Land Fund *Report*, May 1974; *Atlanta Journal and Constitution*, Mar. 17, 1974, p. 10–B.

p. 466: Southern Rural Action: *Atlanta Voice*, Mar. 16, 1974, p. 6; Grayson Mitchell, "Southern Rural Blacks Help Themselves," *Ebony* 30 (Jan. 1975) 78–87.

p. 467: Lockheed aircraft plant: Fishel and Quarles, *Black American*, pp. 510–13; *Ebony* 17 (June 1962) 24; Wilkins, *Standing Fast*, p. 297; Georgia State Advisory Committee, *Unfinished Business*, pp. 48–49.

p. 469: "It was a blockbuster": U. S. Department of Labor, *Negro Employment in the South*, Vol. 3, *State and Local Government* (Washington, D.C., 1973), pp. 16–17; *Atlanta Constitution*, Sept. 4, 1983, pp. 1–D, 4–D; Aug. 11, 1984, p. 24–A.

p. 469: Central State Hospital: *Macon Telegraph*, Jan. 26, 1982, p. 9–B; July 14, 1983, p. 1–A; Jan. 31, 1985, p. 1–A.

p. 470: Macon ratios were fairly typical for the state: Ibid., Dec. 3, 1984, pp. 1, 8–"Business Plus"; Suzanne A. Lindsay, "Georgia's Changing Labor Force: The Expansion of the 1980s," *Georgia Business and Economic Conditions* 49 (July–Aug. 1989) 10 (Table 4).

p. 471: By 1991, there was only one law firm: *Atlanta Constitution*, May 3, 1991, p. 3–E.

p. 472: black in-migration: Marie McGrath Libbey and Suzanne A. Lindsay, "The 1990 Census: Growth and Diversity in Georgia," *Georgia Business and*

Economic Conditions 51 (May–June 1991) 9–17; Douglas C. Bachtel, "Population Growth and Change in Georgia," *Issues Facing Georgia* 1 (Aug. 1981); see also Jack Tucker and Everett S. Lee, *The Distribution of Southern Black Population* (Atlanta: Southern Regional Council, 1973). There was disagreement over the magnitude of a Southern "homecoming" for blacks; see *Atlanta Constitution*, June 14, 1989, p. 1–C; Jan. 10, 1990, p. 1–A; Mar. 16, 1991, p. 3–A.

p. 473: Atlanta has enjoyed a dazzling reputation: "Atlanta: New Mecca for Young Blacks," *Ebony* 28 (Sept. 1973) 63; "Ten Best Cities for Blacks," Ibid., 29 (Nov. 1973) 152.

p. 474: a study...placed Augusta well ahead of Atlanta: *Atlanta Constitution*, June 19, 1986, p. 16–C.

p. 474: "Atlanta has a favorable reputation": Ibid., Mar. 6, 1991, p. 1–C.

p. 474: Recent studies had shown that Atlanta lagged: See Orfield and Ashkinaze, *The Closing Door;* Sjoquist, *Economic Status of Black Atlantans.*

p. 474: "politically empowered yet relatively small": *Atlanta Constitution*, Mar. 3, 1991, pp. 1–A, 12–A.

p. 474: study commissioned by *Georgia Trend:* Allen R. Myerson, "Black Mecca," *Georgia Trend*, Aug. 1987, pp. 52–57; see also "Is Atlanta Really a Black Mecca?" in Ibid., July 1988, p. 66.

p. 474: "The thing about Atlanta": *Atlanta Constitution*, Mar. 3, 1991, pp. 1–A; 12–A.

p. 475: one hundred most influential Georgians: "The *Georgia Trend* 100," *Georgia Trend*, Jan. 1991.

p. 475: Jackson took on the white business establishment: "How Maynard Jackson Changed Atlanta," Ibid., July 1988, p. 67; Orfield and Ashkinaze, *Closing Door*, pp. 54–55.

p. 476: Robins Air Force Base: *Macon Telegraph*, Feb. 9, 1987, pp. 1, 10–"Business Plus."

p. 478: Sweetheart concession deals and favored treatment: Stone, *Regime Politics*, pp. 146–47, 151–53; *Atlanta Constitution*, May 12, 1990, p. 1–B; Dec. 6, 1990, p. 1–E.

p. 479: less than a paradise for black attorneys: "Are Law Firms Color-Blind?" *Georgia Trend*, Jan. 1989, pp. 93–94; *Atlanta Constitution*, Feb. 20, 1990, p. 1–A; July 16, 1991, p. 3–B; July 31, 1991, p. 1–C.

p. 480: *Atlanta Daily World* (and other newspapers): Roland E. Wolseley, *The Black Press, U.S.A.* 2d ed. (Ames: Iowa State University Press, 1990), pp. 99, 124; see also Blackwell, "Blacks and the Media," pp. 77–110, 163–202; *Atlanta Constitution*, Jan. 14, 1990, pp. 1–P, 3–P; June 19, 1991, p. 1–C; July 6, 1991, p. 7–B.

p. 480: WERD in Atlanta: Blackwell, "Blacks and the Media," pp. 122–27, 154–57; Richard Skahlenberg, "Negro Radio," *Negro History Bulletin* 29 (Mar. 1966) 142.

p. 481: Henderson Travel Service: Birmingham, *Certain People*, pp. 268–69.

p. 481: *Ebony's* 1962 list: *Ebony* 17 (May 1962) 130–35.

p. 482: Atlanta Life Insurance Company: See "Insurance: Black America's Biggest Business," *Ebony* 30 (May 1975) 134–36; Henderson, *Atlanta Life Insurance Company*, p. 201; *Atlanta Constitution*, Dec. 3, 1989, pp. 1–R, 6–R; Nov. 10, 1990, p. 1–D.

p. 482: "Revenue is flat": Paul Thiel, "Jesse Hill's Dilemma," *Georgia Trend*, Mar. 1991, pp. 37–40.

p. 483: black bourgeoisie "should push away": Blackwell, "Blacks and the Media," pp. 165–66.

p. 484: 1990 black buying power in Georgia: *Atlanta Constitution,* Mar. 6, 1990, p. 1–B; July 11, 1991, p. 1–E.

p. 484: "Black Dollar Days": *Macon Telegraph,* Sept. 10, 1985, p. 5–C.

p. 484–85: Irvin Betts.... "Redlining is worse": *Atlanta Constitution,* May 2, 1988, p. 5–A (part of the newspaper's "Color of Money" series).

p. 485: Despite the odds: Ibid., Dec. 15, 1974, p. 2–B; July 16, 1987, p. 2–E; *Macon Telegraph,* Oct. 8, 1985, p. 5–B.

pp. 486–87: The Paschal brothers: *Atlanta Constitution,* May 31, 1987, pp. 1–H, 2–H; May 12, 1990, p. 1–B.

p. 487: Georgia... taxed its poor more heavily: Albert Niemi, Jr., "Who Pays: The Sales Tax Increase Hits the Poor the Hardest," *Georgia Trend,* July 1989, p. 11; *Macon Telegraph,* Jan. 15, 1987, p. 1–B; *Atlanta Constitution,* Apr. 23, 1991, p. 2–A.

14
SOCIAL PROBLEMS

p. 489: WIC aid.... food stamp program: *Atlanta Constitution,* Dec. 16, 1990, p. 11–A; June 26, 1991, p. 1–C, 8–C; July 9, 1991, p. 1–B.

p. 490: the "new poor": Ibid., Jan. 29, 1990, p. 1–A; Dec. 6, 1990, p. 1–A; June 3, 1991, p. 1–A.

p. 490: out-of-wedlock birthrate: *Macon Telegraph,* Aug. 29, 1985, p. 2–B; Georgia Department of Human Resources, *1989 Vital Statistics Report,* Vol. 1, *Georgia Births* (Atlanta: DHR, 1990), p. 13; *Atlanta Constitution,* Mar. 25, 1990, pp. 1–D, 8–D, 9–D; Aug. 16, 1990, pp. 1–A, 9–A.

pp. 490–91: Welfare payments in Georgia: Georgia Office of Planning and Budget, *Georgia Descriptions in Data 1986* (Atlanta: OPB) pp. 167, 168; *Macon Telegraph,* Apr. 17, 1986, p. 3–B; Orfield and Ashkinaze, *Closing Door,* p. 226; *Atlanta Constitution,* May 19, 1988, p. 5–C.

p. 491: CETA and JTPA: See Orfield and Ashkinaze, *Closing Door,* pp. 176–77, 181–83. (Chapter 7 deals extensively with job training programs in Atlanta during the 1980s.)

p. 492: "a new kind of slavery": *Atlanta Constitution,* May 12, 1991, p. 1–C.

p. 492: the South's ten "most deadly" counties: See "In Sickness and in Wealth," Ibid., Sept. 30, 1990, pp. 1–A, 10–A, 12–A.

pp. 492–93: Infant death rates: Glen Sisk, "Negro Health in Atlanta," *Negro History Bulletin* 27 (Dec. 1963) 65–66; *Atlanta Constitution,* May 8, 1983, pp. 1–A, 10–A; Oct. 6, 1990, pp. 1–A, 13–A; Georgia Department of Human Resources, *1989 Vital Statistics Report,* Vol. 2, *Georgia Mortality* (Atlanta: DHR, 1990), p. 14.

p. 494: Otis Wesley Smith: *New York Times,* Mar. 27, 1958, p. 28:7.

p. 495: "less of a doctor": Interview with Dr. Johnson in *Macon Telegraph,* June 11, 1984, p. 1–B.

p. 497: city-sponsored study of rental housing: *Atlanta Constitution,* May 14, 1989, pp. 1–A, 8–A.

p. 497: "blockbusters" in the Flat Shoals area: Ibid., June 9, 1974, p. 2–A.

p. 498: only 10 percent of white Georgians: Ibid., June 30, 1991, pp. 1–A, 11–A.

pp. 498–99: "The Color of Money": See *Atlanta Journal and Constitution*, May 1–4, 1988; see also Paul Thiel, "Holding Up a Big Bank Deal," *Georgia Trend*, June 1990, pp. 72–78, and "The Fading Dream of Homeownership," Ibid., June 1991, pp. 82–83.

p. 499: "the dirtiest business in Georgia": William R. Smith, "Easy Credit, Tough Terms," Ibid., Dec. 1989, pp. 73–74; see also *Atlanta Constitution*, Oct. 12, 1990, p. 8–A.

p. 500: The problem of homelessness worsened: Ibid., Sept. 18, 1990, pp. 1–D, 4–D; Nov. 26, 1990, pp. 1–D, 4–D.

p. 501: U. S. Postal Service... curtailed service: See Ibid., Dec. 16, 1988, pp. 1–A, 12–A; Dec. 17, 1988, pp. 1–A, 19–A; Dec. 21, 1988, p. 6–D.

p. 502: "The area's residential streets": Paul Thiel, "Where Money Is Not Enough," *Georgia Trend*, Feb. 1991, pp. 61–63.

p. 502: housing opportunities grew increasingly more limited.... "Unequal housing for those blacks": Orfield and Ashkinaze, *Closing Door*, pp. 81–82, 101–102.

p. 503: throwing money "down a rat hole": *Macon Telegraph*, July 20, 1983, p. 1–B.

p. 503: what black men already knew: *Atlanta Constitution*, June 18, 1990, p. 11–A; Aug. 17, 1990, p. 1–A; Nov. 2, 1990, pp. 1–A, 12–A.

p. 505: sensational CBS television docudrama: For the basis of its story, see Chet Dettlinger and Jeff Prugh, *The List* (Atlanta: Philmay Enterprises, 1983). See *Atlanta Constitution*, June 16, 1991, "Perspective" section for a ten-year retrospective on the Missing and Murdered Children case.

p. 508: "that black life is cheaper": Ibid., Nov. 20, 1990, p. 1–B.

p. 508: he could not print stories of police brutality: "The Police Just Laughed," *Southern Exposure* 8 (Summer 1980) 69.

p. 508: "No account I had read": Watters, *Down to Now*, p. 33.

p. 509: John Wallace... killed Wilson Turner: For an account of the Wallace case, see Margaret Anne Barnes, *Murder in Coweta County* (New York: Readers Digest Press, 1976).

p. 510: tougher training standards for barbers: *Atlanta Constitution*, Sept. 4, 1990, p. 1–D.

p. 512: Savannah's first black policemen: *New York Times*, June 26, 1947, p. 13:1.

p. 514: 64 percent of the men... were unemployed: *Atlanta Constitution*, Apr. 30, 1989, p. 14–A.

p. 514: "patchwork justice": *Macon Telegraph*, March 29, 1987, p. 1–A; see also *Atlanta Constitution*, Dec. 9, 1989, p. 13–C; *Atlanta Journal*, Dec. 14, 1987, p. 1–A.

p. 515: Fulton County Public Defender's Office: *Atlanta Constitution*, Oct. 3, 1990, p. 3–D; Jan. 6, 1991, pp. 1–A, 12–A.

p. 515: disturbing practice in rural Georgia: *Atlanta Journal*, Dec. 14, 1987, p. 1–A.

p. 516: Jasper County was not unique in 1962: *New York Times*, Jan. 7, 1962, VI, p. 81.

pp. 516–17: investigation into sentencing disparities: *Atlanta Constitution*, Apr. 30, 1989, pp. 14–A, 16–A.

p. 517: juvenile justice system was plagued: Ibid., June 21, 1990, p. 1–A; Aug. 14, 1990, p. 1–A; Oct. 19, 1990, p. 1–E.

p. 517: Georgia has never been noted for sparing its children: See Ibid., Feb. 2, 1987, pp. 1–B, 2–B.

p. 518: Over the next ten years, the complexion: See "Who Shall Die?" series in Ibid., Oct. 13–16, 1986.

p. 519: "valley of death": Ibid., July 10, 1991, p. 1–A; July 11, 1991, p. 1–E.

p. 519: Conditions were so bad there in 1957: Gene Guerrero, "Scientific Penology Comes to Georgia," *Southern Exposure* 4 (Winter 1978) 42.

p. 520: guards stood by and watched: *Atlanta Constitution*, Sept. 5, 1982, pp. 1–A, 20–A.

p. 522: "You're dealing with": Ibid., Sept. 15, 1990, p. 1–B.

15
MODERN EDUCATION AND CULTURE

p. 524: Taliaferro County School Board: *Atlanta Constitution*, Oct. 15, 1965, pp. 1–A, 17–A; see also *Time*, Jan. 26, 1976, p. 66.

p. 524: *U.S. v. Jefferson County School Board:* For a history of desegregation cases in the 1960s, see Metcalf, *From Little Rock to Boston.*

p. 527: "a blight on the state": *Macon Telegraph*, Feb. 9, 1984, pp. 1–B, 2–B; Feb. 14, 1984, p. 10–A; Oct. 10, 1986, p. 19–A; see also *Atlanta Constitution*, "Black and White Together," May 16, 1979, pp. 22–23.

p. 528: Atlanta's changes were modified: See Ibid., Nov. 19, 1972, pp. 1–A, 15–A; Mar. 4, 1973, pp. 1–A, 16–A; "Black and White Together," May 16, 1979, pp. 20–21.

p. 530: "a giant powdered-sugar jelly doughnut": Ibid., Oct. 1, 1987, p. 11–A (the article was part of a seven-part series entitled, "Divided We Stand: The Resegregation of Our Public Schools").

p. 531: University of Michigan professor's study: See *Atlanta Inquirer*, Feb. 18, 1978, p. 1; Metcalf, *From Little Rock to Boston*, pp. 53, 92.

p. 533: acts of racism were "more acceptable": *Atlanta Constitution*, Jan. 11, 1991, p. G–2.

p. 534: 99.4 percent...passed: Ibid., Sept. 13, 1990, p. 1–E; Sept. 18, 1990, p. 12–A.

pp. 535: widespread evidence of disparities in school discipline: Ibid., July 10, 1988, pp. 1–A, 6–A.

p. 535: "tracking" students....general diplomas: See Ibid., Oct. 2, 1987, p. 1–A; May 26, 1991, p. 1–A, 6–A.

p. 535: 45 percent of blacks who got college-preparatory diplomas: Ibid., June 6, 1990, pp. 1–A, 8–A.

p. 535: "There are many counties": Alan Ehrenhalt, "The High Cost of No-Frills Education," *Georgia Trend*, Jan. 1990, pp. 50–55; see also Southern Regional Council, *Decade of Frustration.*

p. 536: Our worst schools: Williams, *The Bonds*, p. 174.

p. 537: blacks...would earn 18 percent less: *Atlanta Constitution*, Jan. 24, 1987, p. 1–B.

pp. 539–40: Then the university lost interest in them: A national news magazine in 1990 checked up on the offensive starters for Georgia's 1980 national championship team and reported only three had graduated. See Alvin Sanoff and Joannie M. Schrof, "The Price of Victory," *U.S. News and World Report*, Jan. 8, 1990, pp. 44–50.

16
Civil Rights and Race Relations

p. 551: "The very thought": *Time*, Aug. 18, 1980, p. 24.

p. 551: "worse than Nixon": Ibid., Sept. 7, 1981, p. 9.

p. 551: "The South will rise again": *Atlanta Constitution*, Oct. 16, 1984, p. 1–A.

p. 553: Williams called the King Center elitist: *Atlanta Constitution*, Jan. 17, 1986, p. 1–A.

pp. 553–54: Abernathy...was not invited: See Ibid., Jan. 18, 1986, p. 10–A.

p. 560: "The real threat": Ibid., Nov. 16, 1990, p. 15–A.

p. 560: 1979 and 1991 polls: Ibid., May 16, 1979, p. 1–A; Jan. 9, 1991, p. 3–A.

p. 560: Xernona Clayton was "disinvited": Ibid., Apr. 18, 1987, p. 18–A; Apr. 22, 1987, p. 6–D.

p. 560: Tommie Faye Bateman: Ibid., Aug. 13–16, 1987.

p. 560: letter to the news media: The letter was sent to WAGA-TV and read during a newscast. For its contents, see *Atlanta Constitution*, Dec. 29, 1989, p. 1–A.

p. 561: "entrenched and occasional violent resistance": Ibid., Jan. 24, 1990, p. 1–A.

p. 564: Abernathy was reviled: See Abernathy, *And the Walls Came Tumbling Down* (New York: Harper & Row, 1989), pp. 434–36; *Atlanta Constitution*, Oct. 11, 1989, p. 1–D; Oct. 29, 1989, p. 2–B; David J. Garrow, "The Misguided Sanitizing of King's Image," in Ibid., Oct. 22, 1989, p. 1–H, 2–H; Oct. 25, 1989, p. 5–A; Nov. 11, 1989, p. 5–A; Mar. 18, 1990, p. 1–M. For coverage of Abernathy's death and funeral as well as tributes to him, see Ibid., Apr. 18–29, 1990, passim.

Select Bibliography

Archival Material

Commission for Interracial Cooperation Collection, Trevor Arnett Library, Atlanta University.
George Fort Milton Papers, Library of Congress.
NAACP Administrative Files, Library of Congress.
U.S. Department of Justice Files, National Archives.
U.S. Employment Service, Division of Negro Labor ("Oxley Files"), National Archives.
Carter G. Woodson Collection, Library of Congress.

Government Documents and Publications

40th Cong., 3d sess., House Miscellaneous Document 52, *Condition of Affairs in Georgia* (1869).
42nd Cong., 2d sess., House Report No. 22: *Report of the Joint Select Committee to Inquire into the Condition of Affairs in the Late Insurrectionary States* (Ku Klux Klan Hearings) (1872).
66th Cong., 2d sess., House Document 1027, *Report on the Lynching of Ex-Soldiers* (1920).
67th Cong., 1st sess., House Committee on Rules, *Ku Klux Klan Hearings* (1921).
73d Cong., 2d sess., Senate, *Punishment for the Crime of Lynching: Hearings before a Subcommittee of the Committee on the Judiciary* (1934).
74th Cong., 1st sess., *Punishment for the Crime of Lynching* (1935).
76th Cong., 3d sess., Senate Report 1380, *Lynching Goes Underground* (1940).
90th Cong., 1st sess., House Committee on Un-American Activities, *The Present-Day Ku Klux Klan Movement* (1967).
Congressional Globe
Congressional Record
Georgia House Journal
Georgia Senate Journal

Journal of the Constitutional Convention, State of Georgia 1867–1868.
U.S. Commission on Civil Rights, *Civil Rights Update.*
————. *Perspectives.*
————. *The Decline of Black Farming in America* (1982).
————. *Desegregation of the Nation's Public Schools: A Status Report* (1979).
————. *Statement on Metropolitan School Desegregation* (1977).
————. *The Voting Rights Act: Unfulfilled Goals* (1981).
U.S. Department of Commerce, Bureau of the Census, *Negro Employment in the South,* Vol. 3, *State and Local Government* (1973).

Miscellaneous Reports and Documents

Georgia State Advisory Committee, U.S. Commission on Civil Rights. *The Unfinished Business: Twenty Years Later.* Washington, D.C.: GPO, 1977.
NAACP. "The Lynchings in Brooks and Lowndes Counties, Georgia" (1918).
Proceedings of the Freedmen's Convention of Georgia, Assembled at Augusta, January 10th, 1866, Containing the Speeches of General Tillson, Capt. J. E. Bryant, and Others. Augusta: The Loyal Georgian, 1866.
Sjoquist, David. *The Economic Status of Black Atlantans,* Research Paper No. 3. Atlanta: Georgia State University College of Business Administration, 1989.

Newspapers and Periodicals

African Repository
Atlanta Constitution
Atlanta Independent
Atlanta Inquirer
Atlanta Journal
Broad Ax
Chicago Defender
Civil Liberties
Civil Rights Digest
Crisis
Ebony
Forum
Georgia Trend
Independent
Macon Telegraph and News
Nation
Negro History Bulletin
New York Age
New York Freeman
New York Times
Savannah Tribune
Southern Changes
Southern Exposure
Voice of the Negro

Books

Abernathy, Ralph. *And the Walls Came Tumbling Down*. New York: Harper Collins, 1989.

Allen, Robert L. *Reluctant Reformers: Racism and Social Reform Movements in the United States*. Anchor Books. Garden City, N.Y.: Anchor Press/Doubleday, 1975.

Ames, Jessie Daniel. *The Changing Character of Lynching*. Atlanta: CIC, 1942.

Anderson, William. *The Wild Man From Sugar Creek: The Political Career of Eugene Talmadge*. Baton Rouge: Louisiana State University Press, 1975.

Aptheker, Herbert. *American Negro Slave Revolts*. New York: International Publishers, 1969.

———. *A Documentary History of the Negro People in the United States*. Vol. 1: *From Colonial Times Through the Civil War*. Secaucus, N.J.: Citadel Press, 1971; Vol. 2: *From the Reconstruction Years to the Founding of the NAACP in 1910*. Secaucus, N.J.: Citadel Press, 1972; Vol. 4: *From the Beginning of the New Deal to the End of the Second World War*. Secaucus, N.J.: Citadel Press, 1974.

Arnett, Alex Mathews. *The Populist Movement in Georgia: A View of the "Agrarian Crusade" in the Light of Solid-South Politics*. Reprint. New York: AMS Press, 1967.

Ayers, Edward L. *Vengence and Justice: Crime and Punishment in the 19th Century American South*. New York: Oxford University Press, 1984.

Barbeau, Arthur E., and Florette Henri. *The Unknown Soldiers: Black American Troops in World War I*. Philadelphia: Temple University Press, 1974.

Bardolph, Richard. *The Negro Vanguard*. Vintage Books. New York: Random House, 1959.

Bass, Jack. *Unlikely Heroes: The Dramatic Story of the Southern Judges of the Fifth Circuit Who Translated the Supreme Court's Brown Decision into a Revolution for Equality*. New York: Simon and Schuster, 1981.

Bergman, Peter M., and Jean McCarroll. *The Negro in the Congressional Record*. 8 vols. New York: Bergman, 1969.

Berlin, Ira. *Slaves Without Masters: The Free Negro in the Antebellum South*. Vintage Books. New York: Random House, 1976.

Berry, Mary Frances. *Black Resistance/White Law*. New York: Meredith, 1971.

Berry, Mary Frances, and John Blassingame. *Long Memory: The Black Experience in America*. New York: Oxford University Press, 1982.

Birmingham, Stephen. *Certain People: America's Black Elite*. Boston: Little, Brown, 1977.

Black, Earl. *Southern Governors and Civil Rights: Racial Segregation as a Campaign Issue in the Second Reconstruction*. Cambridge, Mass.: Harvard University Press, 1976.

Blassingame, John. *The Slave Community: Plantation Life in the Ante-Bellum South*. New York: Oxford University Press, 1972.

———, ed. *Slave Testimony*. Baton Rouge: Louisiana State University Press, 1977.

Branch, Taylor. *Parting the Waters: America in the King Years 1954–1963*. New York: Simon and Schuster, 1988.

Broderick, Francis L., and August Meier, eds. *Negro Protest Thought in the Twentieth Century*. Indianapolis: Bobbs-Merrill, 1965.

Brown, John. *Slave Life in Georgia, A Narrative of the Life, Sufferings, and Escape of John Brown, a Fugitive Slave.* Edited by F. N. Boney. Savannah: Beehive Press, 1972.

Bullock, Henry Allen. *A History of Negro Education in the South: From 1619 to the Present.* New York: Praeger, 1970.

Cable, George Washington. *The Negro Question: A Selection of Writings on Civil Rights in the South.* Edited by Arlin Turner. (Orig. pub. 1958) New York: W. W. Norton, 1968.

Campbell, Tunis G. *Sufferings of the Rev. T. G. Campbell and His Family in Georgia.* Washington: Enterprise Press, 1877.

Candler, Allen D., ed. *The Colonial Records of the State of Georgia.* 26 vols. Atlanta: Franklin Printing and Publishing Co., 1904–16.

Carson, Clayborne. *In Struggle: SNCC and the Black Awakening of the 1960s.* Cambridge: Harvard University Press, 1981.

Catterall, Helen T. *Judicial Cases Concerning American Slavery.* Vol. 3, *Cases from the Courts of Georgia, Florida, Alabama, and Louisiana.* New York: Negro Universities Press, 1968.

Cluster, Dick. *They Should Have Served That Cup of Coffee.* Boston: South End Press, 1979.

Coleman, Kenneth, et al. *A History of Georgia.* Athens: University of Georgia Press, 1977.

————. *The American Revolution in Georgia: 1763–1789.* Athens: University of Georgia Press, 1958.

Coleman, Kenneth and Charles Stephen Gurr, eds. *Dictionary of Georgia Biography.* 2 vols. Athens: University of Georgia Press, 1983.

Commission on Interracial Cooperation. *The Mob Still Rides: A Review of the Lynching Record, 1931–1935.* Atlanta: CIC, 1936.

Cook, Raymond Allen. *Fire From the Flint: The Amazing Careers of Thomas Dixon.* Winston-Salem: John F. Blair, 1968.

Cox, LaWanda, and John H., eds. *Reconstruction, The Negro, and the New South.* Harper Torchbooks. New York: Harper & Row, 1973.

Cox, Oliver Cromwell. *Caste, Class, and Race.* Garden City, N.Y.: Doubleday, 1948.

Daniel, Pete. *The Shadow of Slavery: Peonage in the South: 1901–1969.* Urbana: University of Illinois Press, 1972.

Davis, Allison et al. *Deep South: A Social Anthropological Study of Caste and Class.* Chicago: University of Chicago Press, 1941.

Degler, Carl N. *The Other South: Southern Dissenters in the Nineteenth Century.* Harper Torchbooks. New York: Harper & Row, 1974.

Dittmer, John Avery. *Black Georgia in the Progressive Era, 1900–1920.* Urbana: University of Illinois Press, 1977.

Dollard, John. *Caste and Class in a Southern Town.* New Haven: Yale University Press, 1937.

Drago, Edmund L. *Black Politicians and Reconstruction in Georgia: A Splendid Failure.* Baton Rouge: Louisiana State University Press, 1982.

Du Bois, William Edgar Burghardt. *The Autobiography of W. E. B. Du Bois.* Edited by Herbert Aptheker. New York: International Publishers, 1968.

————. *The Correspondence of W. E. B. Du Bois.* Edited by Herbert Aptheker. Vol. 1: *1879–1934.* Boston: University of Massachusetts Press, 1973.

————. *Black Reconstruction in America: 1860–1880.* Reprint. New York: Atheneum, 1973.

————. *The Negro in the South: His Economic Progress in Relation to His Moral and Religious Development.* Philadelphia: George W. Jacobs, 1907.

————. *The Suppression of the African Slave Trade to the United States of America 1638–1870.* Reprint. Millwood, New York: Kraus Thomsom, Ltd., 1973.

Duncan, Russell. *Freedom's Shore: Tunis Campbell and the Georgia Freedmen.* Athens: University of Georgia Press, 1986.

Dykeman, Wilma, and James Stokely. *Seeds of Southern Change: The Life of Will Alexander.* Chicago: University of Chicago Press, 1962.

Federal Writers Project. *Drums and Shadows: Survival Studies Among the Georgia Coastal Negroes.* Westport, Conn.: Greenwood Press, 1972.

Fishel, Leslie H., Jr., and Benjamin Quarles. *The Black American: A Documentary History.* Glenview, Ill.: Scott, Foresman, 1970.

Flanders, Ralph B. *Plantation Slavery in Georgia.* Chapel Hill: University of North Carolina Press, 1933.

Flipper, Henry O. *The Colored Cadet at West Point: Autobiography of Henry Ossian Flipper.* (Orig. pub. 1878) New York: Johnson, 1968.

Fogel, Robert William, and Stanley L. Engerman. *Time on the Cross: The Economics of American Negro Slavery.* 2 vols. Boston: Little, Brown, 1974.

Foner, Eric. *Reconstruction: America's Unfinished Revolution, 1863–1877.* New York: Harper & Row, 1988.

Foner, Jack D. *Blacks and the Military in American History.* New York: Praeger, 1974.

Foner, Philip S. *History of Black Americans.* Vol. 1: *From Africa to the Emergence of the Cotton Kingdom.* Westport, Conn.: Greenwood Press, 1975.

————. *Organized Labor and the Black Worker, 1619–1973.* New York: International Publishers, 1974.

————, ed. *The Voice of Black America: Major Speeches by Negroes in the United States.* New York: Simon and Schuster, 1972.

Forman, James. *The Making of Black Revolutionaries: A Personal Account.* New York: Macmillan, 1972.

Fraser, Walter J., Jr., and Winfred B. Moore Jr., eds. *From the Old South to the New: Essays on the Transitional South.* Westport, Conn.: Greenwood Press, 1981.

Franklin, John Hope. *From Slavery to Freedom.* 4th ed. New York: Knopf, 1974.

Garrow, David. *Bearing the Cross: Martin Luther King, Jr., and the Southern Christian Leadership Conference.* Vintage Books. New York: Random House, 1988.

————. *The FBI and Martin Luther King, Jr.* New York: W. W. Norton, 1981.

Gaston, Paul M. *The New South Creed: A Study in Southern Mythmaking.* New York: Alfred A. Knopf, 1970.

Genovese, Eugene D. *The Political Economy of Slavery.* Vintage Books. New York: Random House, 1967.

————. *Roll, Jordan, Roll: The World the Slaves Made.* New York: Random House, 1974.

Ginzburg, Ralph. *100 Years of Lynching.* New York: Lancer Books, 1969.

Gordon, Asa A. *The Georgia Negro: A History.* Ann Arbor, Mich.: Edwards Brothers, 1937.

Grant, Donald L. *The Anti-Lynching Movement: 1883–1932.* San Francisco: R & E Research Associates, 1975.

Guzman, Jessie P., and Woodrow W. Hall. *Desegregation and the Southern States: Legal Action and Voluntary Group Action*. Tuskegee: Tuskegee Institute Department of Records and Research, 1958.

Hall, Jacquelyn Dowd. *Revolt Against Chivalry: Jessie Daniel Ames and the Women's Campaign Against Lynching*. New York: Columbia University Press, 1979.

Halliburton, R., Jr. *Red Over Black: Black Slavery Among the Cherokee Indians*. Westport, Conn.: Greenwood Press, 1977.

Hanks, Lawrence. *The Struggle for Black Political Empowerment in Three Georgia Counties*. Knoxville: University of Tennessee Press, 1987.

Henderson, Alexa Benson. *Atlanta Life Insurance Company: Guardian of Black Economic Dignity*. Tuscaloosa: University of Alabama Press, 1990.

Henri, Florette. *Black Migration: Movement North, 1900–1920*. Garden City, N.Y.: Anchor Press/Doubleday, 1975.

Higginbotham, A. Leon, Jr. *In the Matter of Color: Race and the American Legal Process: The Colonial Period*. New York: Oxford University Press, 1978.

Holmes, Michael S. *The New Deal in Georgia*. Westport, Conn.: Greenwood Press, 1975.

Jackson, Kenneth T. *The Ku Klux Klan in the City 1915–1930*. New York: Oxford University Press, 1967.

Jones, Jacqueline. *Soldiers of Light and Love: Northern Teachers and Georgia Blacks, 1865–1873*. Chapel Hill: University of North Carolina Press, 1980.

Jordan, Winthrop D. *White Over Black: American Attitudes Toward the Negro, 1550–1812*. Baltimore: Penguin Books, 1969.

Katz, William Loren. *Eyewitness: The Negro in American History*. New York: Pitman, 1967.

Kellogg, Charles Flint. *NAACP: A History of the National Association for the Advancement of Colored People*, Vol. 1, 1909–20. Baltimore: Johns Hopkins Press, 1967.

King, Martin Luther, Jr. *Where Do We Go from Here: Chaos or Community?* Boston: Beacon Press, 1968.

————. *Why We Can't Wait*. New York: New American Library, 1964.

King, Martin Luther, Sr. *Daddy King: An Autobiography*. New York: William Morrow, 1980.

Kluger, Richard. *Simple Justice: The History of Brown v. Board of Education and Black America's Struggle for Equality*. 2 Vols. New York: Knopf, 1975.

Kousser, J. Morgan. *The Shaping of Southern Politics: Suffrage Restriction and the Establishment of One-Party Rule, 1880–1910*. New Haven: Yale University Press, 1974.

Kunstler, William. *Deep in My Heart*. New York: William Morrow, 1966.

Lee, Dallas. *The Cotton Patch Evidence: The Story of Clarence Jordan and the Koinonia Farm Experiment*. New York: Harper & Row, 1971.

Lewis, David. *King: A Critical Biography*. Baltimore: Penguin Books, 1970.

Link, Arthur S., and Rembert W. Patrick, eds. *Writing Southern History: Essays in Historiography in Honor of Fletcher M. Green*. Baton Rouge: Louisiana State University Press, 1965.

Litwack, Leon F. *Been in the Storm So Long: The Aftermath of Slavery*. New York: Knopf, 1979.

Logan, Rayford W., and Michael R. Winston, eds. *Dictionary of American Negro Biography*. New York: W. W. Norton, 1982.

McFeely, William S. *Grant: A Biography*. New York: W. W. Norton, 1981.

McLaurin, Melton Alonza. *The Knights of Labor in the South.* Westport, Conn.: Greenwood Press, 1978.

McMillen, Neil R. *The Citizen's Council: Organized Resistance to the Second Reconstruction, 1954–64.* Urbana: University of Illinois Press, 1971.

Martin, Charles H. *The Angelo Herndon Case and Southern Justice.* Baton Rouge: Louisiana State University Press, 1976.

Mays, Benjamin E. *Born to Rebel.* New York: Scribner's, 1971.

Meier, August. *Negro Thought in America, 1880–1915: Racial Ideologies in the Age of Booker T. Washington.* Ann Arbor Paperbacks. Ann Arbor: University of Michigan Press, 1966.

Meier, August, and Elliot Rudwick. *CORE: A Study of the Civil Rights Movement, 1942–1968.* New York: Oxford University Press, 1973.

————, eds. *Black Protest in the Sixties.* Chicago: Quadrangle Books, 1970.

————. *The Making of Black America.* 2 vols. New York: Atheneum, 1969.

————. *From Plantation to Ghetto: An Interpretive History of American Negroes.* New York: Hill and Wang, 1966.

Metcalf, George H. *From Little Rock to Boston: The History of School Desegregation.* Westport, Conn.: Greenwood Press, 1983.

Mohr, Clarence L. *On the Threshold of Freedom: Masters and Slaves in Civil War Georgia.* Athens: University of Georgia Press, 1986.

Nathans, Elizabeth Studley. *Losing the Peace: Georgia Republicans and Reconstruction.* Baton Rouge: Louisiana State University Press, 1969.

National Association for the Advancement of Colored People. *Thirty Years of Lynching in the United States: 1889–1918.* Reprint. New York: Arno Press and the New York Times, 1969.

Oates, Stephen B. *Let the Trumpet Sound: The Life of Martin Luther King, Jr.* New York: Harper & Row, 1982.

Olmsted, Frederick Law. *A Journey in the Seaboard Slave States.* Reprint. New York: Negro Universities Press, 1968.

Orfield, Gary, and Carole Ashkinaze. *The Closing Door: Conservative Policy and Black Opportunity.* Chicago: University of Chicago Press, 1991.

Penn, Garland I. *The Afro-American Press and Its Editors.* Springfield, Mass.: Wiley and Co., 1891.

Perdue, Robert. *The Negro in Savannah, 1865–1900.* Jericho, New York: Exposition Press, 1973.

Perdue, Theda. *Slavery and the Evolution of Cherokee Society: 1540–1866.* Knoxville: University of Tennessee Press, 1979.

Price, Margaret. *The Negro Voter in the South.* Atlanta: Southern Regional Council, 1957.

Price, Richard, ed. *Maroon Societies.* 2d ed. Baltimore: Johns Hopkins University Press, 1979.

Quarles, Benjamin. *Black Abolitionists.* New York: Oxford University Press, 1969.

————. *The Negro in the American Revolution.* Chapel Hill: University of North Carolina Press, 1961.

————. *The Negro in the Civil War.* Boston: Little, Brown, 1953.

Rabinowitz, Howard N., ed. *Southern Black Leaders of the Reconstruction Era.* Urbana: University of Illinois Press, 1982.

Raines, Howell. *My Soul is Rested: Movement Days in the Deep South Remembered.* New York: G. P. Putnam's Sons, 1977.

Range, Willard. *The Rise and Progress of Negro Colleges in Georgia.* Athens: University of Georgia Press, 1951.

Ransom, Roger L., and Richard Sutch. *One Kind of Freedom: The Economic Consequences of Emancipation.* Cambridge: Cambridge University Press, 1977.

Raper, Arthur F. *Preface to Peasantry.* Chapel Hill: University of North Carolina Press, 1936.

———. *The Tragedy of Lynching.* Chapel Hill: University of North Carolina Press, 1933.

Raper, Arthur F., and Ira De A. Reid. *Sharecroppers All.* Chapel Hill: University of North Carolina Press, 1941.

Rawick, George P., ed. *The American Slave: A Composite Autobiography.* 20 vols. Westport, Conn.: Greenwood Press, 1972.

Redkey, Edwin S. *Respect Black: The Writing and Speeches of Henry McNeal Turner.* New York: Arno Press and the *New York Times,* 1971.

Scarborough, Ruth. *The Opposition to Slavery in Georgia Prior to 1860.* New York: Negro Universities Press, 1968.

Scott, Emmett J. *Negro Migration During the War.* New York: Oxford University Press, 1920.

Sessoms, Josie B. et al. *Jeanes Supervision in Georgia Schools.* Athens: The Georgia Association of Jeanes Curriculum Directors and the Southern Education Foundation, 1975.

Shadgett, Olive H. *The Republican Party in Georgia: From Reconstruction Through 1900.* Athens: University of Georgia Press, 1964.

Shaw, Barton C. *The Wool Hat Boys.* Baton Rouge: Louisiana State University Press, 1984.

Sinkler, George. *The Racial Attitudes of American Presidents from Abraham Lincoln to Theodore Roosevelt.* Anchor Press/Doubleday. Garden City, N.Y.: Doubleday, 1972.

Sitkoff, Harvard. *A New Deal for Blacks: The Emergence of Civil Rights as a National Issue: The Depression Decade.* New York: Oxford University Press, 1981.

Skaggs, William Henry. *The Southern Oligarchy: An Appeal of the Silent Masses of Our Country Against the Despotic Rule of the Few.* New York: Devin-Adair, 1924.

Sobel, Lester. *Civil Rights: 1960–1966.* New York: Facts on File, 1967.

Southern Regional Council. *A Decade of Frustration: Black Belt Schools of Alabama and Georgia in the 1970s.* Atlanta: SRC, 1981.

Stampp, Kenneth M. *The Peculiar Institution: Slavery in the Antebellum South.* New York: Knopf, 1967.

Stone, Clarence N. *Regime Politics: Governing Atlanta, 1946–1988.* Lawrence: University Press of Kansas, 1989.

Taylor, Susie King. *Reminiscences of My Life in Camp.* Reprint. New York: Arno Press and the *New York Times,* 1968.

Thompson, C. Mildred. *Reconstruction in Georgia: Economic, Social, Political.* Reprint. Savannah: Beehive Press, 1972.

Tindall, George Brown. *The Emergence of the New South.* Baton Rouge: Louisiana State University Press, 1967.

Torrence, Ridgely. *The Story of John Hope.* New York: Macmillan, 1948.

Trelease, Allen W. *White Terror: The Ku Klux Klan Conspiracy and Southern Reconstruction.* Harper Torchbooks. New York: Harper & Row, 1972.

Vander Zanden, James W. *American Minority Relations: The Sociology of Race and Ethnic Groups.* New York: Ronald Press, 1966.

Ware, Ethel K. *Constitutional History of Georgia*. New York: Columbia University Press, 1947.

Watters, Pat. *Down to Now: Reflections on the Southern Civil Rights Movement*. New York: Pantheon Books, 1971.

Watters, Pat, and Reese Cleghorn. *Climbing Jacob's Ladder: The Arrival of Negroes in Southern Politics*. New York: Harcourt, Brace, 1967.

Wells, Ida B. *Crusade for Justice: The Autobiography of Ida B. Wells*. Edited by Alfreda M. Duster. Chicago: University of Chicago Press, 1970.

_____. *Southern Horrors: Lynch Law in All Its Phases*. New York: *New York Age* Print, 1892.

White, Walter. *A Man Called White: The Autobiography of Walter White*. New York: Viking Press, 1948.

_____. *Rope and Faggot: A Biography of Judge Lynch*. Reprint. New York: Arno Press and the *New York Times*, 1969.

Wilkins, Roy. *Standing Fast: The Autobiography of Roy Wilkins*. New York: Viking Press, 1982.

Williams, George Washington. *The History of the Negro Race in America from 1619 to 1880*. Reprint. New York: Arno Press and the *New York Times*, 1969.

Williams, Roger E. *The Bonds: An American Family*. New York: Atheneum, 1971.

Wood, Betty. *Slavery in Colonial Georgia: 1730–1775*. Athens: University of Georgia Press, 1984.

Woodward, C. Vann. *The Burden of Southern History*. Baton Rouge: Louisiana State University Press, 1960.

_____. *Origins of the New South: 1877–1913*. Baton Rouge: Louisiana State University Press, 1971.

_____. *The Strange Career of Jim Crow*. 3d rev. ed. New York: Oxford University Press, 1974.

_____. *Tom Watson: Agrarian Rebel*. New York: Rinehart, 1938.

Zangrando, Robert L. *The NAACP Crusade Against Lynching, 1909–1950*. Philadelphia: Temple University Press, 1980.

Zinn, Howard. *SNCC: The New Abolitionists*. Boston: Beacon Press, 1964.

Articles

Bacote, Clarence A. "The Negro in Atlanta Politics." *Phylon* 16 (1955) 333–50.

_____. "Negro Proscriptions, Protests, and Proposed Solutions in Georgia: 1880–1908." *Journal of Southern History* 25 (Nov. 1959) 471–98.

Bailes, Sue. "Eugene Talmadge and the Board of Regents Controversy." *Georgia Historical Quarterly* 53 (1969) 409–23.

Bellamy, Donnie D. "Macon, Georgia, 1823–1860: A Study in Urban Slavery." *Phylon* 45 (Dec. 1984) 298–310.

Belvin, William L., Jr. "The Georgia Gubernatorial Primary of 1946." *Georgia Historical Quarterly* 50 (1966) 37–53.

Bernd, Joseph L. "White Supremacy and the Disfranchisement of Blacks in Georgia, 1946." *Georgia Historical Quarterly* 66 (1982) 492–513.

Bernd, Joseph L., and Lynwood M. Holland. "Recent Restrictions upon Negro Suffrage: The Case of Georgia." *Journal of Politics* 21 (Aug. 1959) 487–513.

Blassingame, John W. "Before the Ghetto: The Making of the Black Community in Savannah, Georgia, 1865–1880." *Journal of Social History* 6 (Summer 1973) 463–88.

Boyd, Willis Delmond. "Negro Colonization in the Reconstruction Era, 1865–1870." *Georgia Historical Quarterly* 40 (1956) 360–82.

Browning, Pamela. "The Erosion of a Scarce Resource." U.S. Commission on Civil Rights *Perspectives* 15 (Winter–Spring 1983) 44–50.

Brundage, Fitzhugh. "The Darien 'Insurrection' of 1899: Black Protest During the Nadir of Race Relations." *Georgia Historical Quarterly* 74 (1990) 234–53.

Clement, Rufus E. "The Historical Development of Higher Education for Negro Americans." *Journal of Negro Education* 35 (Summer 1966) 299–305.

Coleman, Kenneth. "The Southern Frontier: Georgia's Founding and the Expansion of South Carolina." *Georgia Historical Quarterly* 56 (Summer 1972) 163–74.

Crowe, Charles. "Racial Massacre in Atlanta, September 22, 1906." *Journal of Negro History* 54 (Apr. 1969) 150–73.

————. "Racial Violence and Social Reform—Origins of the Atlanta Riot of 1906." *Journal of Negro History* 53 (July 1968) 234–56.

————. "Tom Watson, Populists, and Blacks Reconsidered." *Journal of Negro History* 55 (Apr. 1970) 99–116.

Davis, John W. "George Liele and Andrew Bryan, Pioneer Negro Preachers." *Journal of Negro History* 3 (1918) 119–27.

Drago, Edmund L. "The Black Household in Dougherty County, Georgia: 1870–1900." *Journal of Southwest Georgia History* 1 (Fall 1983) 38–48.

————. "How Sherman's March through Georgia Affected the Slaves." *Georgia Historical Quarterly* 57 (1973) 361–75.

Du Bois, William Edgar Burghardt. "The Freedmen's Bureau." *Atlantic Monthly* 87 (Mar. 1901) 354–65.

————. "Reconstruction and its Benefits." *American Historical Review* 15 (July 1910) 781–89.

Eaton, Clement. "A Dangerous Pamphlet in the Old South." *Journal of Southern History* 2 (May 1936) 323–34.

Edwards, John C. "Slave Justice in Four Middle Georgia Counties." *Georgia Historical Quarterly* 57 (1973) 265–73.

Escott, Paul D. "The Context of Freedom: Georgia's Slaves During the Civil War." *Georgia Historical Quarterly* 58 (Summer 1974) 79–104.

Fisher, James. "Negro Farm Ownership in the South." *Annals of the Association of American Geographers* 63 (Dec. 1973) 478–89.

Fitz Simons, Theodore B. "The Camilla Riot." *Georgia Historical Quarterly* 35 (1951) 116–25.

Flanders, Ralph B. "The Free Negro in Antebellum Georgia." *North Carolina Historical Review* 11 (July 1932) 250–72.

————. "Planters' Problems in Georgia." *Georgia Historical Quarterly* 14 (March 1930) 17–40.

Grantham, Dewey W., Jr. "Georgia Politics and the Disfranchisement of the Negro." *Georgia Historical Quarterly* 32 (1948) 1–21.

Hammett, Hugh B. "Labor and Race: The Georgia Railroad Strike of 1909." *Labor History* 16 (Fall 1975) 470–84.

Harlan, Louis R. "Booker T. Washington and 'The Voice of the Negro': 1904–1907." *Journal of Southern History* 45 (Feb. 1979) 45–62.

Holmes, Michael S. "The Blue Eagle as 'Jim Crow' Bird: The NRA and Georgia's Black Workers." *Journal of Negro History* 57 (July 1972) 276–83.

————. "From Euphoria to Cataclysm: Georgia Confronts the Great Depression." *Georgia Historical Quarterly* 58 (1974) 313–30.

House, Albert V. "Labor Management Problems on Georgia Rice Plantations, 1840–1860." *Agricultural History* 28 (1954) 149–55.

Jennings, M. Kent and Harmon Zeigler. "Class, Party, and Race in Four Types of Elections: The Case of Atlanta." *Politics* 28 (1966) 391-407.

Jackson, Charles O. "William J. Simmons: A Career in Ku Kluxism." *Georgia Historical Quarterly* 50 (1966) 351–65.

Johnson, Michael P. "A New Look at the Popular Vote for Delegates to the Secession Convention." *Georgia Historical Quarterly* 56 (Summer 1972) 259–75.

Jones, Alton DuMar. "The Child Labor Movement in Georgia." *Georgia Historical Quarterly* 49 (1965) 396–417.

Kousser, J. Morgan. "Separate but Not Equal: The Supreme Court's First Decision on Racial Discrimination in Schools." *Journal of Southern History* 47 (Feb. 1980) 17–44.

Lawrence, James B. "Religious Education of the Negro in Georgia." *Georgia Historical Quarterly* 14 (1930) 41-57.

Lesher, Stephen. "Leroy Johnson Outslicks Mister Charlie." *New York Times Magazine*, 8 November, 1970, pp. 34–50.

"Letters Showing the Rise and Progress of the Early Negro Churches of Georgia and the West Indies." *Journal of Negro History* 1 (1916) 69–92.

Levy, Leonard W. "Sims' Case: The Fugitive Slave Law in Boston in 1851." *Journal of Negro History* 35 (Jan. 1950) 39–74.

Libbey, Marie McGrath, and Suzanne A. Lindsay. "The 1990 Census: Growth and Diversity in Georgia." *Georgia Business and Economic Conditions* 51 (May–June 1991) 9–17.

McDaniel, Ruth Curry. "Black Power in Georgia: William A. Pledger and the Takeover of the Republican Party." *Georgia Historical Quarterly* 62 (Fall 1978) 225–39.

McPherson, Robert G. "Georgia Slave Trials, 1837–1849." *American Journal of Legal History* 4 (1960) 257–84; 364–77.

Martin, Charles H. "White Supremacy and Black Workers: Georgia's Black Shirts Combat the Great Depression." *Labor History* 18 (Summer 1977) 366–81.

Martin, Ida M. "Civil Liberties in Georgia Legislation: 1800–1830." *Georgia Historical Quarterly* 45 (1961) 329–44.

Moore, John Hammond. "The Angelo Herndon Case: 1932–1937." *Phylon* 31 (Spring 1971) 60–71.

————. "Communists and Fascists in a Southern City: Atlanta 1930." *South Atlantic Quarterly* 67 (Summer 1968) 437–54.

Moseley, Clement Charlton. "The Case of Leo M. Frank, 1913–1915." *Georgia Historical Quarterly* 51 (1967) 42–62.

————. "Latent Klanism in Georgia, 1890–1915." *Georgia Historical Quarterly* 56 (1972) 365–86.

————. "The Political Influence of the KKK in Georgia, 1915–1925." *Georgia Historical Quarterly* 57 (1973) 235–55.

Poe, William Allen. "Georgia's Influence in the Development of Liberia." *Georgia Historical Quarterly* 57 (1973) 1–16.

Porter, Michael L. "The Auburn Avenue Residential Community: The Formation of the Black Community in Atlanta, Georgia, 1900–1930." *Journal of Ethnic Studies* 6 (Nov. 1978) 48–59.

Proctor, William C, Jr. "Slavery in Southwest Georgia." *Georgia Historical Quarterly* 49 (1965) 1–22.

Rabinowitz, Howard R. "From Exclusion to Segregation: Southern Race Relations, 1865–1900." *Journal of American History* 63 (Sept. 1976) 325–50.

Rable, George C. "The South and the Politics of Anti-Lynching Legislation, 1920–1940." *Journal of Southern History* 51 (May 1985) 201–20.

Raper, Arthur F., and Ira De A. Reid. "The South Adjusts Downward." *Phylon* 1 (1st Quarter 1940) 6–26.

Reed, John C. "What I Know About the Ku Klux Klan." *Uncle Remus's Magazine* 8 parts (Jan.–Nov. 1908).

Rogers, W. McDowell. "Free Negro Legislation in Georgia before 1865." *Georgia Historical Quarterly* 16 (1932) 27–37.

Savitt, Todd W. "The Use of Blacks for Medical Experimentation and Demonstration in the Old South." *Journal of Southern History* 48 (Aug. 1982) 331–48.

Scott, Emmett J. "Letters of Negro Migrants of 1916–1918." *Journal of Negro History* 4 (July 1919) 290–340.

Talmadge, John E. "Georgia Tests the Fugitive Slave Law." *Georgia Historical Quarterly* 49 (1965) 57–64.

Thompson, C. Mildred. "The Freedmen's Bureau in Georgia, 1865–1866." *Georgia Historical Quarterly* 5 (1921) 40–49.

Toppin, Edgar A. "Walter White and the Atlanta NAACP's Fight for Equal Schools, 1916–1917." *History of Education Quarterly* 7 (1967) 3–21.

Wax, Darold D. "Georgia and the Negro Before the American Revolution." *Georgia Historical Quarterly* 51 (1967) 63–77.

Wish, Harvey. "The Slave Insurrection Panic of 1856." *Journal of Southern History* 5 (May 1939) 206–22.

Wood, Betty. "Thomas Stephens and the Introduction of Black Slavery in Georgia." *Georgia Historical Quarterly* 58 (1974) 24–40.

Unpublished Theses, Dissertations, and Papers

Adams, Olin Burton. "The Negro and the Agrarian Movement in Georgia: 1874–1908." Ph.D. diss., Florida State University, 1973.

Averitt, Jack Nelson. "The Democratic Party in Georgia: 1824–1837." Ph.D. diss., University of North Carolina, 1957.

Bacote, Clarence A. "The Negro in Georgia Politics: 1880–1908." Ph.D. diss., University of Chicago, 1956.

Bellamy, Donnie D. "Black Slavery in Georgia." Paper.

————. "The Legal Status of Black Georgians During the Colonial and Revolutionary Eras." Paper.

Blackwell, Gloria. "Blacks and the Atlanta Media." Ph.D. diss., Atlanta University, 1972.

Bolster, Paul Douglas. "Civil Rights Movement in Twentieth Century Georgia. Ph.D. diss., University of Georgia, 1972.

Christler, Edith M. "Participation of Negroes in the Georgia Legislature, 1867–1870." M.A. thesis, Atlanta University, 1932.

Cimbala, Paul A. "The Freedmen's Bureau, Planters, and the Contract System in Reconstruction Georgia, 1865–1869." Paper delivered at the Southern Historical Association, Charleston, South Carolina, 1982.

————. "Reconstruction's Stepchildren: The Freedmen's Bureau and Black Apprenticeship, 1865–1868." Manuscript, Emory University, 1982.

Drake, Richard B. "The American Missionary Association and the Southern Negro." Ph.D. diss., Emory University, 1957.

Ellis, Ann Wells. "The Commission on Interracial Cooperation's Activities in Atlanta." Paper presented at the Second Georgia Studies Symposium, Georgia State University, February 4, 1978.

Farmer, Henry Frank, Jr. "The Negro Exodus of 1879 from the Southeastern States." M.A. thesis, University of Georgia, 1964.

Fish, John Olin. "Southern Methodism in the Progressive Era: A Social History." Ph.D. diss., University of Georgia, 1969.

Fitz Simons, Theodore Barker. "The Ku Klux Klan in Georgia: 1868–1871." M.A. thesis, University of Georgia, 1957.

Fry, Gladys–Marie. "The Night Riders: A Study in the Social Control of the Negro." Ph.D. diss., Indiana University, 1967.

Howard, Cary. "The Georgia Reaction to *David Walker's Appeal*." M.A. thesis, University of Georgia, 1967.

Johnson, Paul Michael. "The Negro in Macon Georgia, 1865–1871." M.A. thesis, University of Georgia, 1972.

McMath, Robert C., Jr. "Profile of Alliance Leadership." Paper presented at Georgia State University, 1975.

Matthews, John Michael. "Race Relations in Georgia, 1890–1930." Ph.D. diss., Duke University, 1970.

Mohr, Clarence Lee. "Georgia Blacks During Secession and Civil War." Ph.D. diss., University of Georgia, 1975.

Mullis, Sharon M. "Black Atlanta Acquires a Hospital: Grace Towns Hamilton and the Hughes Spalding Pavilion." Paper presented at the 2nd Georgia Studies Symposium, Georgia State University, February 4, 1978.

Owens, James Leggette. "The Negro in Georgia During Reconstruction 1864–1872: A Social History." Ph.D. diss., University of Georgia, 1975.

Paulson, Darryl. "Sanitation Strikes, Unionism and Racism in Three Southern Cities—Memphis, St. Petersburg, and Atlanta." Paper presented at the Second Annual Southern Labor History Conference, Georgia State University, Atlanta, May 4–6, 1978.

Pendley, Berry H. "Savannah, Georgia during Reconstruction, 1865–1869." M.A. thesis, West Georgia College, 1969.

Potter, Richard D. "The Georgia Constitution of 1868." M.A. thesis, Florida State University, 1971.

Schinkel, Peter Evans. "The Negro in Athens and Clarke County, 1872–1900." M.A. thesis, University of Georgia, 1971.

Unger, Helen. "Free Negroes in Ante-bellum Georgia." M.A. thesis, University of Georgia, 1949.

Ward, Judson C. "Georgia under Bourbon Democrats." Ph.D. diss., University of North Carolina, 1947.

Wardlaw, Ralph. "Negro Suffrage in Georgia, 1867–1930." M.A. thesis, University of Georgia, 1932.

Wetherington, Mark V. "The Savannah Negro Laborers' Strike of 1891." Paper presented at the Second Annual Southern Labor History Conference, Georgia State University, May 4–6, 1978.

Wingo, Horace Calvin. "Race Relations in Georgia, 1872–1908." Ph.D. diss., University of Georgia, 1969.

Zangrando, Robert L. "The Efforts of the National Association for the Advancement of Colored People to Secure Passage of a Federal Anti-Lynching Law." Ph.D. diss., University of Pennsylvania, 1963.

Index

Aaron, Henry "Hank," 547
Abbott, Robert S., 258, 266, 292
Abernathy, Ralph David, 405, 407, 409, 431, 549–54, 564
Abernathy, Ralph David, III, 454, 458
Abolition Movement, 45, 49, 56, 79, 110; reaction to, 31, 51, 56–57, 74, 77–78
Abolitionists, 45–47, 51, 65, 86
Adequate Program for Education (APEG), 533
Affirmative action, 468–71, 475–78, 496
Africa, 269, 475, 481. *See also* American Colonization Society, Liberia, Sierra Leone.
African American Panoramic Experience (APEX), 543
African Methodist Episcopal (A. M. E.) church, 124, 126, 267–68
African survivals, 43–44
Afro-American Law Enforcement League, 511
Afro-American League 134–36, 215
Agriculture, 347–50, 462–66. *See also* Farmers, Labor, Tenant Farming, Sharecropping.

Aid to Families with Dependent Children (AFDC), 490–92. *See also* Social Welfare.
Alabama, 22, 34, 52, 81, 285, 342, 372, 388–89, 400, 425
Alaimo, Anthony, 519–21
Albany, Ga., 116, 145, 221, 277, 293, 305, 311, 402–13, 495, 506, 524
Albany Movement, 402–13; "Albany Nine," 412
Albany State College, 241–42, 358, 382n, 383, 402, 537–39
Alexander, Cameron, 563
Alexander, Will, 307, 321–22, 327–28, 330–31
All Citizens Registration Committee, 364
Allen, Ivan, 397, 422, 427, 502
Allen, Thomas, 105, 118
Alliance Movement, 173–75, 198, 199
Altamaha River, 4
American Civil Liberties Union (ACLU), 349, 378, 405, 442–43, 514–15, 527–28, 558
American Colonization Society (ACS), 68, 74–76, 286
American Federation of Labor (AFL), 279–80, 282, 354; AFL-CIO, 467
American Legion, 308, 449

American Missionary Association (AMA), 147, 223–26, 228–30, 239, 270
American Negro Academy, 193, 244
American Revolution, 11–20, 21–22, 24–25, 27, 66
Americus, Ga., 130, 135, 166, 229, 283, 289, 292, 312, 377–78, 414, 509, 524
Ames, Jessie Daniel, 322, 329–31
Anderson, William G., 403–407, 409, 412
Andersonville, Ga., 84, 222, 226
Anti-Defamation League (ADL), 559
Antilynching, activities and reform, 126, 135, 316, 321–37, 342; "Before-Day Clubs," 167; Costigan-Wagner Bill, 331–32, Gavagan Bill, 333; state law passed, 168
Anti-Semitism, 351, 355, 399, 561
Appomattox, 82, 91
Aptheker, Herbert, 349
Arlington, Ga., 293
Arnall, Ellis, 357–58, 363, 366, 428–29
Arrington, Marvin, 453, 475, 479, 485
Arthur, Chester A., 132
Artists, 260. *See also* Entertainment.

607

Ashburn, Ga., 510
Associated Press, 164, 187
Association of Colored
    Physicians, Dentists,
    and Pharmacists, 255
Association of Southern
    Women for the
    Prevention of
    Lynching (ASWPL),
    329–31, 333, 356
At-large elections, 441–46,
    451–56, 527, 531
Athens, Ga., 41, 135, 147,
    248, 274, 311;
    elections, 128, 130;
    lynchings, 166, 319;
    schools, 230, 237;
    segregation, 219, 399;
    slaves and free Negroes
    in, 37, 70, 84
Atkinson County, 462
Atkinson, William Y., 158,
    168, 180
Atlanta, antebellum,
    35–36, 68–72; black
    commerce, 248–49;
    475–87; as center of
    black protest and
    education, 167,
    239–41; civil rights
    movement, 388–400,
    421–28; Civil War,
    84–86, 88; crime,
    504–508; employment,
    economic conditions
    for blacks in, 274–83,
    460–61, 472–74, 487;
    government, 470,
    452–53, 475–76; Great
    Depression, 341–43,
    346–48; housing,
    497–502; Ku Klux
    Klan, white
    supremacists, 316,
    319–20, 327–28, 355,
    363; police, 512–13;
    politics and elections,
    127, 200, 352, 364,
    369–70, 372, 437–38,
    451–56, 458; race
    relations, 296, 321–22,
    356; Reconstruction,
    93, 104, 123;
    segregation, 216–221;
    social, fraternal
    organizations, 261–63;
    World War I, 306, 307

Atlanta African-American
    Philharmonic
    Orchestra, 545
Atlanta Black Crackers, 546
Atlanta Braves, 547
Atlanta Business League,
    481
Atlanta Committee for the
    Olympic Games
    (ACOG), 478. See also
    Olympics.
Atlanta Compromise, 238,
    528
Atlanta Daily World, 259,
    391, 480
Atlanta Economic
    Development
    Corporation, 476
Atlanta Hawks, 548
Atlanta Housing Authority
    (AHA), 500–501
Atlanta Independent, 265
Atlanta Inquirer, 391, 480
Atlanta Life Insurance
    Company, 252, 374,
    482–83, 543
Atlanta Loan and Trust
    Company, 251
Atlanta Negro Voters
    League, 370
Atlanta riot, 187, 204–209,
    252, 259, 271
Atlanta schools, 229,
    234–35, 311–12, 370,
    374; desegregation,
    379–82, 527–29, 537;
    school board, 370, 374
Atlanta University, 123, 135,
    163, 168, 205, 208, 226,
    229, 239, 242–46, 270,
    271, 373, 382n; Center,
    353, 540–42;
    Conferences, 244;
    merger with Clark
    College, 541; Studies,
    193
Attaway, Roland, 449–51
Attorneys, black, 256–57,
    479
Auburn Avenue, 249, 262,
    543
Augusta, Ga., American
    Revolution, 14, 19;
    antebellum, 48, 51,
    63–64, 68–70; black
    businesses, 251, 254,
    482; civil rights

movement, 398,
    418–19; Civil War, 84;
    Colonial period, 7, 8;
    economic conditions
    for blacks, 474; labor
    strike in, 279; NAACP,
    307, 311; politics and
    elections, 130, 178–79,
    196, 200; racial
    incidents, 168, 178,
    207, 288, 319, 387, 510,
    558; Reconstruction,
    97, 102; schools and
    colleges, 230–31,
    240–41, 524–25, 530;
    segregation, 216–19,
    221.
Augusta Baptist Institute,
    230, 240–41. See also
    Morehouse College.
Augusta National Golf
    Club, 419, 548

Back to Africa. See
    Colonization.
Bacon, Augustus O., 134,
    151, 197, 218
Badger, Roderick, 71, 256
Bainbridge, Ga., 190, 307,
    315, 333, 368
Baker County, 318, 360, 371
Baker, Ella, 390, 392, 431
Baker, Samuel, 316
Baldwin County, 51, 444
Ballard Normal School, 228
Bankhead Courts, 501
Banks. See Businesses.
Banks County, 133
Banks, Jerry, 513
Baptists, 58–59, 269–270;
    Georgia Convention,
    380; Georgia Negro
    Convention, 269;
    National Convention,
    266, 270, 398–99;
    Southern Convention,
    398, 433; World
    Alliance, 273
Barber, J. Max, 167,
    206–207, 244, 259
Barbering, 218, 251–52,
    254
Barnesville, Ga., 277, 534
Bateman, Tommie Faye,
    560
Battle of Kettle Creek, 17
Battle of Bloody Marsh, 9

Beach Institute, 223, 228, 543
Beal, Alveda King, 456
Beard, Thomas, 114
Beda-Etta Business College, 230
Belcher, Edwin, 105, 114, 150, 157
Bell, Eldrin, 513
Bell, Griffin, 440, 447
Benham, Robert, 458
Berry, Marion, 392
Bethune, Thomas "Blind Tom," 260
Bibb County, economic conditions, 461; job discrimination, 347, 469–70, 511; lynching, 325; politics and elections, 196, 363, 446; schools, 229, 523–24, 526; teenage pregnancies, 490
Birmingham, Ala., 391, 422
Birth of a Nation, The, 190, 315
Black Codes, 22, 95–96, 102, 148, 154
Black Horse Cavalry, 92
Black male, plight of, 492
Black middle class, 205, 247–63 passim, 273, 474–75, 487
Black Power, 426–27, 434
Black press, 164, 187, 205, 207, 211, 216, 257, 289, 314, 480–81; National Afro-American Press Association, 259
Black Shirts, 327–28
Blackwell, Randolph T., 466
Blakely, Ga., 307
Blayton, Jesse B., 480–81
Bleckley County, 444, 446, 463, 526
Blodgett, Lewis Matthew, 288
Blue Bird Body Company, 447, 468
Boggs Academy, 526
Boisclair, James, 71
Bond, Alice, 391, 456
Bond, Horace Mann, 241, 353, 358, 373, 375
Bond, James, 271
Bond, Julian, 391, 393, 397,

406, 418, 427–28, 432, 435–41, 455–56; Bond v. Floyd, 428
Bootle, William, 371, 383–84, 401, 416
Borders, William Holmes, 390, 396, 563
Bourbons, 126, 131, 133, 154–55, 184–86, 196–98, 202–204, 213, 220
Bowen, John W. E., 207–208, 215, 244, 259, 269, 305
Bradley, Aaron A., 101, 104, 107–11, 113–14, 157, 226
Brady, James Calvin, 507
Brawley, Benjamin Griffith, 245
Bronner Brothers, 485–86
Brooks County, 52, 169, 286, 316, 323
Brooks, Tyrone, 446, 457, 459, 475, 491, 524, 550
Brotherhood of Locomotive Firemen and Enginemen (BLFE), 280–82
Brown, Benjamin, 435, 438–39
Brown, H. Rap (Jamil Abdullah al-Amin), 426, 562
Brown, James, 481, 545–46
Brown, Jim, 548
Brown, John (abolitionist), 72, 78
Brown, John (escaped slave), 42, 45
Brown, Joseph E., 73, 79–81, 87, 94, 104, 129, 155–56, 184, 185, 214
Brown, Lee, 505, 513
Brown v. Board of Education, 375–79
Brown, William Wells, 46
Brunswick, Ga., 135, 278, 311, 459, 506, 510
Bryan, Andrew, 59
Bryan County, 37, 228
Bryant, John E., 97, 131, 226, 258, 278
Buck, Alfred E., 132, 180
Buffalo Soldiers, 297
Bullard, Eugene Jacques, 304

Bullard, Helen, 370, 424–25
Bulloch County, 443–44.
Bullock, Rufus, 103, 105, 109, 115–16, 119, 122–23, 126, 154, 157, 196, 226–27
Bunche, Ralph, 374, 400
Bureau of Refugees, Freedmen, and Abandoned Lands. See Freedmen's Bureau.
Burke County, 443–45, 465, 526, 535
Burke, Solomon, 545
Bus desegregation, 389–90, 399–400, 403–407, 415–16, 418–19.
Businesses, black-owned, 247–55, 478–87; financial institutions, 250–51, 483–85; Minority Business Enterprise (MBE) program, 477–78; retail merchants, 254
Busbee, George, 439, 441
Busing. See Schools, busing.
Butler, Pierce, 39, 41
Butler, Thomas M., 157
Button, Daniel, 248
Butts County, 166

Cable, George Washington, 156, 194
Calhoun County, 318, 371, 376, 443–44
Callaway, Howard "Bo," 423, 429
Camden County, 130
Camilla, Ga., 117, 318
Camp Gordon, 303–304, 362. See also Fort Gordon.
Camp Haskell, 301
Camp, Lawrence, 352
Camp Stewart, 362
Camp Wheeler, 361
Campbell, Tunis G., Sr., 101, 106–107, 109–11, 113–15, 120–21, 125–26, 128, 226
Candler, Allen, 161–62, 166–68, 201, 202, 215, 232, 301
Candler, Asa, 306

Candler, Warren A., 168–69
Capital punishment, 517–19
Carmichael, James V., 365
Carmichael, Stokely, 426–27
Carnegie Fund, 261
Carolinas, 4–6, 9–10, 20
Carroll County, 168, 396, 444, 446
Carrollton, Ga., 557, 561
Carson, Rudolph, 448
Carter, Jimmy, 428, 436–37, 439–40, 456, 527, 550–52
Cartersville, Ga., 164, 327, 561
Carver, Daniel, 556, 558
Carver Savings Bank, 483
Cascade Heights, 420, 479
Cater, Nathaniel, 504
Catholic church, 271, 563; desegregation of schools, 381
Cemeteries, segregation in, 221
Central City College, 230
Central of Georgia Railroad, 35, 36, 293
Chain gang, 158–59, 343, 351. See also Convict-lease system, Prisons.
Charitable institutions, 261–62
Charity Hospital, 255
Charles, Earl, 513–14
Charles, Ray, 545–46
Charleston, 8, 27, 36, 46, 62, 72, 220
Charlton, Dimmock, 38
Chatham County, Crusade for Voters, 417–18; free Negroes in, 71–72; land seized by blacks, 138; politics, 109, 116, 129; schools, 529–30; World War I, 306.
Chattahoochee County, 372, 492
Chattahoochee Judicial District, 519
Chattooga County, 125, 160, 170, 228
Chenault, Marcus Wayne, 549
Cherokee Indians, 4, 20–24, 25; black

slavery among, 22; Cherokee War of 1777, 21; Trail of Tears, 24; Treaty of Echota, 23; Treaty of Hopewell, 21
Chicago Defender, 258, 292
Child support, 491–92
Christian League, 208, 209
Christian Methodist Episcopal (C. M. E.) church, 267, 268, 563
Churches, desegregation of, 398, 410. See also Religion.
Citizens Trust Bank, 251, 483, 499
Civil Rights Act of 1866, 212–13, 216–17
Civil Rights Act of 1964, 421–23, 439, 468, 523
Civil Rights Congress, 387
Civil Rights Commission (U.S.), 477
Civil rights movement, 386–433
Civil War, 82–91; prelude to conflict, 77–82; Sherman's march to the sea, 88–91; weakening of slavery during, 83–86
Civilian Conservation Corps (CCC), 347
Civil Works Administration (CWA), 346
Clansman, The, 189–90, 205, 207, 315
Clark College (University), 206, 240, 242, 245, 247, 260, 382n, 541; Clark Atlanta University, 541
Clarke County, 114, 134, 158, 196, 287, 293, 347
Claxton, Ga., 507, 516
Clay County, 371, 442, 444, 461–62
Clayton County, 473, 498, 561
Clayton, Xernona, 472, 560
Clement, George C., 313, 322
Clement, Rufus, 353, 356, 370–73
Clergy. See Religion.
Cleveland, Grover, 186, 203
Clinch County, 401, 492

Clyatt, Samuel M., 150–51
Coal mining, 279; Dade County mining camp, 156
Cobb County, 287, 472, 473, 529, 532, 561
Cobb, Howell, 80, 87
Cocaine, 503, 506–508
Cochran, Ga., 308, 444
Cocking, Walter Dewey, 356–57
Colbert, Ga., 332, 423
Colby, Abram, 106, 119
Cold War, 386–87
Cole, Johnnetta, 475, 541
Cole, Thomas, Jr., 541
Colleges. See Education.
Collier Heights, 420, 479
Colonel's Island, 110
Colonization, 74–76, 286–87
Colored Farmers' Alliance. See Alliance Movement.
Colquitt, Alfred H., 129, 131–33, 155, 157, 184
Colquitt County, 319
Columbia County, 118, 119
Columbians, 363, 512
Columbus, Ga., 248, 287, 293, 311, 506, 519; black employment, 275, 277, 345; civil rights and race relations, 363, 388; desegregation, 377, 395, 419; Ku Klux Klan, 101, 105, 320; lynchings, 56, 326; police department, 511–12; politics, 97, 345; racial violence, 128, 368, 377; schools, 233, 237, 530; slaves and free Negroes in, 38, 69, 84
Columbus Ledger-Enquirer, 480
Commerce, Ga., 558
Commission on Interracial Cooperation (CIC), 319, 321–26, 328–31, 356–57
Communism, Communists, 341–44, 357, 386; International Labor Defense, 342; reaction to, 314, 333, 356–57

Compromise of 1877, 130, 183, 197
Compromise of 1850, 78
Concerned Black Clergy, 492, 563
Confederate battle flag, 378, 565–66
Confederate States of America, 81–91; army, 82, 85, 86
Congregational church, 194, 224–26, 270–71; in Atlanta, 270–71; in Savannah, 270
Congress of Industrial Organizations (CIO), 354
Congress of Racial Equality (CORE), 392, 399–400
Conley, James, 315
Constitutional Convention (federal), 27. See also Georgia Constitutional Convention.
Construction firms, black owned, 478–79
Consumer spending, 483–84
Continental army, 12–13, 15, 16
Continental Congress, First, 12, 27; Second, 12–16, 18, 28
Convict-lease system, 108, 113, 126, 131–32, 135, 153–59, 174, 176, 178–79, 188, 194, 232; abolition of, 158; conditions in camps, 155–56; twenty-year lease, 157
Cook, Eugene, 356, 374
Coolidge, Calvin, 337
Cooper, Clarence, 458
Cordele, Ga., 308, 312, 430, 524, 561–62
Cotton, 31, 33–39, 172, 175, 188, 192, 290, 295–96, 306, 348, 489; effect of boll weevil on, 290, 294–95; overemphasis on production of, 144–45; prices, 146, 173, 178.
Cotton mills, 276–77, 279. See also Textile mills.
Coulter, E. Merton, 192–93

County unit system, 131, 335, 365, 369; demise of, 372; Neill Primary Act of 1917, 335
Covington, Ga., 354
Coweta County, 37, 287, 509
Cox, Eugene "Goober," 350, 354
Craft, William and Ellen, 45–46, 228
Craig, Calvin, 383, 396
Crawford County, 51, 444
Crawford, Jesse, 343
Crawford, Lectured, 174, 178
Crawfordville, Ga., 466
Creek Indians, 20–21, 24–26; Creek War, Battle of Horseshoe Bend, 25. See also Seminoles.
Crim, Alonzo, 528
Crime, 451–52, 502–508; rate, 505–506; black-on-black, 503–504, 508; drugs and, 507–508
Criminal justice system, 54–55, 342–44, 513–22; defense attorneys, 514–17; discrimination, 151, 155, 517; indigent defense, 514–15; jury exclusion, 516; juvenile justice system, 517; and peonage, convict leasing, 151–52, 155
Crisis, the, 243, 309–311, 314
Crogman, William H., 208, 243–245, 314
Crummell, Alexander, 193, 244
Crusade for Citizenship, 390
Cuba, 28, 285, 300–301
Cumberland Island, 25
Cumming, Ga., 170, 554–55
Cumming v. Richmond County Board of Education, 231
Cuthbert, Ga., 99, 117, 248, 370

Dabney, Austin, 16–17, 65
Dahlonega, Ga., 3, 23, 71

Dallas, Ga., 88
Dalton, Ga., 51, 88, 221
Daniels, Grandison B., 229
Danielsville, Ga., 332
Darien, Ga., 4, 9, 88, 109–11, 125–26, 167, 327, 332
David Walker's Appeal, 49–50, 62, 343
Davis, Benjamin J., Jr., 343–44
Davis, Benjamin J., Sr., 259, 262, 265, 336–40
Davis, Jefferson, 82, 91, 113
Davis, Madison, 114, 129, 133, 135
Davis, Ossie, 545
Davison's department store, 396
Dawson County, 473
"Dawson Five," 514
Dawson, Ga., 292, 371, 413, 414, 444
Dawsonville, Ga., 170
Death penalty. See Capital punishment.
Decatur County, 371, 516
Dee, Ruby, 545
DeKalb County, affirmative action, 477; black population, 473; Dr. King arrested, 393; housing, 479, 498, 500; judicial system, 51; politics, 432, 454; schools, 529, 536
Delegale, Henry, 167
Democratic National Convention (1968), 432
Democratic party, 175, 180, 199, 203, 336–40; 352, 356, 363; primary elections, 199–200. See also White primary.
Depression (1893), 254, 275, 300
Depression, Great, 273, 282, 327, 339, 341–55. See also New Deal.
Desegregation, of public accommodations, 391–98, 415–20, 422–23. See also Civil rights movement and specific topics, e.g, Schools.

Deveaux, John H., 129, 135, 169, 180, 187, 196, 258, 262, 300, 336
Dickson, David, 40, 41, 140, 212
Discrimination, in business and contracts, 477; by lenders, 484–85, 498–99; in New Deal programs, 345–48. See also Employment.
Disfranchisement, of blacks, 113, 134, 195–204, 209–11, 312, 334–38; effect on education, 211, 231, 234–35; "grandfather clause," 201, 209–10; of whites, 103–104, 106. See also County unit system, Poll tax, Voter registration, White primary.
"Dixie," 79, 565
Dixiecrats, 67
Dixon, Thomas, Jr., 189–91, 205, 351
Dobbs, John Wesley, 249, 262–63, 370
Dobbs, Mattiwilda, 545
Dodge County, 446
Domestic workers, 141, 277, 341, 360, 468
Dooly County, 318, 443, 462
Dorchester Academy, 226; Community Center, 393, 401.
Dorsey, George, 366
Dorsey, Hugh M., 233, 294, 303, 312, 315, 317, 323–25; Statement from, 324
Dougherty County, 48, 145, 150, 278, 291, 371
Douglass, Frederick, 31, 65, 120, 250
Douglass Theater, 305, 325, 543
Doyle, H. S., 176–78
Dred Scott decision, 72, 78
Drug treatment, 493
Drugs. See Cocaine.
Du Bois, William Edward Burghardt (W. E. B.), 145, 158, 163, 167–68, 190, 193, 201, 215,

238–39, 243, 244, 249–50, 292, 309–10, 313, 330, 353
Dublin, Ga., 175, 275, 283, 312, 368, 497, 532
Durham Statement, 356
Dyer Bill, 271, 322–23, 325–26, 331–32
Dyer, Leonidas, 322, 337

Early County, 261, 316, 371, 402, 443
Eastman, Ga., 317
Eatonton, Ga., 75, 174, 443, 510, 532
Eaves, Reginald, 512–13
Ebenezer Baptist Church, 270, 391, 421, 430
Ebenezer, Ga., 9
Economic Opportunity Atlanta, 491
Education, 61–64, 116, 125, 135, 222–37, 311–12, 330, 356–57, 372–85, 523–42; Atlanta school crisis, 311–12; black educators, 228–31, 238–47, 531, 534; colleges, 238–47, 353, 373, 537–42; dual school system 231–35; Northern philanthropy, 224, 235–36; quality, 533–35; teacher pay, 234–35, 373–74. See also Schools.
Education Review Commission, 533
Edwards, Claybon, 447
Effingham County, 159
Eisenhower, Dwight D., 370, 377
Elbert County, 178, 222
Ellaville, Ga., 165, 325
Elliott, J. Robert, 408–10, 412, 415, 530
Emancipation, 91–92; celebrations, 299–300, 377; Proclamation, 87
Emergency Land Fund (ELF), 464–65
Emory University, 384, 537; Medical School 495–96
Empire Real Estate Board, 481, 497

Employment, government, 282, 283, 468–70; industrial, 276–77; management and professional, 470–72, 475, 479. See also Labor.
Employment discrimination, 274–77, 280–83, 358–59, 467–71, 531; "glass ceiling," 471–72, 475. See also Affirmative action.
Enforcement Acts (1870–71), 127, 129
Entertainment and culture, 260–61, 542–48
Episcopal church, 272
Evans, Hiram, 355
Exodus of 1879, 287

Fair Employment Practices, Act, 441; Office of, 468–69
Fair Employment Practices Commission, 359–60, 369
Fair Housing Act of 1968, 497, 498
Fairburn, Ga., 170
Farmers' Alliance. See Alliance Movement.
Farmers, black, 137–48, 169, 173–75, 249–50, 306, 324, 348–49; decline in number, 295, 462–65. See also Agriculture, Landownership, Sharecropping, Tenant Farming.
Farmers Home Administration (FmHA), 463
Farrakhan, Louis, 561–62
Father Divine, 272
Fayette County, 170, 401, 472
Federal Bureau of Investigation (FBI), 424, 430, 505; wiretapping by, 412
Federal Emergency Relief Act (FERA), 345
Federal Housing Administration (FHA), 348

Federal Writers Project, 30, 41, 347
Felton, Rebecca Latimer, 131–33, 155, 157, 181, 194, 202
Felton, William H., 131–33
Ferris, Christine King, 389, 553
Fifteenth Amendment, 115, 120–21, 125, 127, 130
Fifth Congressional District, 437, 454–56
Finch, William, 123, 229–30, 240
First African Baptist Church, 59, 134, 270
First South Carolina Volunteers, 87, 88
Fisher, A. Franklin, 390
Fitzgerald, Ga., 302
Flag, Georgia state, 378, 565
Flagg, Wilkes, 71–73
Flanagan, Robert, 457, 526
Flint River Farms, 349–50
Flipper, Festus, 62, 297
Flipper, Henry O., 62, 297–99
Flipper, Joseph S., 62, 177, 268, 298, 322
Florida, 3–5, 9, 13, 15, 17, 18, 24–26, 29, 44, 88, 102, 150, 285, 332, 386
Floyd County, 51, 170, 496
Floyd, James "Sloppy," 428
Floyd, Silas X., 258
Food stamps, 489–90
Ford, Gerald, 439
Forman, James, 397, 404, 406
Forrest, Nathan Bedford, 101, 125
Forsyth County, whitecapping in, 170, 290; March for Brotherhood, 554–56
Fort Benning, 361, 383, 387
Fort Gordon, 418, 430. See also Camp Gordon.
Fort Pulaski, 73, 84, 108
Fort Sumter, 87
Fort Valley, 118, 170, 173, 294–95, 430, 446–48, 468, 480, 494
Fort Valley Farms, 349
Fort Valley State College, 241, 246–47, 350, 358,

373, 382n, 447–48, 537–39
Fortune, T. Thomas, 135, 186, 193, 194, 201
"Forty Acres and a Mule," 93, 138, 283. See also Landownership.
Fourteenth Amendment, 102, 106, 114, 125, 127, 130, 212, 445
Fourth Congressional District, 454–55
Fowler, Wyche, 454–55
France, 304–305, 308, 362
Frank, Leo, 315
Franklin County, 165
Fraternal orders, 262–63
Frazier, E. Franklin, 243
Frazier, Garrison, 90, 93
Free Negroes, 64–75; and American Colonization Society, 74–76; apprenticeships for children, 92–93; during Civil War, 82, 84, 86; employment, 36; laws governing, 50, 62; literacy rates, 61; white attitudes toward, 57
Freedmen's Aid Society, 223–24
Freedman's Bank, 250–51
Freedmen's Bureau, 92–99, 101, 107, 111–12, 117–19, 138–39, 147, 149, 196, 223, 255
Freedom rides, 399–400
Fugitive Slave Law (1793) 68; (1850) 47, 78, 81
Fugitive slaves. See Slavery, runaways.
Fulton County, 372, 473, 477, 490, 500, 513; public defender, 515; schools, 533, 535, 542–43
Funderburg, Owen, 483
Funeral homes, 253, 481–82
Fyall, F. H., 114
Fye, Cudjo, 138–39

Gaines, Wesley J., 187, 189, 240, 268
Gammon Theological Seminary, 206, 240, 244, 269, 353, 541

Gangs, youth, 506
Garvey, Marcus, 320
Gate City Bar Association, 481
Genocide, 129, 204, 355, 386–87
George, David, 58–59
George, Walter, 332, 351–52, 377
Georgia Association of Black Elected Officials, 440
Georgia Association of Educators (GAE), 531–32, 534
Georgia Baptist, 258, 269
Georgia Board of Education, 378, 523–24
Georgia Constitution (1865) 212; (1868) 212, 226; (1877) 130–31, 196, 213
Georgia Constitutional Convention, (1865) 94–95; (1867–68) 103–104, 108, 111, 113, 226; (1877) 130
Georgia Crackers, 547
Georgia Education Association (GEA), 226
Georgia Equal Rights Association, 97, 101–103, 226
Georgia Equal Rights League, 205, 215
Georgia Executive Council, 15, 16
Georgia Federation of Colored Women's Clubs, 215
Georgia General Assembly: 15, 77, 79–80, 87, 94, 97, 122, 128, 256, 283, 384, 437, 443, 447, 457, 476, 488, 519, 557, 566; 1865 session, 95; 1868 session, 106, 113–16; 1870 session, 120–121; American Colonization Society, attitude toward, 74; antilynching bill passed, 168; antimask law passed, 370; antimiscegenation law passed, 95, 220; Black Codes passed, 95,

Georgia General Assembly
(cont'd.)
148–49; black colleges, funding, 240, 246; black legislators expelled, 114, reinstated, 120; black militia units restricted, abolished, 100, 299, 300; Bond, Julian, refused seat, 427–28; *Brown* decision, massive resistance to, 377–81; convict-lease system, 154, 156–158; crop lien, landlord-tenant contract laws passed, 142–43; disfranchisement, 180, 196, 201–202, 199, 209; dual school system established, 226–27; education, 236–37, 240, 246, 377–81, 533; "Farmers' Legislature," 174–75, 177; Felder-Williams Bill, 209; "Four-Point White Supremacy Program," 368–69; Fourteenth Amendment rejected, 102, ratified, 106; free Negroes, laws restricting, 50–51, 67–69, 73; Georgia Infirmary chartered, 43; Hardwick Bill, 201–202; King holiday established, 553; Maddox, Lester, elected governor by, 429; Nineteenth Amendment rejected, 335; Quality Basic Education Act approved, 533; reapportionment of, 372; segregation laws passed, 212, 215, 220; Sibley Commission appointed by, 380; sit-in movement, 391, 397–98; slave codes, laws passed, 35, 50–51, 53–54, 63, 67; slave trade, attempt to

reopen, 29; "30 Questions" literacy test approved, 369, 371; "two governors" controversy, 366; white high schools established, 236–37; "work or fight" laws passed, 306. See also Georgia House of Representatives, Senate, Legislators.
Georgia Guard, 23
Georgia House of Representatives, 113, 114, 121–22, 128, 214
Georgia Infirmary, 43
Georgia legislature. See Georgia General Assembly.
Georgia Negro State Fair, 247
Georgia Platform, 78
Georgia Power Company, 475, 477
Georgia Public Service Commission, 458
Georgia Railroad Commission, 214, 215
Georgia Real Estate Loan and Trust Company, 251
Georgia Senate, 100, 109, 111, 114, 122, 126, 128, 421
Georgia state flag, 378, 565
Georgia State Medical Association, 255, 494
Georgia State Patrol, 512
Georgia State Prison (Reidsville), 421, 519–21
Georgia Tech, 383, 385, 537, 540
Georgia Trustees, 4–11, 49
Georgia Voters League, 263
Georgia Workingman's Loan and Building Association, 251
Germany, 302, 355; anti-U.S. propaganda, 305, 359
Gibson, Josh, 546
Gilbert, John Wesley, 243, 269
Glascock County, 526
Glenn Bill, 240

Glover, John, 505
Glynn County, 101, 122, 134, 128, 130, 155, 157, 170, 174, 184, 188
Goldwater, Barry, 423
Golf courses, desegregation of, 377, 379, 417, 548
Gordon, Carl, 481, 495
Grady County, 365
Grady, Henry, 125, 144, 177, 185–87, 206
Grady Hospital, 221, 255, 398, 494–96
Grange, 172, 173
Grant, Edith Ingram, 435
Grant, Ulysses, 87, 89, 91, 93, 98, 100, 118, 120
Graves, John Temple, 187–88, 203, 209, 286
Gray, Ga., 317
Gray, James H., 380, 403, 410, 413, 423, 428; *Gray v. Sanders*, 372
Green, Joseph, 539
Green, Samuel, 367–69, 547
Greene County, 49, 291, 318
Greensboro, Ga., 112, 222, 288
Greensboro, N. C., 391
Griffin, Andrew H., 531
Griffin, Ga., 170, 318, 326, 532, 557–58
Griffin, Marvin, 370–71, 374, 376–77, 379, 390, 416, 420
Grimké, Francis, 164, 190
Guaranty Mutual Insurance Company, 482
Gwinnett County, 472–73, 477, 498, 503, 533

Habersham, James, 19
Habitat for Humanity, 466, 561
Haines Institute, 231
Haiti, 13, 17, 28, 66
Hamilton, Grace Towns, 364, 435, 495
Hammond, John D., 194, 241
Hammonds House, 542
Hampton, Fred, 536
Hancock County, 52, 434–35, 462, 526, 531
Haralson County, 286

Harding, Warren G.,
335–37
Hardwick, Thomas,
201–203, 272, 307, 319,
320, 324, 326;
Hardwick Bill,
201–202
Harlem Renaissance, 309
Harpers Ferry, 72, 78–79
Harris County, 169, 465
Harris, Joe Frank, 469, 533,
553, 558, 565
Harris, Joel Chandler, 163,
191–92
Harris, Julian, 326, 328,
330
Harris Neck National
Wildlife Refuge, 465
Harris, Roy, 366, 380–81,
437
Harrison, Benjamin, 197
Harrison, William H., 101,
256
Hartsfield International
Airport, 437, 475–76,
478, 487
Hartsfield, William B.,
364, 369, 372, 374,
381, 393
Hartwell, Ga., 152
Hawkinsville, Ga., 312
Hayes, Roland, 260, 360
Hayes, Rutherford B., 129,
130, 197
Haygood, Atticus, 191, 228,
268
Health, Education, and
Welfare, U.S. Dept.
of, 525, 538
Healthcare, 42–43, 220–21;
255–56; 492–96; folk
medicine, 42
Healy, Eliza, 271
Healy, James Augustine,
41, 271
Healy, Michael A., 41
Healy, Michael Morris, 40,
271
Heard, William H., 258,
269, 286
Henderson, Fletcher, Jr.,
260
Henderson, Fletcher, Sr.,
260
Henderson, Freddye
Scarborough, 481
Henry County, 245, 513

Henson, Lexius, 254
Herbert, Hilary, 189
Herndon, Adrienne, 243
Herndon, Alonzo F., 243,
251
Herndon, Angelo, 342–44
Herndon Home, 482
Herndon, Norris, 252, 482
Herndon Plaza, 543
Hessians, 12
Higginson, Thomas W., 87,
88
Higher education. See
Education.
Highlander Folk School,
392–93
Hill, Benjamin H., 103, 133
Hill, Betty, 435
Hill, Jesse, Jr., 475, 478,
480, 482–83
Hill, Richmond, 437
Hilton Head, S. C., 110
Hinesville, Ga., 292, 362
Historians, 189, 192–93
Hitler, Adolf, 351, 355
Hogansville, Ga., 128, 282
Holland, Dave, 555, 556
Holley, Joseph W., 241,
357–58
Hollowell, Donald L., 383,
394, 405, 407, 418
Holmes, Hamilton,
383–85, 496, 539
Holsey, Lucius Henry, 241,
267
Holt, Sam. See Hose, Sam.
Holyfield, Evander, 546
Homelessness, 500, 507
Homestead Act, 139
Homicide, 506, 508
Hooks, Benjamin, 440
Hooper, Frank, 379–80,
390, 528
Hoover, Herbert, 338–40
Hoover, J. Edgar, 424, 430
Hope, John, 164, 201, 239,
243–45, 305, 313, 322,
346, 353
Hope, Julius, 563
Hope, Lugenia, 322, 330
Horne, Frank S., 246, 344
Hornsby, Alton, Jr., 397,
540
Hose, Sam, 162–163, 302
Hospitals, 43, 255, 493–95
Hotels, segregation,
discrimination by, 104,

218, 400; desegregation
of, 422–23
Housing, 453, 478–79,
496–502;
desegregation, 497;
discrimination,
496–99, 502; public,
500–502; segregation,
212, 219, 420
Housing and Urban
Development, U.S.
Dept. of, 497, 500, 551
Houston, Charles, 372
Houston County, 128, 152,
233, 442
Houston, Ulysses L., 94
Howard, O. O., 98, 149,
246
Howe, Robert, 13, 14
Howell, Clark, 189,
203–204
Hubert, Benjamin
Franklin, 246, 249, 328
Hubert, C. D., 273
Hubert, Zachary Taylor,
245, 249
Hughes Spalding Pavilion,
495–96
Human Relations
Commission, 475, 561
Humphrey, Hubert H.,
432
Humphries, Solomon, 72,
247
Hunt, Henry A., 241, 246,
294, 344, 353
Hunter, Charlayne,
383–85, 494

Ibo (Ebo) Landing, 48
Income, 197, 205, 460–62,
474, 487–88;
disparities in, 460. See
also Wages.
Independent Movement,
131–33, 142
Indians, 3–5, 8, 13, 19–26
Industrial Revolution, 188,
231
Infant mortality, 492–93
Insurance companies, 250,
251, 482–83
Interdenominational
Theological Seminary,
541
Intermarriage. See
Miscegenation.

Interstate Commerce Commission (ICC), 214–15, 358, 400–403, 411
Ironclad Oath, 103–104, 106, 120, 123
Irwin County, 286

Jackson, Andrew, 23, 25, 29
Jackson County, 75, 171
Jackson, Ira, 475
Jackson, Jesse, 452, 458, 484, 487, 549, 551
Jackson, Maynard, Jr., 437–38, 452, 454, 475–76, 492, 506
Jamaica, 18, 59
Jasper County, 54, 118, 305, 316, 324, 516
Jeanes (Anna T.) Fund, 236
Jeffers, Perry, 117
Jefferson County, 51, 138, 526
Jefferson, Thomas, 12, 20
Jekyll Island, 26, 29
Jenkins, Charles, 95, 97, 103, 104
Jenkins County, 462
Jenkins, Herbert, 512
Jews, and civil rights, 399
Jim Crow. See Segregation.
Job training, 491
Johnson, Andrew, 94, 97–100, 102, 107–108, 112
Johnson County, 367, 443, 449–51, 526, 531
Johnson, Georgia Douglas, 310, 330
Johnson, Henry Lincoln, 243, 336–38
Johnson, James Weldon, 245, 309, 311, 314
Johnson, Leroy, 421, 429, 432, 435, 437–38
Johnson, Lyndon, 371, 422–23, 430, 432, 468
Johnson, Sol C., 258, 262, 313
Joiner, Philip, 116, 227, 277
Jones, Bessie, 545
Jones, Charles, 403–404, 408
Jones County, 51
Jonesboro, Ga., 159, 167, 532
Jordan, Clarence, 377, 465

Jordan, Vernon, 406
Justice system. See Criminal justice system.
Justice, U.S. Dept. of, 349, 371, 412, 437, 443–46, 448–49, 451, 454–55, 477, 530

Kansas, 287
Keith, Leroy, 541
Kelley, Asa, 404, 409–10, 517
Kemp, Jan, 540
Kennedy, John F., 382, 393–94, 407, 409, 414, 422
Kennedy, Robert, 394–95, 410, 412
Keysville, Ga., 445–46, 526
Killens, John Oliver, 544
King, Alberta, 549
King, C. B., 405, 407, 409, 414, 435–36
King, Coretta Scott, 389, 424, 429–30, 433, 549–50, 553, 555, 564
King, Lonnie, 391–92, 396–97, 528
King, Martin Luther, Jr., 270, 388–401, 404–13, 421–26, 429–32, 526, 549, 564; Center for Nonviolent Social Change, 483, 549–50, 553, 563–64; holiday, 552–54, 559, 563; National Historic Site, 552.
King, Martin Luther, Sr., 233, 270, 334, 373–74, 394, 397, 438–40, 549
King, Martin Luther, III, 453–54
King of England's Soldiers, 14, 19
King, Primus, 363–65
King, Slater, 403–404, 409, 412, 465
King, Yolanda, 553
Kingston, Ga., 52
Knight, Gladys, 546
Knights of Labor, 278–79
Knox Academy, 226, 230
Koinonia, 377–78, 465
Korean War, 387
Ku Klux Klan, 92, 105, 117–25, 139; (1915–44)

181, 272, 309, 314–21, 324–25, 354–55, 377; (1945–59) 362–63, 365, 367–68; (1960s) 381–85; 395–96, 422–23, 524; (1980s) 450, 532–33, 555–60; anti-Klan laws passed, 370; black resistance to, 101–102, 109–10, 166, 323–24, 326; black schools attacked by, 222, 228; glorified in The Clansman, 189–90
Kwanzaa, 565

Labor, agricultural, 30–35, 39, 95–96, 139–41, 283–84, 292–94, 462, 466; child, 141, 276, 466; immigrant, 283–84, 295; non-agricultural, 35–37, 84, 274–283, 467–68
Labor agents, 285, 288, 291
Labor shortages, 140, 141, 170, 205, 283, 287, 292–96
Labor strikes, 278–81, 354
Labor unions, 157, 277–82; black, 277–80, 354–55, 467; integration, 280–81, 354
LaBord, Susie, 501
LaFayette, Ga., 279
LaGrange, Ga., 334
Lamar, Charles A. L., 29
Lamar County, 534
Lamson Normal School, 229
Landownership, by blacks, 138–39, 141, 145–48, 248; land tenure during Reconstruction 93–94, 98, 99, 107–108, 110, 111. See also Farmers, Sharecropping, Tenant Farming.
Laney, Lucy Craft, 231
Lankford, Richard, 510
Laurens County, 211
Laurens, John, 16
Law enforcement, 506–13; blacks in, 511–12; police brutality, 508–11. See also

Criminal justice.
Lee County, 130, 316, 371,
    414, 465
Lee, Robert E., 91
Lee, Spike, 541, 544
Legislative Black Caucus,
    439, 457, 459, 469, 476
Legislators, black, 105–15,
    147, 120–22, 134,
    156–57, 214, 227, 421,
    427–28, 432, 435, 439,
    446, 457; expelled,
    113–16; listed, 105;
    reinstated, 120.
Lewis, John, 392–93, 422,
    425–27, 439, 454, 456
Lewis, John Randolph, 118,
    135, 224, 227
Lewis, Marvin E., 526, 531
Lewis School, 228, 246
Lexington, Ga., 102, 313
Liberia, 74–76, 286
Liberty County, 90, 128,
    147, 223, 227, 270, 401
Libraries, 190, 230, 261;
    Carnegie, 205, 217,
    218, desegregation,
    408, 411; read-ins, 392
Liele, George, 58–59
Life expectancy, 492–93
Lincoln, Abraham, 77,
    79–81, 86–88, 94, 110,
    112, 286
Lincoln County, 55, 170
Lincolnton, Ga., 425–26,
    466, 524
Literacy, 228, 230, 237;
    literacy test and
    disfranchisement, 181,
    201, 203–204, 209, 211;
    "30 Questions," 369,
    371, 436
Lodge ("Force") Bill, 186,
    189, 197–98
Lomax, Michael, 453–54,
    475, 502, 542
Long County, 492
Long, Jefferson, 105,
    123–24, 127, 129, 166,
    278
Longstreet, James, 127, 132
Lonnon, Ishmael, 132, 157
Lorick, Oscar, 463–64
Louisiana, 34, 201, 285
Louisville, Ga., 138
Love, Emanuel K., 134,
    174, 230, 269–70, 288

Lowery, Joseph, 450, 470,
    475, 492, 548, 550, 563
Lowndes County, 286, 316,
    323, 444
Loyalty oath. See Ironclad
    Oath.
Lucas, Bill, 547
Lumber industry, 36, 277,
    346
Lumpkin County, 3, 51, 94
Lunch counter sit-ins,
    391–98. See also Sit-in
    movement.
Lyerly, Ga., 170
Lyke, James P., 563
Lynch, James, 92, 223, 267
Lynching, 51, 56, 60–61,
    92, 119, 124, 159–69,
    339, 366, 387; and
    anti-U.S. propaganda,
    305, 359; black
    protests to, 166–67; of
    black soldiers,
    307–308; 314–19, 366;
    in the New South,
    159–169; New South
    mythology concerning,
    164–65; as "push"
    factor in migration,
    284, 289, 291–96; and
    rape myth, 160–61,
    164; resistance to and
    prevention of, 167–68;
    wages, relationship to,
    159; white churchmen,
    attitude toward, 263,
    272; and white
    supremacy, 159,
    164–65. See also
    Antilynching.
Lyons, Judson W., 134–35,
    157, 257, 336

M & M Products Company,
    485
McCown, John, 434–35
McDuffie County, 61, 160,
    176, 526
McGill, Ralph, 356, 370,
    396, 425
McIntosh County, 111, 128,
    166, 401, 464
McKinley, William, 162,
    246
McMillan, Eldridge, 539
McRae, Ga., 351, 377
McRee, Edward, 151

Mableton, Ga., 394, 498
Macon, Ga., 3, 91, 94,
    134–35, 151, 158, 173,
    192, 205, 207, 248, 261,
    274, 278, 280, 281,
    298, 301, 311, 313, 430,
    461, 476, 494–95, 506,
    543, 545; black- owned
    businesses, 481–82;
    black population, 96,
    472; civil rights
    movement, 415–16;
    desegregation, 401;
    election violence,
    127–129; Great
    Migration, 291–92; job
    discrimination,
    469–70; Klan activity,
    101, 320, 368, 558; law
    enforcement, blacks in
    511; lynching and
    whitecapping, 169,
    325; Mercer University
    desegregated, 385;
    politics and voting
    rights, 200, 369, 401,
    446; Reconstruction,
    96–97, 100–102, 112,
    115, 120, 122–23;
    schools, 222, 226–30,
    353, 523–24, 526;
    segregation, 216,
    218–20; slave revolts
    suspected, 49–51, 79;
    slaves and free
    Negroes in, 33, 35, 37,
    39, 43, 58, 63, 69, 70,
    72, 84, 86; World War
    I, 302–306
Macon County, 114, 152,
    349, 526
Macy's department store,
    396
Maddox, Lester, 396, 420,
    423, 428–29, 431–32,
    436–37, 439, 465, 489,
    521
Madison County, 151, 532
Madison, James, 19, 25
Malcolm, Roger, 366
Malcolm X, 426, 564
Mandela, Nelson, 564
Mankin, Helen Douglas,
    370
Mann, Alonzo, 315
Manumission, 38, 64–67,
    72

March on Washington for
     Jobs and Freedom, 422
Marietta, Ga., 51, 171, 315,
     359, 392, 467, 524,
     529, 557–59
Marino, Eugene, 563
Marion County, 249, 492
Maroons, 19, 44, 47, 54
Marshall, Thurgood, 374
Marshallville, Ga., 229
Martin, John Sella, 31, 63
Massive resistance, 375–79;
     Georgia Education
     Commission, 376. See
     also Schools,
     desegregation.
Masters golf tournament,
     419
Mathews, Zeke, 413
Mattingly, Mack, 455
Mays, Benjamin, 190, 265,
     322, 353, 389, 395,
     425, 438, 456, 465
Meade, George, 99
Media, black employment
     in, 479–80; black-
     owned, 480–81. See
     also Black press.
Medicaid, 493
Medical Association of
     Georgia, 494
Memphis, Tenn., 430
Mercer University, 385
Meredith, James, 426
Meriwether County, 79,
     166, 509, 511, 530
Methodists, 58, 60, 225;
     churches, 267–69,
     272–73; education, 230
Metropolitan Atlanta Rapid
     Transit Authority
     (MARTA), 473, 501,
     503
Mexican War, 78
Midway Congregational
     Church, 270
Migration, of blacks from
     Georgia, 285–96; to
     Africa, 74–76, 286; to
     California, 288–89;
     effect on Georgia
     economy, 292–96;
     Great Migration,
     290–96, 306, 321, 323;
     in-migration of blacks
     to Georgia, 472; to
     Kansas, 287; effect on

race relations, 273,
     287, 293–96; during
     World War II, 359
Milan, Ga., 317
Military service, of blacks,
     100, 112, 297–302;
     American Revolution,
     16–17; Civil War,
     86–88; desegregation
     of armed forces, 362,
     387; draft, 302–303,
     361; militia, 100, 111,
     298–301; World War I,
     297–308; World War
     II, 361–62
Milledgeville, Ga., 67, 71,
     75, 78, 81, 90, 94, 101,
     104, 113, 158, 227, 237,
     312–13, 444, 469
Millen, Ga., 318
Miller County, 150, 170,
     318, 371
Miller, Zell, 439, 441, 458,
     488, 565
Milton, George Fort,
     328–29
Mincey, S. S., 339
Minimum Foundation
     Program for
     Education, 374
Minstrel shows, 192
Miscegenation, 40–41, 53,
     69, 95, 113, 129, 212,
     219–20; and lynching,
     164; and "social
     equality," 129. See also
     Race relations, Rape
     myth, "Social
     Equality."
Missing and Murdered
     Children case,
     504–505
Mississippi, 34, 52, 122,
     124, 201, 285, 292, 337,
     347, 387, 400, 426, 461,
     525
Mitchell County, 316, 443
Mondale, Walter, 452, 551
Monday, David, 17
Monroe, Ga., 366
Monroe County, 325, 444
Monroe, James, 29, 74
Montgomery, Ala., 102,
     388–90
Montgomery County, 339,
     368
Monticello, Ga., 316

Moody, Leroy, 560
Moore, Dan, 543
Moore, Romulus, 119
Morehouse College, 230,
     240, 242, 245, 260,
     353, 382n, 540–41;
     Medical School,
     495–96
Morgan County, 128, 288,
     444
Morrill Act, 239, 246
Morris Brown College, 124,
     240, 255–56, 268, 353,
     541–42
Moses, Edwin, 548
Mothers of Murdered Sons
     (MOMS), 508
Motley, Constance Baker,
     379, 383
Mount Vernon, Ga., 368
Movies, 544–45
Muhammad, Elijah, 426,
     562
Mundle, Winfred, 383
Muscogee County, 363,
     473, 530
Museums, 482, 542–43
Musicians, Singers, 260,
     545–46
Muslims, 426, 466, 561–62
Mutual Federal Savings
     and Loan, 483, 499

Napper, George, 503, 505,
     513
Nation of Islam. See
     Muslims.
National Anti-Klan
     Network, 557
National Association for the
     Advancement of
     Colored People
     (NAACP), 211, 245,
     256, 281, 341–42, 440;
     antilynching activities,
     160, 317, 319, 321–24,
     330–34, 337, 366;
     Atlanta branch, 441,
     563; Atlanta school
     crisis, 310–12; capital
     punishment,
     opposition to, 518; civil
     rights activities, 390,
     400–406, 415, 417, 494;
     conventions in Atlanta,
     312, 374, 400;
     economic issues, 463,

465, 467, 478, 484;
education, school
desegregation, 374–77,
379, 383, 528, 530,
534, 538; local
branches, 310–13,
376–77, 415, 447;
offices bombed,
560–61; voting rights,
364, 401, 443, 446
National Association of
Landowners, 465
National Black Arts
Festival, 542
National Industrial
Recovery Act (NIRA),
345
National Lawyers Guild,
405
National Negro Business
League, 209, 255
National Recovery
Administration (NRA),
345–46
National Student Alliance
(NSA), 392
National Youth
Administration (NYA),
345
Negro Labor Union, 278
Negro Leagues, 546–47
Negro Press Association of
Georgia, 258
Negro Transport Company,
216
New Communities Inc.,
465
New Deal, 344–53
"New Negro," 309, 362
New South, 182–95
Newnan, Ga., 162–63, 354,
494
Newspapers, black-owned,
480–81. See also Black
press.
Newton County, 533
Newton, Ga., 331
Niagara Movement, 167,
239, 259, 310
Nineteenth Amendment,
335
Nixon, Richard, 393–94,
432–33, 439, 525
Norcross, Ga., 281
Norcross, Jonathan, 129,
132
Norman, Jessye, 545

North Carolina, 22, 391
Northen, William J., 161,
168, 174, 177, 208–209
Norwood, Thomas M., 132
Nunn, Sam, 478
Nursing schools, 255

Ocilla, Ga., 370
Oconee County, 170, 323,
325
Odd Fellows, 259, 262
Odingsells, Anthony, 72
Ogeechee River, 8, 43
Oglethorpe County, 56,
118, 170, 200, 349
Oglethorpe, James Edward,
4–11, 21, 58
Olmsted, Frederick Law,
33, 39
Olympic athletes, 546, 548
Olympic stadium, 501
Olympics (1996), 473, 478,
501–502, 505, 565
100 Black Men of Atlanta,
492, 536
Oni, Sam, 385
Orr, Gustavus John, 227,
240
Owens, Wilbur, Jr., 443,
468–69, 521

Pace, Harry, 311
Page, Marion, 405–406
Paine College, 241–43,
266–68, 543–44
Palmetto Five, 161
Parks, Rosa, 389
Parks, segregation in, 218,
417
Paschal, James and Robert,
486–87; Paschal's
restaurant, 391,
486–87
Pass and patrol system, 54,
56, 84, 86. See also
Slave patrols.
Payne, Jimmy Ray, 505
Peabody Fund, 236, 357
Peach County, 236, 255,
349, 401, 446–48, 526,
532
Peculiar institution. See
Slavery.
Pelham, Ga., 307, 316
Penn, Lemuel, 423
Penniman, "Little
Richard," 545–46

Peonage, 96, 148–53, 324,
349
People United to Serve
Humanity (PUSH), 550
People's party. See Populist
Movement
Perry, Ga., 442, 495, 524
Perry, Heman, 251–53, 259
Phagan, Mary, 315; Knights
of, 316
Phylon, 243
Physicians, black, 220, 255,
494–96. See also
Healthcare.
Pierce County, 131
Pike County, 170
Pilgrim Health and Life
Insurance Company,
482
Plains, Ga., 527
Pledger, William A.,
131–36, 160, 166, 177,
187, 201, 243, 258, 262
Plessy v. Ferguson, 215, 231
Police. See Law
enforcement.
Politics, (1850–60) 78–82;
(1920–32) 334–40;
(1932–45) 350–52,
357–58; (1945–1960)
363–72; (1960–1970)
393–95, 420–21,
427–29; (1970–90)
434–59; Atlanta school
crisis, 311–12;
disfranchisement,
195–211; Independent
Movement, 131–34;
Populist Movement,
175–81; post-
Reconstruction,
126–36;
Reconstruction,
94–95, 97, 102–26
Polk County, 159
Poll tax, 104, 113, 188, 122,
130, 196–97, 199, 232,
350, 356, 358, 363, 369
Poor People's March on
Washington, 430, 432
Poor whites, 142, 146, 148,
157, 164, 178, 181–82,
199, 202–204, 209,
276, 288
Pope, John, 102, 103
Population, black, 11, 288,
295, 471–73

Populist Movement, 146, 175–80
Port Royal, S. C., 84, 85, 88
Porter, James, 97, 212, 226
Porter, John, 390
Positive Employment and Community Help (PEACH), 491
Potts, Lamar, 509
Poverty, 138–39, 142–45, 460–62, 487, 489–90, 492–93, 500
Powderly, Terence, 279
Powell, Adam Clayton, 383, 388
Presbyterians, 58, 63, 271, 388, 398
Priber, Christian, 21
Prisons, conditions, 342–43, 519–21; convict-lease camps, 155–56; overcrowding, 503, 521
Pritchett, Laurie, 403–13
Proctor, Henry Hugh, 208, 215, 271, 308
Progressive Movement, 198, 199
Project Success, 536
Public defenders, 515
Public Works Administration (PWA), 346
Pulaski County, 446
Pullman cars, 214, 215
Putnam County, 139, 152, 318, 443

Quakers, 61, 223
Quality Basic Education (QBE) Act, 533–36
Quitman County, 371, 436, 462
Quitman, Ga., 128, 229

Race relations, 181–91, 197, 213, 293–96, 313–14, 321–22, 355, 359, 387, 421, 554–61, 565–66
Radio stations, 480–81
Railroads, 35, 278, 280–82, 288, 290–91, 293, 358; convict labor on, 154; corruption involving, 121, 185; racial strife over jobs, 280–82;

recruitment of black workers, 285, 287–88, 290, 293; segregation, 135, 174, 177, 213–15, 322
Rainey, Gertrude "Ma," 545
Randall, William P., Jr., 415, 446, 457, 510
Randall, William P., Sr., 415, 481–82
Randolph, A. Philip, 358, 387, 422
Randolph County, 371
Ransom, Reverdy C., 163
Rape myth, 160–61, 164, 183, 188, 191
Ray, James Earl, 431
Reagan, Ronald, 551–53; administration, 491, 496–97, 536–37
Reagon, Cordell, 403–404
Real estate, 253–54, 527
Reconstruction, congressional, 102–25; 137, 139, 156, 277; New South view of 182–84, 189–90, 192–93 195; overthrow of, 121–31; presidential, 91–102
Reconstruction Acts, 102, 111, 212
"Red Summer," 317, 321
Redding, Otis, 545
Regents, Board of, 539
Regents Test, 538
Reidsville, Ga., 94, 519
Relief, 341, 342, 345, 348
Religion, 57–61, 263–73, 562–63; black churches, 388, 398–99, 454. See also specific denominations, e.g., Baptists.
Republican party, 101, 103, 107, 113, 116, 121, 124, 127–32, 181, 196–98, 336–40, 352, 434, 441; black-and-tan, lily-white division within, 130, 132, 180
Resettlement Administration (RA), 349
Rice, 33, 38, 42, 43
Rich's department store, 396, 473; Magnolia Room, 393, 400

Richardson, Alfred, 120
Richardson, Harry F., 362, 541
Richmond County, 179, 230–31, 511, 525
Ridge, Martin, 23
Rincon, Ga., 318
Rivers, Eurith D., 353
Robber barons, 188, 235
Robins Air Force Base, 470, 476, 539
Robinson, Jackie, 411, 414, 546–47
Rogers, William, 209–10
Rome, Ga., 68, 78, 125, 165, 216, 221, 277, 294, 311, 360, 386, 496, 511, 532
Roosevelt, Eleanor, 351–52, 355, 392
Roosevelt, Franklin D., 331, 333, 340, 344–47, 350–52, 356, 359, 361
Roosevelt, Theodore, 208, 301
Rosenwald Fund, 236, 357–58
Rothschild, Jacob, 399, 425
Royal African Company, 6
Rucker, Henry A., 179, 251, 282, 336
Russell, Herman J., 475, 478, 481, 483
Russell, Richard B., Jr., 332, 350, 367, 369, 379, 387, 395, 401, 409, 524

Salzburgers, 9, 10
Sanders, Carl, 420, 435–36, 438
Sandersville, Ga., 147, 173
Sapelo Island, 110–11
Sasser, Ga., 413–14
Savannah, Ga., 34, 58, 81, 93–94, 124, 127, 143, 151, 159, 202, 248, 261, 286–87, 289–92, 311, 313, 461, 506, 510, 512–14; abolitionists and suspected slave revolts, reactions to, 49, 57, 79; American Revolution, 14, 15, 17–19; black militia units in, 299–300; businesses, black-

owned, 481–83; civil rights movement, 416–18; Civil War, 83–84, 88–91, 267; Colonial period, 6–11; election violence, 118, 128; employment in, 274–75, 277–81, 359; politics, voting rights, 200, 335, 352, 369; racial clashes, 100, 138; Reconstruction, 97–98, 100–102, 108–109, 116, 118; schools, education, 223, 226, 228, 235, 246, 529, 543, 547; segregation, 215–22; slave trade, 27–29, 39; slaves and free Negroes in, 43, 44, 47, 49, 50, 53, 57–59, 62–66, 68–70, 72–76; War of 1812, 25; World War I, 302

Savannah Negro Laborers' Union, 278, 280

Savannah River, 4, 14, 42

Savannah State College, 240, 242, 246–47, 353, 373, 537–539

Savannah Tribune, 129, 258, 480

Saxton, Rufus, 87, 99, 110

Scarborough, William S., 193, 246

Schley County, 165

Schools, busing, 525, 528–30; desegregation, 372–85, 523–32; discipline, racial disparities in, 535–36; "freedom of choice" plans, 524; private, 526–27, black, 536; racial composition, 527, 529, 534; racial unrest in, 532–33; segregation, 213, 227. *See also* Education.

Scipio, Joseph, 17

Scotch Highlanders, 9, 14

Scott, Al, 457–59

Scott, C. A., 480

Scott, Emmett Jay, 259

Scott, W. A., Sr, 259

"Scottsboro Boys," 342

Screven County, 48, 128, 173, 174, 426

Screws, Claude, 360

Sea Islands, 33, 84, 93, 98, 110, 264

Second African Baptist Church, 94

Second South Carolina Volunteers, 88

Secret ballot, 176, 196

Segregation, 86, 129, 211–22, 231; in federal jobs, 282–83; in labor unions, 279–80; of militia units, 300; residential, 348, 363; "separate but equal," 215, 227, 231. *See also* Desegregation, Housing, Schools.

Selma to Montgomery March, 425

Seminole County, 371

Seminoles, 24–26; Seminole Wars, 26. *See also* Creek Indians.

Sengstacke, John H., 258, 266

Seward, William H., 110

Sharecropping, 139–46; "furnish system," 149. *See also* Agriculture, Farmers, Tenant farming.

Sheriffs, 509, 510; posses, 510

Sherman, William T., 88–90, 93, 94, 186, 223, 270; Field Order Number Fifteen, 93–94; march to the sea, 88–91

Sherrod, Charles, 403–14, 465

Sibley Commission, 380

Sierra Leone, 18, 59

Simmons, William Joseph, 316

Simms, James M., 101, 106, 116, 118, 124, 157, 166, 240, 256

Simms, Thomas, 46–47

Singers, musicians, 260, 545–46

Singleton, Benjamin "Pap," 287

Sit-in movement, 391–98

Skidaway Island, 85, 94

Slater Fund, 236

Slaton, John M., 168, 315

Slavery, 4–11, 27–64, 77–90; allowed, 11; among Cherokees, 22; as cause of Civil War, 77–82; during Civil War 82–91; control systems, 52–57; economy and society, 29–44; living standards of slaves, 42; prohibited, 4–10; resistance and rebellion, 44–52; revolts, real or imagined, 28, 48–54, 57, 60, 62, 66, 79; runaways, 4, 9, 13, 16, 18, 19, 24, 26, 31, 44–47, 54, 64–65, 84–85, 87; during Sherman's march to the sea, 88–91; slave codes, 53, 54, 65, 67; slave families, 40, 85; slave narratives, 30, 347; slave trials, 54–55; as viewed by New South propagandists, 183, 189, 192; weakening of, 83–86

Slave patrols, 16, 31, 54, 56, 85, 86

Slave trade, 27–29, 39, 40, 50, 74, 78

Sledd, Andrew, 194

Sledge, Percy, 545

Smith, Charles Henry (Bill Arp), 191–92, 234

Smith, Hoke, 158, 187, 195, 198, 203–205, 207, 209, 216

Smith, James M., 126

Smith, Lillian, 393

Smith, Otis A., 458, 530

Smith, Otis Wesley, 447, 494

Smyre, Calvin, 457

"Social equality," 194, 204, 213, 280, 307. *See also* Miscegenation, Race relations.

Social organizations, 261–63

Social Security, 347
Social welfare, 489–92
Soperton, Ga., 365, 444
Souls of Black Folk, The, 190
South Carolina, 4–13, 16, 21, 33, 49, 53, 57, 66, 75, 84, 110, 124, 201, 300, 304, 396
Southern Christian Leadership Conference (SCLC), 390–93, 405–407, 416–18, 421–25, 430, 431, 435, 450, 451, 465, 470, 543, 549–50, 554
Southern Commission for the Study of Lynching, 328, 330
Southern Conference on Human Welfare (SCHW), 355–56
Southern Manifesto, 378
Southern Regional Council (SRC), 321, 356, 382
Southern Rural Action (SRA), 466
Southern Sociological Congress, 321
Southwest Georgia, 401–15, 461, 467, 493
Soviet Union, 386–87
Spalding County, 308, 497, 532
Spanish-American War, 300–302
Spanish explorations, 3–4
Sparta, Ga., 122, 177, 434–35
Speer, Emory, 131–33, 150–51, 158
Spelman College, 240, 255, 270, 353, 382n, 540–41
Sports, 546–48; college athletics, 539–40
Springfield Baptist Church, 59, 97
St. Augustine, Fla., 3, 4, 9, 18
St. Catherines Island, 4, 110–11
St. Marys, Ga., 25, 51
St. Simons Island, 9, 25, 48, 85, 88, 464
Standard Life Insurance Company, 252, 306, 310

Stanton, Edwin, 90, 100
States' Rights Council, 378, 379
Statesboro tragedies, 165
Steele, Carrie, 261
Stephens, Alexander, 80–81, 91, 127, 133, 185, 197
Stephens, Ed, 556
Stevens, Thaddeus, 93
Steward, T. G., 244, 250
Stewart County, 30, 371, 446, 462, 526
Stone Mountain, 314, 316, 362, 400, 498
Stoner, J. B., 381, 441, 450, 554–56, 559
Stono Revolt, 8, 49, 53
Storrs Academy, 226, 229, 246
Streetcars, segregation on, 215–17
Student-Adult Liaison Committee, 396
Student Nonviolent Coordinating Committee (SNCC), 392, 396, 401–14, 426–28
Styles, William H., 177–78
Sullivan, Herschelle, 397
Sullivan, Louis W., 495, 541
Summerhill, 427, 501
Sumner, Charles, 115, 128
Sumner Civil Rights Act, 128–29, 133, 159, 213–14, 217
Sumter County, 52, 141, 371, 378, 414, 436, 443, 465–66, 527
Swainsboro, Ga., 368
Sylvester, Ga., 307, 316

Taft, William Howard, 247
Tailfer, Patrick, 7
Talbot County, 492, 531
Talented Tenth, 238, 243, 246, 256, 263
Taliaferro County, 303, 442, 466, 514, 524
Talmadge, Eugene, 350–52, 354–58, 360, 364–66
Talmadge, Herman, 366, 368–70, 372–76, 378–81, 387, 395, 421, 423, 437, 455, 547

Tanner, Henry O., 244, 260
Tate, Horace, 438
Tate, James, 229, 253
Taxes, property, 464, 527, 535; sales, 487–88. *See also* Poll tax.
Taylor County, 366
Taylor, Susie King, 39, 63, 83, 223, 248
Teacher Certification Test (TCT), 534
Techwood Homes, 346, 501–502
Teenage pregnancies, 490
Telfair County, 211, 365–66, 443, 532
Tenant farming, 137–48, 348, 462; company store, 143–45, 153, 197; crop liens, 142–43
Tennessee, 22
Terrell County, 371, 404, 413–15, 444, 514, 527
Terrell, Joseph M., 205, 207
Terry, Alfred, 119–20
Test Oath. *See* Ironclad Oath.
Textile industry, 185, 345, 354, 360, 467
Textile mills, employment in, 276–77, strikes at, 276, 279
Third African Baptist Church, 70
Thirteenth Amendment, 95, 108, 149
Thomas County, 264
Thomaston, Ga., 531
Thomasville, Ga., 219, 221, 294, 297, 298, 302, 311, 313, 327
Thompson, Larry, 479, 455
Thompson, Melvin E., 366–69
Threatt, Robert, 542
Tift County, 443
Tifton, Ga., 150
Tillson, Davis, 99, 107, 111, 138, 225
Tilly, Dorothy, 370, 381
Tobacco, 33, 63
Tobias, Channing, 266
Toombs, Robert, 60, 80, 130, 149
Toomer, Jean, 309, 330
Torbert, James H., 246
Townshend Acts, 11

Treutlen County, 444
Troup County, 47, 128, 173
Truman, Harry, 362, 367–69, 387
Tubman, William V. S., 75
Turner, Abram, 122
Turner County, 170, 289, 510
Turner, Hayes, 316
Turner, Henry McNeal, 92, 96, 101, 109, 111–16, 118–22, 124, 129, 133–34, 157, 159, 166, 177, 180, 196, 227, 230, 247, 265, 267, 268–69, 278, 286
Turner, Mary, 316–17
Turner, Nat, 49–51, 60, 62, 68
Turner, Ted, 547
Turner Theological Seminary, 240, 541
Turner, Wilson, 509
Turpentine camps, 145, 150
Tuskegee Institute, 238–39, 357, 362, 372, 377
Tuttle, Elbert, 331, 343, 383
Tutu, Desmond, 553
Twiggs County, 51, 228, 317, 526
Tybee Island, 13, 15

U. S. Employment Service, 348
U. S. House of Representatives, 123, 127
Uncle Remus, 191, 192; Avenue, 219
Uncle Tom's Cabin, 190
Underground Atlanta, 453, 473, 476, 506
Unemployment, 341, 358–59, 467–68
Union army, 83, 87–91
Union Leagues, 103
United Nations, 386–87, 440
Universal Negro Improvement Association (UNIA), 320
University Homes, 346, 501
University of Georgia, 230, 239, 242, 246, 356–57, 373, 378, 382–84, 394, 537–540, 548

Urban League, 289, 313, 332, 359, 364, 391, 491, 495

Valdosta, 85, 203, 312, 444, 532
Vandiver, Ernest, 379–81, 383, 391, 393–94, 404, 408, 409, 523
Vann, James, 22
Venable, James, 532, 556
Vienna, Ga., 237, 332, 510
Vietnam War, 427–30
Vinson, Carl, 387
Virginia, 33, 50, 57, 67
Voice of the Negro, 207, 259
Voter Education Project, 439, 443–44, 446
Voter registration, 364–65, 370–71, 401–403, 413–15
Voting Rights Act of 1965, 425, 437, 442–43

Wages, 141, 275–77, 280, 293, 346, 354, 466–68, 474; agricultural, 141, 143, 159, 160; differentials, 275, 277, 345; standing wage, 139
Walden, Austin T., 257, 304, 328, 331, 366, 370, 374, 393, 397
Walker, Alice, 544
Walker, Charles T., 134–35, 266, 301
Walker County, 170
Walker, David, 49–50, 62. See also David Walker's Appeal.
Walker, Eugene, 457
Walker, Herschel, 539
Walker, Wyatt T., 390
Wallace, Gov. George, 432, 436, 439–40
Wallace, Sen. George, 105, 111, 114, 129, 157
Wallace, Henry, 367
Wallace, John, 509
Walton County, 169, 222, 366
War of 1812, 24–25
Ward, Felker, 475
Ward, Horace, 382–83, 418, 423, 435, 438, 540
Ware, Carl, 437, 475
Ware County, 95, 167

Ware, Edmund Asa, 230, 271
Ware High School, 230–31, 246
Warm Springs, Ga. 344
Warner Robins, Ga., 485
Warren County, 117–19, 146, 349, 526
Warrenton, Ga., 119, 222, 331
Washington, Booker T., 193, 201–202, 208–209, 215, 238–39, 241, 247, 255, 259, 263–64, 312, 336, 483
Washington County, 147, 173, 347, 525–26
Washington, Ga., 317, 524
Washington, George, 12–13, 16, 18
Watkinsville, Ga., 165
Watson, Thomas Edward, 157, 175–81, 202–204, 323
Waycross, Ga., 311, 317, 318, 335
Wayne County, 319
Waynesboro, Ga., 75
Weaver, Robert C., 344
Webster County, 371, 402, 526
Wells, Ida B., 163–64
Wells, Samuel, 408, 412
Weltner, Charles, 421, 429
West Hunter Baptist Church, 431
West Indies, 15, 17, 18, 28, 51
West Point, Ga., 293
Western and Atlantic Railway, 109, 154, 214
Westinghouse Electric Company, 468
Wheeler County, 446, 462
White Citizens' Council, 370, 378, 418
White flight, 452, 472–73, 479, 497, 527–28
White press, 168, 187, 307, 326–27; and Atlanta riot, 204–206, 209; and New South mythology, 191, 204
White primary, 199–204, 363, 364, 366–67
White, Richard W., 116
White supremacist organizations, 92,

White supremacist (*cont'd*)
327–28, 330, 363. *See
also* Ku Klux Klan.
White, Walter, 160–61,
206, 221, 310–11, 317,
330–31, 333–34, 353,
367
White, William Jefferson,
63, 133–34, 157, 164,
179, 205, 207, 226, 230,
258, 269
Whitecapping, 148, 169–71,
290, 323
Whitefield, George,
10, 11
Whitney, Eli, 34
Wilkes County, 60, 122, 524
Wilkins, Roy, 368, 417, 440,
528
Wilkinson, Bill, 450
Wilkinson County, 128
Williams, Adam Daniel,
270, 312

Williams, George
Washington, 193
Williams, Hosea, 416–18,
425, 431, 439, 454–56,
520, 524, 550, 553–56
Williams, Samuel, 390, 428
Williams, Wayne, 451,
504–505
Williamson, Q. V., 437
Wilson, Anthony, 132, 134,
178, 214
Wilson, E. J., 449–51
Wilson, Hercules, 126, 134
Winder, Ga., 272, 532
Woodliff, Edward, 72, 123,
229, 250, 254
Woodruff, Robert, 381
Woodson, Carter G., 540
Works Progress
Administration (WPA),
345–47, 350
World War I, 281, 287, 290,
302–309; "work or

fight" controversy,
306–307
World War II, 355, 358–62
Wright, James, 14, 16
Wright, Louis T., 256, 303
Wright, Richard R., Sr.,
196, 244, 246–47, 251,
291, 301, 336
Wrightsville, Ga., 367,
449–51
Writers, black, 309,
543–44

Yates, Clayton B., 481
Yerby, Frank, 543–44
You and Segregation, 370,
378
Young, Andrew, 388,
409–11, 416, 422, 437,
439–40, 451–52, 456,
458–59, 470, 475–78,
501, 526, 553

About the Author

Donald L. Grant (1919–1988) received his Ph.D. degree from the University of Missouri and was Emeritus Professor of History at predominantly black Fort Valley State College, where he taught for thirteen years. A specialist in black and Latin American history, Dr. Grant was the author of *The Anti-Lynching Movement: 1883–1832* as well as many articles on black history. He was a contributor to the *Dictionary of Georgia Biography* (1983) and *The Encyclopedia of Southern History.*

About the Editor

After Dr. Grant's death in 1988, his son Jonathan edited, revised and updated the manuscript. A former newspaper editor and state government spokesman, Jonathan Grant received his bachelor's degree from the University of Georgia.